Understanding Canada

Understanding Canada

A Multidisciplinary Introduction

to Canadian Studies

EDITED BY WILLIAM METCALFE

Introduction by Roger Frank Swanson
Editorial Assistance: James M. Colthart
Cartographic editor: Edward J. Miles

New York University Press •
New York *and* London • 1982

Library of Congress Cataloging in Publication Data
Main entry under title:

Understanding Canada.

  Bibliography: p.
  Includes index.
  1. Canada—Civilization—Addresses, essays,
lectures. I. Metcalfe, William, 1935–
F1021.U52   971   81-16966
ISBN 0-8147-5382-5   AACR2
ISBN 0-8147-5383-3 (pbk.)

Manufactured in the United States of America
092584

To Richard Seaborn,
who inspired us all to do it

Contents

Contents

Acknowledgments

The opinions expressed in the Introduction and in Chapter 7: *An International Perspective: The Foreign Policy of Adjustment* by Roger Frank Swanson are those of the author and do not represent the views of the Chamber of Commerce of the United States.

We acknowledge permission to publish the following copyrighted material, having made all reasonable attempts to contact present holders of copyright where applicable.

"ANGLO SAXON STREET'", from *The Collected Poems of Earle Birney,* reprinted by permission of The Canadian Publishers, McClelland and Stewart Limited, Toronto.

"Bonne Entente", "Saturday Sundae", by Frank Scott, "Cage d'oiseau", translated by F. R. Scott, "The Sorcerer" by A. J. M. Smith, "The Great Day" by Ralph Gustafson, reprinted by permission of The Canadian Publishers, McClelland and Stewart Limited, Toronto.

"I.O.U." by Neil Tracy, reprinted by permission of Borealis Press Limited, Ottawa.

"L'exigence du pays" and "Tree in a Street" by Louis Dudek, reprinted by permission of the author.

"Poem a Little Chinese", "Faculty Party" by D. G. Jones, and "Speak White" by Michèle Lalonde (trans. D. G. Jones), reprinted by permission of D. G. Jones.

"Erosion" and "Seagulls", from the *Collected Poems* of E. J. Pratt, reprinted by permission of Macmillan Company of Canada, A Division of Gage Publishing Limited.

"The Tragedy" and "Colonial Saturday Night" by Raymond Souster, reprinted by permission of Oberon Press, Ottawa.

"The Skater" by Charles G. D. Roberts, reprinted by permission of
Lady Joan Roberts.

"The Onondaga Madonna" by D. C. Scott, reprinted by permission
of John G. Aylen.

"The Execution" by Alden Nowlan, reprinted by permission of the
author.

"For the Sisters of the Hotel Dieu" from *The Collected Poems of A.
M. Klein* compiled by Miriam Waddington. Copyright ©
McGraw-Hill Ryerson Limited, 1974. Reprinted by permission.

"The Snow Girl's Ballad" from *Collected Poems: The Two Seasons.*
Copyright © Dorothy Livesay, 1972. Reprinted by permission of McGraw-Hill Ryerson

CARTOGRAPHY BY NORTHERN CARTOGRAPHICS, Burlington, Vermont.

Special editorial assistance by Amanda Stedman.

Preface

WHAT HAPPENS WHEN one brings together seven scholars (five Canadian, two American) representing several disciplines and fields of study and asks each to view a nation through his own scholarly lens? In other words, what does Canada look like to a geographer, historian, a political scientist, an economist, an anthropologist, and a literary specialist? The answer can be found in this rather unique book, to which was added a chapter on Canada's international experience, including the U.S.-Canadian relationship.

What emerges is the story of people determined to build their own version of a distinctive nation in North America. Geographically, Canadians attempted to harness an immense and often hostile territory with a relatively small number of people. Historically, Canada gradually evolved into an autonomous nation while simultaneously resisting external U.S. pressures and internal centrifugal regional forces in a quest for national unity. Politically, national institutions were created, combining a federal framework with parliamentary government and requiring highly defined intergovernmental roles at the provincial and local as well as the federal level. Economically, national policies were defined and implemented as Canadians searched for economic growth, efficiency, equity, and stability. Anthropologically, a profoundly multicultural society emerged; and a national consciousness that would be reflected in Canadian literature began to develop. Internationally, Canada gradually took its place as an independent nation on the world stage and came to play an international role far in excess of its real power.

The purpose of this book is to introduce Canada to American college students and laymen by way of seven of the major disciplines and fields of study, all in an easily available and comprehensive source. The usefulness of this collection therefore depends upon the receptivity of the audience, and to maximize this usefulness, a "filter effect" was utilized. That is, the editors brought together U.S.-based scholars representing the various disciplines and fields of study to act as referees, thereby ensuring that U.S. levels of knowledgeability and interest were being met. The hope is to have provided fresh and indigenous Canadian disciplinary perspectives that are geared toward the needs of those unfamiliar with Canada.

In essence, each of the disciplinary chapters constitutes a "starter text" in which the authors explain to the uninitiated what they think is important when applying their fields of study to Canada. At the same time, the book as a whole is intended to provide an overall multidisciplinary introduction to Canada that will be of use, not only to students, but also to laymen and professionals interested in Canada. Each of the chapters reflects the personal and professional bias of its author: the editors have not sought to impose their views or "homogenize" those of the contributing authors.

This project was made possible by the funding assistance of the Government of Canada through the Embassy of Canada in Washington, D.C., and is issued under the auspices of the Association for Canadian Studies in the United States (ACSUS). The editors are especially indebted to Dr. James Colthart, who served as the Canadian liaison officer on this project; to Ms. Linda Ross; and to Mr. Joel Sokolsky. Special appreciation is also extended to the U.S.-based scholars who served as referees on this project: Drs. Edward J. Miles (University of Vermont), Richard A. Preston (Duke University), S. Peter Regenstreif (University of Rochester), John Volpe (Chamber of Commerce of the United States), Mildred A. Schwartz (University of Illinois at Chicago Circle), and Victor M. Howard and Russel B. Nye (Michigan State University).

Dedicated to professors and students of Canadian Studies in the United States, this book was written with the hope that it will encourage a better understanding of Canada as a nation whose national experience is distinct from, but complementary to, that of the United States. Such an understanding is especially compelling for Americans as their closest ally and most important trading partner addresses itself to a national constitutional discussion of historic proportions.

R.F.S.

The General Editor wishes to acknowledge the good offices of the Canadian Embassy in Washington. For many years, primarily through the Academic Relations Officer of its Public Affairs Division, the Embassy has been of immense assistance to ACSUS and to the cause of Canadian Studies in the United States. In particular, two former Academic Relations Officers, Richard Seaborn and James Colthart, have greatly facilitated work on this volume. Special thanks also To Dr. E. J. Miles, Director of the University of Vermont's Canadian Studies Program, for his editing of the cartographic work necessary for Chapter 1, and to Carolyn Perry, who managed to type the lengthy manuscript with skill and good taste without losing her sense of humor.

W.M.

* William Metcalfe is Professor and Chairman of History at the University of Vermont and Editor of the *American Review of Canadian Studies*. He is a Torontonian *errant*.

The Constitution Act
(Canada Act), 1981

ON GUY FAWKES' DAY (November 5), 1981, nine provincial premiers reached a historic agreement with Prime Minister Trudeau on a "patriated" Canadian constitution which could be forwarded to Her Majesty's Government in Britain with a request for speedy action on an ennabling/implementing bill in the British Parliament. Quebec's premier, René Lévesque, stood alone against the agreement, arguing that it would impinge upon Quebec's control of its official language policy (and thus of its cultural destiny), and further that Quebec, claiming to have a veto over constitutional change, would challenge it in the courts. Such a challenge was subsequently brought, but on December 2, 1981, by a vote of 246 to 24, the Canadian House of Commons passed the Constitution Act, 1981 (including a Charter of Rights and Freedoms and a formula for amending the new Constitution in Canada). Six days later the Senate followed suit, and Justice Minister Jean Chrétien was speedily dispatched to Westminster. Despite the continued opposition of Canadian native peoples and the Quebec government, it seemed likely that sometime during the first half of 1982, certainly in time for a July 1 Canada Day celebration, an ennabling act would be passed in Britain, and the Constitution Act (Canada Act), 1981, would come into force. Canada's new Constitution would then consist of the sum total of the British North America Act, 1867, and its subsequent amendments up to and including the Constitution Act, 1981, all these officially referred to as the "Constitution

Acts, 1867 to 1981." Most of the familiar apparatus of Canada's present governmental system (dealt with throughout this book, but especially in Chapter Three) would remain the same under the new Constitution. Its most significant points, however, deserve brief analysis, for although some merely restate or refine existing positions, taken together they present a new image of Canada to itself and to the world.

By the new Act, Canada is officially bilingual; that is, both English and French are official languages federally (and in New Brunswick), and the Constitution itself is legal in both languages. Both French and English minorities, where their numbers warrant provision of public funds for their education, have the right to free public education in their own language. Both languages are legal in Parliament, federal courts and government offices, and federal services must be available in both French and English. The new Constitution may be amended only in Canada, by the Canadian Parliament with the approval of any seven provinces containing fifty per cent of the population; thus Quebec and Ontario will not have veto power over future amendment. No British act passed after the Constitution Act, 1981 comes into effect will have any force in Canada; thus while the institution of the Monarchy will remain, the last theoretical vestige of legislative colonialism will be no more.

The Canadian Charter of Rights and Freedoms will be Canada's first fully-operable, "American style" declaration of rights actually enshrined in a formal Constitution. It guarantees fundamental freedoms (religion, the press, association and peaceful assembly), legal rights (to speedy counsel, against arbitrary detention, against unreasonable search or seizure), equality before the law and equal protection by law, regardless of race, national or ethnic origin, color, religion, sex, age or disability. All rights and freedoms are specifically "guaranteed equally to male and female persons." There is, however, a provision for provincial legislative override of these freedoms, legal and equality rights for a limited, five-year period—it is not *expected* that any provincial legislature would dare to so act.

Finally the Constitution Act contains many clauses dealing with the rights of Canada's aboriginal peoples (Indians, Inuit, and Métis), regional disparities and provincial rights to control natural resources. Although "existing aboriginal and treaty rights" of the native peoples are specifically guaranteed, there is so much controversy over the natural resource implications of those rights that Part IV of the Act stipulates that a special federal-provincial conference must be called within a year to identify and define those rights. The Federal government is specifically bound, by Part III, to minimize the ill effect of regional economic disparities, with equalization payments to the provinces if necessary. To protect the desires of economically depressed provinces to give their unemployed citizens job preference, absolute mobility rights are qualified by an escape clause permitting such discrimination. Provinces may in future decide to opt out of programs which involve educational or cultural matters, receiving compensation from Ottawa when they do so. They may also, with Parliamentary approval, extend their boundaries (a clause which seems ominous to the native and other peoples of the Yukon and Northwest Territories).

Only time—and the vagaries of the legal process—can tell what a constitution really means to the people who are governed by it, and this Constitution will be no exception. Already commentators and analysts, experts and pseudo-experts are in disagreement as to the precise effect which the actual wording of the document *can*, and/or is *likely* to have as the great Canadian game of federal-provincial confrontation is played on throughout the next decades and the coming century. Many worry that the Charter's rights are seriously endangered by the legislative override clause, which is likely to be referred to (cynically? or importantly?) as one of several "notwithstanding" clauses which gladden the hearts of only those who profit from litigation. It has been suggested, in an excellent summary by Robert Lewis in *Macleans* magazine (November 9, 1981), that "a whole generation of activists" may challenge in the courts existing discriminatory laws (the War Measures Act, the Official Secrets Act) and practices (police writs of assistance). In such matters time is the best historian; but for now, many Canadians will be proud to say that for the first time they will have a truly Canadian Constitution.

W.M.

Introduction

ROGER FRANK SWANSON

> You know, I don't believe I ever in my life
> even thought to think about Canada.
> —Anon. American woman to Arthur Phelps,
> quoted in *These United States,* 1941

RELATIVELY FEW AMERICANS have "thought to think about Canada." While this is unfortunate, it is not surprising. It is difficult for Americans to see a Canadian social-cultural distinctiveness because Canadians seem too similar to Americans. The result is that Canada appears to be a copy, reduced in size, to be sure, of the United States. Moreover, there is an extraordinary degree of economic and strategic interdependence between the United States and Canada, which gives Americans the impression that Canada is simply an extension of the United States. Post–World War II rhetorical variations upon the themes of "partner" and "good neighbor" have reinforced America's difficulties in viewing Canada as a separate and distinct nation.

Similar difficulties can be found when Americans attempt to view Canada as a subject for scholarly enquiry. Because many Americans have generally perceived Canada as a replication and extension of the United States, few have discerned a Canadian distinctiveness warranting special or systematic attention. The academic attention paid to Canada in the past half century has tended to be on the individual level, most often among Canadian expatriate teachers who pursued their interest in Canada with little direct institutional support. Such courses on Canada as these pioneers chose to offer usually terminated when they left or retired.

In the 1920s social scientists and historians in the United States began to address themselves to the massive North American impact on Canadian history, society, and culture.[1] Somewhat later, the single most extensive manifestation of academic interest in Canada in the United States was the 25-volume series on Canadian-American relations published from 1936 to 1945 under the auspices of the Carnegie Endowment for International Peace. Here again, the entire project was, to quote one observer, "initiated, largely supervised, and partly written by Canadian-born scholars in the United States aided by scholars who were American-trained and living in Canada."[2]

Although the levels of Canadian activity in U.S. universities increased in ensuing decades, several problems affected the growth of Canada as an area of scholarly enquiry.[3] Canada as a single-nation "area study" had to compete with such regionally oriented programs as European, Asian, Latin American, and Middle Eastern studies, and even when contrasted with such single-nation studies as those involving the Soviet Union or China, Canada seemed less exotic and thus less attractive an area of enquiry for U.S. students. In addition, the fact that Canada apparently lacked the attributes of a "crisis area" gave it a low profile. This precluded its inclusion in governmental and many nongovernmental funding programs that were directed at more "critical" areas of the world. The National Defense Education Act of 1958 (Title VI, Foreign Language and Area Studies), constituting a competitive response to the rise in Soviet leadership, attempted to encourage area and foreign-language studies. Only in recent years has there been an effort to include Canada as an area study within the meaning of this legislation. Nor was Canada—unlike Western Europe, Australia, and New Zealand—originally included within the scope of the 1961 Hayes-Fulbright Education and Cultural Exchange Act. Even the

French content of the Canadian national experience has been largely ignored in the context of U.S. funding assistance.

Notwithstanding these problems (which have tended to militate against the orderly development and sufficient funding of Canadian studies in the United States), several interrelated factors were at the same time furthering an awareness of Canada in U.S. academic circles. Individual course offerings on Canada began to coalesce into formal Canadian studies programs in several U.S. universities. The Canadian programs at the University of Rochester, Duke, and Michigan State were established in 1954, 1955, and 1956, respectively. The momentum continued throughout the 1960s and early 1970s, with various kinds of Canadian studies programs being established at such universities as Vermont in 1963, Harvard in 1967, Maine in 1968, the Johns Hopkins School of Advanced International Studies in 1969, St. Lawrence University and Northwestern University in 1974, Columbia and Yale in 1976, and a host of other institutions.

A second factor encouraging Canadian studies was organizational in nature. In 1971 the disparate Canadian studies programs and individual scholars joined together to form the Association for Canadian Studies in the United States. This was significant in that it provided an organizational focus of activity for heretofore fragmented efforts. The purpose of ACSUS is, quite simply, to promote scholarly interest in Canada at all levels and in all fields and disciplines. This is accomplished through the association's journal, the *American Review of Canadian Studies*, and at its biennial conference and other meetings.

Two additional factors helped to make these developments possible: additional funding and an increasing public awareness of Canada. The William H. Donner Foundation, whose efforts began in the late 1960s, was instrumental in revitalizing and extending Canadian studies in the United States. In the 1970s other foundations became involved, including the Arthur Vining Davis Foundation, the Ford Foundation, and the Andrew W. Mellon Foundation. In addition, several corporations contributed funding for scholarships, guest lecturers, and conferences. The U.S. federal government has recently begun to fund Canadian Studies centers under the NDEA (Title VI) Language and Area Studies Program. This support is significant both for the three (of seventy-six) participating institutions and for the implicit recognition of legitimacy. Last, and importantly, the Canadian Embassy in Washington and the fifteen Canadian consular posts have, since the late 1960s, provided facilitative and modest financial assistance to U.S. scholars. Indeed, this was institutionalized in 1975 with the appointment of an academic relations officer in the embassy specifically charged with coordinating Canadian government assistance and the appointment of consular officials to administer an active program of support for Canadian studies.

All these developments reflect a new and somewhat different public awareness of Canada in the United States. To Americans, Canada increasingly appears less as a sleeping giant and more a dynamic and distinctive North American nation. This heightened awareness of Canada is a result of such forces as the resurgence of a Canadian consciousness during and after the 1967 Centennial celebrations; the 1970 foreign policy review of the Trudeau government that reexamined the foundations of Canadian foreign policy; Canadian disenchantment with the protracted U.S. involvement in Vietnam; the bilateral impact of divergent U.S. and Canadian policy directions in the economic and cultural spheres, ranging from the establishment of a screening device to review foreign investment in Canada to the Canadian deletion of U.S. television commercials; and the drama of the 1976 Parti Québécois election victory in Quebec and the subsequent Referendum on Sovereignty/Association in May 1980. Most recently the possibility of significant constitutional change in Canada has captured some American public attention.

It is ironic that Americans have had difficulty in viewing Canada as a separate nation, since the very essence of the Canadian national experience has been the attempt to create a separate nation in North America. That experience has had two subthemes: the attempt to further national unity in the face of regional fragmentation and the attempt to create national institutions and policies that would both serve Canadian interests and prevent Canadian absorption by the magnetic power of the United States. *Foreign Policy for Canadians*, published in 1970 by the Canadian government, very well summarizes the Canadian position by pointing out that Canada faces "two inescapable realities, both crucial to Canada's continuing existence." First, "there is the multifaceted problem of maintaining national unity. It is political, economic and social in nature; it is not confined to any one province, region or group of citizens; it has constitutional, financial and cultural manifestations." Second, "there is the complex problem of living distinct from but in harmony with the world's most powerful and dynamic nation, the United States. The political, economic, social and cultural effects of being side by side for thousands of miles of land, water and airspace, are clearly to be seen in the bilateral context."[4] It is therefore no accident that all of the Canadian authors in this volume stress these two themes of national unity and the U.S. impact on Canada.

In Chapter 1, Professor Ralph Krueger (Department of Geography, University of Waterloo) assesses the Canadian "man-land relationship." He goes beyond the traditional focus of physical geography to include the interacting cultural, human, and physical processes. Professor Krueger begins by tracing the political geographical pattern now existing across the northern portion of North America, and attempts to describe how and why Canada evolved as a country different from the United States. He then explains Canada's physical geographical patterns and describes how man utilized and was affected by the natural environment, and how the settlement pattern evolved, resulting in the modern, urbanized, industrial nation that now exists. Finally, Professor Krueger describes the general nature of the major regions of Canada and discusses the topics of regionalism and regional disparities. This chapter, given its wide-ranging perspective, is especially useful as a basic introduction to Canada.

In Chapter 2, Professor Gerald M. Craig (Department of History, University of Toronto) presents a comprehensive chronological view of Canada's historical evolution. He stresses the fact that Canadians, both British and French, were determined to create a separate state in North America, examining this theme through four historical periods. Beginning with the struggle for the control of North America (ending in 1818), he then traces the growth of the British North American provinces culminating in the completion of the transcontinental Confederation (in 1873). This is followed by a description of the evolution of the Canadian Dominion and of its emergence with the British Empire/Commonwealth and the world at large. Finally, Professor Craig brings his historical perspective up to the present by reviewing the issues and problems that have faced Canada since 1945, thus providing the reader with the perspective essential to a full understanding of contemporary Canada.

As with any nation-state, one of the bulwarks of Canada as a separate and unified country in North America is its political institutions and system of parliamentary government. In Chapter 3, Professor Robert J. Drummond (Department of Political Science, York University) presents a comprehensive picture of the overall functioning of a government in Canada. He begins by discussing the constitutional bases of Canadian government. He then examines the formal institutions of the Canadian parliamentary system, including the monarchy, the prime minister and his Cabinet, the House of Commons and the Senate, and the public bureaucracy and the judiciary. This is followed by a review of such informal institutions as political parties and analysis of their role in shaping public opinion and electoral behavior. Like the United States, Canada has a federal system, prompting Professor Drummond to conclude with a discussion of its components and their workings, including some perceptive comments on intergovernmental relations and provincial and local politics. This examination of the political framework that Canadians have devised and adapted to give expression to their collective will suggests both the opportunities and obstacles the nation confronts.

If geography and history, natural resources and land settlement have conditioned much of Canada's economic development, Canada's political system and relationships with the Old World and the New have also much to do with her economic situation today. Professor Peter Kresl, of Bucknell University, examines Canada's economic past and present in Chapter 4. Stressing an approach more informed by "political economy" than by pure "economics," he explains the central theses of Canada's economic evolution from colony to a nevertheless interdependent twentieth-century nation. The function of the great staples (fish, fur, timber, and grain), the "National Policy" and its results, branch-plant economics and the modern problems of foreign ownership of Canada's economy are dealt with, as are the long-standing but no less pressing difficulty of regional economic disparity and the much more recent question of the price of petroleum products. Throughout the chapter, the particularly Canadian aspects of the government's role are illuminated, and possible options for future development are discussed.

A major component of Canada's distinctiveness from the United States is the multicultural nature of Canadian society. In Chapter 5, Professor Peter Woolfson (Department of Anthropology, University of Vermont) examines the networks of human interaction and shared traditions of the Canadian peoples. He discusses the traditional lifeways of the native peoples of Canada—Indians, Eskimos, and Métis. The results of acculturation and change among the modern Canadian Indians on and off the reserve is stressed. Professor Woolfson also examines the traditions and problems of the French Canadians, including the role of language, the church and Catholic values, and the family; and the transformation of traditional culture in recent years. He analyzes Canadian immigration and immigrant minorities, concentrating on the Chinese, Blacks, Ukranians, Italians, and Hutterites. The realities of ethnic pluralism are examined, including the role of the English Canadians in Canada's cultural mosaic. The author adds another human dimension to this overall study of Canada by bringing to light the varied social backgrounds of Canada's people.

A major preoccupation of Canadians has been the extent to which they have developed a distinctive national consciousness. In Chapter 6, Professor Ronald Sutherland (Department of Literature, Université de Sherbrooke) examines Canada's national literature in order to better understand Canada's character as a nation. He discusses the preoccupation with the United States found in much Canadian literature, a preoccupation that is characterized by the duality of admiration for, and suspicion of, the United States that can be found in both French and English Canada. Professor Sutherland analyzes Canadian literature by dividing its development into seven chronological periods: the colonial period from 1750 to 1867, the Confederation period from 1867 to 1900, the early twentieth century from 1900 to 1920, the modern period from 1920 to 1945, "the breakup of the old order" from 1945 to 1960, "the search for vital truth" from 1960 to 1970, and "the new hero" from 1970 to the present. Because the thematic evolution of Canadian literature corresponds closely with the development of Canadian national consciousness (which is to say that much of the activity has taken place within the last few years), Professor Sutherland provides the reader with an invaluable perspective on the current Canadian preoccupation with cultural identity and survival.

One of the most basic criteria of a nation is its ability to pursue its interests in the international community as a sovereign actor. In Chapter 7, the present writer analyzes Canadian foreign policy as a twofold process of adjustment. Canadian foreign policy must adapt not only to international forces (given, for example, the vulnerability associated with its open country) but also to those domestic constraints that are imposed by internal forces (e.g., the English-French controversy). The writer begins with the essential historical setting, tracing both the policies and the mechanisms of Canadian foreign policy as it evolved from colonialism to complete autonomy. This process saw Canada emerge from under British tutelage to play an international role that was far in excess of its real power through its active contribution to, and support of, such international organizations as the United Nations and NATO. The writer then assesses the domestic sources of Canadian foreign policy; a discussion of the objectives of Canadian foreign policy includes an outline of the national goals set by the Trudeau government in the early 1970s. These are reviewed by assessing Canada's interest in economic and strategic matters, peacekeeping, arms control/disarmament, and developmental assistance. The next section offers a geographical overview of the range of Canada's relations with other nations and regions, including the Western Hemisphere, Europe, the Soviet Union, the Middle East, Africa, Asia and the Pacific, and the People's Republic of China. Finally, a separate section is devoted to the Canadian-U.S. bilateral relationship, emphasizing the importance of that relationship, not only to Canadians, but also to Americans. What emerges is the picture of a medium-sized nation pursuing its interests through a process of adjustment, both domestically and internationally.

Collectively, the chapters in this book provide the first multidisciplinary introduction to Canada written expressly for Americans. As Canada has evolved from an infant nation to a medium-sized international power with vast resources, and now grapples with the challenges and opportunities implicit in the quest for national unity and survival, the days when Americans could afford to not "think about Canada" are over. The international role of Canada and the future of Canadian federalism are intimately linked with the stability and prosperity of the North American environment. While Canadians have long been regarded as "friends" of the United States, it is time to confer respect on this friendship by better understanding the United States' closest ally and most important trading partner. It is hoped that this book will contribute to such understanding.

Notes

1. It is not irrelevant to note, for example, that in 1925, 600 graduates of Canadian universities held academic positions in the United States. Indeed, much of the seminal work in Canadian history and economics was done in U.S. graduate schools. The *Canadian Historical Review* in 1927 could list 57 doctoral theses in progress on Canadian topics, 44 of which were being done in the United States (33 of the 44 students whose first university degree was Canadian). By 1933, 107 Ph.D. dissertations on Canada were in progress, 70 of which were registered by students in U.S. universities. See Carl C. Berger, "Internationalism, Continentalism, and the Writing of History: Comments on the Carnegie Series on the Relations of Canada and the U.S.," in Richard A. Preston ed., *The Influence of the U.S. on Canadian Development: Eleven Case Studies* (Durham, N.C.: Duke University Press, 1972), pp. 32–38.

2. Ibid., p. 36.

3. See Dale C. Thomson and Roger F. Swanson, "Scholars, Missionaries, or Counter-imperialists," *Journal of Canadian Studies*, vol. V, no. 3 (August 1970), pp. 3–11; and Roger F. Swanson, "The New 'Area Studies': Canada," a paper prepared for the International Studies Association's Conference on New International Relations, November 16–17, 1973. Edward J. Miles, "Canadian Studies in the United States: Challenge and Frustration," *International Journal,* vol. XXVII, no. 2 (Spring 1972), pp. 250–264.

4. *Foreign Policy for Canadians* (Ottawa: Queen's Printer for Canada, 1970), pp. 20–21.

Chapter 1

A Geographical Perspective:

The Setting and the Settlement

RALPH R. KRUEGER*

Introduction

BY WAY OF introduction, and in order to appreciate a geographical perspective of any country, it is necessary to know something about geography as an academic discipline. Geography is the study of the earth as the home of man. It attempts to understand (1) how man interacts with his natural environment; (2) how man interacts with his man-made or man-modified environment; and (3) how and why this interaction differs from place to place (Figure 1). Not all geographers emphasize the three aspects of geography illustrated in Figure 1. Some focus on different parts of the natural environment—such as landforms and climate—seeking to explain their geographical distribution and the way they have affected

---

* Dr. Ralph R. Krueger received his B.A. and M.A. from the University of Western Ontario and his Ph.D. from Indiana University. He has taught in the public school system in Ontario, at Wayne State University (Detroit), Wilfrid Laurier University (Waterloo), and is now at the University of Waterloo, where he was the first chairman of the Department of Geography. Professor Krueger's research interests include urban problems, agricultural geography, the impact of urbanization on renewable resources, and regional disparities and development. He has written several textbooks and coedited several books of readings on Canadian topics for use in both secondary schools and universities, including (with Bruce Mitchell) *Managing Canada's Renewable Resources* (1977).

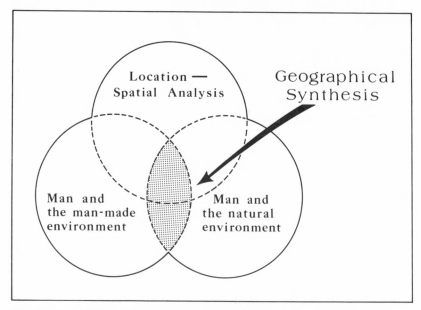

Figure 1. THREE ASPECTS OF GEOGRAPHICAL STUDY. Different geographers emphasize different aspects of the discipline. A geographical synthesis of a country melds all three aspects.

man or how man has modified them. Others concentrate on human use of the earth and the resulting geographical phenomena, including such topics as population, patterns of settlement, cities, economic activities, and political interaction.

Common to all geographical study, however, is the notion of place or location. This emphasis on location has led to an often repeated definition of geography being a study of "why what is where." Some geographers emphasize spatial analysis in their research and, through sophisticated statistical analysis and mathematical models, attempt not only to explain current geographical patterns but also to predict future patterns. A true geographical synthesis of any particular portion of the earth's surface (i.e., a region) must include all three aspects of geographical study.

Another useful definition is that geography is a study of the natural and man-made patterns on the surface of the earth and the processes that produced them (Figure 2). This definition emphasizes the integrated interdisciplinary nature of geography. In order to explain any geographical pattern it is necessary to understand the interlinking and interacting cultural, biotic, and physical processes. The fact that the arrows representing processes are linked illustrates the systems approach taken by geographers, a system being defined as a set of interconnected things each interacting on the other. In

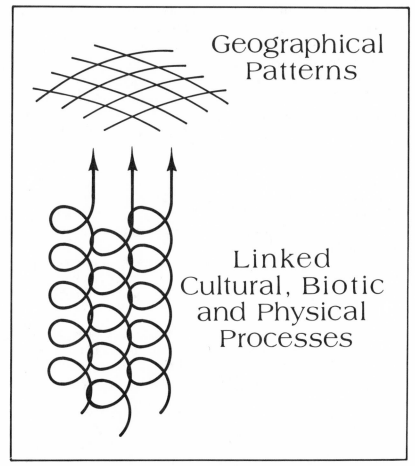

Figure 2. PATTERNS AND PROCESSES IN GEOGRAPHY (after Nostrand.) The patterns illustrate the importance of location in geography. In order to explain "why what is where," geographers must study the linked processes that created the patterns. Thus the comprehensive geographical study of a country or a region must integrate the data used by several other disciplines.

studying these processes geographers find that they are often using the data collected by other scientists and social scientists. By studying process over time, geographers also complement the work of historians.

Because of the breadth of its scope and the integrated nature of its many facets, geography is relevant to many of the issues of greatest concern in the world today. Thus, it is not surprising to find geographers involved in industry, consulting firms, and governments at all levels, working on problems such as environmental degradation, resource management, economic development, and urban land uses. It is also common for academic geographers to comment on environmental and other problems in the public forum. This trend toward relevancy in geographical research has been encouraged by statements of leading geographers in both Canada and the United States:

> Geography is the scientific study of a highly evolved complex—the man-land relationship; and such a study is so intimately bound up with social and economic structure that relevance to national needs ought to be a major determinant in one's choice of research.
>
> —F. K. Hare, from presidential address to the Canadian Association of Geographers, 1964

> Speaking as one individual, I feel strongly that I should not go into research unless it promises results that would advance the aims of the people affected and unless I am prepared to take all practicable steps to help translate the results into action.
>
> —G. F. White, in a paper to the annual meeting of the American Association of Geographers, 1979

These views will provide some insights into the perspectives from which a geographer views Canada. What follows, of course, does not offer a complete geographical synthesis of the country. Because of limited space, many topics of interest to geographers have been omitted. A more comprehensive view of the geography of Canada can be obtained from some of the textbooks listed in the "Annotated Bibliography" for this chapter. This chapter traces processes that led to the political geographical patterns now existing across the northern portion of North America and attempts to describe how and why, from a geographer's point of view, Canada evolved as a country separate and different from the United States. Following the section below on the evolution of Canada, the physical geographical patterns are described and explained in the section "Canada's Physical Geography." The next main section, "Settled Canada," describes how settlers made use of, and were affected by, the natural environment, including a discussion of the ultimate man-made environment, the urban system. The final main section, "Regions, Regionalism, and Regional Disparities, describes the general nature of the major regions of Canada and discusses from a geographical perspective regionalism, separatism, and regional disparities—issues of continuing concern in Canada.

Canada: The Evolution of a Different America

In 1867, almost a hundred years after the American Declaration of Independence, a group of British colonies were transformed into a country called Canada. This was something different in North America—a union of colonies aspiring to become a nation without renouncing political ties to Britain, the "mother country"—and it deserved to be regarded as the "Great Canadian Experiment."

For the experiment to succeed, vast distances and great physical geographical barriers had to be overcome. In addition, to remain unified and become independent, Canada had to repel early threats of American occupation and annexation and, in later times, resist economic and cultural domination by the United States. Also, ways had to be found to evolve from colonial status to national sovereignty, and the aspirations of the French-speaking citizens had to be accommodated within Confederation.

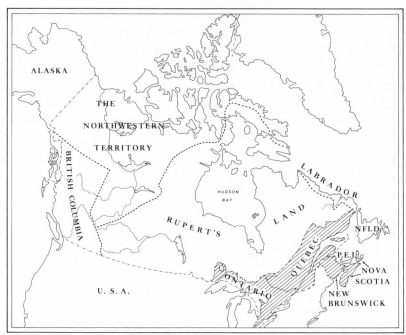

Figure 3. CANADA, 1867. In 1867, the United Province of Upper and Lower Canada became the provinces of Ontario and Quebec and were joined with New Brunswick and Nova Scotia to form a confederated state called Canada. The British North America Act, which created the new Confederation, made provisions for later inclusion of other British territory in North America.

The Dominion of Canada created by the British North America Act of 1867 included only a portion of the then existing British North America (Figure 3). Canadian territorial expansion was not complete until Newfoundland voted to join the Confederation in 1949 (Figure 4). Prior to this achievement, however, Canada formally became a fully independent national state with the passing of the Statute of Westminster by the British Parliament in 1931.

Today Canada is a modern, self-governing industrialized nation whose people live mostly in cities and enjoy one of the highest standards of living in the world. Canada's population of approximately 235 million (1978) is very small when compared with that of other countries, many of which have much less land area and fewer natural resources (Figure 5). However, it must be remembered that vast areas of Canada are not suitable for dense human population. Although Canada's population density per square mile of total area is only one-tenth that of the United States, in the southern, settled areas the density approaches that of the United States.

Canada is an "American" country, since it shares the North American continent with its neighbor to the south. Visitors usually find more similarities than differences between Canada and the United States. A traveler who crosses the border between the two often notices no marked change in the countryside: the architecture is similar; farms look alike; billboards advertise the same products; and people dress in the same way, eat the same kinds of food, play the same

Figure 4. CANADA SINCE 1949. In 1870 Manitoba became a province of Canada. In 1871 British Columbia joined Confederation upon the condition that a transcontinental railway would be built. The Canadian Pacific Railway was completed fourteen years later. Prince Edward Island joined in 1873, followed by Alberta and Saskatchewan in 1905. Newfoundland elected to join Canada in 1949. A second transcontinental railway, the Canadian National [Railways], was completed in the early part of this century, and was taken over by the federal government in 1927.

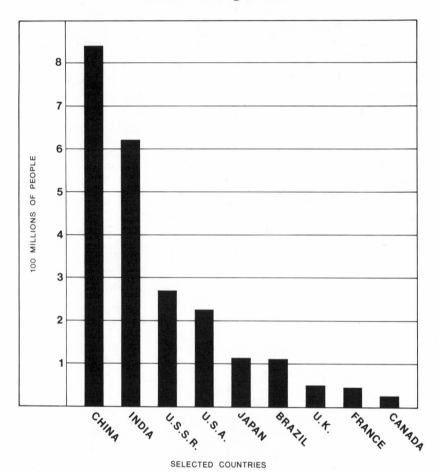

Figure 5. POPULATIONS OF SELECTED COUNTRIES (1976). Although the second largest country in the world in terms of area, Canada is a small country in terms of population.

kinds of games, drive the same kinds of cars, and often watch the same TV programs. Travelers entering the Province of Quebec, of course, will note immediately the prominence of the French language.

There are differences, however, some of them obvious, others more subtle. The parliamentary system of government, the political parties, and the judicial institutions are quite different in Canada, reflecting British more than American influence. The educational system is a blend between the British and American, with some influence from France in the Province of Quebec. There is more government ownership of transportation and communication systems in Canada than in the United States: the Canadian National Railways (CN— its passenger-carrying division now called VIARAIL), the Canadian Broadcasting Corporation (CBC), and Air Canada are all government-owned corporations. Local government reform, including new metropolitan and regional governments, is generally more advanced in Canada. The cores of Canadian cities have tended to remain vital and have not suffered from the physical and cultural deterioration that have occurred in many large cities in the United States.

The French fact in Canada is, of course, one of the most striking differences noticed by an American visitor. In Quebec about 80 percent of the population is French speaking (a majority speak French only). The French names; the long lots running back from the rivers and roads; and the architectural style of houses, barns, and churches give a distinctively Old World character to the landscape. Across a large part of the country outside Quebec the francophone presence is obvious (Figure 6). French-speaking people are not in a majority in all of these areas, but the French influence is noticed in the French place names and street signs and in French-language schools and television and radio programs.

Canada is officially a bilingual country, and federal government services and documents are available in English and French. Money is printed in both languages. All product labels are bilingual. Thus the breakfast food box sitting on the kitchen counter every morning reminds Canadians that they live in a country of two official languages. It should be noted, however, that not all Canadians, especially from the West, feel that such reminders are sensible, or even useful.

Important but very subtle differences between Canada and the United States are the nature, way of life, and attitudes of the people. Although there is a great danger in overgeneralizing on this theme, there do seem to be some differences. First, because of the small number of blacks in Canada, it has not had the same degree of black-white racial tension that has beset the United States. Also, Canada has not been the

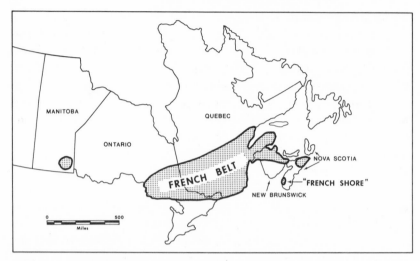

Figure 6. THE FRENCH BELT. The belt of French-speaking Canadians, although centered in Quebec, extends east to include Northeastern New Brunswick, and west as far as Sault Ste. Marie in Ontario. There are small outliers of the French Belt in Manitoba and Nova Scotia. There are also small numbers of French speaking people scattered throughout the rest of the country. Within the French Belt, only in Quebec and Northeastern New Brunswick are the francophones in the majority.

same kind of "melting pot" as has been the United States. Ethnic groups have tended to retain more of their culture and heritage in Canada. Generally speaking, the people of Canada seem to lay less stress on "individual freedom," which is emphasized in the American Declaration of Independence, and appear to be more willing to accept programs "in the public interest." Thus, they have been more willing to accept more "socialistic" governmental approaches, as is evidenced by more government ownership of key industries and by the fact that in several provinces the New Democratic Party (a moderate socialist party similar to the Labor Party in the United Kingdom), and its predecessor, the Cooperative Commonwealth Federation (CCF), have held power.

Above all, Canadians are very conscious of the U.S. colossus to the south. They realize that the United States has a profound economic and cultural influence on their country. Thus, Canadians are very much interested in everything that takes place south of the border. They also feel, rightly or wrongly, that this keen interest is not reciprocated by the people of the United States and that Americans just "take Canada for granted."

Partly because of Canada's proximity to the United States and partly because of the vastness of the country and its great regional diversity, Canadians seem to be obsessed with the fear that Canada lacks a real national identity. This concern about national identity and national cohesiveness may help explain the seemingly "anti-American" statements and actions that sometimes emanate from Canada. Some might argue that perhaps the lack of national self-confidence exhibited by Canadians can be attributed to the fact that Canada is (by comparison with the United States) a young country still unsure of its role and future.

Canada's Physical Geography

Global Location. If one traces on a globe the shortest distance between San Francisco and Moscow, Chicago and Stockholm, or New York and London, one crosses a part of Canada. Canada lies on most of the great circle routes between the United States and Europe—an important fact about Canada's global location. It lies between the two great modern industrial areas of the world, the USA and Western Europe. It also lies between the two most powerful nations of the world, the USA and the USSR. This location explains why the USA has joined with Canada in a North American defense pact (NORAD) and why Canada permitted the United States to build air defense warning installations across northern Canada.

Fortunately, Canada's industrial heartland is located on the Great Lakes–St. Lawrence Seaway, which is on a great circle route to Europe. This provides a great transportation advantage for central Canada. For example, Toronto, which is about one thousand miles from the ocean, is about the same shipping distance from England as is New York, which is right on the Atlantic Coast.

Canada's Pacific neighbors are more distant. For example, Australia and the People's Republic of China are more than seven thousand miles apart. It is true that Alaska separates Canada from the nearest part of the USSR, but the Soviet heartland is not really a Pacific neighbor, but rather lies across the frozen reaches of the Arctic.

Size. One of the most striking geographical characteristics of Canada is its immense size. Canada is second in area only to the USSR, larger than China, the United States, and Brazil, and about the same size as the continent of Europe. The area under Canadian jurisdiction includes the vast saltwater areas such as the Gulf of St. Lawrence, Pacific Coast straits, and the channels of the Arctic Archipelago. The straight-line distance from St. John's, Newfoundland, to Victoria, British Columbia, is more than three thousand miles; the distance from Windsor, Ontario, to Albert, on Ellesmere Island, is almost as great. Canada's longitudinal extent requires seven time zones; its latitude extends from 40°50' north at Pelee Island (which is south of the northern boundary of California) to 90° north (the North Pole).

Canada's vastness is both an asset and a liability. Its size has provided the country with great amounts and varieties of both renewable and nonrenewable resources, including living space and recreational space (which are becoming increasingly important to modern society). However, size has also posed serious cultural and economic problems for a nation with a relatively small population. It is very costly to move people, goods, and services over such long distances. Because of enormous distances between different parts of the country, economic links are difficult to forge and thus regional disparities persist; close social interaction is difficult, and thus attitudinal barriers seem inescapable.

PHYSIOGRAPHIC REGIONS

Landform barriers have added to the problems of great distances in the building of the Canadian nation. The physiographic grain in North America tends to run north-south, but

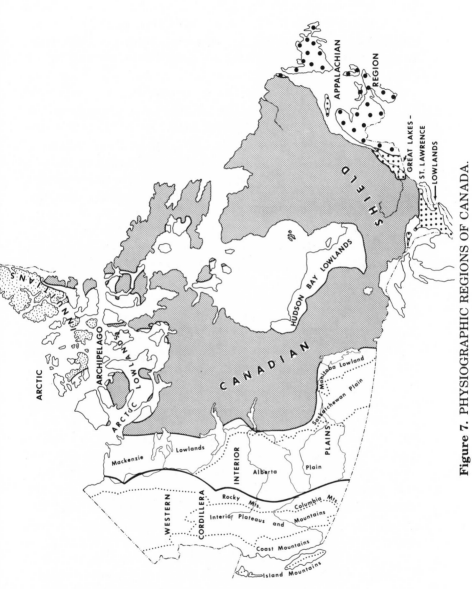

Figure 7. PHYSIOGRAPHIC REGIONS OF CANADA.

Canada had to forge transportation and communication links in an east-west direction, against the grain (Figure 7). The Great Lakes–St. Lawrence Lowlands did provide easy access into the heart of the country. However, the rock, hills, bogs, and lakes of the Canadian Shield were an imposing impediment to building land transportation facilities to the prairie farmlands to the west and the mine and forest resources to the north. The Mackenzie River Valley appears to be a convenient avenue from the Canadian West to the Arctic, but permafrost creates great difficulties in building ancillary roads, railroads, and pipelines. The Western Cordillera, with its seemingly endless systems of towering mountains, presented a barrier that, a hundred years ago, must have appeared almost insurmountable.

The Shield. The cornerstone of Canada's geological foundations is the Canadian Shield (sometimes called Precambrian Shield or Laurentian Plateau). It makes up almost half of Canada's total area. It extends beyond the Canadian boundary into the United States only in two limited areas, at the head of Lake Superior and in the Adirondack Mountains area of New York State. Because of its unique significance to Canada, more space will be devoted to its description than to the other landform regions.

Most of the Canadian Shield is composed of igneous rocks that once were the roots of mountains as high as the present Rockies. During the thousands of millions of years of Precambrian era, mountains arose and were eroded away on three different occasions. During mountain-building periods, there was much folding, faulting, and volcanic activity, and numerous bands and domes of molten rock were intruded into existing rock. Between the mountain-building periods, low-lying land was inundated by the sea and sedimentary rocks were deposited. When the land was uplifted again, these sedimentary rocks were eroded and carried to the shallow seas that completely surrounded the Shield. A few remnants of these sedimentary rock lowlands can still be found within the Shield. The most extensive is the Hudson Bay Lowlands which is of such magnitude that it is usually considered as a separate physiographic region.

Within the last million years, continental glaciers, with ice more than a half-mile thick, advanced over the Canadian Shield, rounding off hills, scouring out valleys, and depositing a variety of glacial landforms such as moraines, drumlins, and eskers. As the glaciers retreated, huge lakes formed at the edge of the ice, resulting in vast glaciolacustrine plains when the meltwaters drained away. The bottom of one of these lakes, called Barlowe-Ojibway, is now known as the Great Clay Belt that straddles the Northern Ontario-Quebec border.

Structurally, the Canadian Shield may be thought of as a huge saucer, primarily of Precambrian igneous and metamorphic rocks, the center of which is occupied by Hudson and James Bay, which have breached the Northeastern rim to drain into the Atlantic Ocean through Hudson Strait. Most of the Shield is relatively level and is less than two thousand feet above sea level. Only along the dissected edge of the "saucer rim" are there major hills and mountains: the Torngat Mountains in northeastern Labrador, the Laurentian Highlands in the Quebec City to Ottawa area, and along the north shore of Lake Superior. Except for the glaciolacustrine plains, the rest of the Shield is composed of undulating terrain with rocky, knoblike hills that range from three hundred to five hundred feet in height. The hollows between the knobs are occupied by lakes of varying shapes and sizes, interconnected by rapid streams seemingly running in all directions. In many areas there are vast stretches of muskeg swamp and peat bog. The helter-skelter arrangement of lakes, bogs, and streams is a result of glacial erosion and deposition that completely disarranged the previously existing drainage pattern.

The history and description of the landforms of the Canadian Shield help to explain its significance to Canada. Its complex geological origins resulted in deposits of metallic minerals such as nickel, gold, silver, copper, and lead. Also in the Canadian Shield are large bodies of iron and uranium ore. Moreover, the lack of sedimentary rock and deep overburden over the Precambrian rock have simplified the finding and mining of minerals. The numerous lakes, rapids, and waterfalls have facilitated the development of numerous huge hydroelectric projects. Because of the short summers and the lack of good soils, farming has been possible only in a few areas (e.g., the Great Clay Belt), and thus the land was not denuded of trees. As a result, the Canadian Shield is a rich source of forest products, particularly pulp and paper.

Most of the economic development and resulting settlement centers of the Canadian Shield have occurred along the southern margin and along the major transportation routes. Only gradually is development penetrating farther north. By the middle of this century there were still vast tracts of land with no economic development and no settlements. However, the search for energy is changing this; mammoth new hydroelectric projects are penetrating farther into the Shield, and the accompanying transportation facilities will encourage mining activity to follow (Figure 8). On the negative side, in the early days the Canadian Shield was a formidable barrier to transportation routes. Even now it is a vast relatively empty area, dividing the more densely settled parts of Canada and adding to transportation and communication costs.

Beyond the Shield. Around the edge of the Canadian Shield is a series of lowlands underlaid by Paleozoic sedimentary rocks and occupied by a series of lake and river systems: the Great Lakes–St. Lawrence Lowlands, the Manitoba Lowland, and the Mackenzie Lowlands. To the north are found the Arctic Lowlands, parts of which have been flooded to form the numerous straits and channels in the Arctic Archipelago. It is in these Arctic Lowlands that oil and gas have been discovered.

Beyond these lowlands, on three sides are found mountain systems. To the southeast are the mountains, hills, and valleys of the Appalachian Mountain system. The landscape here is similar to the Appalachian region in the United States, and the human use of the land is also similar; farming in the lowlands, mining (coal, lead, zinc, gypsum, salt) and lumbering on the uplands, and fishing along the coast. The Appalachian region is composed of a very old folded mountain system that has been eroded down to low rounded mountain ridges with many elongated valleys and low mountain passes. Thus, it has not been a major transportation barrier. Distance, more than rugged terrain, has divided this region from central Canada.

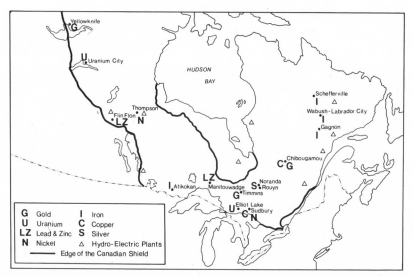

Figure 8. MINES AND HYDRO-ELECTRIC PLANTS IN THE CANA-
DIAN SHIELD. Only a few of the mining towns and hydro-electric plants
are shown on this map. More detail can be found in a geography textbook
or Canadian atlas (see Annotated Bibliography.)

In the extreme North is found the Inuitian region, a system of old fold mountains similar to the Appalachians. Minerals likely exist there, too, but so far climate and remoteness
have prevented them from being exploited.

In the far west is the Western Cordillera, composed of
relatively young, folded, and faulted mountains and plateaus.
The Cordillera is only some five hundred miles wide in Canada, considerably narrower than in the United States. The
major difference results from the fact that the interior plateaus are much less extensive in Canada. Generally, the
mountains are somewhat higher in Canada and contain some
of the most beautiful alpine scenery in the world. This mountainous terrain is a serious barrier to ground transportation
and severely limits agricultural activity, but it also provides
many natural resources: minerals, forests, wildlife habitat,
spawning grounds for salmon, hydroelectric sites, and water
supply and recreational space.

The description thus far of physiographic regions has
omitted much of Canada's West. The Manitoba and Mackenzie
Lowlands mentioned earlier are part of the Canadian Interior

Plains (Figure 7). When Canadians refer to the Western Plains they mean the southern portion of the Interior Plains, including the Manitoba Lowland, the Saskatchewan Plain, and the Alberta Plain.*

The Manitoba Lowland, which is the bottom of glacial Lake Agassiz, is the only part of the Canadian Western Plains that is as flat as a tabletop. The boundary between the Manitoba Lowland and the Saskatchewan Plain is distinctly marked by the Manitoba Escarpment. The Saskatchewan and Alberta Plains are divided in the south by the Missouri Couteau, which is much less prominent in Canada than in certain parts of the United States. The landscape of the Alberta and Saskatchewan Plains is similar to that of the Great Plains in the United States: rolling plains; deeply incised rivers; myriads of water-filled depressions called sloughs; dry streambeds called coulees; and in the drier areas mesas, buttes, and badlands.

Underlaid by sedimentary rocks that were deposited in the bottoms of warm-water seas, the Western Plains have large deposits of the fossil fuels, coal, and petroleum. Large deposits of phosphate, used in making fertilizer, are also found. The level land and fertile soils also make the area valuable for agriculture, although the climate limits crop production primarily to cereal grains, hay, and grass for pasture.

CLIMATE

Canada has a wide range of climatic types. For example, the west coast of British Columbia has moderate summer and winter temperatures similar to those of England and has even more rainfall than on the west coast of England. The central southern part of the Western Plains has great winter and summer temperature extremes and about as much precipitation as the area of Mongolia that is called the Gobi Desert. In the North, winter temperatures plunge to as low as −60° F; but with high humidity, the summer can occasionally make the weather unbearably hot in Southern Ontario.

---

* It should be noted that the Interior Plains of Canada are not exactly an extension of the Great Plains of the United States where the Missouri Couteau is usually considered as the eastern edge of that region.

The general climate of Canada can be described in terms of January (representing winter) and July (representing summer) mean temperatures, annual precipitation, and the number of degree-days in the growing season (Figures 9, 10, 11, 12). The data in these maps represent averages over a long time period. Winter and summer temperatures, precipitation, and the number of degree-days may differ greatly from year to year.

Nevertheless, from these maps one can make some general climatic comparisons. In the interior part of the country the winter temperatures become colder toward the north. The moderating effect of the Atlantic and Pacific oceans is obvious from the way the January isotherms parallel the east and west coasts. The west coast has the milder winters because the westerly winds blow onto the land from across the warm Alaska current. The oceans also moderate summer temperatures on both the east and the west coast. However, in the interior summers become surprisingly warm even at high latitudes. Note, for example, how the 60° F July isotherm reaches as far north as the Arctic Circle in the Mackenzie Valley.

The most precipitation is found on the west coast, the next greatest amount on the east coast. The two driest areas are the south central part of the Prairie Provinces and the Arctic. There is progressively less precipitation from southern Ontario north to the Arctic Archipelago.

The growing season is represented by the accumulated number of degree-days above 42° F (Figure 12). Most Canadian agricultural crops achieve significant growth only when the mean daily temperature is above 42° F. The higher and longer the temperature is above 42° F, the greater the amount of growth. A mean daily temperature of 52° F for one day is equal to a mean daily temperature of 43° F for ten days, both adding up to ten degree-days. Since most grain crops require approximately twenty-five hundred degree-days to ripen, it is clear from Figure 11 where the best agricultural areas in Canada are located. Since trees generally do not grow with less than one thousand degree-days, this map helps explain the location of the tree line as shown in Figure 13.

More comments about the climate of the various regions of Canada are given in the following section.

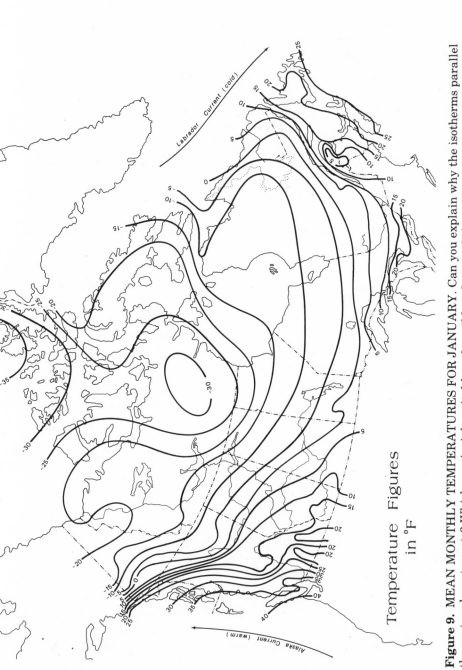

Figure 9. MEAN MONTHLY TEMPERATURES FOR JANUARY. Can you explain why the isotherms parallel the east and west coasts? Which provincial capital has the mildest January? the coldest? Compare the January temperatures of these two cities with your nearest city for which there are climatic records.

Temperature Figures in °F

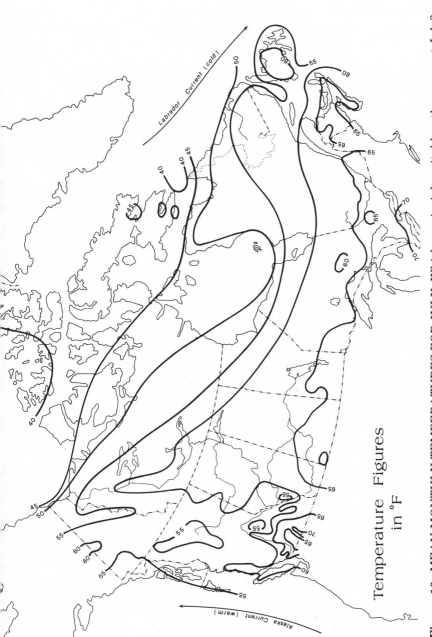

Figure 10. MEAN MONTHLY TEMPERATURES FOR JULY. Which provincial capital has the warmest July? the coolest? Compare the July temperatures of these two cities with your nearest city for which there are climatic records.

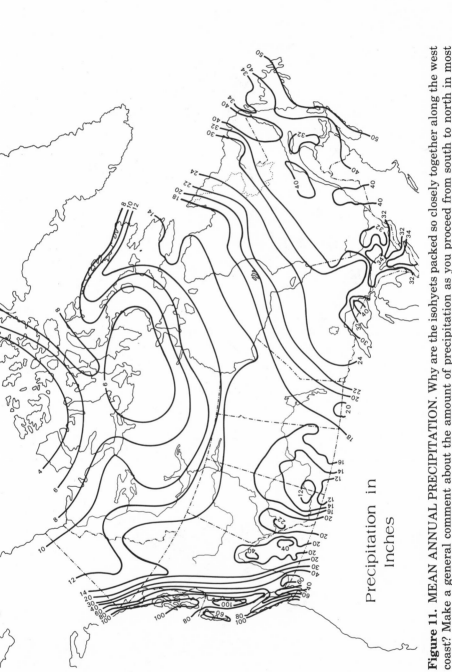

Precipitation in Inches

Figure 11. MEAN ANNUAL PRECIPITATION. Why are the isohyets packed so closely together along the west coast? Make a general comment about the amount of precipitation as you proceed from south to north in most parts of Canada. Which provincial capital receives the most precipitation? the least? Compare the precipitation

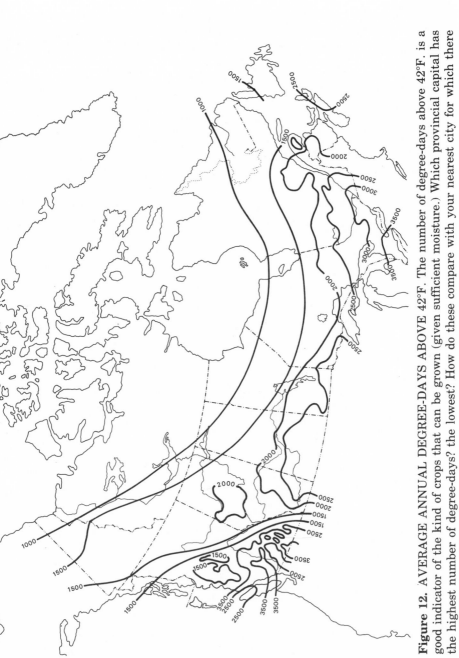

Figure 12. AVERAGE ANNUAL DEGREE-DAYS ABOVE 42°F. The number of degree-days above 42°F. is a good indicator of the kind of crops that can be grown (given sufficient moisture.) Which provincial capital has the highest number of degree-days? the lowest? How do these compare with your nearest city for which there are climatic records?

CLIMATE, VEGETATION, AND SOILS: ECOSYSTEMS

Climate has a direct effect upon the nature and distribution of plants; in turn, climate is influenced by the nature of the vegetative cover. Both climate and vegetation strongly condition the nature of soils. On a more microscale, the texture of the soil (size of the rock particles) and drainage conditions help determine the kinds of vegetation that can survive at a given site. Climate, vegetation, and soils, along with the associated wildlife, are interacting phenomena often referred to as an ecosystem.

Geographers recognize broad ecosystems, or vegetation regions with apparently stable vegetation, each characterized by certain plant species and common climatic and soils properties (Figure 13). These regions are not areas of homogeneous vegetation but rather are zones in which there are recurring plant communities reflecting the various site conditions. The descriptions given here are those of preagricultural vegetation, sometimes called natural vegetation or wild vegetation. For the sake of simplicity, the natural vegetation regions have been divided into three main classes: tundra, grasslands, and forests.

Tundra Region. Tundra is the name given to the true Arctic region, that area north of the tree line, and to the high mountain areas that also have Arctic characteristics. The tundra region is characterized by extremely long cold winters and very short cool summers. Throughout most of the region the annual precipitation averages less than fifteen inches, with the extreme northern portions averaging less than five inches. Thus, the Arctic is not a region of great quantities of snow. However, freezing temperatures and snow occur in every month, and in a large part of the region there is snow cover for about ten months of the year. This is also the land of permafrost, where the lower layers of soil never thaw out. It is this permafrost that makes any construction difficult, because as soon as the top insulation layers of vegetation and soil are disturbed the lower layers melt, resulting in subsidence.

Tundra vegetation consists of low scrubby shrubs, ferns, grasses, mosses, lichens, and numerous colorful flowers such

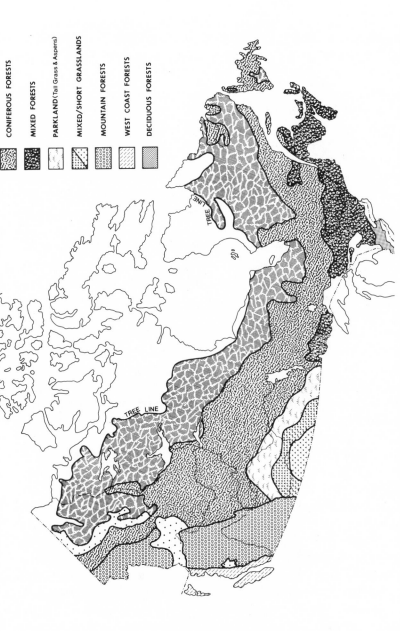

Figure 13. NATURAL VEGETATION REGIONS OF CANADA. These natural vegetation regions are highly generalized. The boundaries between them are usually broad transition zones. The actual plant communities in any one place depends upon the landform, soil and microclimatic conditions of the site. By comparing this map with the previous climate maps, make some general observations between natural vegetation patterns and precipitation and winter and summer temperatures.

CONIFEROUS FORESTS

MIXED FORESTS

PARKLAND (Tall Grass & Aspens)

MIXED/SHORT GRASSLANDS

MOUNTAIN FORESTS

WEST COAST FORESTS

DECIDUOUS FORESTS

TREE LINE

TREE LINE

as the arctic poppy. Because of the continuous daylight during the short summer, the ferns, grasses and flowers grow very rapidly. The brightest colored flowers, fruits, and seeds of the arctic plants make the tundra a colorful landscape in late summer.

A surprising number of wild animals survive the Arctic climate and thrive on the meager food supply there. Among the most important to the natives are the arctic fox and the caribou. There are only a few birds that live all year round in the Arctic, such as the great snowy owl and the ptarmigan. However, many birds that live the rest of the year in warmer climates fly great distances to the Arctic tundra region to nest.

The tundra is the most ecologically fragile and the most hazard prone of all Canadian natural environments. There are relatively few species of plants and animals, and the energy flows and food chains are very simple. Thus, damage to one species or one habitat can have a destructive result throughout the entire web of life. There are great concentrations of wildlife in small areas at particular times of the year, and wildlife tends to move in well-defined narrow corridors. Thus, any development in the wrong place or at the wrong time can have a disastrous effect. Because of permafrost, a bulldozer track across the tundra at the wrong time of year can result in a scar on the landscape that will take years to heal. Oil spills in the Arctic, on the land or in the sea, have a serious environmental effect that lasts several times as long as in a warmer climate. Moreover, many Inuit depend heavily on the land and water resources for their livelihood, so that any damage to the natural environment has an immediate and direct effect upon them. It is for these reasons that the Canadian government has conducted ecological studies, has formulated rules and regulations for development in the Arctic, and has made thorough investigations before authorizing the proposed joint Canadian-U.S. gas pipeline across Canadian territory.

Grassland Region. The grasslands are found where there is insufficient moisture to support continuous stands of trees.

The grasslands are usually called the prairies, and this is where the name Prairie Provinces (Alberta, Saskatchewan, and Manitoba) originated. However, a comparison of the political and natural vegetation maps (Figures 4 and 13) indicates that the Prairie Provinces are really misnamed, because at least three quarters of their territory is covered with forest.

Because of its continental location the grasslands region is both cold and dry. It is influenced mostly by cold dry Arctic and continental polar air masses. Moisture from Pacific air masses is cut off by the Western Cordillera and the warm, humid Gulf air seldom penetrates that far northwest. It is an area of temperature extremes, with temperatures often falling to $-30°$ F in the winter and climbing into the 90s (F) in the summer.

The driest part of the Canadian prairie is in the southwest corner of Saskatchewan. With annual precipitation only around twelve inches, this part of the country is really a semidesert or steppe. The natural vegetation consists mostly of bunches of several types of grasses with some sagebrush and small cactus. Between the bunches of grass bare earth is often visible, and considerable wind erosion is in evidence where the grass has been overgrazed.

Surrounding the dry short grass country is a more humid zone with mixed tall and short grasses. Toward the more moist margins of this area most of the grass is tall true prairie grass. Beyond the mixed-grass zone is an outer crescent with slightly more precipitation, covered with tall grass interspersed with clumps of primarily aspen trees. This parkland zone is a transition zone between the true prairie and the surrounding forest region. Along the outer edges of the parkland zone the vegetation is primarily aspen forest with some prairie openings.

There are three distinct soil zones that correspond with the different vegetation zones (Figure 14). The soils in the short-grass zone are light brown in color and, because of the sparse vegetation, are the least fertile. The drought in this zone causes an upward movement of moisture in the soil, resulting in mineral salts being brought up to the surface. The soils in the mixed-grass zones are dark brown and more

NATURAL VEGETATION

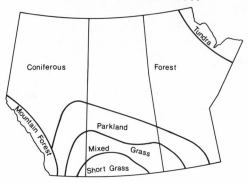

SOILS

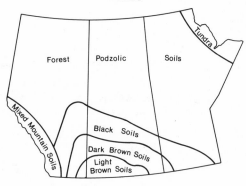

AGRICULTURE

fertile because of the greater amount of humus from the more luxuriant growth of grass. They also contain fewer mineral salts and in general are much better for agricultural purposes. The outer parkland zone has black soil called chernozem. This soil is rich in humus and, because of the moderate amount of precipitation, has not had valuable minerals leached out as happens in the forest soils, nor are there too many mineral salts as in the light brown soils.

The most common wild animals of the grasslands are the gophers, a collective term used for several related burrowing rodent species. Because they eat both grass and ground grain crops, they are considered enemies by the farmers who attempt to eradicate them by various methods including shooting, gas, and poison. Despite these attempts and the work of their natural enemies, the badger, owls, and hawks, gophers can still be seen by the score all across the prairies. Equally ubiquitous across the prairies are wild fowl that are attracted by the numerous sloughs.

The bison, which was seen in countless numbers when the prairies were being settled, is now consigned to a few "buffalo" preserves. The largest wild animals found on the short-grass plains are the mule deer and the antelope, but they do not exist in large enough numbers to be a hazard to farmers.

There are three main types of farming on the prairies: livestock grazing, wheat farming, and mixed farming. The location of these types depends primarily upon the amount of moisture available and thus form concentric zones similar to those of natural vegetation and soils (Figure 14).

The grazing of cattle and sheep is predominant in the short-grass prairie where there is insufficient moisture to support grain crops. Grazing is also important in the Rocky Mountain foothills, but because of rugged terrain instead of lack

Figure 14. NATURAL VEGETATION, SOILS AND TYPES OF FARMING IN THE PRAIRIE PROVINCES. These maps are highly generalized. See the text for more detailed descriptions. The mixed farming area in north-western Alberta is the Peace River district. Figure 10 will help explain why commercial agriculture is possible so far north.

of moisture. Ranching in the dry short-grass country merges gradually into the wheat belt as the annual precipitation increases to about thirteen to fifteen inches. The wheat belt is located primarily on the humus-rich dark brown and black soils. The wheat belt, in turn, merges into the mixed farming belt where the annual precipitation is closer to twenty inches.

These agricultural belts are named after the predominant type of farming found in each, but this does not mean that no other type of farming is practiced in each belt. For example, the grazing belt also has considerable wheat farming, using summer fallow to conserve moisture. In the wheat belt there is also considerable grazing, and other crops are grown on the more humid edge. In the mixed farming belt a great deal of wheat is grown, but it does not predominate over all other crops. Important crops in the mixed farming belt include oats, barley, rye, flax, and rape. Hogs, beef cattle, laying hens, and poultry are the major livestock produced in the zone.

Irrigation has changed the traditional farming pattern in some parts of the prairies. The most extensive irrigated farmland is found in southern Alberta where irrigated hay, grain, sugar beets, potatoes, and other vegetables are grown.

The Forest Regions. Canadian forests are associated with climatic conditions that are warmer than those of the tundra and more moist than those of the grasslands.

The coniferous forest region, sometimes called the boreal forest region (boreal means "of the north"), along with its transition zones to the north and south, constitute the second-largest continuously forested area of the world, second only to the great northern forests of the Soviet Union. The dominant tree species are white and black spruce, balsam and alpine fir, jack and lodgepole pine. Tamarack occupies wet sites throughout the region. Along the southern edge, the broad-leafed species of aspen and white birch are common and often become dominant in fire-swept areas.

It is the coniferous forest region that has made Canada famous as a supplier of pulp and paper. The region is also an important source of lumber, although much of the area is too inaccessible to make commercial lumbering feasible at the present time.

Between the tundra and the coniferous forest region lies a vast transition zone of scattered coniferous trees and tundra, known as the subarctic region or taiga. The subarctic climate with long cold winters, short cool summers and limited precipitation (generally less than fifteen inches) results in small, stunted trees of little commercial value. The area is studded with lakes and muskegs. Much of the region is underlaid with discontinuous permafrost. The subarctic environment is only slightly less ecologically fragile than the Arctic tundra.

The mixed forest region is a transition zone between the coniferous forest to the north and the deciduous forest to the south. Thus, it has a mix of both coniferous softwoods and deciduous hardwoods. The most important hardwoods are the sugar and silver maple, beech, birch, oak, ash, and elm. Unfortunately, the stately, umbrella-shaped elm is fast disappearing because of the Dutch elm disease, which is spreading rapidly throughout the region. In pioneer times the white pine was a very valuable species, and white pine lumber was exported to Europe in great quantities. However, a lack of conservation measures has resulted in a current scarcity of white pine in the region.

The only pure deciduous forest in Canada is found in the most southerly part of Southern Ontario where the growing season is long and the winters are moderated by the surrounding lakes. This is a small part of the broad deciduous forest that extends across a great expanse of the United States. It has the same hardwood trees as the mixed forest region but, in addition, has some species that are commonly found in much milder climates, such as the chestnut, hickory, sycamore, and black walnut. On the lighter-textured soils there is often an association of oak and pine trees. Hemlock is often found in the maple-beech forests.

In the middle of the eighteenth century both the mixed and deciduous forest regions were completely wooded, with the exception of limited areas cleared by the Indians for agricultural purposes. By the turn of this century, all of the deciduous forest region, the Great Lakes–St. Lawrence Lowlands, and the valleys and coastal lowlands of the Maritime Provinces had been cleared for agriculture. The only remnants of the earlier forest is found in farm woodlots and natural parks, but even most of these are not in a virgin state. The Southern Ontario portion of the region is one of Canada's best agricultural areas. The relatively long growing season, the high number of degree-days, and adequate precipitation along with winters moderated by the lakes permit Southern Ontario to grow a wide variety of crops ranging from hay, grain, corn, and soybeans to apples, peaches, grapes, tobacco, and small fruits and vegetables.

The forest region not mentioned so far is that of the Western Cordillera. This western forest region is dominated by conifers. The specific mix of species depends upon elevation and availability of moisture. Some of the interior valleys are in the rain shadow of the mountains and thus have a semiarid climate and steppe vegetation. An example of this is the Okanagan Valley, which has been irrigated to permit the growing of tree fruits.

Because of a longer growing season, milder winters, and an abundance of precipitation, the west coast forest region has the largest trees in all of Canada. The dominant species are western hemlock, red cedar, Sitka spruce, and Douglas fir, all of which are valuable lumber trees. Although the heaviest timber stands of large mature trees in the most accessible areas have been cut over in this century, individual trees in excess of two hundred feet in height and with trunks of more than four feet in diameter are still common. The lower Fraser Delta (the area south and southeast of Vancouver) has been totally cleared for agriculture. As in Southern Ontario, a wide range of crops can be grown there.

The soils of the forest regions are podzolic in nature; that is, they are acidic and the topsoil is leached of certain minerals. The true podzols of the subarctic, and northern coniferous forest are very infertile. The gray and brown podzolic soils of the southern coniferous forest and the mixed and deciduous forest regions are more fertile and produce excellent crops when certain mineral deficiencies are added through natural or artificial fertilizer. The soils of the Western Cordillera region are too complex to describe here. They vary in accordance with the amount of precipitation and nature of the forest cover.

There is not space here to describe the wildlife of the forest regions, except to say that it is abundant and varied and ranges in size from the bear and moose to the squirrel, and from the blue heron to the hummingbird. Insect life is also abundant, as campers will testify with respect to the mosquito and blackfly.

Settled Canada

The previous section briefly discussed Canada's physical geography: its global location, climate, and natural landscape, and only incidentally mentioned some of the implications for Canadians. Perhaps that section comes close to describing the images of Canada held by people not very familiar with the country: Arctic wastes, endless coniferous forests, a rocky lake-studded Canadian Shield rich in minerals, towering mountains on the west coast, a vast expanse of prairies, and above all short summers and long cold snowy winters.

These images are correct, but they are not the Canada known to the vast majority of Canadians who live in the settled parts of the country that constitute only a small part of its total area (Figure 15). In these settled parts of Canada, man has greatly changed the face of the landscape. He has cut paths through the wilderness for highways and railroads. He has cleared vast areas of natural vegetation and has replaced the forests and grass with crops of grain and hay. The wild animals that once stalked through the forests and ranged the plains have been replaced by domesticated animals.

In addition, man has greatly changed the appearance of the natural landscape by the things he has built. Many waterfalls and rapids have been harnessed for hydroelectric power, and canals have been built to let boats bypass them. In the rural settled parts of Canada, it is the road pattern, the type of farm fence, the style of the farmstead, the architecture of the houses, and the general layout of the villages and towns that give character and variety to the landscape. In the larger towns and cities, the natural landscape is

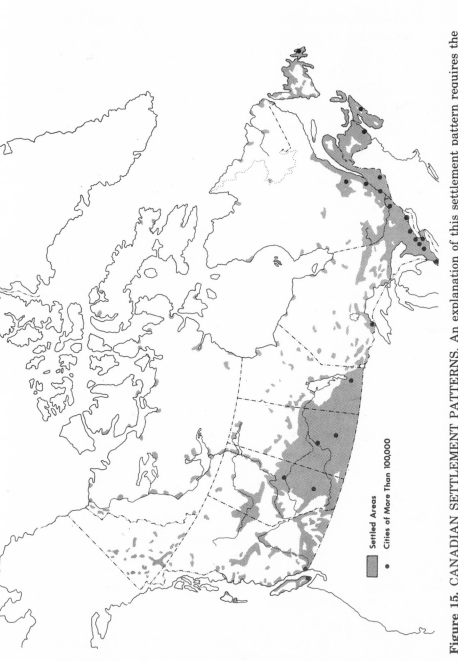

Settled Areas

• Cities of More Than 100,000

Figure 15. CANADIAN SETTLEMENT PATTERNS. An explanation of this settlement pattern requires the consideration of many factors: climate, landforms, soils, renewable and non-renewable resources, comparative

scarcely visible. The urban landscape is a man-made environment of factories, stores, houses, streets, schools, parks, and so forth. The eight of ten Canadians who live in cities would agree with the following:

> The real Canadian scene is a cityscape: smooth pavements and squared-off walls, crowds of people at lunchtime, flowing night-time expressways, and miles of houses elbowing each other. Canadians and their activities are becoming more and more concentrated in a hundred or so urban areas which occupy less than one percent of the land area.

> Gone are the occupations linked to the soil, the rock, and the timber. Canadians are stenographers, dentists, school teachers, salesmen. They depend, not on nature and their own brute strength, but on massive organizations which affect most aspects of their existence. They struggle—more or less—against the giant corporations which employ them, the bank that determines the interest rates on their mortgages, or the city hall which decides the amount of schooling, street washing and parking they may have. Canadians live in close contact with their fellows in a complex, varied, man-made environment called the city. It generates new problems, new solutions, new life-styles.

> The traditional map of Canada with its enormous pastel provinces and tiny dots of cities is not much help in describing Canada in the late twentieth century. The broad sweeping patterns of the distribution of resources which show up on such maps are less relevant, economically, socially, and politically, than the intense variations which take place within the few miles separating city and country, or even the few blocks between different social areas of the city. An accurate map of most of the socioeconomic variables describing Canada would show a few dozen islands of intense activity and great variation, separated by hundreds of miles of low density, homogeneous areas.[1]

Finally, a comment must be made about climate. It is true that the winters outside coastal British Columbia are very cold and snowy. But the vast majority of Canadians do not stay out-of-doors much. Consuming vast amounts of energy to do so, they create (in their often overheated homes, offices, and cars) an environment that ignores the cold and overcomes the snow. The few who do work outdoors keep warm by wearing warm clothing and by keeping active. Many Canadians take advantage of the winter weather to participate in outdoor recreation such as skating, snowshoeing, snowmobiling, skiing, and ice fishing.

Canadians who live in the most southerly parts of the country often complain more about summer weather than they do about winter. For periods of time the summer weather may be too cool for swimming or sunbathing, but then a sudden inversion of humid southern air can feel uncomfortably hot. Homes and workplaces are not as widely air-conditioned as they are in the southern parts of the United States. Thus, for some people in the "land of ice and snow" summer heat is a greater problem than winter cold.

EXPLAINING THE SETTLEMENT PATTERN

A glance at a map of settlement patterns indicates that most of the population has concentrated in a narrow band along the southern border of the country (Figure 15). Within this band there are striking differences in population density. More than half of Canada's population is found within the heartland of the country, in a narrow strip running from Windsor to Quebec City. Within this heartland are the two largest metropolitan centers, Montreal and Toronto, and half of the twenty-four Canadian cities with populations of more than 100,000 (Table 1.1). Outside the heartland, the only city with over 1 million people is Vancouver, British Columbia, and the only cities of approximately a half million are Edmonton and Calgary in Alberta and Winnipeg in Manitoba. The largest city in the Atlantic Provinces is Halifax, with a little over a quarter-million people. Outside these major metropolitan areas are large stretches of rural settlements with numerous villages, towns, and small cities. Beyond the densely settled parts is a vast area, constituting some 90 percent of the country, where settlement is sparse, scattered, or nonexistent.

By comparing the settlement patterns with the physical

Table 1.1 Canadian Cities of Over 100,000 Population

Toronto	2,803,100	Halifax	261,400
Montreal	2,802,500	Windsor	243,300
Vancouver	1,166,300	Victoria	213,000
Ottawa-Hull	672,200	Sudbury	155,000
Winnipeg	570,700	Regina	149,000
Edmonton	543,700	St. John's Newfoundland	140,000
Quebec	534,200	Oshawa	134,000
Hamilton	525,200	Saskatoon	132,000
Calgary	469,900	Chicoutimi-Jonquière	127,200
St. Catharines-Niagara	298,100	Thunder Bay	117,000
Kitchner-Waterloo	269,800	Saint John, N.B.	109,700
London	264,600	Sherbrooke	102,500

SOURCE: Census of Canada, 1976. The populations are for the metropolitan areas and have been rounded to the nearest thousand.

geography of the country, it is clear that physical geographical factors can help explain the distribution of population in Canada. First, the most densely populated areas are located on level plains where the climate is the mildest and where the agricultural land is the most productive. Second, lakes and rivers attracted settlement because they provided water supply, waterpower (later hydroelectric power), and cheap transportation of bulk cargo. The great mineral and forest wealth of the Canadian Shield led to the development of frontier resource-based towns, but the secondary processing, manufacturing, and related tertiary economic activities that led to population growth occurred in the south. Finally, the parts of the country with the most favorable natural environmental conditions were also the closest to the United States. The concentration of settlement along the southern border reflected this proximity: Canadian manufacturing plants were established by industrial firms from the United States, which wanted to locate branch plants as close as possible to the parent company in the areas. Also, many pioneer settlers— including those on the prairies—came from the United States, and they tended to stay reasonably close to the border.

RESOURCES AND THE SETTLEMENT PATTERN

The evolution of Canada's settlement patterns can be told in terms of the development of successive staple resources, primarily for export. This is often referred to as the *staple export theory* of Canada's growth.

Fish. The first settlements were located in the sheltered harbors of southeastern Newfoundland. Europeans, who came to fish primarily for cod on the Grand Banks, used these harbors to make ship repairs, to obtain wood and water, and to dry fish. Some fishermen built cabins, and eventually a few of them began staying in Newfoundland all year, leading to the establishment of fishing villages. In 1583 the explorer Sir Humphrey Gilbert claimed the island of Newfoundland and the adjoining mainland coast (now known as Labrador, a part of the Province of Newfoundland) for the queen of England, thus making it the first British colony in North America. Neither the early fishing villages nor Gilbert's attempts at settlement were successful permanently. Most of the settlers became tired of the difficult life in a harsh environment and returned to Europe.

Many years later new fishing villages, known as outports, were established, with the local inhabitants depending directly on fishing for a livelihood. Many of these outports also disappeared over the years (in recent years with government assistance) because the fishing industry could not support the inhabitants and because there were insufficient other resources that could be exploited competitively. Only St. John's developed into a major city (population 140,000), but its growth was based not only on the fishing industry but also on the provision of port facilities and services to ships from all over the world. Thus, the early fishing industry did little to foster Canadian settlement, the effect being limited entirely to the coastal zone.

After 1800 international export trade of fish (and other products) became the basis of the growth of cities in the Maritime colonies. With the shipping industry subsidized by Britain, the Maritimers assembled large volumes of fish in places like St. John's and Halifax for shipment to the West Indies. By the 1850s fish canneries were established, and the Maritime fish market was expanded. The total settlement impact was many small coastal villages and a few major port cities.

There was no settlement impact on the interior. The same can be said about the settlement impact of the Pacific Coast fishery

Furs. In contrast, the fur trade led to European penetration into the continent on both coasts and resulted in colonization and permanent settlements.

The first permanent settlement in Canada was established at Port Royal (now Annapolis Royal) by the French under Champlain and de Monts. This seemed at first like an excellent site for a colony because the winters were not as harsh as in other parts of the country and there was an abundance of fish, game, and fruit. The soil was fertile and the growing season was relatively long. However, Port Royal had one major locational handicap: it was cut off from the great expanse of the fur-trading country in the interior by the Bay of Fundy and the Appalachian Mountains. For this reason Port Royal did not prosper during the seventeenth century.

Champlain and de Monts soon recognized the locational disadvantages of Port Royal, obtained a charter from France to trade up the St. Lawrence River, and in 1608 established a fortified trading post at what is now Quebec City. From Quebec City the French moved toward the rich fur-trading region of the Great Lakes. Using the natural waterways for transportation, they kept pushing the fur-trading frontier farther and farther into the interior. By 1700 they had built trading posts and forts throughout the Great Lakes drainage basin and had established posts as far west as Fort William and Port Arthur (now Thunder Bay) on Lake Superior and as far south as the mouth of the Mississippi River. In the meantime, the British established fur-trading posts around Hudson and James Bay. Between the British and the French, by the end of the eighteenth century fur-trading posts had been established across the prairies and as far north as Lake Athabasca.

The fur traders did not encourage agricultural settlement because clearing the land for farming would be injurious to the fur-trading industry. Thus, the trading posts in the interior remained small settlements. Population growth resulting from the fur trade occurred at Montreal (founded in 1642). Favorably located at the head of navigation on the St. Lawrence River and at the mouth of the Ottawa River, it became the outfitting center for fur-trading ventures halfway across the continent. Quebec City was still the major ocean port and commercial center, as well as the seat of government. Thus, the exploitation of the staple fur had led to the growth of a couple of large urban centers in the heartland, whereas the hinterland, although supplying the resources, experienced little direct development and remained sparsely populated.

However, the fur trade did set the stage for further development of the interior. The principal waterways had been discovered and used for transportation. The nature of the terrain and climate of the different regions of Canada had been discovered. Agricultural crops had been successfully grown around many of the fur-trading posts. Perhaps most important, it had been discovered that the northern part of North America was of some use and that Europeans could live in it.

The fur trade also had political repercussions. When the English from the Thirteen Colonies started penetrating through the Appalachian Mountains, they found that the French had cut them off from the rich interior by building fur-trading forts along the Mississippi. The bitterness resulting from skirmishes there perhaps was partly responsible for French Canada's resisting later invasions by the United States. When French Canada fell to Britain in 1760, a British presence had been established all across the northern half of North America, thus providing resistance to the northward territorial expansion of the United States after it became independent in 1776. A series of boundary agreements that created most of the present border between Canada and the United States resulted from negotiations that reflected a compromise between American interest in agricultural settlement expansion and British interest (at least initially) in protecting the fur trade. It is interesting to conjecture how the settlement pattern of the northern portion of the continent would have evolved if the Americans had been free to expand into the area.

Forests. In the Atlantic region, forestry was a major growth industry in the nineteenth century. The timber trade was stimulated early in the century when the Napoleonic Wars cut off Britain's supply of wood from the Baltic countries. Additional markets were found in the United States and the West Indies. Lumbering and the accompanying sawmills and small settlements moved along the main rivers deep into the interior of the region. By the latter part of the century most of the softwood forest had been depleted, and there had been no concern for operations that would regenerate the forest resource. Much of the land was not good for agriculture, and thus there was not an alternative resource to help sustain any settlements that had been established. As with the development of the fishing resource, forestry tended to stimulate the growth of the larger port cities.

In the Great Lakes–St. Lawrence Lowlands, lumbering was a temporary economic activity that preceded farming. Lumbering itself had little effect on the settlement pattern. However, in the Canadian Shield, lumbering and the pulp and paper industry became the economic base for numerous towns along the major waterways and rail lines.

In British Columbia the forest industry did not develop until considerably after that of the rest of the country. The California market was closed to British Columbia by tariffs and competition from the states of Washington and Oregon. When markets did open up in the rest of Canada, the United States, and other parts of the world, the towering west coast trees were used first. A number of other small coastal towns developed on the basis of lumbering and pulp-and-paper plants. Forest products remain important export staples for Canada.

Minerals. Mining in Canada has not led to large concentrations of population at the sites of the mines. Instead, small mining towns have developed, and the creation of new, related secondary and tertiary jobs has occurred in one major city in a less remote area. Sudbury, Ontario, is the only city based primarily on mining that has grown to a population of more than fifty thousand. Many mining towns have suffered from the "boom-and-bust" syndrome. After the initial mineral discovery there is rapid growth as the new mines are developed. Then when construction is completed, the mineral is exhausted, or the world market slumps, the mines cut back production or close down, and the town's population declines or disappears completely. In some cases the transportation facilities built to the mining town makes it possible to diversify the economic base by exploiting forest resources or developing a tourist industry.

Mineral discoveries have added greatly to the economic development and growth of cities in southern Canada. The mineral processing, the manufacturing of metal goods, the making of mining equipment, and the provision of financial and other services have greatly stimulated the growth of Montreal, Toronto, and other southern Ontario cities, as well as Winnipeg, Edmonton, Calgary, and Vancouver.

The major growth impetus for Edmonton and Calgary came from the petroleum development in Alberta. The original major western oil and gas "finds" occurred quite near these cities. Ensuing discoveries in more distant places, even in the Arctic, have not led to the growth of new towns but have enhanced the growth of the two large cities. Edmonton and Calgary have been consolidating their predominant position in Alberta by attracting refining and petrochemical industries. It should be pointed out, however, that the urban growth resulting from petroleum development has not been restricted to Alberta. For example, the economy of Sarnia, Ontario, is primarily based on the oil-refining and petrochemical industry, using crude oil and natural gas piped from the West.

British Columbia owed its early settlement boom to the discovery of gold. This precious metal was found in the sand and gravel bars of the lower Fraser River in the 1850s. Within months, thousands of people, mostly from the United States, poured into British Columbia to "strike it rich." A new wave of people came when more gold was discovered in the Cariboo Mountains near the source of the Fraser River. Following the prospectors came merchants, auctioneers, real estate agents, bartenders, entertainers, and others. Everyone spent freely, and while some became rich, most went home penniless. About ten thousand of the newcomers remained as permanent settlers, many as farmers in the Fraser River Delta area.

In the interior of British Columbia it was lode gold, together with lead, zinc, and coal, that became the main economic support for settlement. A number of small mining towns were founded around the turn of this century, many of them later becoming ghost towns. Among those that survived and grew is Trail, on the Columbia River, where huge lead and zinc smelters are located.

Agricultural Land. In some parts of the country agricultural activity merely supplemented the early economic activities; in others, its product became the major export staple on which the economy was based and the settlement pattern determined.

In much of the Atlantic region agriculture has always been relatively unimportant, not the economic base for a dense settlement pattern. Most of the terrain is too rough and the soils too poor to support commercial agriculture. In some parts, particularly Newfoundland, the climate is also marginal. A great deal of the agricultural activity has always been marginal, often a part-time activity in combination with lumbering or fishing. The best agricultural land is found on the coastal lowlands and the major valleys. There are three major commercial agricultural areas: Prince Edward Island, the Annapolis Valley of Nova Scotia, and the St. John Valley of New Brunswick. In Prince Edward Island and the St. John Valley, potatoes are the major export staple; in the Annapolis Valley the specialty is apples. In these three areas there is the expected pattern of rural villages and towns to serve the agricultural community.

In the Great Lakes–St. Lawrence Lowlands, a combination of moderate climate, level terrain, and relatively fertile soils has led to intensive commercial agriculture throughout the region. Whenever the agricultural industry has pro-

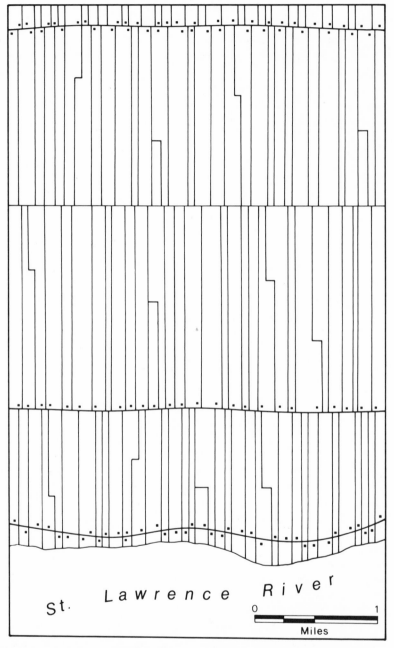

Figure 16. RANG SETTLEMENT PATTERNS IN QUEBEC, A HYPO-
THETICAL MODEL. (After C. Harris and J. Warkentin, *Canada Before
Confederation,* p. 74.) This pattern of long narrow farms with houses close
to one another and very close to the road can still be seen in rural Quebec.

gressed beyond the subsistence level, grain, livestock, dairy products, and apples were exported to Britain and the United States.

In the St. Lawrence Valley, the seigneurial system of landholding led to long lots stretching back from the river with the houses being built along the riverfront. Later houses were built along the roads that paralleled the river, and the long lots extended back from the roads. Each row of long lots became known as a *rang*. As the long lots were divided into smaller units, the farms became very narrow strips with long narrow fields. This resulted in the farmsteads being very close to one another, making the country roads look like a continuous village (Figure 16). To provide services to the farm community, villages grew up at intervals along the roads, usually beginning with a church. Some of the villages with an industrial base such as a sawmill or gristmill, or with a crossroads location, grew into towns and small cities.

In southern Ontario the whole area was divided into counties, and each county was divided into townships. Since the first counties were laid out along the lakeshores, the interior counties and townships became very irregularly shaped. The most common township survey used was that of concessions and lots that divided the land into equal-sized units of land of about one and one-quarter miles square (Figure 17). The original farms were approximately one hundred acres each, and the farmsteads were built along the concession roads. This resulted in farmsteads much farther apart from one another than in the French long-lot system.

In the southwestern part of Southern Ontario a very prosperous agricultural activity led to the establishment of numerous rural service villages and towns, each with a gristmill, a sawmill, a blacksmith shop, other farm service facilities, and commercial services. A railway system and a road network was built throughout the area to connect all of the settlement centers. Some of the earlier villages grew into towns and cities, and new villages and towns arose. Ultimately a central place pattern evolved with numerous villages, many towns, fewer cities and one major metropolis, Toronto. This central place pattern began on the basis of the agricultural

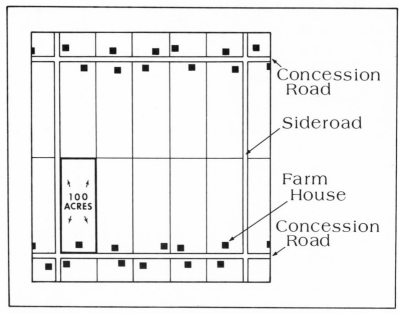

Figure 17. A COMMON SURVEY AND FARM PATTERN IN SOUTH-
ERN ONTARIO. The township concessions (areas between the concession
roads) were divided into blocks by sideroads. Each thousand-acre block was
divided into hundred-acre farms about two-and-a-half times as long as wide.
The farm houses and barns were built along the concession roads, usually
one or two hundred yards from the road.

economy, but soon manufacturing became an important part
of the economic base of the larger towns and cities. Economic
ties within the urban system is very intense.

There is some concern in Canada that urban growth is
now threatening the agricultural land base. Particularly
around the head of Lake Ontario from Oshawa to Niagara
Falls, urban growth is occupying tens of thousands of acres
of prime farmland and ruining tens of thousands more
through low-density urban sprawl. The orchard lands between
Toronto and Hamilton have now disappeared, and the famous
Niagara Fruit Belt seems to be heading in the same direction.
This is serious for Canada, because this is perhaps the best
fruit-growing region in the whole country. Although there is
room in the Niagara Region for both urban growth and fruit
production, effective regional planning may have come too

late to direct urban growth to the poorer land. A regional government with planning control over the whole Niagara Region has been established, in part to limit further urban intrusions into the best fruitland.

In the Prairie Provinces, the major agricultural export has traditionally been wheat. Between 1900 and 1930 the area of occupied farmland in the Prairie Provinces increased from 15 million to 110 million acres. In the same period wheat increased its share of total Canadian exports from less than 5 percent to 40 percent. The prosperous farmers required farm machinery and farm supplies. The wheat-growing boom led to the building of thousands of miles of railroads, which stimulated the production of rails, rolling stock, and building materials; this in turn created new employment, stimulating the economy and urban growth as far east as Toronto and Montreal.

With the exception of the long lots of the French settlers and the farm villages of the Mennonites in Manitoba, the farmland in the Prairie Provinces was divided into square blocks called townships, which measured six miles on each side. The townships were arranged in north-south rows called ranges. Each range and township was numbered for identification purposes, in contrast to Ontario where each county and township was given a name. Each township was divided into 36 one-square-mile units called sections. These sections were further divided into quarter sections of 160 acres each (Figure 18). Although roads were not built around every section, enough roads were built to make it possible to settle all of the land. In the late 1800s and early 1900s quarter sections were granted free to homesteaders. Every other section was given to the railroad company, and when settlers wanted more land they could buy it from the railway company. This was the government's unique way of helping to finance railroad construction. In a similar fashion two sections in each township were reserved as school lands, and when these sections were sold the proceeds could be used to build a school.

As soon as they could afford it, the settlers expanded their farm holdings until the average farm was at least one section (640 acres) in size. Since farming was more extensive than in

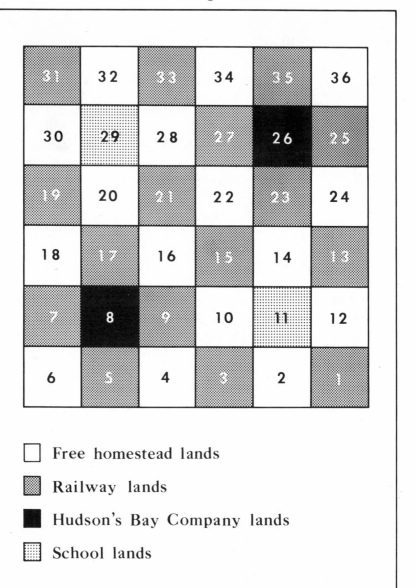

☐   Free homestead lands

▨   Railway lands

■   Hudson's Bay Company lands

▦   School lands

Figure 18. SUBDIVISION OF LAND WITHIN A TOWNSHIP IN THE PRAIRIE PROVINCES. Each township is 6 miles square and is divided into 36 one-square mile sections. Initially, quarter-sections were given to homesteaders, but they soon bought additional land from the railway company. The farms are much larger and the farmsteads much farther apart than in Southern Ontario.

Southern Ontario, the farm population was not as great, and as a result fewer and smaller central places developed. The settlement centers followed the trunk railroads and the many branch lines, since wheat and other crops could most easily be moved out of the region by rail. The major cities were established as railcar repair and maintenance centers. The significance of the railroads to Prairie settlement is illustrated by the fact that in the 1930s more than three quarters of all farmers lived within ten miles of a railway station.

By virtue of its location, Winnipeg became the "gateway" city of the West. In the early part of this century it was the wholesale center for the entire Prairie agricultural region. Around the time of World War I (1914–18) Calgary and Edmonton also began to function as gateways; Calgary to British Columbia and Edmonton to the Yukon and Northwest Territories. The rapid growth of these two cities, which was accelerated by the development of petroleum, rolled back the borders of Winnipeg's dominance over the Prairies.

Both Saskatoon and Regina in Saskatchwan were bypassed as gateway cities. They are primarily service cities, and because their hinterland is truncated on both sides by larger centers and they do not have comparative locational advantages for manufacturing, they have remained relatively small cities (slightly under 150,000 population).

Only 2 percent of British Columbia's land area is considered arable. Mountainous terrain and climate limits agricultural activity to few valleys in the interior, the Fraser Valley Delta area near Vancouver and a small peninsula north of Victoria on Vancouver Island. The most important interior valley is the Okanagan, where a variety of tree fruits (apples, peaches, apricots, cherries) and grapes are grown with the aid of irrigation. The Fraser Valley Delta produces a wide variety of crops and livestock, primarily for the Vancouver market. It cannot be said that agriculture was an engine of growth for British Columbia. However, the industry is the basis of a number of towns and villages in the southern valleys and does reduce the amount of food products that must be imported to the province.

Just as has happened around the head of Lake Ontario,

urban land uses in the Fraser Delta threatened many thousands of acres of prime farmland. In 1972 the British Columbia government passed special legislation to protect its remaining good agricultural land. All land with high potential for agriculture was set aside for farm use only. The government also passed an Income Assurance Act that provides guaranteed returns to farmers for products sold. Thus, the farmers whose land is frozen for agricultural use only are assured of being able to earn a reasonable living.

THE MANUFACTURING AND SERVICE INDUSTRIES

The development of staple resources helps explain the general expansion of Canadian settlement and urban growth, but it does not explain the emergence of an urban system in which is found about 80 percent of the Canadian population. The great urban expansion in Canada was dependent upon the manufacturing and service industries.

The location of manufacturing industry is dependent upon the availability of (1) raw materials including water, (2) power, (3) labor, (4) transportation facilities, (5) market, and (6) capital. Manufacturing firms tend to locate where these ingredients can be brought together most economically.

The Urban-Industrial Heartland The Great Lakes–St. Lawrence Lowlands region has become the urban-industrial heartland of Canada because of its locational advantages over other parts of the country. As noted, it has a wealth of forest, farm, and mineral resources, either within the region or in adjacent areas. The lakes and major rivers provide large volumes of water for industrial and domestic use and are also used to dilute industrial and human sewage. Niagara Falls, the rapid waters of the St. Lawrence River, and the rivers tumbling from the Canadian Shield provide it with significant amounts of relatively inexpensive hydroelectric power, which is supplemented by the thermoelectric power based on coal from the nearby U.S. Appalachian coalfields and on uranium from Elliot Lake in the Canadian Shield. The St. Lawrence River and the Great Lakes provide cheap water transport within the region and to foreign countries. Iron ore from the head of Lake Superior (Atikokan in Ontario and the Mesabi Range in Minnesota) and in the Labrador Trough on the Quebec-Labrador boundary can be transported by boat for most of the distance to the steel plants at Hamilton at the head of Lake Ontario. The steel industry has attracted many other manufacturing industries based on steel products, such as the farm machinery and the automobile industry. Industrialization has led to urbanization, and this in turn has created a large market and a large and diversified labor pool that attracts still more manufacturing. Close proximity to the highly urbanized manufacturing belt of the United States has provided both a market and a supply of capital. Many of the manufacturing companies in the region are branch plants of U.S. firms. Studies have shown that U.S. firms have a strong preference for locating in the region, particularly near Toronto.

In addition to all of these locational advantages, a number of federal government policies encouraged the growth of manufacturing in central Canada. The "National Policy," adopted in 1878, included high tariffs that greatly favored manufacturing in the region. The federal investment in the St. Lawrence Seaway in the 1950s provided an invaluable transportation asset. The 1965 Auto Pact with the United States greatly stimulated that industry, unfortunately only in the short run.

Thus, it is not surprising that the Great Lakes–St. Lawrence Lowlands account for about three quarters of the country's total manufacturing employment. Together, the two largest cities of Montreal and Toronto account for more than one third of Canada's manufacturing production.

Although the original engine of growth of the Canadian urban system was the development of export staples (primary industry)—and manufacturing (secondary industry) reinforced this growth in certain strategically located areas—it is the service activities (tertiary industry) that have shown an almost explosive growth in the largest centers within the last decade. The tertiary industry includes a wide array of governmental, institutional, commercial, and personal services. Once a city reaches a certain size it attracts more specialized services: these services create employment in themselves, but they also attract more manufacturing and commercial enterprises, including the head offices of national firms. Thus, there is a "snowball" or "ratchet" effect. Growth begets growth. Ultimately, the largest metropolis grows so large that there is spillover growth that accrues to the surrounding next-order size of cities, and their growth in turn stimulates growth in the surrounding smaller centers. There is a great flow of people, goods, and services within this urban network.

Nowhere is the growth phenomenon described above as evident as in the urban axis running from Windsor to Quebec City. The urban dominance of this region is so great that one Canadian geographer has termed it "Main Street."

Within the region, the urban system is most highly developed in southwestern Ontario. Metropolitan Toronto has grown at an incredibly rapid rate until in 1976 it became the largest metropolis in the county. Major urban renewal projects and a balanced public transit system (including a subway) and expressway system have kept the central part of the city dynamic and prosperous. A two-tier form of metropolitan government links the economies of the continuous suburban communities to the central city and provides overall control of such essential services as land-use planning, water supply, sewage facilities, education, and police and fire protection. The adjacent steel center of Hamilton and the automobile center of Oshawa are connected to Toronto by fast commuter rail service. The next ring of middle sized cities (Niagara Falls, St. Catharines, Brantford, Guelph, Kitchener-Waterloo, Cambridge, and Barrie) are linked to Toronto by rail and major highways. All of them are experiencing spillover growth from Toronto, and some of them have reached a size where the snowball effect is taking place and they are generating their own growth (Figure 19). London, which is just beyond a hundred-mile radius of Toronto, is not as greatly affected by Toronto but has become an important central place for a large region of excellent farmland and numerous rural service centers and has developed diversified manufacturing and service industries. The economy of the two cities at the wes-

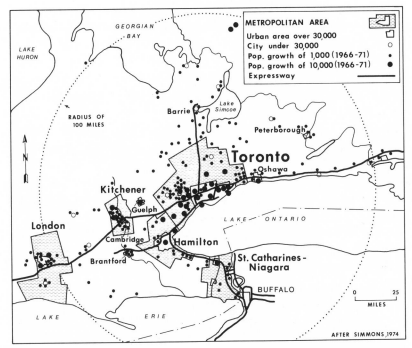

Figure 19. URBAN GROWTH WITHIN A HUNDRED MILES OF TO-RONTO (after J. Simmons and R. Simmons, Urban Canada, p. 61.)

tern end of the urban corridor is primarily single function—automobile manufacturing in the case of Windsor, the manufacture of petroleum and petrochemical products in the case of Sarnia.

For reasons difficult to explain, urban growth has not been as great east of Toronto. Between Oshawa and the Quebec border there are no cities with a population of more than 100,000 and only two (Peterborough and Kingston) more than 50,000. To the north and east, Ottawa has become a large city primarily because it is the national capital.

In the St. Lawrence Valley portion of the region the two cities of Montreal and Quebec City dominate the urban scene. The centers outside these two cities have not grown to the same extent as has happened in southwestern Ontario.

Outside of the urban-industrial heartland only Vancouver (population over 1 million) has reached the size where its growth impetus has become self-sustaining, and its economic influence has spread for hundreds of miles.

METROPOLITAN DOMINANCE

Some urban geographers have predicted that ultimately Toronto will dominate all of Canada via high-order nation-serving functions, while Montreal will dominate the eastern part of the country, including the Atlantic Provinces, and Vancouver will dominate the West. The Montreal sphere of influence will likely extend eastward from approximately the Ontario-Quebec border, and that of Vancouver will extend from the west coast to the middle of Saskatchewan.

If the urban growth trends of the 1960s were to continue, by the year 2000 Toronto would have close to 6 million people, Montreal more than 5 million, and Vancouver more than 2 million. Almost three quarters of all Canadians would live in the largest twelve cities (Figure 20). As a result of this concentrated growth we might expect increased productivity, increased ranges of services, a rising standard of living, and the continued development of advanced technology, all of which would stimulate the national economy. However, on the negative side (as is observable in the United States), social and environmental problems escalate in huge cities. Perhaps, even in economic terms, there is a size beyond which a city cannot provide services efficiently. Moreover, if the major portion of the nation's growth occurred in the major urban-centered regions, the smaller centers remote from large cities would likely suffer from a decline in income, employment opportunities, education, and quality of municipal services. Thus, such a pattern of development would exacerbate the problem of regional disparities in the country.

Predictions of this nature notwithstanding, there are recent indications that the growth rates of larger metropolitan areas have begun to decline. Between 1971 and 1976 nearly one half of Canada's census metropolitan areas grew more slowly than the national average. The growth rates of Toronto and Vancouver declined during this period, and Montreal registered no growth at all. Growth rates were highest among

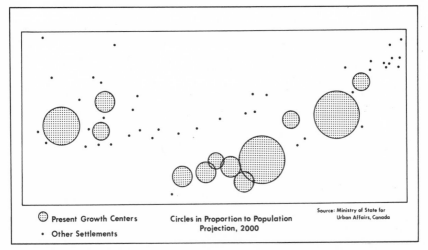

Present Growth Centers   Circles in Proportion to Population

• Other Settlements   Projection, 2000

Figure 20. DIAGRAMMATIC PATTERN OF FUTURE URBANIZATION BASED ON PRESENT TRENDS. By the year 2000, almost three-quarters of all Canadians will live in the twelve growth centers shown here. Can you name each center?

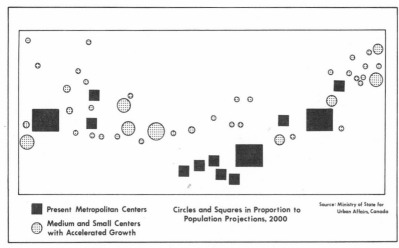

Present Metropolitan Centers   Circles and Squares in Proportion to
Population Projections, 2000
Medium and Small Centers
with Accelerated Growth

Figure 21. DIAGRAMMATIC PATTERN OF FUTURE URBANIZATION BASED ON RECENT TRENDS AND GOVERNMENT POLICY. If recent trends (1971–76) continue and government regional development programs are successful, the growth of existing metropolitan centers would slow down and smaller centers would have accelerated growth, resulting in a more balanced urban pattern by the year 2000. With the help of an atlas, identify the medium and small centers. Which of these had a population of over 100,000 in 1976? (See Table 1.)

the medium-sized cities such as Victoria, Edmonton, Calgary, Kitchener-Waterloo, and Oshawa. Thus, the prediction of the constantly increasing dominance of Toronto, Montreal, and Vancouver may not materialize, and a more balanced distribution of urbanization may occur (Figure 21). Slower growth in the largest cities and increased growth in the smaller cities and towns would help to alleviate many big-city problems and at the same time contribute to the improvement of the lagging economy of some of the hinterland areas. For these reasons, both the federal and the provincial governments have developed policies and programs aimed at encouraging this more balanced urban pattern.

Regions, Regionalism, and Regional Disparities

GEOGRAPHICAL REGIONS
A region is a relatively homogeneous area that is distinctively different from the areas around it. Regions can be defined on the basis of one or more criteria.

Dividing a country into single-factor regions is relatively simple. For example, the physiographic regions (Figure 7) are based upon the composition and structure of landforms, and the natural vegetation regions (Figure 13) are based on the nature of the plant communities. It is more difficult to draw the boundaries of natural regions in which several natural environmental factors combine to give natural unity to certain areas. For example, the Canadian Shield has a characteristically common physiography throughout, but the climate and natural vegetation vary greatly.

Regions based upon natural environmental factors are not adequate for the purposes of geographical description and analysis because geography is concerned with the study of the earth *as the home of man*. True geographic regions must be based upon a blending of natural environmental factors and human activities. This makes the task of "regionalizing" much more difficult. In some cases the dominating factors in delimiting and characterizing the region may be some aspects of

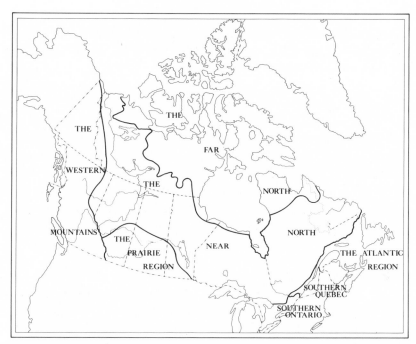

Figure 22. GEOGRAPHICAL REGIONS OF CANADA. What criteria was used to determine the boundaries of these regions? Was the same criteria used for all regions?

the natural environment; in others, it may be the economic activities of man or the way in which he has changed the environment. The boundary lines between geographic regions are often not sharp lines but broad transition zones. Some geographers claim that geographical regions are merely intellectual constructs to assist geographers in dividing a country into manageable units for the purpose of study.

Because of the elusiveness of the concept of geographical region, it is not surprising that different geographers have divided Canada into different sets of geographical regions. One attempt is provided in Figure 22.

There is insufficient space in this chapter for a comprehensive geographical description and analysis of these regions; the "Annotated Bibliography" for this chapter cites several books in which such can be found. Instead, a few key words and phrases that help to characterize each region will be provided. This summary overgeneralizes, does not do justice to the diversity within each region, and may lead to false stereotyping, but it may help to form some mental images of Canada's geographical regions and how they differ from one another.

The Atlantic Region: forested hills and low mountains; rocky shorelines, sheltered coves, isolated fishing villages; ocean fog, port cities, and shipbuilding; Prince Edward Island potatoes and Annapolis Valley apples; French-speaking people in northeastern New Brunswick and the Gaspé Peninsula; below-average incomes. (Note: although the Gaspé Peninsula is part of the Province of Quebec, it is included in the Atlantic Region on the basis of landforms, resources, economic activities, and general standard of living.) Recent oil finds.

Southern Quebec: the St. Lawrence River and Seaway; long strip farms on the St. Lawrence Lowlands; French the predominant language, Roman Catholicism the predominant religion; distinctive culture, language, and heritage; villages and towns visually dominated by large churches with tall steeples; economy dominated by one large city, Montreal.

Southern Ontario: Great Lakes, moderate climate, rich farmlands; complex urban system dominated by Toronto; wide range of manufacturing industries; wealthiest region in Canada. (The above two regions are often considered as one region, the Great Lakes–St. Lawrence Lowlands. They have been separated here on the basis of history, language, and culture.)

The Prairie Region: broad-sweeping plains; continental climate with cold winters, hot summers and little precipitation; grain growing and cattle ranching; large farms; oil, natural gas and potash.

The Western Mountains: scenic snow-clad mountain ranges; wet coast and dry interior valleys; restricted farmland, Okanagan apples; salmon fishing, forestry, and mining; three quarters of population in southwestern corner around one major metropolis, Vancouver.

The Near North: long cold winters, short summers; coniferous forest, minerals, hydroelectric power sites; sparsely populated with vast unsettled areas; resource-based towns near southern edge; native land claims conflict with pressures for development.

The Far North: long harsh winters with very short days and short cool summers with very long days ("land of the midnight sun"); permafrost and tundra; Inuit still making part of living from the land; oil and natural gas discovered.

REGIONALISM

Canada is a very large country with great regional diversity in terms of natural environment, land-use patterns, economic activities, and cultural traits. This regional diversity enriches the Canadian nation both economically and culturally, but the intensity of the differences, reinforced by great distances and physiographic barriers, also has a divisive effect.

Inhabitants of certain regions develop a deep attachment to the land, the people, and the institutions of their region. This identification with a particular region can be termed "regional consciousness." The term "regionalism" is used to describe a state of affairs wherein regional consciousness takes political expression with regions vying with one another and with the central government for certain economic or cultural advantages. To a certain degree regionalism in a large country can be healthy, because it enriches a sense of identity on a smaller and more meaningful scale, and it encourages interregional dialogue and competition. However, in an extreme form (sometimes called sectionalism), the regional interests become paramount despite any negative impact on the nation as a whole. If followed to its logical conclusion, sectionalism could lead to separatism. When separatism is espoused as a political philososphy, it means that the regions

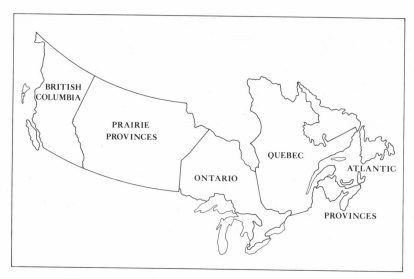

Figure 23. REGIONAL GROUPS OF PROVINCES.

concerned aspire to become separate national states, thus breaking up the original unified nation.

Regionalism has always been an important issue in Canada. Canada was created by joining together a group of separate colonies, some of which have had a longer existence as individual entities than as part of a united country. Confederation did not solve all of the intercolonial differences. In fact, it has been perceived by some that the various national policies have widened the gap between the regions.

(In discussing regionalism in this context, reference is made to regional groups of provinces as shown in Figure 23. Although not geographically as correct as the "physical" regions shown in Figure 21, these regions are more realistic because they represent the political blocs involved. The Yukon and the Northwest Territories are not included.)

Economic disparity and resulting inequity are perhaps the most important underlying reasons for the strength of regionalism in Canada:

In Canada, the physical immensity of the country, the presence of distinct geographic barriers, a narrow, uneven chain of settlement, and a striking diversity of resources and economic structure among our major regions all make for a particularly high degree of regional differentiation. The problem of integration and balance, to assure appropriate participation of each region in the overall process of national economic development, has been an elusive goal and a continuing concern.[2]

Subsequent chapters in this book deal in considerable detail with the problems faced by the people of the various regions of Canada, both historically and at present. Nevertheless, some brief characterization of the nature of these people will not be amiss here.

The people of the Atlantic Provinces, with the longest settlement history, are a relatively homogeneous group, albeit traditional French Acadian-English bitterness persists. Perhaps they are united in their feelings that they were shortchanged by Confederation and by their jealousy of the dominance of Ontario and Quebec in the nation. They feel strongly about the superiority of their less urbanized and "slower" way of life.

Quebec is, culturally and linguistically, predominantly French. Many of the French-speaking, or francophone, Canadians support the concept of a Quebec "nation"—a word that in French refers more to a cultural or social unit than to a political one. This feeling, often both emotional and intellectual in origin, competes with other sentimental and practical attachments to Canada. Many Francophones also feel that they have not been able to participate equally in economic affairs in Quebec and elsewhere.

Ontario, the wealthiest of the provinces, seems to be the most satisfied with its role within Confederation. Although it has had settlers from many different countries (mostly European), it has traditionally maintained a definite British air. There is relatively strong support for the monarchy; the provincial flag has the Union Jack prominently in the upper left corner; and many are proud to be able to trace their ancestors back to the United Empire Loyalists (in the United States, called Tories) who fled to what was then Upper Canada during and after the American Revolution. Heavy immigration and massive urbanization, however, have recently introduced a more marked cosmopolitanism. Residents of Ontario are aware of the importance of Ontario to the Canadian nation and feel that what is good for Ontario is good for Canada.

The Prairie Provinces, with a much shorter settlement history, have an only partially blended culture. Nevertheless, there is a distinctive Prairie regional identity. Like those who live in the Atlantic Provinces, Prairie westerners may feel that national policies usually favor central Canada at their expense. For a variety of reasons, mostly economic in nature, Saskatchewan and Alberta have become aggressive spokesmen in favor of change in this regard. Politically and historically, the regional identity has been demonstrated by the number and strength of western-based, new political parties that have successfully challenged the two traditional parties.

British Columbia, because of its remoteness from much of the rest of Canada, a remoteness reinforced by mountain barriers, has developed a strong regional identity. The people of British Columbia have not felt as "hard-done-by" by national policies, but they do feel a greater affinity for the neighboring states than the distant provinces of eastern Canada. For many of the same reasons it shares, with California, for example, a sense of being different and independent in its interests.

REGIONAL DISPARITIES
Regional disparities of all kinds are widely regarded as serious threats to Canada's integrity:

> The economic prospects of Canadians of certain regions remain more limited than those of people in other regions. If the Canada of the Second Century is to serve the legitimate aims and aspirations of its people, our objective must be to make equality of opportunity real and meaningful. Only through that sense of equality—equality in the opportunities open to all Canadians, whatever their language or cultural heritage, and wherever they may choose to live or move—can we give a purpose to Canada that will meet the proper expectations of our people. And only through measures that will carry this conviction— that we intend to make equality of opportunity an achievement as well as a goal—can we preserve the unity of the country.[3]

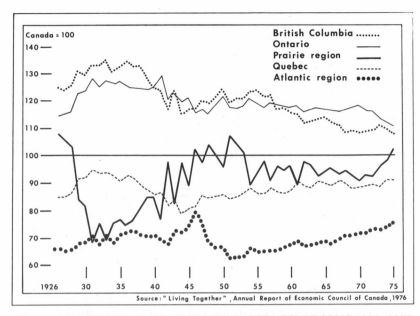

Figure 24. PERSONAL INCOME PER CAPITA BY REGION 1926–1975 (after Economic Council of Canada, *Living Together,* 1977, p. 35). Personal income per capita includes wages and salaries, interest income, welfare payments, pensions and other federal government transfer payments. Regional disparities in income have been persistent in Canada. However there has been a slow convergence since 1955 and an even more pronounced narrowing of the gap since the DREE programs began in 1969. The high variability of income for the Prairie Provinces reflects that region's independence on wheat for export. World wheat prices fluctuate greatly and the amount of production is dependent on the weather. Note the low Prairie income in the early thirties due to the Great Depression and serious drought.

And:

If the underdevelopment of the Atlantic Provinces is not corrected—not by charity or subsidies but by helping them become areas of economic growth—then the unity of the country is almost as surely destroyed as it would be by the French-English confrontation.[4]

Regional disparities as indicated by personal income have persisted for a long time in Canada (Figure 24). Although there has been a general convergence of regional personal incomes over the years, the gap between the richest and poorest regions remain significant.

Income statistics are just a general indicator of regional disparities. The Atlantic Region not only has the lowest per capita income but also has the highest unemployment rate (from 8 to 12 percent since 1970) and the largest proportion of people living in poverty (approximately one third are below the "poverty line"). This means that a substantial portion of the people have a standard of living deemed unacceptable by Canadian society. These economic indicators do not measure the social disadvantages and the mental anguish associated with poverty. Moreover, the income data by region mask the great differences in prosperity within these broad geographical areas.

Some of the reason for persistent regional disparities in Canada can be found in the physical and settlement geography as described previously. Disparities means differences. There are differences in prosperity, not only because some parts of the country have had a relatively stagnant economic growth, but because other parts have had dynamic economic development. Thus, such geographical factors as natural transportation corridors, available natural resources, the pattern of staple resource exploitation, and comparative locational advantage for secondary industry have all been important. Since the employment-generating manufacturing and service industries are attracted to large urban centers, a snowball effect is created and the urbanized heartland continues to grow (and become prosperous) at the expense of the more rural and natural-resource-based hinterland. A succinct explanation for the persistence of this "heartland-hinterland" pattern of development is given by a Canadian geographer:

> Continued and self-sustaining growth depends on a region attaining the threshold size for the internal production of a wide range of goods and services and achieving the associated economies of scale. The region with the greatest initial advantages and achieving sustained growth becomes the economic center or heartland. Centripetal forces are set in motion and leadership in finance, education, research and planning are added to the initial advantages of this heartland. Secondary manu-

facturing and service activity gravitate toward the centre leaving hinterland areas reliant on primary industries which tend to play a diminishing role in national economies. Heartland-hinterland contrasts in regional development are sharpened by the concentration of corporation head offices and the lower interest rates for capital at the centre. The location of corporate control probably influences regional development, decisions made regarding production, sales and research may be strongly influenced by where the key decision-makers live. Likewise, the concentration of corporate offices at the centre of a national territory incurs a flow of corporate profits from the hinterland to the centre and creates an underlying shortage of capital in the hinterland.[5]

This heartland-hinterland theory helps to explain the concentration of wealth in the highly urbanized Windsor to Quebec City corridor. Because of a more widely spread and more integrated urban system in Southern Ontario, the spread effects have been much greater there than in Quebec. A great deal of even the southern portions of Quebec fall within the hinterland category, and thus it does not have as high an income level as one might expect. On the other hand, Vancouver is a secondary heartland of Canada, and since such a large proportion of the province's people live in that metropolis, the average provincial income is considerably above the national average.

It has been argued that, over the years, general government policy has tended to reinforce the geographical factors underlying regional disparities. The National Policy on tariffs following Confederation favored central Canada by protecting its young manufacturing industry. As a result of the protective tariff, both eastern and western Canada have had to pay higher prices for manufactured goods, while their producers of mainly raw or semiprocessed raw materials sell abroad at competitive world prices. Federal government investment in the St. Lawrence Seaway gave advantages to Toronto and Montreal at the expense of Atlantic port cities. During the two World Wars, the bulk of federal government war contracts was given to industries in central Canada, which could quickly gear up to produce war equipment and munitions.

Federal government monetary and fiscal policies may also have tended to discriminate against the less prosperous regions. For example, tight money policies aimed at fighting inflation may slow economic growth and create more severe unemployment in the poorer provinces than in the prosperous ones.

To counter the factors that seemed to encourage regional disparities, the federal government has evolved a number of programs aimed at shoring up the economies of the more depressed regions. Special freight rates have been in effect for many years to subsidize the movement of Prairie grain and the movement of all goods within the Atlantic Region. Subsidies to primary industries have been aimed at stimulating the economy of the hinterland. National social and welfare programs such as universal family allowances and old age pensions, the Canada Pension Plan, unemployment insurance, and manpower training programs have had the greatest impact on the poorer regions of the country. Federal-provincial tax-sharing agreements have resulted in transfer of tax money from the "have" to the "have-not" provinces. Incentives have been given to industries to locate in areas of high unemployment.

Nevertheless, by the late 1960s it was obvious that the income gap between regions was narrowing only very slowly. The many programs to combat disparities had evolved on a piecemeal basis and showed lack of coordination. Actions of different government departments often seemed to run contrary to one another. As a result, in 1969 the federal government established a new Department of Regional Economic Expansion (DREE). This department was given a mandate to coordinate all existing regional development programs and all other programs of government departments that had a bearing on regional development. A new emphasis was to provide subsidies to companies that would locate in growth poles within the depressed regions. This was a reversal of previous policies that tried to attract industry to places with locational disadvantages, high unemployment, and little record of growth. The assumption of the new policy is that investment should be made in the major centers with growth potential in the slow-growth regions; that these growth poles can become engines of growth; and that there will be economic spread effects throughout the surrounding smaller cities and towns, thus stimulating the economy and creating jobs across the whole region.

It is too early to make a definitive evaluation of such efforts. There was a measurable narrowing of the regional income gap between 1970 and 1975. However, much remains to be accomplished. There are few signs as yet that growth poles in the Atlantic Provinces are going to "take off" and have the same impact on the economy of the surrounding area as Toronto has had on Southern Ontario.

Some critics claim that the large amounts of money spent on regional subsidies and regional development programs are poor investments; that the poor regions are poor because they lack either adequate resources or have a disadvantageous location. Therefore, we should not try to buoy up their economy but should let the people move to where jobs are available. Others argue that regional development programs are in the long-run interest of the whole nation; that both the social and economic costs of subsidizing interregional migration would be greater than regional development costs; that even moderate success in regional development programs could add substantially to the gross national product and at the same time reduce the increasing assistance and transfer payments to the have-not provinces.

Finally, it can be argued that failure to be, and to be seen to be, equitable in assuring access to the country's wealth and resources will strain the political fabric. Most Canadians would agree that the cost of such assurance is not too great if reducing regional disparities improves the quality of life of a significant number of Canadians and helps to preserve Canada as a unified nation.

This remains the fundamental challenge that Canada's geography presents to Canadian citizens. The perspective of the geographer therefore is an essential introduction to an understanding of Canada.

List of Figures

Notes

1. James and Robert Simmons, *Urban Canada*, 2d ed. (Toronto: Copp Clark, 1974), p. 203.

2. *Towards Sustained Economic Growth*, Second Annual Review of the Economic Council of Canada, as reprinted in R. M. Irving, ed., *Readings in Canadian Geography*, rev. ed. (Toronto and Montreal: Holt, Rinehart and Winston, 1972), p. 262.

3. L. B. Pearson (former Prime Minister of Canada), *Federalism for the Future* (Ottawa: Queen's Printer, 1968), as quoted in *The Atlantic Economy*, Fifth Annual Review Atlantic Provinces Economic Council, 1971, p. 15.

4. Jean Marchand (former Minister of the federal Department of Regional Eco-

nomic Expansion), "A New Policy for Regional Development," an address to Atlantic Conference 1968, as quoted in *The Atlantic Economy*, Fifth Annual Review, p. 15.

5. D. M. Ray, *Dimensions of Canadian Regionalism,* Geographical Paper No. 49 (Ottawa: Department of Energy, Mines and Resources, 1971). In this book, Ray uses a number of statistical and cartographical devices to measure the heartland-hinterland differences.

Chapter 2

A Historical Perspective:

The Evolution of a Nation

GERALD M. CRAIG*

Introduction

THERE HAVE ALWAYS been two distinct, and separate, schools of Canadian historical writing, one in the English language and one in the French language, and the concerns and interpretative approaches of each have normally been quite different from one another.

English-language historians in the early twentieth century saw Canada as a self-governing Dominion in the British Empire/Commonwealth. Although they were, of course, interested in early exploration and settlement, for them the most significant theme in Canadian history was the transfer of British political, legal, and constitutional institutions and customs to North America and their adaptation to Canadian conditions. The most influential histories of this period stressed the development of self-government, of liberty under law. By the 1930s and 1940s an interest in economic history

* G. M. Craig is Professor of History at the University of Toronto, where his teaching responsibilities have been mainly in the field of American history and, to a lesser extent, in Canadian history. He has also taught American and Canadian history at the University of Colorado and at the University of Maine. Among his publications are *Upper Canada: The Formative Years, 1784–1841* (1963) and *The United States and Canada* (1968).

began to replace the earlier emphasis on constitutional history. The fur trade, the fisheries, the mining and forest industries, and railway building were all studied intensively. Later, in the 1950s, attention shifted to the emergence of distinctively Canadian political traditions, especially as seen through the biographies of outstanding figures such as Sir John A. Macdonald and George Brown. More recently, the focus has shifted again, to urban history, to social history, to the history of women, of the West, and so on.

Canadian historical writing in the French language has concentrated almost entirely on French-Canadian themes and only rarely on the larger Canadian scene. In earlier years two themes predominated. First and foremost was the history of the French regime; few Quebec historians were much interested in the years after 1760. Those who were interested in the post-Conquest years tended to stress the way in which French Canadians had retained their identity while adapting themselves to British political institutions. In the 1920s and after, French-Canadian historical writing became more "nationalistic"; that is, it tended to stress the animosities and antagonisms between English-speaking and French-speaking Canadians, and to emphasize the grievances of the latter, suffered at the hands of the former. Still more recently, younger Québécois historians, while not neglecting the French regime, have increasingly turned to detailed social and economic studies of the post-Conquest years, but still limiting themselves essentially to Quebec themes.

Although their concerns are often different, anglophone and francophone historians share a common interest in writing accurate history based on thorough research. The new stress on social and economic history may break down some of the barriers that have existed in the past between the two language groups. But as long as there is disagreement and uncertainty about the political and constitutional present and future of Canadians, there will be differences in the questions asked of the past by historians.

There are many approaches to history: political, constitutional, social, economic, cultural, and so on. Techniques vary according to the kind of historical writing being attempted. Ancient coins, medieval chronicles, and modern census statistics are only obvious examples of the hundreds of kinds of evidence that a historian can use. In recent years social and economic historians have paid particular attention to the use of the computer for organizing vast masses of material.

The scale of historical writing also varies enormously. Some historians have sought to deal with the whole of world history in a few hundred pages. Others have written hundreds or even thousands of pages on the events of a brief period; for instance, or the origins of the American Revolution or on the outbreak of World War I.

Whatever the kind of history and whatever the scale, all attempts at historical writing usually have two characteristics in common. First, they are concerned with chronology, that is, with movement and change (of whatever kind) over a period of time. Second, historical writing should be more than just a list of dates or a chronicle of events; it seeks to explain how and why events occurred. Accordingly, this chapter seeks to explain how Canada came into being by looking at the evolution of its past. Since the treatment is extremely brief, only some highlights can be mentioned. And since historical writing always has chronology in mind, it is helpful to examine Canada's history in terms of these four periods:

(1) Two centuries of struggle ending in 1818, which resulted in the survival of British North America (comprising the nucleus of what is now Canada) as a separate entity from the United States;

(2) A half century of growth and development in the British North American colonies, which culminated in the establishment of the transcontinental Canadian Confederation (1818–73);

(3) A seventy-year period, which witnessed the maturing of the self-governing Dominion of Canada within the British Empire/Commonwealth (1873–1945);

(4) And, last, the modern era (1945–77), which has seen Canada play its independent role on the world stage as a major industrialized nation.

Colonial Beginnings to 1818

The northern half of the North American continent attracted human activity many hundreds—even thousands—of years before anyone dreamt of the possibility of a Canadian nation. In very early times (twelve thousand or more years ago) the men and women who we have usually called Indians and Eskimos began coming across the narrow Bering Strait from northern Asia and gradually spread across and down the whole of the Western Hemisphere. These people developed societies based on hunting, fishing, and eventually in some instances on agriculture.

The approach to the continent from the northeast came much later. About a thousand years ago, Viking (or Norse) sailors from Northern Europe were reaching out to Greenland and then the eastern coast of North America. By the end of the fifteenth century the maritime countries of Western Europe—Spain, Portugal, England, and France—were ready to strike directly across the Atlantic Ocean in an effort to control and to exploit the resources of the Western Hemisphere. In our attempt to understand the origins and the distinctive characteristics of Canada, we must focus on the long-standing rivalry between England and France.

For more than a century European activity was devoted mainly to voyages of discovery; to unsuccessful attempts to establish settlements; and above all, to fishing for cod. John Cabot reached land at either Newfoundland or Cape Breton Island in 1497 and 1498 and claimed the east coast for England. Verrazano sailed along the New York and New England coasts under French colors in 1524. Of particular importance in Canadian history were the French-sponsored voyages of Jacques Cartier (1534, 1535–36, 1541), especially the second one, which brought him around Newfoundland into the Gulf of St. Lawrence and then to the site of the present city of Quebec. Further geographic knowledge of the continent was acquired by Sir Francis Drake's voyage up the Pacific Coast (1579) and by various early attempts to find the "Northwest Passage," culminating in Henry Hudson's journey (1610–11) into the bay that bears his name.

By this time the French and the English had established their first permanent settlements in North America—Port Royal in Nova Scotia, Quebec on the St. Lawrence, and Jamestown in Virginia. Within another hundred years English colonies stretched along the Atlantic Coast from Massachusetts in the north to the Carolinas in the south. The French established settlements in Acadia (Nova Scotia) and along the St. Lawrence to Montreal; they sent explorers and fur traders far into the interior to claim the upper Great Lakes and the whole of the Mississippi Valley (under the name Louisiana) for France.

From the start the English and the French were rivals for the control of North America. Wars, declared and undeclared, were waged for a century and a half, by regular soldiers and sailors from Europe, by militia from the various colonies, and by Indians enlisted as allies. The two sides fought on Hudson Bay (where the Hudson's Bay Company, chartered by England in 1670, had established control), in Nova Scotia, on the New England frontier, in the Ohio Valley, and in the Carolina back country. After a century of struggle, ending in the Treaty of Utrecht in 1713, the English had forced the French out of the Hudson Bay region, Newfoundland, and had acquired a title to most of present-day Nova Scotia; but the French remained in Acadia as British subjects, and were still firmly entrenched along the St. Lawrence and in the interior. The boundaries between English-held and French-held territories were often vague and disputed.

In the next half century (1713–63) the conflict entered its decisive stage. For the first half of the period there was a peaceful interlude between the wars, a time for growth and consolidation. The English colonies were, to a remarkable degree, self-governing provinces within the British Empire. Their populations grew with great rapidity, far outnumbering the inhabitants of New France along the St. Lawrence. The English colonists (or the Americans, as they can begin to be called) were also relatively prosperous, with increasingly diversified economies and wide trading interests in the Atlantic world. But as thirteen separate colonies, each with a rather parochial outlook, they were poorly organized for waging war against their antagonists to the north, who can now begin to be called Canadians.

As for the latter, in the years approaching the mid-eighteenth century, they were relatively few in numbers: at sixty thousand in 1760, they numbered less than 10 percent of the population of the American colonies. But they were remarkably homogeneous, born in New France for the most part, and firmly established in the St. Lawrence Valley. Beyond the settled region, French and Canadian enterprise had developed a far-flung fur-trading empire, which reached into the prairies beyond the Red River and which in some degree prefigured the transcontinental Canadian economy of a later date. New France was under one government, and thus could mobilize its resources more effectively than could the English and the Americans to the south.

When hostilities resumed in the 1740s, the New Englanders did have one great success; an expeditionary force from Massachusetts compelled surrender of the great French fortress of Louisbourg (on Cape Breton Island); they were greatly disappointed, however, when the peace treaty of 1748 returned Louisbourg to the French.

The last phase of the conflict began in the 1750s in the Ohio Valley. The French regarded control of this region as essential, both for organizing the western fur trade and for maintaining communications between their empire in Canada and their empire in Louisiana. But colonists in Virginia and Pennsylvania were also becoming increasingly interested in land settlement and land speculation schemes in the valley. Soon Virginia and Canada were at war on the Ohio, even though France and England were at peace in Europe.

The conflict quickly broadened, however, when the two mother countries went to war. In Europe it was called the Seven Years' War; in the American colonies, the French and Indian War. In the first years of the struggle the French, better organized and more experienced in forest fighting, had several successes in the interior. In 1755 a panicky Nova Scotian government forcibly expelled most of that colony's Acadian population. The tide began to turn, however, after William Pitt became the British war minister. Louisbourg was again forced to surrender, and French forts along the Ohio, on the Great Lakes, and on Lake Champlain were taken. Most decisive, a British fleet and army entered the St. Lawrence in the summer of 1759 and laid siege to the city of Quebec. On September 13 the British commander, Gen. James Wolfe, succeeded in putting his army ashore on the Plains of Abraham, a plateau upriver from the city. The French commander, the marquis de Montcalm, ordered his troops out from behind their fortifications and engaged the British army in battle. The French were routed and both generals were killed. Another year of fighting confirmed the French defeat in North America.

By the peace treaty of 1763, France ceded to Great Britain all claims to Acadia, Cape Breton, Canada, and all territory east of the Mississippi. Spain succeeded to French claims west of the Mississippi, while Great Britain acquired Florida. Thus, after a century and a half of arduous effort to build New France in North America, to Christianize the Indians, and to explore the remote reaches of the continent, French power was forced to retreat. By contrast, the British saw their moment of greatest glory. The Union Jack was entitled to wave from the southern tip of Florida to the frozen wastes of the Arctic. Everything east of the Mississippi and far into the northwest was now British territory. It was a triumph the American colonists fully shared. They rejoiced in the end of French power and looked forward to a vast future on the continent.

For the British authorities in London, however, victory in North America gave rise to an almost bewildering number of difficult and even embarrassing problems. British inability to find adequate answers to these problems through the next twenty years (the 1760s and 1770s) led to the growth of an American nation and to developments that would eventually make possible a Canadian Confederation. This period is, therefore, in many ways the most important in the history of these two North American countries.

One obvious problem for the British in their greatly enlarged empire was to find a policy for dealing with the sixty-five thousand settlers—*les Canadiens*—who lived along the shores of the St. Lawrence River. Some of the leading figures among them returned to France after "the Conquest" (as it is always called in Canadian history), but the great majority of the Canadians remained in their homeland. By treaty, they were now British subjects, residents of a province of the British Empire, the Province of Quebec. By the Proclamation of 1763 (which defined the boundaries of the Province of Quebec) it appeared that Quebec was to be made into a colony like the American colonies to the south. It was to be ruled by a governor, an appointed council, and an elected assembly. No attempt was made to interfere with the free exercise of the Roman Catholic religion; however, since British law prevented Roman Catholics from holding office, it was evident that the king's "new subjects," the Roman Catholic French-speaking Canadians, would be debarred from any participation in political life. British law and administrative institutions were to be introduced, but French Canadians could not expect to be appointed as judges and justices of the peace or to other such posts. Thus, it would be to their advantage to give up their old language and religion and to adapt themselves to those of the conqueror. In short, this scheme of government was seen as a device for assimilating *les Canadiens* to the English-speaking way of life. From that day to this, this people, who now increasingly call themselves Québécois rather than French Canadians, have seen assimilation as a real or potential danger. For more than two hundred years they have sought, successfully, to survive on an overwhelmingly English-speaking continent.

British hopes for assimilating the French Canadians in the 1760s and 1770s soon had to be set aside or postponed. The first governor, Gen. James Murray, and his closest advisers had much sympathy for the Canadians; accordingly, they refused to call elections for an assembly that would have put legislative power into the hands of a tiny group of English-speaking Protestant merchants. Moreover, the expected influx of English-speaking immigrants from the colonies to the south did not take place; Quebec remained overwhelmingly French speaking. The second governor, Gen. Guy Carleton, was also anxious to win the confidence of the French Canadians, particularly of the seigneurial class and of the clergy. If these groups felt secure under British rule, they would remain cool to any overtures made either by the French or by the "Americans" to the south.

Carleton, therefore, set out to convince the British government that a new policy was needed for Canada. In a memorable despatch he stated: "barring catastrophe shocking to think of, this country must, to the end of time, be peopled by the Canadian Race [i.e., of French descent], who already have taken such firm Root, and got to so great a Height, that any new Stock transplanted will be totally hid, and imperceptible amongst them, except in the Towns of Quebec and Montreal." This line of thought led eventually to the passage by the British Parliament in 1774 of the Quebec Act, one of the most important enactments in Canadian history. This law promised the French Canadians that they could continue to worship freely according to the Roman Catholic faith and that they could hold offices without taking the anti-Catholic oaths still required in Britain. Their clergy would be allowed to collect tithes. The old French civil law would continue, although the criminal law would be British. The seigneurial landholding system, quite different from the freehold system used in Britain and in the American colonies, would continue unchanged. Quebec would be governed through an appointed council, without the representative assembly found in the American colonies. Finally, the boundaries of the province were considerably enlarged, to reach south and west to the Ohio and the Mississippi rivers.

The significance of the Quebec Act has been one of the most hotly debated issues in Canadian history, and it also figures prominently in the history of the American Revolution. For many years the act was seen by many, perhaps most, French Canadians as a sort of Magna Carta that safeguarded their rights and enabled them to survive as a distinct people in North America. More recently, it has been argued that much has been read into the act that was not there, and that the national survival of the French Canadians was not a purpose of its authors. Americans saw the act from a different perspective, as a harsh measure, revealing British contempt for representative government; also, it was regarded as en-croaching on the western land claims of American colonies, and as trying to turn Quebec into a base from which to attack those colonies. Today, however, it is generally agreed that, whatever the wisdom of the act as a solution for Quebec's problems, it did not have an anti-American purpose. Although it was passed at the time of the Coercive Acts, it was not part of that group of measures.

These and other controversies have swirled around the Quebec Act over the last century and more. The immediate question for Carleton in 1774–75 was whether the act would serve to keep Quebec secure against the rising tide of rebellion in the American colonies to the south. Carleton was so con-fident of this that in September 1774 he sent troops from Quebec to assist the British commander in Boston and assured him that the Canadians would remain firmly loyal to the British Crown.

The test came in the following year, 1775. In the autumn two American armies, under Richard Montgomery and Ben-edict Arnold, invaded Canada, proceeding to take Montreal and to put Quebec under siege. This latter assault failed, and in the spring of 1776, with the appearance of a British relief force, the Americans withdrew. In this great contest for the control of Canada, the French-Canadian church leaders and the seigneurial class remained firmly loyal to the British cause, but the great mass of the French-Canadian people stood aloof. Nor did they show much enthusiasm for the American invaders, especially after these soldiers began to seize goods without making payment. In any event, they could hardly be expected to feel very warm toward the predominantly Prot-estant Americans against whom they had fought so often in earlier years.

The American retreat from Canada in 1776 marked the failure of "the struggle for the fourteenth colony." But British efforts to use Canada as a base for attacking the Americans also failed, notably in the defeat of a large British army in 1777 at Saratoga, in northern New York State. The battle proved to have important diplomatic consequences, for it con-vinced the government of France to come out openly as an ally of the Americans; and French support turned out to be crucial in determining the outcome of the fight for independence. The Franco-American alliance may also have played a part, unintended by either party, in ensuring the continued separate existence of Canada in North America. Although the French doubtless wished to regain their lost colonies in America, their American ally had no desire to see a revitalized French empire on its borders. Conversely, the French would not support moves that might place their former colonies under American control. For these reasons, and also because of the unfolding strategy of the war, Canada remained on the periphery of the American War of Independence in its later phases. This statement is also true of another part of the British Empire, namely Nova Scotia. Despite the fact that a considerable proportion of its population had recently emigrated from New England, Nova Scotia was not drawn into the American Revolutionary movement, such was the influence of British seapower and the garrison at Halifax.

Although the French Canadians and the Nova Scotians remained aloof from this movement, it was still not clear what their fate would be after American independence was attained. The phrase "Continental Congress" suggested very broad ambitions, and the Articles of Confederation (1781) contained a section looking to the admission of Canada into the American Union. And when the peace negotiations between the Americans and the British got under way (after the battle of Yorktown, 1781), the American negotiators proposed that all British territory north and west of the Thirteen original states should be given up to the American Union in order to remove any obstacles to a speedy return to Anglo-American friendship. While this was asking too much of the British negotiators, who had little interest in or knowledge of North America, they did agree to very generous boundaries for the United States. Many students of Canadian history have felt that Canada's prospects for growth were crippled from the start because of territory given up by the peace treaty between the United States and Great Britain in 1783. On this occasion, as on others, Americans proved to be astute and hardheaded diplomats.

In particular, the United States acquired title to the vast region bounded by the Appalachian Mountains on the east and the Mississippi River on the west, and stretching from the Floridas on the south to the Great Lakes on the north. Much of this rich region had been tied to the Montreal trading empire for a century. Hence, the boundary settlement in 1783 meant that future Canadian attempts to reach into the Far West would have to be made across the forbidding Precambrian Shield terrain north of Lake Superior instead of across the shorter and easier route south of the Great Lakes.

Another consequence of the American Revolution had an equally decisive influence on the development of Canada. As is well known, perhaps one third of the people in the Thirteen Colonies resolved to remain loyal to the king of England and refused to support the Continental Congress. In some respects, the War of Independence was a civil war, with Americans fighting against Americans. In any civil war the losing side usually suffers bitterly, and this one was no exception. In particular, many thousands were forced into exile or voluntarily chose to leave rather than live under the new Republic.

About thirty thousand "Loyalists," as they became known in Canadian history, were transported in British ships to Nova Scotia. So large an influx of settlers, with an outlook different from that of the existing population of Nova Scotia, led to the formation in 1784 of a new colony, New Brunswick, the Loyalist province par excellence. Far to the west, other Loyalists, mainly from New York and Pennsylvania, moved into the Province of Quebec north of the St. Lawrence River, Lake Ontario, and Lake Erie; some Loyalists also moved west from the Maritimes to join them. These settlers were not as numerous (only about seven thousand) as those who went to the Maritimes, but their coming was nevertheless crucial to the future of British North America, and hence of Canada. They settled west of the Ottawa River (i.e., west of the French-Canadian settlements) and for the first time gave the Province of Quebec a considerable English-speaking population. Here, even more than in Nova Scotia, the newcomers had different customs and aspirations from the older (French-Canadian) settlers, and they insisted on a government of their own.

Again the British had to recognize the reality created by the aftermath of the American Revolution: in 1791, an act of Parliament divided the Province of Quebec into the Provinces of Upper Canada (later Ontario) and Lower Canada (later Quebec). One province was predominantly English speaking and the other (with a much larger population) remained mainly French speaking. The Canadian duality, which has survived from that day to this, thus came into existence. Two different peoples, with different traditions and little understanding of each other, were destined henceforth to live side by side.

At the end of the eighteenth century, then, there were several British North American provinces, each a part of the British Empire but not otherwise joined, politically or economically, to one another. More than that, they were separated from one another by distance, geographic barriers, language, and customs, yet shared certain common political and legal institutions derived from the mother country. Each colony had its own governor or lieutenant governor, sent from Great Britain, and an appointed council. Except for Newfoundland, each had an elected legislative assembly with rather limited powers. English common law prevailed in all criminal cases and in civil matters except in Lower Canada, where French civil law was maintained.

In addition to the two Canadas and the provinces by the sea, British North America also included the vast and largely unknown interior, stretching north to Hudson Bay and the Arctic, and west to the Pacific Ocean. This enormous region was still the preserve of the Indian and the fur trader. As in the days of the French regime, fur-trading organizations from Montreal (especially the North West Company) tried to extend their influence far into the interior. In 1789 one of these "Nor'westers," Alexander Mackenzie, reached the Arctic Ocean via the river that now bears his name. Four years later, Mackenzie arrived at the Pacific after the first overland trip across the continent. Ultimately, however, the Montreal-based North West Company found the expense of its lengthy communications beyond its ability and had to agree to a merger with the Hudson's Bay Company, which enjoyed easier access to the richest fur-trading areas. As a result, control of the fur trade passed to London in 1821, and for the next generation the settled provinces of British North America had little contact with the Far West.

For British North America, the three decades following the treaty of 1783 was a period of tension and then war with the neighboring United States. A whole series of problems, related to Indian wars in the Ohio-Indiana region, continued British possession of certain posts on the American side of the boundary (e.g., at Niagara and Detroit), and disputes over neutral rights on the high seas (following the outbreak of the French Revolutionary wars) nearly brought a renewal of Anglo-American fighting in the early 1790s. But by Jay's Treaty of 1794–95, the main points of difference were either settled or temporarily defused. This treaty was intensely unpopular in the United States, but it did lead to ten years of fairly calm Anglo-American relations; more important for the long run, it helped to set a pattern for the peaceful settlement of disputes relating to the United States, Great Britain, and British North America (later Canada).

That such a pattern would eventually be established was of course not evident in the early nineteenth century, for in 1812 Great Britain and the United States were again at war. The tangled controversy over "the causes of the War of 1812" is beyond the scope of this chapter. From the Canadian point of view, however, one fact stood out: the Canadian provinces were in the front line. There was no other place where the United States could effectively attack Britain, and the Americans believed that these British provinces were vulnerable. Their population was only a fraction of that of the United States, and the Americans believed the French Canadians would not fight to defend British authority. Furthermore, in Upper Canada the original Loyalist population was by 1812 heavily outnumbered by the arrival of later non-Loyalist American immigrants who, it was believed, would welcome invading American armies. Britain, locked in its giant struggle against Napoleon, could spare no reinforcements to strengthen the small number of troops in the colonies; and most of these troops would have to be kept in the East to defend Quebec (the essential port for communication with the mother country) and, to a lesser extent, Montreal (the largest commercial center). Upper Canada to the west was so exposed that it is little wonder that some American leaders said that it would be "a mere matter of marching" to take it.

In fact, despite its much larger population, the United States was not well organized for a war of invasion against the Canadian provinces, a war that one important section of the country, New England, strongly opposed. American generals were elderly; American troops were untrained; and American planning was faulty. As a result, a relatively few well-led British regulars, aided by Canadian militia and Indian allies, not only pushed back the Americans but occasionally took the counteroffensive. After three campaigns (1812, 1813, and 1814), the Americans had only a feeble hold on a portion of Upper Canada east of Detroit, while the British controlled the New York side of the Niagara River and much of the country west of Lake Michigan.

Americans then and later placed great emphasis on single ship naval victories and the rebuff of the British at New Orleans (after peace had been signed, of course); but as Canadians looked back upon it, the essential fact about the war was the failure of the American invasions. A sense of separateness from the United States was reinforced, and the population, both French speaking and English speaking, was more anti-American after the war than before. In fact, the war had a similar kind of importance in both Canadian and American history. Just as Americans saw it as a "Second War of Independence," in which they had successfully defended their rights and their sovereignty against British depredations, so Canadians cherished memories of a patriotic and stout defense against a wealthier and more numerous enemy. It is often claimed that a thriving nationalism requires hostile feelings toward some outside country. Clearly the War of 1812 stimulated national feeling on both sides of the Canadian-U.S. boundary. In the United States other wars (the Mexican War and especially the Civil War) later caused the 1812 war to recede considerably from memory, but it was "*the* war" in the Canadian consciousness for a century.

It is often suggested that the year 1815 ushered in an era

of peace, symbolized by an undefended border, which has now endured for well over a century and a half. The truth is less simple. Threats, rumors of war, and occasional skirmishes persisted for fifty years and even longer. During those years many hundreds of thousands of dollars were spent on both sides of the boundary for the improvement of defenses. Nevertheless, in the years immediately after 1815 a new recognition of the importance of peace began to emerge. The treaty at the end of the war merely brought the fighting to an end and required each side to give up any territory occupied in the other country. A more notable event, though perhaps one of greater symbolic than practical importance, was the signing of the Rush-Bagot Agreement of 1817, by which a limit was placed on naval armaments on the Great Lakes. This averted the possibility of a naval arms race in the interior of the continent, a significant factor in subsequent strategic planning.

Much more far-reaching was the Convention of 1818, which dealt with many important questions, including another effort to determine the right of Americans to engage in the fisheries in Nova Scotian waters. (The fisheries—then of vital interest to New Englanders, including the American secretary of state and later president, John Quincy Adams— have continued to be a point of contention in Canada-U.S. relations to this day.) Also, commissions were to be appointed to settle disputes over the location of the Canadian-American border in the eastern half of the continent, thus strengthening the practice of setting up machinery for the peaceful settlement of bilateral disputes. Finally, and of enduring significance, the western boundary was fixed, at least in part. That boundary demanded attention because, after its purchase of Louisiana in 1803, the United States asserted its claim to western lands already claimed by Great Britain. By the Convention of 1818, it was agreed that the boundary in the west should run along the 49th parallel from the Lake of the Woods to the Rockies; other British and American claims conflicted in the Pacific Coast region then known generally as the Oregon Country, and pending a definite settlement, both Britain and the United States were to have equal rights there.

In retrospect, the year 1818, or thereabouts, brought to

a close one important phase in Canadian development. Nearly two hundred years of intermittent fighting, first during the French regime and then in the first generation of American independence, had failed to impose political unity on the continent. Instead, a boundary line had been agreed upon that stretched from the Atlantic Ocean on the east to the Rocky Mountains on the west. North of that line there was nothing resembling a Canadian nation. It would be the work of the next half century to increase the population, develop the economy, improve communications, and in general provide the underpinning that would make possible the confederation of the British North American provinces that became the Dominion of Canada after 1867.

Evolution of the British North American Provinces, 1818–1873

In recent years an increased awareness of the importance and persistence of regional loyalties and differences has been evident. This awareness helps to better understand the complicated and almost exasperating nature of Canadian history in the half century between the War of 1812 and Confederation in 1867–73. In that period there was in fact no one organizing theme, no single mainstream of development. Instead, several quite separate provinces, each with a distinctive economy and society, developed intensely local ("parish-pump") outlooks and loyalties. These provinces were not politically joined except as constituent parts of the British Empire. Meanwhile, the British Empire itself was rapidly changing. The mother country became increasingly reluctant to pay for the defense of her colonies and more concerned to stress policies that would promote British prosperity, even at the expense of the colonies. Moreover, as the colonies sought to pursue their individual interests, Britain slowly began to accept the growing demand of the provinces for local self-government. Thus, it is helpful to look in turn at the several components that would later be drawn into the Canadian Confederation.

Far to the east was the oldest of the colonies. Newfoundland had been claimed by England since before the end of the fifteenth century. Yet, somewhat paradoxically, for more than three hundred years it was not regarded as a colony at all: permanent settlement was officially forbidden, and instead the island was intended to be used only for the purposes of the fisheries, mainly the cod fishery, which dominated its economy then and afterward. Nevertheless, fishermen and others had tended to stay on over the winter, and gradually a permanent population had settled on the island. Thus, the British government was forced to provide for civil government, and in 1832 a legislative assembly was granted. The debates of the Assembly immediately reflected the often bitter religious and social differences that divided Newfoundland internally and revealed that the people of Newfoundland had their own life, a hard one, remote from the mainland. The remoteness would be seen in the fact that Newfoundland did not join the Canadian Confederation until 1949; and to this day its inhabitants may feel a stronger emotional attachment to the province than to Canada.

In later years people in the Maritime Provinces—Nova Scotia, New Brunswick, and Prince Edward Island—sometimes looked back on the years from the 1820s to the 1860s as a kind of golden age. With the help of trade preference in the British market, New Brunswick began to exploit its vast timber resources, and the returning ships brought thousands of much-needed immigrants. Nova Scotia also flourished in an era of expanding world trade, aided by certain relaxations in the mercantile system. The economies of both provinces led their people to look out across the Atlantic, and sometimes down toward New England, but seldom inland toward the Canadian provinces. In the third of these provinces—tiny Prince Edward Island—the picture was less bright. The development of its excellent agricultural land was hampered by a long-standing class war between the tenant farmers and a small number of proprietors—often absentee landlords—who had title to the land. Politically, these provinces went through a generation of sharp and often acrimonious debate, but by the middle of the century these had achieved substantial constitutional reform, with governments that were responsive to public opinion.

To the west, the Hudson's Bay Company ruled supreme over a vast empire stretching from Hudson Bay to Lake Superior and the 49th parallel on the south, to the Pacific Ocean on the west, and to the Arctic Ocean on the north. The Company had title to a very large part of the region and a trading monopoly over the remainder. It was responsible for law and order as well as for carrying on the fur trade, the foundation of the western economy. Throughout this enormous region there was only one settlement of any consequence—the Red River Colony on the site of the present city of Winnipeg. The Company was not anxious for others to develop, because settlement was harmful to the fur trade. Nevertheless, by the 1840s and increasingly thereafter, the American settlement frontier was reaching into Minnesota Territory and into Oregon. If the British territory north of the 49th parallel remained unsettled, what was to prevent it from being engulfed by the tide of American "Manifest Destiny"? Attempts to answer this question would play an important part in bringing about Canadian Confederation.

The two central Provinces of Lower and Upper Canada both faced serious economic, social, and political problems in the generation after the War of 1812. These engendered a period of extreme tension, culminating in both cases in armed rebellion. There were superficial similarities between the problems in the two provinces, but in many respects they were very different.

In Lower Canada, a relatively small number of English-speaking merchants directed the commercial economy that had earlier been based on the fur trade. With the decline of that trade, the merchants increasingly turned to new opportunities, in particular to the export of square timber and lumber from the Ottawa Valley and of wheat and flour from the Great Lakes region. Major improvements in transportation facilities were required to make this emerging commercial system function efficiently. The situation seemed especially critical after the opening of the Erie Canal in 1825 gave New York a competitive edge in the struggle to control trade from the heart of the continent. It would be necessary to build canals around the rapids in the St. Lawrence River, and that in turn would require the voting of appropriations by the legislature of Lower Canada.

The merchants who supported these improvements were well represented in the executive government and in the appointed upper house of Lower Canada's legislature, but in the Assembly, the elected lower house, the French-Canadian majority was in complete control. The latter did not believe that furthering the commercial ambitions of the English-speaking merchants and their allies (known as the "Château Clique") would do much, if anything, to better the lot of the rural French Canadians. In any event, the leaders of the Assembly had grievances of their own, which they were determined to have removed before they voted money for canals or other costly improvements. Thus, the stage was set for a prolonged struggle in the 1820s and 1830s; the struggle was ostensibly constitutional (i.e., should the majority in the elected Assembly gain effective control over all parts of the government?), but it had strong "racial," linguistic/cultural, and economic undertones.*

Eventually government in Lower Canada came to an almost complete breakdown. The British government tried to find compromise solutions but ran into obstinate resistance from both the English-speaking minority and the French-Canadian Patriote Party, led by Louis-Joseph Papineau. The former were convinced that they were entitled to unwavering support from the mother country in the face of the demands of the French Canadians, who were dismissed as backward, illiterate, and unenterprising. The Patriotes, on the contrary, became convinced that there was nothing to be gained by further constitutional agitation and that more direct action was necessary. The final crisis came in 1837 when the Assembly again refused to vote the funds necessary to carry on the government. The British Parliament then passed Ten Resolutions, one of which might empower the local executive

---

* In mid-nineteenth-century Canada, the term "racial" was frequently used to distinguish French from English, and can be regarded as synonymous with ethnic.

to take money from the treasury without the consent of the Assembly, thus raising memories of the "no taxation without representation" issue of the American Revolution. Out of widespread discontent and frustration came various uprisings north and east of Montreal in the autumn of 1837. After sharp fighting in some places, the rebellion was put down by British troops. Although it had never had the active support of more than a fraction of the French-Canadian population and had been strongly opposed by the leaders of the Roman Catholic church, it became in retrospect a popular uprising looking to national liberation. This reaction was further strengthened by what some regarded as harsh measures of repression that followed the rebellion.

Upper Canada was largely spared the "racial" and linguistic conflict found in the lower province. By the 1820s and 1830s the population, originally almost entirely Loyalists, was extremely diverse. In addition to Loyalist, non-Loyalist, "late Loyalist" and American settlers, a growing influx of English, Irish, and Scottish immigrants from the British Isles added new communities and social groups. There was a great variety of religious sects (in an era when religion was taken very seriously): Methodists, Presbyterians, Baptists, Roman Catholics, Church of England, to name only the most prominent. Moreover, Upper Canada, a colony supposedly founded on Loyalist principles, was, because of its geographic location as well as other factors, more directly exposed to American influences than any other British province, and this in the era of Jacksonian democracy.

Under these circumstances the leaders of the government and their supporters, entrenched in the two appointed councils (the Executive Council and the Legislative Council), felt it their duty to take every measure to keep Upper Canada as British as possible and to repel American influences. The governing oligarchy (which came to be called the "Family Compact") was presently confronted by oppositionists (the "Reformers") who were often in control of the elected Assembly; thus the constitutional aspects of the struggle were similar to those in Lower Canada, although the issues were different. Nor were the two sides as polarized as in Lower Canada. In the province the Patriotes always had complete control of the Assembly; in Upper Canada the Family Compact-led conservatives rivaled the Reformers in their appeals to the voters and sometimes had a majority in the Assembly.

By the middle 1830s the sense of frustration among the leading Upper Canadian radical Reformers, notably William Lyon Mackenzie, was almost as great as that felt by Papineau. The crisis was precipitated by the arrival in 1836 of a new governor, Sir Francis Bond Head, who refused to take the advice of his appointed Council (which for the first time had included some moderate Reformers) and who soon plunged the province into a hard-fought electoral campaign. By making emotional appeals to loyalty, the conservatives managed to win the election. Mackenzie lost his seat and came to the conclusion that there was no hope of effective change within the existing political system. Encouraged by the uprisings that had just occurred in Lower Canada, he led a small band of his supporters against the provincial capital (Toronto). But there was little popular support for rebellion in Upper Canada, and Mackenzie's attempt to establish a republican State of Upper Canada was easily put down despite the absence of the regular troops (who had been sent to Lower Canada).

Nevertheless, in Upper as in Lower Canada, the aftermath of the rebellion troubled the province for months and even years. The victorious conservatives had an opportunity to prosecute (and persecute) their "disloyal" Reform opponents, many of whom were unfairly tarred with the brush of rebellion. More serious were disturbances along the Canadian-American border, caused by escaped Canadian rebels and Americans who sympathized with them. These border raids disturbed the peace more than the actual rebellions, especially in Upper Canada.

The rebellions were past, yet the problems that lay behind them still remained. In some ways those problems were harder to solve than even after the rebellions, because emotions had been raised, hostilities deepened, and men made more obstinate. Most notable, in Lower Canada the elected Assembly had been suspended; for the time being the province would be governed by the appointed Council. In effect, this meant government by the English-speaking minority, leaving the French-speaking majority with a renewed sense of being a conquered people.

A further consequence of the rebellions was that the two Canadian provinces were brought to the attention of the British government as never before. For years that government had paid lip service to the need for political change in the British North American provinces, but, preoccupied with problems at home and unable to come to any agreement in the colonies, the British had done very little to address these issues. Finally, in 1838 the Cabinet dispatched Lord Durham, a prestigious statesman, to be Governor General of all the provinces and to function as High Commissioner to probe into the difficulties in the two Canadas. Durham stayed in North America for only five months; he quarreled with the government at home and resigned. Nevertheless, on his return to England he completed, and submitted early in 1839, the report that at once became the center of great interest and controversy. There is some debate about how much influence the Durham Report had on the actual course of subsequent events, and one can also find numerous errors of fact and judgment in the report; yet it remains a central document for understanding the Canadian past.

In diagnosing the ills of the Canadas, Durham began with a firm belief in the political, the economic, and probably the moral superiority of the English-speaking peoples in the British Empire and in the United States over all other peoples in the world. He was, for instance, an ardent admirer of the great economic progress that Americans were making; and he wanted Canadians to be able to do the same. But, he argued, they would never be able to do so while they were expending so much energy on sterile debates over constitutional forms and on quarrels over language and religion. On the other hand, it was equally clear to Durham that English-speaking people, anywhere in the world, must have control over their government; that is, they were bound to demand that governments change with changes in public opinion. It was even more certain that people of British stock living beside the United States would never be satisfied with anything less than self-government.

Could self-government be reconciled with continued membership in the Empire and with the need to ensure the rights of the English minority in Canada? Durham believed that it could, by the device of reserving a few matters of broad importance to the imperial government and placing everything else under the control of the provincial governments. Nor need the transition to self-government be prolonged by lengthy theoretical debates over forms or a spate of drafting written constitutions in the American manner. A much simpler device was at hand, which could be implemented without any alteration in the formal constitution. That device, known in Canadian history as "responsible government," was to insist that the governor must always act on the advice of the Executive Council and that the Executive Council (later to be known as the Cabinet) would hold office only as long as it could win a vote of confidence in the elected Assembly. Thus, the voters, in choosing the Assembly, would have an indirect but very real control over the executive. This idea was not an original one with Durham. It was derived from British constitutional practices as they had evolved since the American Revolution. Moreover, responsible government had been explicitly advocated by Canadian Reformers, particularly in the upper province, in the 1830s. Nevertheless, Durham's contribution was an important one, since it provided compelling arguments for its adoption that the British government could not dismiss lightly.

In addition to responsible government, Durham also advocated a union of the British North American provinces. He believed union would help to break down the stifling localism that was all too prevalent, and he looked toward the development of another nationality on the North American continent to counterbalance, to some extent at least, the United States.

Durham had another reason for recommending a union of the provinces—his view of the French Canadians. Much as he admired the many fine personal qualities of most French

Canadians, he considered them to be economically backward and, as the recent rebellion had shown, so alienated from Great Britain that they could not be trusted to exercise the kind of political power that the principle of responsible government required. To be sure, since they were British subjects, their political rights had to be restored—but only within a British North American union, where they would be outnumbered and, as Durham expected, gradually assimilated into the English-speaking population, could the interests of the Montreal merchants be protected. From that day to this, French Canadians have been determined to confound Lord Durham's assumption that their distinctive culture could never survive.

Lord Durham's Report ultimately came to be regarded as a major document in shaping the evolution of Canadian government and the transformation of the British Empire into a Commonwealth of self-governing nations. But its immediate influence was more modest. As Durham himself realized, a general union of all the provinces could not be achieved at once. The Atlantic Provinces had so little in common with the Canadian provinces that they lacked any interest in a federation. And in view of the need to return to representative government in Lower Canada, there was no time for the discussions and protracted negotiations. Hence, in 1841 the decision was made to unite Upper and Lower Canada only. In this way, the French Canadians would be outnumbered when the population of Upper Canada was added to the English-speaking minority in Lower Canada.

On the other hand, the British government was initially unwilling to adopt Durham's recommendation regarding responsible government. Although quite ready in principle to see the colonies advance toward self-government, the imperial government believed that in the final analysis the governor appointed by London must be responsible to London. It argued that if the governor received one set of instructions from London and conflicting counsel from his colonial executive advisers, he must obey the former. Otherwise the colonies would be independent, not parts of the Empire. For a half decade after 1841 a complicated partisan struggle dominated Canadian politics with governors trying to stave off the implementation of responsible government, and colonial politicians, at any rate those of Reform outlook, determined to achieve it. The emergence of organized political parties determined the outcome; after 1848 the governor had little or no choice but to bow to the wishes of those who could control the Assembly majority. Nevertheless, certain questions, such as defense and foreign policy, remained in the hands of the British government, and for many years to come the colonial governor remained an influential figure in British North American politics.

While colonial politicians achieved one of Lord Durham's recommendations, responsible government, in another important respect the union of the Canadas worked quite differently from the way Durham had expected. As noted above, he had anticipated that in a united province, with an English-speaking majority that he believed to be more progressive and more vigorous than the French Canadians, the latter would gradually become assimilated by the larger and stronger language group. But French-Canadian identity did not die out. French-Canadian members in the legislature remained united and thus were able to insist upon many of their objectives. Indeed, it proved impossible to carry on the government of the Province of Canada without their cooperation, and this meant accommodations. These compromises were sometimes exasperating to the English majority, especially the Montreal businessmen; their restiveness even produced a short-lived movement for annexation to the United States in 1849. Its supporters hoped that annexation would deliver them from "French rule," but annexation clearly had little popular support, and the movement collapsed almost immediately.

Although responsible government was achieved, and although English-speaking and French-speaking Canadians learned to work together in a functioning political system as the 1850s moved into the 1860s, the union proved to be increasingly cumbersome. The principle developed that a government must have a "double majority"; that is, those who held executive office—the Prime Minister and his Cabinet—must enjoy the confidence of a majority of members of the legislature from both Lower Canada and Upper Canada.* As the government sought to accommodate the divergent interests and ambitions of the two provinces, a delicate balance had to be maintained. When this proved ever more difficult in practice, the result was successive changes in government and frequent elections in accordance with parliamentary tradition. As a result, some were postponed or ignored (although important experience and self-confidence were acquired). Many observers soon concluded that a new political framework was required.

This view was reinforced by the need for new economic policies for which the rapid agricultural and industrial growth of the 1850s called. Large-scale immigration, the advent of the railway era, the spread of wheat farming and of other forms of agricultural activity brought unprecedented prosperity. But these changes also raised the need to find an adequate financial structure to support such new and expensive enterprises as the railways, and also to secure markets for the agricultural surpluses and other products now available for export. The quest for markets was met in part in the negotiation of the Reciprocity Treaty of 1854 with the United States, and for a time north-south trade grew significantly.

Railway building, as mentioned, influenced provincial financial policies. Private companies were chartered to undertake construction, relying on money borrowed abroad, mainly in England; but they also depended upon the provincial government for assistance. Soon the politicians were deeply involved in the railways, both personally and on a policy level. For instance, tariffs were raised to provide revenue to cover the railway loans, which the government guaranteed. Politicians also became interested in schemes that would enable the railways to tap new opportunities—for instance, to extend themselves to the markets in the Maritimes and, in the future, into the Far West.

In fact, the West was coming back into the Canadian range of vision in the 1850s and 1860s. By this time, much of the best and most accessible land was taken up, and the

---

* These terms continued to be used during the union period, although they were formally changed to Canada East and Canada West, respectively.

Province of Canada had nearly reached the limits of its agricultural growth. French Canadians were moving in some numbers to the mills and factories of New England. Upper Canadians were moving into the American Middle West. Politicians, newspaper editors, and other leaders of opinion began to argue that Canada must develop a West of its own and that that West must be joined to the settled regions in the East (thus altering the political balance). These were some of the factors attracting such Canadian politicians as George Brown, John A. Macdonald, and George-Etienne Cartier to the idea of Confederation in the early 1860s.

Still another factor was the outbreak of the American Civil War in 1861. As popular opinion was generally opposed to the institution of slavery, Canadian sympathies were pronorthern when the war began. But these sentiments changed sharply following the Trent affair (December 1861), a matter that provoked a head-on diplomatic confrontation between the United States and Great Britain. Anglo-American diplomatic crises traditionally generated tension along the Canadian-American border, and the Civil War years were no exception. The British sent troop reinforcements to Canada, and both sides strengthened border defenses. Relations were further strained by the activities of Confederate agents in Canada, especially when some of the latter raided St. Albans, Vermont, from a Canadian base in 1864. Northern opinion grew more hostile toward the provinces of British North America, and there was talk of retaliation once the Confederacy was defeated. On the official level, good relations were in fact soon restored with the end of the war in 1865; but the activities of the Irish Americans known as Fenians, who made several raids into Canada just after the war, showed that the border was still disturbed and remained potentially a cause of danger. All of these events lent urgency to the question of how to solve British North America's political and economic problems.

By 1864 it was clear that the French-speaking and English-speaking populations of Lower and Upper Canada were too dissimilar to work harmoniously in one legislature where each had to deal with the local affairs of the other. Under the shadow of the last stages of the Civil War, a truce was called in the constant party warfare, and a coalition government was formed with a commission to try to find a way out of the impasse. One possibility was to look toward a larger union that would include the Atlantic Provinces. In such a union, in the form of a federation, each component could have its own legislature to deal with its own local questions, and there could also be a general legislature to deal with matters relating to the federation as a whole.

At this point a reader may ask himself two questions: To what extent were Canadian politicians of the 1860s influenced by the example of the American federation, which had, after all, been functioning next door to them for some seventy-five years? And also, to what extent were these politicians motivated by a nationalist desire to build a Canadian nation that might set out to realize a Canadian destiny?

In answer to the first question, it appears that the Fathers of Confederation, as they came to be called, were less influenced by the example of the United States Constitution than one might expect. First, the recently ended long Civil War seemed to have revealed serious weaknesses in that Constitution; it seemed to be an example of what to avoid rather than what to copy. Second, the Canadians were not setting out to found an independent country with its fundamental law based on a written constitution. They were perfectly happy with, indeed very proud of, the British constitution, most of which was unwritten. All they wanted to do was to work out certain practical arrangements among the provinces and to continue as self-governing entities within the British Empire.

Regarding the second question, some politicians and some other spokesmen did begin to see the possibility of a federation stretching from sea to sea, and of a new political nationality arising in North America (not, however, politically separated from the British Empire). Certainly, there was a conscious desire on the part of many to create a political structure that could reach out into the Northwest. But again, the concern was more practical than idealist or visionary: to ward off American Manifest Destiny, to strengthen the position of the railways, and above all to find a way out of the political impasse in the Province of Canada.

The process of Canadian Confederation can be summarized briefly; a fuller understanding could require reading hundreds of pages of debates, newspaper editorials, and so on. The chain of events began when delegates from the coalition government in Canada journeyed in the summer of 1864 to Charlottetown, capital of Prince Edward Island, where a conference was considering the possibility of a union of the Maritime Provinces. The Canadians convinced the Maritimers to put this project aside in favor of discussion of a larger scheme—British North American Union. Accordingly, later in the year, a conference was held at Quebec with delegates from Canada and the Atlantic Provinces, including Newfoundland, and within two weeks the delegates agreed upon a scheme of federal union embodied in seventy-two resolutions.

The next stage in the process was to secure approval by the various provincial legislatures of the scheme. Here progress was slower. In Canada there was significant opposition, but under the leadership of Macdonald, Cartier, and Brown the measure was carried in the spring of 1865. English-speaking Canadians, seeking a way out of political deadlock and a framework for more effective economic progress, were, with few exceptions, in favor of the project. French Canadians were more divided, many being fearful of a union that would further erode their minority status. But Cartier convinced a fairly narrow majority of his compatriots that they would be safer inside Confederation that outside. Confederation would be a barrier against annexation to the United States, which, he believed, would destroy the French-Canadian identity. Cartier was sure that the scheme provided adequate safeguards for the protection of French-Canadian interests. Although the new federal government was to have large powers in financial and economic matters, it would have no authority respecting religion and education. French civil law was to continue in the new Province of Quebec, and both French and English would be legal languages in that province as well as in the federal Parliament. Above all, with the dissolution of the union of Upper and Lower Canada and the establishment of the two Provinces of Ontario and Quebec, French Canadians would once again have a province where they were in a majority and where they would have a majority in the legislature. The provincial government would reflect the French fact in Quebec. To be sure, that government would have limited powers and, as the future would reveal, would for many years be comparatively weak and vulnerable to external pressures; nevertheless, it gave French Canadians a commanding voice over their own affairs.

In the Atlantic Provinces many more had doubts about the Confederation project. There it was seen as essentially a scheme of central Canada. The legislatures of Newfoundland and Prince Edward Island decided that those two provinces would not join. The government of Nova Scotia, which favored the project, was so apprehensive of a popular rebuff that it postponed submitting the measure to the legislature. Besides, for geographic reasons, Nova Scotia's adherence would not be very practical without that of New Brunswick; and in that province the measure was submitted to the electorate and was soundly defeated. Most people in the Atlantic Provinces could not see how Confederation could advance their interests; and they had little sense of fellow feeling with central Canadians, either French speaking or English speaking.

Nevertheless, the project survived. Public opinion in New Brunswick and Nova Scotia gradually became more favorable. The British government, for various reasons, endorsed the project strongly and exerted considerable pressure, especially in New Brunswick. Funds sent from Canada, both by the government and by the Grand Trunk Railway, won over some waverers. The threat of Fenian raids from the states across the border persuaded others. The decision in New Brunswick was reversed; and by a very close vote the measure was carried in the Nova Scotia legislature.

The final stages of the process took place in London. Delegates from Canada and from Nova Scotia and New Brunswick revised very slightly the Quebec resolutions, and these so-called London resolutions were then formed into a draft bill. That bill passed through the British Parliament in March 1867, virtually without debate, and the British North America Act became operative on July 1, 1867. The Dominion of Canada—consisting of four provinces, Ontario, Quebec, New Brunswick, and Nova Scotia—had been born. The first of July was its official birthday.

The first half dozen years of the new Dominion were hectic and charged with potential danger. The American Civil War left many problems in Anglo-American and Canadian-American relations that were eventually settled after difficult negotiations led to the Treaty of Washington in 1871. That treaty dealt concretely with a number of specific questions, but its larger significance was that, in a more general (and unspoken) way, it recognized the political division of North America. Individual Americans might continue to have dreams that Manifest Destiny would reach beyond the 49th parallel; but the United States government henceforth acted on the premise that a transcontinental federation functioned in the northern half of the continent.

For by 1871, although the structure was still very frail, Confederation had become transcontinental. The first step came in 1869, when the Canadian government, with British assistance, bought out Hudson's Bay Company claims in the West. The government then proceeded to send out surveyors and other agents, actions that alarmed the population of the Red River Colony. That population, made up mostly of Métis— the progeny of intermarriage among the French, English, and Scottish fur traders and settlers and the Indians—knew little and cared less about Canada; what they did know was that they did not want their traditional way of life disturbed. Under the leadership of Louis Riel, the Métis—determined to defend their rights—established a provisional government. In so doing, the Métis clashed with the representatives of the Canadian government, and one Canadian official was executed. This infuriated Ontario Protestant opinion, but French-speaking Catholic Quebec felt much sympathy with Riel. The new federal government in Ottawa, functioning only since 1867, therefore sought to work out a compromise. On the one hand, the rights of the Red River Colony were recognized, and it was constituted a province to come into Confederation (as Manitoba) in 1870 with the same status as the original four provinces. On the other hand, the federal government appeased Ontario opinion and, at the same time, asserted its own authority by sending troops to the Red River. Métis resistance faded away, and Riel vanished into the United States, only to return fifteen years later when he would again challenge Ottawa's efforts to control the West and its people.

The Canadian Confederation reached the Pacific Ocean with the admission of British Columbia in 1871. This colony had been formed in 1858 when the discovery of gold in the Cariboo triggered a gold rush in the Fraser River Valley. In 1866, in the interests of economy, the colony of Vancouver Island (originally a Hudson's Bay Company outpost) was joined to British Columbia. By then, the quick profits of the gold rush were gone, and the colony found itself unable to stand on its own. The alternatives appeared to be annexation to the United States or entrance into Canadian Confederation. The Canadian Prime Minister, Sir John A. Macdonald, quickly offered inducements to encourage the latter choice; in particular, he promised that a railway to the Pacific would be completed by 1883. This offer brought in British Columbia, but keeping the promise bedeviled Canadian politics for the next decade and a half.

Finally, at the other end of the continent, the tiny Province of Prince Edward Island, faced with insoluble financial problems, entered Confederation in 1873. Thus, through a tortuous, complicated, and most contentious process, the motto on the Canadian coat of arms—*A mari usque ad mare* (from sea to sea)—was verified.

The Dominion of Canada 1873–1945

In the early 1870s the Dominion of Canada, consisting of its seven scattered provinces and several territories, made a brave showing on a map of North America. Its political leaders had found effective answers to some complex and dangerous problems during the previous decade. With an enlarged constitutional framework and broader powers, they would now hope to undertake the task of binding so large a country together. The Dominion was on reasonably friendly terms with its neighbor, the United States. It proudly saw itself as one of the important parts of the British Empire, then at the height of its power and influence: Canadians did not think of themselves as independent of Great Britain, for they valued British friendship and support and admired much that Great Britain represented.

Yet despite these fair prospects, the first generation of the Canadian Confederation was a time of trial, and often of despair. Affecting the whole period was the harsh impact of the sharpest and longest business depression that the modern world had yet seen. It began in 1873 and lasted with some short intervals of recovery until the middle 1890s. It hit Canada with special severity. Markets for Canadian exports, on which the economy heavily depended, declined or dried up. Immigration slowed, and young Canadians left for the States in growing numbers. Thus, there was little population growth.

The gloomy economic scene helped to sharpen the many existing tensions in Canadian life. Sir John A. Macdonald's Conservative government had been forced to resign at the height of its triumph in 1873 because of a scandal over the building of the Pacific railway. But the new Liberal government under Alexander Mackenzie was divided and proved excessively cautious. The two extremities of the country shared the perception that whatever benefits Confederation had brought had accrued primarily to the central provinces: the Maritimes were discontented, and British Columbia was furious that little progress was being made with the railway.

An election in 1878 brought Macdonald and the Conservatives back to power on a platform of implementing a "national policy." Essentially and principally, this policy meant raising the tariff to protectionist levels in order to preserve Canadian markets for Canadian industries. Such a policy appeared to benefit some regions and interests more than others, particularly the industrial and commercial centers of Toronto and Montreal. The result was that trade policy became the most hotly debated question in Canadian politics in the last decades of the nineteenth century.

More generally, the term National Policy came to denote a broadly based program of economic development, involving transportation and settlement as well as tariff policy. Macdonald sought to impose an east-west axis on the country in order to counteract what seemed to be a more natural tendency for trade to flow in a north-south direction. The key question concerned the Pacific railway. All agreed that it should be built. But should it follow a shorter and easier route south of Lake Superior (i.e., through the United States, in part), or should it take the longer and harder route north of the lake? Macdonald determined that it must be an all-Canadian route. After immense effort, the Canadian Pacific Railway was completed by 1885. Canada now had rail links across the continent, for a line to the Maritimes had been completed a few years earlier.

But the goal of national unity proved to be as elusive as ever. In the West, for example, the influx of settlers, and the appearance of government agents, such as surveyors, continued to disrupt the traditional way of life in the territory that now comprised Saskatchewan and eastern Alberta. Most of these inhabitants were Indians, whom the government was trying to move to reserves. There were also considerable numbers of Métis. Many of these had moved west from Manitoba after 1870 seeking to preserve their unique culture. In 1884 the Métis invited Louis Riel to return from exile in the United States to become their leader again.

The problems might have been smoothed over by more understanding on the part of the federal government; but Macdonald failed at first to take the situation sufficiently seriously. Armed clashes occurred and Ottawa sent a few thousand troops to put down what has become known as the Northwest Rebellion of 1885. Riel was captured, tried, and sentenced to hang. Macdonald refused to intervene, and the sentence was carried out in November 1885. The event proved to be one of the most momentous in Canadian history, for it rekindled a sense of French-Canadian nationalism and sharpened and deepened the "racial," linguistic, and religious animosities between French-speaking and English-speaking Canadians. In the long run it helped to weaken the Conservative Party in Quebec and, with other events to come later, opened the way for the stranglehold that the federal Liberal Party came to have in that province in the twentieth century.

Macdonald and the Conservatives won elections again in 1887 and 1891, but after the old leader's death in the latter year the party was clearly falling apart. It was swept out of office by the Liberals under Wilfrid Laurier in 1896.

Thus, notwithstanding the serious difficulties confronting the first generation after Confederation, the Dominion had survived. It had developed essential political and economic institutions and had built a great railway. While still regarded, and regarding itself, as constitutionally subordinate to Great Britain within the imperial family, the Dominion was nevertheless self-governing in internal affairs and had begun the evolution toward distinct nationhood that would be consummated in the twentieth century. Despite strong pressures for free trade with the United States (a step some feared might lead to economic and ultimately political absorption), the Dominion had worked out a national economic policy of its own.

The election of Laurier coincided, accidentally, to be sure, with a dramatic improvement in the economic climate. Canada benefited from the worldwide rise in agricultural prices. Gold discovered in the Yukon (1898), and other, more enduring mining strikes in various parts of the Precambrian Shield (in Ontario and Quebec) and in southern British Columbia did much to stimulate the economy. Canada now became more attractive to settlers, and immigrants streamed in from the British Isles and from Central Europe. Hundreds of thousands of experienced American farmers moved across the 49th parallel into the "last best west." A new mood of optimism encouraged promoters, with government help, to build two additional transcontinental railways, projects that would later be a financial embarrassment. In the East there was a considerable increase in the number and size of manufacturing and other, primarily processing, plants; links with the financial and industrial centers in the United States, and with organized labor, became increasingly important. In a burst of imperial enthusiasm, Canada granted a preferential tariff to British goods in 1897, but because of geography and other factors, trade with the United States continued to grow.

The change in the economic climate eased one set of Canadian problems, but those relating to tensions between French-speaking and English-speaking Canadians persisted. Laurier, the first French-speaking Canadian to hold the office of prime minister, was a man who tried to appeal to moderates of both sides and to find compromises. In the long run, he was overwhelmed by the ethnic and cultural conflict, as were so many others before and after him.

At first, Laurier had some success in finding a modus vivendi with respect to some of the traditional internal tensions between the two linguistic and cultural groups. The new factor that emerged during his years as leader of the Liberal Party was the impact of external events, which lent a new bitterness to the age-old differences. The first of these events was the Boer War, which broke out in 1899. For the first time in its history, Canada faced the question of whether its troops should fight in a British war. The war had come at a time of intense imperial enthusiasm: the most vocal English Canadians insisted that Canada demonstrate solidarity with the empire by coming to the aid of the mother country. French Canadians, however, lacked this sentimental feeling, and many of them also argued that sending troops would set a dangerous precedent for the future. As usual, Laurier sought to find a compromise, which in this case was to authorize a purely voluntary force. This arrangement angered the most brilliant of Laurier's younger followers, Henri Bourassa, who broke with him, yet it failed to satisfy the proimperial English Canadians. The end of the war eased tensions, but bitter memories were left on both sides.

Soon after the Boer War ended, the spotlight shifted to Canadian-American relations, focused by the Alaska boundary dispute. This dispute, turning on the interpretation of maps made nearly a century earlier, affected the ownership of certain harbors along the Alaska Panhandle that were essential for access to the interior. Access was now of increased importance because of the discovery of gold in the Yukon. The American president, Theodore Roosevelt, was completely convinced that his country's claim, inherited from Russia through the purchases of Alaska in 1867, was incontrovertible. Indeed, he believed that the Canadian claim had been trumped up because of the Klondike gold strikes. He talked of putting in troops to run a boundary line according to the American interpretation; but he finally agreed to leave the decision to a group of three "impartial jurists."

Canadians were furious when Roosevelt appointed three Americans not noted for judicial impartiality to sit across the table from two Canadian judges and one English judge. When the decision was announced in 1903—the Englishman, in the interests of a peaceful settlement, had sided with the Americans—Canadians could not decide whether they were angrier with the Americans or with the British.

The incident, perhaps relatively unimportant in itself, throws great deal of light on the development of Canadian attitudes. It significantly advanced the growth of Canadian national feeling, and for once at least it was a feeling shared by both English-speaking and French-speaking Canadians. It afforded further proof that, although Canada would remain friendly with the United States, the two countries had opposing interests on many questions. Canadians also learned that it was necessary to be carefully prepared and toughminded when bargaining with "the Yankees." Finally, however much Canadians favored close ties with the Empire, it seemed clear that Britain could not be implicitly relied upon to defend Canadian interests, especially in negotiations with the United States where good Anglo-American relations could be seen to take priority.

In the aftermath of the Alaska boundary dispute, the need to improve machinery for conducting Canadian foreign affairs was recognized. In 1909 Canada created a Department of External Affairs, which gradually came to serve as its "Foreign Office" or "State Department." In that same year the United States and Canada established the International Joint Commission to study and settle problems arising along the long boundary, especially those concerning waterways. The IJC, which consists of three Canadian and three U.S. commissions plus a technical staff, is busier than ever today in an era of growing concern over pollution.

As the Boer War and the Alaska boundary dispute indicated, in the early years of the twentieth century Canadians were concerned with relations external to North America as well as bilateral Canada-U.S. relations. Problems relating to these two areas of concern coincided in one of the most important of Canadian federal elections, that of 1911. This election vividly highlighted certain persistent features of Canada's political, social, and economic life.

In external relations, discussion continued to center around the nature and organization of the British Empire. Many English-speaking Canadians, who were really ardent nationalists at heart, believed that Canada's destiny could best be fulfilled in close partnership with Great Britain in the larger fellowship of the Empire. These "imperialists" believed that such a partnership would give Canada an opportunity to act on the world stage. In their eyes, the political and military institutions of the Empire had to be reorganized in a centralizing direction. Laurier opposed such views because he knew that they would have a divisive effect in Canada. He stated that Canada would come to the assistance of Great Britain if the latter were threatened; but he refused to commit himself in advance. However, the pressure on him became so strong, particularly after it was evident that Great Britain was involved in a naval arms race with Germany, that in 1910 his government sought parliamentary approval for a small Canadian navy that could be placed under British command in time of emergency. Unfortunately, Laurier had again found a compromise that satisfied neither side. In the election of 1911 Bourassa and the French-Canadian nationalists attacked the prime minister for putting Canadians at the beck and call of the British, while many English-speaking Canadians demanded that Canada do much more to aid the mother country.

At the same time, the perennial issue of trade relations with the United States came back to haunt Laurier and the Liberals. Although Macdonald and the Conservatives had set the country on a protectionist course partly in response to American protectionism, free trade (or rather lower trade barriers) with the United States had been a goal of many Canadian politicians ever since the Reciprocity Treaty of 1854. Now, in 1910, Laurier was presented with what seemed to be a golden opportunity when the American president, W. H. Taft, proposed a reciprocal agreement lowering duties on a broad range of goods. But instead of being widely welcomed by the Canadian public, the agreement became the object of an emotional propaganda campaign: opponents argued that it would be the first step toward annexation by the United States and that it would weaken ties with Britain. In 1911, After fifteen years in power, Laurier was defeated. It is not an excessive oversimplification to say that defeat came because he was thought to be too pro-British in Quebec and too "pro-Yankee" in English-speaking Canada.

Laurier's successor, Robert Borden, dominated Canadian politics in the decade after 1911. A Conservative and a Nova Scotian, Borden nevertheless developed policies that bore some similarity to those of his Liberal predecessor from Quebec. It appears to be almost a law of Canadian politics that prime ministers who have any success seek middle-of-the-road and unheroic policies.

Borden's great test, and also the country's great test, came as a result of participation in World War I (1914–18). It can be argued that this war was the most important event in the history of modern Canada. It brought social change, industrial expansion, a new role in world affairs, a sense of great accomplishment, intense internal bitterness, and of course enormous losses and suffering. There is space here to touch only briefly on a few aspects of this searing experience.

Despite the debates of previous years, there was no disagreement about Canada's course when Britain and Germany went to war in 1914. As a member of the British Empire, Canada was legally at war; but the nature and extent of Canada's contribution would be its own decision. Borden's government elected to raise troops on a voluntary basis. Thousands of young men flocked to recruiting centers, and by early 1915 large Canadian forces were in action on the Western

European front. As the struggle turned into a savage war of attrition, the demands for more troops mounted. By early 1917 the Borden government had to decide whether it could continue to obtain enough men through the system of voluntary enlistments. Discussion of the subject was somewhat sharpened when the United States entered the war (April 1917) and used a draft army from the outset. Eventually the Canadian government made the fateful decision to resort to a similar compulsory method of raising troops. It was fateful because the decision provoked the severest internal crisis in Canadian history up to that time.

It was probably inevitable that French-Canadian attitudes toward the war should be less ardent than those of their English-speaking compatriots. French Canadians did in fact volunteer in considerable numbers, but the community as a whole did not share the same emotional response to the cause as English-speaking Canadians, many thousands of whom were fairly recent immigrants from Great Britain. Moreover, the raising of troops and the organization of the army in Quebec was handled with an obtuseness that alienated many. Finally, in 1917, a bitter dispute over language rights in the schools erupted in Ontario. The stage was set for trouble, and it came in the wartime "conscription" election of 1917. The Borden government was returned to power, but its support now came almost entirely from English-speaking Canada, while the Liberal Opposition was reduced mainly to members from Quebec. Canada was split along linguistic and cultural lines as never before, a particularly bitter result for Laurier, who had devoted his life to attempts to improve relations between the two groups.

The war and its aftermath forced various changes in Canada's international status. Borden proved to be as determined as Laurier had been to find a distinctive role for Canada. During the war he urged that, in imperial and allied discussions and planning, Canada must be treated as an ally and not as a colony. At the Paris Peace Conference in 1919, Borden insisted that Canada should participate (and sign the resulting Treaty of Versailles), both as an individual country and as a member of the British Empire delegations. To some countries, especially perhaps the United States, this dual role appeared anomalous, but the situation arose out of Canada's evolving status. Most Canadians, at least the Anglophones, had no wish to break sentimental and emotional ties with the Empire, particularly with war memories so vivid; nor did Canadians seek all the constitutional trappings of formal independence. At the same time, they wanted international recognition that Canada was no longer a subordinate colony; and they wanted improved machinery for conducting their own external affairs, including membership in the League of Nations.

As a result, the twenty years between the two world wars saw a series of steps, none of them in itself of major impact, by which Canada rather cautiously groped its way toward a changed status in the international community. These steps are discussed in the last chapter of this volume.

The man who was prime minister during three quarters of the interwar period was William Lyon Mackenzie King, one of the strangest yet most successful of all Canadian politicians. King—a grandson, on his mother's side, of the 1837 rebel, Mackenzie—was an extremely respectable and cautious middle-of-the-road politician. A Harvard Ph.D. who had worked for the Rockefellers in the United States, King was a bachelor who found solace in his diary, his dogs, and spiritualism. Although of English-speaking Protestant background, he won the leadership of the badly shaken Liberal Party in 1919 by swearing unswerving allegiance to the ideals of the departed leader, Laurier. During a long career he was to trim his sails on many issues; but he did on the whole try to remain firm to that sworn allegiance. In consequence, he nearly always (except in 1930–35) had a firm base in Quebec. He became prime minister after the election of 1921 and, except for a brief interval in 1926, remained in office until the end of the decade. After defeat in 1930, he returned to power in 1935, to remain there until his retirement in 1948 after a career of unprecedented length as prime minister.

One factor that has been emphasized, perhaps overemphasized, by some historians in discussing Canada's evolving international status is the personal attitude of Mackenzie

King toward Great Britain and the United States. Although he always felt an intense admiration for British political traditions and values, he apparently felt a certain unease, even suspicion, when dealing with British leaders, particularly those of upper-class origin. On the other hand, he seemed to be somewhat more at home with Americans even though there were times when he felt that they too patronized Canadians. In all this, as in other matters, King was a fairly typical Canadian. But probably more important than King's personal prejudices was the fact that Canada was moving toward a new status, yet Canadians remained deeply divided about how fast they should go, and in what direction. Caution, therefore, was probably inevitable.

The trend toward a new status was evidenced by various events of the 1920s and 1930s. In 1922, for example, when the British government asked the Dominions for help in the event that war resulted from a crisis relating to Turkey, King replied that Canada could not be committed in advance. The Canadian Parliament would have to be consulted before any action was taken, a formula that King adhered to until Canada entered World War II in 1939. Then in 1923, Canada signed its first treaty without an accompanying British signature. A formal recognition of the changed status of the Dominions within the Commonwealth (that term was now superseding the world "Empire") came at a conference in 1926 when the leaders of Great Britain and the Dominions declared that Britain and the Dominions were "equal in status and in no way subordinate one to another." This declaration was translated into law in 1931 by the Statute of Westminster, which made it clear that the British Parliament did not have authority to legislate for the Dominions. Even so, there were qualifications arising out of Canadian domestic problems. Since Canadians could not agree on a formula for amending their constitution (as is still the case in 1980), the Canadian government requested that authority to amend the British North America Act should remain with the British Parliament. The Judicial Committee of the Privy Council—a British body—also remained for a time the highest court of appeal for Canadian cases. Only in 1949 were appeals to that court abolished, leaving the Supreme Court of Canada as the nation's highest court.

The search for a new status in the interwar years included a continuing debate over how active Canada should be in world affairs. The fact that Canada joined the League of Nations, and the United States did not, seemed to some observers to indicate that the former country was avoiding the isolationism so increasingly asserted by the latter. In fact, however, Canada showed little enthusiasm for the collective security measures that emanated from the League. Distant from the world's trouble spots, Canada was no readier than the United States to commit itself in advance to come to the aid of countries threatened by aggression. This North American mood of withdrawal from world affairs became more intense after the Great Depression developed out of the stock-market crash of 1929. The 1930s brought long years of misery, poverty, and mass unemployment to both countries, leaving little interest in or energy for efforts at international cooperation.

Instead, in both countries there was a trend toward economic nationalism and also, on Canada's part, a tendency to stress the continental rather than the Commonwealth aspects of Canadian life. Both countries raised their tariff to protectionist levels in 1930 in an attempt to safeguard domestic industries from outside competition. To be sure, by entering into preferential agreements with Great Britain and the Dominions in 1932, Canada made a gesture toward increasing trade with Commonwealth countries, but its practical results were limited. The pull of the continent exerted itself with a greater intensity because of new developments in the Canadian economy. Canada's leading exports were coming to be newsprint, woodpulp, and other forest products, and also various base metals. For these products the leading market was the United States. Thus, while each country was striving to protect its own economy, at the same time the economies of the two countries were becoming more closely tied together.

Yet, despite unprecedented domestic problems, Canada (like the United States) found it increasingly difficult to ignore international problems in the years after 1935. Mussolini's invasion of Ethiopia, Hitler's occupation of the Rhineland, and the outbreak of the Spanish Civil War heralded a succession of crises that were to culminate in the outbreak of World War II in 1939. Mackenzie King realized that Canadians were sharply divided with respect to the policy to be adopted toward European affairs, and he tried to avoid taking any position that would polarize opinion. He refused to support oil sanctions against Italy in 1935 on the ground than Canada was too weak a country to take the lead on so dangerous an issue. While publicly stating that from a purely legal point of view Canada would be at war when Great Britain was at war and privately warning Hitler that Canada would undoubtedly support Great Britain, at the same time he also adhered to his old formula that Parliament would decide. He would take no action to put Canada into war until the Canadian Parliament had an opportunity to debate and vote on the issue. So, at almost all costs, the prime minister was determined to avoid the bitter internal divisions that had marked the years 1914–17.

On September 3, 1939, Great Britain declared war on Germany. Although there was no question that the vast majority of Canadians supported Canadian entry, King stuck to his formula. On September 10 Parliament met and in a voice vote declared war against Germany. Only one member (a pacifist) clearly indicated his opposition; but there was undoubtedly more opposition in the country than this near unanimity in Parliament had indicated. It should be noted that the process was less automatic than in 1914: the issue of neutrality versus intervention had been extensively debated for at least four years. Moreover, there was a gap of one week, even though it was merely symbolic, between the British and the Canadian declarations. Also, it was widely believed (a case of wishful thinking) that the day of large armies was over and that Canada's contribution would be mainly economic. Indeed, there was a commitment by the King government, soon made more explicit, that the government would never resort to conscription. Finally, and perhaps less consciously, Canadian entry was one more way of marking out a different approach to foreign affairs from the neutrality policy of the United States. To follow the American lead would, it was believed, be to fall into the American orbit.

It was of course hard to avoid this latter possibility. After the shattering events in Europe in the spring and summer of 1940, culminating in the fall of France, the very real prospect of a Nazi victory led North Americans to feel more threatened than had seemed at all possible a few months before. The American president, Franklin Roosevelt, moved away from neutrality and called for a rapid military buildup. Bases off the Atlantic Coast were acquired from Britain in exchange for overage destroyers. Most striking from a bilateral point of view was the meeting of Roosevelt and King hastily arranged in August 1940. The two men, after very little consultation with their advisers, signed an agreement to establish a Permanent Joint Board on Defense that was empowered to recommend plans for the cooperative defense of the continent. Construction of a military road in Canada, to link Alaska with the lower forty-eight states, was soon begun; and many other joint projects followed during the remaining years of the war. In April 1941 King and Roosevelt signed the Hyde Park Declaration to facilitate defense-related trade between the two countries and to provide for defense production sharing. These and other measures arising out of the wartime emergency led to an increased intermeshing of the Canadian and American economies. This has continued since the war ended, evoking some concern among Canadians in recent years about Canada's ability to manage its own economic affairs.

The war not only changed the contours of Canadian-American relations; it also revived French-English tensions in Canada despite King's efforts to keep them quiescent. At the outset of the war King had some success when a Quebec government headed by a French-speaking nationalist* (Maurice Duplessis) was defeated and replaced by one willing to

---

* I.e., a spokesman for the interests of the French-Canadian, more recently the Québécois, "nation."

cooperate with the federal Liberals. To attain this result, however, the latter had to reaffirm, more strongly than ever, that they would not introduce overseas conscription. In 1940 the fall of France led many in English-speaking Canada to raise the cry for conscription. King tried to meet it in part by providing for conscription for home (i.e., continental) defense. Those on overseas service would still be volunteers. The question came up again after the entry of the United States into the war (December 7, 1941), with a full conscription law already on the books. King finally resorted to a plebiscite that asked the voters whether the government should be released from its pledges regarding conscription. The result was a crystal-clear demonstration of the division in the country: in English-speaking Canada, 80 percent voted to release the government, but in Quebec 72 percent voted the other way. King's conviction that he must continue to put off the question as long as possible was renewed. But in the autumn of 1944, when the heavy casualties followed the D day invasion of France, he had to give way to mounting pressures. Conscripts were now to become liable for overseas service. In fact, however, the war ended before very many of them saw action. The crisis had been long and at times exceedingly angry, but the country had not been as sharply divided as in 1914–18.

Thus the King government survived. In the summer of 1945 it once more was returned to power. It was not really very popular in any part of the country; but its Cabinet contained many able and experienced men who had conducted the war effort with remarkable efficiency. And in view of the vociferous proconscription stance of the Conservatives (since 1942 called the Progressive Conservatives), Quebec voters, although somewhat disenchanted, had no choice but to support the Liberal Party. Besides, King had found a French-speaking Canadian to serve as a prominent member of his Cabinet: Louis St. Laurent, a man widely trusted in Quebec. St. Laurent, who later succeeded King as party leader and as prime minister, was a man of moderate views who, many Canadians hoped, might be able to restore harmony between the two principal language groups in Canada.

Canada Since World War II

In the earlier sections we have stressed certain continuing and long-range themes in Canada's evolution, such as relations with Great Britain, the United States, and the world generally; problems of the economy and the nature of Canadian regionalism; and finally, relations between language and cultural groups within Canada. These remain important themes in discussing recent Canadian history.

Canada's relations with Great Britain changed drastically in the thirty years after 1945; but the change was so gradual, and so little marked by dramatic events, that its extent often went almost unheeded. At the beginning of the period, Canadians felt very close to Great Britain. Indeed, a few years earlier, in the summer of 1939, King George VI and his wife, Queen Elizabeth, had made a triumphal coast-to-coast tour of Canada that was the occasion for a great outburst of loyal feelings. Such feelings were strengthened through the long years of war, and human ties were further consolidated by a very large British immigration that came in the decade or so after the war. The accession of Queen Elizabeth in 1952, and her coronation the following year, were marked with deep emotion in Canada. For many Canadians the concept of a close tie with Great Britain remained central and has not weakened to this day.

Nevertheless, the tie did weaken, and for various reasons. One of these was the changing composition of the Canadian population. In the quarter century after 1945 there was much immigration from Italy, Germany, several other European countries, and from other parts of the world. When added to the French-speaking population of about 30 percent, the population of non-British origin came to outnumber significantly the population of British Isles origin. Taken as a whole, young Canadians often lacked the sense of identification with the "mother country" that had often been true of their parents and grandparents.

At the same time, Canadian perceptions of Great Britain changed. Until 1939 it had been seen as a great power, the center of a worldwide empire, the home of parliamentary government and of justice under law, and the mother country whose protection had been vital to Canada's survival and growth. But after 1945 the Empire was dismantled; the Commonwealth consisted largely of countries with which Canada had little sense of fellow feeling; and Great Britain was obviously a declining power. A traumatic event came with the Suez crisis in 1956 when the Canadian government felt that it could not support British policy. There was an anguished outcry from some Canadians, mostly of an older generation, who felt that Canada should always stand at Britain's side, but majority opinion was probably with the Canadian government. Furthermore, trade and financial ties between Canada and Britain became relatively less important than in an earlier generation.

Coincident with the decline in the strength of the British tie was the growth of a sense of Canadian nationalism, especially among English-speaking Canadians. (National feeling among French-speaking Canadians is normally, although not always, a different phenomenon, and will be discussed later in this section.) National feeling among English-speaking Canadians had its roots deep in the past, but it took on new characteristics after 1945. Canadian citizenship legislation, in 1946–47 and in later years, sharpened the legal distinctions between Canadian citizens and British subjects. It gradually became accepted (though not legislated) that "O Canada" was the national anthem, not "God Save the Queen." In 1952 a Canadian became governor general for the first time, a precedent that has been followed ever since. In 1965—after a spirited and at times acrimonious debate—Canada adopted a distinctive flag that did not include the Union Jack of Great Britain. These and other matters had as much to do with symbol as substance; but so does so much of nationalism. They indicate that Canadians were searching for an identity of their own, separate from Great Britain as well as from the United States.

Turning to Canadian-American relations, these for the sake of convenience may be divided into two categories: relations arising out of the impact of world affairs on each country and bilateral relations. With respect to the first, the two countries emerged from World War II as firm military allies. Each joined the United Nations and each played a prominent part in programs of reconstruction to deal with the devastation caused by the war. Each was alarmed by the possibility that Soviet influence might become paramount in Central or even Western Europe in the later 1940s. Prime Minister St. Laurent made one of the first suggestions for a binding relationship between the United States and Canada on the one hand and various countries of Western Europe on the other. This idea took form in the North Atlantic Treaty Organization (NATO), ratified in 1949, in which the two North American countries entered into a long-term military-political alliance with the leading countries of Western Europe. From that time to the present, the larger outlines of American and Canadian policy with respect to the defense of Europe have generally coincided, although there have been numerous points of friction about the size of forces and on the question of whether NATO should be seen in primarily military or in broader terms.

With respect to the other side of the world—Asia—there was much more divergence in the policies and attitudes of the two countries. Canada's military alliance with the United States applied only to Europe and did not commit it to support American actions in the Pacific. Nevertheless, the extremely close relations between the two countries, and the great disparity in power between them, meant that Canada had to be extremely cautious in voicing disagreements; conversely, the United States, although it certainly conceded the right of an ally and neighbor to disagree, hoped for understanding and, preferably, support from neighbors in times of great difficulties.

A brief reference to events in China, Korea, and Vietnam will illustrate these general statements. The victory of the Communists in China in 1949 was viewed in Canada as a fact that had to be accepted; Canada was close to extending diplomatic recognition to the Peking regime when the outbreak of the Korean War forced a postponement. In the United States, however, the "loss of China" became central to a prolonged and angry debate, combined with a general determination to protect the Chiang Kai-shek government on Taiwan and even to approve Chiang's use of that island as a base for a return to the mainland; Chinese-American relations remained frozen. After the outbreak of the Korean War (June 1950), Canada agreed to send troops to aid South Korea, but as a member of the UN, not as an ally of the United States. (Of course, it was also important that Canada show solidarity with the United States in a time of great crisis.) Canadians fought to repulse the North Korean invasion, but they strongly disapproved when General MacArthur's actions seemed calculated to broaden the war by bringing in China. Finally, many Canadians came to feel that it was a great mistake for the United States to become deeply involved in civil conflicts in the Indochina peninsula, especially in Vietnam. This issue was also, of course, a source of intense debate within the United States; nevertheless, American leaders, notably President Lyndon Johnson, counted on official Canadian support for, or at least acquiescence in, American policy in Southeast Asia.

If space allowed, this Canadian view could be pursued with respect to other areas—Latin America, Africa, and the Middle East particularly—and to other international topics such as disarmament and developmental assistance. This, however, will be discussed in Chapter 7. Suffice it to say at this point that it is not a simple matter for a Canadian government to pursue an independent policy intended to express Canadian aspirations and protect Canadian interests, and at the same time remain (as it must) on friendly and cooperative terms with the United States.

Turning to bilateral relations between the United States and Canada, we find that these have become so numerous and so complex that it is impossible here to do more than allude to a few highlights. An adequate treatment of any one of these topics would require a lengthy and, in most cases, highly technical treatment. Nevertheless, a few topics that have been prominent in Canadian-American relations during the last generation may be illustrative. We may begin with American cultural penetration of Canada, through the impact of American TV programs, movies, films, and magazines that are widely disseminated in Canada. This is probably the most difficult aspect of Canadian-American relations for Americans to understand. Americans are making these cultural products for their own consumption, and they are not forcing them on Canadians. Canadians should be, and in fact are, quite free to refuse to look at, listen to, or read any American program, film, or magazine.

Despite these facts, the issue is there and has existed from the early years of the nineteenth century, when editors and others complained of "Americanizing" influences. For a long time it was hoped that these might be counterbalanced by the British tie and that, in the meantime, distinctively Canadian forms of expression would emerge. But the advent of radio, mass circulation periodicals, and then television convinced a growing number of Canadians that positive action had to be taken before all opportunity for native Canadian expression would be effectively stifled. During the years 1933 to 1936 a government-owned national radio network had been established, later to be expanded with the coming of television. A National Film Board was established in 1939. In the years after World War II the Canadian federal government sponsored exhaustive studies on the state of the arts, letters, and sciences; on broadcasting; and on publications, out of which came the Canada Council to subsidize and otherwise support Canadian cultural activity.

For the most part such action could not and should not be construed as "anti-American," yet the constantly growing role of the mass media, coinciding with a heightened consciousness of Canadian nationalism, has brought tensions. Most notable, perhaps, was the debate arising from the passage of Canadian tax legislation that effectively convinced *Time* magazine to discontinue publication of its Canadian edition (although the American edition continues, of course, to circulate widely in Canada on the same basis as other American periodicals). Other irritations have been caused by deleting commercials from TV programs emanating from stations at border points—for instance, Burlington, Vermont; Buffalo, New York; and Bellingham, Washington—as a means of attracting advertising revenue for Canadian stations. As long as Canadian national feeling exists, tensions arising out of cultural activity are likely to continue.

A second cluster of issues has been mainly economic in content, although attitudes toward these issues have been strongly affected by national aspirations in both countries; and it is also true that these attitudes have changed with economic change in each country. These general statements may be illustrated by reference to three specific issues, among the many that exist.

First, American investment in Canada. In the nineteenth and early twentieth centuries Canada suffered a chronic shortage of capital and welcomed foreign investment as a means of accelerating the growth of industrial facilities, the exploitation of natural resources, and the building of its transportation system. Investment from the United States seemed particularly desirable because Canada had a persistent imbalance of trade with that country, buying more from, than it sold to, its neighbor. Gradually, however, attitudes changed. It became apparent that a significant part of American investment went into certain sectors of the Canadian economy, especially those relating to natural resources, mainly mining, forest products, and oil. Such resources were crucial to Canada's future, and yet Canadians one day woke up to find them substantially under American control. Moreover, American investment in other areas, such as manufacturing, in addition to generating dividends also resulted in a steady erosion of Canadian ownership and management. The list of small Canadian companies that were bought out and absorbed or eliminated by American giants became longer and longer. Although many Canadians insisted that the free play of market forces should not be interfered with, others demanded some sort of government review of foreign investment to prevent the Canadian economy from becoming a collection of branch plants controlled from outside the country in accordance with policies and decisions not necessarily in Canada's interest.

Second, boundary waters. There is a long history of mutually beneficial cooperation on this subject, but regional and national interests and aspirations in each country have often led to complications. For example, in the early twentieth century Canada pushed strongly for joint Canadian-American development of the St. Lawrence Seaway, but the project was blocked by American east coast interests. In the early 1950s Canada announced that it would undertake an all-Canadian route. Soon afterward the United States announced that it would build two locks on the St. Lawrence. Thus, each country went forward separately. By the end of the 1950s a seaway had been built, but it was not really a joint project and difficulties over matters such as tolls have continued to exist. One could cite similar controversies over hydroelectric power development on the Columbia River. This river rises in British Columbia and then flows to the ocean through the United States. Large power developments have extensive repercussions in adjoining regions, which in this case may lie in separate countries. Moreover, on the Canadian side, it was not always clear whether jurisdiction lay with the federal government or the province. As always, immediate cash benefits had to be balanced against long-term consequences and opportunities. Small wonder, then, that innumerable complications prolonged the Columbia River negotiations for more than twenty years. Other waterways questions, which have sometimes been viewed differently on the two sides of the border, are the diversion of water from the Great Lakes, responsibility for cleaning up these lakes, and dam building on rivers in the Great Plains.

Third and last in this short list of economic issues is energy policy. Canada has long been, and continues to be, a large importer of American coal. For many years Canada also imported oil from the United States, but after the discovery of oil deposits in the Canadian West (mainly in Alberta) in the later 1940s, Canada was not only able to supply its own market as far east as the Ottawa River but also had substantial amounts available for export to the United States.* The American market for Canadian oil was much valued at a time when Canada needed increased exports and when oil reserves

* It was considered to be too expensive to pipe oil from western Canada to the provinces east of the Ottawa River. That market was supplied by imports from overseas, mainly from Venezuela.

seemed to be almost unlimited. Large quantities of natural gas were also discovered in the Canadian West, and that fuel too was moved in volume to both Canadian and American markets. In a relatively short period of time, vast and intricate networks of oil and natural gas pipelines were laid across the continent, crisscrossing the Canadian-American border in many places. The United States and Canada were, on a per capita basis, the world's largest users of energy, but they seemed to be blessed both with large domestic reserves and with readily available supplies from overseas fields in the Middle East and elsewhere.

As is well known, the picture changed quickly and drastically in the 1970s. Domestic reserves proved to be more limited and more difficult to exploit than had been believed or hoped, and overseas imports became more expensive and more uncertain. Both Canada and the United States sought, with growing desperation, sensible energy policies in a rapidly changing situation. In particular, Canada found it necessary to cut back on exports to those very American markets that had come to rely on such supplies. Also, in the new mood of Canadian nationalism (referred to earlier), there was a growing feeling that Canada should not "squander" nonrenewable natural resources by selling them to outside markets when they would be needed at home in the future. There was, however, no single Canadian view. Western producers and eastern consumers saw the matter quite differently.

A further factor was introduced by the discovery of large oil and natural gas reserves along the Arctic shores of Alaska in the late 1960s. The United States assured itself of an all-American route for the transit of some of this oil by building a pipeline across Alaska, and then shipping the oil in tankers to the "lower forty-eight" states. Yet this solution remains of intense concern to Canadians, because an oil spill from any of the tankers could do unpredictable harm to the British Columbia coast.

Similar problems might have emerged in bringing Arctic natural gas to southern markets. One possibility was to adopt the oil precedent: build a pipeline across Alaska and carry the fuel as liquefied natural gas in tankers to west coast ports.

Estimates indicate, however, that gas could be carried more cheaply to the markets where it was mainly needed (the American Middle West) if an overland pipeline from Alaska was built. There were two possibilities, both going across Canada—one down the Mackenzie River Valley and the other along the Alaska Highway route through the Yukon. Thus the transit of Alaska natural gas to the lower forty-eight states became a first-class issue in Canadian-American relations. It was also a domestic issue in Canada, as some Canadians argued that the fragile northern environment should not be jeopardized for the sake of bringing natural gas to American consumers. But the fact remained that in various places pipelines crossed American territory to bring fuel to Canadian consumers. There was also the question of the rights of native peoples, the Indians and Eskimos. Finally, Canada too had extensive oil and gas reserves in the Arctic and thus had a further interest in pipeline routes. The pipeline question became a most dramatic example of the new complications in Canadian-American relations. It was only apparently resolved when, after intense negotiation in the summer of 1977, a formal treaty was agreed to specifying the Alaskan Highway route for a pipeline, and guaranteeing "free transit" for Prudhoe Bay gas. As in the case of Alaskan oil, however, the ultimate solution to the complicated problem of bringing this gas to market remains elusive.

Turning now to internal developments in Canada in the last thirty years, we shall focus on regionalism and the economy, and then on developments relating to language and culture.

Regardless of transcontinental railways, the Trans-Canada Highway, two national airlines, the post office, the Canadian Broadcasting Corporation, and other means of national transportation and communication, and despite the rather striking upsurge of Canadian national feeling in the last two decades, Canada remains a country of regions. The country is so large and the populated areas are so strung out that Canadians often know better (and visit more frequently) nearby American centers than they do other Canadian provinces.

Distance is not the only factor contributing to the strength of regionalism in Canada. Apart from language and cultural differences, there are also sharp disparities in economic growth and achievement. In general, three provinces— Ontario, Alberta, and British Columbia—tend to have higher standards of living, better economic performance, and lower unemployment figures than do the Atlantic Provinces, Quebec, and the two Prairie Provinces of Manitoba and Saskatchewan.* There are many reasons for these disparities. Some of the most important are the central position of Ontario with respect to markets and access to raw materials and good transportation facilities; Quebec's harsh climate and rugged terrain; the distance of the Atlantic Provinces from the main centers of North American economic activity; the still heavy reliance of the Prairie Provinces on one or two agricultural crops; Alberta's good fortune in possessing oil and gas beneath its soil; and British Columbia's excellent coastal location and diversity of natural resources.

It might be argued that such factors are largely beyond the control of man and need not be a barrier to cooperation among regions. It should also be noted that for some years the Canadian federal government has attempted to "even out" the worst of the disparities by transferring tax money from the richer to the poorer provinces. Nevertheless, economic disparities have in fact been the source of recrimination and sharp political debate. For many years it has been widely believed in both western and eastern provinces that economic policy on such matters as the tariff and freight rates has been determined in a way to benefit southern Ontario and certain industrial parts of Quebec. Some Québécois argued that a small group of English-speaking capitalists obtained control of the most profitable parts of the economy at an early stage and have since systematically exploited the majority of the provincial population. Albertans admit their good fortune, but they note that oil and gas are nonrenewable and that unless revenues derived from them are used to diversify the economy, the province prosperity will be brief and fleeting. These are

* Sasketchewan, however, is likely to have a brighter future due to its natural resources.

only a few points in a continuous debate that is troubled and occasionally angry. Although to most peoples of the world Canada appears to be a richly endowed land of vast opportunities, Canadians themselves are preoccupied with the realities of inflation, unemployment, strikes, pollution, lack of industrial competitiveness, foreign control, and the imminent exhaustion of key resources.

Finally, there is the still unsettled question of Quebec in Canada or Quebec versus Canada. On November 15, 1976, a relatively new political party, the Parti Québécois, won the majority of the legislative seats in a Quebec provincial election. The PQ, as its name is often abbreviated, pledged that it would hold a referendum sometime during its term of office to ascertain whether the voters favor the separation of Quebec from the rest of Canada. The party's goal is to obtain political independence for the province, while retaining as yet undefined economic ties with Canada: a position summarized by the term "Sovereignty/Association."

To many Canadians the PQ's electoral success came as both a shock and a surprise. If Quebec becomes independent, could the remnants of Canada—the Atlantic Provinces, Ontario, and the western provinces—continue to function as a viable national state, or would each Canadian region gravitate toward, and eventually be absorbed into, the neighboring American Republic? What response should be made toward the prospect of Quebec independence: a tough, unyielding opposition, or a readiness to compromise and adjust? Why had the independence movement grown in Quebec, despite federal government policies during the previous decade and more, intended to meet the aspirations of French Canadians? The historian cannot answer these questions, but he may be able to put them in some perspective.

It is important to remember that the PQ, although apparently a recent phenomenon, has roots that go deep into Quebec's history. As we have noted in earlier pages, since the time of the British Conquest in 1760, French Canadians have been determined to survive in North America. For economic reasons thousands, even hundreds of thousands, have had to leave their native province to find jobs and homes in the

United States and in English-speaking Canada. Most of these migrants have eventually lost their language and their customs and have blended in with the majority culture. It has gradually become clear that the one certain place where French Canadians could survive as a people—a "nation"— was in the Province of Quebec, where they were in a majority and where they could develop and control institutions needed for ensuring that survival.

For more than a century before about 1960, the strategy of survival was essentially defensive and conservative: keep Quebec as rural as possible, because urban life tended to break down traditional values; keep Quebec as Catholic as possible, because the church provided indispensable leadership in the struggle for survival; build an educational system that gave more stress to the French language and to traditional values than it did to vocational subjects; in federal politics, support the Liberal Party—a factor that has helped to keep Liberal government in Ottawa for all but about ten years since 1921. But after 1960 such attitudes and strategies began to change rapidly in Quebec. A new provincial government led by Jean Lesage came to power, ousting the more Conservative and traditionalist Union Nationale regime. Under Lesage, Quebec experienced "the Quiet Revolution" (*la Révolution Tranquille*), a modernizing of social and economic life and institutions on many fronts. One of the most prominent ministers in the Lesage cabinet was René Lévesque, who shared with others the mood of optimism: Quebec could remain thoroughly French in language, institutions, and outlook, but could also be modern and progressive. Under the federal Liberal government of Lester Pearson (1962–68) there was a sympathetic response in Ottawa to the new aspirations of Quebec. The concept of "cooperative federalism" was formulated, allowing for various accommodations and adjustments between Ottawa and Quebec. Many observers spoke of a "special status" for Quebec, or of Quebec becoming an "associated state," still in Confederation but with special powers, a province "not like the others."

From 1965 the debate went on, and gradually changed in character. In 1968, with the retirement of Lester Pearson,

Pierre Trudeau became Prime Minister. He was a strong believer in a modern and progressive Quebec, but he was equally opposed to "associated state" or "special status" concepts. He argued that they would work to isolate Quebec from the rest of the country, make it into a vast ghetto, and perhaps stimulate further fragmentation. Instead, Trudeau urged that Canada adopt policies that would give French Canadians a feeling of equality with other Canadians, a sense that they were at home in all parts of the country. Hence the Official Languages Act of 1969 sought to ensure linguistic rights, especially in the federal civil service.

On the other hand, René Lévesque and some other Québécois developed a different vision of the future of the province. They did not believe that Trudeau's program would work, if only because English-speaking Canada would never seriously cooperate. In their view, since the rest of Canada was larger and stronger than Quebec, it would always control the Confederation for its own benefit. Besides, Quebec nationalism was a legitimate, inevitable, and necessary force. A strengthened Quebec government offered the only assurance for the survival of the Québécois, a term now preferred to "French Canadians." Lévesque became convinced that Confederation could never be adjusted sufficiently to assure the survival and growth of French culture in Quebec. He left the provincial Liberal Party and with others entered the movement that became the Parti Québécois.

The meteoric rise to power of the PQ in 1976 can be explained by a variety of factors. The incumbent Liberal government under Robert Bourassa was widely seen as tired, arrogant, incompetent, and possibly corrupt. It had made many enemies, especially in dealing with the thorny language issue. On the other hand, Lévesque was an attractive figure who promised competent and honest government. Many voted in the 1976 election simply for change; the question of independence would wait until the promised referendum. Another factor that affected Quebec's political climate was the sizable immigration of the previous two or three decades. Most of the immigrants, of Italian and other European origin, tended in the course of time of integrate into the English-speaking community. Many Québécois felt that this process, combined with their own declining birthrate, might eventually jeopardize their majority position in their own province. Hence, they were ready to support a party that would take strong measures to protect and promote the French language.

Indeed, the PQ did dramatically strengthen the position of French as the required language of work and education (while failing to overcome constitutional obstacles to its being the only official language of the province's laws). Ironically, however, the Referendum of May 1980, asking voters to give Lévesque's party a mandate to negotiate Sovereignty/Association with the resurgent federal Liberals under Trudeau, resulted in a rejection of that mandate by a margin of roughly 59 to 41 percent. Even as experts disagreed as to the precise numbers of francophone (as opposed to anglophone) yes or no votes cast, Prime Minister Trudeau called a conference of Canada's provincial First Ministers to consider once again the possibility of constitutional change.*

At the time of writing, therefore, the debate over the future of Canada goes on, and the discipline of history affords no means of discerning the outcome. The historian's perspective does place emphasis upon certain facts. Canada has never been, and is not now, a homogeneous nation. The country consists of a number of regions that have entered into a working relationship more for reasons of practical convenience than of sentiment. Second, both in times of war and in the long years of peace, Canada and its provinces have retained their separateness from the United States. Close friendship

---

* After a summer's debate, the Premiers and Mr. Trudeau met in Ottawa in September 1980, but failed to agree on formulas for "patriating" the constitution with (as Trudeau insisted it have) a new sharing-of-powers arrangement, an agreeable amending formula and a Charter of Rights entrenched therein. The Prime Minister thereupon introduced (October 6) a repatriation bill into Parliament. By late spring of 1981 the bill had been challenged in three provincial courts, and was subsequently argued before the Supreme Court of Canada. In October of 1981 the Supreme Court ruled, in a split decision, that the Trudeau package *would* change the distribution of powers between Ottawa and the provinces, and that provincial agreement was necessary by *convention* but not by *law* in such a circumstance. At the time of writing, last minute efforts at compromise are being made; but presumably the government intends to send some version of the package to the British Parliament before the end of 1981 (Editor's note.)

with the United States and the impact of many American influences have not diminished the Canadian determination to maintain this tradition of separateness. Finally, with respect to Quebec, the historian might recall the words of Abraham Lincoln during another crisis: "Physically speaking, we cannot separate. We cannot remove our respective sections from each other, nor build an impassable wall between them." Whatever the outcome may eventually be, Quebec and the rest of Canada must continue side by side and find means of coexisting, as they have been trying to do for some two hundred years.

Chapter 3

A Political Perspective:

Institutions and the Canadian

Federal System

ROBERT J. DRUMMOND*

Introduction

THE STUDY OF politics in Canada has always been intimately linked with the study of Canada's history. Canada is a country born of political negotiation and nurtured on political debate. Its development to full nationhood was accomplished through diplomacy; its economic expansion was actively assisted by the state. The social and cultural issues that arise from Canada's diversity have always been objects of political resolution, and its independent existence is frequently justified in political terms. Much of Canada's history is political; it is perhaps not surprising that the analysis of Canadian politics has often been quite historical.

* Robert J. Drummond is an Associate Professor of Political Science at York University in Toronto. He received his Ph.D. from Northwestern University in 1975 and has published in *Current History* and the *Canadian Journal of Political Science*. Some of the research for his dissertation on Ontario voting behavior can be seen in his chapter in Donald MacDonald's *Government and Politics of Ontario*, and he is currently working with his colleagues at York on an extensive analysis of the June 1977 Ontario provincial election.

Canadian political studies from a historical perspective have mainly concerned themselves with the development of the Canadian constitution—the formal institutions of Canadian government, and the traditions that have guided Canadian political life. The importance of convention and usual practice in defining the constituion and the pervasiveness of the common law tradition (at least outside Quebec) necessitate some attention to the history of the country's politics. As well, Canadian scholars have often asserted that contemporary political issues are grounded in social cleavage historically developed. Thus, contemporary discussions of cultural diversity, economic disparity, and national autonomy are regularly supported by reference to historical events.

Following from this historical emphasis has been a concentration on description of the formal institutions of government. The organs of parliamentary government have provided, until very recently, the main subjects of Canadian political scholarship. Out of this tradition of institutional description there has also developed an extensive literature on public administration. The interest in this area has been generally practical, with structures and methods of operation featured, sometimes at the expense of general theory or the analysis of organizational behavior. Parliament and the civil service have received substantial attention in the earliest Canadian political studies, but the courts (perhaps because of their supposed independence from politics) and the analysis of public policy (perhaps because it was felt to be the business of the practitioner rather than of the observer) have received somewhat less thorough scholarly attention. In recent years, that emphasis has changed as the discipline of political science in Canada has expanded. While institutional and historical analysis is far from abandoned, it has been supplemented by attention to a variety of less formal aspects of the political process and to some hitherto neglected institutions.

The courts, for example, had long been the subject of *legal* scholarship concerning constitutional decisions. Now increasingly students of law and politics are coming to realize that, as one scholar has said, "political questions often come to the courts clothed as legal, constitutional questions." Attention has been drawn to the impact that court decisions have on the making and implemenation of public policy. Other aspects of the interface between law and politics, such as the role of the criminal justice system in sustaining social order, or the impact of exposure to the courts on individuals political beliefs, have as yet received little attention in Canada.

The study of public policy in Canada has begun to expand beyond the narrower field of public administration with which it has so often been linked, but it has yet to transcend the case-study approach and provide generalizations applicable across a variety of policy areas. Perhaps because of increased government interest in the field, perhaps because of academic reaction to the discipline's concentration on other (less central) aspects of the political process, this field has become a focus of new and increasing interest among students of politics in Canada.

Renewed interest in public policy has been linked to renewed interest in political economy. The large and pervasive role played by the state in the economic development of Canada has for years attuned Canadian scholars to the interface between politics and economics. This reflects the undoubted significance of economic criteria in any analysis of public policy, and indeed the centrality of economic policy itself in any government's program in the twentieth century.

Since 1950 the most marked reaction against the tradition of institutional description and historical analysis has been the attention devoted to mass political attitudes, beliefs, and behavior. Recent studies, some highly speculative, have explored value differences between Canadians and Americans (on the one hand) and among Canadians themselves (on the other). Attempts have been made to delineate the Canadian political "culture," sometimes conceiving that culture as a pervasive ethos characterizing the political system, at other times deriving the culture from an aggregation of individual findings about the beliefs, attitudes, and values of Canadians. Some scholars have purported to find, implicit in the institutions and behaviors of Canadian politics, a greater deference to authority, less egalitarianism, and more respect for law than is generally present in the United States. Others have found regional differences within Canada that are quite striking with respect to trust in government and feelings of personal efficacy. Canadian scholars continue to pay considerable attention to these aspects of political culture, particularly in attempting to provide them with empirical verification.

At the same time, scholars in Canada have concerned themselves with mass participation in politics, particularly voting behavior, and have undertaken considerable research into the sociological and psychological bases of party and candidate support. Mainly by means of survey research, Canadian scholars have begun to define mass political life and to differentiate it from mass politics in other comparable nations, especially the United States. Further elaboration is under way in such areas as socialization to politics (learning the political culture), recruitment of political elites (how do the influential get that way?), and activist behavior within institutions (how does bureaucratic politics really work?).

Considerable anxiety exists in the Canadian scholarly community that Canadian political science not become a kind of "miniature replica" of American political science. While American students will see many familiar concerns, methods, and models in Canadian political science's approach to the study of Canadian politics, they should be aware that some differences in the systems exist as well. For example, legal and institutional protection for the existence of a sizable linguistic and cultural minority (French-speaking Canadians) has led to the development of an ethic that permits, even encourages the maintenance of widespread ethnic diversity. Where the United States is likened to a "melting pot," Canada is likened to a "mosaic." Equally, operation of a parliamentary system of government has engendered different norms and expectations about central government institutions from those found in a presidential system. The Cabinet may deliberate in secret, but it must defend itself daily in the House of Commons. The Prime Minister may appeal directly to the people, but he will obtain power only if his party colleagues are also approved in sufficient number, each in his own constituency. Also, the national myths of Canada and the United States give different emphasis to the rule of law, the impact of the frontier, and the role of the state in national development. The United States was born in revolution and confrontation; Canada was a creatue of evolution and compromise.

While it is easy to overestimate the consequences of these differences, they should nevertheless not be ignored. Such differences as these have led Canadian scholars to give different emphasis to minority nationalism, regional economic disparity, the decline of Parliament, and the role of the courts, and on occasion to develop new variants of political thought. Thus, the coining, for example, of the term "Red Tory" for persons who combined the egalitarianism of liberal philosophy with the traditionalism and organic conception of society common among conservative thinkers.

Finally, it should be noted that one major difference continues to exist between Canada and the United States that has important consequences for almost all Canadian scholarship. Canada is a small country situated between the two most powerful nations in the world—the Soviet Union to the north, the United States to the south. Geographic and historical factors have combined to make the United States the most significant foreign actor in Canadian life, and a discussion of Canadian politics or economics without reference to the United States would be a distorted one. The reciprocal situation of course does not exist.

This chapter is divided into four sections, the first of which discusses the constitutional bases of Canadian government. An examination of the formal institutions of the Canadian parliamentary system including the monarchy, the Prime Minister and his Cabinet, the House of Commons (often referred to simply as "the Commons") and the Senate, the public bureaucracy, and the judiciary follows. The next section is a review of the informal instituions including political parties, election and voting behavior, and public opinion and the media. A concluding section examines federalism in Canada, it components and their workings including, for example, intergovernmental relations and provincial and local politics.

Constitutional Bases of Canadian Government

The constitution of a country is the set of norms and procedures that delineates the customary ways of transacting public business. The existence of a constitution ensures a clear and shared understanding among the active participants in the political process about the "rules of the game." All systems of government have constitutions in the broadest sense of the term, since all systesm have some principles or norms by which they operate. In a narrower sense, however, states are called constitutional only if those who govern them have agreed to limit their activities in accordance with established customary norms. In such cases, the relations among the organs of government, and between government and the citizen, have been regularized and stabilized. Respect for the fundamental law of the constitution ensures the maintenance of boundaries on the exercise of political power. Thus, a constitution is an important element in the government of all modern, democractic states.

It is also important to recognize that the rules of the game are not inflexible; they do change, and indeed must change, in response to the changing environments in which governments work. It is a constant challenge for modern governments to find the appropriate balance between stability and flexibility in their constitutional arrangements. A constitution that changes too easily provides no security against arbitrary government—the whims of a single administration. A constitution that changes too slowly loses respect, comes to be ignored, and in time may be said to have gone out of existence.

Many countries (such as the United States) have tried to ensure shared understanding of the rules of the game by encapsulating the fundamental law of the land in a single constitutional document. Such written constitutions are naturally subject to interpretation, and the intentions of those who drafted the document may or may not be well served by those who must interpret it subsequently. Other countries (such as Great Britain) have made so little effort to codify their constitutional principles that, at first glance, they appear to have no constitution at all. In fact, the constitution is said to be "unwritten" in such cases (although the traditions of government may really be written down in a number of separate locations). These different forms of constitution seem to give rise to different traditions of "constitutionalism," so that it has been said that:

for the Americans, anything unconstitutional is illegal, however right or necessary it may seem; for the British, anything unconstitutional is wrong, however legal it may be.[1]

Canada's constitution exemplifies a mixture of these two forms, in that it is partly written and partly unwritten. Historically, and still at the time of writing (Spring 1981),* the basic document of the written constitution is the British North America (BNA) Act, passed in 1867 by the British Parliament for the purpose of uniting a number of its colonies to form the Dominion of Canada, and amended by the British Parliament in succeeding years. The document can be understood only as it has been interpreted by the courts, including the Supreme Court of Canada and (prior to 1949) the Judicial Committee of the British Privy Council. Moreover, a literal reading of the BNA Act would give a misleading impression of the nature of Canadian government because of changes that have taken place in the role of the monarch's principal representative (the governor general) since the 1840s but that are not reflected in the language of the act. Also, many of the most important norms, procedures, and powers of Canadian government institutions were not included in the document but have evolved through practice and tradtition; others were merely implied by the statement in the preamble that Canada was to have a constitution "similar to Principle to that of the United Kingdom."[2]

In a sense, the BNA Act can be seen as a kind of "bill of exceptions" indicating the ways in which the Canadian system of government was to differ from that of Great Britain. The main differences resulted from the fact that Canada was to have a federal system of government, with political power divided between the central government and subordinate governments in the provinces. Some additional differences occurred because of guarantees to maintain Protestant and Roman Catholic education rights that existed prior to Confederation, and because of linguistic guarantees (in the federal

---

* But see The Constitutional Act (Canada Act) 1981 analyzed on pp. xvii–xx.

Parliament, the courts, and the legislature of the new Province of Quebec) for the new nation's substantial French-speaking minority.

Similarities with the British model included the principle of "responsible government" (to be discussed later); an independent, nonelected judiciary; retention of the monarch as head of state; a two-house national legislature with a popularly elected lower house; and the doctrine of parliamentary supremacy (explained below).[3]

In addition to the BNA Act, documents that contribute to the Canadian constitution include some statutes of the British Parliament (particularly the Statute of Westminster that markedly altered the relationship of the United Kingdom to her overseas Dominions); some statutes of the Canadian Parliament (such as the Supreme Court Act and the Official Languages Act); the constitutions of the provinces; and some provincial statutes that establish provincial government institutions.

Nondocumentary sources of the constitution reside mainly in the traditions, usages, and conventions of Parliament. These conventions rest not so much on their *legal* enforceability as on the severe *political* consequences that would accrue to any official who breached them.[4]

Apart from disputes about the distribution of powers between federal and provincial levels of government, the main grist for the mills of constitutional lawyers in Canada has been the doctrine of parliamentary supremacy. This doctrine is simply the principle (derived from the British model) that Parliament can make or repeal any law it wishes. In Canada, because the system of government is federal, the doctrine is complicated by the fact that there are two legislative bodies with authority over the same group of citizens. Thus, a law may be beyond the powers of the national government to enact because it is within the powers of the provincial governments (or vice versa), but no law can be wholly outside the competence of *both* levels of government. In practice, however, there are some exceptions to that apparently limitless grant of authority.

First, there are substantial parts of the BNA Act that

can be amended only by the Parliament of Great Britain (although such amendment would be made automatically at the request of the Canadian Parliament, provided no serious objections were lodged by one or more of the provinces).[5] Second, neither level of government has the right to delegate its legislative authority to the other level.[6] Third, it has been argued that there is an implied bill of rights in the statement that the constitution is "similar in Principle" to the British, and the abrogation of those rights would be unconstitutional—no matter how legal.[7] It has also been suggested that where a statute of the federal Parliament cannot be interpreted as being in harmony with the Canadian Bill of Rights (itself an ordinary federal statute), then that statute would be unconstitutional. This last argument has received little support in the courts, however, and must be regarded at this time as a tenuous constraint on the federal government.[8]

The components of the constitution will be made clearer by an examination of the main institutions of Canadian government and of the history of judicial interpretation the constitution has undergone.

Formal Institutions of the Canadian Governmental System

As a North American state with a population one-tenth the size of that of the United States, Canada provides some interesting contrasts with its neighbor to the south. Unlike the United States, Canada is not a republic with a presidential/congressional system of government, but rather is a constitutional monarchy with a parliamentary system. Authority in such a system is said to derive from the Crown, not the people, and there is a fusion of executive and legislative functions (in contrast to the separation of powers that characterizes the U.S. system). Developing the Canadian political system has meant adapting the institutions of monarchy to the realities of a modern, representative democracy. As a consequence, the formal institutions of government generally reflect the differences between Canada and the United States, while the informal processes of politics often highlight the similaries between the two countries.

Canada, like many Western democracies, faces the problem of promoting speed and efficiency in the design and implementation of government programs while at the same time maintaining the accountability of government elites to the mass electorate. The institutions of Canadian government may be evaluated in terms of their ability to resolve this tension satisfactorily in the performance of executive, legislative, and judicial tasks. The most important executive powers are exercised by the Prime Minister and his Cabinet under the authority of the Crown and through the agencies of the federal bureaucracy. However, the Prime Minister and Cabinet are also legislative actors, sitting in and directing the activities of the House of Parliament. Independent of both executive and legislatures is the appointed judiciary.

THE MONARCHY AND THE GOVERNOR GENERAL

The reigning monarch of Great Britain is at the same time king or queen of Canada, but the bulk of the monarch's functions in Canada are performed by his or her representative, the governor general. That Canada is a monarchy has one important technical consequence: all legal authority of the executive arm of government derives formally from the Crown. In reality, of course, the person of the monarch has become increasingly unimportant for political decision making, and the Crown has become a formal institution whose powers are exercised only with or at the direction of the Cabinet—the political executive responsible to Parliament. The governor general, therefore, has become significant mainly for his ceremonial and advisory functions.

The Office of the Governor General evolved from that of the colonial governor of the pre-Confederation period. The governor served as an active head of the colony's government as well as an overseer of the colony reporting to the British Colonial Office. For some years after 1867, the governor general continued to act as if he represented not only the Crown but also the British Imperial government. However, as Canadian autonomy from Britain increased in the twentieth century, the role of the governor general as British supervisor of Canadian government activity declined, as did his special role in relation to foreign affairs. Today the governor general acts in Canada much as the sovereign does in Britain, and generally only on the advice of Cabinet. It should be noted that the Crown is manifested at the provincial level in the person of a lieutenant governor in each province who takes advice naturally from the provincial cabinet. The lieutenant governor performs in each province many of the same tasks performed nationally by the governor general.

The governor general is appointed by the sovereign on the advice of the Canadian Prime Minister for an official term of six years. Customarily the term has been recognized as five years, however, and on occasion it has been as much as seven. The sovereign may remove a governor general on the advice of the Canadian federal Cabinet, but this has never been done in Canada.

The office's powers and functions derive in part from statute law and in part from the remaining prerogative powers of the monarch. Some functions are essentially nominal, being performed in fact by the Cabinet in the name of the governor. Others, however, remain associated with the governor general himself.

First among these responsibilities is the duty of ensuring that there is always a Prime Minister and Cabinet in office. It is the governor general who appoints the prime minister, selecting that person who can form (from among his supporters in Parliament) a Cabinet capable of securing the support of a majority in the House of Commons. It is only when this choice is ambiguous (as when there are two contenders with apparently equal claims, or when the majority party has lost its leader through death or resignation) that the governor general could play an important role. Such instances are rare, of course, particularly since party discipline usually makes Commons support unambiguous, and since all political parties in Canada now have established procedures for the replacement of a leader.

The governor general also has the responsibility to act as adviser to the Prime Minister, but there is no requirement that a Prime Minister heed his advice. The effectiveness of any governor in this circumstance will depend largely on his personal friendship with, or admiration by, the Prime Minister involved.

In times of crisis, the governor general might serve as a mediator between the leaders of contending political parties; however, R. M. Dawson notes that:

> the governor's mediation in the past has been of doubtful utility, and on a few occasions has been a downright irritant; there is nothing to suggest that it will be given encouragement in the future.[9]

The most significant functions of the modern governor general however are ceremonial. The opening of Parliament, the reception of diplomats, the entertaining of distinguished officials and visitors, honorary patronage of the arts and charitable activities, public speeches and tours throughout the country—all these serve to provide a focus for patriotism and national unity that is independent of the political views of a particular elected official. The separation of the appointed head of state from the elected head of government symbolizes the maintenance of the nation and its system of government and the impermanence of changing partisan administrations.

THE PRIME MINISTER AND CABINET

The single most important institution of the Canadian federal government is the Cabinet, selected and presided over by the Prime Minister. This is true despite the fact that all executive authority in Canada is vested by the BNA Act in the queen and is delegated by letters patent to the governor general. The Cabinet's central importance derives from the BNA Act's provision that the queen (and hence the governor) will be advised by a Privy Council appointed by the governor general. By custom, as in Britain, members of this Privy Council are appointed only on the advice of the Prime Minister, and the powers of the Governor-in-Council are exercised by the Council's "efficient" arm—the Cabinet. Since Privy Councillors are appointed for life, the queen's Privy Council for Canada includes all present and former members of Cabinet (together with a number of honorary appointees). However, the Cabinet at any one time contains only those "ministers" selected by the current Prime Minister to be advisers to the Crown, and since the Crown is bound by tradition to take the advice of Cabinet, the *effective* executive power in Canada rests with the Cabinet and its Prime Minister. By the conventions of responsible government, the Cabinet must command a majority of the members of the House of Commons (the elected legislative body). Hence, while the authority of the Cabinet derives from the Crown via the Privy Council, its power ultimately rests with the people via their representatives. Thus is it possible for a representative democracy to operate within the institutions of monarchy.

By convention, members of Cabinet are expected to hold a seat in Parliament; persons appointed to the Cabinet from outside Parliament are expected to secure a seat (either by election to the Commons or by appointment to the Senate) as soon as possible after they are chosen. The longest time a minister has held office without a seat in Parliament, however, is nine and a half months (although there is no specification in law or custom about the maximum length of time possible). It is constitutionally normal that the powerful executive decision makers are members of the Parliament to which they are accountable.

Cabinet Functions. The functions of the Cabinet are both executive and legislative in nature.[10] As the *executive* arm of government, the Cabinet is expected to provide initiative and leadership on matters of national policy. Each member of the Cabinet, as an individual minister, is responsible for overseeing the administration of his particular department of government, and for promoting high morale and an informed perspective among its officials. Most important, perhaps, the Cabinet is collectively responsible for coordinating the activities of its government's departments in the service of the national goals and priorities it has set. Finally, the Cabinet is responsible for exercising specific prerogative powers of the Governor-in-Council, including the summoning, prorogation, and dissolution of Parliament; the appointment of ambassadors and the ratification of treaties; the power of clemency; and certain matters relating to the provinces. These last include the appointment of lieutenant governors, the disallowance of provincial legislation, and decisions on reserved provincial bills (see below).

The *legislative* functions of Cabinet reflect its close relationship with Parliament, particularly the Commons. The Cabinet dominates the timetable and organization of the business of Parliament, as well as generating the vast bulk of legislative initiatives. All money bills (i.e., all measures to spend or raise money) *must* be presented to the House of Commons by a member of the Cabinet and thus always originate in the Cabinet. The Cabinet also legislates more or less directly by enacting subordinate legislation under authority granted by acts of Parliament. W. A. Matheson notes that almost every statute passed by Parliament grants to the Governor-in-Council the authority to make additional rules or "subordinate legislation" to fill in details not considered by Parliament; moreover, the Cabinet is sometimes given the power to act as final court of appeal for administrative decisions.[11] One estimate of the impact of subordinate legislation has suggested that between the beginning of 1965 and the end of 1968, the federal government had published an average of 520 of these regulations per year.[12] Finally, the Cabinet holds a negative legislative authority in respect of provincial legislation. The Governor-in-Council may declare void any act of any provincial legislature within one year of its receipt of the Dominion government. In addition, the Cabinet may be called upon to decide the fate of any bill not signed by the lieutenant governor of a province but reserved for consideration of the federal Cabinet. These powers of reservation and disallowance have been used only rarely in Canadian history; indeed, no provincial act has been disallowed since 1943.

Cabinet Responsibility. Members of the Cabinet are subject to three kinds of responsibility. First, they are responsible to the Prime Minister, who selected them and can remove them from their posts. Second, they are responsible to one another. They must, by convention, maintain a public uniformity on matters of government policy. No Prime Minister expects that all his Cabinet members will automatically agree on every issue. Indeed, one value of the Cabinet is its capacity to consider a variety of views on the proper conduct of the nation's business. However, once the Cabinet has reached a decision on some matter of policy, it is expected that the members of the Cabinet will acquiesce in that decision (at least in public). A minister who feels that he must oppose a decision of Cabinet publicly must first resign from that Cabinet (or expect to be removed). Third, members of the Cabinet are collectively and individually responsible to the House of Commons. A Cabinet that has collectively lost the support of a Commons majority must resign. A minister whose defense of his department's administration is an embarrassment to the government of which he is a member will eventually be removed. It must be noted, however, that party discipline is sufficiently strong that governments rarely lose the confidence of their supporters; as a consequence, a majority government (i.e., a Cabinet whose party holds a majority, and not merely a plurality, of the Commons seats) is rarely defeated in the House. Governments with a secure Commons majority and a comfortable level of public support also seem to be able to accommodate the occasional embarrassing minister. Nonetheless, the responsibility to the Commons is ultimately a responsibility to the elected representatives of the people, and when the Cabinet is called to account by the House of Commons, it must not appear dishonest or ineffectual in its defense or it may lose the support of its voters in the next election.

Personnel. When a Prime Minister comes into office (normally after a general election in which his party has won a plurality of the Commons seats), his first priority will be the selection of his Cabinet. However, there are a number of principles that constrain his selection and therefore condition the quality of his advisers. First, there is the expectation that he will normally select his Cabinet from among his supporters in Parliament. There have been seventy instances (from 1867 through 1979) in which persons have been appointed to the Cabinet from outside Parliament. Also it has become normal that very few Cabinet members will be from the Senate; therefore, almost all Cabinet members sit also in the Commons. When election results in 1979 produced only two Conservative members from Quebec, however, Prime Minister Clark found it necessary to add senators from that province to his Cabinet, a move regarded by some as legitimate but in the light of Canadian parliamentary tradition unfortunate.

Second, it is expected that (as much as possible) the Cabinet will be balanced to reflect some key aspects of the religious, regional, and linguistic diversity of the country. There has been no requirement to give *proportionate* representation to any groups, but every Prime Minister has felt a need to appoint some Protestant and Catholic members, some English-speaking and French-speaking members, and some members from each of the major regions of the country. There have always been considerably more English than French members, and prior to the Pearson administration of 1963, considerably more Protestants than Catholics. The first Jewish Cabinet member was appointed in 1969. The two largest provinces, Ontario and Quebec, have consistently had the largest number of Cabinet representatives, and no other province has had more than three members in any of the "first" Cabinets appointed after a new Prime Minister's selection.[13]

The principle of Cabinet representativeness has not extended to such other characteristics as age, sex, occupation, or educational background (biases in the distribution of these variables occur initially in the selection of candidates for the House of Commons).

The short-lived Clark (1979–80) Cabinet may serve as a representative example. It contained thirty members, of whom four were of French-Canadian origin.[14] Seven members were Roman Catholic, fourteen Protestant, one Mennonite, and one Ukranian Orthodox; seven did not report their religious affiliation in their Canadian Parliamentary Guide biographies. There was but one woman in the Clark Cabinet, and there have never been more than three women in a Canadian federal Cabinet; the *first* female federal Cabinet member was not appointed until 1957. The average age of Cabinet appointees has been around fifty since 1867, and the Clark Cabinet's average age was forty-eight; the youngest member was twenty-nine, the oldest sixty-four. Twelve of these Cabinet members represented Ontario constituencies, three represented Quebec, three were from British Columbia seats, three from Alberta, two from Newfoundland; each of the other provinces and territory is presented by one member.

Roughly half of all Canada's Cabinet members have been lawyers by profession, and fourteen members of the Clark Cabinet were lawyers. Nine members were business executives before entering Parliament; four were teachers, minister, or scientists. All but four of the Clark Cabinet members had some university education, and most of the university trained had degrees (including law) beyond the B.A. (Nearly two thirds of all Cabinet members since Confederation have attended university, and the proportion has been over 80 percent since the 1930s.)

It is clear from these figures that a Canadian Cabinet is, as one might expect, an elite group whose occupational and education characteristics do not perfectly reflect those of the mass electorate. From the viewpoint of a Prime Minister forming a Cabinet, these indicators of achievement signal expertise and high ability—a valuable resource. However, the necessity to choose (almost exclusively) members of the Commons and to represent language, regional, and religious divisions must appear as a constraint on his choice of Cabinet material. Because of these constraints, there is no expectation that Cabinet members will be experts in the particular substantive subjects of their portfolios. Indeed, regional considerations are likely to be more important, so that the minister responsible for fisheries is normally expected to be from a coastal province, and the Minister of Agriculture from one of the Prairie Privinces, regardless of their own occupational backgrounds.[15] Substantive expertise in a department is expected to reside mainly in the permanent staff, headed by its deputy minister, and not in its political head, the minister.

Also, it has not always been the case that ministers have

been chosen because of long parliamentary experience. Often it has been considered more important that an appointee have an administrative background outside partisan politics, either in the public service or in private industry. Of the thirty members of the Clark Cabinet, for example, only three held provincial or municipal offices prior to entering federal politics, and only ten had served more than eight years in Parliament prior to their elevation to the Cabinet.

An office that has sometimes been regarded as a possible training ground for future ministers is that of parliamentary secretary. In December 1976, for example, seventeen of Pierre Trudeau's Cabinet members had been parliamentary secretaries at one time or another. Parliamentary secretaries (sometimes called parliamentary assistants) are appointed from among the members of the government party in the House of Commons for a renewable two-year term.[16] These assistants serve to take some of the administrative burden off the minister's shoulders, and occasionally they may make statements or answer questions about their departments in the House, on behalf of the minister. They are not, however, members of the Cabinet in any sense, nor can all of them expect to attain that rank.

The Cabinet includes all those who are responsible for departments of government[17]; it also includes, from time to time, Ministers without Portfolio. These ministers have no administrative department and in the past were usually appointed with limited duties, principally for the purpose of maintaining regional balance. Recently, however, there has been a tendency to assign such ministers special duties and responsibilities. A third type of minister has also emerged in recent years, "Ministers of State" acting as political heads of agencies created primarily for the purpose of developing policy rather than administering it. Examples include International Trade and Science and Technology.

Presiding over all these ministers, and qualitatively different from them, is the Prime Minister. It is the Prime Minister who chairs Cabinet meetings and generally decides on the consensus reached there. While the style of Cabinet deliberations varies from Cabinet to Cabinet, the Prime Minister is the one who determines the mode of operation. It is he who selects the members of Cabinet, and it is he who can call for their resignations. If the PM resigns, the Cabinet as a whole is presumed to be dissolved. The Prime Minister comes to his position usually by means of prior elections to the leadership of his party, and therefore the selection of the Prime Minister is best discussed in the section on political party operations (see p. 188–191).

Organization. The organization of Cabinet activity has altered considerably as government in Canada has evolved since Confederation. These alterations have involved mainly the use of Cabinet committees, and the expansion of the Privy Council Office (or Cabinet Secretariat) and the Prime Minister's Office.

Prior to World War II, Cabinet committees were generally ad hoc and few in number, although from the beginning they were used to take some of the decision-making burden off the full Cabinet. Following World War II, however, greater use was made of standing committees, although most of the matters discussed in committee were still discussed again in meetings of the full Cabinet. Under Prime Minister Pearson in the early 1960s, a large number of standing committees were created, with membership on the committees reflecting departmental responsibilities and not (as in the past) regional representation. As in previous years, committees could operate more informally than full Cabinet, sometimes hearing arguments from civil servants and others, but most of their decisions were again raised for consideration in full Cabinet meetings. Prime Minster Trudeau reduced slightly the number of Committees, and during his first administration (1968–79) many decisions taken in Cabinet committees did not receive further discussion in the full Cabinet. Some of the committees are intended for *coordination* of government activity; others have primarily a *substantive* policy discussion function. The two most important coordinating committees are Priorities and Planning (chaired by the Prime Minister) and Treasury Board (the Oldest Cabinet committee and one of two given statutory recognition). The other coordinating committees are Legislation and House Planning and Federal-Provincial Relations. The substantive committees usually include External Policy and Defence; Economic Policy; Social Policy; Government Operations; and Science, Culture and Information. The membership and organization of Cabinet committees are internal matters for Cabinet decision; therefore, membership is often kept secret, and committee names and functions occasionally change.

One of the most noted innovations of the first Trudeau administration was the increase in size and importance of the Privy Council Office (PCO) and the Prime Minister's Office (PMO). The PCO, with some 350 employees in the late 1970s, is responsible not only for the preparation and circulation to ministers of the agendas and supporting documentation for Cabinet and Cabinet committee meetings. It has also become a kind of policy refinery, in which information about policy proposals is gathered, summarized, and circulated to Cabinet members. In addition to providing clerical assistance to the Cabinet and keeping records of Cabinet decisions, the PCO is expected to brief the Prime Minister on matters coming before the Cabinet and to advise him on the allocation of governmental responsibilities among departments and agencies. In discussing the changes in organization and size of the PCO, W. A. Matheson writes:

> These changes represent an attempt to rationalize policy-making, but it should be noted that the process has added immensely to the influence of the Prime Minister, to whom the Privy Council Office is directly responsible. By providing a source of policy input independent of the government departments, the role of departmental civil servants has been greatly reduced.[18]

The potential policymaking importance of the Prime Minister's Office was also enhanced under Mr. Trudeau's direction. The staff of the PMO, around forty when Trudeau took office, reached about ninety by 1977. While in the 1930s and 1940s the PMO's role was primarily clerical, concerned mainly with routine correspondence, in the 1970s it became a larger operation, at least partly concerned with policy advice to the

Prime Minister. Since one of the prime functions of the office is liaison with the political party of which the PM is the leader, most of the PMO staff personnel are political (rather than public service) appointees.

These changes in the size and organization of the executive bureaucracies were intended to increase the efficiency of Cabinet decision making, but they have been criticized by observers who feel that the changes have also reduced the Cabinet's accountability to Parliament and the people. Indeed, such changes, together with an alteration in the work load and procedures of the Commons, have led one observer of Canadian politics to conclude that we have created in Canada "a presidential system without any of its congressional advantages."[19]

THE HOUSE OF COMMONS

An assessment of the power of the Prime Minister and the Cabinet cannot be complete without some understanding of their relationship to the main legislative bodies of the parliamentary system. Canada's federal Parliament contains a bicameral legislature—the lower chamber, the House of Commons, is popularly elected; the upper chamber, the Senate, is appointed. (Senators were appointed for life prior to 1965; senators appointed after 1965 must retire at age seventy-five.) The importance of the Commons relative to the Senate is enhanced not only by its elected character but also because it has the function (under the conventions of responsible government) of sustaining the Cabinet in office, or of removing the Cabinet when the Commons's confidence in that Cabinet is lost. The Senate can amend legislation passed in the Commons (it may merely *suggest* amendments to money bills), but in general it may be said, in the long run, the Senate must assent to legislation that has the Commons's support.

Representation in the House of Commons is intended to be roughly proportionate to population, but special provisions in the distribution of seats among the provinces, as well as the allowed variation is constituency size, necessitate some departure from the ideal. For example, no province may have

fewer Commons seats than the fixed number of Senate seats
to which it is entitled. Moreover, when the redistribution of
seats occurs (normally after each decennial census), no province may be assigned more than 15 percent fewer seats than
it was entitled to at the previous redistribution. At present,
there are 282 members in the House of Commons. Any re-
drawing of constituency (sometimes called "riding") boundaries is conducted by nonpartisan boundary commissions in
each province under the supervision of a federal Representation Commissioner. All constituents now elect a single member to the Commons (prior to 1966 there were some two-member constituencies). The population of each constituency may
vary by as much as 25 percent from the provincial quota (the
population of the province divided by its allocated number of
seats). The combined effect of these rules is that substantial
variations in constituency population remain despite the intention to represent each citizen equally.[20]

Except in cases of war or other national emergency, when
special arrangements may be made, the life of a Parliament
may not extend beyond five years. However, since the Prime
Minister may at any time request the dissolution of Parliament (and consequently initiate a general election for the
House of Commons), Parliaments have frequently been of
shorter duration. A dissolution will generally be requested if
the Cabinet loses the confidence of the House, but a Prime
Minister may also choose to "go to the people" whenever he
feels that the time is propitious for improving his party's position in the Commons.

Parliament must meet at least once each year, but there
is no requirement as to the length of each session. Some sessions have been more than a full year in length, while one
(in unusual circumstances) lasted only a few hours. As the
business of government has increased in recent years, it has
become normal for sessions of the federal Parliament to run
for the whole year with breaks in the late summer and at
Christmas and Easter.[21]

Functions. Constitutionally the most important function
of the Commons is to produce and sustain a government in

office—the Cabinet, to retain its executive authority, must maintain the support of a majority in the House. Except in the most extraordinary circumstances, however, members of the Prime Minister's party in the Commons will not vote against the government. Thus, a government is rarely defeated in the House, and then only by agreement among the opposition parties when a government does not have a majority. This situation highlights the fundamental duality of the House of Commons—the division between the "government" party (which will do all in its power to sustain the Cabinet in office until the Prime Minister requests dissolution) and the "opposition" (usually a temporary alliance among a number of parties bent on forcing the current government out of office).

The dichotomy of the government and the opposition is visible in all of the functions of the House of Commons. For example, the Commons is expected to authorize the appropriation of funds through the tax system for the conduct of government, to approve the allocation of those funds among the various departments and programs of government, and then to review or postaudit the expenditures to ensure that efficiency has been served. This function derives from the centuries-long struggles between Crown and Parliament in Great Britain, through which the monarch was eventually forced to call Parliament into session and hear the grievances of the people before being supplied with the funds he required to carry out the executive acts he had planned. In the modern Canadian Parliament, this process of "supply" is played out between the Cabinet and its supporters (i.e., the government) who propose and defend taxes and expenditures and the opposition who present grievances and call the legislative program of the government into question, before eventually acquiescing to the provision of funds.

A third and related function of the Commons is to provide a forum for the discussion of public issues and problems to which the government might be expected to respond. While this discussion can go on in both the Commons and the Senate, the elected nature of the former body ensured that its members have a more direct interest in promoting the concerns and demands of the mass public. Here again the dichotomy of government and opposition appears. The government supporters will be intent on demonstrating that the major issues of the day have been anticipated by the Cabinet and that Cabinet proposals represent the best solutions currently available to the problems of the nation. It is the role of the opposition to expose the flaws in government policies, and also to bring to the attention of government and electorate alike the neglected problems of society.

The fourth and most commonly mentioned function of the Commons is, in cooperation with the Senate, to pass legislation. Since the bulk of the legislation proposed in the Commons derives from the deliberations of the Cabinet, the failure of any major legislative proposal would normally signify that the Cabinet had lost the confidence of the House. As a consequence, the debate surrounding any legislation once again pits government against opposition. The task of the opposition parties will always be to seek amendments to bring the legislation more into line with their policies, or to defeat the legislation entirely. However, given the rare occurrence of government defeat, the most successful task the opposition can take may to be delay the passage of legislation until such time as public opinion can be marshaled, or until the parliamentary session ends and the legislation "dies on the order paper."

The constant struggle between government and opposition that results from the performance of the Commons's functions ensures that a more or less continuous election campaign takes place throughout the life of Parliament. Each opposition party must not only cast doubt on the ability of the current Cabinet to govern but also provide evidence of its own ability to form a successful Cabinet after the next election. In an era when representative assemblies in all Western democracies seem to have been weakened in their capacity fundamentally to affect social and economic policy (in the face of initiatives from increasingly powerful executives), the "election campaign" function of the House of Commons may be its most significant one. Assessment of its organization and procedures should therefore focus predominantly on the extent to which they facilitate the performance of that function.

Organization and Procedures. At the beginning of each parliamentary session, the members of the House of Commons are summoned to the Senate chamber where, together with the senators, they listen to the governor general read the Speech from the Throne.[22] This speech outlines in general terms the legislative program of the government for the coming session. Although the fiction is maintained symbolically that the speech is the governor general's statement of his reasons for calling Parliament into session, the statement is in fact prepared by the Prime Minister and approved by Cabinet. Upon returning to the Commons chamber, the House exercises what R. M. Dawson calls "its immemorial right to attend first to its own business before considering the affairs of the Crown" by giving first reading to a *pro forma* bill that does not exist except by title.[23] The Speaker of the Commons then presents the Speech from the Throne to the House, and a time is set for its further consideration. A striking committee of government and opposition members is formed to draw up the membership of the standing committees of the House.

At the next sitting of the House, an address in reply to the Throne Speech is moved and seconded by two government backbenchers.[24] The address is then debated for no more than eight days, at the end of which debate it is passed by strict party vote. The Throne Speech Debate provides the first and most general opportunity for opposition members to criticize government policy. The subject matter on which the debate can touch is virtually unlimited, and in the course of an eight-day debate many speakers can be accommodated. However, because the debate is so wide ranging and its eventual outcome is never really in doubt, it does not attract much public attention once the Prime Minister and the leaders of the opposition parties have been heard. Criticism by the opposition leaders generally takes the form of amendments to the main motion, and of course the passage of any of these amendments would constitute an indication of nonconfidence in the government.

A second significant opportunity for opposition criticism occurs on each sitting day of the session (normally every weekday). Following opening prayers, the tabling of government reports and motions, and the reading of ministerial answers to written questions (placed on the order paper by members), there begins a forty-minute oral question period. During this period, ministers of the Crown are expected to answer questions regarding the policy and administration of their departments. These questions often provide the opportunity for opposition members to surprise and embarrass the government by pointing out problems or errors that have escaped Cabinet's attention or that reflect badly on the government's administrative competence. The question period is normally well attended, both by members of the House and by reporters in the press gallery. Moreover, Commons's proceedings are now televised; thus, a minister who performs badly in question period cannot hope to have his misfortune overlooked.[25] Although ministers are not compelled to answer, and questions may not be argumentative or provocative, the question period still provides one of the most direct and dramatic points of confrontation between the government and the opposition.

A further opportunity for general criticism is provided three days a week, when a thirty-minute debate (consisting of three short debating periods) is permitted on the motion to adjourn the House at the end of the evening sitting. This "late-show" debate is one instance of a common phenomenon in Canadian parliamentary procedure—the use of an ostensibly procedural motion as the occasion for a substantive debate on some aspect of the government's policy or performance.[26]

The other opportunities for carrying on the "continuous election campaign" arise in connection with the passage of legislation on the one hand and the surveillance of government finance on the other. Legislation coming before the House can be divided into two classes—private and public bills. Private bills are those that aim at some narrow purpose regarding a particular person or corporation, and these seldom occasion much conflict between government and opposition. Public bills fall into two subclasses—government bills and private member's bills. The latter are bills introduced by individual members of the House without the expressed support of Cabinet, and the time afforded these bills is extremely limited. They almost never secure successful passage through the House. Government bills, on the other hand, make up the legislative program of the Cabinet, and they occupy nearly four fifths of the Commons's legislative timetable.

All bills go through five stages in the Commons, and the same five stages in the Senate, before they are passed on to the governor general for royal assent. The first stage is a motion for leave to introduce the bill, together with first reading. When a bill is read the first time, it is given an identifying number and is printed for all members of the House to scrutinize it. Normally a time is then set for second reading. Debate at second reading concerns only the principle of the legislation, and no amendments are permitted. When the bill has passed second reading, it is referred to one of the standing committees of the House for clause-by-clause examination. At this third stage, the members are free to suggest amendments the government may accept or reject, but since membership on the committees reflects party balance in the Commons, a party that controls the House will also control its committees. Nevertheless, a minority government may be constrained to accept some amendments to preserve the confidence of the House. When a bill has been debated in committee, it is reported back to the Commons. At this fourth stage, debate again proceeds on a clause-by-clause basis, and amendments may once again be suggested (including some which may have been rejected at the committee stage). The fifth and final stage is third reading, and debate is generally very brief at this point. If a government does not feel it can secure passage of bill at any stage, it will probably withdraw the legislation rather than face the possibility of defeat in the House—a clear indication of nonconfidence.[27] The opposition thus has a number of opportunities to attack the principle and the details of each piece of government legislation and to suggest amendments to it. At the very least, it has the opportunity to delay implementation of government policy.

With respect to financial surveillance, there are three points of confrontation between government and opposition: supply (or estimates); ways and means (the budget); and post audit (the report of the Auditor General).

Spending estimates for each fiscal year are prepared in government departments by civil servants, coordinated by

Treasury Board, and approved by Cabinet before introduction in the House. Once introduced, they must be referred to standing committees for scrutiny before March 1 and reported back to the House by May 31. Interim supply (to permit the government to function during the period before final approval of main estimates) must be approved by March 26. Supplementary estimates may be introduced at any time, but these must be approved by June 30, December 10, or March 26, depending on the time at which they are introduced. The scrutiny of departmental estimates in committee provides an opportunity for opposition members to criticize, and government members to defend, the spending programs of the administration. It is worth noting, however, that the time limit on consideration of estimates may allow the government simply to "wait out" opposition critics.

Before the adoption of this system, estimates were debated in the full House, organized as the Committee of Supply. Debate ranged over all aspects of the policy and administration of a department whose estimates were being scrutinized, and grievances could be vented before supply was approved. When scrutiny moved from the whole House to more efficient committees, this ancient privilege of "grievances before supply" could have been lost. To avoid this eventuality, the Commons now sets aside twenty-five "allotted days" during each session (five on or before December 10, seven more by March 26, and thirteen more by June 30) in which only opposition members can present motions, on "any matter within the jurisdiction of the Parliament of Canada ." A maximum of six of these motions may be motions of nonconfidence (up to two in each of the aforementioned periods). Other motions brought forward are debated, but not normally voted on.

When the main estimates are reported back from committee, they are presented to the House of Commons as an appropriations bill, which then goes through the same Commons stages as any other piece of legislation (except that in the committee stage it is normally dated in Committee of the Whole House). The opposition thus has three opportunities to criticize the government in connection with the supply procedure—the scrutiny of estimates, the debates during the allotted days, and the debate of the appropriations bill.

The taxation proposals of the government are also debated in the Commons, first in connection with the presentation of the budget—the balance of expenditure with revenue and loans—and second when the budget proposals are formulated as legislation. The presentation of the budget by the Finance Minister generally includes an assessment of the general economic condition of the country, and this presentation provides the occasion for a debate to which six days are allocated. The opposition and government confront one another on the general budgetary policy of the government and its strengths and weaknesses in meeting the economic needs of the nation. The motion supporting the government's budgetary policy is eventually approved, or else the Cabinet must resign, having lost the confidence of the House.

The postaudit function is carried out by an official of Parliament (not of the Cabinet) called the Auditor General, who reports to Parliament primarily through the House of Commons Standing Committee on Public Accounts. The Public Accounts Committee is always chaired by a member of the opposition, and its function is to scrutinize the past fiscal year's expenditures and to seek remedies for such waste or inefficiency as the Auditor General may have found. As may be expected, opposition members will attempt to link budgetary problems to the government's administrative performance, while government members will seek to defend the administration against these opposition attacks. Thus, government and opposition confront one another at each stage of the financial surveillance process.

Presiding over the House and responsible for its orderly conduct of public business is the Speaker, who is assisted by a deputy. Although the Speaker is traditionally a member of the governing party, he is expected to maintain impartiality in his rulings.[28] Unusually, the Conservative Clark government retained the previous Speaker, James Jerome, although he was a Liberal member. Upon his return to power in the spring of 1980, Prime Minister Trudeau appointed Canada's first woman Speaker, Mme. Jeanne Sauvé (also a Liberal).

Each political party in the House can play its part in the "continuing election campaign" only by maintaining solidarity in speech and action. This solidarity is directed by the party House leader (as distinct from the leader of the party) and his staff of party whips (who are also members of the House).[29] The maintenance of a common front can be assured only if members have an opportunity to discuss policy issues openly within party ranks: to this end, each party meets in secret as a party caucus, to plan strategy and resolve differences, each week when the House is in session.

THE SENATE

Senators are appointed by the Governor-in-Council (effectively the Cabinet) to serve until age seventy-five. They must be at least thirty years of age and British subjects, hold real property in the province they represent to a net value of $4,000, and be worth $4,000 above all debts and liabilities.[30] Senate representation is distributed among the provinces as follows: Ontario and Quebec each have twenty-four senators; the four provinces west of Ontario have six each, as does Newfoundland; Nova Scotia and New Brunswick have ten each; and Prince Edward Island has four; and the Yukon and Northwest Territories have one each. Provision exists for the Senate, currently at 104 seats, to be enlarged by four or eight members, but no Prime Minister has taken advantage of this opportunity. The Senate of Canada has a position analogous to that of the House of Lords in Great Britain, in that it is by far the weaker of the two chambers in Parliament.

Legislation other than money bills may be introduced in either House of Parliament, and all legislation must be passed by both the Commons and the Senate. In the event of disagreement, however, it is usually the case that the will of the elected Commons will prevail. The Senate can act to amend legislation (often with Cabinet approval) so that "sober second thought" is sometimes brought to bear by Senate deliberations. It has become the practice in recent years to introduce virtually all *private* bills in the Senate, since the Senate can devote considerable time to investigating them while it awaits public bills being sent up from the Commons in the early weeks of each session.

The committees of the Senate, like those of the Commons, are empowered to subpoena documents and call witnesses.

Unlike Commons committees, those of Senate are not required to devote large amounts of time to the scrutiny of estimates. As a consequence of this leisure, and of the ability of their members, standing and special committees of the Senate are uniquely qualified to engage in the investigation of social or political problems. In recent years, major Senate committee reports have been published on such subjects as poverty in Canada, the mass media, and government science policy. As an investigatory body, however, the Senate has on occasion been seen as excessively conservative, especially when the interests of Canadian businessmen have been in question.

Appointment to the Senate is generally reserved for persons who have served the government party in some notable way. Because of this patronage function, the Senate has been criticized for being the last reward of old politicians rather than an active legislative body. There have been a number of suggestions as to how the Senate might reasonably be reformed (including the suggestion that it be abolished entirely); however, there has as yet been little change in its constitutional form apart from the introduction of the compulsory retirement provision.[31]

THE PUBLIC BUREAUCRACY
It has been estimated that roughly one in twenty Canadians works for some level of government, and that roughly one in fifty works for a department or agency of the federal government. As demands for increased social services multiplied in the postwar period, and as government expanded its role in the stabilizing and developing of the Canadian economy, the public service was expanded to take account of these new tasks. Critics of this expansion have objected to the bureaucratization of many aspects of political and social life, but is is not at all clear that the tasks demanded could have been performed without recourse to large organizations, whether of the public or private sector. By their very nature, many social service programs did not attract the participation of private investment, so that the expansion of public involvement was almost inevitable.

More telling than this attack on growth per se, however,

are some other criticisms of bureaucratic development in Canada. For example, the massive size of the bureaucracy makes it difficult to ask Parliament (let alone the responsible Cabinet minister) to scrutinize and control effectively the full range of administrative activity in a department. The increasing delegation of decisions on legislative detail to administrative officials has largely removed such detail from public debate. By the time government policy is applied in an individual case, it may be specified not simply in the legislation of Parliament, or even the Orders-in-Council drafted by Cabinet, but in intradepartmental memos, guidelines, or handbooks. Moreover, when an administrative department or tribunal acts in a judicial or quasi-judicial capacity, it is not always the case that safeguards are present of the kind taken for granted in the formal legal system of the regular courts.

At the top of the civil service pyramid, bureaucrats exercise a significant policy role. The development of substantial expertise (and personal contacts) in the senior levels of a "permanent" civil service gives the bureaucracy considerable influence in the formulation of government policy. The elected "masters" may have to defer to their nonelected "servants" on technical questions so frequently that the policy is markedly altered in its development and application. The consequences are summarized by Mallory as follows:

> The close connection between "politics" and "policy" means that the distinction between the minister who takes decisions for political motives and the official who advises him in complete ignorance of the political facts of life, is artificial and can no longer be maintained.[32]

Yet one of the strongest norms of the Canadian public service is that it must be nonpartisan. Civil servants are to be hired and promoted in accordance with principles of merit rather than by recourse to a "spoils" system in which the winning party in an election rewards its supporters with patronage appointments. Nevertheless, the strong connection between policy development and policy implementation means that in practice the civil service is expected to be partisan in favor of the government—no matter which party forms the Cabinet.

The assumed close agreement between a minister and deputy (and, by extension, his department as a whole) permits the maintenance of the tradition that civil servants do not respond to public criticism. The minister is responsible for the operation of his department, and he must be prepared to defend his staff.

When one party has been in control of the government for a long period of time, therefore, it is not surprising that there grows up a similarity of thought between the bureaucrats and the party in power. Some critics have alleged that the senior civil service in Canada has been generally more sympathetic to the Liberal Party, which controlled the Canadian government for all but twelve of the last sixty years.

The assumption that the civil service is nonpartisan and expert justifies the further assumption that public servants enjoy security of tenure and can be removed only for malfeasance or demonstrable partisanship. Whenever a civil servant finds that he cannot agree with his minister, he does have the option of resigning and thereby making public the cause of his disagreement. Given his security of tenure, however, he will usually prefer to wait until events prove him right by giving him a new minister. If he chooses to frustrate the minister or does not respond to orders, the prime minister and Cabinet may act to move him to another department. Such an action would not be deemed to be a breach of his tenure.

Each department of government is organized hierarchically under a deputy minister. The deputy is appointed by the Governor-in-Council on the recommendation of the Prime Minister, but other members of the staff are appointed and promoted by the departments under the direction of the Public Service Commission, an independent agency broadly responsible for the selection and training of staff in accordance with the merit principle. More recently the Commission has also been responsible for developing an internal management consulting service for promoting the capacity of the public service to operate effectively in both official languages.

With the introduction of collective bargaining in the public service in the mid-1960s, the Treasury Board was recognized as employer with respect to most of the public service. It determines the terms and conditions of employment throughout the federal government, subject to the collective gargaining provisions of the Public Service Staff Relations Act.

Some government functions are not performed by regular departments but rather by semiautonomous agencies or by so-called Crown corporations that are created by government to perform advisory or regulatory functions or provide essential services. The former include, for example, the National Energy Board, which regulated the production and sale of certain forms of energy, and the Canadian Transport Commission, which regulates international and interprovincial transportation. Crown corporations operate like private sector corporations in most respects, providing a public good or service. Examples are the Canadian Broadcasting Corporation, the national government-owned radio and television network; and Air Canada, the national government-owned airline. Their relationships to Parliament and their organizational structures are as varied as the reasons for setting them up as independent bodies. Generally speaking, while each reports to Parliament through a minister of the Crown, the minister is not responsible for them in the same way as he is for his department. Some critics have been alarmed at what they perceive to be a proliferation of such semiautonomous agencies (the tendency to use them is even greater at the provincial level). It is argued that their independence of Cabinet control often means that they are accountable to no elected official at all.

Despite the pervasive influence of nonelected officials in the making and implementing of government policy, it is clear that some matters inevitably require the attention of the Cabinet. These include matters that are perceived to be controversial and the subject of the partisan division, policies that will establish new government programs, and policies that will involve significant expenditures of funds (some very large contracts in fact require Treasury Board approval).

There remains, finally, a constant, unresolved tension in Canadian politics between the desire to maximize the public accountability of government departments and agencies, and the need to develop a secure, experienced, expert, and non-partisan civil service.

THE JUDICIARY

Canada's legal system is customarily divided into two major parts—one dealing with the civil law, the other with the criminal law. Broadly speaking, criminal law is that body of law which assesses penalties for the commission (or omission) of specific acts, whereas civil law is a body of rules for the regulation of such matters as personal, family, or property relations. The BNA Act assigned jurisdiction over the criminal law (including procedure in criminal cases) to the federal government, while matters involving property or civil rights were assigned to the provinces (with some few specified exceptions such as banking, interest, promissory notes, and bankruptcy). Thus, while there is a unified criminal law for all of Canada, civil law may vary from province to province.[33]

The provinces were also given jurisdiction over the establishment of civil and criminal courts and over procedure in civil matters, while the federal government was given authority to establish a general court of appeal for Canada and any additional courts "for the better administration of the laws of Canada." In addition, the federal government was made responsible for the salaries of judges in the main provincially established courts.

This situation is further complicated by the fact that the Province of Quebec has developed its civil law out of a wholly different legal tradition from that which underlies both the criminal law and the civil law of the other nine provinces. Quebec civil law derives, through original importation from France, from the Roman Law tradition, and it is much more dependent on codification than on the precedents set by previous court decisions. The criminal law derives from the English common law tradition, as does the civil law of the other provinces. Under this tradition, law is contained not only in codified statutes but also in the decisions and interpretations judges have made in cases before the courts.

The Federal Courts. Under the general authority to establish courts, the federal government has created two main courts—the Supreme Court of Canada and the Federal Court—and a number of minor courts (such as the Court Martial Appeal Court, the Tax Appeal Board, and the territorial courts of the Yukon and Northwest Territories).

The Supreme Court is a general court of appeal for Canada, composed of a Chief Justices and eight puisne (or associate) judges; it hears appeals in civil or criminal cases from the provincial courts on matters it considers of legal importance.

Since the abolition (in 1949) of the right of appeal to the Judicial Committee of the Privy Council of Britain, the Supreme Court has been the final court of appeal for Canada. Except in cases of great importance, the full Court does not normally hear appeals; most cases are decided by panels of five or seven judges. In addition to hearing appeals on specific cases, the Court is required to give advisory opinions on matters referred to it by the Governor-in-Council. As a consequence, the Court may rule on the constitutionality of a statute even if no case challenging that statute is before the courts.

Justices of the Supreme Court are appointed by the governor general on the advice of Cabinet and hold office during good behavior to age seventy-five. In order that their independence from political pressure might be preserved, they may be removed only upon a joint address from both houses of Parliament, and their salaries may not be reduced during their terms of office. At least three of the judges must be appointed from the Bar of the Province of Quebec, and informal representation is also given to other regions.

The seventeen-member Federal Court of Canada consists of a Trial Division and an Appeal Division. The Appeal Division is composed of six justices, including the Chief Justice; the Trial Division includes the nine remaining judges and the Associate Chief Justice who presides. Four of the judges must be from the Bar or Bench of Quebec, and all enjoy tenure during good behavior until age seventy. The court deals with appeals from the judicial or quasi-judicial orders of federal tribunals, boards, and agencies. It is the court that adjudicates suits against the Crown in right of Canada,[34] and it has jurisdiction over matters (including admiralty law) outside the competence of provincial courts. In addition, it has concurrent jurisdiction with provincial high courts over matters within the competence of the federal Parliament (such as promissory notes, aeronautics, and interprovincial works).

The Provincial Courts. There are three broad classes of provincial courts. First, the provincial superior courts, normally including a trial and an appeal division in each case, are appointed by the federal government,[35] and their judges hold office during good behavior until age seventy-five. Their removal requires a joint address of both Houses of Parliament. Second, the district or county courts are also federally appointed, but judges may be removed for cause by the Governor-in-Council without a parliamentary resolution. The third class of courts includes such inferior provincial courts as a province may establish. Their judges are normally appointed during good behavior by the Lieutenant-Governor-in-Council (in effect, the provincial cabinet).

The appeal division of a province superior court may hear appeals from the lower courts, or from its own trial division that acts as court of original jurisdiction for most civil and criminal cases of substance. The county or district courts deal normally with civil suits involving smaller amounts of money, or with lesser criminal charges. The lower courts created by the province may include such things as surrogate courts (dealing with estates), family and juvenile courts, and magistrate's courts (whose duties might cover hearing charges on petty offenses, conducting preliminary hearings, issuing warrants, etc.).

The system of courts is somewhat more complicated in Quebec, where the superior court is divided into two branches, one of which (the Court of Queen's Bench) is both the appeal court and the court of original jurisdiction in criminal matters.

The other branch (the Superior Court) is a court of civil jurisdiction.[36]

Canadian judges have traditionally been appointed from among those engaged in the private practice of law (as in the United States and Britain), and not from a career civil service judicial stream (as in some European systems). Judges are appointed rather than elected (following British practice) in order that the independence of the judiciary from partisan political control may be maintained. This principle has been somewhat impaired, however, by the custom of appointing judges at least partly as a reward for past service to the party in power. Some critics argue that this procedure sacrifices valuable legal scholarship in favor of the pragmatic perspective of the former politician. However, the norm of nonpartisanship is so strong among judges that probably the only effect of partisan appointment is to narrow the range of available talent.[37]

THE COURTS, THE CONSTITUTION, AND CIVIL LIBERTY

In Canada, as in the United States, a system of judicial review exists, by which courts are given an important constitutional responsibility when deciding the cases that come before them. They must assess whether or not the law applying to a particular case is within the lawful powers of the government that passed it, and in so doing they help to establish the legitimate boundaries of government authority. In carrying out this responsibility, they can provide protection for individuals against the abuse of authority; in other words, protection for civil liberty.

In the United States, many civil liberties are expressed in a Bill of Rights, which is entrenched in the Constitution and thus can be changed only with great difficulty. Canadians also share most of these rights, since they derive largely from bases common to both countries—British constitutional tradition and the common law. However, Canada's Bill of Rights is not entrenched in a constitutional document, and protection of civil liberties depends largely on an agreement among Canadians that certain rights have been traditionally established and shall continue to exist. Moreover, while a U.S. court may declare a law invalid if it violates a provision of the Bill of Rights, Canadian courts operate under the assumption of parliamentary supremacy and have generally been reluctant to suggest that any act is beyond the competence of *both* levels of government. Thus, the courts have sometimes overturned abuses of personal freedom by provincial governments only on the grounds that the legislation required fell within the criminal law power of the national government.

What are the civil rights of Canadians, and how may the courts act to protect them? The present Chief Justice of Canada, Bora Laskin, some years ago suggested a useful classification of civil liberties.[38] His four categories included political liberties, economic liberties, legal liberties, and egalitarian liberties. The first category, political liberties, comprises such things as freedom of assembly, association, and utterance; freedom of the press and other communications media; and freedom of conscience and of religion. These liberties, essential to the maintenance of a free democracy, are protected in the United States principally by the First Amendment to the Constitution. In Canada, there has been some suggestion that these freedoms are implicit in the preamble to the BNA Act (which states that Canada's constitution is to be similar in principle to that of the United Kingdom), but the courts have given only very limited support to that view.[39] They have preferred to find other grounds on which to invalidate laws that have abrogated those rights.

The second category, economic liberties, includes such things as the right to own property and not to be deprived thereof without compensation, the right to withhold one's labor, and freedom of contract. While there is some reference to property rights in the Fifth Amendment to the U.S. Constitution, economic liberties in both Canada and the United States have depended for protection mainly on convention, and on common law as it applies to torts and contracts.

The third category, legal liberties, is perhaps the most important for individual freedom, and it is thus not surprising that the rights it comprises are the subject of the Fourth,

Fifth, Sixth, Seventh, Eighth, and Fourteenth Amendments to the U.S. Constitution. In Canada these rights—the right to a fair hearing, freedom from arbitrary arrest, access to counsel, protection of an independent judiciary, and so forth— are protected primarily by the common law, and by the traditional expectation that the courts are to operate according to the principles of fundamental or "natural" justice.[40]

The fourth category, egalitarian liberties, includes such matters as the right to employment, education, accommodation, and so on, without discrimination on the basis of race, color, creed, sex, or economic circumstances. These rights are the subject of the Fourteenth and Fifteenth Amendments to the U.S. Constitution. In Canada most of these matters come within the jurisdiction of the provincial governments. Several provinces have passed Human Rights Codes, but these ordinary statutes are not in any way entrenched. Thus, they could be repealed or altered by any succeeding legislature. It is probably fair to say that egalitarian liberties remain the ones that are least well protected by legislation in Canada and thus are the most dependent on the goodwill and fair-mindedness of the general population and its legislators.

In 1960 the Canadian federal government passed a statute called the Canadian Bill of Rights. This statute was intended to specify the rights and liberties of Canadians, but it was passed only as an ordinary statute of the federal government, and as such it could not bind succeeding Parliaments. The law exists as a guide to statutory interpretation, so that judges are expected to interpret all other federal laws so that they are not in conflict with the Bill of Rights, but it is not always clear what is to be done if a statute *cannot* be so interpreted. The use made of the statute by the courts has been quite limited to date, and most of the rights it enumerates already are derived from customary practice or from the common law.[41]

Because of the doctrine of parliamentary supremacy, the courts have generally declared laws invalid only when they were found to be outside the legitimate jurisdiction of the legislative body that passed them, or when their application abrogated the principles of fundamental justice. The most fundamental freedoms of Canadians rest, like much of their constitution, on tradition and convention. It is not at all clear that having such freedoms written down would make them more secure.

Informal Institutions of Canadian Politics

POLITICAL PARTIES

Origins of the Two-Party System. In the colonial legislatures prior to Confederation, the development of responsible government led to the formation of two more or less disciplined groups—one in support of the current government and one in opposition to it. With the formation of the House of Commons in 1867, similar parliamentary groups appeared in the national legislature, and they reflected, in their origins and operation, the politics of the pre-Confederation period. As time passed, the loose parliamentary groups became more disciplined and institutionalized and thus developed into the two major national parties, the Liberals and Conservatives.[42]

The national Conservative Party began as a coalition of interests in support of the first Prime Minister, Sir John A. Macdonald, and included: representatives of the commercial interests of Toronto and Montreal; descendents of Loyalist families who had fled the United States during and after the American Revolution and thereafter established themselves prominently; propertied interests who had supported the colonial aristocracy in the struggle over responsible government; and Tories advocating a strong central government with a powerful executive. In Quebec particularly, the Conservatives enjoyed the support of the hierarchy of the Roman Catholic church; elsewhere, the Anglicans predominated.

The Liberal Party, which had originally been called the Reform Party, combined agrarian interests from western Ontario, the anticlerical Parti Rouge in Quebec, and some reformist elements from the Maritime Provinces of Nova Scotia and New Brunswick. The dominant element in this coalition at first was the Ontario group, nicknamed "Clear Grits" because of a remark by one of their founding members that they wanted candidates who were "all sand and no dirt, clear grit all the way through." This wing of the party favored free trade and free land policies that would promote the individualistic development of the western frontier, and they have been compared in their views to the Jacksonian wing of the U.S. Democratic Party. In later years, this Ontario dominance was supplanted by the growth of Liberal support in Quebec under the direction of the second Liberal Prime Minister, Sir Wilfrid Laurier.

It should be noted that party lines were so vaguely drawn in this early period that one could offer oneself as a candidate for election with a promise to support the ministry (or Cabinet) no matter which party formed it. In that heyday of patronage politics, a constituency could so benefit by supporting the government that its voters might be willing to overlook the absence of party labels in selecting a representative. Moreover, elections were scheduled by the government of the day, and voting in "safe" government seats might take place days before voting in more insecure areas. Voters in marginal seats thus had a clear idea which way the wind was blowing before they had to make a choice. From 1878 on, however, all constituencies voted on the same day, the secret ballot was introduced, and property qualifications for the franchise began to disappear. Parliamentary groups then saw a need to develop campaign organizations that could mobilize the votes of the new mass electorate. It is at that point that the ad hoc parliamentary groups began to resemble modern, democratic parties.

For fifty years following Confederation, the evolution of loose parliamentary groups into two national parties resulted in relatively close competition. Both parties sought to form governments based on grand coalitions of English and French, urban and rural, Protestant and Catholic interests, and each was for a time successful. In the twelve elections prior to 1917, the Conservatives averaged 48.96 percent of the popular vote and the Liberals averaged 48.93 percent, from 1867 to 1896 the Conservatives held a slight edge; and from 1896 to 1911 the Liberals were marginally ahead. The Conservatives, however, won the election of 1911.

At the next election, in 1917, a "Union" government under the Conservative prime minister (Sir Robert Borden) received more than 60 percent of the vote in every province west of the Quebec border; two-party competition remained strong in the Atlantic Provinces; but in Quebec, the opposition took 73 percent of the popular vote and sixty-two of the province sixty-five seats. Before 1917, the Conservatives have only twice risen above 35 percent in that province. The strong links between Quebec and the Liberal Party, which had been developing during the years of Sir Wilfrid Laurier's leadership, were firmly forged in the election of 1917.

The Beginning of the Multiparty System. The next federal election, in 1921, reflected another shift in the national party system with the growth of agrarian parties, primarily in the Prairie Provinces. Building on provincial roots in place before 1900, "third" parties began to provide possible alternatives to the Conservatives and Liberals. A farmer-labor government came to power in Ontario in 1919, and in 1921 the United Farmers Party took control of the provincial administration of Alberta. The United Farmers of Manitoba became the governing party in that province in 1922, and agrarian parties also displayed some strength in the Atlantic Provinces of Nova Scotia and New Brunswick in the same period. In the national election of 1921, the Progressive Party (a coalition of United Farmers groups from several provinces) won sixty-four seats to the Liberals' 116 and the Conservatives' fifty; farmer and labor candidates won forty of the forty-three Prairie seats. Because many Progressives distrusted organized parties, however, they declined to form the Official Opposition (a role normally played by the largest opposition party). At least partly as a consequence of this fact, their support gradually dissipated in the succeeding three general elections (1925, 1926, and 1930), two-party competition was gradually reestablished, and many voters returned to their former parties. (Indeed the Manitoba Progressives entered a formal coalition with that province's Liberal Party. When, in 1942, the former leader of the Manitoba Progressives became leader of the national Conservative Party, that party was renamed the Progressive-Conservative Party—the name it formally retains today.) Since the 1920s, however, the Canadian party system has included two significant third parties: the example of the United Farmers was not forgotten by the men and women who exploited regional discontent to build two new national parties in the mid-1930s—the Social Credit League and the Co-operative Commonwealth Federation (which later developed into the New Democratic Party).

The Social Credit League was formed during the Great Depression of the 1930s and advocated reform of the monetary system as a solution to the economic problems of the time. In succeeding years the party abandoned some of its monetary proposals and developed into a conservative, populist party, concerned mainly with the problems of small businessmen and farmers, but drawing considerable support from blue-collar workers as well. The party formed the government in Alberta in 1935 and in British Columbia in 1952, and prior to the 1960s these two provinces provided the bulk of the party's electoral support in federal campaigns. Since 1962, however, Social Credit has enjoyed some support in Quebec, where the party's representatives briefly formed a separate organization known as the Ralliement des Créditistes before eventually rejoining the main party. Social Credit is currently the governing party in British Columbia and the Official Opposition in Alberta; but in the 1980 election it lost all six of its House of Commons members (who had been sitting for Quebec ridings).

The Co-operative Commonwealth Federation was a democratic socialist party formed in the early 1930s and dedicated to the creation of a "co-operative commonwealth" through social ownership of productive enterprise and centralized economic planning. Its limited electoral success (despite a hopeful beginning) led its leaders to formalize links with the trade union movement in the hopes of expanding the electoral and financial base of the party. In 1961 elements of Canada's main union organization (the Canadian Labour Congress) joined with the CCF to form the New Democratic Party—a social-democratic party similar in style to the British Labour Party or the social-democratic parties of Sweden and West Germany. The NDP currently is the governing party only in Saskatchewan and is the Official Opposition in Manitoba and British Columbia. In Ottawa, it holds thirty-two seats in the Canadian House of Commons.

Neither Social Credit nor the NDP has ever formed the government at the national level, although one or the other has from time to time held the balance of power in a minority government situation. In the federal election of 1972, these two parties polled more than 25 percent of the popular vote and obtained 46 of the Commons's 264 seats. In 1974 they polled more than 20 percent of the vote for 27 seats. In 1979 they polled 22.49 percent of the votes, controlling 32 seats. Thus, they held the balance of power in the Commons. In 1980, however, their influence diminished substantially as a result of Liberal sweeps of the East and the Conservative sweep of the West.

Minor Parties. The Communist Party of Canada and a Maoist party called the Communist Party of Canada (Marxist-Leninist) each ran more than fifty candidates in the 1979 federal election, but none was elected.[43] The last Communist member of the Commons was elected in 1945 and resigned his seat when he was convicted of espionage in 1946. One of two Communist members have appeared more recently in provincial legislatures occasionally under the name Labour-Progressive. Apart from independents, all members of the Commons since the election of 1949 have been members of one of the four principal parties—Liberal, Progressive-Conservative, New Democratic, or Social Credit/Créditiste.[44]

Provincial Parties. Albeit with varying strength, the four major parties are also active at the provincial level. In addition, in Quebec, the Union Nationale, formed originally as a coalition between the Quebec Conservative Party and some dissident Liberals in that province, provided either the governing or main Opposition Party in Quebec from 1936 to 1973.

It is now being reorganized, and may reemerge as a Conservative party. The Parti Québécois was founded in 1968 to coalesce separatist strength in that province. It won the provincial election of November 15, 1976, and has formed the Quebec government ever since. Despite losing the Referendum vote (on giving it a mandate to negotiate Sovereignty/Association with the rest of Canada) in May 1980, the PQ remains in office, having won its second electoral battle in April 1981 by a wide margin (while promising not to hold another sovereignty/association referendum during its term in office, should it be reelected).

Party Structure. A primary structural function of the major national parties is to provide an electoral organization—selecting candidates, designing platforms, organizing campaigners, and mobilizing voters for the purpose of placing the party's representatives in office. To some extent, parties also operate between elections to build support for their viewpoints and to develop party policy through internal discussion of public issues. However, these political education and policy development functions are increasingly being performed between elections by an elite or oligarchy within the party— even in parties of "movement" or extraparliamentary origin. In fact, despite differences in party origin and ideology, the organizational charts of the principal parties display striking similarity. The older, "cadre-type" parties have made moves in the direction of mass organization in an attempt to build effective campaign machinery.[45] The "movement" parties that *began* as mass organizations have had to accept more centralized direction from party elites. Hence the similarity in current organizational form.

Each of the major national parties is organized as a federation of provincial parties, but the provincial wing of any party may be practically moribund in a province where that party has not enjoyed much electoral success. Thus, for example, strong provincial Social Credit organizations exist really only in Alberta, British Columbia, and Quebec.

The centerpiece of each provincial party is its annual or biennial convention to which delegates are elected from the constituency associations that form the basic units of the party organization. (Also chosen as delegates are certain party officials; legislators; and, occasionally, defeated candidates.) Party constitutions generally also provide for a large executive body responsible to the convention and a smaller executive responsible to the larger body. In addition, each provincial office is served by a small bureaucracy headed by a director or provincial secretary. Parallel forms of these structures can be found at the national level as well. In addition to these extraparliamentary structures, there exists a party leader and (when the party has legislative representation) a parliamentary caucus. It is often the case that the parliamentary wing of the party has much more influence on party policy and operation than the extraparliamentary wing, even in parties like the NDP where extraparliamentary control is an article of faith for party activists.

Despite these structural similarities, there are some differences in the organizations of the main parties. These differences occur mainly between parties of movement origin (such as the NDP, Social Credit, and the Parti Québécois) and those of parliamentary origin (like the Liberals and PCs). The constitutions of the movement parties generally spell out in considerable detail the qualifications and responsibilities of members; those in the older, cadre parties often do not. A somewhat greater degree of ideological commitment seems implied in membership in the movement parties. The NDP, for example, explicitly requires that its members not belong to any other political party (a device often used to expel suspected Communists, but also effective in forcing a dissident wing of the organization to stop acting as a "party within the party"). Membership in the NDP, moreover, requires a rather different financial commitment from that required by membership in the older parties. The Liberals and Conservatives have generally not been as dependent as the NDP or Social Credit on individual membership fees to finance party activities, and their dues have therefore usually been lower. All of the parties provide for direct membership by individuals, but the NDP also allows for members who join indirectly by virtue of their membership in an affiliated trade union local or farm organization.

A final difference between the movement and cadre styles

of organization involves the importance accorded the party convention in their operation. In the parties of extraparliamentary origin, the convention is said to be the supreme governing body of the party. Debate on policy resolutions often takes up a much larger proportion of the time at such conventions than it does in conventions of the older parties. In fact, the final policy decisions will still be heavily influenced by party elites, including the parliamentary caucus. However, the elites always feel constrained to explain in detail to the convention any deviation from the preceding convention's guidance. Some critics have suggested that close adherence to convention-established policy is easiest in opposition, when the party does not have the responsibility of forming and operating a government.

It is also worth noting that the NDP recognizes no difference (as the older parties do) between regular conventions and those called to select a leader. Leadership conventions are called only rarely in the major parties; every NDP convention selects a new leader or confirms the old leader in office.[46]

Financial support for the Liberal and Conservative parties has traditionally come mainly from a few corporations and wealthy individuals. That for the NDP has been drawn from individual membership fees and from affiliated trade unions. Social Credit has been able to secure corporate donations only where it has been electorally successful, otherwise, it has been dependent on individual members. Recent federal legislation provides financial support from public funds for candidates who receive 15 percent or more of the vote in a federal election, and free broadcast time is provided, during election campaigns, to representatives of recognized parties.[47] The legislation also requires disclosure of the source of large donations, makes donations tax deductible (up to a point), and provides ceilings on the levels of campaign spending. This legislation has helped somewhat to reduce the inequality of resources available to parties during campaigns, but not all party fundraisers have been happy with the new rules. One reason is that some corporations that previously donated to both the Liberals and the PCs have reduced or eliminated their contributions because of the disclosure legislation.

A number of provinces have passed similar legislation, and Ontario has limited the amount a person or corporation may donate. Parties that previously depended on a small number of large donations in that province now find that they must exert the effort needed to attract a larger number of smaller gifts.

Party Functions. Although only a small proportion (less than 10 percent) of the Canadian population belongs formally to any political party, the party system provides important linkages between the ordinary voter and the government. Parties act to mobilize voters in election campaigns; they provide platforms and resources for candidates to make themselves and their views known to the public. Parties provide a symbol around which voters can rally to simplify the complex issues of politics and resolve them into a decision on election day.

Perhaps more important, the parties select the leaders and candidates who constitute the elected decision-making elite. They then generally provide a means for rank-and-file members to advise their leaders about their policy preferences—an important opportunity for the aggregation of diffuse public opinion into usable policy proposals. Even if the bulk of policy initiatives comes from parliamentarians or civil servants, the party rank and file can at least provide a valuable sounding board against which such proposals can be tested.

ELECTIONS AND VOTING BEHAVIOR

The Election System. Members of the House of Commons, and members of the provincial legislatures in all but three provinces, are elected according to a simple plurality system in single-member districts. This means that each voter has one vote in his district of residence and the single candidate with the most votes wins the seat for that district, regardless of how many votes are distributed among other candidates. An exception is Prince Edward Island, where all provincial legislators are elected in two-member districts, and each voter has two votes.[48] There are also three two-member districts in the Nova Scotia legislature and seven in that of British Columbia.

Admirers of the single-member, simple plurality system—a "first past the post" or "winner take all" system—credit it with the production of stable majority government, through its underrepresentation of splinter parties and its exaggeration of the winning party's margin of victory. Critics of the system argue that it is artificial and unfair in its translation of votes into seats. One critic in particular[49] has suggested that the distorting effect of the system on the distribution of seats in the House of Commons has clearly altered the style and content of Canadian political debate and perhaps impeded national integration. Because a party will receive more seats for a given number of votes if the votes are concentrated in a particular region than it will if the votes are spread out across the country, parties have been rewarded for making regional appeals. Parties appealing on other grounds (e.g., social class) have been disadvantaged. Even the parliamentary caucuses of the major national parties display regional biases, as parties tailor their campaign appeals to those regions where the chance of gain is greatest. Also, argues this critic, the appearance of political instability is created artificially because the electoral system translates a small change in votes into a large change in seats. While the system is credited with producing majority government, it has done so only rarely, and then often at the expense of effective opposition. In spite of these conclusions (which other scholars have disputed), there has been very little support for changing to any alternative system.[50] Nevertheless, persistent regional disparities in representation in the Commons—exceedingly few Conservatives are elected in Quebec, exceedingly few Liberals west of Ontario, for example—are prompting renewed interest in possible changes.

At one time or another, the right to vote has been restricted in Canada, or in one of the provinces, according to age, sex, property ownership, citizenship, and ethnic or racial origin, but most of these barriers no longer remain. The only major restrictions on the franchise currently are related to age, citizenship, and length of residence.[51] All Canadian citizens eighteen years of age or older (nineteen in British Columbia provincial elections) may vote if they have been resident in the country (or province, in the case of provincial elections) for the required period—six months for provincial elections in Newfoundland, New Brunswick, and Saskatchewan; twelve months for all other provincial and federal elections. Some provinces have also extended voting rights to British subjects (i.e., citizens of other Commonwealth countries) and to citizens of the Republic of Ireland.

Voters lists are prepared at the federal level, and in all but three provinces, by means of a door-to-door canvass prior to each election. British Columbia operates a permanent voters list for which the prime responsibility to register rests with the individual elector. Quebec has begun to use a permanent list updated annually in the late summer or early fall, and Prince Edward Island has also adopted a permanent list with frequent opportunities for updating.

The campaign period in federal elections is normally fifty-eight days; provincial campaigns tend to be somewhat shorter. Turnout in federal elections is usually 70 to 80 percent of the eligible electorate; turnout in provincial elections varies from province to province, being slightly higher than federal turnout in some, and slightly lower in others.

Since there is no fixed term for either the House of Commons or the provincial legislatures, elections can be held virtually at any time. However, climate and normal vacation periods make late spring and early fall preferred times. National and provincial elections are administered by different electoral officers and administrative machinery, and balloting for the Commons never coincides with that for a provincial legislature. Also, since the Prime Minister and his Cabinet run for office as ordinary members of Parliament and not separately as executive officers (the same is true in the provinces), each voter has only one choice to make at each election—for which candidate will he vote to represent his constituency. As a consequence, voting machines have not been needed in Canada for general elections, and paper ballots bearing the names of candidates are used. Voters are simply required to place an X next to the name of the candidate for whom they wish to vote.[52]

Voting Behavior. In some countries, voters' choices among political parties can be linked to membership in social categories that reflect important political cleavages. In Canada, as in many of the Anglo-American democracies, such linkages are far from clear. The social group variables that appear most obviously connected with voting choices in Canada are region, ethnic background, religious affiliation, and social class.[53] However, the proportion of variation in party choice association with these variables is generally quite low, and considerable research remains to be done to elaborate our understanding of the bases of party support in Canada. There is some evidence that voting and party indentification are quite volatile in Canada (with as many as 60 percent of voters in some surveys indicating that they have previously identified with a different party from the one they now support). The complexity of Canadian voting comes in part from the existence of a federal system in which the national party system is overlaid on ten very diverse provincial ones.

There are considerable regional variations in Canadian federal party support (see Table 3.1). Close, two-party competition involving Liberals and Conservatives exist only in the Atlantic Provinces. Quebec has long been a Liberal stronghold, with only a small, Créditiste rump and major breakthroughs for the Conservatives only in the elections of 1930 and 1958. Ontario, which has fully one third of the Commons representation, displays fairly clear three-party competition involving the Liberals, Conservatives, and New Democrats in several areas, and the same is true for votes (if not seats) in Manitoba and Saskatchewan. Alberta has been a Conservative stronghold since the early 1960s, although prior to that it displayed considerable Social Credit strength. British Columbia has moved from a period of national four-party competition to one of three-party struggle, since the decline of Social Credit support in that province in *federal* contests.

The principal ethnic cleavage in Canada has been that between Anglophones and Francophones. The Liberal Party

Table 3.1 Distribution of Seats in the House of Commons and in the Provincial Legislative Assemblies Following the 1980 General Election

Legislature	Last Election	Government	Official Opposition	Other	Total
House of Commons	Feb. 11, 1980	Liberal — 147	Prog/Cons — 103	NDP — 32	282
Alberta	Mar. 14, 1979	Prog/Cons — 74	Socred — 4	NDP — 1	79
British Columbia	May 10, 1979	Socred — 31	NDP — 26		57
Manitoba	Oct. 11, 1977	Prog/Cons — 33	NDP — 23	Liberal — 1	57
New Brunswick	Oct. 23, 1978	Prog/Cons — 30	Liberal — 28		58
Newfoundland	Jun. 18, 1979	Prog/Cons — 33	Liberal — 19		52
Nova Scotia	Sep. 19, 1978	Prog/Cons — 31	Liberal — 17	NDP — 4	52
Ontario	Jun. 9, 1977	Prog/Cons — 58	Liberal — 34	NDP — 33	125
P.E.I.	Apr. 23, 1979	Prog/Cons — 21	Liberal — 11		32
Quebec	Nov. 15, 1976	Parti Québécois — 69	Liberal — 28	Un-Nat — 11, Socred — 1, PDP* — 1	110
Saskatchewan	Oct. 18, 1979	NDP — 44	Prog/Cons — 17		61

* Popular Democratic Party.

Note: The customary designation for members of the Commons is MP (member of Parliament); since most of the provincial legislatures are called formerly Legislative Assemblies, their members are customarily known as MLA's. Exceptions are the legislatures of Ontario, Newfoundland, and Quebec. Ontario's legislature is sometimes called the Provincial Parliament, and the designation MPP is often used for its members. The Newfoundland legislature is called the House of Assembly—hence the designation MHA for its members. The legislature of Quebec is called the National Assembly, but (following French practice) its members are usually called deputies.

has been consistently best able to attract the support of the latter group, while Conservative support tends to come more from persons of British ethnic origin. In terms of religious cleavage, the Liberal Party received disproportionate support from Roman Catholics and Jews, while the Conservatives receive substantial Protestant support. NDP support does not appear to be related to religious affiliation directly, and while provincial support for the Social Credit Party in the West is mainly Protestant (often fundamentalist), national support for the party in Quebec comes mainly from Roman Catholic French Canadians.

The New Democratic Party is strongest among unionized, industrial workers in urban areas (although in Quebec, much blue-collar support goes to Social Credit in rural, primary-industry regions and to the Liberals in urban constituencies). Middle-class voters tend to divide nationally between the Liberal and Conservative parties, with Liberal strength being somewhat greater in urban areas and Conservative support being highest in rural regions.

The Liberal Party has been most successful in aggregating diverse interests into a kind of "grand coalition" center party. The ideological differences with the Conservative Party have become somewhat blurred in recent years, and both Social Credit and the NDP have adjusted their initial movement positions somewhat in an attempt to attract wider support.

INTEREST GROUPS

Private associations in Canada make considerable attempts to influence government policy. The pervasive nature of such pressure-group activity can be gauged from the fact that a recent study of voluntary associations by Professor Robert Presthus found that more than two thirds of a sample of 639 interest-group directors could recall attempting to influence government directly.[54] In another study Professor Presthus found that 93 percent of a sample of Commons members agreed most legislators did not find pressure-group activities improper, and 85 percent felt that pressure groups were necessary to make government aware of the needs of the people.[55]

Interest groups may direct their appeals to a variety of government actors. The Cabinet and its surrounding bureaucracy seems to be a more sensible target than legislators in Canada, since the Cabinet is the central decision-making body in the parliamentary system. However, by virtue of its broad public support, its centrality to the system, and above all the secrecy of its deliberations, the Cabinet may more easily resist the persuasion of most lobbyists. Access to the Cabinet and legitimacy in the eyes of Cabinet ministers are themselves resources that, like time, money, and membership, are not evenly distributed among all groups. Some organizations may find it most to their advantage to seek influence through the civil service or through regulatory agencies. If a group can convince bureaucrats of its value as a source of expertise, it may be able to provide much of the information on which civil service decisions are made. It may even be able to place a representative on the board of an agency designed to regulate the sector, industry, or collectivity for which the group speaks.

Appeals may also be made to individual members of Parliament or to parliamentary committees. Given the importance of the Cabinet and bureaucracy, however, resort to legislators may reflect a failure to receive a favorable hearing at other levels. Similarly, a group that appeals to government only through a brief to a legislative committee or a letter-writing campaign aimed at members of Parliament, or through newspaper advertisements or public protest demonstrations, may be indicating its failure to receive access to key decision makers through the less formal channels of friendship and preexisting similarity of viewpoint.

Large budgets and memberships, lobbying experience, and substantive expertise may be necessary, but not sufficient, conditions for effectiveness. For example, Presthus found that political elites believed large business and labor organizations would be the most effective lobbyists; but his case studies demonstrated that welfare and educational groups were almost as successful as business groups and that labor was often not as successful, despite its large membership and budget, because it lacked "the popular legitimacy often described to business, welfare, and educational groups."[56]

Moreover, he concluded:

> Labour and welfare activities . . . have at best a precarious legitimation in capitalist societies. Thus, whereas business, religious, and educational groups tend to focus on the apex of political power, the Cabinet, labour and welfare groups turn mainly to the legislature and the civil service.[57]

Business and industrial groups and trade union organizations make up the bulk of interest-group activity in Canada, although there remains a considerable degree of organization in the agricultural sector (reflecting the significant role played by that sector of the Canadian economy in the last one hundred years). A considerable number of fraternal/service and social/recreational groups exist in Canada as well, but they tend to be less significant in relation to government lobbying than business, professional, labor, or agricultural interests. The main national associations of business groups include the Canadian Chamber of Commerce and the Canadian Manufacturers Association; a number of business organizations exist in particular industrial sectors as well, such as the Canadian Petroleum Association and the Canadian Construction Association. Trade unions in Canada are organized in two main groupings—the Canadian Labour Congress and the Quebec-based Confederation of National Trade Unions, and appeals to government are normally, though not always, channeling through these organizations.

PUBLIC OPINION

One of the strategies open to interest groups in a democracy is the attempt to mobilize public opinion in support of their views. Indeed, the basis of democratic government is the recognition that those in office are dependent on the good opinion of the public in order to retain their position. As a consequence, the capacity to measure and utilize public opinion has become an important consideration for participants in the process of Canadian government. The support of the public can be a valuable political resource; the possibility of public censure is a significant political constraint.

The effectiveness of public opinion as a resource or a constraint depends on the degree to which it can be mobilized. The opinions of a very few people cannot generally have an impact on decision makers unless the opinions reflect expertise the decision makers value. To be felt, usually public opinion must be organized; it must be presented as the view of a significant proportion of the relevant public (usually the electorate). While politicians are interested in discovering the public will in regard to an issue, they are also interested in using expressions of that will in support of positions derived from other information. The concerned observer must be able to make sense of contending measures of public opinion if he is to assess politicians' claims to represent that opinion.

A variety of indicators of public opinion are used regularly in political debate; their impact will depend not only on the number of opinion holders they indicate, but what they indicate about the resources of those opinion holders and the likelihood that they will be moved to action by the intensity of their views. A favorite means of expressing opinion, often employed by interest groups, is the organized letter-writing campaign. Public officials are bombarded by letters, telegrams, and postcards in support of a particular view. Such campaigns will be effective only if policymakers are convinced that the letters are not fraudulent—not all composed by a very few people claiming to represent thousands more. Also they must believe that the opinion has not been "created" by an organization that prodded its members to express a view the members did not hold intensely enough to express on their own.[58]

Public meetings or demonstrations are less effective in impressing policymakers than they are in publicizing a cause or grievance to solicit the support of the mass public. Politicians are generally aware of how easy it is to get a small crowd together in support of virtually any position. At the same time, since demonstrators are always few in relation to the whole public, they can always be labeled unrepresentative by their opponents.

The public will can be most directly effective if it is expressed in a referendum—a vote in which a policy proposal is submitted to the whole electorate for a binding decision. To date, referenda have rarely been used in Canada, except at the municipal level where they have concerned such issues as local implementation of liquor-licensing laws and fluoridation of water supplies. There have been a few referenda of national importance, however. One, concerning conscription during World War II, provided support for the Canadian government to change an arrangement it had firmly promised to maintain. Another, in the British colony of Newfoundland, enabled that colony to enter Canada as the tenth province. The recent Referendum on Sovereignty/Association in Quebec (May 1980) has already been referred to (see p. 141). Local referenda are sometimes hedged with restrictions against the expression of "unrepresentative" opinion, so that a referendum to be binding must sometimes win the support of two thirds or more of the electorate rather than the simple majority. (This was not the case in the Quebec Referendum.) Such restrictions may arise from the conviction that it is easier to mobilize forces for change in an existing situation than it is to mobilize the contented in support of the status quo. Also, it is sometimes argued that issues important enough to be submitted to a referendum should be seen to succeed by a "clear" and not a "narrow" majority; otherwise, they should fail.

The government itself will often solicit information on the opinions of that portion of the public it considers relevant to a particular policy issue. Committees of Parliament solicit briefs, as do Royal Commissions (special investigatory bodies established from time to time to explore a matter of public importance and make recommendations to the Crown). Again, completing interests vary in the resources they can bring to bear in presenting such briefs. Also, submissions of opinion will be solicited by civil servants or elected officials only if they already accord the group concerned a degree of legitimacy.

Public opinion polls may provide the best indicator of public viewpoints to the independent observer, but they too can be flawed in their representation of the public will. A number of government departments now conduct surveys to gather opinions and other information in particular policy areas,[59] and there are frequent privately conducted soundings as well. The most frequent and well-known Canadian private poll is probably the Gallup poll, administered monthly by the Canadian Institute of Public Opinion.[60] The government studies may be unsatisfactory for the general public because they are usually conducted with a narrow purpose in mind and for private consumption of the department concerned. The Gallup poll, although more frequent than in the past and improved in character, still has some shortcomings. For example, the concern of public issue pollsters is to measure opinion quickly and simply with respect to some matter that is in the news (their main "customers" are the media). Questions may therefore be simplified to get a quick and consistent response from as many people as possible, and the nuances of an issue can be lost in the process. Also, the poll and its main consumers have little interest in plotting changes in opinion (except of the largest magnitude); therefore, questions are not always repeated exactly in succeeding polls. Moreover, a problem with all polls is that opinions may change so rapidly that last month's poll is not a good indicator of this month's opinion. Finally, dramatic events at the time of a poll may introduce short-term fluctuations into the measurement of long-term attitudes. Of course, all of these problems are compounded by the need to ensure that the sample selected for interviewing in a poll is genuinely representative of the population about whom one wishes to generalize.

Even if one concludes that, taken together, these various measures can provide a pretty clear picture of public opinion, one must recognize that only a small segment of the population is ever fully active, knowledgeable, and concerned about political issues. It is necessary to consider the ways in which the attentive public forms its opinions and the means by which those opinions then circulate in the society at large. Central to both these concerns are the structure and operation of the mass media of communication.

THE MASS MEDIA

The Canadian mass media system has been characterized as being

marked by cultural dualism, a significant degree of public ownership, the absence of a national press, and a substantial communications overflow from the United States.[61]

The most broadly pervasive actor in the system is probably the publicly owned Canadian Broadcasting Corporation (known in French simply as Radio-Canada). Founded as a radio network in 1932, the CBC now provides radio and television services in English and French to almost all Canadians. CBC-TV provided the first television service in Canada in the early 1950s. A privately owned television network, Canadian Television (CTV) was formed in 1961 and operates nationally in English; there are also three regional networks and several independent outlets. (Most Canadians, of course, are able to watch U.S. network television—cable TV services are available to 83 percent of Canadian households—and it must be admitted that many prefer to do so.)

There are no truly national newspapers in Canada, at least partly because the costs of distribution to a small, highly dispersed population make such newspapers economically unfeasible. The paper that most aspires to national status, the *Toronto Globe and Mail*, sells only around 3 percent of its circulation outside the Province of Ontario. For a national picture of news events, Canadians must rely on the CBC and CTV national newscasts, or on the wire service, Canadian Press, which is a national news-gathering and distribution agency owned cooperatively by the major daily papers. Its subsidiary, Broadcast News, provides teletype and tape service to the major networks and to more than 300 private radio and TV stations.

There are at present over 110 daily newspapers in Canada with a combined circulation of some 5 million; roughly 80 percent of those dailies are owned by newspaper chains, and the three largest chains control roughly half the total circulation. Two of those chains, Southam and Thomson, maintain news bureaus in Ottawa, the national capital.

In addition to the daily newspapers, there are more than 1,000 other papers, some 100 television stations (not including repeater or rebroadcasting stations), and about 500 radio stations. A study done in 1969 for the Senate Committee on the

Mass Media found that about 96 percent of a national sample of Canadians owned a television set, 98 percent owned a radio, and around 88 percent subscribed to at least one newspaper.

Cultural dualism in the media system results from a number of facts. First, apart from correspondents in Ottawa, most Quebec news outlets do not have correspondents outside that province (where 80 percent of Canada's French-speaking population lives). The exception is Radio-Canada, which does have correspondents across Canada, but stories without an angle of relevance to Quebec or to French-speaking Canadians may receive less attention for the network. Second, the personnel and content of the CBC's English and French news services are completely separate. Third, while Canadian Press translates material for its members, the French media tend to rely heavily on their own personnel. Thus, English and French Canadians may get quite different pictures of the same political event.

Finally, it is important to recognize the pervasive influence of the United States in Canada's media system. More than three quarters of the magazines bought by Canadians are published in the United States, and most of Canada's population now has direct or cable access to U.S. television programs and news. The Canadian Press is dependent for much (although not all of its foreign news on the American news agency, the Associated Press; Canadian television networks often purchase U.S. networks' news films of foreign events. The Canadian public thus has potentially greater exposure to American issues than to Canadian ones, and there is a degree to which Canadian politicians and reporters have begun to emulate American media practices.

Apart from free-time broadcasts and paid advertising during election campaigns, the most direct impact the media have on politics is in their reporting of political news. The highly partisan press that characterized nineteenth-century Canada, and still exists in some European countries, is no longer a reality in Canada today. Although newspapers often endorse candidates or parties during elections, they generally aim for neutrality in their news stories, and the same is true of the television networks. Of course, reporters and editors develop prejudices about what is newsworthy, as well as views of politicians and issues, and they convey these views to some degree in whatever they write. If reporters and editors develop an image of a particular politician, for example, they will (almost unconsciously) select material for publication that reinforces the image and reject material that calls the image into question.

Most of the news about national politics that the average citizen hears or reads is collected and reported by the members of the Ottawa Press Gallery—named for the special observation gallery of the Commons reserved for reporters. Since members of the Gallery see one another daily while the House is in session, and since they have ample opportunity to discuss among themselves the events they are all observing, a kind of collective conventional wisdom is easily developed. There will be deviations within the broad range of this consensus, but an editor is likely to find a reporter's perception or interpretation questionable if it does not accord with what other reporters are saying, or if it is incompatible with his own beliefs about political figures.

During an election campaign, the media take on increased importance. In many respects, the campaign becomes a contest for media attention, especially from the minor parties, which do not have as large budgets as the major parties for campaign advertising. A party which does not provide access for reporters may suffer in this contest, but a party will suffer equally if its leaders and candidates grant ready access but do not provide the basis for colorful copy. Professor Fred Fletcher quotes one journalist as saying that:

> There is a natural alliance between news makers and news reporters. The news maker wants publicity and the reporter needs a steady flow of usable copy. . . . The press gets angry when the politicians don't make news.[62]

One fairly significant aspect of press coverage in election campaigns is its concentration on party leaders. News stories, particularly those about the government party seeking reelection, do not usually mention a party without mentioning the leader. By contrast, the Prime Minister, or an opposition leader, will occasionally be featured in a story that scarcely mentions his party at all. Indeed, parties with a popular leader may make the media leader focus an aspect of their campaign strategy.

The media inevitably performs a "gatekeeper" and "agenda-setting" role in their selection of material to report, and there are always accusations leveled at newspapers, radio, and television that they ignore or undervalue certain issues, institutions, or political viewpoints. Some bias is unavoidable of course; for example, the media outlets are all large corporations, and it would be surprising to see them espousing anticorporate views. They are in the business of providing information, but they must be attentive to the public's desire for certain kinds of information or they risk going out of business. Finally, both reporters and the public have an interest in the simplification of issues in the news; the reporters will seek the simplest means of presenting the most "newsworthy" material, and the public will usually welcome the resolution of complex matter into simple categories. It may be the case that more "bias" in reporting results from the desire to produce colorful, interesting, easily understood news stories than from any desire to promote or hinder particular political interests.[63]

The Canadian Federal System

In 1837 rebellions had broken out in Upper and Lower Canada, and when the fighting had ended, the British authorities sought to prevent further unrest by changing the governing structures of the two colonies. One of the changes they made was to join the two Canadas into a single legislative union, which lasted until Confederation in 1867. As a consequence of this union, many of the statesmen who helped form the new nation in 1867 possessed considerable experience with the difficulty of combining two large, culturally diverse entities under a single government. Many representatives of the largely English-speaking, Protestant Canada West (later Ontario) believed that the frustrations of the pre-Confederation union could be avoided only if they could established control (through alliance with their counterparts in Nova Scotia and New Brunswick) over a commerce-oriented unitary government. To the representatives of largely French-speaking, Catholic Canada East (later Quebec) a federal form of government was preferable so that at least one level of government would exist which was responsive to French Canadians' hopes for cultural survival.

A federal solution was eventually adopted, but with the example of the U.S. Civil War fresh in their minds the founding fathers sought to establish a very powerful central government. In order to build a strong, industrial nation, capable of providing for the common defense and able to resist secessionist sentiments in the peripheral members of the union, they gave the central government control over the major sources of revenue and most aspects of commercial life. To the provinces they left those matters of property, civil law, local government, and education that seemed essential to the maintenance of cultural diversity.

As noted in the previous chapter, there have been substantial changes in the conditions that guided the intentions of the founding fathers, and judicial review and intergovernmental negotiation have often considerably shifted the distribution of power between the levels of government. New provinces have been added; the concentration of population has altered; the importance of particular sources of revenue has changed. Federal power was enhanced by the necessity of directing the nation's military effort in two world wars; the importance of some provincial areas of jurisdiction was demonstrated during the Depression; and attempts to alleviate regional economic distress have highlighted the need for government cooperation. The evolution of Canadian federalism has been conditioned mainly by three sets of factors: (1) the demands for government services made by the Canadian people; (2) the varying interpretations of each level of government's legislative authority; and (3) the availability of fiscal resources to meet demands within legitimate areas of authority. The result has been the development of a highly interpenetrated system that has sometimes been labeled "co-operative federalism."

THE CONSTITUTIONAL BASIS
A federal system always creates at least two levels of government with legislative jurisdiction over the same body of citizens. It becomes necessary to divide the known areas of legislative activity between the two levels, and to provide a means of assigning unanticipated areas (or residual powers) to one level or the other. It is also necessary to establish which level's legislative authority is to prevail in cases of conflict within areas of concurrent (or shared) jurisdiction. The principal statement of the division of powers between the federal and provincial levels of government is found in sections 91 and 92 of the BNA Act; section 93 makes special provision regarding the protection of education rights for Protestant or Catholic minorities, notwithstanding the provinces' right to legislate on educational matters; and sections 94A and 95 indicate the areas of concurrent jurisdiction.[64]

Section 91 was intended to be a clear grant of general and residual powers to the federal government, and section 92 was intended to enumerate exhaustively the classes of subjects within which only the provinces could make laws. However, section 91, after assigning the federal government the authority to "make Laws for the Peace, Order, and Good Government of Canada, in relation to all Matters not coming within the Classes of Subjects by this Act assigned exclusively to the Legislatures of the Provinces," went on to enumerate "for greater Certainty" twenty-nine specific areas of jurisdiction. Subsequent judicial interpretation has usually sought to justify federal legislation by reference to these twnety-nine specific headings and has relegated the general grant of authority to the status of an "emergency powers" clause. At the same time, the courts have tended to construe federal powers such as authority over interprovincial trade and commerce very narrowly, while giving a broad construction to the provincial field of property and civil rights.

The evolution of the Canadian federal system has proceeded by several means, including formal amendment of the BNA Act, judicial interpretation, and negotiation between levels of government.

FORMAL AMENDMENT

Since 1949 the Parliament of Canada has been able to amend portions of the BNA Act by ordinary statute, but the sections dealing with educational or language rights, the requirement of a yearly session of Parliament, the normal life of Parliament, and the division of powers between the two levels of government may still be amended only by the Parliament of Great Britain. It would be unthinkable for the British government to refuse an amendment requested by the Canadian Parliament; the difficulty in making such amendments lies in the moral and political necessity of securing agreement first among affected parties in Canada.[65] The British government would find itself in an untenable position, for example, if the Canadian Parliament requested an amendment to the BNA Act that was strongly opposed by one or more provinces.* Thus, it has been customary to consult the provinces when their interests are likely to be directly affected by a proposed amendment.[66]

There have been three occasions in which formal amendment of the BNA Act was used to produce explicit changes in the division of powers between the federal and provincial governments. In 1940 the national government was given exclusive legislative jurisdiction over unemployment insurance; in 1951 and 1964, the national government was given concurrent jurisdiction with the provinces over old age pensions and supplementary old age pension benefits, respectively. In the latter two cases, unlike the situation with other areas of concurrent jurisdiction, provincial legislation was given paramountcy— that is, in cases of conflict, provincial legislation was to prevail.

* This is precisely the situation of 1981's federally proposed patriation of the Constitution, with its amending formula and new Charter of Rights, opposed by eight provinces! Canada's Supreme Court ruled (October 1981) that provincial consent was necessary by convention but not by law (Editor's note.)

JUDICIAL REVIEW

A much more significant role in the evolution of Canadian federalism has been played by judicial interpretation than through formal amendment. Indeed, many Canadian Scholars have blamed (or credited) the Judicial Committee of the Privy Council (JCPC) of Britian with the transformation of a highly centralized federation envisioned in the BNA Act into the highly decentralized federation that is Canada today. Some critics of the JCPC have accused it of misreading the intention of the founding fathers, clearly expressed in the words of the act; others have indicated it for taking too rigid a view of the constitution and not being flexible in the face of changing circumstances, or simply for ignoring Canadian events and attitudes.

Beginning in the 1890s, and culminating in the rejection of the "New Deal" legislation in the 1930s,[67] the decisions of the JCPC tended to restrict the powers of the national government by enhancing those of the provincial authorities. Through a series of decisions, the Privy Council destroyed the apparently general grant of power in the preamble to section 91 and restricted the federal government's legislative authority to the enumerated examples in that section. Only if a matter could *not* be encompassed under a provincial power enumerated in section 92 (and there was little that could not be assigned to "property and civil rights" or "matters of a merely local or private nature") could the national government legislate in that field. Later it was suggested that the "Peace, Order, and Good Government" portion of section 91 gave the national government the authority to exceed its enumerated powers only in case of national emergency. The fairly clear "residual powers" clause implicit in the preamble to section 91 was effectively ignored in favor of the "property and civil rights" head of section 92.

It is perhaps unfair to be too critical of the results of these decisions. Conditions and events in Canada were probably not so unambiguous that consideration of them would have led in every case to a clear and universally approved decision. After all, there was some dispute about the desired outcome of every case before the JCPC, or there would have been no case in the first place. Also, despite the clarity of the wording in section 91, the act gives little guidance about the disposition of matters between "trade and commerce" (federal) and "property and civil rights" (provincial). Nor does it make clear what kinds of property-relevant questions are so central to the peace, order, and good government of Canada that they cannot be encompassed by the provincial power over property and civil rights. Finally, there remains considerable dispute over the effects of the JCPC's decisions. Some scholars argue that the federation was benefited by the opportunity to decentralize; they believe the courts merely facilitated a desirable, perhaps inevitable process.

INTERGOVERNMENTAL NEGOTIATIONS
While the courts may have created the decentralized federalism of the 1930s in Canada, that of the 1960s and 1970s (following a period of renwed centralism during and immediately after World War II) appears to be largely the result of intergovernmental negotiation. The decisions of the Judicial Committee served to indicate that the activities expected of government in the later twentieth century were mainly within the legislative competence of provincial governments whose revenue sources were not equal to the task. In the 1940s, that conclusion led to demands for constitutional reform, combined with occasional willingness to abdicate responsibility to the central government. In the 1960s and 1970s, while demands for constitutional reform have not disappeared, there is a greater acceptance of the need for cooperation between levels of government. From the viewpoint of the provinces, such cooperation has often meant the securing of funds from central government revenues to provide services that fall within areas of provincial jurisdiction. From the national government standpoint, cooperation provides the possibility of influencing provincial priorities and establishing national standards of social services through the application of the federal spending power.[68]

Largely because of the lack of coincidence between revenue sources and legislative responsibilities,[69] the expansion of government that has characterized many Western nations in the postwar era has necessitated in Canada a substantial degree of intergovernmental consultation and coordination. As a consequence, considerable institutional machinery has been developed (with varying degrees of formalization) to facilitate such consultation.

The bulk of the consultation between the provinces and the federal government (and among provinces) occurs at the level of the executive. Contacts occur very frequently among bureaucrats, somewhat less frequently among Cabinet ministers, and least frequently among First Ministers (Prime Minister and Premiers). Various estimates of the frequency of contact exist, but it may be said with some confidence that between 100 and 200 formal meetings between or among governments occur yearly in Canada, with two or three of these being meetings of all provincial premiers and the Prime Minister (together with supporting bureaucrats and some Cabinet ministers) in a full Federal-Provincial Conference. Informal contacts are of course even more frequent.

Prior to the 1960s, senior-level consultation was relatively rare and involved mainly conditional grant programs and tax agreements.[70] In the 1960s, however, a considerable expansion in the number of such meetings occurred, and the scope of their deliberations widened. In addition to shared-cost arrangements and tax proposals, they began to examine consitutional reform, as well as a number of areas of shared interest such as environmental pollution, Indian affairs, energy policy, and foreign investment. Some of these discussions took place in subcommittees established at Federal-Provincial Conferences and involved senior civil servants as well as elected officials. To coordinate these efforts, the federal Cabinet now has a Standing Committee on Federal-Provincial Relations, and there is a Federal-Provincial Relations Secretariat within the Privy Council Office. Ontario, Quebec, Sasketchewan, and Alberta have also established executive machinery to facilitate intergovernmental cooperation, and other provinces may follow suit if the trend in expanding such consultation continues.

Of course, these meetings do not only allow for cooperation. They also provide an arena for airing the major conflicts between governments. It used to be said that the only time provincial governments agreed was when they went to Ottawa to bargain with the central government, but recently the lines of conflict have occasionally placed Ottawa on the side of some provinces in opposition to others. For example, recent "energy conferences" tend to find the central government agreeing with those provinces that are principal consumers of fossil fuels, in opposing to the major "producing" provinces, but on occasion even this posture is reversed. The development of Canada within a federal political arrangement has allowed diversity on economic lines to flourish, as well as the cultural diversity the system was originally designed to protect. As a consequence, many of the political disputes among provincial governments in Canada today have their roots in differences of economic interest.

POLITICAL ECONOMY OF FEDERALISM
From the start, Confederation was at least partly an economic bargain, and the participants were far from equal in their economic resources. The BNA Act sought to make provision for the absorption of the colonial debts by the new central government and provided in addition that yearly payments be made from the central government's revenues to the provinces for the support of provincial government. These unconditional grants were to be in full settlement of all future demands on the government of Canada, but within two years the schedule of subsidies was increased, and from then on (until World War II) that section of the BNA Act became a flexible portion of the constitution. It is little wonder that R. M. Dawson said, in writing of this area:

> The world of Dominion-Provincial finance has for much of its history had an air of grotesque unreality, untrammelled by logic and the ordinary restrictions and meanings of world.[71]

Following the Great Depression of the 1930s, the central government moved to take exclusive control of the personal and corporate income tax, in order to effect fiscal control to promote stable economic growth. Because the BNA Act restricted the provinces to direct taxes,[72] the federal government felt some necessity to compensate the provinces for its exclusive occupation of what was becoming, potentially, the preeminent revenue field. For some time therefore they "rented" the indirect tax fields from the provinces by paying each province an unconditional grant. Until the early 1950s, equalization payments (money from central government revenues paid to only some of the provinces unconditionally on a fiscal need basis) were tied to tax-rental arrangements. Beginning in 1962, the federal government was forced to end the tax-rental agreements and permit the provinces to reenter the personal corporate income tax fields (indeed, Quebec had begun to levy its own income tax in 1954). The central government adjusted its own income tax rates to permit the provinces to levy income taxes without adding an unreasonable burden on the individual taxpayer. This system of tax abatements effectively ended in 1972, and both levels of government now adjust their rate and scope of taxation in accordance with their needs and resources.

Another aspect of federal-provincial financial arrangements that was a prominent feature of Canadian politics in the 1960s was the development of numerous shared-cost programs, in which the federal government provided funding for national schemes (such as health insurance and pensions) to provinces whose governments agreed to take part. Such provinces were expected to provide a portion of the funds themselves in the case of some programs. In 1965 the federal government responded to provincial objections that such conditional grants were unwarranted interference in provincial legislative priority setting. They allowed provinces to "contract out" or "opt out" of certain shared-cost programs and to receive from the federal government an abatement of income tax rates (up to 20 percentage points) in lieu of the conditional grants they would have received. Only Quebec took advantage of this offer, and later adjustments to the tax system did not make the offer available, despite indications from Ontario and Alberta that they might take advantage of such a scheme.

Virtually all that now remains of the highly interpenetrated tax system of the early 1960s is an agreement that Ottawa will collect provincial personal income tax for the provinces (Quebec collects its own), provided that such taxes are calculated on the federal base; the provinces, of course, may set their own rates of tax. The central government also collects corporate income tax for a number of provinces.

This rather confused set of relationships and agreements is regularly renegotiated among the governments involved, customarily at five-year intervals. The system of tax agreements, conditional grants, and unconditional payments, derived through executive-level negotiation, must generally be given force by legislation passed by Parliament and the provincial legislatures. Accordingly, these arrangements form the focus of an important part of Canadian politics.

The fiscal aspects of Canadian federalism reflect some basic economic realities about the provinces. First, some provinces are very poor in relation to others; their revenue-producing capacity cannot support social services that are easily provided in the wealthier provinces. If national uniformity in standards of health care and social welfare, for example, is deemed desirable, then a redistribution of funds must be accomplished through the agency of the central government.

Second, the spending priorities of the wealthier provinces will not be as directly affected by conditional grant or shared-cost programs as well those of the poor provinces. The "have" provinces can afford to opt out of programs or to provide their own; the "have-not" provinces will need the cooperation of the central government if they are to contemplate the provision of high-cost services. Indeed, the cost-sharing arrangements which may be essential for the smaller, poorer provinces, if they are to offer such services, often require the participation of the larger, wealthier provinces (who have least to gain from them) before they are economically feasible.

Third, since provinces may wish to accomplish other aims through the tax system besides the raising of revenue (e.g., incentives to various kinds of economic activity), they may not remain content to adjust merely the *rates* of tax, but may also concern themselves with modifications of the *base* on which the tax is calculated.

Finally, it should be noted that revenue sources and fiscal effectiveness are not primarily constitutional issues but are matters for negotiation and political debate. The capacity of the central government to stabilize the fluctuations of the economy by taxing and spending will be heavily dependent on its capacity to secure the cooperation of the provinces. Since all the provinces taken together now tax and spend more than the federal government, and since they sometimes act at fiscal cross-purposes (as well as competing with one another to borrow in the bond markets), the capacity of the central government to deal with unemployment and inflation may be severely impaired. The economic differences between rich and poor provinces, between producer and consumer provinces, and among agricultural, resource-extractive, and industrial provinces remain so prominent that the consultations and negotiations some authors have called "cooperative" federalism might better be called "competitive." Indeed, one student of Canadian federalism has drawn attention to the decentralized nature of the Canadian system by employing the metaphor of relations among sovereign states, calling the system "federal-provincial diplomacy."[73]

PROVINCIAL POLITICS
As has been implied previously, the political systems of the provinces are quite distinct, despite marked similarities in the formal institutions of government. Moreover, their much larger contemporary roles also invite attention. Accordingly, a few comments on provincial diversity are in order. Population size is a political resource in any system based on representation by population, but for provincial governments, a large population may be most significant because of the demands it generates for government services. The *economic* impact of population size will be dependent to some extent on the skill levels and productivity of the population in question. Almost two thirds of the total population of Canada can be found in the two largest provinces, Ontario (around 36 percent) and Quebec (around 27 percent), and less than 10 percent in the four Atlantic Provinces (Nova Scotia, New Brunswick, Newfoundland, and Prince Edward Island). British Columbia,

the third most populous province, contains a little more than
10 percent of the population, while the remainder can be found
in the three Prairie Provinces (Alberta, Saskatchewan, and
Manitoba) and in the Yukon and Northwest Territories. Ontario has been the preferred destination of most (roughly 55
percent) immigrants to Canada in recent years, with Quebec
and British Columbia preferred by about 15 percent each.
Newfoundland and Alberta have benefited most by natural
increase, having high birthrates and low death rates, while
Ontario and British Columbia have benefited most from interprovincial migration.

In addition to population size, the resource based and
industrial capacity of a province may affect its economic development, which in turn will have consequences for its politics and government. The Province of Alberta, for example,
is responsible for between 70 and 80 percent of the crude oil
and natural gas production in Canada, but Ontario and Quebec have between them some 60 percent of Canadian crude-
oil-refining capacity. This situation has led to conflict over
pricing policies and the location of new industrial development. Ontario and Quebec also have around 64 percent of the
electricity-generating capacity and account for more than 80
percent of the total value added in manufacturing activity.[74]
The Prairie Provinces for many years were heavily dependent
on agricultural activity, and Alberta still accounts for a large
proportion of beef cattle production in Canada, while all three
Prairie Provinces (Saskatchewan in particular) contribute the
bulk of Canada's wheat crop. The Atlantic Provinces are most
clearly involved in fisheries (Newfoundland accounted for 36
percent of total poundage of fish in 1969, and the other Atlantic Provinces combined for 45 percent), while British Columbia's fishery, especially Pacific salmon, accounts regularly
for a large proportion of the *value* of fish landed (17 percent
in 1969). British Columbia and Quebec are also major forest
product centers, with nearly 70 percent of wood cut in 1969
coming from those provinces (British Columbia 44 and Quebec
24 percent). It should not be difficult to imagine differences
in wealth, as well as differences in economic interest, that
derive from figures such as these and are reflected in federal-

provincial relations. On a variety of measures, Ontario, British Columbia, and Alberta appear as "have" provinces, whereas Saskatchewan and the Atlantic Provinces sometimes appear in the "have-not" column. Manitoba and Quebec vary, depending on the measure used, but both have disadvantaged regions that sometimes place them on the "have-not" side of the ledger. One illustration of economic regional differences can be seen in a comparison of unemployment rates. In 1974 the seasonally adjusted average annual rate was 4.2 percent in Ontario, 2.7 percent in the Prairie provinces, 6.1 percent in British Columbia, 7.3 percent in Quebec, and 9.7 percent in the Atlantic Provinces. Naturally, these economic differences are reflected in the tone and focus of provincial politics, and in policy decisions taken by the government.

The formal institutions of government in the provinces are quite similar across provincial boundaries. All have representative, responsible government, parliamentary systems with a unicameral (one-house) legislature.[75] Each province has a lieutenant governor appointed by the central government who is responsible, if only in theory, for overseeing provincial activity for the federal authorities. Increasingly the provincial governments have been independent of direct federal intervention, except through the use of the spending power. Like the federal Parliament, the provincial legislatures operate according to practices derived originally from British tradition, and all are similar to the federal House of Commons in terms of parliamentary control of finance, responsible government, the rights and immunities of members, the role of the Speaker, the normal term (five years), and the legislative process. They all now have oral question periods, and all have some provisions for limiting debate and for emergency debates. All provincial legislatures delegate some functions to committees, but committee activity has not been as extensive in most provinces as it has been at the federal level.

The cabinet in each province looms a little larger in relation to the legislature than the federal Cabinet does in relation to the Commons. Cabinets normally range between fifteen and twenty-five members (in 1975, Prince Edward Island had the smallest with ten; Quebec, the largest with twenty-seven); and thus, while the federal Cabinet is usually 10 to 12 percent of the Commons, the provincial cabinets are generally closer to 30 percent of the membership of their legislatures. Outside Ontario, cabinet committee systems are not usually very highly developed. Most cabinets have a treasury or management board; some also have a committee concerned with general policy and priority planning; a few have more specialized committees as well.

The legislative sessions in the provinces used to begin generally in the early spring and last for three or four months. In several provinces (notably, Alberta, Newfoundland, and Quebec) the sessions are now ten months to a year in length. Ontario, Nova Scotia, and Saskatchewan sessions usually run more than four or five months now, and British Columbia has begun to employ more frequent special sessions, thereby extending the activity of the legislature beyond the customary three months. The rest average from three to five months. The normal expectation used to be that serving as a provincial legislator was a part-time job, and remuneration was accordingly low. As legislative sessions are extended, the situation is gradually changing.

Like the formal institutions of government, the spending priorities of the various provinces are also remarkably similar—partly because of the legislative fields entrusted to the provinces, and partly because of national shared-cost programs. Health and social services represent around 30 to 40 percent of all but the Atlantic Provinces' budgets, and 25 to 30 percent in the Atlantic Region. Education costs constitute 25 to 30 percent of the government budgets in all provinces, and transportation and highways account in all provinces for 8 to 12 percent. In Ontario (because of size) and in the Atlantic Provinces (because of low revenue bases) between 5 and 10 percent of the provincial budget normally goes to service the public debt.

Revenue sources include direct taxation (personal and corporate income tax, sales taxes, and occasionally succession duties), unconditional and conditional federal grants, licenses and fees, premium income in some cases from compulsory insurance schemes, and sales through provincial enterprises (such as liquor stores and provincial utilities). Since the provinces are responsible for municipal government, the property taxes collected to support local administration may also be seen as a provincial revenue.

LOCAL GOVERNMENT

By 1976, 75.5 percent of the Canadian population resided in (statistically defined) "urban" areas; nearly 56 percent lived in twenty-three urban centers of more than one hundred thousand population.[76] Urban concentrations are prominent in the lower Great Lakes and St. Lawrence Valley regions of Ontario and Quebec, the lower Fraser Valley of British Columbia, the Assiniboine and Red River valleys of Manitoba, and the St. Lawrence Gulf coastlines of the Atlantic Provinces. Thus, while only 37 percent of Prince Edward Island is urban, 81 percent of Ontario is so described. Consequently, municipal politics also varies considerably in scale and importance.

Local government in Canada tends to be formally non-partisan, but most municipal politicians have affiliations with one or another of the major national parties. Several attempts have been made to run candidates in municipal elections under national party labels, but these have generally been unsuccessful, and politicians tend to keep their affiliations quiet at election time. As a consequence of the need to organize for municipal elections, and because of the desirability of uniting for concerted action on municipal councils, a number of strictly municipal political parties have arisen without provincial or federal counterparts. Such parties have tended to arise on opposing sides of specifically municipal issues (often related to what one author has called the main business of local government—the property industry).[77]

Since many of the functions of local government relate to the use and value of real estate, the participation of persons involved in the real estate business has been notable in Canadian local government. Since most municipal revenue comes from property taxes (a tax on the value of land), there is an incentive from municipal governments to act in ways that will increase the value of the land in their areas. This will be especially true when increases in the mill rate (the amount of tax per unit value of real estate owned) are politically infeasible. This incentive results in a skewing of local government policy, because the provision of needed housing, for example, may be in conflict with the need to increase municipal revenues, perhaps through the construction of luxury dwellings.

A further revenue crisis arises for local governments because most of the services they provide are labor intensive. As the cost of labor increases, the cost of services may rise without a coincident rise in output. Major urban centers become increasingly dependent on provincial aid to carry such services as education, urban transit, roads, public health, and social welfare. As a result, one tends to find little interest-group activity at the municipal level. Provincial dominance is also reflected in the fact that to date the role of the federal government has been relatively small in Canada (especially when compared with the situation in the United States), and federal involvement has been limited pretty much to the provision of funding for housing programs and to research on urban problems.

It appears likely that some challenges to the maintenance of the present federal system will come in the future from problems arising at the municipal level. Provinces may press for a greater central government role in the funding of municipal services, while at the same time they may seek greater provincial involvement in the location of population through immigration controls and in the location of industry through tax and other incentives. The increasing concentration of Canada's population in urban centers may pose problems of mass democratic participation, and of policing and social control, that will have consequences at all levels of the political system. In addition, the fact that such concentrations are almost all within a couple of hundred miles of the U.S. border has some bearing on the problem of maintaining Canadian cultural independence.

Notes

1. J. R. Mallory, *The Structure of Canadian Government* (Toronto: Macmillan, 1971), p. 2.

2. The British North America Act, 1867, 30 and 31 Victoria, c. 3, preamble.

3. These institutions and principles will be treated in greater detail in later sections.

4. For a fuller treatment of these matters, see R. M. Dawson, *The Government of Canada*, 5th ed., rev. N. Ward (Toronto: University of Toronto Press, 1970), pp. 57–75.

5. See Mallory, op. cit., pp. 375–377.

6. R. I. Cheffins and R. N. Tucker, *The Constitutional Process in Canada*, 2d ed. (Toronto: McGraw-Hill Ryerson, 1976), p. 33.

7. This view is supported really only by an *obiter dicta* statement by Mr. Justice Abbot of the Supreme Court of Canada in his judgment of a case decided essentially on other, more traditional grounds. As a consequence, it is not binding on lower courts. See Ibid., pp. 43–44.

8. Ibid., pp. 46–47.

9. Dawson, op. cit., p. 155.

10. Much of what follows is based on Dawson, op. cit., pp. 197–217.

11. W. A. Matheson, *The Prime Minister and the Cabinet* (Toronto: Methuen, 1976), p. 14.

12. Canada, House of Commons, *Debates*, January 25, 1971, p. 2738, quoted in Matheson, op. cit., p. 15.

13. Matheson, op. cit., Table 2-1, p. 26. No person of other than British or French origin was appointed to the Cabinet before 1926. The first native Indian was appointed in 1976. The first Cabinet member of German origin was appointed in 1926; of Ukrainian origin, in 1957; of Italian origin, in 1976.

14. The information on the current Cabinet was taken from biographies in P. G. Normandin, ed., *The Canadian Parliamentary Guide, 1975* (Ottawa, 1975).

15. Mr. Clark's minister of agriculture was not from the prairies, but was a former farmer from Ontario. However, responsibility for the Canada Wheat Board was left in the hands of a Cabinet minister from Saskatchewan, the minister of transport.

16. The number of parliamentary secretaries is limited to the number of ministers established under the Salaries Act. Parliamentary secretaries are deemed to go out of office with the dissolution of Parliament.

17. From time to time, there have been ministers responsible for departments who were not included in the Cabinet. Examples include the controllers of customs and of inland revenue in the 1980s, and the solicitor general for numerous periods prior to World War II. See Dawson, op. cit., p. 170.

18. Mstheson, op. cit., p. 95.

19. Denis Smith, "President and Parliament: The Transformation of Parliamentary Government in Canada," in T. A. Hockin, ed., *Apex of Power* (Scarborough, Ont.: Prentice-Hall, 1971).

20. An indication of the imbalance can be seen be comparing the smallest constituency (outside the Yukon) with the largest in the 1974 election. The number of eligible electors in Malpeque (Prince Edward Island) was 13,609. The number in York-Scarborough (Ontario) was 122, 578.

21. During the breaks within a session, Parliament is said to be in recess; between sessions, it is "prorogued"; and between Parliaments, "dissolved."

22. When a new Parliament is beginning, the first act of the new Commons will be the selection of a speaker. Only when a speaker has been chosen will the Speech from the Throne be delivered. See Dawson, op. cit., pp. 344–348.

23. The Senate also has a *pro forma* bill of this kind. For the details of this tradition and the exceptions to its application, see Dawson, op. cit., p. 348.

24. The term "backbencher" refers to a private member of the Commons who does not sit on the front bench of the government party (occupied by the Cabinet) or that of the Official Opposition (occupied by the men and women who would form a Cabinet if the main opposition party came to power—the so-called shadow cabinet).

25. Of course, questions may be asked genuinely for information-gathering purposes. Indeed, questions may even be asked by government supporters who presumably have a stake in not embarrassing their ministers!

26. A similar opportunity occurs when a member moves the adjournment of the House to debate a matter of urgent importance. There are restrictions on the effectiveness of this technique that cause it to be used only rarely. See Dawson, op. cit., pp. 371–372.

27. Minority government has led to some ingenuity in the interpretation of this constitutional tradition. On occasion in recent years, when a government has been defeated in a vote on some portion of a bill, the government has asked for, and received, a vote of confidence from the House. The defeated legislation is still lost, but there is then no need for the government to resign.

28. There have been occasional suggestions that British practice be emulated and a permanent Speaker be chosen, who would run for election unopposed. To date, efforts to secure all-party agreement to such a scheme have failed.

29. The organization of the House timetable is facilitated by informal, but generally binding, agreements among party House leaders. Like most legislative bodies, the Commons has numerous rules limiting debate, including closure. The less drastic forms of debate limitation require the agreement of party representitives—i.e., the House leaders.

30. This was quite a substantial property qualification in 1867 when it was introduced; however, succeeding Parliaments have not seen fit to alter it in keeping with rising costs.

31. See Mallory, op. cit., pp. 238–241.

32. Mallory, op. cit., p. 115.

33. There is a sort of provincial criminal law as well, in which penalties are assessed to make effective legislation whose "pith and substance" falls within provincial jurisdiction (e.g., fines imposed for driving offenses under acts intended to regulate highway traffic in a province).

34. Effectively these are suits against the federal government or one of its agencies. Because of the ancient presumption that the Crown can do no wrong, it used to be necessary to seek permission of the Crown to bring suit against it! Since the simplification in 1970 of procedures for suing the Crown, the Crown has had the same position before the Federal Court as an ordinary litigant.

35. The appointment of the Chief Justice of each province is a prerogative of the Prime Minister; other justices are normally appointed on the recommendation of the Minister of Justice.

36. For a more detailed treatment of the structure of Quebec's court system, see Mallory, op. cit., pp. 297–298.

37. It has become the custom to submit the short list of candidates for a new judicial appointment to the Canadian Bar Association and ask that the candidates be divided into three categories: well qualified, qualified, and not qualified. The appointment is then made from among candidates in the first two categories.

38. Bora Laskin, "Note on Civil Liberties and Legislative Power," *Canadian Constitutional Law*, 3d ed. (Toronto: Carswell, 1966), pp. 970 ff., quoted in W. S. Tarnopolsky, *The Canadian Bill of Rights*, 2d ed., rev. (Toronto: McClelland and Stewart, 1975), p. 3.

39. No court *majority* has ever used these grounds to decide a case in Canada, but a number of individual judges have cited the grounds among those on which they have decided, or cited the doctrine in an *obiter dicta*. See Peter H. Russell, *Leading Constitutional Decisions*, rev. ed. (Toronto: McClelland and Stewart, 1973), chap. V.

40. The concept of a "fair hearing" is thought to include such things as notice of intention to make a decision, sufficient information to permit an adequate reply, an opportunity to answer allegations, a right of cross-examination, reasonable time to prepare a case, and the assumption that the composition of the deciding tribunal will be the same as that of the tribunal that heard the evidence and arguments.

41. For an extensive treatment of the Bill of Rights and the issues of civil liberties in general in Canada, see Tarnopolsky, op. cit.

42. For a fuller treatment of this development, see G. Hougham, "The Background and Development of National Parties," and E. M. Reid, "The Rise of National Parties in Canada," in H. G. Thorburn, ed., *Party Politics in Canada*, 3d ed. (Scarborough, Ont.: Prentice-Hall, 1972), pp. 2–22.

43. Fifty candidates has been established as one of the criteria for recognizing a political party eligible to be registered under federal legislation and therefore entitled to free-time broadcast privileges.

44. For simplicity's sake, the 1963 split in the Social Credit Party has been ignored. The Quebec wing of the party became a separate entity, known as Ralliement des Créditistes. The rift was healed in 1971, at which time Quebec had the only Social Credit representation in the Commons.

45. For the distinction between "cadre" and "mass" parties, see Maurice Duverger, *Political Parties*, trans. Barbara and Robert North, 3d ed. (New York: Wiley and Sons, 1963), pp. 63–71.

46. Both major parties now have procedures for calling leadership conventions, although it has been customary to await the death, retirement, or resignation of a sitting leader before calling a convention to select his successor. Votes for the leadership in all the four principal parties are by secret ballot; the lowest candidate on each successive ballot is normally dropped before the next vote is taken. The first Liberal leadership convention was in 1919; that of the Conservatives, in 1927. Prior to that time, and on two subsequent occasions in the Conservative Party, the parlimentary caucus chose the leader.

47. Recognized parties are those registered under the legislation. Parties are eligible to register if they have fifty candidates in the election, or if they have twelve representatives in Parliament. See Canada Elections Act, *Revised Statutes of Canada*, 1st Supplement, C. 14 (1970). See also *Statutes of Canada*, 21–22 Eliz. II, 1973–74, C. 51.

48. Half of the legislators are elected as councillors and half as assemblymen, reflecting the fact that Prince Edward Island once had a bicameral legislature. There is effectively no difference in the legislative position of the members, however, one councillor and one assemblyman being elected in each district.

49. See Alan C. Cairns, "The Electoral System and the Party System in Canada, 1921–1965," *Canadian Journal of Political Science*, vol. I (March 1968), pp. 55–80. For a response, see J. A. A. Lovink, "On Analysing the Impact of the Electoral System on the Party System in Canada," *Canadian Journal of Political Science*, vol. III (December 1970), pp. 497–516, and reply from Cairns, pp. 517–521.

50. British Columbia experimented briefly in the early 1950s with a preferential voting system. It was introduced by the Liberal-Conservative coalition government, with the intention of ensuring the government's reelection. It failed to do so.

51. There are certain administrative restrictions as well, such as those barring prisoners and district returning officers from voting.

52. Voters in federal elections, and in some provinces, may use a checkmark or other indication to mark their ballot in place of an *X*; however, no mark may be made on the ballot that would identify the voter. In many provinces, the party affiliation of the candidates are not included on the ballot.

53. For a comprehensive review of the literature on Canadian voting behavior see Mildred A. Schwartz, "Canadian Voting Behavior," in Richard Rose, ed., *Electoral Behavior: A Comparative Handbook* (New York: Free Press, 1974), pp. 543–618.

54. Robert V. Presthus, *Elite Accommodation in Canadian Politics* (Toronto: Macmillan, 1973), p. 142.

55. Robert V. Presthus, "Interest Groups and the Canadian Parliament: Activities, Interaction, Legitimacy, and Influence," *Canadian Journal of Political Science*, vol. IV (December 1971), p. 455.

56. Presthus, *Elite Accommodation*, p. 207.

57. *Ibid.*, p. 154.

58. For examples of such a campaign, see Ron Haggart, "The Strange Case of the All-Alike Letters" and "The Brilliant Campaign to Make Public Opinion," in Paul Fox, ed., *Politics: Canada*, 3d ed. (Toronto: McGraw-Hill, 1970), pp. 175–180. The articles originally appeared in the *Toronto Daily Star*, February 28 and March 1, 1962, respectively.

59. Information on government surveys can be obtained from a periodical published by Statistics Canada called *New Surveys* (Cat. No. 11-006), which appears quarterly.

60. A discussion of some of the weaknesses of public opinion polls can be found in Hugh Whalen, "The Perils of Polling," in Fox, op. cit., pp. 223–227.

61. F. J. Fletcher, "The Mass Media in the 1974 Canadian Election," in Howard R. Penniman, ed., *Canada at the Polls* (Washington: American Enterprise Institute for Public Policy Research, 1975), p. 245. Much of what follows is based on Professor Fletcher's account.

62. Anthony Westell of the *Toronto Daily Star*, quoted in Fletcher, op. cit., p. 285.

63. For discussions of some sources of bias and examples of selectivity, see Fletcher, op. cit., and Conrad Winn and John McMenemy, *Political Parties in Canada* (Toronto: McGraw-Hill Ryerson, 1976), pp. 129–150.

64. The areas of concurrent jurisdiction are old-age pensions and supplementary benefits, agriculture, and immigration. Provincial authority is paramount in the first area; federal authority, in the second and third. Education is made partially concurrent by the provision of federal authority to pass remedial legislation to block provincial abrogation of denominational education rights previously established. See D. V. Smiley, *Canada in Question*, 2d ed. (Toronto: McGraw-Hill Ryerson, 1976), p. 6, and R. M. Dawson, *The Government of Canada*, rev. N. Ward (Toronto: University of Totonto Press, 1970), pp. 84–85.

65. The customary method of requesting an amendment has become the passage of a joint address by the Canadian House of Commons and the Senate. No formal requirement exists that any other party be consulted, and indeed it would not be *legally* impossible for the request to come from a Canadian Cabinet acting on its own. Obviously, agreement on an amending formula is essential to any plan for repatriating the Canadian constitution, and several possibilities have been suggested. The two most well known were the Fulton-Favreau proposal, which emanated from a round of intergovernmental negotiations in 1964, and the Victoria Charter formula developed in 1971 after a series of constitutional conferences. Both formulas appeared to have achieved agreement from all eleven governments at first, but eventually both ran into difficulty (mainly from the government of Quebec). For discussions of these formulas, see Smiley, op. cit., chaps. 1 and 2, esp. pp. 9–11 and 40–49. 1981 has seen yet another formula as part of Prime Minister Trudeau's patriation plan.

66. For a discussion of the procedures and practices regarding formal amendment, including consultation of the provinces, see Dawson, op. cit., pp. 123–128.

67. The legislation, introduced by the Conservative government of R. B. Bennett, was intended to stimulate the economy by means of central government intervention. Because of its similarity to the New Deal introduced by the Roosevelt administration in the United States, the same term has been applied to the legislative program suggested for Canada.

68. Since the courts have distinguished between the right to make a law and the right to make a gift, the federal government has had the opportunity to influence provincial legislative priorities by offering conditional grants—i.e., money that may be used by the provinces for specified purposes only. This legal power of the central government to make payments to people, institutions, or governments for purposes over which it has no constitutional lawmaking authority is what is meant by the spending power.

69. These "responsibilities" arose because of demands that the central government undertake responsibility for stability of the national economy and the promotion of economic growth, as well as demands that social services be expanded, preferably with some uniformity across the country. At the same time, many of the necessary legislative powers to accomplish these ends were in the hands of the provinces.

70. For a discussion of this period and the development of federal-provincial financial relations, see Smiley, op. cit., pp. 117–123.

71. Dawson, op. cit., p. 103.

72. It is sometimes difficult to distinguish direct from indirect taxes, but broadly speaking, a direct tax is one that is clearly levied on the person or corporation on whom the incidence of the tax falls. For example, the provinces may levy sales taxes on consumers when they make a purchase, but they may not levy sales taxes at the wholesale or manufacturer level. If the eventual payer of the tax will be the consumer, then the tax must be levied at that level.

73. Richard Simeon, *Federal-Provincial Diplomacy* (Toronto: University of Toronto Press, 1972). Professor Simeon's account of federal-provincial relations centers on three issue areas: development of the Canada and Quebec pension plans, working out of federal-provincial financial arrangements in 1966, and the debates concerning the constitution between 1967 and 1971.

74. These figures, and others in this paragraph, are taken from *Canada Year Book 1972* (Ottawa: Queen's Printer). The unemployment figures are from the 1974 edition of the same annual.

75. Five of the provinces had second chambers after entering Confederation.

Manitoba abolished its upper house in 1876, New Brunswick in 1892, Prince Edward Island in 1893, Nova Scotia in 1928, and Quebec in 1969.

76. The Economic Council of Canada and Leroy O. Stone, "From the 1960's to the 1970's: Urban Growth," in L. D. Feldman and M. D. Goldrick, eds., *Politics and Government of Urban Canada*, 2d ed. (Toronto: Methuen, 1972), pp. 13–14.

77. James Lorimer, *A Citizen's Guide to City Politics* (Toronto: James Lewis and Samuel, 1972).

Chapter 4

An Economics Perspective:

Canada in the International

Economy

PETER KARL KRESL*

Introduction

For this brief introduction I have three objectives in mind. First, I would like to specify for the noneconomist reader those aspects of a multifaceted, complexly interrelated reality which the economist picks out for his special focus: What is it that makes an economist distinctive as a social scientist? Second, we shall give some consideration to the development of the study of economics in Canada, especially as this relates to, or is reflective of, the development of Canada as a society. Third, I mean to ask whether there is anything about the Canadian economy per se that is of interest to a non-Canadian economist.

* Peter Karl Kresl is Associate Professor of Economics at Bucknell University. American by birth and education (his Ph.D. is from the University of Texas), he studies Canada purely from interest, and finds doing research on Scandinavian economic problems a valuable complement. The author of a monograph on *Norway's Foreign Capital Policy,* he has published articles in several journals, including the *American Review of Canadian Studies,* the *Journal of Interamerican Studies,* the *Journal of Radical Political Economics,* the *Review of Industrial Management,* and *Comparative Social Research.* He has served on the Executive Council of the Association for Canadian Studies in the United States (ACSUS).

WHAT IS ECONOMICS?

The standard response to this question is as follows. Economics concerns itself with the study of the production of goods, the allocation of resources and the distribution of income; that is, with *what* is produced, *how* it is produced, and *for whom* it is produced. Economists begin with the notion that all societies have differing amounts of the various resources at their disposal: each society organizes itself in such a way that those resources are allocated in production so as to give both the combination of goods and the distribution of those goods which that society will find most desirable. In evaluating the performance of an economic system, economists place primary emphasis on two criteria, efficiency and equity. The definition of the first criterion is rather straightforward: efficiency concerns itself with getting the maximum output from a given set of resources. Attaining efficiency in production requires that attention be given to the organization of production and social institutions, and to an incentive system (the incentives may be material or nonmaterial) that will make the people in that society want to participate in production. Equity, however, is a much more ambiguous concept, since it involves considerations of "fairness." Some people believe the fairest or most equitable system distributes the production of society in accordance with each individual's productivity or contribution to production; others argue goods should be given to each member of society in equal amounts; still others feel each individual should be paid according to the intensity of his or her need. Economists are no more united on this than is any other group in society, but most would agree that there is a basic incompatibility between achieving either efficiency or equity in many, but not all, situations in which we find ourselves. Making the economy more efficient may create inequities, or vice versa.

Although there is some fundamental divergence of views on the definition of equity and, therefore, on the nature of the relationship between equity and efficiency, economists do generally agree upon this latter as the central focus of their study. However, economists are very sharply divided into two main groups on the issue of the breadth of that central focus. One's group is determined by one's answers to two broad questions: (1) What methodology is appropriate for the economist (and what data or evidence can be used in economic analysis)? (2) What questions is it legitimate for an economist to ask? Those who believe in something they call "economics" answer these questions differently from those who practice "political economy."

Those economists who practice "economics" argue that we should concern ourselves only with marginal or incremental changes. Since we exist in an economy that is essentially a market economy, economists should confine their study to questions of production, allocation, and distribution in an interrelated network of markets. These questions are in practice resolved by individuals and firms responding to changes in relative prices (the price of one good in relation to all other prices); thus, it is argued, economists should limit themselves to studying the underlying conditions of supply and demand that generate prices and price changes. Market transactions are expressed in terms of prices for different quantities of various goods and services, so many economists argue we must be content with studying questions for which we can obtain these kinds of objective data. This of course has methodological implications. If economists consider only questions that can be analyzed using price and quantity data, then they must be well versed in the use of mathematics, statistics, and computers.

Economists who, on the other hand, practice "political economy" do not accept these limitations on either the questions considered legitimate to ask or the methodology deemed appropriate. They begin by arguing that the data to which "economics" limits itself in many cases only loosely conform to the reality they purport to capture. This can be due simply to problems of definition and data collection, but more tellingly it may be because imperfections in the market, such as ignorance, monopoly power, or collusion between buyer and seller, may be causing observed prices and quantities to diverge from what they ought to be, given economic conditions.

Moreover, political economists view the policy options of today as being to a significant degree determined by the events of the past and by the interaction of existing social institutions. Thus, economists of the "political economy" camp see the decisions of production, allocation, and distribution as being the result of a multifaceted decision-making process that can only be studied meaningfully if sufficient attention is given to history, politics, sociology and culture, as well as to responses of consumers and producers to changes in relative prices. As a final point, political economy explicitly sees the economy as being in a state of evolution and asks, not questions that are incremental, but rather those which focus on the longer-run nature of that evolution, and even that question which is taboo for economics: What kind of an economic society should we be creating?

ECONOMICS IN CANADA

In order to work as an economist, whether in teaching, government, or business, one must earn an advanced, graduate university degree. Because of the size of Canadian society and the nature of its relationship to the United Kingdom and the United States, there was little graduate education in the social sciences in Canadian universities until the 1950s.[1] The typical experience was for an aspiring Canadian economist to follow an undergraduate education in Canada with three or four years of graduate study at a major American or British university. This meant that Canadian economists were familiar with the foremost practitioners of a discipline that has been dominated by Americans and Britons. It also meant that along with the latest techniques and theories, Canadian economists also absorbed the politics and ideology that were then current in these two citadels of liberal thought.

Prior to the late 1940s, with few exceptions, the vast majority of all economists took the political economy approach to their work. But with the development of Keynesian analysis came the understanding that government could and, perhaps, ought to intervene in the functioning of the economy in the pursuit of full employment and economic growth. Such intervention, however, required (or implied) greater certainty about actual economic conditions, and economists were urged to become more data oriented and quasi scientific in their analysis. The result was a rapid move of the profession, during the 1950s and 1960s, from political economy to economics. This transition was delayed among Canadian economists—not simply because, as has been said, "everything happens in Canada six months later," but because of the strength of the traditional political economy approach in Canada and the apparent appropriateness of that mode of analysis to the study of the Canadian economy.

One could argue, indeed, that "economics" is particularly appropriate to American economists. They function in the largest single industrial economy and in a society that expresses so much attachment to free enterprise liberalism. In this country, with a vast number of producers and consumers, a uniquely large percentage of economic decisions are made on the basis of responses to relatively freely fluctuating prices. But smaller countries, such as Canada, usually have little power in international markets and, rather than finding themselves continually making major adjustments in reaction to seemingly random events in the international economy, they adopt institutions or mechanisms that act to control price changes. Hence, in smaller societies the state usually has a greater role to play, as does collective action by producers and consumers. In Canada this phenomenon has produced, among other things, state support for transportation (canal and railroad construction), communication (the Canadian Broadcasting Corporation), and industrial activity (the Canadian Development Corporation), cooperative ventures (marketing boards for commodities such as wheat and fish), and provincial governmental activities of central economic significance (hydroelectric corporations). Historically, then, when Canadian economists studied a question of economic performance or policy it made a great deal of sense for them to ground their analysis in an understanding of the evolution of the Canadian economy and to take into account the functioning of the relevant social institutions. In the next section of this chapter, on Canadian economic development, we shall discuss the "staples" theory or approach. This is the work of the dominant Canadian economist to date, Harold Innis, and it is solidly in the tradition of political economy.

During the 1950s and 1960s, Canadian economists increasingly went to the United States rather than to the United Kingdom for their graduate education, and for the most part they came back more fascinated with American economics than with political economy. As graduate education expanded in Canada, this American influence was solidified through informal, "old-boy" hiring practices and the clear inability of the growing Canadian departments to satisfy their own staffing requirements. As departments of economics in Canada became Americanized, political economy gave way to economics, and institutions such as the Economic Council of Canada concerned themselves with more highly technical studies of narrowly perceived questions of economic policy.

The political economy tradition did not fade for long, however, as many economists chafed at the limitations placed on them by the narrow focus and methodology of economics. It was felt that the political economy approach was needed if economists were to grapple with pressing problems of regional economic expansion, foreign domination, and industrial development. Today both approaches thrive in Canada, in a healthy and lively division of labor. If economics tends to be supportive of the existing economic system and to concern itself with making marginal adjustments to a continually changing economic reality, political economy is always willing to look to larger issues such as structural change and significantly different ways of making decisions about production, allocation, and distribution.

WHY IS CANADA OF INTEREST TO A NON-CANADIAN ECONOMIST?

The discussion thus far has touched upon two aspects of the answer to this perennial question. The first is the staples theory of, or approach to, economic development. This product of Canadian economists can be seen either as a description of what took place in Canada during the past three centuries or, when generalized as a theory of export-led economic growth, as a prescription for countries of the Third World that have yet to achieve sustained growth of incomes and production. The second is that, lacking the laboratory experimentation methodology of natural and physical scientists, economists learn much through comparative studies, and Canada provides an alternative to the U.S. model of society—the current U.S. fascination with the provision of medical services in Canada is a good example of this.

As a third item, we should note that no two industrial societies are as closely related economically as are Canada and the United States. This means that for many interesting economic questions—such as the effects of international movements of goods, capital, or people; the transmission across national borders of inflation or unemployment; and problems of policy coordination between countries—the effects on Canada are more significant and easily measured than they are elsewhere. Furthermore, the unique relationship of Canada to the United States facilitates comparative study of the subtly different development of social and cultural institutions that have played a part in the economic policy-making processes of both countries.

There are a number of ways one could provide an overview of the Canadian economy. The approach taken here will be that of combining descriptive material about the development and structure of economic activity with a focus on some key problem areas. The first substantive section highlights some aspects of Canada's economic history—aspects that give a character to today's economic activity. The next two sections cover the struggle for autonomy by a society that is continually prone to being dominated by a larger neighbor, and the strong regional character of Canada. They lead directly into a discussion of the role of the state in the economy, followed by sections that describe the structure of economic activity and relate this to the international economy that so powerfully affects Canadians. In the final section we briefly discuss some of the most pressing problems of economic policy for Canada in the near future.

The Development of Canada's Economy

The primary orientation of economic activity in Canada has always been the exploitation of raw materials for export to some other specific, originally European economy. There are a number of significant implications of this. It has meant certain opportunities for Canadians in their work, but it has also placed limitations on what they have been able to do. The availability of both natural resources and a profitable export market for them has attracted capital, labor, and imagination (which might otherwise have been employed in manufacturing) to the exploitation of raw materials. The external market for Canada's resources was generally determined by economic and political events occurring in Europe or the United States, over which Canada had no control. Hence, it was frequently necessary for the Canadian economy to make major internal adjustments as demand in this market fluctuated. Out of this experience of more than three centuries of economic history, Canadian economists have developed their own approach to economic growth and development. It is called the staples theory because its central focus is on the extraction of staple commodities (also referred to as raw materials, or primary goods) for export, and the implications this has for the sort of economy and society that can be created in conformity with this production.[2]

There have been four great Canadian staples that have, in turn, provided the basis for economic activity. The first resource Europeans found attractive was fish taken from the rich waters off the coast of Newfoundland and Nova Scotia. As they penetrated the interior, however, they discovered North America was amply endowed with fur-bearing animals, in particular the beaver, and the fur trade was dominant through the eighteenth century. The Napoleonic blockade of the Baltic opened the British market to Canadian timber in the first half of the nineteenth century. The final great staple was grain, with the wheat boom lasting from the 1890s through the 1920s. Each of these staples placed different demands on capital, labor, and land and required that different institutions be set up to facilitate that production: it is this that provides the material for staples theory and analysis.

The staples theory has been referred to as a theory of investment demand because of the highly individualized impact each specific staple has on the structure of production. Investment occurs when a society allocates a portion of its total production, not to consumption, but to the creation of the capability to produce other goods. This investment demand can be broken down into three distinct "linkages" of backward, forward, and final demand. The backward linkage refers to investment in the production of goods that are used in the industry; for example, in steel production backward linkages might refer to development of coal and iron mines and of transportation needed to get the raw materials to the mills. Industries that then use the steel produced—for example, to make automobiles or machinery—provide the forward linkage. Investment in production of the whole range of consumer goods purchased by the workers in the industry constitutes the final demand linkage. The richness of this approach to economic history, and the nature of these linkages, will become clear if we examine each of the four staples and its significance in the development of Canada's economy and society.

There is no contesting the fact that fishing has been a mainstay of the economy of the Atlantic Provinces, but it is equally true that this industry does not provide a good base for economic development, because the linkages between fishing and the rest of the economy are minimal. Until the development of modern freezing techniques, fish was either salted down right on the ship (the green cure) or taken to facilities on shore where it was dried in the sun on drying racks (the dry cure). The French had an abundance of salt, whereas the English had little; thus, the French had no need to establish bases or settlements on land, and the impact of their fishing activity on Canada was next to nil. However, because of technology of production in the English fishing industry (the use of the dry cure), England was forced to make contact with the land. Even for the English, however, the linkages were very weak. There was some boatbuilding and small-scale settlement (backward linkage), very little activity involved in processing (forward linkage), and because settlements were small and not concentrated in one area, there was little final demand linkage. Fishing tended to be very much an enclave activity, with its focus entirely on the sea rather than on the vast continent that lay to the west.

The fur trade provided a sharp contrast with fishing in at least two ways. From the standpoint of industrial organization, fishing was dominated by small-scale firms—usually one-man owned, and operating only one boat. However, again owing to the nature of the product, the fur trade was best carried out if one firm could have a monopolist's control over all aspects of production and marketing. Fur was a luxury good, and therefore small shifts in fashion (demand) would have a sharp impact on price and total revenue, unless the quantity of fur brought to market could be manipulated to counter such shifts. Given these uncertainties in demand, there was a great incentive to take the surprises out of as much of the rest of the activity as was possible. Only a monopoly, such as the Hudson's Bay Company, could do away with price competition in the purchasing, in England, of the manufactured trading goods and in their rate of exchange when traded to the Indians for fur. This generally successful experience with a large monopoly organization provided Canadians with a precedent for an alternative to the competitive industry (composed of many small firms) that is so much a part of the social philosophy of Americans.

It is also of significance that the fur trade was not an enclave activity, as was fishing, but rather expanded its vision and organization to encompass the entire breadth of the continent. The competition that did exist between Montreal and Hudson Bay as trading centers was resolved when it became clear that the Hudson's Bay Company was better able to organize trading and transportation over an area hundreds of thousands of square miles in size. The entire Canadian West was seen as the proper sphere of the Company's operation, and after its transportation lines extended to the Rockies and beyond it was possible to think of a Canada stretching "from sea to sea." For all this, the actual demand linkages of the fur trade were rather weak. Manufactured goods continued to be imported from Europe, and little investment was called for in Canada (with the exception of trading posts). While the fur trade was large scale in organization and in vision, there was nothing in it that would cause Canada to develop anything other than a fur-trading economy.

This was not the case with the third staple, timber; and the crucial factor here was transportation. Ships that carried fur from Canada could return fully laden with goods to be traded to the Indians who supplied the furs, but timber shipments resulted in an "unbalanced cargo"—bulky timber leaving Canada, much smaller cargoes returning. Shippers were anxious to take any cargo they could on the return voyage to Canada, and it soon developed that the most suitable cargo was settlers. With the exception of the American Revolutionary War, this was the first positive stimulus to large-scale migration of Europeans to Canada. Whereas the fur trade had discouraged settlement since agriculture took land from fur-bearing animals, the production of timber was complementary to settled agriculture, since cutting timber resulted in cleared land. And while most of the settlers did engage in agriculture, they brought the full range of skills and interests and ambitions found in any group of immigrants, and this helped to "flesh out" Canadian society and its economy.

The increase in population which was an indirect result of timber production meant that the final demand linkage was far stronger here than with either fishing or the fur trade. But the other linkages were stronger as well. Sawmills had to be constructed, and there was a demand for a variety of metal tools, such as saw blades and axes. Since timber was low in value and bulky in volume, it was profitable to process it into goods, such as furniture and boats, in Canada. Additionally, the timber industry and the production it stimulated generated new demands for commercial and financial services and institutions. In brief, timber was in many respects a very desirable staple for a new society, and much of the very significant transformation and growth of Canada during the first half of the nineteenth century was attributable to the development of this industry.

Agriculture was an increasingly important industry throughout the nineteenth century as settlers migrated to Canada and forest gave way to farmland, especially in southern Ontario. Toward the end of the century newly developed strains of wheat allowed the opening of the northern prairies to agriculture and this then became the "engine" of Canada's expansion until the Great Depression of the 1930s. Filling prairies with settlers meant, of course, that there was a significant final demand linkage. Western Canada's economy of single-family farms presented a large and broadly based market for the whole range of household and personal consumption goods. Each farm needed productive implements, such as plows, wagons, harvesting equipment, and small tools. Moreover, there was a great need for rails and rolling stock for the railroad network that would take the grain to eastern and foreign markets—in short, a tremendous demand for iron and steel and machine tools. The challenge to the rest of the economy was one of producing domestically the goods to meet these final demand and backward linkages. The success of firms like Eaton's (mass retailing) and Massey-Harris (farm equipment), and of the steel industry in Hamilton, Ontario, attest to the impact of the "wheat boom" early this century.

Wheat's forward linkage was limited to flour mills and forwarding companies, but wheat production had one other important impact on Canada. Each successful farmer saw himself as a productive businessman whose contribution to society was an important one. Western farmers have been very forthright about demanding their share of government services and their right to share in the process of governance. They have demanded, from whichever government (federal or provincial) was ready to listen to them, government support for transportation, communication, and education, and they have pressed strongly for the democratization of government.

In the introduction to this chapter it was stated that the staples theory was a product of the tradition of political economy. The preceding discussion of the four staples of Canada's economic development should have made that clear to the reader. While allowing for ample concern with more narrowly focused economics—the demand, supply, and price for various goods and resources—staples theory analysis additionally relates developments in the economy, narrowly perceived, to the development of social, political, and cultural institutions and perceptions. The fur trade left Canadians with an increased acceptance of monopoly industrial organization under certain conditions and what can be called a continental vision; timber led to immigration and pressures for financial and commercial institutions; and single-family farm agriculture generated pressures for a particular set of government services and a broadly participatory political process. The staples theory also transcends the self-proclaimed task of economics, that of simply describing "what is," and permits normative judgments about "what ought to be or not be." This is seen most clearly in two concepts that are part of the staples literature: the "staples trap" and the "export mentality."

Standard economic theory argues that both efficiency and equity will be best served if each country determines its comparative advantage and fits its economy into the resulting international division of labor.[3] By comparative advantage we mean that, owing to the availability of resources and skills, each economy is best suited to produce certain goods and should obtain all other goods through exchange—some countries will then grow coffee and others will produce computers. In the process total world incomes will be maximized, and one need only be sure that monopoly power does not cause an "inequitable" share of that total income to be appropriated by individual nations or producers. The staples theory does not argue with this as a theory; but it does find that in the context of Canadian economic development the actual results fall far short of the goal. The term "staples trap" refers to an inflexibility or a rigidity that is a feature of a staples-producing economy. Even if it could be objectively determined that Canada's comparative advantage had shifted from staples production to manufacturing, such a transformation in the Canadian economy would not in fact take place. In the years when revenues are good there is no incentive to make the change, and if the economy is in a slump there are no revenues to finance it. Rather than take the risk and make the effort to transfer resources from one industry to another, the country takes the safe, easy route. Production of the staple is a known thing; there is a considerable investment of time, resources, and imagination in the staple; and economic activity is therefore "trapped" in a pattern that has worked in the past, is comfortable, and, it is hoped, will continue to work again soon.

A concomitant to the staples trap is the preoccupation of a staples economy with producing raw materials for the export market. As a society develops with this as its predominant focus, financial and commercial institutions become geared to meeting the needs of a staple-exploiting, staple-exporting economy (during the nineteenth century in particular merchants could generally get short-term financing to support their exports of staples, but there was little long-term "venture capital" available for new manufacturing projects). Individuals become blinded to opportunities for another type of economy that periodically present themselves—this is the "export mentality."

As evidence that the staples trap and the export mentality have been of significance in Canada we can refer to three separate but interrelated phenomena. The first, and most noticeable, is the high degree of foreign ownership of the Canadian manufacturing sector. We shall discuss this at length later in this chapter, but cite here the fact that foreign ownership exceeds 50 percent as an indication of the extent to which Canadians confined themselves to exploiting and exporting raw materials and left other activities to be developed by outsiders. Second, Canadians have been described as a nation of "satisficers." By this it is meant that economic decision makers tend to be content with a pace of economic activity and a degree of efficiency that is not the maximum possible but is rather one that is "adequate," or that suffices. It suggests that Canadians have been willing to leave the innovation and extra effort to others and, more or less, to be pulled along. Hand in hand with this is the third phenomenon, the frequently observed lack of aggressiveness and competence on the part of much of Canadian industrial leadership.[4]

Some ascribe this to insufficient graduate training in business management; however, others see it, and the "satisficers" characterization, as symptomatic of something deeper—a historical proclivity to accept, and to accommodate one's activities to, decisions made in a foreign "center" to which Canada was a reactive and subordinate "periphery." It is generally argued that these three phenomena are complementary to, and/or reflective of, Canada's traditional reliance on raw materials exports.

Until the 1840s, whether the staple of primary importance was fish, fur, or timber, Canada was tightly integrated into the international economy. This was not, however, the essentially market economy that exists today but rather Britain's mercantilist system. The division of labor under mercantilism was not one that evolved in accordance with principles of comparative advantage. Britain simply allocated roles to each part of the system, and peripheral areas (i.e., the far-flung colonies) were developed primarily for their supplies of raw materials and foodstuffs. This allocation of production was buttressed by parliamentary measures such as the Navigation Acts and the Corn Laws. Moreover, military and, more broadly, strategic considerations were of major, at times overriding concern. Thus, privileged access to the central market for the staple exports of the peripheral area was not something that could be taken for granted. Staples exporters were continually obliged to curry favor in Britain and to accept conditions that were not to their advantage if their livelihood and place in the system were to be assured. The early struggle to establish a resident fishery in Newfoundland in opposition to Britain's West Country fishing interests and their supporters in Parliament is an example of this; another occurred during the 1840s when free trade policies supplanted those of traditional British mercantilism.

Until the 1850s Canada produced goods, not for the world market, but for Britain. Even after 1848, when it was no longer mandated by statute that peripheral areas such as Canada feed raw material to Britain's manufacturing industry, the relatively underdeveloped nature of Canada's economy encouraged the maintenance of this division of labor. The advantages to Britain of a new, freer international economy were that the cost of mercantilist tariffs and preferential bounties was avoided, and Britain could now choose to obtain primary goods from the lowest-cost supplier, whomever that might be. To Canada this meant that what to that time had been the only market for its exports could be totally closed owing to some event in, say, Australia, the United States, or Argentina that the Canadians had no power to influence. In short, it resulted in a very precarious and uncertain economic condition.

Feeling abandoned by Britain, on whom they had come so much to rely, Canadians turned their attention to the other large market available to them—the United States. This was partly out of necessity and partly as a natural consequence of historical dependence upon the external market, of which the export mentality and staples trap are symptoms. In 1849, in the Annexation Manifesto, prominent Montreal merchants argued for integration with the United States. Then in 1854 Canada and the United States signed a Reciprocity Treaty in which free trade for some agricultural goods, freer access to coastal fishing waters, and an opening of water transportation along the border were agreed upon. American grain could now be taken to Chicago, transported through the Great Lakes and U.S. and Canadian canals to Kingston, through Montreal to Portland, Maine, where it might be shipped to Halifax, Nova Scotia, for use there or export to Britain. From an economic standpoint the border was becoming blurred. At the conclusion of the American Civil War, however, the United States abrogated reciprocity, leaving Canadians very divided (as they remain divided to this day) on the pros and cons of freer trade with the United States.[5]

In a matter of two decades Canada had gone from being a dependency of Britain, with its economy almost totally locked into the needs of British mercantilism, to being an economy in the process of being integrated with that of the United States. Having been forced to adjust to a different set of economic needs and opportunities, Canada then found itself twice rebuffed and very unsure about its economic future. Readers of Chapter 2, on Canadian history, will recall that economic uncertainty contributed to the move toward Confederation (achieved in 1867); and they will know that a decade later the government of John A. Macdonald embarked on a set of policies, the so-called National Policy, with the aim of creating a transcontinental economy. This will be discussed in the section that follows, but for now let us simply characterize this period as one of nation building and of attempts to make Canada less vulnerable to the sort of uncertainty and radical restructuring of the economic environment that had been a feature of the first two thirds of the nineteenth century.

The two themes on which we have focused our attention in this short examination of the development of Canada's economy do not cease to be important after 1879 and the implementation of the National Policy. To this day, Canada continues to be heavily reliant upon the exploitation of staples for export to an external market, and as long as this is the case Canada will be in a subordinate and dependent position vis-à-vis that external market. What is of particular significance about Canada's historical position is that it has not been integrated into the world economy, as might have been encouraged by liberal, free trade economics; on the contrary, Canada has been a supplier of primary goods to one specific economy, first the United Kingdom and then the United States. This is never a situation in which a country has significant bargaining power or control over its actions.

The Struggle for Autonomy

The last third of the nineteenth century has been charcterized by one writer as a period of "nationalism in search of a nation."[6] In other words, many Canadians had a sense that they were somehow distinctive from other societies and that their distinctiveness was something in which they could take pride, but that the nation that conformed to that society was lacking in political and economic substance. In this section we are going to examine the strategy followed by the federal government to create a transnational economy and to make that

economy less a colonial appendage of another more industrialized nation.

John A. Macdonald, considered to have been the chief
father of Confederation, served as Prime Minister for most of
Canada's first three decades after 1867.[7] After a six-year period of getting government in Canada established, the Conservatives were caught being overzealous in soliciting financial support and were thrown out in disgrace in 1873. The
Liberal Mackenzie government faced a period of economic
recession but was too committed philosophically to noninter-
ventionist, free trade policies to do much about it. The Conservatives were voted in again in 1878 and promptly introduced a multifaceted development program that has come to
be known as the National Policy. It consisted of three mutually supportive policies: construction of a transcontinental
railway, increased immigration, and a protective tariff on
manufactured goods. The railway, it was hoped, would carry
the new immigrants to the Canadian West; their production
of grain would provide freight for the rail system; and the
tariff would protect the "infant industries" in Canada from
"mature" foreign competition and allow the Canadian manufacturing sector to feed upon the linkages created by railway
construction and the expansion of the Prairies agriculture.

Before we make any evaluation of the National Policy we
ought to distinguish between two terms economists frequently
use: "economic growth" and "development." Economic growth
is a purely quantitative phenomenon. If we say an economy
has experienced significant growth, we mean that the output
of goods and services is larger at the end of the time period
being considered than it was at the beginning. This growth
can be generated domestically through changes in technology
or resources, or it may be a function of the external demand
for what that country produced. Development is a rather more
complex concept and has reference to the maturation of a
society and of its social institutions. It is quite possible for a
country to have a high rate of economic growth for a long
period of time and yet to have very little development.

The National Policy seems to have been partially successful, initially at least, in attaining either growth (the cre-

ation of a transcontinental economy) or development (the movement "from colony to nation."). The period of the 1870s and 1880s is generally taken to have been one of slower growth, if not stagnation for much of the European and North American economy. Nevertheless, it must be noted that the Canadian Pacific Railway did reach the Pacific Ocean in 1885; employment in manufacturing more than doubled between 1880 and 1910; and a great stream of immigrants did begin to flow into the Canadian West. By 1905 Manitoba, Alberta, and Saskatchewan had become provinces, and between 1867 and 1896 Canada's population increased from 3.5 million to more than 5 million. By the beginning of World War I, the population of Canada was about 8 million, an increase of 3 million souls in just under twenty years. Small wonder that Wilfrid Laurier could hope, at the turn of the century, that the next century would be Canada's! Of course this expansion and economic growth were caused partly by a stimulative government policy, but also partly by general world economic conditions.

When we consider the National Policy according to the development criterion, its accomplishments are less impressive. The Canada of 1900 or 1910 was arguably not much different in terms of its relative autonomy than that of 1880. (For details, see Chapter 2.) Indeed, one of the three planks of the National Policy actually had long-run effects that worked against Canadian autonomy in a subtle but very significant way. The intent of imposing a high protective tariff was to increase the viability of manufacturing domestically and to reduce Canada's traditional reliance on imports of finished goods from Britain and the United States. The tariff did increase the price in Canada of foreign manufactures. This allowed producers in Canada to sell their goods at higher prices—prices that gave firms just getting started sufficient profits for survival and expansion. Ideally, such tariffs are reduced to zero as the firms grow in competence and size until finally they are capable of meeting foreign competition at home and even in markets abroad. But in Canada this did not happen: one legacy of the 1879 tariff has been an economy characterized by firms that sit comfortably behind the protective tariff, content to produce at a small scale appropriate to the size of the Canadian market rather than competing aggressively in world markets. If tariff created the firms, the firms then became dependent on the continuation of the tariff. To this day, exports of Canadian manufactured goods are low, consumers pay high prices, and the manufacturing sector is composed of weak and inefficient producers.[8]

Shortly after World War I some Canadians became aware of another factor that was depriving Canada of the autonomy that is a part of nationhood. In developing manufacturing behind the tariff wall insufficient attention had been given to the nationality of the investors who were building the factories and mills. Earlier investment by foreigners had been in railway, canal, and government bonds. Bondholders had a first claim to a fixed stream of the borrower's income, but they neither owned the assets of the borrower nor actively participated in management decisions. But foreign investment in manufacturing enterprises that began to be significant around the end of the nineteenth century took the radically different form of direct investment. Direct investors own equity in the enterprise (or shares of its assets), and as owners of the firm they can influence decision making to the extent of their ownership. What early critics of the growing foreign ownership of Canadian manufacturing found objectionable was that the power to make basic economic decisions about the structure of production in Canada, the rates of economic growth and unemployment, and the types of jobs that would be available to Canadians (what, how, and for whom goods would be produced) was increasingly being concentrated in the hands of foreigners. In 1920 such critics were very few in number; but this issue grew, slowly at first, in subsequent decades. By the late 60s it had assumed critical proportions in the eyes of many Canadians who were aware of a decision-making process of vital importance, over which they felt they did not have sufficient control.[9]

The twentieth century is characterized, for Canada, by a transition from formal membership in the British Empire to an informal position in an economic order almost totally dominated by the United States. Occasionally this transition has become a partisan political issue in Canada. In 1911 the Liberals and Wilfrid Laurier ran, in part, on the issue of free trade with the United States, and Conservatives were elected on the slogan: "No truck nor trade with the Yankees." This is the last time economic (i.e., tariff) integration with the United States has been formally considered, but in the ensuing years what one writer has referred to as "creeping Continentalism" has without fanfare brought the reality of Canada's economic life a good distance toward overall economic integration therewith.[10] Laurier's position in 1911 was consistent with the arguments of writers of that period, such as Goldwin Smith, who articulated the "Continentalist" view that the political boundary dividing the United States and Canada was an artificial and arbitrary device imposed on the population to enrich a parochial and inept Canadian business elite that would not be able to survive if they were deprived of the protection of the state. At the heart of this debate is the question of whether it matters who, Canadian or American, makes the decisions. One's response is determined by whether one believes individuals differ regarding their basic values according to the society and culture in which they live. Liberals may say, "No, it doesn't matter, because we all want the same thing—more material well-being." Conservatives are much more prone to see individuals as being enmeshed in a set of traditions and institutions, from which they derive positive benefits, which affects the preference they have for various policies and, thus, their behavior.[11]

That which may tip the balance in favor of a gradual process of informal, *de facto* integration into the U.S. economy is the evolving relative position of the U.K. vis-à-vis the United States. The seeds of Britain's decline as a world economic power were planted in the 1870s as its standard of living increasingly became dependent, not on domestic production, but on inflows of wealth from foreign territories under its control and the earnings on investments around the world. Simultaneously, the United States had completed its continental expansion; and the abundance of natural resources, prime agricultural land, and a constant inflow of cheap immigrant labor led to a rapid rise in American strength and influence. The period of World War I marks this shift in relative positions.

Data depicting trade and investment relations show clearly when, and the extent to which, the United States replaced the United Kingdom as the central external focus of Canada's economic activity. Between 1901 and 1960 (see Table 4.1) the positions of the two countries are almost perfectly reversed as sources of capital and as markets for Canada's exports. Import figures show a movement that is in the same direction, albeit far less striking. Table 4.1 also indicates the clear preference of British investors for portfolio and of American investors for the direct form of investment. So in the years following World War I, the United States takes over from Britain as chief investor in Canada and portfolio investment gives way to direct investment. This is of major importance because of the ownership, and control over decisions that are part of direct investment. Not only is more of Canada's capital American in origin, but the Americans exercise an influence that was never a feature of previous in-

Table 4.1 U.K., and U.S. Trade with and Investment in Canada, Various Years

	1901	1926	1939	1945	1955	1960
Total foreign capital in Canada—	(1900)					
Percentage from U.K.	85	44	36	25	18	15
Percentage from U.S.	14	53	60	70	76	75
Percentage from Other	1	3	4	5	6	10
U.S. capital in Canada—						
Percentage in direct form		44	45	47	62	63
U.K. capital in Canada—		(1930)				
Percentage in direct form		14		20	38	46
Total Canadian exports—						
Percentage to U.K.	60	36	37	30	18	18
Percentage to U.S.	27	37	42	38	60	56
Percentage to Other	13	27	21	32	22	26
Total Canadian Imports—						
Percentage from U.K.	24	16	15	8	8	11
Percentage from U.S.	60	66	66	77	73	67
Percentage from Other	16	18	21	15	19	22

SOURCE: M. C. Urquhart and K. A. H. Buckley, *Historical Statistics of Canada* (Toronto, Macmillan, 1965), pp. 169, 173

vestment. This transition is especially noticeable between 1939 and 1955, during which years Britain's figures fall by 50 percent. These are, of course, dramatic years, but the single most important event of them, for our purposes, is the immediate postwar period and, specifically, the "Dollar Crisis" of 1948.

World War II had caused such extensive destruction and disruption of economic relationships that the concern that was foremost in the minds of the leaders of all the affected nations for the decade that followed was reconstruction and the creation of the international institutions (specifically, the International Monetary Fund, General Agreement for Tariffs and Trade, and the International Bank for Reconstruction and Development) that, it was hoped, would ensure a peaceful and prosperous future. Neither Canada nor the United States suffered war damage to their economies. The United States was catapulted into leadership of the Western world; Canada, because of its historical position in the "North Atlantic Triangle" (Canada, the United States, and Britain) was caught between a strong and aggressive United States and a weak and foundering United Kingdom—the result was the dollar crisis. Canada had a balance-of-trade surplus (exports in excess of imports) with Britain, but a deficit in her trade with America. Ordinarily this would have been a perfectly viable situation—her pound earnings would be exchanged in the currency market for U.S. dollars to cover the deficit with the United States—but during the postwar reconstruction of Europe's economy currencies were not convertible, so Canada's deficit with the United States could not be offset with earnings elsewhere.

At this point Canada faced a clear choice between two fundamentally different solutions. The liberal, free trade option is always to increase a country's integration into the world economy, and in this case it meant increasing exports to America. Conversely, one could opt for reduced imports from the United States—this would channel domestic demand to domestic producers and stimulate Canadian manufacturing. Either increased export revenues or reduced import expenditures would balance the trade account with the United

States. But what could Canada sell to the Americans? Minister of Finance Douglas Abbott specified "farm products, lumber and wood products, and base metals," and both he and the Minister of Supply and Reconstruction, C. D. Howe, also saw the possibility of increased manufactures "through the existing branch plant system" (i.e., through production by American-owned plants in Canada). Thus, the government's forecast was for a continued emphasis on Canada's traditional exports of raw materials or staples, and an increase in foreign ownership and control of Canadian manufacturing.

There was some reaction against the "Abbott Plan" in Parliament. One member asked:

> Does this mean that we in Canada are to become hewers of wood and drawers of water for United States industrialists by sending them our natural resources, while they fabricate them and send them back to us in the form of manufactured articles? Does it mean the merging of ourselves with the United States economy so that we become an economic colony?[12]

There were a few other critics who voiced similar reservations to Abbott's plan, but they fell on deaf ears. It would not be an exaggeration to say that given the choice between increased Canadian autonomy and a reaffirmation of the customary subordinacy to another more powerful economy, Canada chose the latter. Shortly thereafter Canada had accomplished its transfer from the British to the American orbit, as the data in Table 4.1 show.

After a decade of rebuilding, however, the voices of the critics of the close relationship between the two economies grew both in number and in stature. In 1958, for the first time, a government document focused attention on the high levels of American ownership. Walter Gordon's Royal Commission into Canada's Economic Prospects[13] did little more than raise the issue, but it was followed by a series of other reports that did try to examine specific concerns and articulate policy alternatives. The Watkins Report, in 1965, and the report of the Wahn Commission, in 1970, were issued during a period of increasing worldwide restlessness with the dominant position and leadership of the United States. The extraterritorial application of U.S. law, and the effects of foreign ownership (both broadly political and cultural and narrowly economic) were studied. After a period of intense study of foreign ownership and of the operations of U.S.-based multinational corporations that was reported in the scholarly and popular press, the Canadian government commissioned a report by Herb Gray, the minister of industry, trade and commerce, that was published in 1972 under the title "Foreign Direct Investment in Canada."

At the time of the Gray Report, foreigners owned 58 percent of manufacturing assets. Americans alone owned 44 percent of Canada's manufacturing sector and more than half of the key resource sectors, mining/smelting and petroleum/natural gas. No other country in the world has either this high a percentage of foreign ownership or such a dominant position occupied by the investors of a single foreign country. Of the key manufacturing industries, foreign ownership exceeded 50 percent in rubber products, primary metals, machinery, transport equipment, electrical products, nonmetallic mineral products, petroleum and coal products, chemicals and chemical products, and miscellaneous manufacturing.[14] Canadian ownership was high only in food and beverages, leather products, textile industries, wood, furniture, printing and paper. We shall discuss the effects of high foreign ownership later, but note in passing that foreigners had high ownership positions in the high-technology, dynamic industries that would be the most important in the future, while Canadians were in control of the low-technology, slow-growth industries.

The authors of the Gray Report were sufficiently concerned about the long-run, detrimental effects of high foreign (and U.S.) ownership that they recommended the establishment of an agency that would be charged with examining, or screening, all future investment proposals by foreigners. The Foreign Investment Review Agency (FIRA) began operation in 1974. Opinions differ on the effectiveness of the FIRA, but whether seen as successful or not, the FIRA does represent an attempt by the government to reduce the power of the United States and of American institutions in economic decision-making processes in Canada.

A second action in this recent assertion of Canadian autonomy is the establishment of the Canadian Development Corporation (CDC). Whereas the FIRA was set up to reduce the effects of high foreign ownership, the CDC had as its charge the provision of venture capital to Canadian industry in hopes that this would strengthen individual Canadian-owned manufacturing enterprises, and the gaining of control of key foreign-owned corporations that have their major operations in Canada—its purchase of a controlling interest in Texas Gulf, whose major source of revenues is mines in Ontario, is a good example of this.

In this section we have seen Canada vacillate between an essentially liberal position of opening her borders to "economically rational" movements of goods and capital, and attempts to gain control over the structure of the economy and over economic decision making. Given that about two thirds of Canada's trade is with the United States and given the extraordinarily high percentage of foreign ownership, Canada's option may be rather limited; it may now be a question of closing the barn door after the horse has run away. Nonetheless, the struggle to gain economic autonomy is likely to continue to be a recurring policy issue in the years to come.

The Regional Character of Canada

When outsiders study Canada, one of the features they find most fascinating is the uniqueness of each of Canada's regions and the strength of the regional identities and loyalties of the people who inhabit them. Each discipline of the social science has its own explanation for this diversity, but perhaps the most sensible way of looking at this is to view Canada, not as a vast land stretching to the Arctic, but rather as it is demographically—four thousand miles wide and seventy-five miles deep. From this perspective, Canada is similar to a string of beads, each region having only limited contact with only its contiguous neighbors. The anglophone regions are separated from each other by francophone Quebec and by great physical barriers, the Rockies and the Canadian Shield. Thus, no one region feels any strong affinity or shared interest with any of the others. This contrasts sharply with the United States in which the "beads" are arranged more or less in a square matrix, with each region having a less sharply defined identity and each region blending into each of its multiple neighbors. (Do Texans identify most strongly with the South, the Great Plains or the West? It is difficult to say.)

For Canada the "national" orientation must be east-west, and much of Canadian history since Confederation is concerned with the attempt to reinforce this orientation in the face of north-south pulls that are of considerable strength. Is it not understandable if Atlantic Canada feels a stronger affinity with New England than with the Prairies? or Manitoba with the upper Midwest than with Quebec? In this section we are going to examine the evolution of these regional characteristics and the economic relationship between them and the policies of the federal government.

Canada was, of course, first settled in the East; and as successive waves of immigrants came from Europe, the center of both population and economic activity was pushed westward. As can be seen from Table 4.2 the Maritimes' share of the Canadian population has declined steadily for the past century and a half as Ontario; then the Prairies; and finally, as the last column shows, British Columbia have, in turn,

Table 4.2 Percentage Distribution of Population by Regions, Various Years

	1825	1851	1871	1921	1961	1978	% change, 1961–71
The Maritimes (excl. Newfoundland)	24	22	21	11	8	7	8.4
Quebec	58	37	32	27	29	27	14.6
Ontario	18	39	44	33	34	36	23.5
The Prairies	—	—	2	22	17	17	11.4
British Columbia	—	2	1	6	9	11	34.1
Canada	100	100	100	100	100	100	18.3

SOURCES: W. T. Easterbrook and H. G. J. Aitken, *Canadian Economic History* (Toronto, Macmillian, 1963) M. C. Urquhart and K. A. H. Buckley, *Historical Statistics of Canada* (Toronto, Macmillan, 1965), p. 14.

been peopled. We get a similar picture if we consider the evolution of economic activity during this period. Since data are difficult to get on a regional basis for the early nineteenth century, it may be more informative to take three very general (and admittedly impressionistic) glimpses at Canada in 1830, 1900, and 1970.

In 1830 the Maritime Provinces were the center of the British North American economy. Timber was the major staple, shipbuilding was the major industry, and Halifax was a thriving center of finance and commerce. The St. Lawrence economy was suffereing from the transfer of the major fur-trading center from Montreal to Hudson Bay and a new central focus, and heart of economic activity had not yet emerged. The fact that Upper and Lower Canada were not under a single government made it difficult to plan or finance the internal improvements (primarily transportation facilities) that would facilitate the creation of what historian Donald Creighton has called the "Empire of the St. Lawrence." What is now Southern Ontario was still only lightly settled, and the West not at all.

The golden period of the Maritimes had ended by Confederation, and by 1900 the commercial and financial center of a Canada stretching from the Atlantic to the Pacific had moved to Montreal. The National Policy had begun to have its effects, with industry in the belt from Hamilton, Ontario, to Montreal being fueled by the demands of western agriculture. The Maritimes' share of the population had fallen by 50 percent since 1867, and the causes of the region's perennial stagnation were already beginning to have their effect.

By 1970 the decline of Canada's old East had extended to Montreal as the business community transferred the seat of its operations to Toronto. British Columbia and southern Ontario had become the high growth areas, but the energy resources of Alberta and Saskatchewan were about to change the economic status of the western Prairies. The position of the various regions today is graphically shown in Table 4.3. Unemployment ranges between averages of 12.4 percent for the Atlantic Provinces and 5.4 percent for the Prairies, and per capita income in the poorest region is only 63 percent of

Table 4.3 Some Regional Statistics

	Unemployment (1978)	Per Capita Income (1978)	Per Capita Federal Transfers to Provinces (1971–75)
Newfoundland	16.4%		$701
Prince Edward Island	9.9		713
Nova Scotia	10.6	$1948	515
New Brunswick	12.6		562
Quebec	10.9	2489	461
Ontario	7.2	3097	252
Manitoba	6.5		406
Saskatchewan	4.9	2453	356
Alberta	4.7		335
British Columbia	8.3	3000	240
Canada	8.4	2700	

SOURCES: *Canadian Statistical Review* (Ottawa, Information Canada), and Economic Council of Canada, *Living Together: A Study of Regional Disparities* (Ottawa, Economic Council of Canada, 1977).

that with the highest income. The federal government has responded to these regional imbalances with a system of transfers of tax revenues back to the provinces; the last column of Table 4.3 indicates there is a systematic transfer from west to east with the Ottawa River being the line of demarcation between givers and receivers, at least for this category of funds.

In part, this pattern of regional imbalance is in conformity with what one would expect. In a country as demographically long and narrow as Canada one would hardly expect the heart of economic activity to be located at either of the extremities—transportation, locational theory, and simple "gravity" all point to the center being the locus of decision making, manufacturing, and commerce. But regions other than central Canada (Southern Ontario and Montreal) have argued that they have been impoverished by the policies of the federal government, beginning with the infamous (in some places) National Policy. Maritimers argue that the NP's high tariff and focus on western development have built up central Canada at the expense of what had been, prior to Confederation, a thriving manufacturing economy in Nova Scotia and

New Brunswick. Canada's system of a handful of nationwide chartered banks has meant that the savings of Maritimers have been channeled westward to finance economic expansion there rather than remaining in the cities and towns in which the savers work and live. High tariffs have meant that farmers in the Prairies have been forced to pay higher prices for farm implements, and all manufactured goods, than have their counterparts across the border in the Dakotas and Minnesota. There, combined with high interest rates for loans and "unactual" freight rates that have been set by bankers and bureaucrats in Toronto, Ottawa, and Montreal, have caused western farmers to feel that their interests, and incomes, have been sacrificed to further the economy of Ontario. We have, in addition, heard much recently of the economic domination experienced by Francophones in Quebec. But "regional gripes" have been very much a part of Canadian politics since Confederation, and one should not for a moment forget that Maritime and Prairie provincial governments have frequently and very strongly voiced their own dissatisfactions.

Of the three major sets of regional economic problems, those of the Atlantic Provinces are the most difficult to discuss in a brief space. The decline of this region in relation to the others has been in progress for the better part of the past century. This is in part a question of resources that face stagnant or deteriorating markets, and in part a question of being physically on the periphery of a critical mass of economic activity and being separated from it by too many dollars of "dead" transportation expense. To study this adequately would require far more space than we have here; so for the rest of this chapter we shall examine the two other salient regional stresses facing Canadians today.

Most of the provinces have at least at one time in their history been rich in resources—perhaps the only exception is Prince Edward Island. One thinks of Nova Scotia's coal; of the minerals of Quebec, Ontario, and British Columbia; and of petroleum/natural gas in nineteenth-century Ontario. In recent years attention has been turned to the vast reserves of petroleum/natural gas, coal, and potash of Alberta and, to a lesser extent, Saskatchewan.

The Prairie Provinces have always been very articulate in expressing their belief that they have been manipulated by bankers and politicians "back east." Western economic frustration and dissatisfaction have generated a series of reactions—the Winnipeg General Strike in 1919, farmers' marches on Ottawa in the 1920s, and in 1934 the formation of Canada's socialist party, the Cooperative Commonwealth Federation (now the New Democratic Party). The Prairies' complaint is not, then, a recent development; as an agricultural region, they had little with which to bargain and no power that would allow them to impose solutions to economic problems that would work to their advantage. The recent virtual explosion in the value of Prairie resources on world markets has changed this situation dramatically.

The petroleum and natural gas era began for Alberta with the discovery in 1947 of major, exploitable reserves in the Leduc field. Pipelines linking this resource to central Canadian markets were built during the early 1950s. Although there have been significant oil and gas discoveries in the North and off the Atlantic Coast, the Alberta fields (spilling over into British Columbia and Saskatchewan) remain the source of almost all of Canada's current production, with Alberta itself contributing about 85 percent of that total. The British North America Act (Canada's "constitution") gives control of resources to the provinces, but once they are transported across a provincial border they are considered interstate commerce and fall under the power of the federal government. However, production and distribution of oil and gas were totally controlled by the major companies, the so-called Seven Sisters. Throughout the 1950s and 1960s there was a worldwide surplus of oil and gas, as is indicated by the fact that prices for both products fell by about one third between 1950 and 1970, so there was not much struggle between the provincial and federal governments over policies in this area.[15]

In the 1970s, however, as a result of actions of the major producing countries, the OPEC group, prices have risen dramatically—from about $3 per barrel of oil in 1970 to more than $20 per barrel for some shipments today. This rapid rise in world oil prices created a tremendous stream of revenues, and it was over the disposition of these revenues that the two levels of government in Canada began a sometimes very heated discussion.

The position of the federal government was predicated on two assumptions: (1) all Canadians ought to pay the same price for oil and gas; and (2) Canadians should pay lower than world prices for oil and gas as a means of gaining a competitive advantage in world markets for exports of manufactures. Western oil and gas was shipped only as far east as Ottawa, while Quebec and the Maritimes got their supplies from world markets. This meant that the ideal federal policy would be to limit Alberta's exports (roughly, to equal what was imported in the East) and to impose an export tax, the proceeds of which would be used to subsidize eastern oil and gas users. That is, if the world price were $12 per barrel, all Canadians could have oil at, say, $8 per barrel.

Alberta has countered with its own argument, which is basically that all resources should be sold at world market prices and that the provincial governments should receive the major share of tax revenues. This, they argue, is in conformity with practice in the past. Since Albertans never enjoyed access to Ontario's minerals, food, or manufactures at subsidized prices, why, then, should Alberta's resources be sold at a discount? It is also clear that oil and gas are in finite supply and that at some point in the future Alberta's reserves will be depleted—what will there be to maintain the economy of Alberta when oil and gas are depleted? Is it not only fair, they ask, that Alberta be allowed to maximize its oil and gas revenues so that investments can be made today that will establish the basis of tomorrow's economy?

In fact, the export tax and subsidy to eastern users have been in place for over five years, so the federal government has been able to implement its policy. Alberta has accumulated its immense revenues from oil and gas taxes in the Alberta Heritage Fund. This fund (some $5 billion in early 1980) is making investments and funding research and industrial expansion in Alberta that, it is hoped, will provide future generations of Albertans with a viable economic base.

Continuing discussion between Ottawa and Alberta (complicated by the twofold change of governments in Ottawa in
1979–80) now tend to concentrate on the relative shares of
the benefits accruing to the two governments rather than on
the principle of the sharing. Negotiations can be expected to
continue for years to come.

A separate and very important issue has arisen from the
fact that petroleum is the raw material input to the petrochemical industry. Both governments agreed that Canada
needed a "world-scale" petrochemical facility—one that would
produce at a large enough scale of operations that its costs of
production would be minimized and its output be competitive
in world markets. Premier Peter Lougheed of Alberta wanted
the plant to be located in his province so that the industrial
jobs involved with processing Alberta's resources would be
open to Albertans. This would contribute to their objective of
building on industrial base for the Alberta of the future. The
federal government's position was that it made more sense to
put the facility at the end of the pipeline, in Sarnia, Ontario,
where the petrochemical output would be closer to ocean
transport and to industrial users in central Canada. To Albertans this sounded like yet another ploy to build up Ontario's industrial economy at the expense of the other regions,
and Lougheed threatened that it might not be able to assure
supplies of oil needed (percent of the province daily production) if the plant were not located in Alberta. The company
involved, Petrosar, did in fact get permission in 1975 to locate
the facility in Sarnia; however, Alberta has been successful
in getting other corporations to establish smaller petrochemical plants in the province.

Issues such as oil and gas pricing and taxation and the
location of the petrochemical industry have served to keep
alive the sense of western regional identity and of exploitation
by central Canada that had in earlier years been fed by farmer
complaints about freight rates and interest charges. The sheer
magnitude of the revenues involved and the dependency of
the rest of Canada on continued supplies of energy have given
Alberta a strength in bargaining that is of an entirely different order than was the case when agriculture was the industry

involved. Economic power has perceptibly shifted westward in recent years, and this is sure to have an impact on federal-provincial relations. Premier Lougheed has been a strong and articulate spokesman for increased provincial rights in certain areas. One can only speculate as to the long-run impact this will have on the Canadian Confederation.

Quebec's economic grievance is quite different and must be seen in the context of the experiences of a people over a period of more than two centuries.[16] Intellectuals who support Quebec's present aspiration for Sovereignty/Association speak of a continuing history of subordination within an anglophone community, of which the most important events are: the Conquest on the Plains of Abraham in 1759, the rebellions of 1837–38, the execution of Louis Riel (1885), the conscriptions of both World Wars and provincial legislation (primarily in Manitoba and Ontario) that has restricted the language rights of Francophones outside Quebec. This history of Quebec/Canada, French/English, or francophone/anglophone relations is presented elsewhere in this book and will not be covered again here. The nonmaterial dimension of the dissatisfactions many Quebecers have with Confederation may not seem as significant to non-Quebecers, as do the more easily dealt with economic issues, but nonetheless any discussion of Quebec's future relationship with the rest of Canada, and for that matter North America, must give them serious consideration. It is this that provides the contrast with Alberta's position.

Whereas Alberta's concern is primarily (although not exclusively) one of revenues and industrialization, the material aspect of Quebec's frustration is one of access to positions of power and decision making, of being locked into a situation of economic inferiority. In brief, the argument of Québécois nationalists has been that Anglophones control the economy and make decisions that benefit (chiefly) Anglophones. The remedy for this situation must be to become francophone "Masters in our own house," or, in contemporary, Parti Québécois terms, "Sovereign." Not all Quebecers share in these feelings—clearly not the English-speaking minority (in whose hands economic control was once lodged), nor some French speakers to whom the present relationship has been very good, nor most recent immigrants to the province. But it is fair to say that the three quarters of Quebec's population who are middle- and lower-income Francophones share some, if not all, of the Parti Québécois' sentiments (even if they themselves may vote Liberal at election time).

We have already presented data that indicate that unemployment is higher, and per capita incomes lower, in Quebec than in Canada as a whole. Within Quebec, Francophones have still higher unemployment and lower incomes than do other language groups. These figures reflect the fact that Anglophones own, control, and to a large extent manage the great majority of corporations in Quebec that are large, that are in the growing industries, and that extend their operations beyond Quebec to Canada, the United States, and world markets. These corporations have determined the nature of the evolution of the Quebec economy. Historically, Francophones have not been welcomed into this world, except in noncrucial, cosmetic positions. As a result of this lack of opportunity in the private sector, francophone Quebecers sought employment, not in business, but in government, teaching, and the professions—this was complementary to the traditional Catholic emphasis on a "classical" rather than a "practical" education. Francophone Quebecers still disproportionately find employment in jobs that entail less responsibility, require less skill, and provide less income. They tend to own, control, and manage firms that are smaller in size, more confined to sales within Quebec, and are not in the most rapidly growing sectors of the economy. This point has elsewhere been made at greater length and supported with a barrage of statistics[17]—we will be content with having made the point that francophone dissatisfaction with *les anglos* concerns control over the basic institutions of their society and a historic struggle to avoid assimilation into anglo North America. What has been written here about the economy is also true in the areas of culture and politics, and no one area can be dealt with in isolation from the others.

From what has been said it should be clear that the Quebec "gripe" is far less tractable and easily resolved than is Alberta's. Ottawa is discussing with Alberta the question of who gets what share of a new, large, and growing stream of income—the basic point remains that both will get "more." With Quebec it is not a case of determining shares of the pie. Power and control tend to come in fixed quantities, and their allocation tends, therefore, to be a "zero-sum game." As Francophones gain more control over the basic institutions of their society, the anglophone community will have to give it up. This factor combines with the historical and psychological dimensions of the question to produce an issue that is extremely difficult to negotiate. Supporters of Sovereignty/Association argue that the history of these negotiations has been that only symbolic gestures are made by the anglophone elite and that further discussions about marginal changes in these relationships will never effect substantive transfer of power and control; therefore, a complete break must be made.

Sovereignty/Association has been at the core of the program of the Parti Québécois since its founding in 1968. It is a concept that is unique to this particular issue, so its precise definition has evolved and been refined in response to events and as the political situation has changed since that time. "Sovereignty" refers to the notion that Quebec must: (1) attain complete political sovereignty so as to break the legacy of conquest and domination of the past two centuries; and (2) structure the political reality so that control over the basic institutions of their society can be maintained in the future. "Association" refers to the economic relationship Quebec will have to the rest of Canada (and of course, by extension, to the United States)—this entails agreements treating "international" movements of people, goods, and capital; the currency to be used in Quebec; the disposition of jointly owned institutions such as Air Canada; and a host of other similar issues. Although much ink has been spilled on the question of whether or not Sovereignty/Association is economically (let alone politically) viable, it would be idle to speculate here on various scenarios for negotiations that might make it appear more, or less, viable to those Canadians and Québécois who *might* have to try to make it go in a future unknown to us at present.

This section, on so-called regional gripes, has focused on

two fundamentally different problems that are pressing economic and political concerns today and that promise to continue in the near future. In conclusion, it should simply be reiterated that the strong regional identities and attachments that persist throughout Canadian history provide one of the aspects that make the study of the economy of Canada so fascinating.

The Role of the State in the Economy

There is in previous sections of this chapter ample material in support of the proposition that the state ought to play a more significant role in the Canadian economy than is the case in the United States. The two most prominent themes thus far have been: (1) the need to formulate policies that would nurture an autonomous national economy in the face of great and continual pressures that would make Canada the appendage of either the United Kingdom or the United States; and (2) the role of the federal government as arbiter of regional grievances. Without a strong, central force, either of these pressures would have produced a Canada that is markedly different from the one that exists today. This section will pursue the historical need for significant governmental intrusion into the workings of the economy and will discuss some of the specific policies and institutions that define this governmental role and that differentiate the Canadian experience from that of the United States.

In this context it is interesting to examine the argument of one social scientist, Louis Hartz, which provides a very general, philosophical explanation of these differing approaches to government.[18] Hartz noted that emigrants from Britain settled in the various "lands of recent settlement" (Canada, the United States, Australia, Rhodesia, etc.) at different periods of time and that the individual areas attracted emigrants of different characteristics. The United States was settled by large numbers of British people earlier than was Canada, and those who came were largely middle-class settlers who were anxious to maintain the rights of individuals, seeing government as the chief threat to those rights. The United States adopted, from the beginning, a democratic,, one-man, one-vote political system, and much of the political history of the past two centuries concerns attempts to keep power from being appropriated by a small elite. This is not to say that the United States is not a society with classes and that class does not matter, but from Andrew Jackson to Jimmy Carter populism has been a force to be reckoned with and a force that has worked to keep political processes open, in a relative sense. Finally, America is politically a "liberal" society and one that resorted to a War of Independence to break the constraints that were inherent in a colonial relationship to the mother country.

Canada was settled later, and by people who looked to the United Kingdom and its government as a source of support and sustenance, a guarantor of a way of life rather than as a threat to it. Canadians never rebelled against mercantilism, with its emphasis on the state as the central organ in society, but were perfectly comfortable with it. When the mercantilist system was dismantled by Britain, in the 1840s, Canadians entered upon a period of thirty years of searching for a suitable replacement—reciprocity with the United States, Confederation, and, finally, the National Policy. In the light of this we could characterize Canadians as a people who prefer a society in which the individual is more completely integrated in a web of tradition and social institutions, and less an atomistic maximizer of his own, individual material well-being. This suggests to political scientists the reason for the greater strength in Canada than in the United States of conservative and socialist political parties. To the economist it suggests that free enterprise will not be quite as free in Canada and that government will more closely monitor and alter the workings of market forces.

When we turn to strictly economic considerations, there are two general forces at work that have produced an active government. The first is Canada's physical location, next to the United States, and the second is Canada's historical focus on staples production. Being next to the United States meant that Canada was not able to develop according to its own pace. The United States was a dynamic and aggressive economy; almost uniquely endowed with resources; and always with larger and more advanced commercial, financial, and industrial sectors. The United States could expand settlement with little obstruction as far as the Rocky Mountains, and this expansion could progress along a thousand-mile-wide frontier. Canadians settled among the river valleys and Lakes Erie and Ontario, but then faced the formidable barrier of rock and forest that stretches from Ottawa to Winnipeg—eight-hundred miles of land that would not support agricultural settlement. The effect of this was to force Canada to play "catch up" to the United States. This was particularly true during the great push westward and the internal-improvements era of the nineteenth century, and is most clearly represented by Canada's experience with canal and railroad construction.

Early in the fur trade era there was intense competition between the Montreal–St. Lawrence and the Albany-Hudson systems as gateways to the interior. When the northern trade was shifted to Hudson Bay in 1820, the St. Lawrence forwarding economy was left high and dry. The new strategy for commercial survival put grain in the place of fur, with Montreal simply adapting itself to a different staple. Immediately Albany emerged to threaten this plan with the completion of the Erie Canal in 1825. Midwestern grain could now be shipped through the Great Lakes as far as Buffalo or Oswego and then sent down through a man-made waterway to the Hudson and then to world markets through New York. This was an all-year port, and traffic could go in both directions; Montreal was closed during the winter, and a series of rapids made the river navigable only by rafts floating downstream. So the Erie system had a natural advantage, and it was not until more than twenty years later that Canada had a comparable system.

The land in upstate New York was very flat, so that the Erie Canal was relatively easily and cheaply constructed. The Canadians were not so fortunate and faced two major cost-increasing, physical difficulties. The first was the need to make the three-hundred-foot drop from Lake Erie to Lake

Ontario less abrupt and more suitable to navigation than was Niagara Falls. This was accomplished with the Welland Canal in 1829. The second difficulty was the need for a series of short canals along the St. Lawrence. (The first response was to avoid the problem entirely with the Rideau Canal that, in 1834, linked Lake Ontario with the Ottawa River and avoided the St. Lawrence above Montreal. This was a militarily attractive project, since it kept traffic far from the New York border, but it never was of much commercial importance.) Not until 1848, however, was the St. Lawrence system itself finished.

These canal projects were very large ventures for a small colony, and the private sector was not capable of operations on such a scale. On the one hand, there was insufficient private capital in Canada; on the other hand, a canal in the wilderness of Canada looked to be a rather risky investment to those in England and elsewhere who did have the funds. So government was needed in one way or the another. The difficulty with this was that while Upper Canada was eager to see the canal system built, since it was primarily Upper Canadian farmers, millers, and forwarders who would derive the benefit, Lower Canadians, with the exception of the English mercantile establishment in Montreal, were reluctant to commit or tax themselves for this purpose. The inability of these two governments to join in a single coherent plan for the development of the St. Lawrence economy meant that Upper Canada bought canal company stock, borrowed on its own account, and guaranteed borrowings of private companies until at the end of the 1830s it was on the edge of bankruptcy, with the system still incomplete. The British government intervened in 1840 and with the help of a sizable loan negotiated the union of Upper and Lower Canada. The new government had considerably more power to tax and to borrow, and eight years later the canal system was finished.

We have already mentioned that 1848 was also the year in which the dismantling of British mercantilism was completed, thus depriving Canada of the protection in that market which to a large degree justified the canals, and we have also noted the confusion this generated in Canada. A fact of equal importance was that, while Canadians had been building canals to meet the competition of the Erie and other U.S. canals, the Americans had gone on to develop a network of railroads, which by the end of the 1840s consisted of almost nine thousand miles of track (Canada had by then built less than one hundred miles). Just as one enormous project had been finished, then, the government was obliged to undertake another, and moreover a project that would actually compete with the one it had just completed.

In 1849, with existing railroad projects in serious difficulties because of the inability to secure adequate financing, the government passed the Guarantee Act, which allowed for public support of railroad construction projects that met certain conditions. From this date on the federal government was heavily involved in the development of Canada's rail system. Private companies were formed, and government guaranteed some of their interest payments, subscribed to their bond issues, and wrote off some company obligations to the government. This was satisfactory for the eastern railways, but when it came to building an all-Canadian line from the Atlantic to the Pacific—the great promise of Confederation—this was a project that required even more government support. In addition to the usual difficulties in railroad construction, the line to the Pacific had to content with eight hundred miles of forest and muskeg between Ottawa and Winnipeg and the uncertainty of finding a suitable pass through the Rocky Mountains. Some private syndicates were interested in building the line, but none were willing to include the link north of Lakes Superior and Huron—they proposed to use existing U.S. track through Detroit, Chicago, and Minneapolis. The government insisted on an all-Canadian route, and only government could make such a contract profitable. In addition to direct financial support, the Canadian Pacific Railway Company was given a vast land grant, control over its freight rates for a period of time, and a guarantee of monopoly in the territory it served.[19] The monopoly clause was initially aimed at keeping smaller feeder lines from being built to channel grain south to the American rail system. An additional intervention of the government in Canadian transportation occurred in 1920 when several smaller railroads in financial straits were merged into the Canadian National Railway and run as a Crown- or government-owned, corporation.

The importance of resource development throughout Canada's history has generated additional pressures for an active government. In relation to its land space and resource endowment Canada has a very small population with an insufficient ability to generate savings for investment. Resource projects tend to be large and capital intensive. Because they require tremendous amounts of capital, even if the Canadian capital market is able to provide the necessary financing, the occasional large research project tends to absorb all the funds available, thus starving out worthwhile industrial projects. The only alternative for these companies or entrepreneurs is to raise capital in other countries, and to the extent that they rely on share or equity financing this only exacerbates the very significant problem Canada has with foreign ownership.[20] Because they are large projects in a rather small economy, some resource developments have powerful impacts on other industries and on governments themselves. Resources are inputs for other industries, and the pricing and production policy for certain strategic raw materials can determine the viability of some manufacturing lines. This bull-in-the-china-shop potential has led both the federal and several of the provincial governments to place some key resource areas under government ownership. Because of the size and diversity of the U.S. economy, Americans are not confronted with this situation, and government ownership is not a feature of our economy.

One sector of the economy in which these concerns can be seen clearly is hydroelectric power generation and transmission. Owing to glacial action, much of Canada's surface is rock, either bare or thinly disguised with soil. Thus, rainfall tends to run off in rivers rather than soak into the earth. These rivers can be dammed for the generation of hydroelectric power in many parts of the country. This source provides more than 90 percent of the electricity of Newfoundland, Quebec, Manitoba, and British Columbia; more than 50 percent for New Brunswick; and about 44 percent for Ontario. Only

Saskatchewan, Nova Scotia, Alberta, and Prince Edward Island derive less than 40 percent of their electric power from hydroelectricity. In Ontario the potential of hydroelectricity was seen very early, and control over this source of energy became a political issue around the turn of the century.

The American approach to this sort of an industry has been to allow privately owned companies to exploit the resource and provide it to the public. Because of the technology and economics of the industry, local monopolies are usually formed and a public commission is established to regulate the industry and to assure that the public's needs are met and its interest protected. It is said that "politics make strange bedfellows," and this was certainly true in Ontario with regard to hydroelectric power. A municipal reform movement, composed in part of mayors of cities in southern Ontario, argued for public ownership so as to guarantee that citizens of this region would not be vulnerable to price or supply decisions made by a power monopoly, one that would in addition probably have been owned by Americans. They were supported in this instance by Ontario industrialists who believed a publicly owned corporation would be more likely to provide electricity at low rates, thus giving them a slight cost advantage. The alliance was successful when the Conservative Party established the Ontario Hydro-Electric Commission upon taking office in 1905. In subsequent years the Ontario model of public ownership of hydroelectric generation and transmission has been adopted in other provinces.

Another telling example of the Canadian model of government intervention in the economy if provided by provincial and federal ownership of industrial concerns, primarily those closely related to major resources in the purview of the government concerned. Recent years provide three major examples, one provincial, one federal, and one proposed provincial. The provincial example in being is Saskatchewan's ownership and producing position in its potash industry. Alarmed by the high degree of American ownership of one of the province' major sources of wealth, the Saskatchewan government enacted the Potash Development Act in 1976, giving the province the power to expropriate the assets of existing companies.

The Potash Corporation of Saskatchewan was formed and proceeded to purchase, for fair market value, several mines. It is now well on its way to meeting its objective of ownership of 50 percent of the potash-mining capacity in the province. There have been some stormy legal and political battles, as is the case whenever government moves into what has hitherto been considered to be the private sector, but observers within the industry have concluded that the government has conducted its operations in a managerially sound way and has not used its power to unfair advantage.

It was a New Democratic government that got the Province of Saskatchewan into the potash industry, and when the federal Liberals were returned with a minority government in 1974 one price of NDP support was the establishment of Petro-Canada. This corporation is the keystone fo the federal government's position in the oil and gas industry. The legislation passed in 1975 allows Petro-Canada to engage in all activities from exploration to marketing finished products, but in fact its operations are largely confined to the crucial areas of exploration and obtaining crude oil. It began by taking over the government-held shares of Panarctic Oils and Syncrude, two companies that operate in the Far North and in the tar sand deposits of northern Alberta. These are not activities that yield quick returns, and the corporation required an annual infusion of government money. However, it has recently purchased companies, such as Pacific Petroleums, which already have sizable incomes, and it is expected that Petro-Canada will soon be independent of federal financing.

After the election of 1976 the Quebec government made good a long-standing campaign promise of the Parti Québécois by announcing its intention to take over a major element in the asbestos industry, Asbestos Corporation, a subsidiary of the U.S. firm General Dynamics. Although action on the takeover was delayed by a court battle over the compensation proposed, by mid-1981 it appeared that expropriation might actually take place in the near future.

One common thread that runs through each of these recent examples of government ownership (or proposed ownership) is the unwillingness on the part of Canadians to allow the private sector to have a complete monopoly of knowledge and decision making with regard to key resources. Without independent knowledge of an industry—its reserves and the costs of various aspects of operation—it is impossible for society to enact rational policy measures. There is also the belief that the interest of the private company does not always coincide with the interest of society as a whole: thus the perceived need for a strong government position in the economy, which is quite antithetical to prevailing attitudes in the United States.

The Structure of the Economy and Production

We have hitherto been concerned primarily with discussing four major aspects of Canadian economic history: the staples theory, the struggle for autonomy, regional stresses, and the evolving role of government in the economy. In this and the following sections we turn our attention to the present and the future. First we shall examine the structure of economic activity today, concentrating on aspects that are of special interest to policymakers. These aspects are so highly interrelated that it is difficult to treat them in isolation from each other; nonetheless, we can pick out four specific aspects as being of particular significance:

(1) the effects of high tariffs on production
(2) foreign ownership and its effects
(3) the composition of output
(4) international trade relations

The past twenty-five years have seen a great outpouring of studies of economic activity in Canada. This is probably the result of two factors: first, there are now more economists who have been educated in Canada; they have written dissertations of Canadian issues and have used Canadian data and resources. Thus, they have an intellectual investment in studying the Canadian economy. Second, as the focus has shifted from economic history and refining the staples theory to questions of economic performance, economists have come to see the Canadian economy as one that does not operate very efficiently, and this has led to a very active debate about the optimal policy prescription for its ills. Efficiency relates ends to means and, in the context of an essentially individualist, materialist Western culture, is measured by the incomes generated out of a given set of resources. Inefficiently organized production encourages much waste and a lowered standard of living. It is also possible, however, that an economy that is efficiently organized on a global or North American basis may systematically drain income from Canadians to some other "more deserving" people, and thus from a Canadian perspective the utilization of their resources will be "inefficient." Two major factors that immediately come to mind in this context are the tariff and foreign ownership.

We noted earlier that Canada had imposed a high tariff in the latter part of the nineteenth century in an attempt to create a more autonomous national economy. Manufacturing was thereby assisted, but much of that activity was carried out with foreign capital and, in many instances, by foreigners. Thus one result of the tariff was a high degree of foreign ownership of Canadian industry. Once foreign-owned companies were producing in Canada, they argued for the retention of the tariff so as to protect their positions in the Canadian market. Thus, both factors in question here are inextricably interrelated.

A tariff is essentially a tax on foreign-produced goods, and as such its primary effect is to increase the selling price of these goods. As the price rises, it becomes possible for domestic producers to compete with foreigners in the home market. In theory the tariff is imposed in hopes that new producers will be able to become skilled and competent in this industry—technology, expertise, and marketing skills will all develop, and as the firm grows larger it will achieve economies of large-scale production. As the cost of production falls, the tariff is reduced toward zero; and after a period of ten to twenty years a mature industry is in place, capable of meeting foreign competition in its home market, without further assistance, and perhaps even of exporting its products to other countries. This theory seldom works in practice. Rather, the protected industry prefers to remain sheltered, and its forecast of significant job losses and unemployment in the wake of tariff reduction is usually enough to convince political leaders to keep the tariff in place.

The Canadian case is even worse, because of what economists have called the "miniature replica effect."[21] Because of the unusual proximity of the two economies and the emphasis of firms within an industry on maintaining or increasing their shares of the market, when one firm in an industry begins to produce in Canada the others tend to follow. Thus, if an industry in the United States has five large producers, so will Canada. This is fine in a market of over 200 million people, but for the Canadian market (one-tenth that size) it means that each producer may be operating with a plant that is not large enough to take advantage of all the economies of large-scale production. Hence, they cannot, and indeed do not wish to, compete with foreign producers in an open market; they demand the tariff; and Canadian consumers are faced with prices that may be 20 or 30 or more percent higher than in the United States (and higher than would be charged in Canada without the tariff).

For this kind of inefficiency the high degree of foreign ownership of Canadian manufacturing has become a very hotly debated policy question during the past ten or fifteen years. The data given in Table 4.4 show how extensive this foreign ownership is and where it is concentrated. Of this foreign ownership, about 85 percent is of U.S. origin. The good, or bad, effects of this situation are debatable, but it remains true that no other industrialized country has either such a high percentage of its economy owned by foreigners or such a high share of that ownership in the hands of citizens of one individual country.

It is a common misconception that this situation has developed only in the post–World War II period; as early, as 1919 figures showed ownership percentages almost as high, and a handful of individuals were alarmed at that time. Telling data have been made public periodically since that time,

Table 4.4 Foreign Ownership of Canadian Industry, 1968

| Industry | Percentage Majority of Foreign Ownership as Measured by | |
	Assets	Profits
Food and beverages	31.2	30.1
Tobacco	84.3	82.7
Rubber products	93.1	90.0
Leather products	22.0	25.2
Textile industries	39.4	54.4
Wood	30.7	23.6
Furniture	18.9	20.8
Printing, publishing and allied	21.0	22.3
Paper and allied products	39.4	40.6
Primary metals	55.3	62.4
Metal fabricating	46.9	65.0
Machinery	71.8	78.9
Transport equipment	86.6	89.9
Electrical products	64.2	78.2
Non-metallic mineral products	51.5	47.0
Petroleum and coal products	99.5	98.6
Chemicals and chemical products	81.5	89.6
Miscellanious manufacturing	53.9	72.1
Total—All Manufacturing	58.0	63.6

SOURCE: Government of Canada, Privy Council, *Foreign Direct Investment in Canada*, Otttawa (1972), p. 21.

but it was not until the late 1960s that foreign ownership and control became an issue of wide political concern.

As to the effects of this foreign ownership, economists are not really able to "prove" very much. To test our hypotheses ideally, one would have to find an economy with no foreign ownership, introduce to it a high degree, and then observe the changes in a variety of different aspects of economic activity. Lacking this opportunity, we tend to fall back on lesser methodologies. One is to "build a model" of an economy, effect the desired change, and then "observe the impacts." But this involves critical, and arguable assumptions as to how the economy fits together and functions. We can also do comparative studies in which we try to determine whether high foreign ownership economies have anything in common. This approach is only as good as the quality and quantity of the

economies one has to compare. Finally, we can take an economy such as Canada's, observe that it has certain characteristics, and then inquire as to whether economic theory would
suggest a causal relationship between them. (It is best to fix
upon only two characteristics at a time.) This last method has
been the primary mode of enquiry in the foreign ownership
debate.

Economists who have been critical of foreign ownership
have presented the following arguments. The essence of foreign ownership is that the locus of decision making is transferred, in this case from Canada to the United States. The
"branch plant" is a subsidiary of a foreign corporation, and
the internal logic of long-run profit maximization on a global
basis dictates that the Canadian subsidiary function in a
manner that is different from that of an independent company
owned locally. This point can be made most clearly when we
consider the likely export/import performance of the two
firms. The locally owned firm will aggressively seek to sell
in any and all markets, subject to its financial abilities. The
subsidiary may well be constrained: (1) to not export into
certain markets that have already been allocated to either
the parent firm or another subsidiary in some third country;
(2) to purchase components from another entity in the multinational corporation rather than open the contract to competitive bidding; and (3) if it produces raw materials, to export
those goods in an unfinished state rather than process them
into final goods in the economy in which they are found. To
the extent that these constraints are exhibited in reality, the
host country would tend to have a balance-of-trade deficit, to
have a weakened manufacturing sector, and to export raw
materials and import manufactured goods. These effects are
important because of the financial implications of, and the
burdens imposed on, the rest of the economy, by a trade deficit,
and because manufacturing tends to generate the high-skill,
high-paying jobs. They are also, in fact, features of the Canadian economy, and many economists assert high foreign
ownership is the causal factor.

There have been three Canadian government studies of
the activities of foreign investors in Canada. A brief summary

of their conclusions will enable us to get a sense of the effects
that have been most bothersome to Canadians. The first report
was that of the Watkins Commission of 1968.[22] This study
singled out the extraterritorial application of U.S. law as
being the "most serious cost to Canada of foreign ownership
and control"; for example, the prohibition of exports by U.S.
subsidiaries producing in Canada to countries listed in the
American Trading with the Enemy Act. The commission also
took note of several effects that tended to make the Canadian
industrial sector less efficient, and they argued that more and
better data about the activities of foreign-owned companies
were needed before a rational policy could be adopted. The
major significance of this report was that it alerted Canadians
to an issue that clearly ought to be examined to a far greater
degree than it had been in the past.

One year later (1969) the House of Common's Standing
Committee on External Affairs and National Defense, chaired
by Ian Wahn, issued a report on *Canada-U.S. Relations* that
while giving less economic analysis than the Watkins Report,
was rather more critical in its conclusions. Its general position
was that there was a danger that Canada "might drift into
such a position of dependency that it will be unable, in practice, to adopt policies displeasing to the United States because
of the fear of American reaction which would involve consequences unacceptable to Canadians";[23] and they broadened
the concern to encompass political, military, economic, and
cultural independence. To support this wider perception of the
threat of American ownership, the committee discussed the
undesirable effects of the subordination of Canadian trade
unions to American-based "internationals," the U.S. presence
in Canadian communications and "culture industries," and
endorsed all of the Watkins Report's reservations about the
effects of foreign ownership on economic efficiency and performance. Their recommendations were a series of steps they
felt would reassert Canadian control over these institutions
and sectors of society. The provincial and federal governments
were specifically asked to become more involved and interventionist in determining and asserting the Canadian interest.

Finally, in 1970 the government of Canada published

Foreign Direct Investment in Canada, the so-called Gray Report.[24] Here for the first time was a mass of data and economic analysis devoted to an examination of the issue, in the context of Canada, leading to a specific policy prescription. We shall consider this policy in the next section, but the analysis is pertinent here. The Gray Report confirmed the existence of the inefficiencies suggested by the earlier reports. The "miniature branch plant replica" effect refers to the duplication in Canada of the industrial organization of the United States— each U.S. firm in an industry gets a share of the Canadian market, with the result being too many small-scale, high-cost, inefficient plants for the smaller Canadian economy. U.S. antitrust law makes mergers and coordination of the operations of these branches difficult. The report also noted the low level of processing of raw materials in Canada and the frequent transfer of that processing, and the industrial jobs that go with it, abroad. Two other serious problems derived from foreign ownership: "the stultification of domestic capacities and the possibility of unbalanced development of the resource sector"—in short, pressures that lead Canada to be, to use the well-worn phrase, a "hewer of wood and drawer of water" for the industrial economy of the United States.

The basic point of all three reports is that foreign ownership, on the scale found in Canada, does cause significant problems—economic inefficiencies and a broader political and cultural dependency—and that positive policy measures are required to counter these effects.

When we examine the structure of production—that is, what Canadians produce—it is most interesting to look at the trend in industrial employment since World War II. This gives us a clue as to what Canada is becoming. From the data in Table 4.5 it is clear that since 1946 jobs have been undergoing a shift from agriculture and manufacturing to trade and service. This is a common phenomenon that has occurred in all developed economies. As incomes rise, people spend a greater proportion of their incomes on having things done for them rather than on purchases of more material goods; as agricultural technology advances, fewer people are needed to produce a given quantity of good.

Understanding Canada

Table 4.5 Employment by Industry

	1946	1960	1976
Agriculture	29.6	11.3	4.9
Other Primary Goods	3.0	3.1	2.5
Manufacturing	26.2	24.9	20.3
Construction	5.0	7.2	6.7
Trade	12.0	16.2	17.3
Transportation, Communication, and Utilities	7.8	8.6	8.7
Finance, Insurance, and Real Estate	2.6	3.8	5.2
Service and Public Administration	16.4	25.0	34.3

SOURCES: *Canada Year Book, 1978–79,* and M. C. Urquhart and K. A. H. Buckley *Historical Statistics of Canada* (Toronto, Macmillan, 1965).

We get an insight into some of Canada's regional differences from Tables 4.6 and 4.7 that present data for only the goods-producing industries (i.e., we exclude services). In Table 4.6 the data show, for each province, the distribution of goods produced by each of seven industries. Of goods produced in, for example, Newfoundland, 29 percent are in the mining industry, 22 percent in manufacturing, and so on. A somewhat different look at the same data, in Table 4.7, tells us that of Canada's agricultural output 54 percent is generated in the Prairies, 3 percent in the Atlantic Provinces, and so forth.

Tables 4.5–4.7 facilitate some interesting observations. The employment figures show that agriculture has been in decline throughout the post–World War II period. From Table

Table 4.6 "Value Added" in Goods-Producing Industries, 1975

	Ag.	Forestry	Fish.	Mining	Elec. Power	Manuf.	Const.
Newfld.	—	4	4	29	12	22	30
PEI	29	—	8	—	5	25	34
N. Scotia	4	1	6	6	6	50	28
N. Bwck	4	5	2	6	6	46	32
Quebec	5	2	—	4	5	64	21
Ontario	6	1	—	5	3	71	15
Manitoba	25	1	—	8	6	43	17
Saskatch.	51	—	—	20	2	12	14
Alberta	13	—	—	50	2	15	19
Br. Col.	4	7	1	11	4	49	25
Canada	9	2	1	13	4	53	19 = 100

SOURCE: *Canada Year Book, 1978–79.*

Table 4.7 Regional Distribution of Production, by Industry 1975

Region	Ag.	Forestry	Fish.	Mining	Manuf.	Const.
Atlantic	3	10	56	6	4	8
Quebec	13	20	5	11	27	22
Ontario	26	14	3	20	54	36
Prairies	54	4	2	53	6	19
Br. Columbia	4	52	34	10	9	14
	100	100	100	100	100	100

SOURCE: Economic Council of Canada, *Living Together: A Study of Regional Disparities* (Ottawa, Economic Council of Canada, 1977).

4.6 we note that Prince Edward Island, Manitoba, and Saskatchewan are essentially agricultural provinces. It should not surprise us then that during these years these provinces have been losing population to provinces that produce other goods. We can observe the heavy concentration of manufacturing in Quebec and Ontario, the only provinces in which manufacturing accounts for a greater percentage of goods produced than the Canadian average (53 percent). This concentration of manufacturing has, of course, given rise to much criticism (in other regions) of the policies of the federal government. As a final point, we should mention the continued importance of staples or raw materials in defining the provincial or regional economies: more than 50 percent of Canada's agriculture is done in the western grain belt, British Columbia accounts for over half of forestry output, as do the Atlantic Provinces for fish and Alberta and Saskatchewan for mining (including petroleum).

An additional factor in the determination of the structure of Canada's production has been the opportunities made available through international trade. (Between 1960 and 1978 exports rose from 18.3 to 26.7 percent of goods and services produced in Canada; thus, this factor has become increasingly important.) As producers have met the demands of foreign markets, certain industries have been stimulated, and those which have not been able to take advantage of this growing demand have found it less and less possible to grow. The structure or composition of exports has therefore had a direct impact on the structure of domestic production and the employment options open to Canadians.

Table 4.8 Exports and Imports, by Degree of Processing

	1963		1969		1978	
	Imports	Exports	Imports	Exports	Imports	Exports
Food	21.5	11.9	10.7	7.8	11.0	7.7
Raw Materials	27.7	13.9	25.4	8.6	21.1	13.1
Semi-manufactures	39.1	23.9	30.2	20.9	33.5	16.5
Manufactures: ex. trans.	10.5	40.1	12.2	36.9	8.2	36.5
Transportation goods	1.3	10.2	21.5	25.7	26.2	26.1
	100.0	100.0	100.0	100.0	100.0	100.0

SOURCE: Department of Finance, *Annual Review* (April 1979), p. 207.

Table 4.8 gives us the breakdown of exports and imports during the past fifteen years, and the trends that are indicated here tell a story that has characterized Canada's trade experience since World War II. Many economists perceive the Canadian manufacturing sector to be underdeveloped, and it is clear that trade relations have only worked to exacerbate this situation. Canada continues to specialize in the exporting of food, raw materials, and semimanufactured goods, and in the importing of manufactured items. We have made a separate entry for transportation equipment because of the enactment in 1965 of the Canada-U.S. Auto Pact, which created a free trade area between the two countries for automotive goods. The effect of the Auto Pact shows clearly (in the 1969 data) that by far the major component of Canada's manufactured exports is the result of a continental specialization in automobile production. Other manufactured goods are actually a smaller share of total exports in 1978 than in either of the two earlier years. This suggests an inability of Canadian manufacturing to compete in international markets, and it is in conformity with the tariff and foreign ownership concerns noted earlier.

Canada and the International Economy

In this last substantive section we shall examine Canada's relationship to the international economy and some of the pressing policy questions that come out of this relationship. We are concerned here with issues that arise from the movement of goods across a national boundary. We have already given some background to two of these issues, and the third is very much in the news media today.

We have seen how international trade and foreign capital affect the performance and character of the Canadian economy; the policy issue here is whether existing controls ought to be released or tightened further. One group argues that only freer trade and fewer restrictions on capital will revitalize Canadian industry. This is the standard "liberal" position in favor of the free market as a solution to virtually any economic problem. Another group (the "political economists" in our earlier terminology) believes that a more activist leadership by the state is required and concludes that the "liberal" solution leads to dependency and less attractive options for Canadians. Although a similar philosophical split occurred when foreign investment was discussed in the early 1970s, a new policy is now in place—the Foreign Investment Review Act—so we shall confine our comments to the operation of this act. The third issue is energy policy and the continental sharing of resources. The question here is whether Canada has energy to export to the United States, and if so whether those resources should in fact be exported or used domestically.

Once again, the context for this discussion of policy is a manufacturing sector that is perceived by many to be stunted in development and inefficient in performance. Producing behind a tariff wall, with many factories owned and/or controlled by foreign investors, individual plants tend to be smaller than optimal in size, turning out high-cost goods that cannot compete internationally. This means lower incomes for Canadians, a limited decision-making possibility, and a concentration of manufacturing in central Canada that contributes to regional stresses.

The argument in favor of free trade is a simple one to state. It was initially advanced in the late eighteenth century as a reaction to intervention by the government in the operation of the economy. Since this intervention was usually for military or political reasons, the consequence was inevitably economic inefficiency and citizens were obliged to accept lower incomes. Free traders argued that if the state would allow individuals to manage the economy in an environment of free competition, we would all be better off. Consumers would determine with their buying power which goods ought to be produced, producers would choose the most profitable technology and product, and the economy would be operated most efficiently—people would have maximum incomes, lowest prices, and the specific goods they wanted. When we extend this argument to the world economy, each nation should leave itself completely open to worldwide demands for goods, and supplies of resources and technology. Each nation will then find it is most capable of producing some of the goods it consumes and will export some of those goods "in trade" for the ones it does not produce. That is, each nation will specialize in producing those goods in which it has a "comparative advantage." If each producer is doing that task for which he is best suited, the output and incomes of the entire world will be maximized, and governments need only work to guarantee that monopoly power does not develop that could allow some individual class or nation to appropriate a larger share than it ought to get . Any intervention in this competitive, market world economy will cause output and incomes to fall; hence, there is a general argument against the state's presence in economic affairs.

The free trade prescription for Canada today suggests generally that the most beneficial option would be multilateral free trade through the General Agreement for Tariffs and Trade (GATT); failing that, bilateral free trade with the United States. In either case, with free trade Canada would specialize in producing and exporting only a few goods, produce many goods for the home market only, and import the others from countries that could produce them at lowest cost. As an example, Canadians today pay rather high prices for wine because of a tariff that is used to protect the domestic wine industry. The domestic wine is thought by most people to be inferior to the imported wines. With free trade, the Canadian wine industry might disappear, and vineyards could be converted to the growing of peaches and apples. As a result, Canadians would have lower prices for better wine, and lower prices and greater quantities of top-quality peaches and apples. The only people injured would be the Canadian wine producers. Free traders feel that protective tariffs merely tax all consumers to give a benefit to a small segment of society.

In a free trade economy the surviving manufacturing industries would be characterized by larger plants having open access to a greatly expanded market. They would be able to take advantage of all the economies of large-scale production; thus, costs and prices would be lower and incomes would be higher. But would Canada specialize in manufacturing at all? Or would the entire manufacturing sector succumb to foreign competition and Canada become even more than now an exporter of food, raw materials, and semimanufactured goods? (There would, of course, still be manufacturing of goods that were not traded internationally.) This is one question that has been widely studied, and there are two conflicting answers. The free trade position has been most convincingly presented in a number of articles by R. J. Wonnacott. One of the most convincing counterarguments has been given by a geographer, John H. Britton.

Wonnacott's 1967 study,[25] using 1958 data, showed that manufacturing costs in Canada's industrial belt, from Windsor, Ontario, to Montreal, were lower in five of seven major industries than were costs in all U.S. regions. This suggested to him that with free trade, when industry began to rationalize its production on a continental basis, much manufacturing would choose to locate in Canada. In a 1975 study for the Economic Council of Canada he repeated this conclusion, but softened it somewhat by stating "that the free trade prospects for Ontario and Quebec are better than the prospects of the U.S. regions outside the great industrial triangle (Chicago-Washington-Boston). They may be better or worse than the prospects of the U.S. regions within the triangle."[26] Even with this weaker statement Wonnacott felt he could conclude that Canadian incomes would rise by between 10 and 15 percent following the enactment of Canada-U.S. free trade.

Britton argued that this conclusion was questionable on

at least two grounds.[27] First, Canadian costs had increased considerably since 1958, and it was doubtful that it would now make economic sense to manufacture in Canada when the Canadian market could be reached from a plant in the United States. Data from a recent Department of Finance report support this contention, showing that between 1969 and 1976 Canada's competitiveness in manufacturing had deteriorated by 23 percent. Thus, this part of the free trade argument cannot be accepted without further study. In addition, Britton noted that the industrial belt in the U.S. Northeast has been steadily losing ground to competition from the South and Southwest—the Sun Belt. Even if Windsor-Montreal had some advantages vis-à-vis declining Cleveland and Pittsburgh, could the same be said with regard to the rapidly growing, largely nonunion industry of Georgia and Texas? Could it not be that under free trade Canada's future might take on the complexion of West Virginia or upstate New York, both low-cost yet economically depressed areas close to the market? What likelihood is there that Windsor could compete with Atlanta or Dallas?

As a final reservation to a policy of free trade, we could add the uncertainty about the duration of any political argument. How long would both governments continue to adhere to free trade? This uncertainty alone would be enough to cause some industries to concentrate their production in the United States and export to Canada. Should this occur, Canada would have to pay for these manufactured imports with whatever was marketable—probably food and raw materials. Thus, the result of free trade could well be that Canada would be trapped in the old staple economy of the nineteenth century, increasingly dependent on the United States.

What is the alternative?[28] Certainly, few economists would argue that a high tariff is a sensible policy for Canada. Perhaps the state should have considerable power to intervene in the economy, but contrary to the eighteenth-century mercantilist approach this intervention should be carried out with economic rather than military or political objectives in mind. Implicit in this argument are the notions: (1) that free trade may leave Canada with a smaller manufacturing sector; and

(2) that Canadians have a strong preference for an industrialized rather than a staples-oriented economy. In a free trade economy market forces reflecting the underlying conditions of supply and demand direct the flow of resources from one sector to another; with the interventionist alternative the state would provide that guidance with the advantage being that the pace and extent of adjustment could be controlled. For example, Canada's textile industry is heavily protected, and some segments of it are obviously inefficient and inappropriate for Canada, whereas others are, or are capable of becoming, able to meet competition in world markets. The state would provide capital and consultants to the strong areas to get them to reorganize into large economically efficient units and to adopt the latest technology. Thus, parts of this industry would be systematically phased out, while other parts would be reorganized. With a free trade pact it would be difficult to get a comprehensive set of government interventions accepted by the trading partners, since these measures are often seen as subsidies and unfair practices.

The last aspect of trade policy we should mention is the overwhelming share of Canada's trade that is done with the United States. The Trudeau government became concerned that Canada was too reliant on one market and in 1972 launched, with much publicity, the "Third Option"[29]—this being essentially a rejection of autarky and closer ties with the United States in favor of reaching out to Europe and Japan. The data in Table 4.9 indicate that Canada is indeed tied to the U.S. market. Some other things to note:

- about two thirds of Canada's exports of finished goods consist of automotive shipments to the United States and its general weakness in competing in manufactured goods markets even extends to "other countries";
- the emphasis on exports of food, raw materials, and semimanufactured goods and imports of manufactures is as characteristic of Canada's trade with the EEC as it is with the United States;
- the reliance on the U.S. market is as strong today as it was when the Third Option was pressed.

Table 4.9 Canadian Trade Data, 1967–77 Combined

	Imports			
	Total	*U.S.*	*EEC*	*Other*
Food	6179 (7.7)	3255 (5.9)	708 (10.4)	2216 (12.7)
Raw Materials	10397 (13.0)	3197 (5.8)	185 (2.7)	7015 (40.2)
Semi-manufactured	13228 (16.6)	9385 (17.0)	1648 (24.1)	2195 (12.6)
Manufactured (excl. Transp.)	23755 (36.3)	17017 (30.6)	3142 (46.1)	3596 (20.6)
Transport goods	25076 (26.0)	21833 (39.3)	995 (14.6)	2248 (12.9)
	79535	55289	6818	17428
Per cent of total	100.0	69.5	8.6	21.9

	Exports			
	Total	*U.S.*	*EEC*	*Other*
Food	8794 (10.8)	2300 (4.1)	1766 (19.3)	4728 (28.6)
Raw Materials	17105 (21.0)	10792 (19.4)	2359 (25.8)	3954 (23.9)
Semi-manufactured	27075 (33.3)	19231 (34.6)	3997 (43.8)	3850 (23.3)
Manufactured (excl. Transp.)	6535 (8.0)	4266 (7.7)	631 (6.9)	1638 (9.9)
Transport goods	20950 (25.8)	18587 (33.5)	361 (3.9)	2002 (12.1)
	80957	55320	9126	16511
Percent of total	100.0	68.3	11.3	20.4

SOURCE: *Canada Year Book, 1978–79.*
Note: the figures in parentheses are the percentage breakdown of goods traded by degree of processing.

Part of the reason for the failure of the Third Option is in the competitive weakness of Canadian manufacturers, but it should also be noted that Europe and Japan are much more aggressive than are North Americans in restricting their imports to primary and semimanufactured goods and keeping the home market for their own producers. By now most observers would agree that the Third Option has little future and that Canada must either resign itself to being pretty much confined to the North American market or to mounting a massive campaign to restructure and revitalize domestic manufacturing.

We have already discussed the problems Canada faces as a result of its high degree of foreign ownership, and have noted that the policy response to this situation was the Foreign Investment Review Act of 1974. This act established an office, the Foreign Investment Review Agency (FIRA), to evaluate the benefit to Canada of any new direct investments. An investment proposal would be approved if it could be shown that this investment would create new jobs and/or exports for Canada, reduce imports, bring to Canada new technology, and so forth. Thus, the central thrust of the FIRA is not that of limiting foreign investment but rather of assuring that Canadians are demonstrably better off as a result of the additions to foreign capital in Canada. This has made the FIRA acceptable to the business community, since it does not really present a threat to either domestic or foreign investors. About 10 percent of the petitions coming before the FIRA have been rejected; others have been withdrawn, presumably because the petitioners perceived that a refusal was likely.

The primary difficulty with any foreign investment policy for Canada is that so much of Canadian industry is already owned or controlled by foreigners. With almost 60 percent of manufacturing in foreign hands, only a very radical departure from current practice can have anything more than a very marginal impact. The most convinced critics of foreign ownership have suggested other strategies. One would be to declare certain industries or sectors of the economy to be "key" and to require majority Canadian control of any enterprise producing those goods. Another would entail the Canadian government's buying back (or nationalizing) the resource sectors, forestry, mining, and so forth. The government could then be in a position to mandate that those resources be processed in Canada to a greater degree than is now the case, and the historical pattern of staples exporting could be broken. The difficulty with these proposals lies in the vast amounts of capital which "Canadianization" would require. If foreign assets were to be repurchased, it would so completely drain Canadian capital markets that funds for other investments would be impossible to find. The unavoidable conclusion seems to be that Canada was too late in implementing controls on foreign ownership and may simply have to live with its consequences.

Finally, for the critics the essential point is that even if some jobs, technology, and exports are gained, the decision-making capability and responsibility has shifted out of the country to the home offices of the multinational corporations who own Canada's branch-plant economy. Without control over decision making, no society can avoid existing in a condition of dependency.

Most Americans have the impression that Canada is a vast storehouse of resources, the owners eager to sell to the highest bidder. This is very understandable because it is only since the early 1970s that this has not been the case. As late as the 1960s Canada was interested in getting the United States to purchase vast quantities of oil and gas. The actions of OPEC, of course, changed all of this, but there has also been among Canadians a gradually rising concern that their resources ought to provide a basis for manufacturing in Canada rather than elsewhere. Although this concern extends to almost all resources—nonferrous minerals, potash, asbestos, timber, and so on—it is oil and gas that have received the most publicity and that seem to give the most possibility for government policy.

As recently as 1973 Canadians were told they had enough oil and gas to last well into the next century. Now, although natural gas reserves do seem to be sufficiently large to allow exports to the United States, Canada is a net importer of crude oil, and it will increasingly be so for the near future. Canadians continue to be the world's heaviest per capita users of energy, and the "energy crisis" is finally being felt in Canada, albeit not as powerfully as it is in the United States. Several years ago one U.S. oilman was quoted as saying that he liked to invest in wells in Alberta because he did not want to become dependent on "foreign" supplies. It has come as a surprise and a shock to Americans that we can no longer consider Canadian reserves as extensions of our own—as a backup reservoir.

Canada actually does have an abundance of petroleum and natural gas, but much of it is very expensive to get to market. There are major reserves in the Far North, in the Beaufort Sea, and the Arctic islands, but their exploitation requires pipelines that would literally be sink holes for scarce capital—upward of $5 billion each. Other reserves are off the

Atlantic Coast and require relatively expensive drilling procedures. A third known and rather vast reserve is the tar sands of Alberta; but here, too, exploitation is both technologically difficult and financially very costly. A final consideration that must be taken into account when discussing supply, especially with regard to the reserves of the Far North, is the ecological damage that will be done, not only to the physical environment, but also to the lives of the native peoples who now have a viable, functioning economy and society that is based on traditional culture and ways of living. The conclusion of Mr. Justice Thomas Berger, who was appointed to study the impacts of a pipeline to the Beaufort Sea, was that a moratorium of ten years ought to be placed on this sort of intrusion by the "Southern economy" into the Far North.[30] For the next decade or so Canadians will experience some of the same difficulties with regard to petroleum as the rest of us.

Given the pressure of demand against available supplies of oil and gas, Canadians must decide how they should plan to use these scarce goods, and whether to sell the raw materials for what they can get in world markets or to insist they be processed into finished goods first. There is yet another issue that must be taken into account—that of the impact of resource policy on the exchange rate for the Canadian dollar. When Canada exports oil and gas, or other raw materials, the purchasers have to buy Canadian dollars to make payment. This increased demand forces up the value of the Canadian currency, increases the prices to foreigners of all Canadian goods, and lowers the prices of imports to Canada. Thus, a policy of allowing increased raw material exports has the effect of lowering foreign and domestic demand for Canadian manufactured goods. In the short run Canada gets revenues that allow Canadians to have more imported manufactured goods, but in the long run it makes them even more dependent on foreign producers, increases pressure for high tariffs to protect the remaining Canadian manufacturers, and probably lowers incomes.

Although one must be rather pessimistic about the ability of Canadians to do much about the basic nature of their trade and investment situations, there is considerably more room for maneuver regarding energy policy. The federal government, through the National Energy Board, must now sanction every contract to export oil and/or gas. Policy must usually content itself with operating at the margin and, although existing contracts do make claims on future supplies, new supplies continue to be discovered. If Canada wishes to reserve those supplies for processing and use at home, this can be a significant policy decision. Another encouraging factor is the existence of Petro-Canada, the Crown corporation operating in oil and gas exploration and development. With this corporation Canada is in a much better position than the United States to get a firsthand understanding of the technology and economics of the industry, without the intercession of the major private petroleum companies, and has an instrument for assuring some control over supplies and prices of crude oil. Topping this is the fact that Canadians seem today to be more aware of the alternative futures and the policies needed to get to them than was the case in the past.

Conclusions: Current Problems of Economic Policy

Throughout, we have tried to focus on those aspects of Canada's economy that would be of most interest to American readers, on policy areas that are most likely to have an impact on our own economy. As was stated at the beginning of this chapter, the choices available to a society today are in large part defined by what has happened in the preceding decades and even centuries. The staples model provides us with an alternative to the more balanced American experience with economic development, yet it still gives a perspective that yields valuable insights into present-day Canada. In spite of the development of manufacturing and the service sector, raw materials remain vital to Canadian economic activity today. Worldwide resource and energy shortages of increasing intensity promise to make staples even more important in the

future. The struggle for autonomy has been refined conceptually in recent years to give recognition to the less obvious
cultural and economic threats to national sovereignty. Study
of this dimension of the Canada-U.S. relationship should give
Americans a better understanding of the position of the
United States in the community of nations and an awareness
of the subtler international impacts of actions the United
States undertakes. The evolving interplay between an economically active central government, on the one hand, and
strong regional identities and provincial political powers, on
the other, makes the Canadian Confederation both distinctive
and fascinating to study. Americans are aware of the international economy only occasionally and when circumstances
force us to take notice. As a contrast, the interaction between
the international economic environment and the structure
and performance of Canada's domestic economic activity is
both strikingly direct and of increasing importance. This interaction is, however, also of growing importance to the
United States as trade and capital movements become freer
over time; although we will never experience Canada's multifaceted exposure to the world economy, we can learn much
from that experience.

Probably the most widely discussed policy issue for the
next few years will be Canada's uneasy relationship with the
United States, but curiously enough there is not likely to be
much change in this area. We have already noted that the
FIRA was established after the fact; and that unless a *radical*
change were to occur in the federal government there is not
much likelihood that the extent of foreign ownership will be
significantly reduced. Canada is already so closely integrated
into the U.S. market that trade with Europe and Japan would
have to at least double before that relationship could be altered much. The reluctance of these other countries to reduce
quotas and other "nontariff barriers" makes it unlikely that
Canada will increase its exports abroad of anything but scarce
raw materials. Nonetheless, the Canada-U.S. tariff issue is
being hotly debated. In 1979, while the newly elected Conservative Finance Minister, John Crosbie, was suggesting
that Canada ought to have another look at free trade with the

United States, Gérard Pelletier, Canada's ambassador to France, was detailing for a meeting of French economists the dangers (for Canada) of close relations with the Americans.[31] The recently concluded Tokyo Round of GATT negotiations seems, if anything, to have drawn Canada closer to the U.S. market. But with three fourths of Canadian-American trade already duty free and with 70 percent of Canada's trade taking place with the United States, there really is not much room for maneuver in tariffs; and, as we suggested, energy and resource use are more likely to be areas in which the important decisions could be made.

The energy policy announced by President Carter in July 1979 included increased use of Canadian natural gas, a pipeline to carry Alaskan gas through Canada to U.S. markets, and stepped-up development of coal gasification and oil from tar sands and oil-bearing shale. Canada will have to be aware of the effect of major capital-intensive projects on the value of the Canadian dollar, and hence on the international competitiveness of Canadian manufactures and the future availability of hydrocarbons for industrial use. This presents an opportunity for Canada to bargain this cooperation for increased exports of manufactured goods, access to technology, and whatever else they might wish. This could be done in conjunction with the "industrial policy" that has been debated so much in recent years—federal government policy initiatives aimed at strengthening the manufacturing sector and reversing the historical dependence on raw materials exports.

Natural resources in Canada are, as we noted earlier, under the jurisdiction of the provincial governments; thus, if the federal government is to bargain effectively with the United States, continued accommodation with the interests and demands of the regions will have to be made. The future status of Quebec is certainly a question of primary importance, but Alberta, Newfoundland, Saskatchewan, and British Columbia have also articulated positions that require major policy responses from Ottawa. Indeed, virtually all of Canada's provinces continue to demand a greater role in the making of policy decisions that most powerfully impinge upon their interests, and to call for a more even distribution of manufacturing and incomes. The ongoing federal-provincial debate has always been characterized by the notion that "the squeaky wheel gets the grease," and it will continue to be a challenge to Ottawa to make necessary concessions to the regions without in the process reducing its own ability to bargain for the interests of Canada as a whole.

Questions of economic policy ultimately depend on the capability of the central government to provide the leadership that is required by an economy such as Canada's. We have seen how an industrial, national economy was created in the face of very significant geographical obstacles. This was accomplished because the state supported and subsidized the development of a nationwide transportation network and an industrial economy. If there is one challenge today that stands out from the others it would be that of gaining control of the pace and direction of this economy. For this to be done the state will once again be required to articulate a vision of what can be achieved, specify what policies this vision requires, and demonstrate the leadership ability to implement those policies.

Notes

1. Mel Watkins discusses this in his "The Dismal State of Economics in Canada," in Ian Lumsden, ed., *Close the 49th parallel, etc.* (Toronto: University of Toronto Press, 1970), pp. 197–208.

2. For the economics of the various staples, see part I of W. T. Easterbrook and M. H. Watkins, *Approaches to Canadian Economic History* (Toronto: McClelland and Stewart, 1967), pp. 1–98. Mel Watkins's article, "A Staple Theory of Economic Growth," pp. 74–98 in this book, examines the theory itself.

3. Any principles of economics or international economics textbook will give an adequate discussion of comparative advantage and international trade. One such source is Tom Riddell, Steve Stamos, and Jean Shakelford, *Economics: As if People Mattered* (New York: Addison-Wesley, 1979).

4. See, for example, Pierre L. Bourgault, *Innovation and the Structure of Canadian Industry* (Ottawa: Government of Canada, 1972), Science Council of Canada, Special Study No. 23, chap. 6; and A. E. Safarian, *The Performance of Foreign-owned Firms in Canada* (Montreal: Private Planning of Canada, 1969), chap. 2.

5. Robert E. Ankli, "The Reciprocity Treaty of 1854," *Canadian Journal of Economics* (February 1971), pp. 1–20.

6. Malcolm Ross, ed., *Poets of the Confederation* (Toronto: McClelland and Stewart, 1960), p. x.

7. A fascinating account of this whole period can be found in Donald Creighton's two-volume biography, *John A. Macdonald* (Toronto: Macmillan, 1952–55).

8. The Canadian tariff and its effects are studied in: Economic Council of Canada, *Looking Outward* (Ottawa: Government of Canada, 1975), esp. chapts. 2, 3, and 6.

9. Peter Karl Kresl, "Before the Deluge: Canadians on Foreign Investment, 1920–55," *American Review of Canadian Studies* (Spring 1976), pp. 86–125.

10. John A. Fayerweather, "Nationalism or Continentalism? Canadians React to U.S. Investment," *Challenge* (September–October 1973), p. 42.

11. More extensive discussion of the terms "liberal," "conservative" and "nationalist," as used in this chapter, is found in Peter Karl Kresl, "The 'New Nationalism' and Economic Rationality," *American Review of Canadian Studies* (Spring 1974), pp. 2–19.

12. *Canada Gazette* (1948), p. 400.

13. Royal Commission on Canada's Economic Prospects, *Preliminary Report* (Ottawa: Government of Canada, 1956).

14. Privy Council, *Foreign Direct Investment in Canada* (Ottawa: Government of Canada, 1972), p. 21.

15. A brief summary of this relationship is given in Ed Shaffer, "Oil and Class in Alberta," *Canadian Dimension* (June 1979), pp. 42–45.

16. René Lévesque has stated this position clearly in "For an Independent Quebec," *Foreign Affairs* (July 1976), pp. 734–744.

17. See, for example, *Report of the Royal Commission on Bilingualism and Biculturalism,* book III, *The World of Work* (Ottawa: Government of Canada, 1969).

18. Louis Hartz, *The Founding of New Societies* (New York: Harcourt, Brace and World, 1964).

19. For a "heroic" account of this see Pierre Berton, *The National Dream* (Toronto: McClelland and Stewart, 1970).

20. The development of Canada's private sector is examined in a very readable book by R. T. Naylor, *The History of Canadian Business, 1867–1914* (Toronto: James Lorimer, 1975). See also the Drache, Bliss, and Gonick articles in Ian Lumsden, ed., *Close the 49th parallel, etc.* (Toronto: University of Toronto Press, 1970), pp. 3–73.

21. This and other aspects of tariffs are discussed in R. J. Wonnacott, *Canada's Trade Options* (Ottawa: Government of Canada, 1975), chap. 2.

22. Task Force on Foreign Ownership, *The Structure of Foreign Ownership in Canada* (Ottawa: Government of Canada, 1968).

23. House of Commons, *Canada-U.S. Relations* (Ottawa: Government of Canada, 1970), p. 33.

24. Privy Council, *Foreign Direct Investment in Canada* (Ottawa: Government of Canada, 1972).

25. R. J. and Paul Wonnacott, *U.S.-Canadian Free Trade: The Potential Impact of Free Trade on the Canadian Economy* (Washington: National Planning Association, 1968).

26. R. J. Wonnacott, *Canada's Trade Options* (Ottawa: Government of Canada, 1975), p. 207.

27. John N. H. Britton, "Locational Perspectives on Free Trade," *Canadian Public Policy* (Winter 1977), pp. 4–19.

28. The options are discussed in a special "An Industrial Strategy for Canada" issue of *Canadian Forum* (January–February 1972).

29. Mitchell Sharp, "Canada-U.S. Relations: Options for the Future," *International Perspectives* (Autumn 1972), pp. 1–24.

30. Justice Thomas R. Berger, *Northern Frontier/Northern Homeland: The Report of the Mackenzie Valley Pipeline Inquiry* (Ottawa: Government of Canada, 1977), vol. 1, pp. vii–xxvii.

31. Minister of Finance John Crosbie's remarks were made at a press conference at the Economic Summit in Tokyo and were reported in the *Ottawa Citizen,* June 29, 1979. Ambassador Gérard Pelletier's speech was to a meeting of French economists in Paris, June 12, 1979, and is available from the Department of External Affairs, Public Relations Office, in Ottawa.

Chapter 5

An Anthropological Perspective:

The Ingredients of a

Multicultural Society

PETER WOOLFSON*

Introduction

MANY ANTHROPOLOGISTS HOLD that culture is the key concept in anthropology. The cultural perspective is one that focuses on the blueprints of human behavior; that looks for networks of human interaction and shared traditions.

Although anthropology as a discipline has many areas of research, this chapter focuses on ethnographic descriptions of some of the groups that make up Canadian society. The primary thrust of these descriptions is persistence and change: To what extent are traditions associated with a group being maintained, and to what extent are they being lost or changed?

* Peter Woolfson is Associate Professor of Anthropology at the University of Vermont. He received his B.A. and M.A. (in English) from the University of Toronto, and his Ph.D. in anthropology at the State University of New York at Buffalo. A member of Vermont's Canadian Studies Program, he has previously taught at SUNY/Buffalo and Wayne State University, and has been a visiting researcher at the International Center for Research in Bilingualism at Laval University. His principal research is on rural French-Canadian society in Quebec and Vermont, and he has published articles in the *American Review of Canadian Studies*, the *Louisiana Review*, *Franco-American Overview*, and *Vermont History*.

Is there such a thing as "Canadian anthropology"? Louise Sweet, in an article in the *American Anthropologist*, writes:

Canada is at once a past and present victim of a sequence of imperialism: feudal French, mercantile British, and now a capitalist American, last and most destructively of all. . . . More than 60% of academic anthropology positions (in Canada) are held by foreigners, mostly Americans. . . . Canada is a colony in the American neocolonial empire, the closest one, the most affluent one, and the one least able to break the bonds of dependency. Thus the concern of the Canadian academics (and Americans in Canada) particularly in the social sciences, is understandable. There are many aspects of concern: one is that the very content of the Canadian social science curriculum is less about Canada than about the United States. . . . Negler's *Natives Without a Home* uses without a flick of hesitation the 'culture of poverty' myth transposed from American to Canadian cities uncritically.[1]

This statement, to be sure, represents an extreme position, but it clearly expresses one of the concerns Canadians have about social science done in Canada. The 40 percent of Canadian anthropologists actually born in Canada could also be said to have been "tainted" by "American neocolonialism." A large number of them have at least one degree from an American university. They belong to American anthropological associations, and they subscribe to those American journals that are at the hub of current interests and research. They submit articles to these same prestige-conferring journals that reach large audiences. All this suggests that anthropologists working in Canada are very much influenced by what happens in the United States.

The last decade, however, has seen a burgeoning of studies of Canadian immigrant and ethnic minorities. At the same time, Canadian governments, federal and provincial, have been very supportive of social science research. Royal Commissions, such as the famous Royal Commission on Bilingualism and Biculturalism in Canada (1963–67), have commissioned important studies pertinent to their concerns. A Ministry of State for Multiculturalism was established in

1971—its mandate includes the encouragement of research on native and ethnic cultures.

Canadian anthropologists, however, have been reluctant to do studies of modern groups. Louise Sweet writes:

> Canada, under the bland courtesy that prevails in public places, has scarcely been accounted for . . . much less deeply analyzed, particularly by anthropologists who, with a few conspicuous exceptions, have until recently seemed to regard salvage ethnology [the study of what is left of native cultures] among the Inuit and Native Peoples as the only true field for anthropological research.[2]

The study of small, homogeneous Indian and Eskimo groups has been the major concern of anthropologists in North America throughout much of anthropology's development as a legitimate field of study. Anthropologists considered Indian and Eskimo communities as natural laboratories in which the diversity of human experience can be explored. Consequently, although the native peoples of Canada represent only about 1.2 percent of the total population, anthropologists have considered them to be a major area for research. For this reason the discussion of the native peoples has a prominent place in this chapter.

Increasingly, anthropologists are applying the cultural perspective honed in the description and analysis of small homogeneous societies to that of factories or ethnic enclaves: that is, anthropologists are no longer limiting their efforts to the study of remote and exotic "simple" societies. Anthropologists also pursue the study of other aspects of Canada's social fabric, as well as many sociological studies of ethnic and native groups. These studies will also be discussed in this chapter.

Canada became a nation in 1867. Recently, there has been tremendous concern with whether that nation will continue to exist. An anthropological-cum-sociological perspective on the history and present state of the peoples of Canada can shed some light on Canada's crisis of unity.

The conflicts between the two founding peoples of Canada

have come to a head with the election of the Parti Québécois in Quebec. Together, those of British descent (44.6 percent) and of French descent (28.7 percent) make up nearly three quarters of the population of Canada. The challenge that the conflict between the two major ethnic groups in Canada presents is one those in favor of Canadian national unity are only now beginning to face squarely.

Another challenge to Canadian unity comes from regional interests. Most Canadians orient themselves toward the natural geographical axis of the land—from north to south. Because of both geological and climatic limitations, the majority of Canadians live within a hundred miles of the American border. Travel across the border for many Canadians is both easy and profitable. In the first half of this century, thousands of French Canadians left their rural homes for jobs in the mill towns of New England. The Maritimes have always had a natural working relationship with Boston.

Some of the reasons for Canadian Confederation were the result of negative feelings about the United States. Mildred Schwartz writes:

> Prior to Confederation, the United States represented a special bogey, the victim of its own defective federal union, angry with Britain for its sympathies with the southern states, and possessed of a large and threatening army. After introducing the Quebec Resolutions to the Legislative Council, Premier Taché warned, that without Confederation, 'we would be forced into the American Union by violence, and if not by violence, would be placed on an inclined plain [sic] which would carry us there insensibly.'[3]

Behind much of the urgency for Confederation was the fear of being swallowed up by a potentially militant United States. Such a motivation produced problems of national unity and national identity. Schwartz writes:

> Unity might be achieved where there is virtual absence of those historical cleavages that have regularly been associated with sharp and even violent conflicts. This is obviously not descriptive of Canada at its birth. Confederation was proposed

just because of such cleavages, and the economic stagnation and political deadlocks they produced. Agricultural versus manufacturing interests . . . Catholics versus Protestants, the Maritimes against the Province of Canada (now Ontario and Quebec)—What more could one ask for as a scenario for conflict? Initial unity did not lie in the population make-up, nor could it be expected to emerge from that composition.[4]

Canadians have been obsessed with making Canada a unified nation "from sea to sea." Recognizing this need to develop the Canadian identity, the governments of Canada have given massive aid to systems of communication. Canada nationalized its railways, created a national airline, and developed a national ratio network. Nevertheless, Canada remains "a collection of economically and socially diverse regions." J. F. Graham continues:

A central question is whether . . . there is a Canadian spirit that can transcend regional attachments. Can this spirit be developed to establish a strong sense of Canadian unity and sense of purpose, so the people will see value in, and have loyalty to, Canada as an entity and be able to achieve both local and country-wide aspirations?[5]

Traditionally, Canadian identity has been expressed in terms of contrasts with the United States. Ask Canadians about what they think a Canadian is, and they will answer, "*Unlike Americans*, we are . . . we believe . . . or we have . . ." One of the stock images Canadians use to describe themselves is something called the "cultural mosaic." What many Canadians believe is that the United States is a "melting pot" while Canada is not. Canadians believe that the Americans have assimilated their ethnic and racial minorities into a single North American culture, while Canadians have allowed their ethnic minorities to retain their ethnic identities. Yet both these symbols of "melting pot" and "cultural mosaic" are myths, more indicative of ideology than fact. Americans have begun to set aside the mythical metaphor of the "melting pot" in favor of the "tossed salad" or "stew." They are beginning to appreciate American's culturally pluralistic society that, like a salad, allows each vegetable to retain its identifiable taste. Moreover, the Canadian metaphor—cultural mosaic—suggests that each tile in the mosaic makes an equal contribution to the overall effect of the whole. But sociologists like John Porter suggest that the "mosaic" is a vertical one in which some Canadians are more equal than others. Those Canadians of British descent (now broadened to include the Irish—of Anglo-Celtic descent) were traditionally expected to be the bulwark of the new Canadian nation. The fathers of Confederation believed that they were creating a British nation in North America. Schwartz writes:

> Canada could be nothing but British, because it was already peopled predominantly by those of British origin, and it soon would be a welcome haven for others like them.

> In 1871, in a population of almost three and one-half million, those of British origin represented just over sixty percent of the population, almost double the size of the French.[6]

And historically, Canadians either born in the British Isles or descended from them, have been the favored group in Canada economically, educationally, and politically. Nevertheless, even though the cultural mosaic is not the perfect example of what many Canadians believe to be Canada's superiority to the United States, there is some truth in its assertions of a difference in the racial and ethnic minority treatments in the two countries.

Canada began with a large French population. Schwartz writes:

> There was, of course, already one embarrassing exception to the British enclave, and it was one that would not disappear. Yet it was also recognized that while the rights of the French must be protected, it was because they would be a vulnerable minority, and could never expect to be augmented through immigration.[7]

The British, however, never foresaw that the French Canadians would maintain their one-third share of the population of Canada. Nor did they foresee that the French would maintain their linguistic and cultural identity with an almost unimaginable tenacity. There remain in Canada today two "founding peoples" with distinct linguistic and cultural traditions, both of whom feel that they are the ones who are truly Canadian.

In addition, although the fathers of Confederation believed that Canada would attract many emigrants from Great Britain, the immigration of people from the British Isles did not reach the hoped-for proportions. By the turn of the twentieth century, the need for settling the West had a higher priority than finding immigrants who could augment the "good" British stock. And so, immigration from Eastern Europe, including the Ukraine, was encouraged. As a result, many Eastern Europeans found themselves in western Canada on prime farmland. Having very little contact with either Canadian governmental representatives or settled Canadian communities, they were forced to develop their own communities and resources. They did not assimilate to a "Canadian way of life" because there was no institutional or social pressure to do so. They were able to transfer cultural patterns and beliefs without any interference, and thus the transplanted ethnic communities put down solid roots in the West. Today almost one quarter of Canada's population has origins other than English or French—the largest number being from Germany (6.1 percent), Italy (3.4 percent), and the Ukraine (2.7 percent). Immigration has continued to be a force in giving Canada its distinctive flavor—since the end of World War II (1945), more than 3.8 million immigrants have come to Canada to form an important segment of Canada's relatively small population of 22 million people.

The government of Canada has officially recognized the culturally pluralistic nature of its country by making multiculturalism an official national policy. A government brochure put out by the Minister of State for Multiculturalism begins:

Multiculturalism is an important dimension of national policy. This program was originally announced by the Prime Minister in 1971 in the House of Commons. Since that time the concept has grown and flowered into an operational Directorate whose responsibility is to ensure that all Canadians regardless of their cultural background have equal opportunity in Canada.

The multiculturalism policy also recognizes the fundamental right of Canadians to retain and preserve their cultural background. This right stems from the free nature of our society.

The retention of cultural values is important to Canadians as individuals and it is important to the nation as a whole. Canada as a nation clearly has benefitted from the diversity of its people. When this cultural pluralism is retained by Canadians and shared in an integrated society all of us benefit. Canada, in light of its bilingual and multicultural nature, is provided a unique opportunity and challenge to show to itself and to the world that we, as Canadians, are capable of living together in a spirit of understanding and mutual appreciation.[8]

Not all Canadians know that multiculturalism is an official policy of their country. A recent survey of national attitudes states:

Knowledge of the multiculturalism policy was not widespread and most people perceived the government's policy to favour 'permissive' rather than 'supportive' integration. Despite this low level of knowledge and the inaccurate perception of the policy, multicultural attitudes were generally positive.[9]

Nevertheless, there is also strong opposition to the policy within Canada. This opposition is especially vocal in Quebec. Guy Rocher, a Quebec sociologist, maintains that Canada is not uniquely multicultural; many nations are. He also argues that Canada is multicultural only in its largest cities such as Montreal and Toronto: "there are large areas of the country in which multiculturalism remains an abstraction."[10] He suggests that multiculturalism has no political meaning for Canada. What makes Canada distinct is its two cultures: French and English. He writes:

From the political standpoint, it is the existence of the two principal cultural and language communities, anglophone and francophone, and the give and take between these two communities which is, and will continue to be, the significant factor in the decisive events of Canadian politics.[11]

Rocher considers that the policy of multiculturalism has relevance only for the Canadian anglophone community. In actuality it is a threat to the Francophones of Canada because it will destroy the recognized reality that French Canadians are partners along with the community of English speakers in forming the country's sociological structure. He writes:

> Canada, as the Trudeau government defines it, no longer has a clear identifiable cultural nucleus. It is a kind of Grand Central Station for all the nations of the world, and regardless of their numerical importance they are all entitled to the recognition and financial support of the Canadian government. Canada could probably have gained a great deal culturally if it had retained the idea of two central cultural communities serving as a focal point around which the other ethnic communities could group and find support. Instead the Trudeau government envisages a sort of nebula consisting of countless cultures which are expected to interact although no common denominator exists.[12]

Nor do all Anglo-Celtic Canadians fully support multiculturalism, although they may be willing to accept it, if Anglo-Celtic Canadians are recognized as the most important force in Canada. Senator Eugene Forsey writes:

> For the Anglo-celtics are not only one of the largest and longest established of our ethnic groups. History and circumstance have made them also the group which has had, and will probably continue to have, the most decisive influence on Canadian culture and institutions.[13]

It seems inevitable to Senator Forsey that British cultural traditions are, and should continue to be, the dominant cultural force in Canada. English is spoken by two-thirds of Canadians and is not likely to be superseded. The laws of Canada, except for civil law in Quebec, are English. The political system, that of responsible Cabinet government, is primarily English. He writes:

> And their importance is almost incalculable. For they really determine the essential character of our political institutions. . . . It is the Queen, or her representative, the Governor-General, whom she appoints and can remove who, in strict law, appoints the Prime Minister and all the other ministers . . . and who can dismiss any or all of them. It is the Queen who, in strict law enacts statutes. . . . It is the Queen's representative, the Governor-General, acting in the Queen's name, who, in strict law, appoints all the members of the Upper House of Parliament. It is the Queen's representative . . . who, in strict law, appoints all judges of our courts. . . . To cap it all, it is the Queen, or her representative, who declares war, makes peace, appoints ambassadors, negotiates, signs and ratifies treaties.[14]

Forsey believes that the contribution of Anglo-Celtic Canadians is both a fundamental and inescapable aspect of Canadian life that has been "too often unknown, or ignored, or misunderstood, or derided and despised."[15]

He holds that it is the ideals of British liberty and justice that are at the base of the Canadian way of life:

> I am 'proud of the imperial fountain of our freedom'; I hope all of us may be 'worthy' of those ideals of British liberty and justice which have sent their light forth . . . across this Dominion, 'from sea to sea,' and from the river unto the end of the earth.[16]

Nor are Canada's native peoples totally accepting of the new government policy of multiculturalism. They believe that they are, and will continue to be, distinct nations within Canada and that Canada must honor the treaties that were signed with them; that is, native peoples have a special status in Canada, and they want to maintain that special status. They feel that the new multicultural policy is not for them. Clive Linklater states:

> The intent of the European immigrants is to exterminate, to terminate, to dispossess, to extinguish and alienate us from

our lands and to make us beggars, strangers and outcasts in our own lands.

But for yourselves, you now seek to establish a nation with a multiplicity of races, cultures and languages.

You would leave us, the indigenous owners of this land, out of such an arrangement.

We consider such an action to be immoral, illegal, unethical, unChristian, undemocratic and contrary to all the values and mores you profess to believe.[17]

This chapter will present an anthropological perspective on Canadian society. Such a perspective of the ingredients of Canada's multicultural society must, of necessity, be selective for reasons of space; and this discussion is limited to the Indians, Anglo- and Franco-Canadians, and five immigrant groups. The fifth and concluding section of this chapter briefly examines the Canadian identity by asking the question: Can these different cultural groups enriched by a variety of linguistic and cultural traditions be integrated into one overall Canadian identity?

Native Peoples of Canada

The decision to distinguish native peoples of Canada from native peoples in the United States is an arbitrary one. The borders are, for the most part, artificial ones that were drawn by Europeans, not the native peoples themselves; thus, they have little relevance for the discussion of traditional life styles that follows. The Iroquois, for example, found themselves in a difficult position as a result of the American Revolution. They found their former English allies split into two hostile groups and were forced to make choices as to which of their former allies they would join. Some, like the St. Regis Iroquois, decided to stay where they were. Today, the reservation is divided into an American half in New York State and a Canadian half in both Ontario and Quebec. Other Iroquois decided to stay with their British allies and moved to the Six

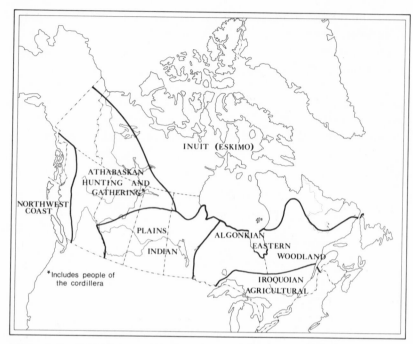

Figure 25. NATIVE PEOPLES OF CANADA AT THE TIME OF EU-
ROPEAN CONTACT.

Nation Reserve at Brantford, Ontario. With this in mind, we
shall nevertheless limit our discussion to those bands and
reserves that are on the Canadian side of the border. The
accompanying map (Figure 25) shows the location of Canada's
native peoples at the time of the European contact.

THE FIRST NORTH AMERICANS

Amerindians (North American Indians) bear a striking re-
semblance to East Asians. In color, they range from a yellow-
ish white to a light brown. The majority, however, are bronze
or copper-toned. The term "red Indian," however, did not refer
to this copper quality. The early visitors to Newfoundland
gave the name to the Beothuk Indians because they smeared
their bodies and clothing with red ocher. The eyes of Indians
are dark brown, and their hair is thick, coarse, straight, and
black on their heads, other body hair being sparse. The clear-

est link with Asian populations is the incidence of shovel-shaped incisors: the inner surfaces of the front teeth are concave in shape. This trait is very common among Asians but rare among other racial groups.

There are, however, differences in the physical appearance of Amerindians and modern Asians: many Amerindians have aquiline or hawklike noses, while most Asians have flat noses; many Asians have fleshy eyefolds called the epicanthic fold, while most Amerindians do not. These physical features suggest that Amerindians are related to Asians but of a physical type that separated from Asians before these distinctive Asian traits developed. The Inuit (more familiarly known in the United States as Eskimos) are much more closely related in physical features to modern Asians.

Another problem in identifying the source for Amerindians is the question of language. The Inuit speak a language—Eskimoan—that is clearly related to some Northeast Asian tongues like Kamchadal and Chukchi. No clear relationship, however, has been found between any Amerindian tongue and Asian languages.

Most anthropologists believe that the first North Americans entered the North American continent through the Bering Strait, a narrow body of water that separates the USSR from Alaska. The same anthropologists, however, disagree both on how these people crossed the strait and when they did it. Many believe that these Indians walked across the strait when a land bridge was opened approximately twenty-eight thousand years ago.

Culture and Culture Areas. In order to understand the modern native peoples of Canada, we must put them in their historical context: What were their cultures like at the time of European contact and what was the result of that contact? The discussion begins with an examination of the cultures of the native peoples at the time of contact with the Europeans, or shortly after. Each native culture area is also discussed in terms of the impact of early European contact, especially the fur trade.

The concept of culture includes beliefs, values, artifacts,

subsistence techniques, folklore, music, art, child raising, burials, and anything else modified or manipulated by human beings who share traditions and interact with each other. The concepts of "culture type" and "culture areas" developed out of the need to display ethnographic materials in museums. One could arrange artifacts by types, that is, in groupings that reflected usage—hunting tools, horticultural tools, religious paraphernalia—or one could organize artifacts by the geographical areas in which they appeared. The concept of culture area resulted from the discovery of similarities in artifacts of a number of groups that occupied the same basic geographical region. The Plains Indians, for example, although quite diverse in language and origins, followed similar life styles: they lived in conical skin tents, hunted the buffalo with bows and arrows on horseback, and maintained many similar customs and beliefs.

Because of the wide variety of Canadian physical environments and distinct regional orientations, many anthropologists have found it useful to classify the native peoples of Canada according to the principle of culture area. Diamond Jenness, for example, notes seven culture areas:[18] the migratory tribes of the Eastern Woodlands, the agricultural tribes of the Eastern Woodlands, the Plains tribes, the tribes of the Pacific Coast, the tribes of the Cordillera, the tribes of the Mackenzie and Yukon River basins, and the Eskimos along the Arctic Coast. With the exception of the tribes of the Cordillera, who live in the mountainous region between the Northwest Pacific Coast and the Mackenzie and Yukon River Basin, we will utilize these culture areas in our discussion of the traditional native cultures of Canada. The tribes of the Cordillera appear to share many cultural traits with both the Northwest Coast Indians and the Indians of the Mackenzie and Yukon basins and thus do not stand out as distinctly as the other six culture areas do.

THE ALGONKIAN TRIBES OF THE NORTHERN WOODLANDS

The Indians of the Eastern Woodlands, including the Beothuk, Micmac, Naskapi, Cree, Montagnais, Algonkin, and Ojibwa, inhabited the northern part of what is now Ontario and Quebec (underlain by the huge rock formation called the Laurentian Shield) and the Atlantic Provinces of Newfoundland, New Brunswick, Nova Scotia, and Prince Edward Island.

Cultural Ecology. The term "cultural ecology" in the anthropological sense, refers to the relation among culture, social institutions, and the environmental setting. In this discussion, however, we will limit our description to the way in which the native peoples of Canada used the resources of their environment for subsistence.

The Algonkians followed the game according to the seasonal movements of the particular quarry. Living beyond the region of effective maize horticulture, they focused their subsistence activities on hunting, fishing, and collecting. Animals in the region were varied—moose, deer, bear, beaver, otter, mink, various kinds of fish, and flocks of waterfowl during their migratory flights. Despite this, the Eastern Woodlands were not optimal hunting territories. The winters were harsh and often the available game was sparse. Hunting animals like the moose is very different from hunting herd animals like caribou and bison. Hunters, either alone or in small groups, usually stalked their quarry with bow and arrow, although snares and deadfalls were frequently used to catch smaller game. The hunters also used a variety of devices for imitating the calls of various animals to lure them within shooting range. The Indians of the Atlantic Province, such as the Micmac, considered fishing as important as hunting and used spears, traps made of baskets, and nets for catching fish. Both fish and meat were dried for winter use. The Ojibwa, who lived in the territory around Lake Superior, harvested wild rice. The headman of the Ojibwa divided up the rice beds into family units. Each family would first tie several stems of the rice plants into bundles—a practice that enhanced the ripening process. At harvest time a man and a woman would paddle into their rice beds. The man paddled while the woman struck bent rice clumps so as to cause the grains to fall into the bottom of the canoe. The rice, once husked, became the major vegetable of the group during the winter months.

The hunting and gathering societies of the Eastern Woodlands used birchbark extensively. They stripped the bark from large trees in huge sheets. The bark was used in a variety of ways for containers, canoes, and the familiar birchbark wigwam. They even used the birchbark as utensils for cooking. They would fold a rectangle of birchbark into an envelope, fill it with water, and drop small heated stones into it. The *babiche* or rawhide line was another feature of their material culture that was of universal importance. A skilled worked stripped a single moose hide into a thin continuous spiral while the hide was still green. The *babiche* was used for a number of purposes, including lashings and snowshoes.

All Algonkian hunting groups wore the same type of apparel—tailored clothing of tanned skins and soft-soled moccasins.

Social Organization. [19] The basic family unit was the nuclear family—a man, his wife, and children who occupied a family bark wigwam. Kin groups often remained together in the same vicinity for mutual support; but because of the seasonal and scattered nature of the fish and game, the groupings were quite small for much of the year. Larger gatherings, however, were common for brief periods during some seasons at a favored hunting or fishing ground, and for trade or festivities. Each family and band had a leader, usually charismatic in nature—chosen for his individual characteristics of courage, character, or hunting skill. Larger gatherings also displayed the same loose organization.

Religion. The Algonkians believed in a higher supernatural force called Manito. There were other supernatural forces as well. Frequently they were personified in animal form and played the trickster role—the trickster was a figure whose appetites dominated his behavior; his only purpose was to gratify his needs and in doing so he passed from one mischievous exploit to another. They also had culture heroes: among the Micmac it was Gluskap who was responsible for the introduction of most arts and crafts. The Algonkians, like most other Canadian Indian groups, believed in guardian spirits. They would gain spiritual power with the aid of a spirit who had come to them in a vision. They often wore tokens or amulets of objects they had seen in their visions. For example, an Algonkian Indian carefully preserved a single hair he pulled from the mustache of the Manito.

Medicine men or shamans of the Algonkian tribes of the Eastern Woodlands often played significant roles both spiritually and politically. The medicine men had particularly powerful guardian spirits who aided them in healing the sick. The Ojibwa and the Central Algonkians had, in addition, Grand Medicine Societies, or Midwewin, that functioned as curing societies. The initiated were not shamans, because they did not have power to cure. However, initiation could cure the illness of the initiated and give them strength for a long life.

European Contact. The Algonkian Indians of the Eastern Woodlands became intensely involved in the European fur trade. The rapid development of trade relied upon the Indian's hunting ability, his knowledge of animal habits, and his familiarity with the country. In the long run, the effect of this European contact was overwhelming. Indian craftsmanship became a lost art as trade goods replaced the ancient tools. As the supply of pelts decreased in an area, the hunters were forced to wander farther and farther from the areas they knew well. This traveling weakened cultural orientations and stability. In addition, it created both economic and political pressure on surrounding groups that revived intertribal warfare now made devastating by the introduction of guns. Guns also increased the deadliness of the hunt. Food supplies as a result became increasingly scarce. The hunters became more and more dependent on European foodstuffs, which in turn produced an unbalanced diet and increased chances of disease. European communicable diseases spread like wildfire through the Indian populations—measles, scarlet fever, smallpox, typhus, typhoid, and venereal disease. Medicine men were helpless in curing these European diseases, and their failures further weakened traditional values. The fur trade also had tremendous effects on social organization—property became more like that of Europeans with territories becoming owned by individual families. A new type of chief arose: the commercial representative of the fur traders.

THE IROQUOIAN HORTICULTURALISTS OF THE EASTERN WOODLANDS

The Iroquois and related groups like the Huron, Neutrals, and Tobaccos lived in more or less settled communities in the fertile lowlands of Ontario between the Great Lakes and the Laurentian Shield.

Cultural Ecology. Iroquois villages, of between three hundred to three thousand inhabitants, were usually situated beside a lake, stream, or spring surrounded by a trench with a high palisade of stakes. The villages were near timbered lowlands where maize horticulture was practiced in cleared garden plots that sometimes extended for several hundred acres. The staple crop was Indian corn: flint corn, starchy corn, sweet corn, and popcorn. The Iroquois planted beans, squash, and pumpkins in the same hills where they planted their corn. They cultivated tobacco, melons, and sunflowers in separate plots.

Tracts of land were prepared by the slash-and-burn method: parcels of land were burned and trees were felled by an alternate use of ringing with fire and chopping with stone axes. The digging stick made of wood or bone was the major horticultural tool. Although the Iroquois understood the principles of transplanting and seed selection, they did not practice either crop rotation or fertilization; as a result, land became exhausted every ten years and the whole village was forced to move to a new site. The only domesticated animal was the dog. The horticultural activities (mainly done by the women) were supplemented by the hunting and fishing of the men.

Social Organization.[20] The major social unit of Iroquois society was the household composed of a maternal lineage: the women who occupy a single longhouse and trace their descent in the female line from a single ancestress. The longhouse was a rectangular building large enough to accommodate several families. Throughout the longhouse ran a corridor in which fires were laid at twenty-foot intervals: each fire served two families who occupied apartments on either side of the fire. The apartment was little more than a platform of bark, twelve by six feet, raised a root or two off the ground, and covered with mats and skins: it served as a seat by day and a bed by night.

The husband had no authority over his wife in the household: the principal authority rested with a chief matron, most often a grandmother or maternal aunt. She not only supervised the domestic life of the household but exercised important political functions assisted by a council of all the women in the longhouse of childbearing age.

A number of households, united in the same maternal lineage, formed a clan that functioned as a mutual-aid organization to redress injuries and avenge deaths. Each clan had a body of chiefs and a council on which both sexes were represented—these clans bore animal names; for example Bears, Turtles, Eels and Snipes. These animals were not totemic in the strict sense of the word, since there were no taboos on eating them and they were not worshiped or treated like ancestors. Normally a clan was part of a larger unit, the moiety, or phratry, that operated as social and ceremonial units, to conduct funerals, for example.

A still larger and more important level of social organization was the Iroquois Confederacy composed of the five Iroquois tribes: Seneca, Cayuga, Oneida, Onandaga, and Mohawk—others were added later. This confederation operated under a council of fifty sachems, or councillors—each of these sachem positions were named and had particular duties and responsibilities. Sachems were always male, although a woman could act as regent for a young boy who belonged to her clan. Sachems were selected by the matron of the household at a council of the women of her clan, she had the power to depose a weak sachem as well. The fifty sachems, all of equal rank, administered the affairs of the Confederacy, deliberating on matters of war and peace, and other problems common to all. They did not have any voice, however, in the internal affairs of the individual tribes. Decisions had to reflect a consensus, and the skillful orator who could persuade his colleagues was highly valued.

Religion. The Iroquois had five great deities: Ataensic, the grandmother of the gods and goddess of death; Taronhai-wagon, the benevolent national god who created humans and animals; his brother, Tawiskaron, who represented the destructive side of nature; Heno, an agricultural deity who brought rain and ripened crops; and Agreskew, the sun god who was the patron of war and who occasionally received human sacrifices. There were other gods as well: an Earth Mother and the Three Sisters representing the spirits of maize, bean, and squash.

There were also malevolent spirits like the hideous flying heads. The Iroquois believed that a dead person's soul became a ghost which haunted graves by day and wandered at night in search of food. They were dangerous because they caused sickness and often desired human flesh. Youths received guardian spirits through dreams brought about by rigorous fasting in a period of seclusion. If a youth dreamed of an animal like a muskrat, it became his mentor and he wore its skin as his personal medicine.

A class of special medicine men claimed to possess supernatural power. Through their special spirit helpers they were able to control the weather, prophesy the future, and injure an enemy. They also practiced more standard healing through bleeding and herbal medicines. If the illness was the result of hostile magic, they held shamanistic seances to discover the cause and then removed the offending objects from their patient's body.

European Contact. The Iroquois became bitter enemies of the French when Champlain aided the Montagnais against them in 1609. The Iroquois, who became allies of the English, acquired firearms from the Dutch and gradually overwhelmed their enemies. Some of the Onandaga and Mohawk, however, were missionized by the French Jesuits and accepted Christianity. Their descendants still live in Quebec at Caughnawaga and St. Regis.

From 1642 to the end of the century, the Confederacy suffered tremendous losses through war and disease. The Iroquois reacted strongly to the pressures caused by European contact and involvement. One effect was that of a revitalization movement. Revitalization movements represent extreme reactions to European domination. They are deliberate efforts by members of society to construct a more satisfying culture. About 1800 a Seneca sachem, Handsome Lake, during a period of illness, had a series of supernatural visions in which he was taught how to bring the Iroquois back to their former cultural traditions. He traveled from village to village preaching his message to each tribe. The message was simple: act according to the traditional Iroquois ways. They were especially cautioned to hold on to their lands and to reject the white man's liquor. Like many revitalization movements, the message showed elements of acculturation—where traditional beliefs are mixed with Christian ones. Handsome Lake was like the Messiah, and his rules of conduct were like Christian commandments. The longhouse tradition started by Handsome Lake still has adherents today.

THE INDIANS OF THE PLAINS
The Indians of the Plains, the Assiniboine, the Plains Cree, Blackfoot, Sarcee, Gros-Ventre, and Sioux were migratory hunters who ranged through the Canadian prairies, now called Manitoba, Saskatchewan, and Alberta.

Cultural Ecology. The prairies, although more varied in appearance than most people assume, are characterized by long stretches of flat, treeless plains, with occasional valleys, lakes, streams, and clumps of trees. They are a land of extremes, with breathlessly hot summers and bitterly cold winters—spring brings a variety of flowers, and autumn has an abundance of wild fruits. The territory once abounded in large game: elk, deer, antelope, and especially the bison (buffalo).

Life on the plains did not represent the typical patterns of the Indians before the coming of Europeans—the Cree had been forest dwellers before they took to the plains; other groups had been corn growers and village dwellers before their move to the plains. The Plains Indians developed their unique life style as an adaptation to the Euro-American frontier. It is ironic that the Plains Indians became symbols of the quintessential Indian, since their cultures were in fact aberrations produced by culture contact and the changes it engendered.

The people of the plains were primarily large-game hunters, especially of the buffalo. They made little use of fish or small game. The only aboriginal domesticated animal was the dog who, although eaten by a few tribes, was primarily used for transporting loads by means of the *travois*—a special harness attached to two poles. The Spaniards introduced the horse to the plains and thus revolutionized the hunting, fighting, and traveling patterns of the Indians. The transformation, however, was not sudden: the Blackfoot apparently did not get horses before 1730.

There were several methods of hunting. A hunter would don a wolfskin and sneak up close enough to his quarry to shoot it. Individual Assiniboine hunters tracked buffalo on snowshoes (buffalo embedded in the snow became easy targets), but the most important hunting was done collectively. The "surround" became the most popular method of collective hunting. Hunters, mounted on their ponies, would surround a herd of buffalo and then shoot them down with bows and arrows. Impounding—the use of a corral where two fences channeled the herd of buffalo toward the entrance—was often used by the Cree, Assiniboine, and the Blackfoot. The buffalo was the principal source of food—both fresh and dried or mixed with fat and berriers to make pemmican. The skins were used for a number of purposes—as covering for the *tipis*, for bedding, for containers, and for some clothing. The horns were made into cups and ladles and tools were made from the bones. The Plains Indians used every part of the animal: its tail for a fly whisk and its dung for fuel.

The Indians, thus dependent on the buffalo, were forced to follow the migratory patterns of the animals. They hunted the buffalo on the open plain, slaughtered and prepared the hides of the animals in wooded and well-watered ravines, and spent their winters close to the edge of the forests where they trapped and hunted.

Social Organization.[21] The smallest unit of Plains Indian society was the individual household—the inhabitants of a single *tipi*: parents, children, and perhaps a grandparent or unmarried aunt. The band, however, was the basic economic and political unit of the tribes. Band membership was based on kin ties, although there were no hard-and-fast rules of descent. Wives usually joined the bands of their husbands, but the reverse could occur as well. The tribe was an organization unit that functioned only for a few weeks of the summer, the time of the communal hunt.

One characteristic of Plains Indians' social organization was the societies that cut across the ties of kinship and band affiliations. There were various kinds: warrior societies, religious cults, and dancing associations. The warrior societies, often age-graded (where boys of similar age became members and moved from rank to rank together) were important because they did the policing at the large summer encampment.

Religion. The dream or vision played an extremely important role in the lives of the Plains Indians. The youth who sought a vision (which could be merely auditory, not visual at all) would seclude himself in a lonely spot, fast, and mutilate himself (e.g., by cutting off a finger). In his heightened emotional state, he experienced the visitation of his guardian spirit. The form of that spirit could vary enormously: buffalo, deer, elk, eagles, flies, or mosquitoes. Some youths, however, never succeeded in having a vision: they were the unlucky ones. Those who had a special gift for attracting supernatural helpers became medicine men or shamans. Spirits were highly specialized and could be used for only specific ailments: some shamans treated only snakebites or problems of childbirth. The usual cure was to find the cause and extract it from the body. The shamans also did more regular doctoring, such as prescribing potions and liniments.

Plains Indians believed in souls but did not concern themselves with what happened in the afterlife except for vague notion of a "happy hunting ground." Rituals were important in their lives. Of special importance were the bundle ceremonies and the Sun Dance. The owner of a pipe bundle enjoyed considerable prestige. Medicine bundles were usually purchased. Among the Hidatsa children some inherited the prerogative of buying a medicine bundle from their father. A bundle could include the fetus of a deer, muskrat, and deerskins, as well as the tobacco pipe. The owner of a pipe bundle was obligated to open it at the first thunder of spring. The owner had some unusual taboos to maintain: for example, he could not point with any finger other than his thumb, and he could not sit on his bedding. The pipe bundle ceremonial itself was very simple: one opened the bundle and sang some songs in sets of seven, and then did some simple dances.

The Sun Dance was the most conspicuous religious ceremony for many of the Plains Indian tribes. The dance did not center on the sun as a particular god. It was a dance that occurred annually in the late spring or early summer. However, it was an individual Indian who pledged to have the dance in order to relieve some distress. An important aspect of the ceremony was the search for a suitable tree that was chopped down by a chaste woman and treated like a fallen enemy. Before the three was raised again for the ceremony, offerings were placed in the fork of the trunk. Generally the pledger, and those accompanying him, fasted for several days while they stared at the top of the tree. They also performed a simple dance. Some of the Plains tribes had a practice whereby the participants put skewers through their breasts or backs and attached them to ropes leading to the central pole. The dancers then strained against the ropes until the skewers were torn loose.

Effects of European Contact. The most important result of the European contact was the extinction of the bison: they were gone by the late 1870s. The second was the great smallpox epidemics of the late eighteenth and early nineteenth centuries which came as the result of increased European contact and larger aggregates of Indians brought together for the bison-hunting expeditions. The whiskey trade became an additional factor in the debilitation of the Indians, and the Indians began to congregate around the forts and trading posts. Major destructive Indian wars did not occur on the Canadian Plains. But in 1885, Louis Riel rallied the métis and their Indian allies to battle against the government. (The métis are people of mixed Indian-Caucasian descent, many of whom are descended from French-Canadian *coureurs des bois* and Scottish fur traders.) They were defeated by General Middleton and Riel was hanged. With this defeat, the Indians were rounded up and placed on northern reserves, where they became "nontreaty" bands.

THE INDIANS OF THE NORTHWEST COAST
The Indians of the Northwest Coast like the Tsimshian, Haida, Kwakiutl, Bella Coola, and Nootka lived in a narrow coastal area stretching from southeastern Alaska to the redwood forests of California.

Cultural Ecology. The Northwest Coast Indians settled on the river mouths, beaches, fjords, and coastal islands near the Pacific Ocean. The climate is essentially a warm one where the warmer air is brought in by the Japanese current and the mountains form barriers protecting the coastal regions from the extremes of winter. Rainfall is considerable, and there is dense growth of forests of firs, spruce, cedar, and yew. The forests and rugged terrain made travel difficult, and the Northwest Coast communities traveled from one place to another, primarily by sea. There were many animals in the region: deer, elk, bear, wolf, grizzly, mountain sheep, beaver, mink, and farther interior, moose and caribou. Waterfowl flew along the coast in their annual migrations and were plentiful. Land animals did play a part in the economy of the Northwest Coast Indians, but the communities were principally oriented toward the sea. Fishing of the basic crop, salmon, was much more like harvesting. The salmon, although an oceangoing fish, spawns in freshwater streams. During the five to seven salmon runs during the year, the Indians could collect unbelievable quantities of the fish. The problem was not where to find the fish but what to do with the surplus. There were other kinds of fish as well: herring, halibut, smelt, and *oulachon* (candlefish).

Permanent houses and settlements resulted from the obligations of capturing, cleaning, and preserving the catch at several periods during the year.

Although there are several differences between various Northwest Coast groups, the Haida are representative of the native cultures in the area.

The Haida had no domestic animals except the dog and did not until recently practice agriculture. Their subsistence activities were quite varied: they gathered clams, mussels, crabs, birds' eggs, wild roots, herbs, fruits, berries, and seaweed, which they made into cakes. In addition to collecting, they trapped birds and small animals, hunted deer with bows and arrows, and killed bears with traps and snares. But the Haida derived most of their food from the sea. They hunted all sea mammals, except the whale, which they used for skins as well as meat. Using screens, hunters approached the sea mammals in shallow water and dispatched them with bows and arrows. They also surrounded mammals in a circle of canoes and harpooned them when they came up to breathe. Excellent fishers, the Haida used hook and line to catch cod and dogfish; they used dipnets, open-mesh baskets, large floating nets, and rakes to secure herring; and they used dams and specially spaced wicker fences to catch leaping salmon.

There was always a considerable surplus of food. Quantities of berries, bark, and fish were dried and stored away in boxes. The flesh of fish was cut into thin strips and either dried in the sun or smoked over a low fire. Oil and grease were used as a sauce with all the fried food, the grease being obtained by boiling the partially putrefied flesh of sea mammals and fish.

Wood became the major material for building and manufacturing. They built their huge rectangular houses out of planks of cedar. The beds in their houses were raised plank platforms covered with mats and fur. They made their canoes by digging out huge logs. Baskets were made from cedar bark and spruce fibers. They ate from wooden plates, and they used spruce fiber to make thread and ropes.

Social Organization.[22] The Haida were divided into two exogamous moieties: that is, members of a moiety (or half) sought mates in the opposite moiety. The moieties did not perform any governmental function: they functioned only for regulating marriage and descent. Each moiety was further divided into twenty matrilineal clans: the clan was a localized segment of the moiety that inhabited or was connected to a single village from which it derived its name. The clan owned property: hunting grounds, camping and village sites, salmon streams, berry patches, and strips of beach. The chief of the clan held the land in trust for his members. The clan also owned nonmaterial property: names, ceremonial house titles, songs, dances, ceremonies, and special crests that they tatooed on their bodies, carved on their boxes, and painted on their houses. Each clan was made up of about a dozen separate households that numbered as many as thirty people each. A household usually consisted of a house chief, his wife or wives, his young sons and unmarried daughters, a married daughter, her husband and children, the chief's sister's sons married and unmarried, a poor relative, and one or two slaves.

Any man who owned a house, either through inheritance or construction, was a house chief. He directed all the economic activities of his household and protected and served as the formal spokesman for its members. The richest and most powerful of the house chiefs was usually the clan chief. His position was inherited, but his authority was dependent on his wealth, personality, and prestige. He had authority but no power; that is, he could command obedience or punish subordination in the other house chiefs. Chiefship was also hereditary in the households: inherited through the female line passing to a younger brother or the eldest son of an eldest sister.

The most important event in Haida life was the potlatch. Before an heir to a house succeeded to the position of house chief, he must have validated his claims by holding a funeral potlatch, where he distributed goods to members of the opposite moiety while they erected a mortuary column to the deceased. The most important potlatch, however, was the house potlatch. The event was anticipated long in advance, because it took about ten years to amass the required amount of property for distribution. The members of the opposite moiety were invited by the host to spend the winter constructing a house for them. Following the completion of the construction, a totem pole was erected and a special day was set aside for the tattooing of the hostess and the children.

The actual potlatch occurred in the new house after all of the work had been completed. The guests were seated in the house according to rank. The host and hostess (the woman is really the donor of the potlatch) threw back a curtain that had concealed a huge pile of furs, blankets, and other property. The host and hostess conferred names on their children, which thus changed their status from commoners to nobles. Each guest then received property according to his rank and contribution. There was no bickering, because each person knew exactly what he was entitled to. The house chief and his wife were completely divested of all their material resources, but they gained tremendously in rank. The more potlatches one gave, the higher would be the rank. As a result, competition was keen, not only for the numbers of potlatches given, but also for the splendor of the chief's generosity at these potlatches.

Religion. The Haida believed that a great divinity lived under a bowl like earth with his dog. When the dog shook itself, earthquakes occurred. Raven played a major role in their account of the creation of the world, and there were several legends about him, like the time he stole the moon. The Haida peopled the world around them with a myriad of supernatural beings who might or might not be of help to humans. The most important deities were those of the fish and sea mammals. They believed in a sky god which ruled over life and death, a thunderbird who caused thunder by flapping its wings; and Creekwoman who lived at the source of streams. There were few rituals attached to these deities: to appease killer whales, a man out in the sea would put a feather, some deer tallow, and tobacco on the end of a paddle and lower it in the water. In order to communicate with spirits, one must have purified oneself, through fasting and abstaining from water and by purging the stomach of its contents.

There were two kinds of religious practitioners: a class of seeresses who possessed the power of prophecy, through dreams, and a class of shamans. The shamans could summon their familiar spirits to aid them at any time. Shamans knew considerable practical treatments for diseases, but they were particularly effective in cases of sorcery. A sorcerer was discovered through the aid of a captured mouse that nodded its head at the sound of the sorcerer's name.

THE ATHABASKANS OF THE MACKENZIE AND YUKON BASINS

The Chipewyans, Beavers, Slaves, Yellowknives, Hares, Sekani, Dogrib, Nahani, and Kutchin occupied the great basin of the Mackenzie River in the Canadian Northwest Territories.

Cultural Ecology. The Athabaskans live south of Arctic at the tree line. It is a region of cold winters and hot summers. The game is of various kinds: caribou, moose, deer, elk, bear, wolves, and foxes. The caribou and the moose, however, were the chief sources of food. The caribou moved to the tundra, the vast treeless plains, in the spring and to the edge of the forest in the late fall. The Yellowknives had their caribou drives in the late fall and early winter as the caribou came back to the forest. They strung lines along fenceposts to lead the animals to a corral. They also pursued the caribou in the water where they lanced them with spears. In addition, they used snares to catch the antlers of the animals as they ran through the woods. The snares and lines were made of semitanned caribou hides cut into strands to form the *babiche*. The Athabaskans could not store meat like the Inuit (who had permafrost storage), so they dried and smoked their meats or made it into pemmican.

The slaves hunted moose rather than caribou, and the moose, not a herd animal, called for a different hunting technique. While the caribou drive required cooperative efforts by groups, the moose was hunted by one or two men. The Dogrib pursued caribou herds in sleds or on foot but in a less organized way than the Yellowknives. Bear, beaver, and rabbit were also important animals to be hunted. Both birds and their eggs were eaten; fishing under the ice in winter and by dams in the summer was done. Interior Athabaskans collected berries and the tender shoots of various plants.

During the winter, hunting on foot was done with the aid of snowshoes. The Dogrib and Yellowknives used frozen beaver skins as sleds that were pulled by dogs. Summer travel was by canoe made of birchbark or spruce. The Dogrib canoe was quite small so that it could be carried by one man on the frequent portages.

The Athabaskans lived in conical skin tents similar to those of the Plains Indians but wider and more squat. The *tipi* could be covered with ice and snow in the winter. The Dogrib and Yellowknives did not sleep in their *tipis*, but rather slept outside in skin sleeping bags.

Social Organization.[23] For most of the Athabaskans, the band was the largest unit of social organization. The band consisted of little more than related or friendly families or a single extended family. The band leader was generally its chief hunter whose skills and personality kept the group together. The Dogrib and Yellowknives had hunt leaders, however, for their communal hunts. The Dogrib had two kinds of bands: the local band and the regional band. The local band was made up of close kin, while regional bands were made up of relatives tied together through blood and marriage.

Warfare was common among the Athabaskans, and the need arose for war leaders. Not surprisingly, they were usually aggressive men who were physically quite strong.

Religion. The Northern Athabaskans had myths about the Raven and various tricksters, but animals important in the food quest dominated their world of the supernatural. Care had to be taken to avoid offending the spirits of various animals. The Athabaskans believed that animals allowed themselves to be captured. A successful hunter could command the game to go to certain places to be captured. Shamans were usually males among the Athabaskans, but it was possible for a woman to have shamanistic power. Shamans, like other men, sought spirit helpers through visions; the powerful shaman was able to acquire a variety of spiritual helpers. The primary duty of the shaman was to cure disease, which he usually did by removing an object from the patient's body. He, like other shamans elsewhere, went into trances and asked his spiritual helpers to help him find out the cause of the illness. Shamans also foretold the future and brought game to the hunters.

The Athabaskans did have some ceremonials like the ceremony of the first salmon where the fish were placed on fresh grass in front of the houses. The people, after purifying themselves, would clean the fish without breaking the backbones. The entrails were thrown back into the water. Some of the Athabaskans also had potlatches.

European Contact. The Northern Athabaskan Indians did not wage war with the Europeans, nor were they removed from their lands. The land, moreover, had little appeal for European settlers. The major contact of the Athabaskans with Europeans was with the fur traders. European goods reached the Indians before actual contact with Europeans was made. The Indians particularly desired iron goods: knives, chisels, and axes. The North West Company and the Hudson's Bay Company were in fierce competition for the furs the Indians had for trade. The competition had a double effect: it brought alcohol in large quantities to the Indians and depleted the population of the beaver in some areas. Like other Amerindian groups, Athabaskans were ravaged by European diseases: influenza, tuberculosis, and smallpox.

About 1910, a Sarsi Indian named Cough brought a variant of the Ghost Dance to the area. The Ghost Dance derives its name from the belief that the Indians would be reunited with their dead. It was originally developed in Nevada where a Paviotso Indian went into trances and preached that the dead were about to return to the earth to enjoy both the ancient life and plentiful game. Cough's message was to return to the religion as it existed before Christianity had come and destroyed its power. He had power to heal diseases, and his fame spread widely. While his movement died out after ten years, other nativistic movements in the area have prospered.

THE INUIT (ESKIMOS)

The Inuit live almost entirely north of the timberline along the Arctic Coast and Arctic islands. The most important Canadian Inuit are: the Mackenzie Inuit who live near the mouth of the Mackenzie River; the Copper Inuit who live around Coronation Gulf, the Central Inuit who live on Baffin Island, Southampton Island, and the Melville Peninsula; and the Labrador Inuit who live on the coast of Labrador and the Ungava Peninsula. The term "Eskimo" means "eater of raw meat" and was derived from Abenaki and Cree. The natives prefer to be called Inuit, which means something like "human beings."

Cultural Ecology. The climate of the Arctic is extremely hard with long cold winters where fierce storms attack the rocky and treeless land. The summer, however, from July to September, is pleasant and may go up to 70° Fahrenheit. The coastal area where the Copper Eskimo or Inuit live varies considerably from huge cliffs to low beaches with many bays, inlets, rivers, and fjords.

The Copper Inuit had distinctly different summer and winter sites. They spent the longest time, however, at the winter site. During the late fall, the different family groups headed for the sealing grounds, which were in an area protected from the wind. The ice was smooth and accessible. Ice hunting for seals became the dominant winter activity, although the men would occasionally go on a bear hunt. The Inuit hunted seal by waiting patiently by a seal's breathing hole. The seal is an air-breathing mammal and must return to the surface several times during the day to breathe. The motionless hunter waited until the seal came to the surface to breathe, when he harpooned it. Since the seal had several breathing holes, the vigil might last for hours, even days. After harpooning a seal, the hunter played the seal like a large fish until he had exhausted it. Then the air hole was enlarged, and the animal was hauled out. The seal was the Inuits' most important animal: it provided the greater part of their food during the winter; its blubber lighted their lamps and warmed their igloos; its hides were used to make water-proof kayaks and boots.

As the days grew longer, the community began to move to the hunting grounds farther inland. Larger groups of Inuit were able to congregate together in the warm seasons, but the size of the group depended on the resources of the area. The Inuit did some springtime hunting of caribou, but the animals were thin and not as desirable as they are later in the season. Although there was some individual hunting, the Inuit preferred communal drives where everyone played a role herding the caribou into an accessible area like a blind ravine, swamp, or lake where the hunters could easily lance them.

The main summer activity, however, was fishing for salmon trout, lake trout, and coast tomod. Great quantities of salmon trout were caught with nets or dams during the spawning season. The Inuit were able to collect few fruits or vegetables except for some berries at the end of the summer. To get vegetable matter they would eat the digested contents of a caribou's stomach when an animal was butchered. Between the fall hunting season and the winter seal fishing, there was little to do but wait. Larger quantities of caribou meat were stored in stone cairns to keep scavengers away. Most of the time was spent in preparing winter clothing and making and repairing sleds and tools.

The Inuit did not use snowshoes or skis, but they did use dogsleds made of whalebone or driftwood. The sled dogs were used as pack dogs during the summer and to aid in hunting in the winter, especially for finding the breathing holes of seals. The Copper Inuit generally had three dogs on a team; they were harnessed three abreast rather than in single file. When necessary an Inuit wife helped the dogs pull the sled while the man pushed. The Copper Inuit used the small kayak for water travel. The kayak was used by a single paddler who was snuggly waterproofed in the interior. This boat was used mostly for spearing caribou in the freshwater lakes during the summer.

The Copper Inuit, unlike some other Inuit in the area, lived in igloos during the winter. An igloo might be twelve feet or more in diameter and ten feet high. Sometimes the igloos of a community were connected by passages that also led to a large community dance house. In summer, the people lived in tents of caribou hide or sealskin. Most Inuit clothes were made of caribou skins.

Social Organization.[24] The Inuit had very little recognizable governmental structure. The basic unit was the band, which was made up of kin who were related by blood or marriage. Larger bands became associated with an area and were named often by directions, although the Copper Inuit are named for their distinctive artifacts. The Copper Inuit were divided into about fourteen bands of about fifty persons each in the years 1913 to 1916. Leadership was charismatic— some outstanding hunter would be listened to.

Religion. The Inuit believed that malevolent spirits were everywhere. These spirits were powerful and could entice or steal the soul of a sick person. Aches and pains were caused by objects placed in one's body by the spirits of an evil shaman. A friendly shaman went on a magical spirit flight to discover the cause of the illness. If it was an implanted foreign object, he removed it. Like other shamans in North America, the Inuit shaman summoned his spirit helpers while in a trance.

Although there were spirits everywhere, some spirits were more important than others. The most important to the Copper Inuit was Sedna, the female spirit of the sea. She hated people because her father threw her overboard to avoid the wrath of a vengeful bird spirit. According to the legend, her father cut her fingers off at the first joint as she was holding on to the side of the boat: these joints became the whales of the sea. He then cut off the second joints of her fingers, which became the seals of the sea. He then cut off the third joints of her fingers, which became the walruses. With her fingers gone, she sank to the botton of the sea and began her reign over the animals of the sea. She must be carefully appeased; when ritual taboos were broken, she withheld the sea animals from the hunters.

Another important spirit was Sila, a sky god who controlled the sun but did not provide any aid to the Inuit.

European Contact. The earliest contact of the Inuit with Europeans was with the Noresemen of Greenland. The search for the Northwest Passage brought many explorers to the region: Frobisher, Davis, Baffin, Hudson, and others who had repeated contact with the Inuit.

The first known contact of the Copper Inuit with Europeans was when Samuel Hearne came with a group of Chipewyan Indians in search of copper. These Chipewyans massacred a settlement of Inuit. As a result, the Copper Inuit fled from Europeans for some time after that.

Eventually the fur trade was introduced. It had similar acculturating effects there, as elsewhere. The trader became the de facto ruler of the land. The Inuit traded furs for rifles, cartridges, traps, knives, and other goods the trader would lend as credit to induce greater trapping of fur-bearing animals. The Inuit became dependent on the trading post not only for supplies but for food, since there was little time for subsistence hunting. Moreover, the natural food supply became rapidly depleted because of the devastating efficiency of the rifle. The Inuit became more dependent on the store-bought food and other goods: flour, sugar, coffee, tea, alcohol, and tobacco. The generally healthy Inuit were weakened by this unbalanced diet and became more susceptible to the newly introduced European diseases.

INDIANS AND MÉTIS: PROBLEMS OF IDENTITY

In the United States an Indian, legally, is someone whose ancestors lived in America before its discovery by Europeans, and an individual who is considered to be an Indian by the community in which he lives (Federal Indian Law 1958:6). Some Indian groups, like the Blackfeet of Montana, require that to be considered an Indian one must have at least one-quarter Indian blood. The situation in Canada is quite different. A Canadian Indian is a real or legal Indian if his name and number are written on a list in Ottawa and posted in a conspicuous place in the superintendent's office that serves his band. A number was given to each Indian who took treaty status at the time a treaty was signed. The number is handed down in the male line: the wife takes the number of her husband. One can lose one's number if he becomes enfranchised which means denying his special status as an Indian.

Enfranchised Indians, at one time, received the privilege of voting and of drinking. But both those rights were granted to all Canadian Indians in 1960. What an enfranchised Indian receives today is the chance to sell his land to the band or receive compensation from the government. He may, however, retain his property by a special location ticket, rent the land from his former band for ten years, and then own it outright. But once he has done this he receives no special considerations as a treaty Indian. He is, in effect, no longer an Indian.

The people of the North consider the Métis to be nontreaty Indians and unlisted Eskimos: persons who do not have the legal status of an Indian. Generally speaking, however, Métis are persons of known Indian-European or Inuit-European ancestry who, although occupying the status of whites, consider themselves to be Métis. It is not enough to have both European and native ancestry, because some who have this background are identified by themselves and others as Indians, while others, especially if urbanized, are to all intents and purposes Euro-Canadians.

The Métis were and are a product of acculturation. The fur traders, the *coureurs des bois* of the late seventeenth to early nineteenth centuries, frequently lived with or married Indian women and developed a life style that was peculiar to the fur trade: partly Indian and partly European, yet distinctive. A Métis sense of "national" identity developed in the middle of the nineteenth century, resulting in the declaration of a Métis Nation, and the two insurrections of 1870 and 1885.

At the present time, there are about sixty-thousand Métis in Canada. From the earliest times, the Métis were at the heart of the transportation industries in the North. Many of them are still trappers, but a number of them are employed in construction industries.

The Native Peoples and the Canadian Government

Having examined the traditional cultures of Canada's Indians, let us now turn to a discussion of the contemporary relationship between the Indians and the government of Canada.

The Treaties. Formal arrangements between the native peoples and the Canadian government took the form of treaties, most of which were similar. Heather Robertson, in her book, *Reservations Are for Indians,* uses the one at Lake of the Woods, Manitoba, signed on October 3, 1873, as a typical example.[25] The Indians ceded some five-thousand square miles of northwestern Ontario and received in return some gardening supplies and tools, one plow for each ten families, one chest of tools for the entire band, one yoke of oxen, one bull, and four cows. These tools and supplies were to encourage the Indians to become settled farmers in the European sense. They were, however, given $1,500 and a year's worth of ammunition and twine for nets so that they could continue to do some hunting and fishing. Reserves were set aside for the Indians on the scale of one square mile for each family of five, more or less, depending on the number of children.

The government reserved several rights to the land established for reserves, including the right to sell, lease, or otherwise dispose of it. The government also reserved the right to allow settlements, mining, lumbering, or other activities on the reserves. As a reward for signing the treaty the chief received an annual salary of $25 a year, a new suit of clothes every three years, and a "suitable flag and medal." Each Indian received $5 a year for signing the treaty.

Robertson reports that there were four important agreements that have been at the heart of much controversy and bitterness: the government agreed to provide schools on the reserve whenever the Indians desired it; the Indians were forbidden to drink alcohol on the reserve; the Indians had the right to hunt and fish throughout the surrendered territory; and the government reserved the right to appropriate sections of the reserve for public works or buildings.

Hunting and fishing rights were particularly difficult for the Indians to maintain: much of the ceded territory became occupied and unsuitable for the hunt. In addition, there were regulations like the Migratory Birds Act that forbade whites and Indians to shoot birds out of season. Provincial rules were developed that further restricted the rights of Indians to hunt and fish: they were required to have licenses like everyone else.

Heather Robertson maintains that the treaties were not really treaties, because the Indians had no rights at all: they were living on government land that was administered by government agents. The Indians had no rights of self-government. She argues that the reserves were intended as government-owned and -operated farms that would support the Indian population, to be administered for them by "Her Majesty's government." The reservations are administered today by the Minister of Indian Affairs and Northern Development. There are about 230,000 Indians in Canada and 2,241 reserves. Sixteen percent of the Indians who are entitled to live on the reserves do not.

In addition to regulations administering the running of the reserves, the Indian Act contains various regulations concerning the individual conduct of Indians. For example, there are special regulations concerning Indians and alcohol. Section 95 of the act states:

An Indian who

    (a) has intoxicants in his possession,

    (b) is intoxicated, or

    (c) makes or manufactures intoxicants,

off a reserve, is guilty of an offence and is liable on summary conviction to a fine of not less than ten dollars and not more than fifty dollars or to imprisonment for a term not exceeding three months or to both fine and imprisonment.[26]

The case of Joseph Drybones, a Dogrib Indian, centered on this section of the Indian Act and has had major implications for the legality of the act itself. The incident underlying the case occurred in April 1967. Joseph Drybones was found "dead drunk" on the steps of a hotel in Yellowknife. The Royal Canadian Mounted Police (RCMP), following the regulations of the Indian Act, carried him to jail, a commonly accepted police procedure with intoxicated Indians. After sleeping it off, Drybones was brought before the territorial judge who fined him ten dollars. After paying the fine, Drybones was released from jail.

A young lawyer, Brian Purdy, read the court record in Yellowstone and became interested in the Drybones case. He was struck by the injustice of the Indian Act, which had more stringent penalties for intoxicated Indians than those applied to intoxicated Euro-Canadians under the Ordinances of the Northwest Territories. He decided to challenge the legality of that particular section of the Indian Act. The appeal was heard in Yellowknife in June of that year, and Justice Morrow allowed Drybones to change his plea to not guilty in the new trial.

Brian Purdy argued that this section of the Indian Act violated Canada's Bill of Rights, which guarantees in part I, section 1(b), "the right of the individual to equality before the law and protection of the law." In other words, Joseph Drybones had been denied this protection guaranteed by the Bill of Rights. He further argued that the Bill of Rights should take precedence over every other act in Canada, and in this case, the Indian Act. The judge agreed with the young lawyer. In agreeing with Purdy, Judge Morrow established a new precedent: that the Bill of Rights took precedence over a bill of Parliament. Following that decision, Purdy pleaded the case before the Northwest Court of Appeals and finally before the Supreme Court of Canada. The Supreme Court made its ruling in the Drybones case on November 20, 1969, the majority opinion being that the section of the Indian Act under which Drybones was convicted infringed upon one of the basic rights and freedoms set down in the Bill of Rights.

The decision in the Drybones case has put into question not only the whole legality of the Indian Act as it applies to the freedom of the individual but also the legality of any parliamentary act if the Supreme Court interprets it as an infringement of the Bill of Rights.

In 1969 the Minister of Indian Affairs, Jean Chrétien, came out with a White Paper that would integrate the Indians into the mainstream of Canadian life. The purpose of the law was to end the legal distinctions between Indians and other Canadians and transfer the administration of Indian affairs to other federal and provincial agencies. Most of the Indian leadership renounced the White Paper because they saw it as a way of nullifying the special status of Indians as a result of their treaty rights. The government's new policy was applied to integrating Indian children in provincial schools. It was, for example, applied to the Blue Quills Residential School in Northeastern Alberta near the Saddle Lake Athabaska Reserve. The Indians, under the leadership of Stanley Redcrow, chairman of the Native Educational Council for the Schools, used sit-ins and other forms of protest to get the government to change its position. His goal was to place the school under complete Indian control. Chrétien announced in August 1970 that Blue Quills School was to be transferred to the local Indians to be administered by Stanley Redcrow and the Native Education Council as board of trustees. Indians for the first time were given responsibility for the education of their own children.

A MODERN MICMAC RESERVE

Fred Gross, in an article called "Indian Island: A Micmac Reserve," describes a modern Maritime reserve of about two hundred persons divided into about forty nuclear families.[27]

There are few opportunities for work on the reserve, and except for brief stints as migratory workers picking blueberries or potatoes in Maine, the majority of the residents get their support from government-sponsored assistance programs such as an Indians Affairs Welfare Program; old age, veterans', and other pensions; and salaries for educational and occupational training programs. Some crops are grown by the residents, but they do not produce cash incomes. The Micmac also do some collecting of shellfish and some fishing for eels, mackerel, and smelt, but there is not enough fishing equipment to make fishing commercially profitable.

The policy of Canada since 1970 has been to encourage Indians to assimilate into the larger Canadian society, but the rate at which the Indians leave the reserve is about the same as that of the birthrate, and so the reserve is not likely to disappear in the near future. There are some people on the reserve who have little desire to leave the reserve: it is not only their home but it provides them with welfare and other benefits they could not get elsewhere.

Gross maintains that the combination of government paternalism and traditional Micmac values has resulted in a "culture of poverty" where there is high unemployment and underemployment of unskilled workers; little social, political, and economic organization other than welfare to aid low-income people; and an attitude of outsiders to the effect that Indians are poor because they are personally inadequate, or inferior.

Although there are other poor Maritimers, there are some differences. Gross demonstrates that the Micmacs on the reserve live in a welfare state: they get free education through college; they receive free medical attention, when available; they receive free on-reserve housing if unable to obtain their own; and they receive welfare payments to cover the cost of food and clothing.

There are other differences: the Indians have less well developed political organization, more sporadic cooperative activities, and less well defined leadership.

This may be because they have maintained the traditional orientation toward charismatic leadership and group cooperation. They also have not accepted the Euro-Canadian standards of future planning, especially in saving money in the bank for some future goal.

A CREE INDIAN RESERVE

John Bennett has described a Cree Indian reserve in Sas-katchewan.[28] The population on the reserve when Bennett studied it in the 1960s had few connections with the original groups who had inhabited the region: only two of the families were considered to be descendants of the original band. The remainder on the reserve had "drifted in" over the years. The Department of Indian Affairs considers this reserve to be marginal: too small for large amounts of support and too dis-organized to benefit from the little aid the Department can give them.

At the time of Bennett's study there were about one hundred Indians on the reserve: twenty-five children under five; forty-six from six to twenty-five; twenty-four people from twenty-six to fifty-five; and four who were fifty-six or older. There were more males than females on the reserve. The re-serve was divided into twelve fluid households, half of them with parents and children. One pattern, which was produced by a government policy fobidding unlisted Indians or Indians listed in another band from living on the reserve, is that of "visiting" where relatives may visit the reserve for periods up to five years. This results in much overcrowding, since houses for visitors cannot be built. While the band exists as an official entity, there is no band chief, nor is there any real band fund. The cohesiveness of the group, Bennett maintains, is more the result of white discrimination, some sharing of language and traditions, and some sharing and transferring of possessions.

The looseness of social organization was reinforced by what has been called the "jalopy culture," a transference of the Cree migratory patterns from horses to cars. Bennett writes: "The car is not only a means of transportation, but a means for amusement, a way to kill time, and on occasion, a place to live and sleep."[29]

None of the Indians was a Christian. The majority kept fragments of Cree and Assiniboine folklore, magic, and spells. They maintained some idea of their traditional spirits, but rituals were changed considerably: they would pour a little beer on the ground before drinking it as an offering to the generations of dead Cree. They did give a powwow in which both Cree and Assiniboine songs and chants were sung and drums were beaten. They also held rain dances on the reserve yearly. The Department of Indian Affairs built a school on the reserve in 1958, but the experience was not considered successful by the white teacher, and the children were bused to the town schools after 1963. The effect on the Indian children was one of rapid assimilation to the white model.

The Indians receive a small cash income from government family relief allowances, some manual labor for ranchers or the highway department, rents from white ranchers for use of Indian pastureland, illegal sale of cows given to the Indians by the department, some borrowing and begging, and the occasional trapping of animals. The annual income in 1960 for an Indian family with five children ranged from $1,000 to $1,500 dollars but fluctuated considerably.

The surrounding ranchers consider the Indians to be childish and irresponsible. The Mounties, who arrested them most often for drunkenness or traffic violations, considered them to be irresponsible kids, even "savages." The whites exploit the Indians in the area: they have bought and sold Indian land illegally; they made unfair deals with the Indians for use of their pastureland; and they bought their cows illegally. The Indians retain some sense of self-respect by riding broncos or steers in rodeos and occasionally by swindling the whites.

MODERN INUIT SOCIETY

Jack Ferguson has coined the term "the satellite society" to describe the relationship between the Inuit and Euro-Canadian society.[30] He sees the Inuit as a powerless minority, physically and economically separated from Euro-Canadian society, with an alien government imposed on it.

Until the 1960s, the RCMP and traders were the only Euro-Canadians with whom the Inuit had contact. However, during the late 1950s and early 1960s the Department of Northern Affairs and National Resources expanded its Arctic administration: it sent a Northern Service Officer into most Arctic communities. In addition, engineers came with the construction of the DEW line and its radar station sites, which, in turn, drew a large proportion of Inuit to the sites as laborers. The Inuit workers assimilated rapidly to Euro-Canadian food, housing, and standard of living. However, when construction ended, the labor force was reduced. The Inuit who stayed on as maintenance workers were, for the most part, those who spoke English well and had some education. Education became a higher priority, and many Inuit stayed in the settlements because of the day schools. The nursing stations were a further enticement to stay.

Settlement soon followed a typical pattern of urbanization where communities developed two hundred to five hundred permanent residents made up chiefly of a large native population and a small European population consisting of traders, missionaries, and RCMP who represented the government. At first the Inuit did not participate in the political process, but in the middle 1960s many communities had village councils. By then the European population had increased dramatically, as well, to more than twenty percent. Most of them were civil servants, their housing segregated from that of the native population. There has been little opportunity for the native people of these permanent villages to earn their livings by traditional methods: seals cannot be hunted there, and the whale population is remote and sparse. The boats of the fishermen have deteriorated, and there is little possibility for commercial fishing. Fur-bearing animals are few and far away. At any rate, fur prices fell as store goods increased in price. There have been some efforts to establish workshops for making of fur garments, but the products were not very marketable owing to inferior furs and "lack" of originality of design. Soapstone carving, although more successful than the manufacture of fur garments, benefited only about three or four skilled workers in each settlement.

As a result, most of the Inuit are supported by relief and other welfare payments. Without any meaningful economic activities, the Inuit community becomes more of a "satellite" to the Euro-Canadian community. Further deterioration of Inuit self-pride and identity was produced by the schools, which devalued Inuit culture and made English the sole language of the schools.

INDIAN ACTIVISM

It would be a mistake to view the Indians and Inuit of Canada as an impoverished and totally demoralized remnant of peoples and cultures who were once thriving and viable. There are Canadian Indians who take great pride in their heritage and have organized themselves for effective action. In November 1965, for example, the Indians of Kenora, Ontario, marched down the main street of the town and confronted the town council with several demands: radio-telephone equipment to improve communication with the larger communities; a lengthened trapping season with a shortened time between the fishing and trapping season; the availability of services of the Alcoholism Research Foundation; and the establishment of a process to air grievances between the Indians and the town. The town council granted all their requests. It was the beginning of a growing self-respect, pride, and hope.

Political activism has been common on other reserves as well; in 1968 the Mohawks of St. Regis conducted an effective boycott against the Salmon River School District in New York State in order to keep their own Indian school. Their Canadian counterparts tried their hand by blockading the International Bridge across the St. Lawrence in protest against the deprivation of their rights (under Jay's Treaty of 1794) of free passage across the U.S.-Canadian border. There developed, as Jack Frish states, "a new sense of unity" and a "new feeling of tribalism."[31]

One of the St. Regis Mohawks to come to the force during and after the demonstration at the International Bridge was Ernest Benedict, an electrician with a degree in sociology. He is not a leader in the accepted European sense. He holds no official position, since he resigned from the Band Council in protest of its policies, particularly the firing of the band secretary, John Booth. Moreover, he is very unassuming. Loren Lind writes:

> Mr. Benedict sat balancing on a backless bench, eyes closed, waiting patiently his turn to talk. This meeting had no chairman and he didn't attempt to speak until Mr. Mitchell, a young Indian dancer, called his name.

Then he smiled sheepishly and stood up with a deprecatory wobble. Both hands were in the pockets of his tassled jacket. . . . A chubby man, father of four, he seemed more a travelling salesman than an Indian statesman.[32]

Since 1967, Ernest Benedict has been going to the eastern reserves with his North American Indian Travelling College. The Travelling College promotes consciousness and awareness of Indians in Canada for both Indians and other Canadians. They have promoted films and other media presentations of Indian activities, including a National Film Board picture called *You are on Indian Land,* documenting the demonstration on the International Bridge at Cornwall.

The Canadian government is becoming more sensitive to Indian demands, but there are still many hurdles to overcome. Two of the most recent episodes where Euro-Canadian values and economic aspirations came directly in conflict with those of native peoples are the James Bay Hydroelectric Project and the Mackenzie pipeline.

More than 6,000 Cree Indians live in the James Bay Region where the Quebec government constructed a massive hydroelectric plant through diverting a thousand-mile river system and creating a system of dams to contain the water in vast man-made lakes. The building of this hydroelectric project flooded much of the land on which the Cree lived.

The Cree have never signed any treaties with either the federal or provincial governments that could cede their lands. Until the initiation of the James Bay Project, Indian claims, although never having been resolved, were not at a critical stage. The Cree continued to live much as they had for many years—hunting, trapping, and fishing on a relatively successful subsistence basis. Like many other Indian groups, they felt that the land was important, not only for maintaining traditional subsistence patterns, but also for maintaining other aspects of their traditions, culture, and identity. For example, the Cree consider the bodies of their dead as sacred and were opposed to having their burial grounds flooded.

The Quebec government did little to consult with the Indians about the project. A Cree version of an ecological report was sent to them, but it was in dialects which the Cree of this region could not understand. In addition, the Cree version was fifteen pages long, an obviously shortened one, since the English one was fifty-five pages. In frustration, the Indians burned the report in a woodstove.

In May 1972 the Cree took their claims to court, specifically on the question of ownership of the James Bay Region. The Quebec Superior Court ruled in their favor. The Cree then sought an injunction against the James Bay Development Corporation to halt all construction. In the end, however, the project could not be stopped, and the Indians had to accept a cash settlement. Although the settlement was large, in the millions of dollars, it was not what the Cree wanted: the Cree wanted to be left alone, to hunt, trap, and fish; and to maintain the traditions of their people.

In 1977 Mr. Justice Thomas Berger published a report on his enquiry into the effects of the Mackenzie Valley pipeline on both the ecological system and the social lives of native peoples of the Mackenzie Valley. Berger heard the testimony of three hundred experts on northern conditions and visited thirty-five communities. The Mackenzie Pipeline is a major construction project that required the construction of many buildings, wharves, airstrips, hundreds of miles of roads, as well as thousands of workers and pieces of heavy equipment. Berger reported that in addition to the irreparable damage the pipeline could have on a rich and varied ecosystem, the pipeline would have a tremendous impact on the native peoples who call it their homeland. He considered the native peoples to have a culture and traditional life amounting to "a great deal more than crafts and carvings."[33] He writes:

> Their respect for the wisdom of the elders, their concept of family responsibilities, their willingness to share, their special relationship with the land—all of these values persist today, although native peoples have been under almost unremitting pressure to abandon them.[34]

Berger maintained that Euro-Canadian society has refused to take the native culture seriously. He saw the role of

Euro-Canadians as a negative one—depreciating native cultures in favor of the Euro-Canadian ones:

> Native institutions, values and language were rejected, ignored or misunderstood and—given the native people's use of land—the Europeans had no difficulty in supposing that native people possessed no real culture at all. Education was perceived as the most effective instrument of cultural change: so, educational systems were introduced that were intended to provide the native people with a useful and meaningful cultural inheritance, since their own ancestors had left them none.[35]

He maintained, however, that the native peoples did not see themselves as simply lamenting the loss of their traditional way of life. The native peoples wanted to be able to "shape their own future, out of their own past."

They especially did not want settlements in the old tradition of the treaties in which they extinguished their rights. They wanted a settlement that ensured their rights to the land and that laid the foundation of native self-determination under the constitution of Canada. Berger concluded:

> The native people of the North now insist that the settlement of native claims must be seen as a fundamental reordering of their relationship with the rest of us. Their claims must be seen as the means to establishing a social contract based on a clear understanding that they are distinct peoples in history. They insist upon the right to determine their own future, to ensure their place, but not their assimilation in Canadian life.[36]

Berger argued that if the native people were to achieve their goals, the pipeline should not be built for at least ten years. In July 1977, Canada's National Energy Board endorsed the building of the pipeline along the Alaska Highway to carry natural gas from the Prudhoe Bay area south to Edmonton, where it can be fed into the existing pipeline system. If and when it is needed, a spur will be constructed from Dawson in the Yukon to the Mackenzie Delta to tap natural gas from that region. The concerns for the ecology and native peoples of the Mackenzie Valley are being reflected and, to some degree, met.

The building of the pipeline underlined the limitations of Canada's multicultural policy. The native peoples of Canada would like to be proud partners with the other peoples of Canada, but they see little hope for a real assurance of cultural freedom within the framework of Ottawa's conception of multiculturalism.

Philip Blake, a representative of the Dene (a grouping of Indian tribes of the Northwest Territories), states:

> If your nation chooses . . . to continue to try and destroy our nation, then I hope you will understand why we are willing to fight so that our nation can survive. It is our world.
>
> We do not wish to push our world onto you. But we are willing to defend it for ourselves, and our children, and our grandchildren. If your nation becomes so violent that it would tear up our land, destroy our society and our future, and occupy our homeland, by trying to impose this pipeline against our will, then of course we will have no choice but to react with violence.
>
> I hope we do not have to do that. For it is not the way we would choose. However, if we are forced to blow up the pipeline . . . I hope you will not only look at the violence of Indian action, but also on the violence of your own nation which would force us to take such a course.[37]

There have been a few incidents of sabotage to the pipeline, but there are some hopeful signs. A Council of Indians in the Yukon representing forty-two hundred native people in the area have agreed to participate in a planning council with representatives of the federal government to settle land claims. Negotiations are continuing.

The Founding Peoples: Anglo-Canadians and Franco-Canadians

While the native peoples of Canada constitute an essential ingredient of that nation's multicultural society, much of the concern in Canada today is over the "two solitudes"—the

French and the English peoples of Canada. In some accounts, the gap between the two groups is felt to be so strong that they are referred to as the "Two Founding Races" of Canada. From the anthropological point of view, this is utter nonsense: both Anglo-Canadians and Franco-Canadians are classified as members of the Caucasoid subpopulation of the human species. Beyond that, the gene pool shared by these two cultural entities is very similar if not the same: Celtic, Roman, and Germanic. After 1066 when the Normans invaded England, there was an even greater mixing of genes between the two peoples. The differences between the French and English of Canada, in short, are cultural, not racial.

There have been several attempts at discovering how deep these cultural differences go. Stephen Richer and Pierre Laporte presented a contrasting picture of the two ethnic groups.[38] They described the French Canadian as dominated by his religion, educated by his church, rural, raised in an authoritarian family structure, submissive in relationships, living in the present, and means rather than goal oriented. On the other hand, the English Canadian, not dominated by his religion, was educated in secular schools, urban, raised in an egalitarian family structure, individualistic, competitive in personal relationships, living for the future, and goal oriented.

Although this characterization is a common one applied to the two groups of Canadians, it is somewhat out of date when one considers the changes that have occurred in Quebec in the last twenty years. Nancy Frasure and Mary Louise Kirby (1974) suggest that in the Canada of today, it is the English who are more conservative and the French who are more liberal, at least in the Province of Quebec:

> It is possible that there are two breeds of Canadians being formed: an English Canadian who is relatively more traditional and conservative than his forefathers, and a French Canadian who is more liberal and doctrinaire than his parents.[39]

One study of values of grade four children in Anglo-Protestant and French Catholic schools in an industrial community in the eastern townships of Quebec showed that most of the characterizations of French-Canadian and Anglo-Canadian differences described by Richer and Laporte do not hold up, for these children at least.[40] Both French-Canadian and Anglo-Canadian children, in some instances, prefer an authoritarian family structure; look toward the future, are both goal and means oriented; and, in spite of differences in religious training, feel about the same on the basic goodness of human beings. The study shows, however, that there are differences in value orientations between the two groups of children. The French-Canadian children, for example, feel that the influence of heredity on performance is more important than environmental opportunities, while their Anglo-Canadian counterparts feel otherwise. The francophone children moreover value peer-group interrelationships more than their anglophone counterparts, who more often choose dependence on authority or self-reliance.

Some Anglo-Canadians are descended from United Empire Loyalists who left the Thirteen Colonies at the time of the American Revolution; some have other American roots: many Americans immigrated to the Eastern Townships of Quebec at different periods of history in search of farmlands rather than of political compatibility. Other Anglo-Canadians are immigrants or descendants of those who came from the British Isles and can be further categorized as Scots, Welsh, English, and Northern Irish (the Orangemen). In addition to having different geographical origins, they also show regional distinctions based on where they settled: Maritimers, westerners, and easterners. Each of these differences in regional and historical origins should be examined in any account of the Anglo-Canadians of today.

The remainder of this section, however, is devoted to the French of Canada, who although constituting a unique component of North American society, have largely gone unnoticed by Americans. Moreover, the Anglo-Canadians are covered in other chapters in this book, less through their social organization than through the political and economic culture of which they largely constitute the elite.

The French Canadians

The French of Canada number more than 5 million people, most of whom are descendants of colonists who settled in Canada more than three hundred years ago. The original settlers of New France, as it was then called, were mainly from northwestern France: Normandy, Pays-d'Aunis, Brittany, and Paris. The push toward immigration to New France came from three sources: mercantile interests—especially the fur trade—the military, and the French Catholic church. The mercantile companies had the obligation of encouraging colonists to New France in order to establish a French Catholic state in the New World. In addition, officers and soldiers were encouraged to become settlers when they were discharged: they were offered both large tracts of land and money to remain in the colony. After an initial debacle involving the sending of one hundred women from the Hôpital Général de Paris (a large pauper's home) to become mates for the single soldiers, many peasant farmgirls were sent as marriage partners for the bachelor colonists: *demoiselles*, ladies of breeding, were also sent for the officers.

Horace Miner, in his classic study *St. Denis: A French Canadian Parish*, suggests that the drive toward populating the new colony set some patterns of family life and farm settlement that became the basis of the traditional culture of French Canada.[41] The French government, in the first place, did everything it could to encourage large families: bounties were paid for early marriages to both boys and girls, and special bounties were paid to families having from ten to fifteen living children not in religious orders. In the second place, the manner in which land settlement was prescribed set the pattern for the French-Canadian farm. The initial land distribution was based on the French feudal system, but with some differences. The greater part of the land was given to the *seigneurs*, or feudal lords, as grants by the king of France. Although a *seigneur* had land, he did not have any voice in the government, nor did he have the right to use his *censitaires*, or vassals, as a private militia. Moreover, many of the *seigneurs* were former officers who did not have any major sources of funding to draw upon. To make matters more difficult, the Crown imposed a stringent time table for clearing the land. As a result, the *seigneurs* were obliged to grant land to their farmers for a small perpetual rent in order to encourage them to clear the land quickly. The grants to the farmers, or *habitants* as they were called, were usually four or five arpents wide—an arpent is about 192 feet—and forty arpents long.

These family farms initially bordered the St. Lawrence River because of its importance as the major route for traveling from one place to another. Individual farms ran back for about a mile and a half, providing the settlers with a variety of terrain: cleared fields, meadow, and wooded uplands.

These farms were to be ceded freely to the *habitant's* heirs, but there were fines—a little over 8 percent of the purchase price that was to be paid to the *seigneur* if a farm were sold. One result of this practice was to encourage the tradition of keeping a farm in the family. The survival and security of the family farm became a major value for the French Canadians throughout much of their history. In addition, because of the variety of uses to which the terrain on the narrow strip farms originally ceded could be put, and the large number of children in the farm family, the French-Canadian *habitant*, except for such obligations as grinding his grain in the *seigneur's* mill, could take care of most of his family's needs without recourse to outside help. Another French-Canadian tradition resulted: a strong desire to maintain the independence of the family. Except for the *premier voisin*, the neighbor next door, and the occasional *corvée*, or barn raising with the aid of one's neighbors, there was little need for contact with outsiders. As long as there was more land available, fathers could provide for their sons by building a new row of farms (the second *rang*) behind the first. However, because of geological and climatic factors, there was not an inexhaustible source of new land. Moreover, farm management, such as crop rotation and fertilization, was not widely practiced; eventually, once productive land became less fertile even while farms were being divided into smaller parcels to accommodate heirs. An added factor was the Industrial Revolution of the nineteenth century (and, in its effects, the twentieth), which lured the sons and daughters of farmers to the growing metropolis of Montreal and the mill towns of New England. At the present time, only about 5 percent of the land of Quebec is under cultivation, and less than 3 percent of Quebec's population works in agriculture. Yet the traditional farm values of independence and security remain high, especially among the modern farmers of the Richelieu Valley.

The fur trade, however, was another way of making a living in New France. Consequently, another tradition developed: that of the *coureur des bois*, the fur traders. If the *habitants* represented stability and security, the *coureur des bois* represented the spirit of adventure. Unlike the *habitants*, wrote Donald Creighton, the *coureurs des bois* were "irreverent, impatient of authority, extravagantly friendly and violently quarrelsome by turns, they were spendthrifts who squandered their money in the taverns along the riverbank."[42] French participation in the fur trade declined after the French were defeated by the English in 1759 on the Plains of Abraham (the Conquest). However, a new tradition developed which roughly corresponded to that of the fur trader: *le bucheron*, the lumberjack. The timber industries required men who could make trails to new lumber and camp sites; men to cut down the trees; men to haul the logs to the rivers; and *les draveurs*, men to float the logs down the rivers. These men retained many of the personality characteristics of the former *voyageurs* (explorers) and *coureurs des bois*. But an interesting duality of life style eventually developed for many farmers, especially as farming shifted from subsistence to cash economies during World War I (1914–18). When the war was over, farmers who had geared crop production to the war effort found themselves with few buyers. Men whose families had become used to some of the luxuries cash could buy went to the woods during the winter to compensate for the loss in income. The farmer and the lumberjack became one.

Habitant, coureur de bois, bucheron, and *draveur* take on mythic proportions for the French Canadians in the same way the cowboy does for the Americans, and the Northwest (not Royal Canadian) Mounted Police do for the Anglo–Canadian.

The Church. Because of the structure of the *rang* (the system of farm management), municipal organizations like towns never became as important in New France as in France of the period. Later, when *seigneurs* and merchants left after the Conquest, the only major social institution other than the family that remained intact was the parish, which served as the framework for the civil administration. According to Jean-Charles Falardeau:

> The clergy was . . . the sole guide and the real leader of the population, the main unit that integrated social life in the parish. Although the seignoir was master of his censitaires . . . very few seignoirs fulfiled their obligations, including that of living on the estate. . . . The uncontested leader of the parish was the priest, whose role as spiritual minister and moral arbitrator of his flock developed into that of a natural protector, adviser.[43]

At the time of the Conquest, this impact must have been minimal: there were only 138 prients for 70,000 people. The strength of the Church, nevertheless, continued to grow until it became a major force in French-Canadian life in the 1840s. Up until the Révolution Tranquille (the "Quiet Revolution") of the 1960s, the Church pervaded every aspect of French-Canadian life. Schools, for example, were distributed by parish and, for Catholic students, were controlled by the Church in Quebec. This control extended all the way into higher education where the universities of Montreal and Quebec had the archbishops of their respective cities as chancellors as well as a high proportion of clergy among their faculty. Nuns and congregations of brothers dominated the welfare and charitable institutions: hospitals, orphanages, rehabilitation centers, sanitoriums, and other kinds of charities. Even in the areas of work were to be found the hand of the Church: mistrusting secular unions as communistic and atheistic, the priests organized their own unions, unions of young agricultural Catholics, young Catholic workers, young Catholic students, and the Union of Catholic Cultivators.

However, the impact of French-Canadian Catholicism went beyond the control of social and cultural institutions; it permeated the everyday life of its parishoners. In talking about the daily lives of the French-Canadian farmers of St. Denis, Miner saw the role of religion as pervasive:

> Life in St. Denis is a flow of traditional behavior. Upon rising there are family prayers: then the animals must be fed and the cows milked; the workers return to cross themselves and sit down to breakfast. . . . Incidents in this stream of events can be singled out as sacred and secular, but such distinction is not part of the native's own conceptualization of life.[44]

The calendrical cycle revolved around religious events. The Mass of St. Mark's day at the end of April was a call for divine blessing of the seeds for planting; at the end of May the ceremony of *fête-dieu* for the blessing of the newly sown crop; the first of November brought All Saint's Day, or *Toussaint*, in which the dead were remembered. Christmas called for a number of religious ceremonies as well as *veillées*, or social evenings—Christmas Eve, with its midnight mass followed by *Réveillon*, the special midnight supper; New Year's Day when a father blessed his children; and the *jour des rois*, the day of the kings, the first week of January. Mardi Gras (Shrove Tuesday) and *Les Cendres* (Ash Wednesday) came in February or March; *Les Rameaux* (Palm Sunday), *Vendredi Saint* (Good Friday), and *Pâques* (Easter) occurred in mid-April. These religious events were rites of intensification that reinforced the religious values of the *habitant* during the year.

But the various stages of an individual's life were also punctuated by religious rites of passage where the changes in status were marked by religious ceremony. Horace Miner described these events as a journey along a road "from the secular world into the sacred."[45] The journey began with the baptism of the infant signifying the first rite of entrance into the Catholic community. It was followed by the *petite communion*, or first communion, when the child entered school, at which point the child began to become a practicing Catholic; full membership in the community of Catholics came with the *grande communion*, or Confirmation, when the child was eleven or twelve. This rite of passage could be considered as a change to the status of religious adulthood. Miner wrote:

After the festive *grande communion* the status is that of a participating member of the society demanding a Mass for burial, mourning, and requiring of the individual full participation in the religious activity of the community.[46]

Marriage was common for couples in their twenties. A young man would call upon the family of the young woman he had selected: the young lady in question sat inconspicuously in the room without saying anything. After a period of time, sometimes as little as a month, the young man asked the father of the woman for his daughter's hand. Then the marriage contract was arranged between the two sets of parents and the bond was sealed. The parish was then informed of the actual date by the reading of the banns, the notice of an intended marriage. The marriage mass took place in the parish church of the bride. Before the service was read, the bride deposited her blue membership ribbon in the Enfantes de Marie on the alter; thus, she signified her departure from the group of unmarried girls and women.

Death brought the final series of rites of passage. Death came in two stages—apparent death and real death. Real death came about two hours after a person had been judged dead, that is, when the sacrement of extreme unction was given. Ultimately bells were rung to notify the parish of the death. The body of an adult was laid out in a coffin in the home for three days, dressed in dark clothes. Each night until the burial there was a wake during which friends and relatives congregated at the house. The funeral mass was followed by the funeral procession to the cemetery, in which the person's most intimate friend carried the cross draped in black crepe. Wives wore mourning clothes (a completely black dress and veil) for about a year and a half. Masses were sung often for the deceased to ensure the voyage of the soul from purgatory to heaven.

With the impact of urbanization and modernization, the

power of the Church in Quebec has weakened considerably. The Quiet Revolution of the 1960s was heralded by the slogan, *Maîtres chez Nous* (Masters in our own house). To be masters in their own house, the Liberal government of Jean Lesage believed it was necessary to control the economic life of the province. Therefore, one of the major thrusts of the government in the early 1960s was to revolutionize the educational system in the province. The traditional educational system under the control of the Church had previously been oriented toward a classical education with an emphasis on the arts and literature. The classical colleges were attuned to the professions: the church, the law, medicine, and letters. As a result, the government felt the need to secularize the educational system. The new system would train French Canadians to be engineers and business administrators so that they would, in reality, be masters in Quebec. A Minister of Education was named in 1964, and new kinds of educational institutions appeared: the comprehensive high school and the CEGEP, or general and vocational college (roughly equivalent to the American junior college).

In addition, the provincial government became more involved with social services. In 1970 a Department of Social Affairs was created with responsibility for health and social services in Quebec, including unemployment insurance, comprehensive pension payments, and family allowances. These governmental services lessened the role of the church as an agent of charitable and social services.

But an even more significant factor in the weakening of the role of the Church in Quebec has been the change in life style. The simple life of the *habitant* has been replaced by the complex one of the urban and suburban dweller. Colette Moreaux, in an article called "The End of Religion," has argued that:

> The declining recruitment rate in monasteries and the priesthood and the abandonment of the religious and ecclesiastic state are recent and serious problems in Quebec. The secular world is being put on an equal footing with the formerly well-protected ecclesiastical hierarchy through a questioning of the religious state, its definition of itself and its place in a secular

society. . . . The community based on faith no longer acts as a principle of cohesion. . . . Essentially secular values are being progressively established and structured by institutions which are increasingly freed of confessionals and clerical personnel.[47]

The Family. French-Canadian families have a structure similar to that of other Western European groups: a bilateral kinship system in which family members relate to close relatives on both the mother's and father's side. Like other Western European systems it, too, is patronymic: children take the surname of their fathers; wives take the surname of their husbands. French Canadians are well aware of their more than three hundred years of history in North America. This awareness is reflected in the pride that many French Canadians have in the history of their family names: many keep detailed and extensive genealogical charts and records.[48]

In spite of this detailed consciousness of extended kin, most French Canadians have closer social contact with relatives in the same generation: siblings and cousins. Certain rites of passage such as baptism, confirmation, marriage, and death involve participation of the larger kin network. For example, grandparents often assume the responsibility of godparents for the firstborn children of their sons or daughters. Friendship, however, most often comes from the large network of cousins: one does not go to the mountains to enjoy the fresh air but to see Cousin Luc, who happens to live there.

For most matters it is the household itself that is at the center of French-Canadian family life: a man, his wife, and any other close relatives who may happen to live with him (his parents, a maiden aunt, or a younger brother). As Horace Miner described the division of labor in *St. Denis*, farm responsibilities were clearly defined. Women did the spinning, weaving, knitting, making of clothes, cooking, serving at the table, washing, vegetable gardening, milking; men raised the hay and grain, cut the wood, kept the house in repair, and attended to business contacts. The sexual dichotomy was so pronounced that the men and boys sat on one side of the large kitchen table, while the girls, with the exception of the mother and perhaps an older daughter, sat on the other.

The rural Quebec farm was, unless the owner had the misfortune to be childless, strictly a family affair. The hiring of outsiders was unusual. As a result, large families remained a necessity: a man needed at least three ablebodied sons to help him with his work; a wife needed the same number of daughters to help with the chores in the barn and around the house. Many farm families had eight or more children. At the same time, only one of the boys could inherit the family farm. And, contrary to English tradition, it was rarely the eldest son who did so. The eldest son would be ready to assume responsibility for the farm while the father was in his fifties, still in his prime.

The father was most definitely the head of the household. His authority was sanctioned by the Church and modeled on the Holy Family. As God was the director of their lives, from whom they could expect justice, so were their own fathers the directors of their secular lives. As the Virgin Mary was the mother of them all, compassionate to all, offering intervention with God, the Father, on their behalf, so it was their own mothers who were compassionate confidantes from whom they could expect advocacy of their wishes with their own fathers, the heads of the household.

The father's authority was so extensive in the period prior to World War II (1939–45) that all members of the family were expected to proffer any money earned outside the household for his disposition. It was his responsibility to see to the welfare of his family, and especially to see that his daughters were settled and his sons established. If the father was provident and just, his children were willing to accept this paternal control with little hesitation.

Philip Garigue, in an article entitled "The French Canadian Family," based on research among urban French-Canadian families in Montreal in the late 1950s and early 1960s, showed that many of the orientations and values of family life in the rural parish studied by Miner were maintained in the urban setting. He interviewed seventy people on the obligations and responsibilities of fathers and mothers within the Quebec household: sixty-eight out of the seventy saw the roles of the husbands and wives as being complementary. The

husband exercised the traditional role of punishing misbehavior, providing protection, and giving economic support.
The wife exercised her traditional role in the household: raising children, seeing to their spiritual and secular education,
and planning the family's leisuretime activities. Although
these roles were seen as complementary, it was understood
that the wife complemented the husband and not the husband
who complemented the wife. Until the Quebec Civil Code was
modified in 1964, the man exercised the legal rights of his
family: he had legal control of his wife's property and was
expected to conduct her financial transactions. This legal control was so inclusive that a mother could not sign consent
forms that would authorize emergency surgery on an injured
or seriously ill child. The father was the sole legal guardian.

Although the father had the ultimate responsibility for
punishing misbehavior, he did not, in actuality, devote much
time to disciplinary action. As one would expect, it was the
mother, in more frequent daily contact with her children, who
dealt with the everyday infringements. Her punishments
were rarely physical. In punishing her children, she did so
clearly as the father's surrogate, in his name.

It would be a mistake, however, to view the French-Canadian woman as powerless. Wives often were better educated
than their husbands, who had left school earlier to work on
the farm or in the lumber camps. Often a man deferred to his
wife in educational and religious matters, although the final
decision was always his. He could, however, be influenced by
a persuasive and reasonable wife. Yet French-Canadian men
of this period maintained the traditional stereotypes of the
woman as the "weaker sex." A good husband tried to create
a climate of security for his more emotional and sensitive
spouse. He saw his role as one of firm support in times of
difficulty, a protector for his dependent and attentive wife.

Garigue's respondents also discussed the relationships of
parents and children. The father, as head of the family, was
supposed to introduce his children to their family responsibilities. The best father was one who was impartial, just, and
firm. The mother was first and foremost a mother: this was
her primary vocation, her happy duty.

The French-Canadian family has been described as rigidly authoritarian, but at the same time, both individualism and personal independence of family members were recognized and valued. Although most French-Canadian children had more obligations and responsibilities than most Anglo-Canadian and American children, nevertheless they had more leeway in the performance of a task than is general in these other families. Once a child had demonstrated competency, then parents felt no further need to intervene in the performance of a task. French-Canadian parents felt strongly about recognizing the specific strengths of a child and encouraging his independent development. In the final analysis, barring a serious moral or legal breach of norms, parents regarded the child's happiness as a major consideration.

The expectations of a child of its parents varied with both the sex of the child and the sex of the parent. The majority of children, however, had a stronger emotional attachment to the mother: she was the one who displayed affection, the one who shared their triumphs and defeats, the one who interceded with the father on their behalf. The father, at best, was one for whom the children felt a great deal of respect. But he also engendered hostility: he was the one who most often represented an obstacle to a particular aspiration of the child. At the same time, fathers and daughters had very strong ties, while fathers and sons did not; mothers and sons had a special bond, while mothers and daughters did not. Garigue suggested that it was the pressure of role modeling that produced this division. The son's role was to become like his father as quickly as possible, but according to his mother's interpretation. The daughter was to become a woman according to the model and ideal of the mother with the consent of the father.

In addition, relations with siblings were for the most part supportive rather than competitive. The strong sense of individual worth and respect for the independence of one's brothers and sisters was coupled with an equally strong sense of the family as the source of one's security. The result was a high degree of responsibility toward one another; and aid was rarely denied to one another. In large families where there were many children, not only were older siblings expected to look after younger siblings, it was a necessity that they do so.

The Quiet Revolution brought changes in the Quebec urban family in the years after 1960. Marc Adélard Tremblay maintains that "French Canadian families are engaged in the process of freeing themselves from the authoritarian structure of the patriarchal system."[49] One of the elements of the "New Quebec" was the development of the women's liberation movement. Quebec women are now more conscious of having occupational status outside the home, of family planning, and of being au courant in politics and world affairs.

Québécois children are now being reared much more permissively than were their parents. The school and the mass media, especially television, have increased modern Quebec children's intellectual and emotional scope, and they are more apt to express values and attitudes that are contradictory to those of their parents.

The Language: A Sociolinguistic View of Quebec. In 1969 when Canada passed its Official Language Act, Canada became, officially, a bilingual nation: English and French are the two official languages of Canada. Not everybody, however, or even a majority of Canadians, can speak both French and English. In fact, according to the latest census, of the 14 million Canadians whose mother tongues are other than French, only 3 percent claimed to be bilingual in French and English: fewer than 400,000 people. Most of the French-English bilinguals of Canada are people whose mother tongue is French. Moreover, if one ignores Montreal where there is a large English population, a large majority of the people of Quebec speak only French. William Mackey maintains that more people who are fluent in both French and English can be found in a monolingual nation like France than in bilingual Canada. Officially, bilingualism within the national government means only that Canadians have the right to communicate with, and be served by, federal agents in either English or French.

Richard Joy in an article, "Languages in Conflict: Canada, 1976," sees Canada as becoming polarized with French in Quebec and English elsewhere.[50] One important issue for

Canadians, both French and English, is whether there is something one could call French Canada. Marcel Rioux writes:

> To speak of French Canada (or of the French people of Canada) is to speak of Canadians who speak French and who live in all parts of Canada. . . . Federalists are happy to grant the name of French Canada to the totality of French-speaking people scattered throughout the Canadian territory. . . . In the 1960's a great change occurred, revolutionizing the situation. In Quebec, people began to make a distinction between Quebec and French Canada. . . . Federal government statistics show that outside of Quebec this population—speakers of French—is becoming anglicized at various rates of speed—The steamroller of English-speaking North American culture will soon leave nothing but a few remnants of this language and culture.
>
> On the other hand, there is a vast land three times larger than France, where the French-speaking people are a great majority, namely Quebec.[51]

This distinction between French Canada and French Quebec is an important one. The issue for the people of Quebec is not whether they can get federal service in French or English anywhere in Canada, but whether the French language and culture can survive, and even flourish, within Quebec itself. In 1974 Quebec passed its own Official Language Act, Bill 22 (in 1976 replaced by Bill 101), making French the only official language of Quebec.

The clash of English and French in Quebec has taken place mainly in two arenas: the world of work and the world of education. Many French-speaking Québécois use French as the language of the home, neighborhood, social gatherings, and shopping; however, because many of the firms for which they work are owned or managed by Anglophones—speakers of English—they must work in English. The result is a classic example of diglossia where one set of behaviors, attitudes, and values is expressed in one language; another set of behaviors, attitudes, and values is expressed in the other.[52] However, the diglossia of Quebec is not fully accepted as culturally legitimate and complementary by the Québécois: they see themselves as "menaced." "In the working world, they occupy, even in Quebec, a position inferior to the English Canadians and to every immigrant group with the exception of the Italians."[53] The conflict is especially strong in the middle and higher levels of Quebec's manufacturing industries because these levels showed, according to the Gendron Commission (appointed by the Quebec government in 1968 to investigate French-language rights in Quebec), that:

> the primary and secondary industry in Quebec was dominated by English speakers at the top and French speakers at the bottom. In addition, there appeared to be a direct relationship between the low level of use of French in functional communications in any given sector and the overrepresentation of English people—especially in administrative and professional positions.[54]

Québécois believed that they had the right to expect that they could use the French language everywhere, in all levels of economic activity in the province. Chapter VII of Bill 101, Quebec's present language act, requires that employers must write all communications to their employees in French; they must render all results of arbitration and collective bargaining in French; they cannot dismiss or demote an employee simply because he speaks only French; and they must prove to all interested persons and government agencies that knowledge of a language other than French is necessary in a particular job. French has become the only official language of work in Quebec. The results of this language policy have been predictable. Some Anglo-Canadian companies (e.g., Sun Life Assurance of Canada) have announced that they are moving their headquarters to Ontario because they cannot accept the terms of this language policy. The change in official policy is eliminating the need for diglossia in Quebec, and with it the need to be bilingual in French and English; the strongest reason for Quebec's Francophones to learn English—economic advantage—is being eliminated.

The most vehement battles over language have been fought in the sphere of education. The major issue is whether immigrants have the right to be educated in English rather than French in the Province of Quebec. The Francophones of

Quebec feel that the French language will not even survive in Quebec unless immigrant families send their children to the French-language public schools. There are a number of factors to be considered: the birthrate of French-speaking Québécois has been reduced to the lowest of all Canada; few French-speaking people from France, Belgium, Switzerland, or other French-speaking areas of the world immigrate to Quebec; and most immigrants, including some French-speaking ones like the Moroccan Jews, want their children to be educated in English because they recognize that mobility in work and on the North American continent depends upon the ability to communicate in English. As a result, the desire of immigrants, especially that of Italian Catholics, to have their children receive English instruction in school has angered many francophone Québécois, even to the point of violence. The riot in St. Léonard, a small Montreal suburb, on September 10, 1969, is a case in point, albeit an isolated example.

The issue of English-language rights is not only a question of the language to be used in school, but also a matter of contrast in orientation between anglophone Canadians and francophone Québécois. Anglophones see the issue as one of the rights of the individual: parents have the right to choose the language in which their children are educated. Francophones argued that the rights of the collectivity—the majority of French speakers in Quebec—need to be protected. If immigrants are allowed to continue to educate their children in English, French as the language of Quebec is doomed. The most recent language legislation, Bill 101, strongly asserts the rights of the collectivity: instruction in all levels of education from kindergarten through secondary school must be done in French. Only children who have at least one parent educated in English in Quebec, or whose parents were educated in English outside Quebec but came before the law went into effect, or those children who are already enrolled in English classes and their younger brothers and sisters may be educated in English in Quebec. All other children must enroll in French-language schools. Many parents have refused to comply with the law and have enrolled their children illegally in English-language schools. In the eyes of the law, these children are nonstudents, and they cannot officially graduate from school in Quebec. Language rights in Quebec remains a highly emotional issue.

Another sociolinguistic question is what kind of French Québécois French is. Several varieties or dialects of French are used in Quebec. There is *la langue soignée* of formal French, which is very close to the standard French spoken on the European continent, especially in vocabulary and syntax, although there are some differences in pronunciation. It is the variety used from the pulpit on Sunday and in the editorials of such newspapers as *Le Devoir* as well as by the announcers on Radio-Canada, the French-language network. *La langue populaire,* or popular French, is spoken by the majority of Québécois. Popular French has some archaic forms like *piastres* for dollars and a number of words borrowed directly from English, such as *un party* instead of *une soirée,* or *une shop* instead of *une boutique.* There is also *le joual,* a variety of French originating in Montreal, which has many borrowings from English, especially slang, in both words and constructions. This language contains a number of contractions of syllables and dropping the sounds that make it almost impossible for outsiders to understand.

The issue at stake is more than communication. It is a question of identity. Many nationalists in Quebec feel that *joual* is the real Québécois, a distinct language that represents their uniqueness as a culture. In the last ten years plays, novels, and poems have been written in *joual* and are quite popular. The education hierarchy, however, considers *joual* an aberration, a historical accident. Signs on the buses and subways tell Québécois to be proud to speak good French— that is, standard French. *Joual* as a literary dialect has gained some legitimacy in Quebec, then; but standard French, the language of the educated, is the one that is taught and tested in the schools.

The Quest for National Identity. It is necessary to make a distinction between French-Canadian culture and Quebec society. French-speaking minorities in Canada and the United States can share in ideas, beliefs, and behavioral patterns that are similar to those practiced in Quebec. However, militant Québécois see their role as one of liberating Quebec society from the economic and political domination of the rest of Canada, especially Ontario. The liberation of Quebec is to be realized by a synthesis of two conflicting tendencies: survival of the language, traditions, and ideals of the Québécois; and the modernization of the economic, political, and educational life of its people. They do not see the Anglo-Canadian or American models of modernity as appropriate to their own development. The current party in power in Quebec is the Parti Québécois (PQ) under René Lévesque's leadership. Lévesque sees the resolution of the tendencies for conservation of a unique way of life and modernization of the political, social, and economic institutions in Quebec as coming through a new kind of structure: a Sovereignty/Association in which Quebec would be free to develop its own institutions and cultural life while sharing in the economic growth of modern North America through investment and trade.

It is no accident that license plates in Quebec have changed from the slogan *La Belle Province* to that of *Je me souviens*: from "the beautiful province" (part of Canada) to "I remember"—a reminder of more than three hundred years of history. For many Québécois, the future is an extension of the past; for some Anglo-Canadians, however, it appears to promise a dissolution of the present.

The Immigrants

Nearly 30 percent of Canada's population is of other than British or French origin. Twenty percent of these are immigrants to Canada, many of whom, more than 3 million people, came to Canada after 1945 and represent more than fifty different ethnic groups.

In 1966 a government White Paper, indicating governmental policy, contained the following resolution: "There will be no discrimination in immigration by reason of race, colour or religion."[55] This was not always the case in Canadian history.

A BRIEF HISTORY OF CANADIAN IMMIGRATION POLICY

At the time of Confederation, 1867, only 8 percent of Canada's population were other than French or English. The fathers of Confederation concentrated on the British-French duality and ignored any other kind of ethnic diversity, although British North America already contained "significant numbers of people of German and Dutch origin, well-established black and Jewish communities."[56]

At the turn of the century, economic conditions improved and Wilfrid Laurier's Liberal government actively promoted immigration to Canada, especially by those who wished to farm in the newly opened lands of the western prairies. Between 1896 and 1914, 3 million immigrants, many of whom were British, came to Canada. As discussed above, a large number of Eastern Europeans came as well. The growth of the population of Canada in this period was substantial: it increased 43 percent, 22 percent of which was the result of immigration. The Canadian prairie west began to take on a distinctive flavor with more than one third of its population other than English or French in origin.

The predominant view toward immigrants was in support of assimilation. Howard Palmer, a historian, writes:

> Throughout the period of the first large influx of non-British, non-French immigrants (indeed up until World War II) anglo-conformity was the predominant ideology of assimilation in English-speaking Canada—Proponents of anglo-conformity argued that it was the obligation of new arrivals to conform to the values and institutions of Canadian society—which were already fixed. During this period when scarcely anyone questioned the verities of God, King, and country, there was virtually no thought given to the possibility that "WASP" values might not be the apex of civilization which all men should strive for.[57]

Palmer goes on to point out that Anglo-Saxon white superiority was taken for granted. The closer the immigrant in physical and cultural similarity to Englishmen, the more desirable he was as an immigrant. The hierarchy of desirable immigrants began with English and American whites, then Northern and Western Europeans, then Central and Eastern Europeans, excluding Jews; then strange religious sects like the Hutterites, Mennonites, and Doukhobors; and last,

> the Asian immigrants—the Chinese, Japanese, and East Indians. . . . Running somewhere close to last were black immigrants, who did not really arise as an issue because of the lack of aspiring candidates, except in 1911, when American blacks were turned back at the border by immigration officials because they allegedly could not adapt to the cold winters in Canada.[58]

The 1920s brought another wave of non-English, non-French immigrants into Canada. These years brought even greater restrictions on Oriental and Central and Eastern European immigration to Canada. However, a shift in attitude began in the mid-1920s. Palmer writes:

> Several powerful sectors of Canadian society, including transportation companies, boards of trade, newspapers and politicians of various political persuasions, as well as ethnic groups, applied pressure on the King government to open the immigration doors. These groups believed that only a limited immigration could be expected from the 'preferred' countries and that probably only central and eastern Europeans would do the rugged work of clearing marginal land.[59]

The government made arrangements with the railroads to bring in a number of Central and Eastern European immigrants to settle as farmers, farm workers, or domestic servants. One hundred and sixty-five thousand Central and Eastern Europeans as well as twenty thousand Mennonites were brought to Canada. At this time the non-British, non-French population was more than 18 percent of the total Canadian population. The prevailing view toward these new immigrants was that of R. B. Bennett, who became Prime Minister of Canada during the 1930s:

> These people [continental Europeans] have made excellent settlers . . . but it cannot be that we must draw upon them to

shape our civilization. We must still maintain that measure of British civilization which will enable us to assimilate these people to British institutions, rather than assimilate our civilization to theirs.[60]

The depression of the 1930s saw a severe decline in immigration into Canada. It was not until after World War II that another large wave of immigration began with "the influx of refugees from war-torn Europe and thousands of German, Dutch, and British immigrants seeking better economic opportunities."[61] The postwar immigration policy of Canada gave preference to immigrants of either British or French origin—and to those others who could be easily absorbed into the Canadian mainstream. Asians and West Indians were not included in this category.

However, the size of the postwar immigration to Canada had a tremendous impact on the character of Canada's society, particularly on the large cities like Toronto and Montreal. By 1961, the proportion of the non-British, non-French population of Ontario was nearly a third of the total population. The city of Toronto was soon transformed from a relatively small, conservative British city ("Toronto the Good") to a cosmopolitan metropolitan area with a variety of cultures and languages enlivening its streets.

The 1950s and 1960s saw greater acceptance of both new immigrants and existing ethnic minorities. Nazi racism had shocked Canadians who did not want to be associated in any way with the racial and ethnic intolerance of Hitler's regime. In addition, the civil rights movement had begun in the United States and had an influence on Canadian thinking. The economic prosperity Canada enjoyed contributed in turn to a much more relaxed attitude toward racial and ethnic minorities—they were no real threat to employment or wages. In 1962 Canada's immigration law was changed to allow for the admission of an immigrant to Canada regardless of nationality, so long as he had "sufficient means of support to maintain himself in Canada until he has established himself."[62] The immigration law was amended so that immigrants who passed an assessment (made by immigration officers on a point system) could be admitted into Canada. The immigration officers assessed each immigrant on the basis of skills, occupational demands in Canada; age; knowledge of English and French; as well as other factors such as "personal" assessment, presumably "personality and appearance."

Most recently the Immigration Act of 1978 attempts to tie the number of immigrants to long-term demographic planning and the needs of the labor market. However, it also establishes a new "family class" allowing Canadian citizens to sponsor a wider range of relatives.

The situation of Canada's immigrant and ethnic minorities has improved. The WASPish vertical mosaic has begun to break down as the media, professions, governmental positions, and political parties have become more open. Canada has had a reputation for liberal and fair treatment of refugees such as Hungarians in the mid-1950s and more recently the Moroccan Jews and Vietnamese. But it would be a mistake to think that there has not been, or does not continue to be, racism and discrimination against minority groups in Canada. As Palmer puts it, "Much of the rhetoric [about being a cultural mosaic] has simply been wishful thinking. There has been a long history of racism and discrimination against ethnic minorities in . . . Canada, along with strong pressures for conformity to WASP ways."[63]

Throughout much of Canada's history, it has been assumed that those immigrants who needed to change their ways the least made the best immigrants, particularly those from the British Isles. Of the 3.5 million immigrants who came to Canada in the years before 1972, more than 26 percent came from the United Kingdom, and nearly two thirds came from either Britain, the United States, or Western Europe.

The evidence, however, points to a different conclusion than that anticipated by those who made immigration policy. Anthony Richmond writes:

> This assumption and the policy conclusions drawn from it have not been fully supported by experience. In fact, the studies of post-war immigrants in Canada and of the return movement to the former country support the view that return migration

tends to be highest among 'those who will have to change their ways least in order to adapt themselves.' There is some truth in the proposition 'easy come easy go'. Immigrants who have first to make a major effort to adapt themselves, once they have overcome initial difficulties, tend to put down roots and be more likely to stay permanently.[64]

It would be impossible to describe the experiences of all the ethnic and racial minorities of Canada within the scope of this chapter. The rich and varied life of the many immigrant groups will be restricted to a somewhat arbitrary few: Chinese, Blacks, Ukrainians, Italians, and Hutterites. The Blacks and the Chinese, although small in number as a result of Canada's nonreceptive immigration policy for many years, represent Canadian minorities that have experienced, and continue to experience, treatment as deprived and excluded minorities. The Hutterites have preserved their distinctive cultural patterns through a separately lived communal life; they are, as a result, of great interest to anthropologists and other social scientists. The Ukrainians and the Italians are two of the largest immigrant groups in Canada and have had, and are continuing to have, an important impact on Canada's "cultural mosaic."

THE CHINESE

Although there have been claims that the Chinese reached North America in the thirteenth century, the story of Chinese immigration into British North America began with the Fraser River gold rush of 1858. They came, as they did in California, to work as laborers in the gold mines. Moreover, large numbers of Chinese men came to British Columbia during the period from 1881 to 1884 to work on the building of the Canadian Pacific Railway. These early immigrants had no intention of staying in Canada. They were peasants from the south of China who came to North America simply to make money, "to dig gold," and then to be "homeward bound." Their desires to return to China were reinforced by the attitudes of Anglo-British Columbians. The latter discriminated actively against the Chinese, whom they called "yellow bellies," "chinks," and "monkeys." Ethnocentric Anglo-British Columbians, like their California counterparts, considered the Chinese as treacherous and dishonest by nature—even though there was contrary evidence that a Chinese businessman's word was as "good as gold." In 1860 Sir James Douglas of Vancouver Island reported to the Colonial Office in London that "the Chinese were certainly not a desirable class of people as a permanent population but were, for the present, useful as laborers and consumers." Certainly their hopes of retiring in China with their earnings were dashed when neither their employers nor the government were willing to take the responsibility of sending them home after the completion of the railway. The hapless Chinese workers found themselves stranded in a foreign country without food, money, or the support of their families—they had left their wives and children behind in China. They took jobs where they could: as houseboys at $5 a month, lumberjacks, miners, laundrymen, workers in restaurants, farm laborers—and many went to clear and farm land on the banks of the Fraser.

In response to the needs of these unemployed Chinese men, the Chinese Benevolent Society came into being in 1889. Its first function was to provide food, hospital care, and shelter to those who were in need. It became an important protective and mutual-aid society for the Chinese, was incorporated under British Columbia law in 1907, and later opened branches in other parts of Canada.

In 1884 there were about sixteen thousand Chinese in Canada, the majority of whom were in British Columbia. The labor unions, who feared the competition of Chinese laborers, pressured the Canadian government to restrict stringently the immigration of Chinese into Canada during the period from 1885 to 1947. From 1885 until 1923, Chinese immigrants were required to pay a head tax that began as $50 a head in the 1880s and increased to $500 a head in 1903. In 1923 the federal government passed what was euphemistically called the Chinese Immigration Act. It was in reality a "Chinese Exclusion Act": all Chinese except for students and missionaries were excluded from entering Canada. Vivian Lai writes,

"Only forty-four Chinese were allowed into Canada between the years 1923 and 1947."[65]

The Chinese who came to Canada before 1923 were both culturally and socially isolated from Anglo-Canadian society. They maintained their language and their dress—the typical straight-cut Chinese jacket buttoned from the throat to the hem and hanging loosely over their cuffless trousers. They wore their hair in the long queue or pigtail that signified their submission to the Manchu dynasty. Their separateness was noted by a *Caribou Sentinel* editorial of 1867 that criticized the Chinese because they were "aliens in nationality, habits, religion; they never became good citizens; they dealt entirely with their own countrymen; they hoarded their money and sent it home; . . . and they were inimical to immigration."[66]

In addition to such organizations as the Chinese Benevolent Society, the Chinese formed many other clubs and societies. District organizations were formed to look after the welfare of those Chinese who came from specific localities in China.

The majority of Chinese in Canada before 1947 were Buddhists or Taoists in religion and Confucian in orientation. Chinese Buddhism was influenced by the Zen sect that stressed enlightenment through meditation and insight. The Chinese, however, replaced meditation with hard work and rugged self-reliance. Taoists, also stressing the independence of the individual, believed that one should be in harmony with the great pattern of nature—the Tao, which is a mutually complementary and balancing dualism: the yang that is male, light, hot, and positive, and the yin that is female, dark, cold, and negative. Confucianism was an ethical philosophy that stressed harmony in human relations—a recognition of the principles of order and authority in family, society, and the state. Beginning in 1889, the traditional Chinese of Vancouver's Chinatown sent their children to a Chinese-language school two hours a week to learn the Chinese language, good manners, and Confucian ethics.

Because of the strong anti-Chinese feeling in Canada, there were all kinds of restrictions on Chinese employment. Until the British Columbia legislature granted "its coloured minorities" the vote in 1947, Chinese were without voting rights. They could not practice law or any other licensed profession. Many Chinese were confined to occupations in laundries and restaurants. According to Rose Hum Lee, "The host Canadian society would only tolerate the Chinese serving minor 'woman's functions, cooking, washing, and domestic work' while the other occupations were not tolerated."[67]

But with a change in attitude reflected in the more liberal immigration act of 1962, a new group of Chinese immigrants came to Canada, mainly from Hong Kong. Vivian Lai describes these new immigrants as refugees who came to Hong Kong after the Communist takeover of China in 1949 and who subsequently left there for permanent settlement in Canada because they feared the political future of Hong Kong, especially following the Communist riot in 1967. They also felt they could not better themselves economically in overcrowded Hong Kong.

A slight majority of Vivian Lai's sample were single (51 percent) and female (57 percent). About half of her sample were between the ages of twenty-five and thirty-four. The majority of these new Chinese did not believe in any religion; the rest were either Protestant or Catholic. Almost half of these immigrants had university education—40 percent of the males had postgraduate training. Only about 10 percent could not speak, read, or write English. On the other hand, only 40 percent felt that they could speak English fairly fluently. Compared with their occupations in Hong Kong, the new Chinese immigrants are underrepresented in the professional, semiprofessional, and business categories and overrepresented in the clerical, sales, skilled, and unskilled jobs.

These Chinese immigrants from Hong Kong retain some traditional values but also show some assimilation of urban or Canadian ones. Fifty-eight percent of Vivian Lai's sample believe in the traditional pattern of giving a part of their salary to their parents, and 36 percent believe that a son should live, according to tradition, with his parents after marriage. The majority of immigrants—unlike the traditional Chinese—would allow women to remarry: the traditional Chinese wife was to remain loyal for life. However, they are much more conservative, they feel, than other Canadians regarding public kissing and virginity.

The majority of the new immigrants do not go to church or belong to voluntary associations. Very few of the new immigrants had Canadian friends. Vivian Lai concludes:

> The Canadian immigrants who came to Canada after the change of the immigration law in 1962 differ greatly from the previous Chinese immigrants who came to Canada in the nineteenth century with respect to such factors as occupation and motivation for emigration. They came from the cosmopolitan, international city of Hong Kong instead of the agrarian villages in Southern China . . . their life style and attitude . . . were either in a state of flux or had already been changed before coming to Canada. In any case, it could be said that this new group of Chinese immigrants appears to be more 'at home' in Canadian society than their nineteenth-century precursors.[68]

However, not all of their integration into Canadian society has been smooth. From 1960 to 1963, the Canadian government sent the RCMP accompanied by Hong Kong police to raid homes and offices in the Chinatowns in search of illegal aliens. It was another reminder that Chinese Canadians were not just Canadians like everybody else. There are only about fifty-eight thousand Chinese in Canada today.

BLACKS
Blacks in Canada have diverse historical origins. Robin Winks[69] isolates eight distinct historical groups: those who came as slaves with the United Empire Loyalists such as the Sewells, Wentworths, Parrs, or Smiths; the Black pioneers who came to Nova Scotia as freemen skilled as sawyers, caulkers, and coopers; the maroons, descendants of the fierce Jamaican rebels who were deported to Halifax; the refugee Blacks, "a disorganized, pathetic, and intimidated body,"[70] who were brought to Nova Scotia between 1813 and 1816; the fugitive slaves who made it to Canada via the Underground Railway; the contemporary West Indian migrants who began to arrive during World War I and landed at Halifax or St.

John to take up work in the coal mines and shipyards; and the urban American Blacks who came to work as porters on the railroads as well as the Harlem Blacks who came to Montreal to avoid Prohibition.

Winks contends that these groups had little to do with each other. The Loyalist Blacks, for example, considered themselves "founding fathers" and thus superior to the others. However, one factor unified all Blacks: Canadian prejudice and discrimination. There is no reason to assume that white Canadians have been any more enlightened about race relations than their American counterparts. Clairmont and Magill write:

> The history of the blacks in Nova Scotia has not been pleasant. Blacks have been poorer than the average white Nova Scotian who, in turn, over the past hundred years has been poorer than the average Canadian. Throughout their settlement in Nova Scotia blacks have had to carry a special burden, the burden of the white man's prejudice, discrimination, and oppression.[71]

Discrimination against Blacks in Canada can be found at many levels: immigration, education, land purchase, housing, public accommodations, employment, and social services.

Canada likes to point with pride to its abolitionist tradition and its part in the Underground Railway, and thus, by implication, its superiority to the United States. But slavery existed in Canada for more than two hundred years, from as early as 1628 in New France until the abolition of slavery by the British Emancipation Act of 1833. Moreover, Canada's racial policies have been very similar to those in the United States. Winks writes: "Much of Canada's participation in the abolition movement resulted from geographical proximity rather than from ideological affinity. Negroes fled to Canada . . . for negative rather than positive reasons, and once there they encountered race and color prejudice not unlike they found in Massachusetts or Ohio. Free they were but equal they were not."[72]

As late as the 1950s Canada had discriminatory regulations in its Immigration Act prohibiting the admission of persons who were unsuitable because of problems of adjustment to the Canadian climate. Of the 3 million immigrants that entered Canada between 1925 and 1964, only a little more than seventeen thousand were known to be Negroes. The present Black population of Canada is estimated at about 1 percent of the total population.

Segregated schools were legalized in the Province of Canada—now Ontario and Quebec—in 1849 by a statute that authorized municipal councils to establish separate schools for Negroes. In 1859 the Separate School Act was passed: it stated that any five Negro families could petition their local school officials for the establishment of their own separate schools. Davis and Krauter argue that this "voluntary" procedure was a device to force all local Blacks into segregated schools.[73] Black separate schools began to disappear from Ontario after 1910. The last separate school in the province, however, did not close until 1965. Moreover, in Nova Scotia, although legally separated Black education was ended in 1963, there are still some all-Black schools to be found in the province today. There is little doubt that Black schools have been both separate and unequal. Barbara Clark maintains that the elementary schools were unable to provide Black children with adequately enriched curricula even after they had made striking gains in a headstart program.[74]

Traditionally, Blacks are generally confined to segregated residences in the poorest areas of cities (even in Toronto and Montreal where well-defined ghettoes are missing). Better housing opportunities are not available to them. There are considerable restraints on employment opportunities for Blacks as well. Davis and Krauter point out that the Blacks who came as slaves worked primarily as household servants. The refugee slaves of the nineteenth century primarily found employment as farm laborers, although a number worked with railroads. In more recent times, Blacks still occupy the lowest levels of the occupational scale: 50 percent of Montreal Black males in the 1940s were railway porters, and 80 percent of the working females were domestic servants. Today, a number of West Indian women, many with good educations, work as domestic help in Toronto and Montreal. The worst employment opportunities, however, for Blacks are in Nova Scotia.[75]

There are many examples of discrimination against Blacks in public accommodations and services in Canadian history: restaurants and taverns refused to serve them in various cities during the 1930s and 1940s; they were denied the right to join the Boy Scouts or the YMCA in places like Windsor, Ontario. They not only could not go to beaches, parks, and theaters in some cities, but in Halifax they could not be buried in Anglican cemeteries.

But being an excluded minority did not seem to provide the Canadian Blacks with any impetus toward unified action. Until recently, it was outside organizations like the Canadian Jewish Congress that championed the rights of Blacks and other minorities. However, the Black revolution in the United States has had a tremendous impact on Canadians in recent years, especially the visit of Stokely Carmichael to Nova Scotia in 1968 and his message: "Be Black and be Proud."

Clairmont and Magill describe changes in racial identity and pride in Halifax through the adoption of Afro dress, natural hairstyling, and

a song about Black pride developed by Black youths in the town of Truro, and the 'we're Black and we're proud' chant of the youth in the urban fringe community of Cherrybrook.[76]

The center of Black Canadian life was the church, especially the African Baptist Association. The wider Canadian society saw the religious leaders of these churches as the spokesmen for the whole Black community.

There are some differences between the cultural patterns in white Baptist churches and Black churches in Canada: one of the principal differences is the Black "expressive style" as a heightened emotional involvement with congregational participation. As one former deacon described the service in the old church in Africville, a former Black community within the city of Halifax, Nova Scotia, "People would get together and sing and clap and have a great time and when the Church would really get emotional the whole congregation would get up and lock hands and dance around."[77]

The church was also a place where people could "bear one another's burden." People would tell their problems to a sympathetic congregation on Sunday morning. After church people would open up their houses, and members of the congregation would go from one house to another.

There were distinct rites of passage and intensification connected with Canadian Black religious traditions. Only adults were eligible for baptism, and they became members through a vision. Having a vision meant that one had been "saved." Many of the visions had a sea orientation, not surprising in a community close to the sea. Not everyone, however, had a vision, and those who did not were not eligible for membership in the church.

An important rite of intensification was the Sunrise Service on Easter Sunday morning. Clairmont and Magill report that the church members led by the deacons went into the church singing spirituals around four or five o'clock in the morning when the sun came up and did not come out until 3:00 P.M. They write, "When the people came, they would just flop with the spirit."[78]

Black churches were the most conspicuous Black institutions in Canada, but their influence has often been over-emphasized. Generally, the church members formed a small group with limited wider influence. Most community members did not go to church, and many, as Clairmont and Magill suggest, were cynical about the role of the church and its leaders in making significant social progress or in displaying real rather than ceremonial power.

The Canadian Black churches had their origins in the Great Awakening that swept across the American colonies during the late 1700s. They retained both their relationship and similarity to their sister churches in the United States. Martin Luther King, Jr., for example, was as much an inspiration to Canadian Blacks as he was to Americans.

Canadian Blacks, Robin Winks maintains, are different from American Blacks in two respects. In the first place, Black Canadians had to fit into the cultural mosaic of transplanted Europeans: that is, to be black tiles, or hyphenated Canadians, in the Canadian conglomeration of other hyphenated Canadians. The second was that Canadians wanted the Black to "take pride in his ethnic heritage, to embrace his negritude,"[79] just as French Canadians valued their origins.

Some social scientists disagree with Winks's interpretation. They suggest that the establishment merely wanted the Blacks to keep their place. Certainly there still remains considerable latent prejudice against Blacks and other racial minorities in Canada.

UKRAINIANS
Many Ukrainians came to Canada in the 1890s without a clear national identity: some were recorded as Austrians, Galecians, Bukowinians, and Ruthenians. The first Ukrainian settlers, however, came from the Catholic western Ukraine.

In the middle of the nineteenth century, when Ukrainians began to immigrate to the Americas, the Ukraine was divided between the Austro-Hungarian and Russian empires. After a brief period of independence during the years 1917 to 1921, the Ukraine was again divided, this time among the Soviet Union, Poland, Romania, and Czechoslovakia. After World War II (1939–45) all the territory that historically and culturally could be considered Ukrainian was united in the Ukrainian Soviet Socialist Republic.

For much of their history, then, the Ukrainians were a political, social, and economic minority under severe restrictions. Most lived in considerable poverty, lacking land, political freedom, and educational and social opportunities— these factors led to widespread emigration. There were three waves of emigration from the Ukraine to Canada: the first from 1896 to 1914, the second during the 1920s and 1930s, and the third from the late 1940s to the early 1950s.

After 1896 the immigration policy of the government of Prime Minister Wilfrid Laurier was implemented by Clifford Sifton, Minister of the Interior, and promoted by the efforts of Josef Oleskow, a Ukrainian agriculturalist who encouraged Ukrainians to come to Canada. In order to settle the empty prairies, the Canadian government initiated the free homestead system and the railway land-grant system—the immigrants could have very inexpensive land, much of it free for the settling.

The first Ukrainians arrived in their new homes in the Prairie Provinces with virtually no support. They were dropped off the trains without any Canadian agencies to help them adjust to a new way of life, and also without any Ukrainian leaders to take control. In particular, there were no clergy with them, so they had to establish not only their own homes and farms but also their own religious services (which they held in one another's homes).

The traditional Ukrainian village communities, closely built villages of whitewashed cottages, were not practical in Canada. Under the Homestead Act each farmer had 160 acres of land, which isolated him more than a half mile from his nearest neighbor. Successful farmers in the Ukraine, these immigrants were not familiar with farming on such large lots, but they soon adapted to the western methods of farming by horse, harness, and agricultural machines. The soil was rich, and they had bountiful crops of wheat, plus potatoes, cabbage, and other vegetables. They supplemented their vegetable diets with the abundant wild game of the region and with eggs and milk from the few livestock they brought with them.

Their first houses were made from mud applied to a wooden frame. The main building was a single combination home-and-barn structure where the stock was housed in one end and the family in the other. They slept on large mattresses of hay covered by coarse linen and covered themselves with their sheepskin coats. The only other furniture was simple wooden benches and tables. Families brought their own spinning wheels and looms on which the women made the cloth for their traditional brightly colored and embroidered costumes.

The Ukrainians only slowly established their own churches and congregations. As a result, many of them initially called upon religious leaders of various denominations—Russian Orthodox, Roman Catholic, Presbyterian, and Baptist—for aid in baptizing their babies, marrying their daughters, and burying their dead. Their relationship with the Russian Orthodox church, with rites similar to that of their own church, was most successful. However, many Ukrainians were suspicious of Russians and preferred to go to the Roman Catholic church, even to other denominations. Today, there are two major Ukrainian church systems: the Ukrainian Greek Orthodox church and the Ukrainian Greek Catholic church. The majority, however, belong to the Orthodox church.

The Ukrainians also had difficulties establishing educational institutions for their children. Few of them knew English, while few Canadian teachers knew Ukrainian or were willing to come to these isolated communities. The Province of Manitoba recognized the need for teachers for the Ukrainians, but few were available or acceptable in terms of the standards of the province. The Ruthenian Training School was established by the Province of Manitoba in 1905 to help train young Ukrainians to teach in the Ukrainian schools and thus alleviate the problem. Eventually about two hundred teachers were trained in the school, and many went to the universities where they developed into a Ukrainian intelligentsia in Canada. The abolition of this training school and bilingual schools in 1916 was of deep concern to the Ukrainians, who established Ukrainian student hostels in Saskatoon, St. Boniface, and Edmonton. Students were allowed to live there and go to the city schools if they studied Ukrainian language and culture in their free time. They also established vernacular schools for other children after school.

The communities, although split by religious divisions, remained relatively homogeneous, speaking Ukrainian and practicing subsistence farming. But the homogeneity of the Ukrainian communities began to break down in the 1920s and 1930s. The second generation was becoming better educated and better speakers of English than their parents. David Millet noted that:

> Unsatisfied with their rural life and deprived of cultural ties with the homeland, the second generation drifted into the prairie cities or left the West for industrial work in Ontario, particularly in Toronto. In the cities the Orthodox and Greek Catholic churches became hives of political activity, as the population divided into pro-communist and anti-communist factions or movements of cultural nationalism.[80]

Some second-generation Ukrainians considered these movements to be barriers to their progress at school and at work: they feared that the maintenance of the national and religious prejudices brought over from Europe left "the young Ukrainian-Canadian ignorant of and therefore unaccepted by the society in which he lived."[81] Many of these Ukrainians married outside the church. Their children, however, although they do not speak Ukrainian, are now attracted to the Ukrainian churches because they see them as treasure troves of Ukrainian lore.

In addition to generational acculturation, the homogeneity of Ukrainian society and culture suffered because of the differences in the kind of immigrants who came at different periods of time. Between 1918 and 1939, a new class of immigrants, many former soldiers with high school and advanced degrees, came to Canada. They worked on farms for only a short period and then gravitated to the cities. They were highly nationalistic and felt that the existing Ukrainian organizations such as schools and newspapers were too "Canadian." They then developed their own institutions and organizations. Inevitably, rivalry between old settlers and new settlers developed. Another wave of immigrants came after 1945. They came as refugees and were drawn from yet another segment of society: craftsmen, technicians, and professionals. A number of intellectuals were among them, and they too established their own institutions and organizations.

There were several factors that militated against complete assimilation into mainstream Canadian life. Many of the immigrants maintained their mother tongue within the family circle: Ukrainian in the home and English elsewhere. The establishment of Ukrainian churches and Ukrainian parochial schools helped to maintain language and traditions for some Ukrainian Canadians as well. There was also the development of the Ukrainian press in Canada: there have been some 135 Ukrainian newspapers in Canada, many of which are still being published. However, it is the community centers that appear to be the most important of all Ukrainian institutions for cultural maintenance. It is at the community centers where the Ukrainians keep up their drama, folksongs, dances, and handicrafts and introduce them to their children.

Among Ukrainian Canadians there are widely different attitudes toward their own heritage. At one extreme are those who believe that Ukrainians should assimilate completely into the Canadian way of life; others believe that Canada is only a temporary residence that they will give up when the Soviets get out of the Ukraine. There are some who are indifferent, and still others who want to establish a Ukrainian separate province in Manitoba. There are about five hundred thousand Canadians of Ukrainian origin in Canada today.

THE ITALIANS OF MONTREAL

A study done for the Royal Commission on Bilingualism and Biculturalism on the ethnography of the Italian immigrants to Montreal by Jeremy Boissevain stands out as one of the best. The description of the Italians of Montreal that follows is based on his ethnography, published in 1970.

Italian immigration to Canada becomes noticeable toward the end of the nineteenth century. Economic and political conditions in Italy were unsettled between 1859 and 1870, the period of Italian unification. The situation in southern Italy was particularly difficult because of a chronically large impoverished population. Simultaneously, Canada needed unskilled workers to build the Canadian Pacific Railway and other projects. Many Italians responded to these pressures and opportunities.

The first arrivals came without any support systems and found that the English Canadians and French Canadians controlled the economic and political life in Montreal; they showed little concern for these new immigrants. In 1901 there were about sixteen hundred Italians in the city.

Before and after World War I, more Italian immigrants arrived, and by 1921 there were fourteen thousand Italians in the city. When the government of Mussolini abolished its Commissariat for Emigration and replaced it with its General Agency for Italians Overseas in 1927, all Italians overseas were then considered as citizens of Italy "temporarily abroad."

At that time the Italian consul took an increasing interest in the Italian community of Montreal. Italian fascists organized a number of national-political societies similar to those in Italy. By no means were all the Italians in Montreal fascists; however, the Order of Italo-Canadians split with the Sons of Italy over the issue.

Boissevain says that many of the older Italians in Montreal would like to forget the war years. He writes:

> In 1940, almost overnight the Royal Canadian Mounted Police wiped out the leadership of the Italian community by sending virtually all the leaders to the internment camp at Petawawa. Italians who up until then had been increasingly accepted by the French and English-speaking communities were suddenly shunned. Italians themselves played down or hid their Italianness; they had suddenly become enemy aliens. The Church was also affected. Its leaders had been among the most vocal partisans of Mussolini's policies.[82]

When World War II ended in 1945, thousands of Italians came to Canada. The old leadership that had disappeared was replaced; old associations, like the Sons of Italy, were reactivated. An Italian background became an asset because of knowledge of the language and the culture of the new immigrants. Italian contractors and shopkeepers became prosperous. There are well over half a million Italians in Canada today.

Most of the immigrants who settled in Montreal came from southern Italy, and they brought with them many of their traditional institutions. The central institution, as it is for many cultures, is the nuclear family: a husband, wife, and their children. Other kin on both the father's and mother's side are important as well as support systems, but rights and obligations rarely extend beyond second cousins and are usually limited to first cousins. The strongest obligations are to the members of one's own domestic family: a man has the obligation of maintaining or improving the economic life of the family and the duty to defend the virtue of the women of his household.

Boissevain suggests that to the Italian breadwinner the

world was divided into kin and nonkin: kin were allies and friends who engendered rights and obligations; nonkin were potential or real enemies with whom he was in competition. This view of family was retained by the Italians of Montreal. Italian families kept in close contact with each other even when they lived some distance apart. Many of the later immigrants were helped to ease into the new society by their relatives in Canada: 91 percent of the Italian immigrants have had family members who sponsored them.

Another Italian tradition brought to Montreal was that of the *paisan,* or countryman. Most of the immigrants who came to Montreal were from small villages where face-to-face contact was frequent and intimate. New immigrants gravitated to Montreal neighborhoods where former villagers and friends lived. These neighborhoods centered around an Italian parish church and soon attracted a cluster of small Italian shops and businesses. The neighborhoods became "Little Italies" similar to those in Boston and New York.

A third tradition was that of the Italian parish. In Canada, Italian parish churches are mission churches run by Italian missionaries for Italian immigrants. These priests preach and carry out all activities in Italian. Some first-generation Italo-Canadians stop to chat with the priests in order to practice their Italian. Ninety-seven percent of the Italians in Montreal are Roman Catholic and are members of a parish. The role of the Italian parish is similar to that of the traditional French-Canadian parish, presiding over the essential religious rites of passage: baptisms, marriage, and funerals. The Italian mission churches, however, reinforce some different rites of intensification than the French-Canadian church: the feast of Sant-Antonio of Padua is more important than the celebration of St. Jean-Baptiste (the patron saint of French Canada).

Italian clubs are another place where old country traditions are maintained. There are many different types of Italian associations: mutual aid, church, regional, occupational, and social. The oldest are the mutual-aid societies that function like insurance companies: they provide modest unemployment and funeral expenses for families. Boissevain points out, however, that there are not any associations to aid the needy, like those of Montreal Jews who have active charitable organizations. Most charitable work, as it is among the French Canadians, is seen as the preserve of the church.

At the time Boissevain wrote his ethnography there were four Italian weeklies as well as daily radio programs and weekly television programs, including the mass, in Italian in Montreal. These too aided in the maintenance of cultural traditions.

In spite of these institutions there are mechanisms that are leading toward assimilation. Most of the Italians who came to Montreal were farm laborers. They became factory workers and unskilled laborers in an entirely different environment: a large urban metropolis. They left Italy to make a better life for themselves, and everyone in the family worked to make it possible, especially to buy a home. The children of these immigrants have better educational opportunities than their parents, and they may (if they learn French as well as English) move from laboring jobs into white-collar work. As they move with relative ease in Canadian society, they see the involvement of their parents in Italian societies and traditions negatively: as impediments to success in Montreal.

There are also tensions between "old-timers" (those who came before World War II) and those "newcomers" who came after the war. Many of the former feel that the new, brash immigrants do not feel appreciative enough of the sacrifices old-timers were forced to make.

Boissevain reports that Canadian-born Italians often are embarrassed by recent "immigrants" and are concerned that they will give all Italian Canadians a bad name:

> Very often the immigrants' manners, level of education, even standards of personal cleanliness are criticized by Canadians of French and British origins with whom Italians born in Canada are trying to establish contact.[83]

The relationship between the French Canadians and Italian Canadians has several points of friction. Boissevain reports that many Italians consider the French profligate idlers:

This condemnation becomes acute when French and Italians live side by side as the French are often tenants of the Italians. For many Italians this is sufficient proof that the French are lazy spendthrifts.[84]

The French, on the other hand, see the Italians as assimilating to Anglo-Canadian language and culture and thus weakening the French culture and language in Quebec. The tension was dramatically demonstrated in the incident at St. Leonard mentioned in the last section.

HUTTERITES

One of the Canadian ethnic groups most studied by anthropologists and other social scientists is the Hutterites. The Hutterites did not come directly to Canada from Europe, but rather came to the Canadian Prairies because of difficulties they had in South Dakota as conscientious objectors during World War I.

Hutterites are a sect of Anabaptist Christians, similar to Mennonites and Amish. They differ from both these others because of their insistence that all major property must be shared by the community as a whole. Moreover, they believe that children should be raised communally.

Anabaptists believe in a return to the doctrines expressed in the Acts of the Apostles. They particularly object to hierarchies of church organization and to the pomp and ceremonies of organized churches. They believe in "egalitarian social relations, a sharing of possessions, charity and brotherly love for all, and a life of austerity and simplicity."[85]

The Hutterian Brethren, named after Jacob Hutter, were a loosely federated Anabaptist group that fled the Austrian Tyrol because of persecution and entered Moravia, now part of Czechoslovakia, at the invitation of some local lords around 1530. They prospered in Moravia until 1622 when the Catholic church had them driven from their estates. The Hutterites, reduced in size, fled to Romania where the Russians protected them and invited them to settle in southern Russia as models for the more backward Russian peasant farmers. The Hutterites lived in Russia in relative peace until some 250 years later when the Czarist officials attempted to draft the Hutterite men into the army. The Hutterites are committed pacifists and consequently fled to North America during 1871 and 1879, where they finally settled in South Dakota. They remained there until 1916 when the American government tried to draft them into the army. In addition, local patriots persecuted them in the belief that they were German enemies. Canada, in its concerted effort to people the Prairies, invited them to Canada. Most of the Hutterites live in the Province of Alberta today, although there are Hutterites in Montana and the Dakotas. The Alberta government's limiting of the establishment of new colonies has also led to the establishment of colonies in the more receptive farmlands of Saskatchewan.

Canadian Hutterites are one of the immigrant groups most successful in maintaining their cultural traditions. They have assimilated modern techniques in farming and farm management with little hesitation but have strongly resisted other areas of cultural change. They believe that official churches and secular state governments are evil and contemporary life styles sinful temptations of the devil. They avoid contact with the outside world as much as possible. They will not hold public office, but they will vote if the issues affect their interests.

One of the strongest institutions of cultural persistence is the colony itself. The colony is a kind of movable village that has its own equipment, funds, and labor force. The Hutterites divide their colonies in two when the population exceeds 125 or 130 because they have found management difficult above that number. Although the Hutterites believe strongly in communal sharing, including the communal raising of children, they respect the nuclear family each of which has its own private apartment of from two to four rooms in the communal row houses. Marriage is by love match. When a couple marry they are given basic furniture, a clock, and a sewing machine.

Children are usually born in the local hospital. The Hutterites, as always, respect scientific and technical expertise.

The children are raised by their own parents until they reach the age of three, when they enter the colony school system. Children, however, return to their parents' apartments at night. There is a public school built on the land owned by the colony, but the teacher comes from the town. Education of Hutterite children abruptly stops at grade eight, further education being deemed unnecessary.

Although communal and collective solidarity is an ideal, male siblings have strong bonds that often develop into "brother cliques." Each Hutterite is also related to other Hutterites in other colonies, and there are bonds that cut across colonies. Large extended families are called *Leutes,* or branches of the family: Hutterites marry inside their own *Leutes* and, generally speaking, have closer relations with members of the same *Leut.*

Colony leadership is at two major levels: the elders or executives and the managers. The farm boss and the German teacher, however, combine both levels: the farm teacher directs the activities of the field and the personnel; and the German teacher directs the garden activities and the women who work in the nursery school and kindergarten. The Hutterites also have a council that considers issues raised by the Assembly, which is composed of all the men twenty years of age or older. Hutterites elect officeholders, but once elected the officeholder has considerable authority—a kind of "managed democracy."[86] Everyone in the colony works, but there is a division of labor where the women are subordinate to the men. The head cook, however, has managerial responsibilities and is elected to her office. Women are not forced into marriage, and spinsters often work in the nursery and kindergarten.

The Hutterites have made successful adjustments to life in Canada because of their skills in managing, their acceptance of all kinds of technological advances, and their orientation toward conservation. They seem to have a high motivation to succeed without the usual competitive and cash incentives.

John Bennett points out that the Hutterites are seldom welcomed by the other Canadian groups in their areas. He writes:

> The local inhabitants . . . fear their powerful competition, irresistible ability to buy land, and alleged failure to spend money. . . . Most of these accusations are misleading, since essentially Hutterites add greatly to local productivity, buy large quantities of special equipment. . . .
>
> But the non-Hutterites in Jasper had other criticisms as well. They noted that the Hutterites stood aloof from the rest of society and social relations, and refused to take part in the churches and in politics—hence were not fully participating members in the community—Hutterites seemed to belong to another race, another world.[87]

The future of Hutterite settlements may be jeopardized by the difficulties of finding new lands for establishing future colonies. In order to maintain their traditions, they may have to once more move to another country, perhaps in Latin America.

THE SOCIAL ADAPTATION OF IMMIGRANTS TO CANADA

In recent years immigrants to Canada have fit into two categories: independent or nominated. Independent immigrants were admitted to Canada because they met the nine-point selection criteria of the immigration officers. Nominated immigrants were admitted to Canada on a less stringent point system, because they were nominated by a close relative who was, in most cases, a Canadian citizen.

The Department of Manpower and Immigration undertook a "systematic study of immigrants who arrived in Canada during the years 1969 to 1971."[88] Their first study concerned three groups of immigrants who arrived in Canada in 1969. The researchers used questionnaires with a representative sample to ascertain their economic and social adaptation. Although the initial sample included approximately 5,000 immigrants, the actual sample used was based on 2,037 immigrants who remained in the survey for the full three years.

Economically, the immigrants in the sample fared relatively well. Although only 25 percent had prearranged jobs, most of the immigrants who sought work were employed in four weeks. To a large extent, they were a highly skilled group of workers: "the largest proportion of all the new workers entered managerial, professional, or technical fields, followed by craftsmen and clerical and sales occupations."[89] Most of the immigrants were able to find the kind of jobs they wanted, although in some cases there was no demand for their special skills. In addition, some others did not have their qualifications accepted. Language also proved a problem for some initially, but after three years was no longer one. A larger percentage, 47 percent, did not change jobs during the first three years of their arrival in Canada, and 25 percent of the others changed their jobs only once.

Wives of immigrants in the sample did not follow the more general pattern of immigrant working wives: most of them did not take jobs during the three years of the survey.

Those immigrants who had occupational skills in demand made, as one would expect, a more successful adaptation economically than others. Those who did not have these skills had an unemployment rate of 10 percent during the three years of the survey.

Many of the immigrants made successful adaptations to Canadian social life, although 20 percent thought that they had better social positions in their countries of origin, and half thought it was about the same. Ninety percent of the sample, however, believed that they were either well or generally accepted in their communities.

In spite of an increasing emphasis on multiculturalism in Canada, these immigrants showed both a desire and interest to belong to the mainstream of Canadian society. The report states:

> There was an increasing tendency to marry across ethnic lines with the passage of time, with the young, the independent immigrants, and the immigrants from English-speaking countries leading the way. The number of immigrants speaking a mother tongue at home other than French or English dropped by only six percent in two years, but the number with a working knowledge of one of these languages increased by 10 percent. By the end of their second year, 31 percent of the sample were participating in voluntary associations in which, in close to

two-thirds of the cases, Canadians constituted the majority. After three years' residence in Canada, 55 percent of the immigrants polled reported that they felt at home . . . in Canada; only 14 percent felt more attached to their country of origin, while 31 percent were undecided.[90]

However, a study by Anthony Richmond points out that this somewhat positive picture of successful adaptation to Canada may be misleading. His study shows that "approximately one in every three immigrants who entered the country since the end of the Second World War is no longer resident in Canada."[91] He maintains that the efforts of either the federal or provincial governments, including language classes, were minimal: "The large majority of immigrants were compelled to make their own way in Canadian society with little institutional support."[92]

Most of the immigrants eventually came to the large Canadian cities because of the greater opportunities for employment. Although the attitude toward ethnic minorities and the level of tolerance for their distinct cultural traditions have improved since the new bilingual and multicultural policies have been put into effect, there still remains considerable latent prejudice, especially toward blacks and Asians among "the older and less educated sections of the population."[93] Blacks and Asians, in particular, reported difficulty in having their professional and technical qualifications recognized as well as difficulty in finding housing.

Richmond says that although it is unreasonable to suppose that immigrants fit into a singular mold, there seem to be some general trends. He writes:

Studies in Toronto suggest that education and length of residence, combined with personal and ethnic preferences for maintaining cultural differences and ethnic social distance, determine the main patterns of immigrant adaptation. Many immigrants originating in rural areas of southern Europe, have re-created social networks in Canadian cities based on close relatives and others from their own country and region of origin. Although their economic status is low by Canadian standards they are well satisfied and committed to Canada. . . .

Others from various parts of the world who have come as independent immigrants or as refugees, and have a higher level of education, can be divided into two types. They are the anglo-conformists (or franco-conformists in some parts of Quebec) who seek to assimilate into a Canadian middle-class way of life as quickly as possible and others who prefer a pluralistic form of social integration, in which some aspects of the former language and culture are maintained.[94]

Canadian Identity?

In 1977, From January 24 to April 7, a Symposium on 20th Century Canadian Culture was held in Washington, D.C. Northrop Frye, one of Canada's leading literary critics, gave the keynote address. His speech demonstrated Canadian preoccupation with identity; and, as one might expect, his address began by contrasting Canadians with Americans. His opening remarks are worth repeating here at the end of this chapter. He states:

> It is generally assumed that English-speaking Canadians cannot be told apart from Americans. My American students often ask me if I notice much difference between teaching them and teaching Canadians in Toronto. They usually expect the answer to be no, but my answer is yes. American students have been conditioned from infancy to think of themselves as citizens of one of the world's great powers. Canadians are conditioned from infancy to think of themselves as citizens of a country of uncertain identity, a confusing past, and a hazardous future.[95]

In the last seventeen years, the Québécois—the French of Quebec—have, in contrast, developed their own distinct identity. Unlike Anglo-Canadians, they seem to know why they are. Michel Tremblay, a leading Quebec playwright, says:

> It is true that when a Québécois chooses to write about his own people, he chooses to limit himself. Perhaps this is a problem

in terms of culture. Personally, I don't care about culture. My main concern in writing is to talk to the people I live with, and the rest of the world is not very important. The important thing is that a man or a woman from the east end of Montreal can go to a theatre and look at himself or herself cry and laugh. People should have that basic right to see themselves.[96]

Tremblay's statement is an eloquent example of what cultural identity is all about—commonly shared attitudes, emotions, and ideas forming a psychological membrane that separates those within from those without.

The native peoples of Canada are beginning to get the message across to Canada that they too have an identity. Clive Linklater began his address to the Multiculturalism Conference in 1976 with these words:

From time immemorial our forefathers have lived on this land. This is our land. This is our home. We have no memory of existence in any other lands across the oceans. Our history and our allegiance is to this land and to no other. Today, we still live in this land that belonged to our forefathers, that still belongs to us, and that we will pass on to our children yet unborn.[97]

In evoking the Indian's connection with the land, Linklater gives another example of what we would call Canadian identity, an equally eloquent description of cultural identity.

The question for Canada remains—Can these different cultural identities, enriched by the language and cultures of many immigrant groups, be integrated into one overall identity that can be called Canadian? We may not have to wait very long for the answer.

Notes

1. Louise Sweet, "What Is Canadian Anthropology?" *American Anthropologist,* vol. 78, no. 4, (December 1976) pp. 846–847.

2. Ibid., p. 846.

3. Mildred Schwartz, "The Social Make-up of Canada and Strains in Confederation," *Canadian Public Policy,* vol. III, no. 4 (Fall 1977), p. 481.

4. Ibid., p. 483.

5. J. F. Graham, "Comments," in *Canadian Public Policy,* vol. III, no. 4 (Fall 1977), p. 474.

6. Schwartz, op. cit., p. 480.

7. Schwartz, op. cit., p. 480.

8. Norman Calif, *Multiculturalism and the Government of Canada* (Ottawa: Minister of Supply and Services, 1978), p. i.

9. J. W. Berry, R. Kalin, and D. M. Taylor, "Summary—Multiculturalism and Ethnic Attitudes in Canada," *Second Canadian Conference on Multiculturalism* (Ottawa: Minister of Supply and Services, 1976), p. 160.

10. Guy Rocher, "Multiculturalism: The Doubts of a Francophone," *Second Canadian Conference on Multiculturalism* (Ottawa: Minister of Supply and Services, 1976), p. 48.

11. Ibid., p. 48.

12. Ibid., p. 62.

13. Eugene Forsey, "Multiculturalism: An Anglo-Celtic View," *Second Canadian Conference on Multiculturalism* (Ottawa: Minister of Supply and Services, 1976), p. 61.

14. Ibid., pp. 62–63.

15. Ibid., p. 64.

16. Ibid., p. 61.

17. Clive Linklater, "Special Presentation," in *Second Canadian Conference on Multiculturalism* (Ottawa: Minister of Supply and Services, 1976), p. 177.

18. Diamond Jenness, *Indians of Canada,* 6th ed. (Ottawa: Queen's Printer, 1967), pp. 12–14.

19. With respect to the life cycle, every society had rites-of-passage ceremonies that recognized the change of status of an individual in the cycle of life. Notes 19–24 give life-cycle information for five Indian tribes and the Inuit. Ojibwa children early in their life, for example, took part in a naming ceremony where relatives and friends gathered at a feast to watch the child's grandfather or other elderly kinsman take the child in his arms and call on all the great spirits to bless its names.

Micmac mothers strapped their babies to wooden cradles where they accompanied their mothers while they did their chores. Montagnais, however, carried their babies in moss bags that served to keep the infant dry. Naskapi girls made and played with dolls, an activity rare among Indian children.

Puberty brought changes in status and new responsibilities. Montagnais and Naskapi girls passed a period of seclusion at the first menstruation. At about the same time, boys fasted in order to obtain a guardian spirit. Parents among the Montagnais and Naskapi gave their daughters away without any ceremony or consultation with them. A son-in-law, however, had to give bride service for a year with his parents-in-law before he could take his wife back to his own family. The Montagnais and Naskapi had different burial practices: the former wrapped their dead in birchbark and buried them in the ground; the latter deposited their dead in trees or suspended them on scaffolds.

20. An Iroquois infant is given a name shortly after birth by its mother: it is later confirmed at an assembly of the entire clan to ensure that the name does not belong to anyone living.

The mother wraps her baby in skins and lashes it to a cradleboard, which she carries on her back with the aid of a tumpline; often the baby hangs from a tree limb in its cradle while she works.

A girl is isolated during her first menstruation, at which time she must do arduous labor and avoid special foods. Boys at puberty, however, remain isolated for a year in a hut where they are tended by an old man and woman. Boys must undergo various tests of endurance during this period, such as having to swim in ice-cold water. Both boys and girls receive new names during this period of adolescence.

A young man's mother selects his bride without consulting either her son or her choice of bride. The interested families exchange food and gifts, and the couple is informed that they are husband and wife.

The Iroquois take great care of their aged. At death, the dead person's body is painted and put in its finest clothes. There are two types of burial: in a circular pit in the ground or on a scaffold or tree branch. A dead man is given some food and tobacco to help him on his way. Then a fire is built on the grave, and a captive bird is released to carry the soul away.

21. During childbirth, a Cree women knelt and gave birth attended by midwives. One midwife cut the umbilical cord, wrapped it in hide, and hung it on a tree. Eventually the cord was put in a decorated skinbag, which the child wore around its neck. Soon after birth the child received a name at a feast by a godparent chosen for his or her supernatural powers: the name was derived from an event or character in the name giver's vision.

Children were weaned gently—sometimes as late as four years of age. At puberty, a girl was secluded for four days under the care of an old woman. She had a number of arduous tasks to perform such as chopping wood and sewing hides. She ate little, cried a lot, and scratched her head with a stick. Girls usually had their visions during this period. After four days, the women came to the camp, knocked down her carefully constructed woodpile, and led her back to her home. A feast followed where the parents distributed presents to the guests. No comparable ritual accompanied the maturity of boys; they were usually told to fast and seek a vision.

An Indian male sought a wife by offering horses as prized objects of exchange and prestige to the bride's family—the brideprice; or in some instances gave bride service, where the prospective groom worked for his bride's family for two years. The Plains Indians practiced both the sororate, where a dead wife was replaced by her unmarried sister, and the levirate, where a dead husband was replaced by his unmarried brother. Polygyny, or marriage to more than one wife, was practiced, but the majority of marriages were monogamous. Marriages did not have religious sanctions, and divorce was easy.

Most corpses were buried, but in winter a body was placed in a log chamber covered by brush or placed on a platform in the fork of a tree. A dying man could request to be left seated inside a tipi on a hill to be later surrounded by a stone wall. The dead man received a can of grease and a filled pipe for his journey. A braid was cut from the hair of the deceased, and it became part of a sacred bundle. These bundles were highly prized.

22. The Haida take special care of pregnant women both before and during childbirth, which takes place on a soft bed. The birth is assisted by a paternal aunt of the child; she severs the umbilical cord with a knife of the father's, if it is a boy; one of the mother's, if it is a girl. The mother remains quiet for a period of ten days. Mothers nurse their babies for two years or more. The children are kept in cradles padded with soft moss. The mother, in consultation with the father and the grandparents, names the child at a feast in its honor. It is usually named after a deceased ancestor who is believed to be reincarnated in the child. A girl often remains with her parents even after marriage. A boy, however, takes up residence with his mother's brother and assists him in his endeavors after the age of ten. The uncle toughens the

nephew by various trials. There are no special puberty rites for males, but a girl is isolated behind a curtain in the home for a month after the first menstruation and has various taboos to observe. She is visited during the period by her paternal aunts, who take care of her and instruct her. At the end of the month she gives them all her childhood toys, dresses in new garments, and attends a feast in her honor. Shortly after, she marries.

The preferred marriage pattern is for a man to marry a cross-cousin—his father's sister's daughter—although he will marry his maternal uncle's daughter if he is to succeed his uncle as house chief. The mother of the boy arranges the marriage after consultation with her relations, the girl's mother, and the intended. The boy works for his potential in-laws for a year before the marriage. The wedding takes place in the home of the bride. The bride is escorted to the side of the groom, who is seated in a place of honor. Speeches are made, gifts are exchanged, and a feast follows the wedding. The couple visit the groom's sisters for an entire season in rotation; then they take up residence in the bride's father's household.

Old people are respected and well cared for by their relatives; they are never abandoned or killed. The Haida believe that the soul flies away when a person dies and enters the body of a pregnant women to give life to her unborn child. There is another soul, the dream soul, which has adventures while the person sleeps. The dream soul, at death, falls to an underworld where it is welcomed with a feast and dance by the spirits there. It can, however, occasionally return to the earth as a ghost and is heard in graveyards or "ghost towns." Those who die by drowning become killer whales and live in villages under the sea.

When a person is at the point of death, his possessions are piled around him. A male cross-cousin makes his coffin in his presence. His body is decorated and propped in a lifelike position on a box in the position of honor by the hearth, where it remains four days. Vigils are kept by male and female cross-cousins for four nights. The body is then placed in a cedar chest and buried in the burial hut of the clan. All of his property is distributed.

23. Birth, as it did among many Plains Indians, took place apart from the men in a special lodge constructed for the purpose, although the hut was also used as a place of menstrual seclusion. Women were believed to be potentially harmful when menstruating or giving birth. There was little ceremony attached to giving birth.

Children were kept in a skinbag lined with moss or rabbit fur for about two years. As they grew, boys were instructed in hunting, and girls were instructed in cooking and sewing.

There were no specific puberty rites for boys except to go out and seek "spirit power." A girl, however, was given considerable attention at the first menstruation. She left the camp; built a brush shelter; and, as among the Slaves, she stayed in the hut ten days. Girls were considered ready for marriage soon after; boys, however, married somewhat older than girls. The mother of the girl selected the husband of their daughter; the best potential sons-in-law were those older men who were wealthy and established. Polygyny occasionally occurred, with older wealthy men having several wives and younger men unable to find any. The Slaves preferred marriages with their parallel cousins; i.e., the daughter of a father's brother or a mother's sister. The Athabaskans required the men to do a period of bride service for up to two years before the couple could be married.

Death was feared. A whole camp stayed up when someone was dying. Death was never considered a natural state; it was always the result of strong witchcraft. The Athabaskans gave up the dwelling in which the death occurred. The body was placed on a burial platform. There were only vague notions of an afterlife.

24. Children, both boys and girls, are welcomed at birth by the Inuit, but sickly or deformed babies are not allowed to live. Babies are nursed for more than two years and then gently weaned. Training is informal and often in the form of games.

The Inuit do not have puberty ceremonies for either girls or boys. Adulthood comes gradually and is not fully realized until marriage and the establishment of an independent household.

There is considerable freedom of choice in marriage partners and place of residence after marriage. Cousin marriages are common; but there is no distinction between parallel cousins and cross-cousins. The levirate and sororate are practiced, but there are no definite rules requiring them. There are no elaborate ceremonies for marriage, although some groups on Inuit practice a "simulated marriage by capture" ceremony. Monogamy is common but a man can have more than one wife. Husbands will lend their wives to other men, but women are not treated as pieces of property. Wife lending is more important for the necessary sharing of labor than it is for sexual relations.

Old people are loved but senilicide will occur in times of famine if the survival of the group is threatened. Actually, the old people themselves decide to stay behind rather than jeopardize the group as a whole.

Once a person dies, the spirit of the dead person is feared regardless of the kind of life the deceased lived: all ghosts are malevolent. The survivors abandon the area where the person died as quickly as possible: it is believed that the ghost remains in the area for five days before departing for the spirit world. The name of the deceased is so charged with power that it cannot be mentioned until it is given to a new baby.

25. See Heather Robertson, *Reservations Are for Indians* (Toronto: James Lewis and Samuel, 1970).

26. *Revised Statutes of Canada,* vol. IV, 1970.

27. See Fred Gross, "Indian Island: A Micmac Reserve," in Jean Leonard Elliot, ed., *Minority Canadians I,* (Scarborough, Ont.: Prentice-Hall of Canada, 1971).

28. See John W. Bennett, *Northern Plainsmen* (Chicago: Aldine-Atherton, 1971).

29. Ibid., p. 158.

30. See Jack E. Ferguson, "Eskimos in a Satellite Society," in Jean Leonard Elliot, ed., *Minority Canadians I* (Scarborough, Ont.: Prentice-Hall of Canada, 1971), pp. 15–28.

31. Jack Frish, "Factionalism, Pan-Indianism, Tribalism and the Contemporary Political Behavior of the St. Regis Mohawk," *Man in the Northeast,* no. 2 (November 1971), p. 80.

32. Loren Lind, "Common Sense in Iroquois Land," in *Issues for the Seventies: Canada's Indians* (Toronto: McGraw-Hill, 1970), p. 67.

33. Thomas R. Berger, *Northern Frontier Northern Homeland* (Toronto: James Lorimer and Co., 1977), p. xviii.

34. Ibid.

35. Ibid.

36. Ibid., p. xxxiii.

37. Ibid., p. 198.

38. See Stephen Richer and Pierre Laporte, "English-French Competition," in Jean Leonard Elliot, ed. *Minority Canadians II,* (Scarborough, Ont.: Prentice-Hall of Canada, 1971).

39. Nancy E. Frasure and Mary Louise Kirby, "English and French Canadian Children's View of Parents," unpublished manuscript, Department of Psychology, McGill University, 1974, p. 25.

40. See Peter Woolfson, "Value Orientation of Anglo-Canadians and French Canadian School Children in a Quebec Community Near the Vermont Border," *American Review of Canadian Studies,* vol. IV, no. 1, pp. 75–88.

41. See Horace Miner, *St. Denis: A French Canadian Parish* (Chicago: University of Chicago Press, 1939).

42. Donald Creighton, *Dominion of the North* (Toronto: The Macmillan Company of Canada Ltd., 1957), pp. 81–83.

43. Jean-Charles Falardeau, "The Role and Importance of the Church in French Canada," in Marcel Rioux and Yves Martin, eds., *French Canadian Society I,* (Toronto: McClelland and Stewart, 1971), pp. 345–346.

44. Ibid., p. 91.

45. Ibid., p. 92.

46. Ibid., p. 93.

47. Colette Moreaux, "The End of Religion," in Gerald L. Gold and Marc-Adelaid Tremblay, eds., *Communities and Culture in French Canada* (Toronto: Holt, Rinehart and Winston, 1973), pp. 333–334.

48. See Philippe Garigue, "The French Canadian Family," in Bernard R. Blishen, ed., *Canadian Society: Sociological Perspectives,* 2d ed., (Toronto: Macmillan of Canada, 1968), pp. 151–166.

49. Marc-Adelaid Tremblay, "Authority Models in the French Canadian Family," in Gerald L. Gold and Marc-Adelaide Tremblay, eds., *Communities and Culture in French Canada* (Toronto: Holt, Rinehart and Winston, 1973), p. 116.

50. See Richard Joy, "Languages in Conflict: Canada, 1976," *American Review of Canadian Studies,* vol. VI, no. 2 (Autumn 1976), pp. 7–21.

51. Rioux and Martin, op. cit., 1971, pp. 112–113.

52. Fishman, Joshua A., *The Sociology of Language* (Rowley, Mass., Newburg House, 1972), p. 92.

53. Rioux and Martin, op. cit., p. 99.

54. John R. Malea, *Quebec's Language Policies: Background and Response* (Quebec: Les Presses de l'Université Laval, 1977), p. 12.

55. "Immigration," *Canada Today/D'Aujourd'hui,* vol. 5, no. 1 (January 1974), p. 3.

56. Howard Palmer, "Reluctant Hosts: Anglo Canadian Views of Multiculturalism in the Twentieth Century," in *Second Canadian Conference on Multiculturalism* (Ottawa: Minister of Supply and Services, 1976), pp. 84–85.

57. Ibid., p. 85.

58. Ibid., p. 86.

59. Ibid., p. 91.

60. Ibid.

61. Ibid., p. 98.

62. Statutory Regulations 62–36, February 14, 1962.

63. Palmer, op. cit., p. 84.

64. Anthony Richmond, *Aspects of the Absorption and Adaptation of Immigrants* (Ottawa: Information Canada, 1974), p. 14.

65. Vivian Lai, "The New Chinese Immigrants in Toronto," in Jean Leonard Elliot, ed., *Minority Canadians II* (Scarborough, Ont.: Prentice-Hall of Canada, 1971), p. 120.

66. Sien Foon, "The Chinese in Canada," essay submitted to the Royal Commission on Bilingualism and Biculturalism, 1967, p. 16.

67. Lai, op. cit., p. 133.

68. Lai, op. cit., p. 139.

69. Robin W. Winks, "The Canadian Negro: The Problem of Identity," in Jean Elliot Leonard, ed., *Minority Canadians II* (Scarborough, Ont.: Prentice-Hall of Canada, 1971), p. 102.

70. Robin W. Winks, *The Blacks in Canada* (New Haven, Conn.: Yale University Press, 1971), p. 117.

71. Donald H. Clairmont and Denis W. Magill, *Africville* (Toronto: McClelland and Stewart, 1974), p. 39.

72. Winks, *The Blacks in Canada*, p. 270.

73. Morris Davis and Joseph K. Krauter, *The Other Canadians* (Toronto: Methuen, 1971).

74. See Barbara Clark, "Preschool Programs and Black Children," in Jean Leonard Elliot, ed., *Minority Canadians II* (Scarborough, Ont.: Prentice-Hall of Canada, 1971), pp. 106–119.

75. Davis and Krauter, op. cit., p. 47.

76. Donald H. Clairmont and Denis W. Magill, "Nova Scotia Blacks: Marginality in a Depressed Area," in C. L. Boydell, C. F. Grindstaff and P. C. Whitehead, eds., *Critical Issues in a Canadian Society* (New York: Holt, Rinehart and Winston, 1971), p. 308.

77. Davis and Krauter, op. cit., p. 79.

78. Davis and Kranter, op. cit., p. 83.

79. Winks, "The Canadian Negro," p. 105.

80. David Millet, "The Orthodox Church: Ukrainian, Greek, and Syrian," in Jean Leonard Elliot, ed., *Minority Canadians II* (Scarborough, Ont.: Prentice-Hall of Canada, 1971), p. 57.

81. Ibid.

82. Jeremy Boissevain, *The Italians of Montreal* (Ottawa: Information Canada, 1970), p. 7.

83. Ibid., p. 83.

84. Ibid., p. 84.

85. Bennett, 1971, p. 248.

86. Ibid., p. 262.

87. Bennett, op. cit., p. 87.

88. Canada, Department of Manpower and Immigration, *Three Years in Canada* (Ottawa: Information Canada, 1974), p. 1.

89. Ibid., p. 6.

90. Ibid., p. 12.

91. Richmond, op. cit., p. 45.

92. Richmond, op. cit., p. 45.

93. Richmond, op. cit., p. 45.

94. Richmond, op. cit., p. 47.

95. Northrop Frye, "Canadian Culture Today," in Judith Webster, ed., *Voices of Canada* (Burlington, Vt.: The Association for Canadian Studies in the United States, 1977), p. 1.

96. Michel Tremblay, comment in "The Cultural Renaissance of Quebec," in Judith Webster, ed., *Voices of Canada* (Burlington, Vt.: The Association for Canadian Studies in the United States, 1977), p. 12.

97. Linklater, op. cit., p. 177.

Chapter 6

A Literary Perspective:

The Development of a National

Consciousness

RONALD SUTHERLAND*

Introduction

PHILOSOPHICAL BACKGROUND
OF CANADIAN LITERATURE
THE STUDY OF literature, when properly conducted, is an
experience of beauty and insight—the beauty of sound,
rhythm, structure, of language skillfully and sensitively
molded to a purpose, coupled with insight into individual and
collective human nature. The study of a national literature,
therefore, besides giving aesthetic pleasure, provides the key
to understanding the character of a nation, its conditioning

* Ronald Sutherland completed his B.A. and M.A. at McGill University, then went
to the University of Glasgow as the McGill-Glasgow Exchange Scholar. Since receiving a Ph.D. from Wayne State University in 1960, he has been Professor of
English and Comparative Literature at l'Université de Sherbrooke, Sherbrooke, Quebec. He has served as Commonwealth Visiting Professor at the University of Leeds,
England, and has frequently been an invited lecturer at American colleges and
universities. His books include *L'Esprit de la langue anglaise* (1965), *The Romaunt
of the Rose and Le Roman de la Rose* (1967), *Frederick Philip Grove* (1969), *Second
Image* (1975), *The New Hero* (1977), and two novels: *The Snow Lark* (1975), and
Where Do the MacDonalds Bury Their Dead? (1976).

forces, its formative myths, its dreams, its nightmares, its successes, its failures, and the extent to which its more impressionable and creative people have been able to realize themselves. A national literature is a record of ideas. But unlike textual history, it dramatizes rather than describes, exploring motivations and reactions at the human level, incorporating psychology, theology, philosophy, and prophecy. The greatest writers of a nation transcend the factual and the temporal by articulating basic values. They respond to the forces that condition a nation's philosophy of life, and they in turn condition that philosophy; in other words, the major themes of a national literature are the essence of the nation itself. American classics—*Moby Dick, Huckleberry Finn,* the Leatherstocking Tales—have all, for example, focused upon the communion between persons of different races, and the theme has persisted in the works of Faulkner, Porter, Baldwin, Ellison, Kesey, and many others. American writers have sensed from the beginning that the survival of the United States would ultimately depend upon the capacity of people of different races to find a mutually acceptable means of coexistence.

It is not surprising, then, that Canadian literature has from the beginning reflected a preoccupation with the United States of America, as if Canadian authors sensed that the survival of Canada would depend upon its capacity to coexist continentally with a nation many times more populous and enormously greater in power and influence.

Consciousness of the United States and of Americans in Canadian literature is marked by duality—admiration for American dynamism and knowhow tempered by fear of American license and extremism. This dual attitude can be seen in the works of the first significant Canadian writer, Thomas Chandler Haliburton, who was born in Windsor, Nova Scotia, in 1796 of United Empire Loyalist stock. In histories of American literature, Haliburton is sometimes referred to as the "Father of American Humor"; he is one of many writers whose influence has been unrestrained by the international border. His first book, a descriptive history of the Province of Nova Scotia, contained his own sympathetic account of the expulsion of the Acadians, original French settlers who were dispossessed and deported as far as Louisiana by the British, and this account was later to be echoed in Henry Wadsworth Longfellow's *Evangeline*. But Haliburton is best known for the creation of the character Sam Slick, the Yankee trader who from the viewpoint of his Canadian customers is at once admirable and despicable. It is of interest to note that in his *Dictionary of Americanisms* (1859) John Barlett included a number of Sam Slick's sayings.

The Canadian dual attitude of admiration and suspicion has recurred in various forms throughout the literature of both French and English Canada. It can be found in the Quebec classic *Maria Chapdelaine,* the story of a farmgirl written by an immigrant French novelist, Louis Hémon. Maria, who symbolizes the determination of French-speaking Canadians to preserve their culture, resists the temptation to leave the bitter hardships of rural Quebec and go with a suitor to the relative affluence of a New England mill town, which has sidewalks and streetlamps and other amenities undreamed of in the frozen North. In another Quebec classic, *Trente Arpents—Thirty Acres,* by Philippe Panneton, a number of characters give in to the drawing power of the prosperous nation to the south, but the fear and suspicion remain, as they do in recent works by Michèle Lalonde, Jacques Godbout, Réjean Ducharme, and countless other Quebec writers.

The same duality of attitude can be found in Canadian literature in English, such as Hugh MacLennan's *The Precipice* or even Stephen Leacock's humorous *Sunshine Sketches of a Little Town.* Lately there has been a wave of novels dealing directly with American-Canadian relations, all of them either based upon or containing sinister American plots, still characterized by a combination of ruthless and impressive efficiency, to take over Canada and its resources. Richard Rohmer's two potboilers, *Ultimatum* and *Exxoneration,* are examples: Patrick Watson's *Zero to Airtime* is another. Less direct treatments of the United States in the Canadian consciousness are found in André Langevin's *L'élan d'Amérique—The Moose*—and Margaret Atwood's *Surfacing.*

For an American making a first approach to Canadian

letters, however, the works that deal specifically with American-Canadian relations are not likely to present a challenge. After all, the most effective critics of materialism and the dehumanization of the technological state are still American writers themselves, and the only extra dimension brought by a Canadian author is a bitter indignation that somehow the border has not protected his interests. And he does not necessarily blame the United States for this shortcoming; more often than not the bitterness is directed against Canada for its failure to maintain the integrity of an independent nation.

Self-blame, incidentally, has been a major trait of Canadian writing, and it is here that the literary traditions of the United States and Canada show a marked divergence, a divergence that has its roots in the early history of each nation. Both countries were strongly influenced by Puritanism, but the Puritan ethos developed and transformed itself quite differently in Canada than in the United States, and an awareness of this difference is prerequisite to understanding the evolution and import of Canadian literature.

The effects and aftereffects of Puritanism on American thought and institutions have been thoroughly documented. In Canada, Calvinistic doctrines also prevailed, both among Protestants (Scottish Presbyterianism being especially strong) and among Roman Catholics—Jansenism, or *Rigorisme* as it is sometimes called in French Canada, conditioned both Irish and French Catholicism. Introduced to Europe by Cornelius Jansen, bishop of Ypres, at the beginning of the seventeenth century, Jansenism, like Calvinism, was based upon predestination and used the rather imaginative, if perhaps a bit sinister, symbol of a crucifix with the arms of Christ only partially spread, embracing the "elect" but rejecting all others. One such crucifix, incidentally, can still be seen at the Old Fort Beauséjour Museum near Sackville, New Brunswick. Undoubtedly many others were destroyed as a result of a papal bull called *Unigenitus,* which condemned Jansenism in 1713, but the effects of the doctrine in Canada could not be so easily erased.

The basic rationale of Canadian Jansenism and Calvinism may be summarized as follows. Man in himself is insignificant and deserves nothing better than damnation unless the grace of God has been bestowed upon him. There is nothing he can do to bend the divine will—either he has been elected for salvation or he has not. However, the inclination, abundantly demonstrated, to attend church regularly and to do one's duty on earth diligently and without complaint—"la résignation chrétienne" as it was called in Quebec—can be indicative of the prepossession of God's grace. Contrary tendencies, especially idleness and the wish to pursue personal comfort and pleasure, are the symptoms of predestined doom. An interest in art that is not patently moralistic or didactic is at best highly suspicious. Being after all only flesh and blood, man must be expected to have the occasional fling—a roaring drunk or a roll in the hay—but if he has God's grace in his bones, then the fling will result in misery rather than joy. He must never delude himself into thinking that the so-called sins of the flesh are satisfying at a level other than that of the primitive beast. To succumb to the fires of passion is understandable and possibly even excusable; but to enjoy it is a certain indication of different and everlasting fires to come. Saturday night, being followed so closely by Sunday morning and the moment of truth in God's house, is commonly accepted as the most appropriate time for flings. Man's role on earth, then, is to follow the prescribed rules, to do his duty and to suffer his "purgatoire sur terre."

Now, anyone who has examined accounts of early American Puritanism will immediately recognize the similarities with the Calvinist-Jansenist set of precepts just outlined, attitudes reflected over and over again in the works of Canadian writers. But American Puritanism was more severe and demanding than Canadian Calvinism. The major Puritan thinkers of New England, Jonathan Edwards in particular, put far more stress on the depravity of man and the graphic qualities of hell than apparently did their counterparts in the North. What is more important, however, is that American Puritanism underlined self-reliance and the responsibility of the individual. In a natural reaction to the idea of an Established Church, which was what drove the Pilgrims from England in the first place, there was in the colonies an aversion to any

hierarchical, centralized, or extensively structured ecclesiastical system. Canada, by contrast, had relatively sophisticated,
firmly established church systems among both Protestants
and Catholics. While New England Puritanism called for individual self-examination and commitment, working out one's
own salvation through "fear and trembling," Canadians always had the security of reliance upon a church institution,
detailed codes of behavior, a controlling system. And in general until the 1970s Canadians have tended to depend upon
and to trust systems that control their lives, whether religious,
governmental, social, educational, or more recently, labor
union.

Being less extreme than the early American variety, Canadian Puritanism colored life in grays rather than in black
and white, which explains why Canadian literature did not
produce a Melville or a Hawthorne. Moral issues, as distinct
from conventional morality, did not preoccupy the significant
writers of the nineteenth century in Canada. Nature poetry,
heroic verse, historical and idyllic romances—these were the
stuff of Canadian literature of that period. But although Puritanism was milder in Canada than in the United States, it
was more stubborn—lasting longer and changing less.

Benjamin Franklin is often regarded as the man who split
American Puritanism in two, appropriating the principles of
industry, efficiency, self-reliance, and worldly success as sig-
nals of God's grace, then dropping God from the picture to
create the rationale of American materialism. Having abandoned the Puritan God, the materialist tradition then proceeded to invent a succession of its own deities from Irving's
"almighty dollar" to the current status symbol. Meanwhile,
Jonathan Edwards went to the other extreme, moving further
and further away from the pragmatism of the Pilgrim Fathers,
tormenting himself with the impossible task of harmonizing
dark Calvinism with enlightened rationalism, and inadvert-
ently promoting a tradition of highly disciplined intellec-
tualism. With boosts from immigrant scholars and the frontier, this tradition has also flourished in the United States.
It too, of course, soon dropped the old Puritan deity as well
as the notion of the innate depravity of man (had already done

so by the time of Emerson and Thoreau), but it has retained an obsession with ethics. The American artist-intellectual tradition, in reaction to the increasing conformism of the materialism stream, has elevated and glorified the principle of self-reliant individualism, the capacity and the right of each person to think for himself and to act accordingly.

Awareness of a fundamental dichotomy has always been a powerful motivating and conditioning force in American literature. Like the general theme of racial coexistence mentioned earlier, tension between two poles, between individualism and conformism, between a natural, commonsense view and a distorted, conformist view of life, has characterized most of the great literary works of the United States. *Moby Dick* and *The Scarlet Letter,* for instance, place the old Puritan obsession with sin and the compulsion to see all things as either good or evil against the simple desire to live and to let live and to accept the world as it is. By the time of *Huckleberry Finn,* the parallel streams have become more defined, and the tension is between a morally decadent, materialist society and the will of natural man to act upon his natural impulses. The same polar tension can be seen in many other works, notably Faulkner's *As I Lay Dying,* Porter's *Ship of Fools,* Ellison's *The Invisible Man,* Kesey's *One Flew Over the Cuckoo's Nest.* What is arresting, perhaps even alarming about the contemporary literary representation of the conflict between individualism and conformism in American literature is that the self-reliant individualist, once the ideal and winner, is now becoming the loser. In the latest of the novels mentioned above, the protagonist McMurphy, possibly the toughest individualist of them all, is finally crushed by a thoroughly regimented system—Big Nurse and the state asylum.

Now, Canadisn literature, in contrast to American, has not been dominated by tension between two opposite poles, for the Jansenist-Calvinist ethos of Canada never split in two as did American Puritanism. Consequently, Canada did not witness the emergence of the two extremes of materialism and intellectual individualism, and the proximity of the United States provided a safety valve against anyone who happened to develop a taste for one or other of the extremes.

Canadian churches, as suggested earlier, were careful not to risk cutting their own throats by encouraging self-reliance. The stress, in fact, was evidently placed upon the human-insignificance-and-impotence part of the Puritan ideology, making man more than ever dependent on the church as custodian of God's grace. And the harsh climate of the country, the early frosts that could destroy in minutes the back-breaking labor of a whole season, the winter blizzards that could freeze a man to death on his way from the house to the barn did nothing to dispel the notion of human dependence and impotence. While the great split had the effect of releasing Americans from the stifling aspects of the old Puritan theology, Canadians remained enslaved until only a few years ago. This fact is probably the reason why Canada, compared with the United States, has never produced within its boundaries a proportionately impressive intellectual-artistic elite or a proportionately efficient business machine. Instead of undergoing a dramatic transmogrification, the Calvinist-Jansenist attitudes of Canada slowly eroded, growing weaker and toothless with age but still snarling into the second half of the twentieth century. Rather than a mutation, they left a memory, as well as an indelible mark upon Canadian literature.

The lingering hangover of Puritanism in Canada and its devolution in the United States are closely related to the development of respective national myths. In contrast to the positive, expansionist thrusts of American "Manifest Destiny" and "Garden of the World," Canadian myths were modest and low keyed. Rather than "life, liberty and the pursuit of happiness," the fathers of Confederation opted for "peace, order and good government." The pioneers of Canada—United Empire Loyalists forced out of the United States, dispossessed Scots, the French after the Conquest, Irish and Eastern Europeans—were not, after all, riding on the wave of victory. What positive myths existed in the country at one time or another, the dream of the old French regime to branch out from a chain of forts stretching from the mouth of the St. Lawrence down the Mississippi to the Gulf of Mexico, the vision of a shipping and shipbuilding empire among the seafarers of Nova Scotia, even Quebec's "Revenge of the Cradle" as a means to repossess the land through weight of numbers were all thwarted sooner or later.

There has never been a strong pan-Canadian nationalism. Confederation was a marriage of convenience, a stratagem to protect the family interests against an uncle to the south whose power and territorial acquisitiveness were increasing at an alarming rate—Florida, Texas, California, "54-40 or Fight!" Even the poets who sang the new nation generally did so with the bilateral sentiments of Helen Johnson's "Our Native Land," which goes in part:

> How many loving memories throng
> Round Britain's stormy coast!
> Renowned in story and in song,
> Her glory is our boast!
> With loyal hearts we still abide
> Beneath her sheltering wing;
> While with true patriot love and pride
> To Canada we cling.

Like the Canadian boatman in a well-known verse of the same name, the hearts of Canadians were "in the Hebrides," or possibly in the slums of Glasgow, Dublin, and Liverpool. Naturally, the fact that each of the two major linguistic groups of Canada derived from an overwhelmingly powerful cultural tradition did not expedite political nationalism of a native variety. Indeed, to protect itself from the other and from the United States, each group constantly reaffirmed its links with its ancestors, and terms like "our martial sires," "founding races," "nos aieux," and "notre maître le passé" became the lexicon of nationalism in Canada. And as will be seen, the theme of exile was strong in Canadian poetry.

Another of the major conditioning forces that made American literature different from Canadian is the idea of the "frontier," which in turn is a ramification, or perhaps more accurately a deformation of, the earlier "Manifest Destiny" and self-reliant individualism in the United States. Canada, too, had a frontier, but it never acquired the mythic associations of the American West. Relatively speaking, peace and order prevailed in the northern plains and mountains, symbolized of course by the red-coated Royal Canadian Mounted Police. Generally the Mounties, if not always in the spectacular manner of romantic Hollywood movies, succeeded in establishing the law of the land. The one significant rebel of the Canadian West, Métis leader Louis Riel, was captured and executed in due course, and settlement took place in a quite orderly fashion.

Taking into consideration, then, the different forces that have shaped the values and outlooks of the United States and Canada, it is not difficult to understand why mainstream American literature should be different from both French-Canadian and English-Canadian literature. Neither is it surprising that two subdivisions of American literature—the black and the southern—should have certain characteristics in common with Canadian literature, for American blacks and southerners have been conditioned by a negative "loser" syndrome that in some respects is similar to that of Canadians. The main bodies of American and Canadian literature, however, are quite distinct from each other. Moreover, considering the absence of positive Canadian myths and the labored development of Canadian nationalism, it is understandable that a distinctive Canadian literature took so long to emerge in force. Even today, incidentally, there is controversy as to who precisely is a Canadian author, a problem that rarely occurs in a country of strong national identity such as the United States. Canadian anthologies, for instance, sometimes include the works of writers who lived in Canada for varying periods of time. Brian Moore, 1975 winner of the highest Canadian literary distinction, the Governor General's Award, for his novel *The Great Victorian Collection,* who was born in Ireland and now lives in California, is an example. Malcolm Lowry, author of the highly acclaimed novel *Under the Volcano,* is another.

The most evident differentiating feature in the literature of Canada and the United States, a feature clearly resulting from the divergence of national values, is in the character of fictional protagonists. The traditional American hero is defiant, self-reliant, hurling challenges not only at the system but sometimes even in the face of God. The Canadian, until certain works of recent years which will be considered later, is self-effacing, struggling within himself to find an accommodation of some sort. Not only is the traditional Canadian hero a loser, he is a determined loser, albeit beautiful at times. Often enough he is in confrontation with system (whether religious, social, or other), but unlike the American hero he is seldom in conflict. Because of the peculiar Canadian Calvinist-Jansenist conditioning, when he discovers that he is in disagreement with the dictates of the system, instead of defying it or fighting it as do American protagonists from Hester Prynne and Huckleberry Finn to Sister Carrie and Mc-Murphy, the Canadian protagonist blames himself. The tension thus becomes internalized, the character engaging in painful and destructive soul-searching in an attempt to discover his own deficiencies. Many examples of this type of hero will be examined in detail when the works of Hugh Mac-Lennan, Morley Callaghan, Sinclair Ross, Gabrielle Roy, and André Langevin are presented in the perspective section of this survey.

The thematic evolution of Canadian literature corresponds closely with the development of Canadian national consciousness—most of the activity, that is to say, has taken place in the last few years. The Calvinist-colored notions of *Divine Order and the Land* dominated largely from the colonial period right up to World War II. In both prose and poetry the most commonly recurring theme is submission to God's design and acceptance of one's duty, because the individual is considered insignificant compared with the system ordained by God and the king. The purpose of man on earth is not the pursuit of happiness or personal success as in the United States, but rather the fulfillment of the divine plan, whatever suffering or earthly purgatory be required. The struggle is between man and the land, a cruel land often enough, but one that nevertheless operates according to God's will, the seasons changing and life itself progressing in obedience to immutable laws. Man need only follow the cycles, fit into the design and become part of the *Divine Order*.

World War II triggered a disenchantment with the tra-

ditional system in Canada, long after the same type of disenchantment had taken place in Europe and the United States.
Canada had its own "Lost Generation," but generally its components were lost at home. Through the late 1940s and 1950s,
the theme that dominates Canadian literature is the *Breakup
of the Old Order*. To some extent there is a parallel between
works in this thematic category and American writing that
treats the disintegration of the American Dream. An important distinction, however, is that the American character—
in Fitzgerald, Miller, Salinger, Baldwin, for instance—is disillusioned, and he blames the nation, society, the system for
cheating him. In keeping with the Calvinist-Jansenist rationale, the Canadian protagonist is not disillusioned. Rather
he is confused, and more often than not he suffers from a guilt
complex. The old Order is falling apart, the old values do not
seem to make sense anymore; and the Canadian character
blames himself for his disbelief. He still thinks of the established system as far greater than he is. He has not been, like
the American, seasoned in self-reliance, individualism, and
distrust of authority.

It is in the 1960s that the third major thematic division
of contemporary Canadian literature—*Search for Vital Truth*—
begins to take shape. What distinguishes this category from
the *Breakup* is the final disappearance of guilt feelings about
the invalidity of the Old Order. A number of writers present
characters for whom the traditional values mean nothing at
all. They are not sorry about their inability to adapt, nor are
they intent upon making an accommodation. But although
these characters have found a cure for the Calvinist-Jansenist
hangover, they still have problems. They begin at zero; they
have no values, and they are searching for some kind of vital
truth or substitute raison d'être. For some of the poets and
novelists of Quebec the idea of an independent nation—separatism—provides a temporary solution. But even the revolutionaries in Quebec novels, as will be seen, do not find the
separatist cause sufficient to provide a complete and satisfying life direction. The hero of each book is confused to begin
with, then he becomes even more confused. It is a big leap
from the total-life-controlling Old Order to a state of noth-

ingness. Then added to this shock is the problem of identity, both group and personal. For some writers of the *Search* category, the personal raison d'être of their fictional characters is tied up with the raison d'être of the nation itself, a questioning of whether Canada does, can, and should exist as a nation. It would seem, by contrast, that no major American writer, even Mailer or Faulkner or the most disillusioned black poet or novelist, has had quite the same sentiment. American writers question and lament what the United States has become, to be sure; they call for changes, revitalization and rededication, or else they despair that deterioration is too far gone, but never do they question their nation's existence or their own identity as Americans, however much they may resent both. Even Ralph Ellison's "invisible man" knows who he is—the problem is that others do not really see him.

Finally, a fourth major thematic category—*The New Hero*—has now emerged in Canadian literature of the 1970s. It was mentioned earlier that the traditional American hero, the self-reliant individualist, has in recent years tended to be less successful than he used to be, becoming the victim rather than the conqueror of the social system. Intriguingly, the very reverse is happening in the literature of Canada. A new hero has, as it were, suddenly exploded from the pages of Canadian fiction. In many respects he is an exponent of traditional American rather than Canadian values—self-reliance, individualism, independence, self-confidence. But in contrast to the American hero, he is not consciously embracing accepted national virtues with the resulting tendency to self-righteousness; actually, he is ignoring his own national virtues, or perhaps simply recognizing that they are no longer valid and therefore he must depend on his own resources. He is neither defiant nor domineering, but he is determined to follow his own convictions; and manifestly unlike the former Canadian hero, he has no Calvinist-Jansenist guilt complex or feelings of insignificance. Clear examples of the new hero are found in novels from both French and English Canada, indicating that Canadians of each major language group are simultaneously and at long last creating a new image of themselves.

The implications of the new Canadian hero, who like all distinctive characteristics of a national literature undoubtedly reflects the changing nature of the nation itself, could be profound and far-reaching indeed. There is food for thought, perhaps, in the statement of the giant Indian in Ken Kensey's *One Flew Over the Cuckoo Nest*—after he has mercifully put the crushed American hero out of his misery, he speculates that he will travel for a while in the Northwest, eventually to find his way over the border to Canada.

PERSPECTIVE

For the purposes of clarity and convenience, it is expedient to look at Canadian literature chronologically; although the following periods, if the first four are grouped together under *Divine Order and the Land,* also correspond to the thematic development of both poetry and prose: This chapter is therefore divided into the following sections:

- The Colonial Period (1750–1867)
- The Confederation Period (1867–1900)
- The Early Twentieth Century (1900–1920)
- The Modern Period (1920–1945)
- The Breakup of the Old Order (1945–1960)
- The Search for Vital Truth (1960–1970)
- The New Hero (1970–   )

The Colonial Period (1750–1867)

Like the settlers of the United States, the people who first cleared the land and built farms in the Canadian wilderness did not have a great deal of time for literary pursuits. In the English-speaking areas of Canada, it was not until the American Revolution pushed some thirty thousand United Empire Loyalists north that significant cultural activity began to take place. And it was not until the second generation of Loyalists, in the 1820s and 1830s, that Canadian literature as such began to appear.

In French Canada, outside of accounts of trips and exploration during the French regime (1534–1759), little of literary significance was produced for several decades after the Conquest. The British, of course, had cut off all relations with France, and *les canadiens* as they then called themselves, were culturally isolated, something that relatively speaking did not happen to Americans after the Revolution. Interestingly enough, the first newspaper to appear in French in Canada, the *Gazette littéraire* of Montreal, was founded in 1778 by Fleury Mesplet, a Frenchman whom Benjamin Franklin had met in London and persuaded to immigrate. But much as in English Canada, it was not until the 1830's that a significant native literature began to take shape.

Halifax, in the Province of Nova Scotia, was the earliest cultural center of English Canada. The first Canadian book-length poem was written by a Haligonian (native of Halifax) called Oliver Goldsmith (1794–1861), whose grandfather Henry was the brother of the famous Oliver Goldsmith of England. Beginning a pattern of derivation that would haunt Canadian letters for a long time, the Canadian poet was much inspired by his granduncle's *The Deserted Village,* and the uninspiring title of his own major work is *The Rising Village* (1825).

Undoubtedly, however, Thomas Chandler Haliburton (1796–1865), the satirist mentioned in the introduction, was the dominant literary figure of the Colonial Period in Nova Scotia. He was of the staunch Loyalist, Tory (conservative) establishment, his father a judge and his mother the daughter of parents who had died for the Crown during the War of Independence. But after becoming a lawyer and a member of the Nova Scotia government, Haliburton developed a number of liberal ideas, including freedom for Roman Catholics to hold public office and free public schooling. Haliburton's *The Clockmaker; or, The Sayings and Doings of Samuel Slick, of Slickville* began serially in the *Nova Scotian* in 1835, then was published in book form in three series (Halifax, 1836; London, 1838, 1840).

Besides formulating the Canadian dual attitude toward Americans already discussed, *The Clockmaker* provided Haliburton with a platform to criticize Nova Scotian habits and policies. Hector St. Jean de Crèvecoeur, in his *Letters of an American Farmer* (1776), had commented that the people of Nova Scotia lacked amibition and a spirit of industry. Through Sam Slick, Haliburton sought to improve the situation, using the drive, hard work, and ingenuity of the Yankee as a model. Another model that provided Haliburton with ideas, including the use of vernacular speech, was the popular New England book by Seba Smith entitled in the manner of the times: *Life and Writings of Major Jack Downing, of Downingsville, Away Down East, in the State of Maine* (1833).

The Clockmaker is simply a series of episodes involving the narrator and Sam as they travel around Nova Scotia selling clocks. It is Sam Slick who holds the reader's attention, and Haliburton's skillful presentation of his vanity, resourcefulness, and "gift of the gab" have sustained the book through at least seventy editions. Professor Fred Cogswell, in a chapter of the *Literary History of Canada,* describes Haliburton's protagonist as follows:

> In point of fact, Sam Slick's versatility is an artistic reflection of the spirit of New England. The Yankees were the Greeks of the New World, and Slick is a folk hero, an Odysseus of their commercial frontier. In their excursions by land and sea, the Yankees not only acquired knowledge of men and affairs, but they also picked up their language where they found it, appropriating picturesque phrases much as they appropriated ideas that could later be turned into dollars and cents. In Haliburton's time, Slick was a credible New Englander; if he is a stage character today, he is one at least in the same brilliant sense as the characters of the Molière and Dickens.

Thomas Haliburton went on to write other books, including *The Attaché; or Sam Slick in England* (1843), which may have given Mark Twain the idea; but *The Clockmaker,* which effectively illustrates the budding divergence of national philosophies between Canada and the United States as well as the emergence of the two contrasting types of protagonist discussed above in the introduction, remains his major accomplishment.

While Goldsmith, Haliburton, Joseph Howe (essayist and

magazine editor who first published *The Clockmaker*), and a number of others were establishing a literary circle in Nova Scotia, Ontario (or Upper Canada as it was then known) and Quebec (Lower Canada) were also witnessing the early signs of a nascent literature. Perhaps the best-known example is Susanna Moodie's *Roughing It in the Bush* (1852), a documentary study of the hardships of pioneering. But Moodie (1803–85) was a transplanted Englishwoman of genteel pretensions, forced by circumstances, it would seem, to live among, as she put it, "semi-barbarous Yankee squatters who had left their country for their country's good." If Thomas Haliburton lays emphasis on the one side of the twin Canadian attitudes of admiration and suspicion regarding Americans, Moodie certainly underlines the other. Speaking of the cholera doctor Stephen Ayres, she comments: "A friend of mine, in this town, has an original portrait of this notable empiric— this man sent from heaven. The face is rather handsome, but has a keen, designing expression, and is evidently that of an American from its complexion and features."

Besides Americans and upper-middle-class English (halfpay officers attracted by generous land grants), there were other people settling in Canada—Scots, Irish, Germans, East Europeans, mainly of the peasant and laboring classes— and they too produced literature. Alexander McLachlan (1818–96) composed three volumes of verse, not unexpectedly patterned after the works of Robert Burns, and Charles Heavysege (1816–76) wrote poetry and a novel called *The Advocate* (1865). His verse drama *Saul* (1857) was extravagantly praised by Longfellow, who went so far as to pronounce its author "the greatest dramatist since Shakespeare." For the modern reader, however, Longfellow notwithstanding, a far more enduring and captivating work is *The Backwoods of Canada* (1836), written by the sister of Susanna Moodie, Catherine Parr Traill (1802–99). Like *Roughing It in the Bush, Backwoods,* contains detailed and perceptive accounts of the life of settlers, but it is not so burdened by self-pity and conviction of social superiority.

Two native-born Canadians, both of Loyalist descent, made their marks in Upper and Lower Canada during the

Colonial Period. John Richardson (1796–1852), a much-traveled adventurer, based his long narrative poem *Tecumseh* (1828) on personal experiences in the War of 1812, but he is best known for the Gothic tale *Wacousta* (1832), about Pontiac's siege of Detroit in 1763. Charles Sangster (1822–93) won considerable popularity among his contemporaries with his descriptive verse, notably *The St. Lawrence and the Saguenay* (1856), but modern readers are likely to find his work excessively ornamented and idealized.

In French-speaking Lower Canada, the first novel to appear was Philippe Aubert de Gaspé's (1814–41) *Le Chercheur de trésors ou l'influence d'un livre* (1837)—*The Treasure Seeker or the Influence of a Book*—which is based upon the superstitions and folklore of rural French Canada. Closer to a novel of manners and containing dramatization of the repercussions of the Conquest for *canadien* society is *Charles Guérin* (1846) by Pierre Chauveau (1820–90).

What really provided the literary spark in French Canada, however, was the celebrated *Report on the Affairs of British North America* (1839) by the earl of Durham, which advocated massive British immigration to effect the assimilation of *les canadiens,* whom the report described as a people without a history or a culture. The first reaction was François-Xavier Garneau's (1809–66) monumental *Histoire du Canada* (1845–48), which did much to implant a sense of collective pride and mission in francophone Lower Canada. A little later came the novel *Les Anciens Canadiens* (1863)—*Canadians of Old*—by Philippe Aubert de Gaspé (1786–1871), father of the author of *Le Chercheur.* This novel is one of a group that, symbolically to offset the humiliation of military defeat, present love affairs between British men and alluring *canadienne* maidens, each of who, after having reduced her suitor to blubbering incapacity, haughtily refuses to marry him. *Les Anciens Canadiens,* a book rich in detail about early Quebec life and mores, tells how the handsome Archibald Cameron of Lochiell, desperately in love with Blanche d'Haberville since the prewar days when he had lived in Quebec as a guest of her family, is by duty obliged to take part in the defeat of the French and consequently loses his true love.

Among other significant contributions to the Colonial Period literature of Lower Canada are the long poems of Octave Crémazie (1827–79), poems that embody a somewhat glorified image of mother France. Ironically, Crémazie, who expressed an exile spirit while in Canada and who, despite being a writer himself, despaired of French Canadians ever producing a literature of any but regional interest, became disillusioned by the real France when he went there in 1862. He ended his days in the old country feeling an exile all over again. Antoine Gérin-Lajoie (1824–82) had more positive inclinations. His two novels of the soil, *Jean Rivard le défricheur— John Rivard the Settler,* and *Jean Rivard economiste,* published in 1862 and 1864, articulated many of the motifs that would recur in Canadian novels during the next half century and longer. Gérin-Lajoie was worried about the exodus of French Canadians to the mill towns of New England, and his novels are attempts to demonstrate how the honest, industrious farmer can succeed if he sets his mind to the job.

Like Thomas Haliburton, then, Antoine Gérin-Lajoie was acutely aware of American dynamism and accomplishment, and he is another prominent example of how consciousness of the United States has been a conditioning force on Canadian literature. The sense of collectivity, as opposed to the American spirit of independence and individualism, and the need for adherence to the dictates of the established system and God's design are also strongly expressed in Gérin-Lajoie's two didactic novels, as in other minor works of the time. Thus even before the end of the Colonial Period, the first comprehensive theme of Canadian literature—*Divine Order and the Land*—had been firmly established.

The Confederation Period (1867–1900)

Canadian Confederation, however reluctantly and negatively instituted, created high excitement in the new nation. There was a spirit of challenge throughout the land, a certain awe at the vastness of its territory both actual and potential (today second only to the Soviet Union in geographical size). Besides large tracts remaining in the Maritimes, Ontario and Quebec, the West was now opened up to settlement, and there were plans to build a transcontinental railroad, a condition for bringing British Columbia into the fold in 1871. The railroad, incidentally, despite an alleged conspiracy by American interests to sabotage the project because it would compete with the Union Pacific, was finally completed in 1885 by another, transplanted, American, William Van Horne.

The excitement of Confederation was reflected in an explosion of cultural activities, including the founding of new journals, expansion of universities, and the writing of a great deal of poetry. Here, as elsewhere in this brief perspective, it is of course impossible to comment on all the literature produced. In English Canada, four poets are generally considered to have dominated the period between Confederation and the end of the nineteenth century: Charles G. D. Roberts, Bliss Carman, Duncan Campbell Scott, and Archibald Lampman.

Charles Roberts (1860–1943) was born near Fredericton, New Brunswick, and through his mother could trace his lineage back to the grandfather of Ralph Waldo Emerson, the Reverend Daniel Bliss, who was a United Empire Loyalist. Roberts's first book, *Orion and Other Poems* (1880), had a tremendous influence, particularly on other poets such as Lampman and Carmen, and is credited with initiating the first consequential poetic movement in English Canada. He was essentially a landscape poet, heavily influenced by the British tradition, and his particular landscape was the region of the Tantramar marshes and St. John River Valley in New Brunswick. The bulk of Roberts's ten volumes of poetry is now forgotten, but some of his descriptive sonnets are still memorable for their success in capturing a mood, a fleeting moment, or a picturesque scene. "The Skater" is one of his best-known poems:

> My glad feet shod with glittering steel
> I was the god of the winged heel.
> The hills in the far white sky were lost;
> The world lay still in the wide white frost;

And the woods hung hushed in their long white dream
By the ghostly, glimmering, ice-blue stream. . . .

And the wandering wind was left behind
As faster, faster I followed my mind;

Till the blood sang high in my eager brain,
And the joy of my flight was almost pain.

Then I stayed the rush of my eager speed
And silently went as a drifting seed,

Slowly, furtively, till my eyes
Grew big with the awe of a dim sunrise,

And the hair of my neck began to creep
At hearing the wilderness talk in sleep.

Shapes in the fir-gloom drifted near.
In the deep of my heart I heard my fear

And I turned and fled, like a soul pursued,
From the white, inviolate solitude.

Roberts's cousin, Bliss Carman (1861–1929), who was also from New Brunswick, studied philosophy for a time at Harvard University and spent most of his adult life in the United States. His poetry, like that of Roberts, is close to nature, but whereas the latter depended on his eye for minute detail, Carman leaned more toward the lyrical reaction evoked by natural phenomena. Here is part of his "A Vagabond Song":

The scarlet of the maples can choke me like a cry
Of bugles going by.
And my lonely spirit thrills
To see the frosty asters like a smoke upon the hills.

A difference between the first two Confederation poets and Duncan Campbell Scott (1862–1947) is that the latter more often took human beings and life situations as his inspiration. The son of a Methodist minister, Scott moved among several communities as he was growing up, then he went to work for the Department of Indian Affairs. His sympathetic interest in, and his knowledge of, native peoples is reflected

in his best poems, which are certainly among the more realistic and perceptive representations of the North American
Indian to be found in either Canadian or American literature.
"The Onondaga Madonna," for example, makes poignant and
ironic use of traditional Christian symbolism:

> She stands full-throated and with careless pose,
> This woman of a weird and waning race,
> Where all her pagan passion burns and glows;
> Her blood is mingled with her ancient foes,
> And thrills with war and wildness in her veins;
> Her rebel lips are dabbled with the stains
> Of feuds and forays and her father's woes.
>
> And closer in the shawl about her breast,
> The latest promise of her nation's doom,
> Paler than she her baby clings and lies,
> The primal warrior gleaming from his eyes;
> He sulks, and burdened with his infant gloom,
> He draws his heavy brows and will not rest.

Born in Morpeth, Ontario, Archibald Lampman (1861–99)
is another Canadian poet of Loyalist descent. Although he
completed a degree in classics at Trinity College, Toronto, he
spent his short adult life working for the Post Office Department of the Canadian civil service. Like Roberts and Carman,
Lampman was mainly a nature poet, but his work is marked
by greater emotional intensity than can be found in that of
his two fellow poets. He too was influenced by the English
Romantics, especially Keats and Wordsworth; his poetry reveals a keen eye for detail combined with a Wordsworthian
faith in the power of nature as a transcendental lever to spiritual insight.

In addition to the four major poets of the Confederation
Period in English Canada, there were many lesser lights, Is-
abella Valancy Crawford (1850–87) and William Wilfred
Campbell (1861–1918) prominent among them. Curiously,
however, outside of the historical romances of William Kirby
(1817–1906) and Gilbert Parker (1862–1932), the period witnessed very little long prose fiction of note. The same situation
largely obtained in French Canada.

Louis Fréchette (1839–1908), the leading figure of Quebec letters in the last quarter of the nineteenth century, was born in Lévis, near Quebec City, and went to work in the United States at the age of fifteen. He returned to finish his classical studies, subsequently pursuing careers as a lawyer, journalist, and politician, spending several years in Chicago along the way. Like the English-speaking Confederation poets, Fréchette was inspired by the great writers of Europe, in his case Lamartine and Hugo. Unlike Carman, Roberts, and Lampman, however, his imagination was more attuned to his people's history than to landscape, and his greatest volume is entitled *La Légende d'un peuple* (1888)—*The Legend of a People*. More romantic in temperament was Pamphile Lemay (1837–1918), who translated Longfellow's *Evangeline,* and his sonnets are not unlike much of the poetry of his compatriots Carman, Roberts, and Lampman.

Completing the parallel between English and French Canada is Laure Conan (1845–1924), who like Parker and Kirby wrote several historical romances. Another prose writer of the Confederation Period has the distinction of having produced the first nationalistic novel with racist coloring. Jules-Paul Tardivel (1851–1905) was actually born in Covington, Kentucky, and did not learn French until he came to Quebec at the age of seventeen. He was a religious fanatic, and his *Pour la patrie* (1895) is filled with distortions of every kind. Curiously enough, Tardivel saw France as a major threat to Quebec—"La France mondaine, sceptique, railleuse, impie et athée. . . . La France ennemie déclarée de Dieu et de son Eglise a fait irruption au Canada" (Worldly, skeptical, jeering, wicked and atheistic France. . . . declared enemy of God and His Church, has invaded Canada).

The Confederation Period in both English and French Canada started with much hope and enthusiasm, but by the end of the nineteenth century the honeymoon was over. The great depression that began in 1873 undoubtedly helped to cool the ardor of many Canadians. There were threats of secession as early as 1886 (Premier Fielding of Nova Scotia) and loud protests that the country was being dominated by the central provinces. Goldwin Smith, a distinguished political scientist, even went so far as to declare in his *Canada and the Canadian Question* (1891) that Canada as a nation had failed. He advocated annexation to the United States as the only reasonable solution. And indeed more than a million Canadians, including poets Carman and Roberts as well as thousands of young men and women from Quebec, personally made that choice and emigrated over the border, leaving fewer than 5 million countrymen to face the new century.

The Early Twentieth Century (1900–1920)

Desmond Pacey, a pioneer of Canadian literary history, noted in his *Creative Writing in Canada* that "if the last three decades of the nineteenth century to some extent deserved the popular epithet of 'the golden age' of Canadian literature, the first two decades of the twentieth were without doubt the age of brass . . . an era of best sellers." Now, Pacey was referring only to English Canada, but the latter part of his statement is in a way also true of Quebec writing of the period. The dominant figures of the beginning of the twentieth century in both English and French were, from the standpoint of their literary production, somewhat unique virtuosos. They composed works that stand alone and are distinguished by either great popular and international success or extraordinary impact and influence.

Among the poets there were Robert Service, Emile Nelligan, Albert Lozeau, and William Henry Drummond. Prose writers included Stephen Leacock, Louis Hémon, Lucy Montgomery, Ralph Connor, and Albert Laberge.

Robert W. Service (1874–1958) made a fortune with his barroom verse of the Canadian North and the gold rush, then sensibly retired to the French Riviera to enjoy it. He was working as a clerk for a bank in Whitehorse, Yukon, when, tired of endless repetitions of "Casey at the Bat" and "The Face on the Bar-room Floor," he decided to compose his own ballads. *Songs of a Sourdough* (1907) was an immediate success, followed by several more volumes, and soon Service's ballads were being repeated endlessly. Probably the most popular of them are "The Cremation of Sam McGee" and the rollicking tale of "The Shooting of Dan McGrew," which begins:

A bunch of the boys were whopping it up in the Malamute
  saloon;
The kid that handles the music-box was hitting a jag
  time tune;
Back of the bar, in a solo game, sat Dangerous Dan
  McGrew,
And watching his luck was his light-o'-love, the lady
  that's known as Lou.

When out of the night, which was fifty below, and into
  the din and the glare,
There stumbled a miner fresh from the creeks, dog-dirty,
  and loaded for bear.
He looked like a man with a foot in the grave, and
  scarcely the strength of a louse,
Yet he tilted a poke of dust on the bar, and he called
  for drinks for the house.
There was none could place the stranger's face, though
  we searched ourselves for a clue;
But we drank his health, and the last to drink was
  Dangerous Dan McGrew. . . .

Popular success, of course, is hardly an indication of excellence, and no one, including Service, pretends that he was a practitioner of high art. It must be said, nevertheless, that he had a sure sense of rhythm and narrative interest, and that what he set out to do, he did well.

A complete contrast to Robert Service is Emile Nelligan (1879–1941), son of an Irish father and French-Canadian mother, who has been generally accepted as the most gifted and original poet of the "Ecole littéraire de Montréal," a literary group at the turn of the century. While Service lived to the age of eighty-four, sunning himself in southern France and traipsing around the world, Nelligan's career was over at the age of twenty, when he was committed to an insane asylum. His poetry is intellectual, of intense subjectivity and sensibility. The critic and literary historian Gérard Tougas, in his *Histoire de la littérature canadienne-française* (1964), says of Nelligan: "Romantic in sentiment, parnassian in form, symbolist in vocabulary, at his best Nelligan fuses these elements through his imaginative power." Here is a translation by P. F. Widdows of one of the most widely acclaimed of Emile Nelligan's poems, "Le Vaisseau d'or"—"The Golden Ship":

> There was a fine Ship, carved from solid gold,
> With azure-reaching masts, on seas unknown.
> Spreadeagled Venus, naked, hair back-thrown,
> Stood at the prow. The sun blazed uncontrolled.
> But on the treacherous Ocean in the gloom
> She struck the great reef where the Sirens chant.
> Appalling shipwreck plunged her keel aslant
> To the Gulf's depths, that unrelenting tomb.
>
> She was a Golden Ship: but there showed through
> Translucent sides treasures the blasphemous crew,
> Hatred, Disgust and Madness, fought to share.
>
> How much survives after the storm's brief race?
> Where is my heart, that empty ship, oh where?
> Alas, in Dream's abyss sunk without trace.

Albert Lozeau (1878–1924), who was crippled by tuberculosis of the spine while still a teenager, joined the "Ecole littéraire de Montréal" about five years after mental illness had caused Nelligan's departure, and like Nelligan he distinguished himself from the other members of the literary society. More conventional than the hypersensitive Nelligan, he nevertheless succeeded in writing love poetry of unusual sincerity and originality. At the time that he fell in love, both he and his sweetheart believed, on medical advice, that his paralysis could be cured. But the hopes were ill founded, and Lozeau lived through the whole spectrum of emotional turmoil associated with young love, hope, disappointment, and eventually having his loved one marry another suitor. All these emotions, unsentimentalized and skillfully dissected, are reflected in Lozeau's poetry.

Quite distinctive in still another way is the work of William Henry Drummond (1854–1907). Born in Ireland, he came to Canada at the age of ten and eventually became a doctor in the Eastern Townships of Quebec. Like Service, he wrote popular verse rather than serious poetry. He had been captivated by the broken English dialect of *canadien* lumbermen and farmers, and he composed in that dialect, blending humorous characterizations with descriptions of the Quebec landscape. "The Wreck of the Julie Plante," which appeared in his *The Habitant, and Other French Canadian Poems* (1897) is one of Drummond's best-known efforts. It begins:

> On wan dark night on Lac St. Pierre,
> De win' she blow, blow, blow
> an' de crew of de wood scow Julie Plante
> Got scar't an' run below—
> For de win' she blow lak hurricane,
> Bimeby she blow some more,
> An' de scow bus' up on Lac St. Pierre
> Wan arpent from de shore.

The poem goes on to describe how the captain tries to save the cook, Rosie, by lashing her to the mast, but alas all are killed. Hence the last verse entitled "Moral":

> Now all good wood scow sailor man
> Tak' warning by dat storm
> An' go an' marry some nice French girl
> An' leev on wan beeg farm.
> De win' can blow lak hurricane,
> An' s'pose she blow some more,
> You can't get drown on Lac St. Pierre
> So long you stay on shore.

Turning to fiction, *Sunshine Sketches of a Little Town* and *Maria Chapdelaine*, which first appeared in 1912 and 1913, respectively, and have subsequently gone through numerous editions in many languages, are doubtless two of the most enduring of Canadian classics. Both were written by men who were born outside Canada, Stephen Leacock (1869–1944) in Hampshire, England, and Louis Hémon

(1880–1913) in Brest, France. Leacock crossed the Atlantic as a child, was educated at the Universities of Toronto and Chicago, then taught economics and political science at McGill University until he retired in 1936. Hémon, on the other hand, came to Canada at the age of thirty-one, in 1911, and he barely had time to complete his famous novel before he was killed in a railroad accident at Chapleau, Ontario, in 1913. It is possible, nevertheless, that in the short time he spent on Canadian soil, Hémon became more attuned to the distinctive qualities of the national consciousness than did Leacock in his long and productive life.

Stephen Leacock's humor is partly in the general North American tradition that traces back through the comedy writers of American newspapers and Mark Twain to Thomas Haliburton and Seba Smith, and that leans on dialect or accent, exaggeration, and the naive or "queer" character to achieve comic effect. But Leacock also exploits the methods of British humor, which tends to depend upon urbanity, irony, and straight-faced, often elaborate presentation of the absurd as commonplace. Understandably, then, Leacock's own two favorite humorists were Charles Dickens and Mark Twain; obviously, he learned from both of them.

Most of Stephen Leacock's many volumes, which appeared regularly each year from 1910 to his death, are collections of separate, brief sketches or vignettes. Unity of theme is found in *My Discovery of England* (1922) and *College Days* (1923), while *Arcadian Adventures of the Idle Rich* (1914) is a portrait of life in a big city, which could be New York or Chicago. *Sunshine Sketches of a Little Town* describes a small Ontario town with a combination of satire and nostalgia. And as the author himself remarks in the book's preface: "These works are of so humorous a character that for many years it was found impossible to print them. The compositors fell back from their task suffocated with laughter and gasping for air. Nothing but the invention of the linotype machine—or rather, of the kind of men who operate it—made it possible to print these books. Even now people have to be very careful in circulating them, and the books should never be put into the hands of persons not in robust health."

Sunshine Sketches reveals the complete Leacock, the kindly humorist chuckling over human foibles and the lethal satirist striking at hypocrisy and pretentiousness. Politics and politicians are among his targets, and the last part of *Sunshine Sketches* concerns the "Great Election" and the defeat of the longtime incumbent John Henry Bagshaw. Toward the end of the campaign, Bagshaw begins to realize that he might be defeated, and as Leacock puts it: "'I am an old man now, gentlemen,' Bagshaw said, 'and the time must soon come when I must not only leave politics, but must take my way towards that goal from which no traveller returns.' There was a deep hush when Bagshaw said this. It was understood to imply that he thought of going to the United States."

As pointed out in the introduction, Maria Chapdelaine also thinks of going to the United States, but Louis Hémon's heroine finally rejects the idea and remains in Quebec to follow in the footsteps of her long-suffering mother. The novel *Maria Chapdelaine* is a vivid representation of the values that kept French-Canadian society static for such a long time. Samuel Chapdelaine, Maria's father, is the prototype of the traditional Canadian character discussed earlier—he accepts hardship, indeed he invites it, moving to the wilderness all over again once he has cleared and established a farmstead. *Divine Order and the Land* prescribe the lives of all the Chapdelaines. When, for example, the handsome adventurer François Paradis is lost in the bush, Maria is upset, but she takes the appropriate measures. She knows that if one repeats a thousand *Ave Marias* on the day before Christmas and asks a favor of God, then barring extraordinary alternate plans on the part of the divinity, the favor will be granted. Unfortunately, it appears that God does have alternate plans in this instance, and François freezes to death in the forest. At first it is hard for Maria to accept. "Christ Jesus, who hold out your arms to the unfortunate," she says to herself, "why didn't you deliver him from the snow with your pale hands? Why, Holy Virgin, didn't you permit a small miracle when he stumbled for the last time?" But Maria's doubts do not last long, for like her father and mother she knows the deep satisfaction of being sure: "Oh! Certainly! The contentment of an august promise which dispels the terrible fog of death. While the priest was performing the holy rites . . . Samuel Chapdelaine and his children prayed without lifting their heads, almost consoled, free from doubt and worry, certain that whatever happened was according to a pact with the divinity, which made the blue heaven sown with stars of gold an authentic blessing." The Chapdelaines thus accept their lives as ordained, and the novel exemplifies the long-lasting belief that French Canada would be preserved only by adherence to the status quo and resistance to all social change.

Contrasting with the social realism and group psychoanalysis of *Maria Chapdelaine* are the many rural idylls that appeared across the country in the early twentieth century. Prominent among the writers of these regional romances was Lucy Maud Montgomery (1874–1942), of Prince Edward Island, who achieved great popular success with her children's classic, *Anne of Green Gables* (1908). Mark Twain himself, not given to generous handouts of praise, called Anne "the dearest and most moving and delightful child since Alice in Wonderland." Even greater popular acclaim was accorded Ralph Connor (1860–1937), a clergyman-novelist who wrote moralistic romances such as *Black Rock* (1897) and *The Man from Glengarry* (1901). Critic Desmond Pacey has aptly explained Connor's success: "There was in Connor's novels, though in very mild form, the appeal we find in *Moll Flanders*: readers could comfort themselves with the thought that they were being instructed in virtue while at the same time getting some glimpses of vice."

On the other side of the ecclesiastical fence and the opposite of the authors of idyllic romances was Albert Laberge (1871–1960), an anticlerical novelist who purposely limited publication of his work because he disdained to bring the wrath of Quebec's powerful church establishment down upon his head. A sports writer by profession, Laberge was the first Canadian naturalist. His novel *La Scouine* (1918)—*The Slovenly Woman*—which appeared in but sixty copies, can be compared in terms of its position in Canadian literature with Zola's *La Terre*. In contrast to the works of Gérin-Lajoie, Montgomery, Connor, and a host of others, it dwells upon the ugliness of farm life, the grotesque deformation of the human spirit that can be brought about by constant and unrewarding hard labor. Unlike Louis Hémon, Albert Laberge saw no redeeming qualities, and he looked upon religion as a stifling force. In these respects he resembled the American naturalists of a decade or so before him—Stephen Crane, Theodore Dreiser—but Canadian society, still locked in the trammels of Calvinist-Jansenist values, was not ready for him. Compared with Crane or Dreiser, the impression he made was minuscule, and he remained in almost total obscurity until 1963, when critic and novelist Gérard Bessette rescued him in his *Anthologie d'Albert Laberge*. In fact, however, Laberge is the true precursor of contemporary Quebec writers such as Marie-Claire Blais and Roch Carrier, who will be discussed later.

The age of the virtuosos was brought to a close by the Great War, which temporarily turned the eyes of the nation away from Canada itself. The war also had the effect of stimulating the desire for a separate and distinctive national identity, as Canadians in large numbers went off to prove themselves on the battlefields of Europe.

The Modern Period (1920–1945)

Canada's impressive performance in World War I was justification at last for the untying of the British apron strings, and in 1926 the nation was officially recognized as equal partner to Great Britain in the Commonwealth. Soon afterward Canadian diplomats were sent to Washington and other capitals; the national interests of Canada would no longer be handled by the British foreign embassies. Coupled with these political developments, there was a renewal of the Confederation spirit of nationalism and widespread efforts to promote Canadian culture. In painting, the "Group of Seven" began to gain international fame. A number of literary and scholarly journals were founded, and publishing houses began to spring up. Unfortunately, the Great Depression of the 1930s brought an end to many of these endeavors, but not before a few Canadian writers had become commercial successes, something that competition from the United States, Great Britain, and France has made virtually impossible since. Canadian writers have little hope today of breaking into the vast and tightly controlled paperback trade that markets in bookstands rather than bookstores. A lamentable and increasingly serious (for Canada) consequence of the current situation is that many Canadian writers of high caliber are barely known and rarely sold beyond the nation's borders.

Mazo de la Roche (1879–1961) is probably the most illustrious of the commercially successful authors of the pre-paperback period. In 1927, her novel *Jalna* won the *Atlantic Monthly* $10,000 prize over twelve thousand entries from all over the world. This achievement initiated a whole series of "Jalna" novels, sixteen romantic idylls of rural Ontario life describing the saga of the Whiteoaks family. Another commercial success was Henri Grignon's (1894–   ) *Un homme et son péché* (1933)—*A Man and His Sin,* although for quite different reasons. Grignon's comic story of a miser named Seraphin (a name that has become part of Quebec French) was transformed into a radio series of long-lasting popularity.

Meanwhile in the realistic and naturalitistic modes, the impact of *Maria Chapdelaine* brought forth seemingly countless novels of the soil, or *romans du terroir* as they are called in French. Two writers, one in Quebec and the other in the Canadian West, stand out as having brought the genre to a climax: Philippe Panneton (1895–1960), who wrote under the nom de plume Ringuet, and Frederick Philip Grove (1917–48), who in a way also used a pseudonym, for recent research has convincingly established that he was really Felix Paul Greve, an immigrant from Germany. Greve, apparently an accomplished linguist, had previously written novels and poetry in German, worked as a translator, and frequented illustrious European literary circles that included such notables as André Gide and Oscar Wilde. In Canada, Grove produced several volumes, novels, essays, sketches, and his autobiography. His *Master of the Mill* (1944), which resembles the novels of industrial-commercial empires by Upton Sinclair, Frank Norris, and other American naturalists, has proved to be highly prophetic in its analysis of labor relations and the effects of automation.

The two books that bring the Canadian novel of the soil to culmination are Grove's *Our Daily Bread* (1928) and Ringuet's *Trente Arpents* (1938)—*Thirty Acres*; in dramatizing the theme of *Divine Order and the Land* they are much alike. As a matter of fact, the two novels are so similar in theme and plot and even in certain details and scenes that one wonders if Panneton had ever read Frederick Philip Grove. On the other hand, the books are quite different in atmosphere and technique, so that in the unlikely event that the Quebec writer did borrow certain ideas he subjected them thoroughly to his own creative process. *Trente Arpents,* it should be pointed out, is a better novel than *Our Daily Bread.* Its rhythmic prose and skillful use of the colloquial diction of rural Quebec contrast with Grove's stiff, often lumbering style. Ringuet had a genius for selecting the kind of small detail that brings a character to life, engaging the imagination and sympathy of the reader. When Phydime Raymond, for example, visits neighbor Euchariste Moisan to negotiate for Moisan's half of a small wood, which he desperately wishes to buy, the ancestral Norman propensity for circumlocution is illustrated in a manner worthy of Maupassant at his best. Raymond explains that he has come to see if the sick cow is getting better. Then the conversation, between drags on their pipes, proceeds to diseases in general, the weather, the icy road that is becoming dangerous, the elections. On his way out the door, Raymond enquires about the fence bordering the two properties and who should repair it that year. Then he, who is the one wanting to buy Moisan's half of the wood, offers to sell his half to Moisan, remarking that it isn't worth ten dollars to him; whereupon Moisan, who has not the least notion of buying land, says that such a purchase might not be a bad idea. And on they go, each somehow divining exactly what the other had in mind. Compared with Ringuet's technique of characterization, Grove's is stark and clinical. Nonetheless, considered as an artistic whole, despite its obvious shortcomings *Our Daily Bread* does make a deep impression upon the reader, an impression of magnitude of vision. It may well have as permanent a place in Canadian literature as *Trente Arpents*.

The parallels between the two novels are manifest. Both stories concern a man obsessed with the idea of building a dynasty upon the land in fulfillment of God's design. Euchariste Moisan and John Elliot both have loyal, long-suffering wives, each of whom was chosen to bear children and each of whom brings four sons and six daughters into the world. Alphonsine Moisan dies in delivery, while Martha Elliot is a victim of cancer of the womb, making both of them martyrs to their husbands' obsessions. Like the mother in Hémon's *Maria Chapdelaine* and Alphonsine, Martha has always harbored a sense of frustration, but she alone of the three gets a chance to make a small gesture of defiance against the joyless Jansenist-Calvinist rationale. In a memorable scene, one of Grove's best, she rises from her deathbed and goes to a dance, the loose, heavy folds of her dress draping shroudlike about her wasted body.

Samuel Chapdelaine, John Elliot, and Euchariste Moisan have identical attitudes toward the land. Elliot's daughter Cathleen has a university professor as suitor, and of this man Elliot says: "Woodrow Ormond, a sensible man, mature beyond his years. But unanchored in the soil." In *Trente Arpents*, speaking of the farm establishments, a similar statement: "La patrie c'est la terre, et non le sang" (The land is more important than even the blood). And coping with the harsh land of Canada isolates the Elliots and Moisans from even the most monumental events of the outside world. Hearing of the prospects for a great war in Europe, Moisan is baffled: "These people," he says, "how can they think about fighting when the harvest isn't in yet." He begins to see how war fits into the *Divine Order* when the local priest explains to him that France is being punished for mistreating the clergy.

At the end of *Our Daily Bread* Elliot staggers across miles of country, crawling the last few yards on his hands and knees, to die on his own piece of land. At the end of *Trente Arpents* Moisan is still alive, working as a watchman in a New England garage and dreaming of his thirty acres, but earlier in the book there is a scene much lke the climax of *Our Daily Bread*. Ephrem Moisan, the uncle from whom Euchariste inherited his farm, is found lying on one of his fields: "Il était mort sur sa terre, poitrine contre poitrine, sur sa terre qui n'avait pas consenti au divorce" (breast against breast, on his land, which had not consented to divorce).

It is perhaps Grove who best sums up the values of the Old Order when he has John Elliot say, "I don't want my children and sons-in-law to be rich. But I want them to show me to my satisfaction that they can make their daily bread." In other words, the purpose of life is not the pursuit of comfort or happiness according to one's personal lights, but rather to fit into the design conditioned by the *Land and Divine Order*. When Elliot rationalizes with the words, "If God had ordained things that way, perhaps there was a meaning to it, a purpose," he is professing the same almost masochistic resignation as the Chapdelaines, the same "acte de soumission à la volonté divine" (act of submission to the divine will). Ringuet and Grove, however, foresee the *Breakup of the Old Order,* for in both their novels not one of the many children adopts the values of the father.

The theme of *Divine Order* nevertheless persists through the Modern Period and can be found in various forms in the works of other major novelists such as Morley Callaghan, Sinclair Ross, and Roger Lemelin. In fact, it is in the novels of these writers that the typical protagonist of the Canadian Jansenist-Calvinist tradition is most completely delineated.

Morley Callaghan (1903–   ), born in Toronto, studied for the bar, but was steered toward a literary career by Ernest Hemingway. Both men were on the staff of the *Toronto Star* at the same time, and Hemingway, after he had gone to Paris, was able to place some of Callaghan's stories in little magazines. Callaghan was also encouraged by Scott Fitzgerald, who urged Scribner's to publish his first novel, *Strange Fugitive* (1920), and first collection of short stories, *A Native Argosy* (1929). Callaghan then went on to write a steady series of novels and short stories, as well as a description of his experiences in Paris with Hemingway, Fitzgerald, Joyce, and the other "Lost Generation" writers of the time: *That Summer in Paris* (1936).

Probably the most psychologically penetrating of Callaghan's novels is *Such Is My Beloved* (1934), the story of a young priest. Father Dowling begins his career with a highly idealized vision of the sacerdotal role he will enact. He is intellectually inclined, gentle, hypersensitive, and genuinely intrigued by the religious mystique. But contrary to his expectations, he soon finds a panorama of sordid realities when he is assigned to a church in a working-class district. He tries to do his best, but his well-intentioned efforts are ineffectual, if not actually detrimental to the welfare of the people involved. Prevented by doctrine from advising the desperate mother of too many children that she should have the common sense to practice birth control, he must fall back on the barren plea for "Christian resignation to a life of misery." After the initial shock of being propositioned by two young prostitutes as he is walking along the street with his clerical collar hidden by a scarf, Father Dowling starts a campaign to "save" the girls. He gives them money, buys them gifts, attempts to find them jobs, even succeeds in winning their confidence—which is quite an accomplishment, considering that the closest either of the girls has come to any kind of male concern for her welfare has been with a pimp. But the whole project falls through when the girls are run out of town through the intervention of the local bishop, who fears that a scandal would ruin his current charity drive and tarnish the image of the church. And the bishop, of course, is quite right. Obviously it will not do to have a priest spending too much time with prostitutes—how are people to know that the motivation lies in his profession and not in that of the women? Father Dowling, in effect, has acted naively and in a manner inconsistent with established church policy, placing a little too much confidence in his personal judgment and will. And in keeping with the character of the Canadian *Divine Order* protagonist, he reacts to censure not by defiance, not by an attack upon the system he has found inadequate. He withdraws into a profound depression, undergoing the familiar process of tormented soul-searching, seeking the personal deficiency that will explain the tension between the institution and himself. He is eventually removed to an asylum for the mentally disturbed.

Two other typical Canadian protagonists of the Old Order are also clergymen—there must be more men of the cloth, both as characters and writers, in Canadian literature than in any other, a clear indication of the special impact of the church on national consciousness. Reverend Philip Bentley is the protagonist in *As For Me and My House* (1941), a powerful novel of the Prairies by Sinclair Ross (1908–   ). Bentley continues for many years to practice a ministry in which he cannot fully believe. He lacks the confidence and self-reliance necessary to break away, and he spends his time sitting at his desk sketching people without faces (absence of individualism?) and the false storefronts of his sterile little prairie town. When finally his frustration and convenient opportunity lead him to seduce an infatuated and equally frustrated choir girl, the act is not a grand passion, a defiance of conventional morality in the manner of Hester Prynne, nor even an expression of affection or physical desire. It is an empty and self-punishing gesture, its punitive aspect further heightened by adoption of the resultant illegitimate child as a seemingly charitable intervention. The adoption, in fact, is doubly punishing, for Bentley's struggle, like Dowling's, is essentially interior, which is also the case for Pierre Boisjoly in Roger Lemelin's *Pierre le magnifique* (1952).

Roger Lemelin (1919–   ) was brought up in a working-class district of Quebec City, the oldest of ten children, and he drew upon his experiences of urban life to write *Au pied de la pente douce* (1944)—*At the Foot of the Gentle Slope*—a novel that has become a landmark of Canadian literature in terms of social sature and realism. From the point of view of psychological analysis, however, *Pierre le magnifique* is probably Lemelin's best work, and once again the protagonist emerges as a typical self-effacing, system-haunted Canadian. After he has been put through a seminary by a kindly old priest, Pierre rejects the idea of taking holy orders. Eventually he finds himself alone with the woman he loves, Fernande.

The two declare their love to each other passionately, and the reader says to himself, "This is it." But it isn't. In fact, the episode leads Pierre to decide on the priesthood after all.

It is of course impossible here to touch upon more than selected highlights of Canadian literature, and numerous authors and works must perforce be left for the student to discover for himself. Before leaving the fiction of the Modern Period, however, it should be mentioned that a few writers were beginning to react against the religious restraints and consequent hypocrisy of Canadian society. Among these writers was Jean-Charles Harvey (1891–1967), who for a time was the editor of *Le Soleil* in Quebec City. Harvey's rather poor novel, *Les Demi-civilisés* (1934), achieved the distinction of being banned by His Eminence Cardinal Villeneuve. "Son decret," wrote Harvey in the Preface to a reissue of the book, "défendait aux fidèles, sous peine de péché mortel, de lire ce livre, de la garder, prêter, acheter, vendre, imprimer, ou diffuser de quelque façon" (forbade the faithful, under pain of mortal sin, to read, keep, loan, buy, print or distribute the book in any way). Shortly afterward Harvey lost his job at *Le Soleil,* and when Maurice Duplessis became premier of Quebec in 1937, Jean-Charles Harvey was told to leave the capital city.

Les Demi-civilisés is by modern standards a mild novel. It does openly question certain practices of the church, the government, and the law profession, and it calmly asserts that sex can be pleasurable. Although it is directed mainly at the situation in Quebec, Harvey is careful to note the trans-Canadian nature of the Calvinist-Jansenist philosophy of life. "Nous avons des affinités," he points out, "avec les puritains de Toronto, qui péchent en jouant au bridge le dimanche, mais qui ne se feront pas scrupule de passer cette journée ivres au fond d'une chambre, volets clos" (they regard it as sinful to play bridge on Sunday, but they have no scruples about spending the day dead drunk behind closed shutters). Harvey, thus, along with Ringuet, Grove, Callaghan, Ross, Lemelin, and other major novelists of the years between 1920 and 1945, underlined the distorting and stifling effects of the Old Order on the Canadian character. They saw that society was in need of change, and by articulating what they saw they helped to bring about the changes that were soon to begin sweeping across the land.

Poets, too, were aware of the need for change in Canadian society. In the 1920s and 1930s, there was a dramatic shift away from the romanticism, metrical regularity, dutiful complacency, and especially the subject matter of the nineteenth and early twentieth centuries. Nature was replaced by everyday life, flora and fauna by the flaws of human beings and society. Canadian poets suddenly became conscious of the "new poetry" of Britain and the United States, the works of Sandburg, Frost, Stevens, Yeats, Pound, Eliot, Cummings, Auden, and Lawrence, and they began to experiment with form and meter. Generally regarded as the signpost of the poetic revival in English Canada is the anthology *New Provinces: Poems of Several Authors* (1936), which includes the work of A. M. Klein, Leo Kennedy, F. R. Scott, A. J. M. Smith, Robert Finch, and E. J. Pratt. In French Canada, the two poets most influential in promoting the break with convention were Hector Saint-Denys-Garneau and Alain Grandbois.

A. J. M. Smith (1902–1980), critic as well as poet and professor of poetry at Michigan State University from 1936 until his retirement in 1975, was a major pioneer in introducing modernist poetry to Canada. Smith set high standards for himself, and in his many articles and anthologies he urged the same standards on others. His careful craftsmanship can be seen in any of the numerous published volumes of his poetry. "The Sorcerer," a poem that has often been anthologized, is an appropriate illustration of Smith's work, for it reflects the desire for freedom from convention and tradition and from the inhibiting self; Lachine, incidentally, is a suburb of Montreal and the birthplace of Saul Bellow:

> There is a sorcerer in Lachine
> Who for a small fee will put a spell
> On my beloved, who has sea-green
> Eyes, and on my doting self as well.

> He will transform us, if we like, to goldfish:
> We shall swim in a crystal bowl,

And the bright water will go swish
Over our naked bodies; we shall have no soul.

In the morning the syrupy sunshine
Will dance on our tails and fins.
I shall have her then all for mine,
And Father LeBeau will hear no more of her sins.

Come along, good sir, change us into goldfish.
I would put away intellect and lust,
Be but a red gleam in a crystal dish,
But kin to the trembling ocean, not of dust.

A longtime friend of Arthur Smith, Frank R. Scott
(1899–   ), has combined a distinguished career as professor
and constitutional law expert at McGill University with that
of poet. Scott also was involved in the creation of Canada's
socialist political wing, now called the New Democratic Party,
and he represented the United Nations in Burma. His poetry,
in contrast to Smith's symbolist and metaphysical bent, is
marked by directness, wit, comedy, and social criticism. "Saturday Sundae" is an example:

The triple-decker and the double-cone
I side-swipe swiftly, suck the coke-strawy dry.
Ride toadstool seat beside the slab of morgue—
Sweet corner drugstore, sweet pie in the sky. . . .

I swivel on my axle and survey
The latex tintex kotex cutex land.
Soft kingdoms sell for dimes, Life Pic Look Click
Inflate the male with conquest girly grand.

My brothers and sisters, two by two,
Sit sipping succulence and sighing sex.
Each tiny, adolescent universe
A world the vested interests annex.

Such bread and circuses these times allow,
Opium most popular, life so small and slick,
Perhaps with candy is the new world born
And cellophane shall wrap the heretic.

The cores of the kingdoms have become considerably

harder and the prices have gone from dimes to dollars since Scott wrote this poem in the 1940s, but otherwise his observations on the "new world" are more than ever relevant. The same is true of his brief "Bonne Entente," which illustrates Scott's capacity to find humor and irony in the commonplace:

> The advantages of living with two cultures
> Strike one at every turn,
> Especially when one finds a notice in an office building:
> "The elevator will not run on Ascension Day";
> Or reads in the *Montreal Star*:
> "Tomorrow being the Feast of the Immaculate
> Conception,
> There will be no collection of garbage in the city";
> Or sees on the restaurant menu the bilingual dish:
>> DEEP APPLE PIE
>> TARTE AUX POMMES PROFONDES

Frank Scott's poetry is as varied as the man himself, whose interests also include translation of leading Quebec poets, in particular the work of a man completely his opposite in life style and temperament, Hector Saint-Denys-Garneau. Great-grandson of historian François-Xavier, Saint-Denys-Garneau (1912–43) was a tragic figure, withdrawn from human companionship and tormented by a puritan conscience. Much of his work was published after his death (possibly by suicide) at the age of thirty-one, and his intimate *Journal,* which complements his poetry, was translated by another poet and novelist, John Glassco (1909–1981), who is perhaps best known for his *Memoirs of Montparnasse* (1970), a charming account of his experiences in the Paris of Callaghan and Hemingway. Garneau's poetry is the product of his solitude, symbolist and introspective, somber and often macabre. Here is an excerpt from Scott's rendition of "Cage d'oiseau"—"Bird Cage":

> I am a bird cage
> A cage of bone
> With a bird
>
> The bird in the cage of bone
> Is death building his nest

When nothing is happening
One can hear him ruffle his wings. . . .

It is a bird held captive
This death in my cage of bone . . .

He cannot fly away
Until he has eaten all
My heart
The source of blood
With my life inside

He will have my soul in his beak.

Although also concerned with the theme of death, more positive and far less limited than Saint-Denys-Garneau is Alain Grandbois (1900–   ), whose collection *Les Iles de la nuit* (1944)—*The Islands of Night*—with its free verse and distinctive imagery, has had a tremendous influence on younger poets. Other Quebec poets who achieved prominance between 1920 and 1945 include two women, Rina Lasnier (1915–   ), who often chooses religious themes, and the cousin of Saint-Denys-Garneau, Anne Hébert (1916–   ), who shares to some extent his troubled sensibility. There is also poetnovelist Robert Choquette (1905–   ), who was born in Manchester, New Hampshire. His first volume of poems, *A travers les vents* (1925)—*Across the Winds*—was hailed as a breakthrough for modernism, although shocking some critics of the time. Even more controversial is his much later *Suite marine* (1953), a 6,000-line epiclike composition of much complexity.

One Canadian poet of the Modern Period did succeed in writing epic poetry. He is Edwin John Pratt (1882–1964), who came from Western Bay, Newfoundland, and eventually settled in Toronto, where he was appointed professor of English at the University. Like Choquette, Pratt has been the subject of considerable controversy among critics, although all have been forced to recognize that he is a major poet. The problem, it seems, is that Pratt with his eighteen volumes of poetry is something of an anachronism. Poets of the twentieth century do not generally write epics; yet Pratt's work includes several, and what is more, they are all of high quality. There is robustness, zest, great magnitude, and accuracy of observation in his poems. *The Titanic* (1935), for example, is an exciting account of the famous marine disaster, ironically and effectively underlining modern man's overdependence and subservience with respect to the machine. *The Witches' Brew* (1925) is an amusing satire against prohibition, describing how the fish of the sea hold a monumental spree with the vast quantities of exquisite wines and spirits that have gone down with ships. Among Pratt's other epics or epiclike poems are *The Roosevelt and the Antinoe* (1930), which with his usual attention to details on seamanship tells of a rescue during a North Atlantic storm; *Dunkirk* (1941), about the storied evacuation of British troops from the continent at the beginning of World War II; and *Brébeuf and His Brethren* (1940), about the Jesuit missionaries in Canada.

The sea, of course, dominated the imagination of this man from the shores of Newfoundland. As in his long poems, Pratt's short poems of the sea are marked by accuracy of detail, vivid imagination, and directness. Here is "Sea-Gulls":

> For one carved instant as they flew,
> The language had no simile—
> Silver, crystal, ivory
> Were tarnished. Etched upon the horizon blue,
> The frieze must go unchallenged, for the lift
> And carriage of the wings would stain the drift
> Of stars against a tropic indigo
> Or dull the parable of snow.
>
> Now settling one by one
> Within green hollows or where curled
> Crests caught the spectrum from the sun,
> A thousand wings are furled.
> No clay-born lilies of the world
> Could blow as free
> As those wild orchids of the sea.

But Pratt was far more than a descriptive poet. Human beings, the tensions between man and his creations and the struggle within man between the primitive and the civilized, are found throughout his work. "Erosion," another short poem, provides an example:

> It took the sea a thousand years,
> A thousand years to trace
> The granite features of this cliff
> In crag and scarp and base.
>
> It took the sea an hour one night,
> An hour of storm to place
> The sculpture of these granite seams
> Upon a woman's face.

Canadian critic Munro Beattie perhaps best sums up E. J. Pratt when he says in *The Literary History of Canada:* "In Canadian literature the poems of E. J. Pratt are an isolated spendour . . . since 1920, Pratt's work has counted for more than any other man's—counted by virtue of its craftsmanship, its breadth of subject-matter, its competence in dealing with the devices and phenomena that engage the interest of twentieth-century men and women, its uninhibited and exhilarating vision of life."

Another example of somewhat isolated splendor is the poetry of Abraham Moses Klein (1909–72), whose rabbinical studies gave him the rich knowledge of Jewish theology and culture that is reflected in his work. Klein also saw affinities between the Jewish people and the French Canadians, a people set apart because of language and religion but determined to preserve their identity. This attitude is seen in poems such as "For the Sisters of the Hôtel Dieu":

> In pairs
> as if to illustrate their sisterhood,
> the sisters pace the hospital garden walks.
> In their robes black and white immaculate hoods
> they are like birds,
> the safe domestic fowl of the House of God.
>
> O biblic birds,
> who fluttered to me in my childhood illnesses
> —me little, afraid, ill, not of your race,—

the cool wing for my fever, the hovering solace,
the sense of angels—
be thanked, O plumage of paradise, be praised.

The period from 1920 until 1945 thus witnessed Canadian writers' branching out in many new directions. In particular there was a vastly increased awareness of what was happening on the international literary scene—the time lag between new movements outside the country and their effects within was considerably shortened. World War II would shorten this time lage even more.

The Breakup of the Old Order (1945–1960)

Between the two world wars, as so many works of literature indicate, Canadians had begun to feel uneasy with the Old Order. Society was evolving rapidly, and the Jansenist-Calvinist values that had so long conditioned life in Canada were being seriously questioned. With their insistence on self-effacing dependence and adherence to the established system, these values were actually part of a colonial mentality, or "garrison mentality" as the esteemed critic Northrop Frye has described it. World War I had done much to weaken the spirit of colonialism in Canada, and the new freedom and broadening horizons of Canadian writers had reinforced the process. It was World War II, however, that administered the coup de grâce, both for the Old Order and its concomitant colonial mentality. As a result, significant Canadian novelists and poets began now to become concerned with the disappearance of traditional values. Novelists everywhere, to be sure, had the same concern, but it seems likely that in Canada, where the two major ethnic groups had tried so long to outdo each other in conservatism, where the old values were so strongly entrenched and where much of the literature right into the twentieth century was a celebration of them, the concern has been greater and more agonizing than in other Western countries. Undoubtedly World War II, which in proportion to population involved many more Canadians than Americans, had a profound and general effect of disillusionment. Two novels that deal specifically with the war, *Les Canadiens errants* (1954)—*The Wandering Canadians* by Jean Vaillancourt (1923–61) and *Execution* (1958) by Colin McDougall (1917–   ), provide penetrating analyses of the phenomenon.

Both novels, after presenting the initial idealism of Christian soldiers marching off to war, describe the reaction of these soldiers to the brutality and horrors of actual military operations. The first phase of this reaction is a blunting of the sensitivity, the building of a shell around oneself. But the shell can never be perfect. In *Execution* there is an episode where the soldiers are in a barnyard with an old farmer. Suddenly a mortar explodes, killing one of the soldiers and the farmer's son. The Canadians have tried to condition themselves to such happenings. The dead soldier's best friend is quietly ordered to collect his gun and personal effects. But then after a few moments of stunned silence, the farmer begins to scream hysterically. "Mio bambino!" he cries to the heavens, "Morto! Morto!" And because the protective shell of the soldiers is not perfect, they cannot endure this demonstration of natural despair. Finally the farmer is silenced by a hard slap in the face.

Neither McDougall nor Vaillancourt is interested in singing the heroics of war. In fact, the two books clearly illustrate that men confronted with brutality are invariably reduced to perpetrating the same kind of brutality. When, for example, a German prisoner spits in the face of Lanthier, one of Vaillancourt's characters, he can no longer control himself: " 'Ah, mon enfant-de-chienne,' he hissed. He had grabbed his Sten by the strap. . . . The German's body quivered, then for a few moments went through a hideous convulsion, twisting like a worm."

In *Execution* there are a number of similar incidents. In short, for a man to be a competent soldier he must also be an efficient killer. And this bitter realization sooner or later leads the more philosophical natures to a redefinition of traditional values, even of the hallowed notions of courage, goodness, justice, decency, and mercy. Richard Lanoue, in Vaillancourt's book, is typical. For a time he hangs on to his Christian beliefs; then he begins to think of God as playing cruel games with human beings, as a cat does with a mouse. Finally he is crushed, not knowing what sense to make of life and death. McDougall's Padre Philip Doorn is likewise crushed, but not before he decides that a just God, the God of his childhood and seminary days, would never permit such depraved activities and insane slaughter to take place. Deciding to bring the matter to God's attention, he steals a piece of wood said to be part of the true cross and carries it with him onto a battlefield. While the shells are bursting around him, he holds the precious relic in the air. But nothing happens. The battle continues. And the piece of the true cross is ground into the dust with the rest of the debris.

For many of its participants, then, the war creates an existential vacuum—a frame of mind in which all values have lost their significance, leaving people with a sense of emptiness and despair. The war, of course, is an excellent means to speed up the process of value disintegration, and in the case of McDougall's *Execution*, incidents such as the senseless killing of two Italian prisoners of war and later that of a young Canadian soldier, all three victims strikingly simple and innocent, further expedite the process. In Canadian novels of the late 1940s and 1950s that do not deal directly with the war, the same process takes place, but more slowly and usually involving a greater confrontation between the traditional views and the new absence of values.

The confrontation can be seen in the works of almost all prominent novelists of the period, including Hugh MacLennan, Yves Thériault, Robert Elie, Mordecai Richler, André Langevin, Jean Simard, and W. O. Mitchell. Gabrielle Roy (1909–   ) in her classic *Bonheur d'occasion* (1945)—*The Tin Flute*, and Adele Wiseman (1938–   ) in her comparable novel *The Sacrifice* (1956) treat the theme with artistry and skill. Roy's heroine, Rose-Anna Lacasse, finds herself in the Montreal slum of St. Henri with a big family and an unemployed husband. Yet she continues to order her life according to the old rural practices, producing a child regularly every spring, enduring her purgatory on earth. She has a few moments of doubt as to the extent of God's interest in her affairs, visualizing the deity as being tired and harassed as she herself is and therefore unable to attend to all human needs. But she remains convinced of the necessity for Christian resignation even when her baby son dies and her family is falling apart before her eyes.

The protagonist of Wiseman's *The Sacrifice*, an immigrant butcher from the Ukraine called Abraham, is an even more tragic figure than Rose-Anna. Before his arrival in the Canadian West, he had witnessed the brutal pogrom murder of his two sons, Moses and Jacob. He is strictly Orthodox, and like Rose-Anna he is ready to endure all tribulations rather than modify his attitudes toward the role of man on earth. Rose-Anna and Abraham, therefore, are staunch adherents of the *Divine Order,* which the society around them has rejected.

Abraham's remaining son, Isaac, like the Lacasse children, adopts a philosophy of adapatation to the realities around him. The old man had concentrated all his hopes and dreams in Isaac, and this creates tension between father and son when Isaac does not conform. Nevertheless, Abraham adores Isaac, and Isaac has much respect and affection for his father. When the family synagogue catches fire, Isaac rushes into the building and saves the holy Torah, despite a heart ailment. But the strain takes its toll, and after a few months of illness he dies. Abraham, who has also lost his wife shortly before, is a broken man.

It is during this period of despair and after a violent quarrel with his daughter-in-law that Abraham's employer asks him to deliver a package to Laiah, a lady of easy virtue who is attracted to the still robust butcher. She makes the mistake of flirting with him. But all he can comprehend is that she, a depraved Jezebel, barren, lascivious, the antithesis of all he holds to be sacred, is alive, whereas his three sons, his wife, his hopes, and his dreams are dead. And unfortunately for Laiah, a freshly honed carving knife is on the table nearby. Repeating to himself the word "Life," Abraham cuts the woman's throat with professional expertise.

In *Bonheur d'occasion* there is no climax of comparable

intensity. Rose-Anna's daughter Florentine simply refuses to follow in her mother's footsteps. Rather than suffer, like Isaac she would like to pursue happiness and some of the good things of life as she conceives them. Pregnant by one man (a scheme that did not work out as planned), she salvages the situation by marrying another who will be able to take her out of the slums. She is thus the complete reversal of Maria Chapdelaine. And Rose-Anna and Abraham, incapable of making the necessary adjustments in the confrontation between the old and the new, are tragic losers, their fate symbolizing the dissolution of the old *Divine Order* concept of life.

Gabrielle Roy, incidentally, wrote several important novels after *Bonheur d'occasion*. She and Hugh Maclennan, who also brought out a Canadian classic, *Two Solitudes,* in 1945, dominated the field of Canadian fiction in the postwar period. Born in Nova Scotia, MacLennan used Halifax and the great explosion of 1917 as the setting for his first novel, *Barometer Rising* (1941). *Two Solitudes* concerns the relations between the French and English in Quebec, but all of MacLennan's novels also focus of the tensions between generations, the Old Order versus the new spirit of independence, and the problems of Canadian national identity. *The Watch That Ends the Night* (1959), probably MacLennan's most powerful book, deals specifically with the phenomenon of changing values. Ranging over a half century, it is a symposium of ideas, forces, and Canadian cultural evolution. The protagonist, George Stewart, is in many respects the archetypal Canadian character, while Jerome, the doctor whose life resembles that of the famed Norman Bethune, the Canadian medic who worked with the Chinese Red Army and is regarded as one of the heroes of the Revolution in China, is a forerunner of the new Canadian hero of the 1970s.

The Watch That Ends the Night describes how for many people in the 1930s the ideals of socialism provided a temporary substitute for the fading Old Order. Jerome is convinced that the world can be changed and that a new and equitable distribution of the good things of life can be effected if only the capitalist system, together with fascism, can be destroyed. George, on the other hand, is conservative, unwilling to take changes or to embrace new causes. He meets his future wife, Catherine, while he is still a boy, but the girl is suffering from a heart ailment, and George's authoritarian aunt warns him not to become involved. Catherine has been told by doctors that she cannot expect to have a normal life and that certainly she will never be able to risk having a baby. But she is defiant, and on one occasion she attempts to make George a gift of her naked young body. He resists, not for lack of desire, but because his affection is so strong that he cannot chance putting the girl's health in danger. Jerome has no hesitation in taking the risk, and Catherine's wish for a child is granted. She and Jerome have a reasonably happy marriage, while George waits in the sidelines, until Jerome decides to go to Spain to serve the socialist cause in the civil war.

Because he has lost his faith in the old values yet cannot accept any of the available substitutes, George becomes increasingly demoralized as life to him appears more and more absurd. He has, however, retained his capacity to love, and that is precisely the force that sustains him. When Jerome has disappeared and is officially declared dead, Catherine finally accepts George as her husband. By that time she is helpless, but George, despite the fact that he knows she still loves Jerome, takes it upon himself to care for her and her daughter.

Never having imagined that the world could become utopia, George can continue when his dreams evaporate because his resources include a willingness to accept life as it is and a capacity to love. Such is Hugh MacLennan's solution to the *Breakup of the Old Order* and the resultant existential vacuum. It is the same solution suggested at the end of McDougall's *Execution*, and it can also be found in *Mon fils pourtant heureux* (1956)—*My Son Happy in Spite of Himself*, by Jean Simard (1916–   ). An iconoclastic novel, *Mon fils* is the story of another young man who finds himself in the value vacuum. Like the hero of Harvey's *Les Demi-civilisés*, he comes to view the religion and morality of his society as hypocritical and destructive. "What sad marriage," he asks himself, "between Puritans and Jansenists has brought about this false austerity which has perverted so many of our human relations, all our joys?" It is through a chance meeting with a man who has truly suffered hardships and rebounded from them that Simard's hero acquires the capacity to accept life and emotional involvement.

There are a number of similarities between Hugh MacLennan's protagonist George Stewart and Alain Dubois in *La Poussière sur la ville* (1953)—*Dust Over the City*, by André Langevin (1927–   ). *Poussière* is about a newly married couple and a company town, and although the marital problems of the couple appear at first sight to be the author's predominant concern, the mining town of Thetford Mines, Quebec, functions at once as locale and major character in Langevin's novel. The town surrounds the couple both horizontally and vertically, the reader being kept aware of it through repeated references to asbestos dust in the air and to the miners, on round-the-clock shifts, constantly burrowing underground. The rural town, quite backward compared with large urban centers like Montreal, also symbolizes the restraining forces of Canadian society, the smothering dust of rigid convention.

Another prime example of the typical Canadian hero, Alain Dubois, like George in *The Watch,* is determined to blame himself and suffer quietly rather than to strike at the cause of his miseries. He spends a lot of time speculating on what might be wrong with himself, and he punishes himself, even to the extent of permitting his errant wife to entertain her lover in the public privacy of his own parlor while he sits in his doctor's office listening to creaking springs and gleeful laughter. Alain Dubois does show defiance, but his defiance is like that of Father Dowling when he ignores the bishop's warnings and continues to help the two prostitutes he has befriended. It is a defiance that is guaranteed to increase his own suffering, that is bound to bounce back on himself like a rubber ball tossed against a wall. What Dubois defies is the virility principle upheld by the townspeople that male dignity, manhood if you will, ought not to be seen to be demeaned. If Alain's wife Madeleine had been having a discreet affair, meeting a lover for weekends in Montreal or Quebec City perhaps, few people would have known, and even those who knew would have smirked and not have been overly concerned. But that she should go to a restaurant and pick up a local man, then carry on with him openly, is definitely not acceptable. It is expected that Dubois will take the necessary steps to correct the situation.

Langevin's triumph of characterization in *Poussière* is his success in engaging the reader's sympathy for Madeleine. Both Alain and George Stewart are patient and long-suffering to the point of irritating the reader perhaps; certainly, it seems, they would irritate the American reader accustomed to Hemingway, Kesey, Miller, or any of a number of novelists of the United States. Madeleine, it must be admitted, is impossibly obstreperous by any standards. She is neither abused nor neglected. She can spend what money she wants, although her husband is in debt. She has a maid, and as a doctor's wife her social status has risen considerably from what it was when she grew up in a working-class family. Alain caters to her whims and fancies, including pop music and melodramatic double features, neither of which he has much stomach for himself. One almost wishes that Alain would assert himself, would slap down his outrageously brazen wife, once in a while at least. As the book progresses, however, one is drawn more and more into seeing Madeleine as Alain sees her and into sharing his emotional reaction to her.

Langevin repeatedly uses animal imagery when referring to Madeleine. She is a "jeune fauve" (a wild creature). She is physically splendid, uninhibited, sexually enticing. Like a cat, she is domesticated and wild at the same time, and there is a beauty, a fascination about her wildness. Her acting on impulse and complete unpredictability are an antidote to the drab, humdrum, robot existence of the people around her, and especially to the endless routine of the asbestos miners, who punch the clock and descend into the suffocating pits day after day as the shifts change. Madeleine is simply not capable of submitting to extended curtailment of her liberty; she can neither be trained or tamed. She is a child in the body of a woman, for somehow she has preserved the innocence, the excitability, the belief in magic, the desire for life and adventure of a child. As Alain notes, she wants to try everything, experience everything. The problem is that even if he is willing to let her do so, the community around her is not. Her woman's body disqualifies her from the privileges accorded a child.

Poussière sur la ville ends in tragedy for both Madeleine and Alain. He turns to alcohol, but he cannot escape the curse of having to come to grips with the meaning of life and the question of divine justice. He rejects the local priests's Jansenist conviction—"Je n'ai jamais cru et je ne croirai jamais au bonheur sur terre" (I have never believed and will never believe in happiness on earth). But unlike the heroes of MacLennan, McDougall, and Simard, he finds no solution to the existential vacuum. He can only envy his wife's capacity to live from sensation to sensation, not knowing and not caring to know about the philosophical issues of being.

In *Bonheur d'occasion,* Gabrielle Roy suggests that some people can escape the trauma of the *Breakup of the Old Order* by simply becoming complete materialists; that is to say, by devoting themselves to the acquisition of material possessions and comforts. Both Florentine Lacasse and her first lover, Jean Lévesque, adopt the principle, which of course has already been established for generations in the United States. But somehow Canadian characters do not seem to enact it quite so spectacularly or successfully as American characters. Alex Hunter, in *Under the Ribs of Death* (1957) by John Marlyn (1912–   ), achieves only modest success. Duddy Kravitz, in *The Apprenticeship of Duddy Kravitz* (1959) by Mordecai Richler (1931–   ), accomplishes a great deal more. Through cunning, determination, boundless energy, and innocence of any scruples about exploiting his friends, Duddy makes money and eventually acquires valuable development land in the resort area of the Laurentians. But the exploit proves hollow in one important respect. Duddy's obsession stemmed from his grandfather's remark that a man without land was a nobody. When Duddy finally offers his granfather a house and lot, the old man, who has found out about the wheeling and dealing, rejects him with bitter disdain. By then, however, Duddy is so totally devoted to the principle of material success

that he soon gets over the shock. Richler offers no philosophical solution to the disappearance of the old values.

Neither does Gérard Bessette (1920–   ) in his *La Ba-
garre* (1958)—*The Brawl*, although the novel is a remarkable
study of the social upheaval taking place in Quebec. Through
protagonist Jules Lebeuf, an adult student who supports himself working nights as a sweeper for the tramway company,
the reader witnesses drastically changing attitudes toward
religion, education, sex, and the colloquial language of Quebec. The book is uncannily accurate in its analysis of labor
relations, presenting a state of dissatisfaction and indirection,
but prophesying the widespread troubles to come in the 1960s
and 1970s. Bessette symbolically refuses to suggest solutions
to the confused situation of Quebec by having an American
character, Weston, who is in Montreal to write a thesis on
French-Canadian society, abandon the project as impossible
and return to his home in St. Louis.

Cabbagetown (1950), a novel set in the slum district of
Toronto, written by Hugh Garner (1913–1979), covers much
the same period as MacLennan's *The Watch* and also explores
the substitute orders of socialism and fascism as they make
brief appearances on the Canadian scene. Basically the novel
concerns the growing-up process of a boy from late childhood
to maturity and is one of many Canadian novels that do the
same. The most celebrated of these books is *Who Has Seen the
Wind?* (1947) by W. O. Mitchell (1914–   ), who traces the
evolution of a child in a small prairie town from the age of
four to about twelve. Mitchell's novel is a tour de force in that
it is presented entirely from the viewpoint of the child with
no trace of banality or sentimentality. The author becomes
totally immersed in the mind and body of the child, and he
has a gift for linguistic virtuosity and humor. The result is
a sensitive and perceptive analysis of a universal human experience, as well as a series of insights into a society wrestling
with its basic standards.

Little has been said so far about Canadian drama, mainly
because little of any import, aside from a few ponderous verse
plays, was created during the nation's formative years. Drama
depends on the theater, and for a long time the Canadian

theater was either nonexistent or presented the works of the great European playwrights, a difficult act to follow. Before World War II a few Canadian dramatists began to appear with the spread of the Little Theater Movement. Merrill Denison (1893–1974), Detroit born, wrote realistic and satirical plays using the North and Canadian history as subject matter. Four of his plays were published in *The Unheroic North* (1923). Poet Duncan Campbell Scott and novelist Mazo de la Roche also enjoyed some success as dramatists, as did two Quebec priests, Emile Légault, whose touring company Les Compagnons de Saint-Laurent lasted from 1937 to 1952, and Gustave Lamarche, who founded and wrote for another group, Les Parboliers du Roi. But the prewar Little Theater Movement and touring companies failed to generate a great deal of interest, and it was not until the 1945–60 period that Canadian drama, with an important assist from radio, began to come into its own.

Among the playwrights who gained distinction in the postwar period are Robertson Davies (1913–   ), some of whose ironic, witty plays are collected in *Eros at Breakfast and Other Plays* (1949), and Gratien Gélinas (1909–   ), whose *Tit-coq* (1950), about a soldier and his feelings of insecurity over his illegitimacy, has become a Quebec classic. Gwen Pharis Ringwood (1910–   ), author of *Dark Harvest* (1945), and Lister Sinclair (1921–   ), who has had a long career as a radio dramatist, are also worthy of mention. In Quebec, Paul Toupin (1917–   ) and Marcel Dubé (1930–   ) began the dissection of society that would flower in the dynamic Quebec theater of the 1960s and 1970s.

The years after World War II were highly productive for Canadian poets. Smith, Scott, and Pratt continued to publish regularly, while many others, including Earle Birney, Ralph Gustafson, Irving Layton, Louis Dudek, Dorothy Livesay, P. K. Page, Miriam Waddington, and Fred Cogswell either established or consolidated their reputations. In French Canada, there was a veritable explosion of poetic activity during the same period, underlying once again the parallel, though often mutually isolated, development of Canadian literature in English and French, with Roland Giguère, Pierre Trottier,

Gatien Lapointe, Jean-Guy Pilon, Micheèle Lalonde, and Gaston Miron, among others, coming to the fore.

Proliferation of little magazines and anthologies did much to foster poetry and encourage young poets. Ralph Gustafson (1909–   ), who wrote poems and short stories for many years in New York City, prepared several anthologies, including *Penguin Book of Canadian Verse* (1958). A. J. M. Smith's *The Book of Canadian Poetry*, originally published in 1943, was revised in 1948 and 1957, and in 1960 Smith brought out *The Oxford Book of Canadian Verse; in English and French.* Smith and F. R. Scott coedited a book of satirical and humorous verse, *The Blasted Pine* (1957). *Other Canadians* (1947) was prepared by John Sutherland (1919–56) to introduce new poets of the 1940s. Louis Dudek (1918–   ) worked as an editor for journals and as a publisher with Contact Press, founded in 1952. He and Irving Layton (1912–   ) brought out *Canadian Poems: 1850–1952* in the same year. *Twentieth-Century Canadian Poetry* (1953) was edited by Earle Birney (1904–   ), and Milton Wilson (1923–   ) compiled *Recent Canadian Verse* (1959). Fred Cogswell (1917–   ) is another Canadian poet who has worked tirelessly for the cause, editing the magazine *Fiddlehead* and publishing individual poets through Fiddlehead Press.

Turning to individual poets, Dorothy Livesay (1909–   ), who is still teaching and writing poety as vigorously as ever, has had an impressively sustained career. She was in her teens when the Macmillan Company published her first volume, *Green Pitcher* (1928). She studied at the University of Toronto and the Sorbonne, did social work in the United States and Canada, taught high school, worked for UNESCO in France and Africa, all the time continuing to write poetry. Her *Selected Poems* appeared in 1957.

Dorothy Livesay absorbed a variety of influences on the way to developing her own methods—the French symbolist poets, Americans Edna St. Vincent Millay, Dorothy Parker, and Emily Dickinson. Like Robert Frost, she prefers speaking tones to a singing voice, and her social work was undoubtedly instrumental in making her a writer of protest on many occasions. Yet she is probably at her best communicating emotion in sharp images and simple language. Here is "The Snow Girl's Ballad":

> I should have let you lay me in the snow
> then lift me back
> so that my body's trace
> might still be there
> come spring
> a power in the grass
> my bones
> firing the stones
> my eyes
> anemones
>
> O brightly would I lie
> the body that you traced
> with your fine fingers
> the gaze entranced
> from my garden place
> up to your story windows
>
> I should have let you know
> more things about me
> and never let you find
> a world within
> without me.

Earle Birney and Ralph Gustafson are two other poets who have enjoyed long and prolific careers. Birney's service in the armed forces during the war resulted in his comic, picaresque novel *Turvey* (1949) and in several poems. He has always been experimental, willing to explore any of a variety of possibilities and often emerging with surprising success. His ingenious adaptation of Old English word formation, alliteration, and cadence to a Toronto tenement district, "AN-GLOSAXON STREET," is a case in point:

> Dawndrizzle ended   dampness steams from
> blotching brick and   blank plasterwaste
> Faded housepatterns   hoary and finicky
> unfold stuttering   stick like a phonograph
>
> Here is a ghetto   gotten for goyim

O with care denuded   of nigger and kike
No coonsmell rankles   reeks only cellarrot
attar of carexhaust   catcorpse and cookinggrease
Imperial hearts   heave in this haven
Cracks across windows   are welded with slogans
There'll Always Be An England   enhances geraniums
and V's for Victory   vanquish the housefly

Ho! with climbing sun   march the bleached beldames
festooned with shopping bags   farded flatarched
bigthewed Saxonwives   stepping over buttrivers
waddling back wienerladen   to suckle smallfry

Hoy! with sunslope   shrieking over hydrants
flood from learninghall   the lean fingerlings
Nordic nobblecheeked   not all clean of nose
leaping Commandowise   into leprous lanes

What! after whistleblow!   spewed from wheelboat
after daylong doughtiness   dire handplay
in sewertrench or sandpit   come Saxonthegns
Junebrown Jutekings   jawslack for meat

Sit after supper   on smeared doorsteps
not humbly swearing   hatedeeds on Huns
profiteers politicians   pacifists Jews

Then by twobit magic   to muse in movie
unlock pictureboard   to lope to alehall
soaking bleakly   in beer skittleless

Home again to hotbox   and humid husbandhood
in slumbertrough adding   sleepily to Anglekin
Alongside in lanenooks   carling and leman
caterwaul and clip   careless of Saxonry
with moonglow and haste   and a higher heartbeat

Slumbers now slumtrack   unstinks cooling
waiting brief for milkmaid   mornstar and worldrise

Toronto 1942

Like MacLennan in fiction, Birney in his poetry has often
attempted to come to grips with the national consciousness
and the peculiarities of Canada. His "Canada: Case History"
effectively summarizes the country and the Old Order and
makes a wry comment on relations with the United States:

"His uncle spoils him with candy, of course, /yet shouts him down when he talks at table." A later poem, called "Can. Lit.," is arrestingly perceptive with respect to the differences between Canada and its continental neighbor, revealing again Birney's gift for memorable epigram:

> We French, we English, never lost our civil war,
> endure it still, a bloodless civil bore:
> no wounded lying about, no Whitman wanted.
> It's only by our lack of ghosts we're haunted.

Ralph Gustafson has never been as demonstrative or adventuresome as Birney. His strength lies in metrical craftsmanship, the communication of a visual effect or an idea through unusual positioning of words and ironic imagery. "The Great Day" is an example:

> A long wait for the last
> trump with nothing else
> to do but rot. The best
> nilly must put a false
> face on the matter, think
> of heaven, that day when all
> is risen in the just wink
> of a lid and rearward hal–
> lelujah, the joyful body
> back, Byron his limp
> and Socrates his beauty,
> patient Pope his hump.

Another poet of quiet intensity is Neil Tracy (1905–   ), who has been blind since his early twenties. His best work distills deep personal feeling with almost disarming candor and simplicity. Here is a sonnet entitled "I.O.U.":

> You granted me a shrine where I may go
> To meet the soul I loved before you came.
> Strong winds blew down that idol long ago,
> Potpourri strong with bittersweet, no blame.
> For it was I who kissed her eyes asleep

And closed the small white fingers that contained
Life's ivory ebony in such a sweep.
Outside, the wind blew keenly and it rained.
How many times have hands and spirit met
Across the debts and credits of a life,
Hot anger flashed, dark moods then quick regret,
Humor and truth that shape a man and wife?
Hers are the golden fragments of a chain.
You sewed the buttons on my life again.

Comparable to Smith, Gustafson, Cogswell, and Dudek as a motivating force in the promotion of poets and poetry, Jean-Guy Pilon (1930–　) has worked in editing and publishing as well as supervising cultural programs for the French network of the Canadian Broadcasting Corporation. At the same time, he composed four volumes of poetry between 1953 and 1960, and he has continued to produce since then. Like the other writers of the *Breakup* period, he too is concerned with the transformation of moral values and with comprehension of the nation itself. Louis Dudek translated "L'Exigence du pays!" "The Needs of the Land":

Who am I then to take on such expanses of space, to comprehend a hundred thousand lakes, seventy-five rivers,
　　　　　ten
chains of mountains, three oceans, the North Pole and
　　　　　the sun
that never sets on my country?

Where shall I plant my home in this infinitude and these great winds? In what corner place the vegetable garden?
　　　　　How
shall I say, in despite of the seasons, those everyday
　　　　　words, the
words of life: woman, bread, wine?

There are countries for children, and others for men,
　　　　　some
few only for giants . . .
Before we can learn the words necessary to live, it is
　　　　　already
time to learn to die.

Dudek himself, incidentally, besides his editing, translating, teaching, publishing, and critical work, has produced a dozen volumes of poetry since *East of the City* appeared in 1946. His poems range from the complex and intellectual travel sequence *Europe* (1955) to short, trenchant thrusts at modern civilization such as "Tree in a Street":

> Why will not that tree adapt itself to our tempo?
> We have lopped off several branches,
> cut her skin to the white bone,
> run wires through her body and her loins,
> yet she will not change.
> Ignorant of traffic, of dynamos and steel,
> as uncontemporary
> as bloomers and bustles
> she stands there like a green cliché.

Jean-Marie Lapointe, born in 1929 in the Lac Saint-Jean area of Quebec described in *Maria Chapdelaine,* is another exponent of the rejection of the old Jansenist value system. In response to the negation of the flesh, Lapointe is often deliberately sensual, beginning with his first volume, *Le Vierge incendie* (1948)—*The Flaming Virgin*. The following untitled and free-form poem, a subjective catalogue of the parts of the girl's body, will serve to illustrate:

> leg with foot calf knee and thigh and belly a-
> bove pussy warm little leg and rustle of silk and
>   other
> leg two legs and two hands on the two legs
> and up and down the two legs and the belly at the end
>   of the legs
> and the breasts and shoulders and the shoulders' arms
>   with hands at the
> end and the head with the mouth and the eyelids and
>   hair
> on the temples a whole body a whole woman a whole
>   other
> body and my own both bodies mine the other one which
>   is not
> mine and yet is mine

Another Quebec poet who vividly expressed the suffocating effects of the old values and the spirit of renewal is Roland Giguère (1929–   ), who is also a painter and graphic designer. Giguère's poetry suggests the need to break entirely with the past and to create a new order by means of the artistic imagination. Here is a partial translation of "Continuer à vivre" "In Order to Carry On":

> Advancing on the thin table-cloth of now
> a thousand images already thrown away
> and continuing to entreat us these images
> of a world we knew was sunken in decay
>
> and the cancer was flourishing invulnerable
> it was not the fear but the disgust
> which put lumps in our throats . . .
>
> we felt that we were guilty
> guilty and burdened
> with all the blood spilt and encrusted
> of the disfigured animals of inanimate nature
> of the breadless days of black years
> of a life distorted in the end
>
> we felt that we were guilty
> in the disaster body and soul
> and in order to carry on
> in our solitary silent little cells
> we began to build a new world of our own
> with the colors and the forms
> which we had found for it in dreams

Thus, Roland Giguère, along with the other poets, dramatists, and novelists discussed, and many more omitted because of limitation of space, records the passing of the old *Divine Order*. By 1960, the guilt feelings which Guiguère describes, the Calvinist-Jansenist hangover, have all but disappeared, and the search for something to replace the former raison d'être, a new vital truth, becomes the predominant theme of Canadian writers. This search takes many forms, and essentially it represents the need for a new identity, either personal or national.

The Search for Vital Truth (1960–1970)

The decade of the 1960s was an exciting one for Canadians, highlighted by the countrywide Centennial celebrations and Expo '67, Montreal's huge world's fair. It was a surprise for some, perhaps, to realize that the country had lasted for a century, and for others it was the occasion for the emergence of a new kind of nationalism.

Nationalism can be a loaded term. To different people it has come to mean entirely different things, some of them pleasant and many of them unpleasant. Nationalism as we know it today, moreover, is not necessarily confined to a political nation according to the standard concept. Within large nations there are ethnic groups frantically trying to maintain or to create distinctive cultural identities. Expanding communications, trade, and travel have immensely enlarged man's consciousness of the world and of important events everywhere, moving people closer to Marshall McLuhan's "global village." At the same time, such advances coupled with the rapid expansion of international corporations have helped to promote cultural domination by the more powerful and dynamic nations of the world, without benefit of old-style colonization or the river gunboat. Nowadays the process is far more subtle and efficient. The spread of the so-called American way of life—Coca-Cola, supermarkets, Playboy bunny clubs, Poulet frit à la Kentucky and McDonald's hamburgers, the lifetime goal of a chicken in the pot and at least one car in the two-car garage—provides an obvious example, an example of which Canadians are acutely aware. The opposite trend, the nationalistic urge for a singular and distinguishing cultural identity among new nations and ethnic groups—Canadians know something about that too.

In fact, by dint of circumstances Canada has become a microcosm of the opposing trends mentioned above, an arena for the play of various centripetal and centrifugal forces. The new nationalism that took shape in Canada in the 1960s is both cultural and political (and economic to the extent that anything can be done), but in effect it is clearly more cultural than political; and since Canada is a multicultural country, it has sometimes seemed that the Canadian, like the horse-man in one of Stephen Leacock's sketches, has jumped on a horse and ridden off in all directions.

The new nationalism in Canada differs from that of Con-federation in that it does not look backward for justification; it is a native product, springing from the actualities of con-temporary Canada, and in essence it blends with the *Search for Vital Truth*. Jacques Godbout (1933–   ), novelist, poet, and filmmaker, neatly sums up the situation of French-speak-ing Canadians in the Preface of his *Le Couteau sur la table* (1965)—*Knife on the Table*: "Mais plutot qu'être Français, d'une façon personnelle, nous préférons maintenant être nous-mêmes en français" (but rather than being Frenchmen in any personal sense, we now prefer to be ourselves in French). Iron-ically, perhaps, the new Canadian nationalism, which is the keystone to the literature of the 1960s, began to gain strength when nationalism was declining in the nations that founded Canada. In his controversial volume, *Without Marx or Jesus,* French scholar Jean-François Revel writes of the "cultural colonization of European life by U.S. values, language and patterns of behavior." He goes on to say that the European elite have lost their ability to initiate or to define; they "no longer feel at ease as anything but disciples," and the new attitude means the death of nationalism and the establish-ment of world government. However accurate Revel's views are, certainly the opposite is true for Canadians both fran-cophone and anglophone: they have stopped being disciples.

The phenomenon is more apparent in Quebec than in other parts of the country, mainly because of the "Quiet Rev-olution" that began in 1960. At that time the reactionary and repressive provincial government of Maurice Duplessis, a true disciple of the Old Order, was replaced by a reformist, Liberal administration under Jean Lesage. Among numerous other things, the new government wrested control of education away from the church and created tuition-free, American-style jun-ior colleges to replace the old elitist classical colleges. Sub-sequently the influence of the church in Quebec, which had prevailed for so long and is so strongly reflected in literature, seemed to evaporate like mist in the sunshine. Cultural activity—writing, painting, sculpture, music—at the same time expanded with the effect of a volcano.

The cultural nationalism of Quebec was concomitant with a new desire for political independence—separatism—which has greatly conditioned Canadian literature in both English and French. Ever since Confederation there had been separatist leanings in Quebec, but the erstwhile nationalists, in keeping with the Old Order, were reactionary rather than revolutionary. As intimated in books such as *Jean Rivard* and *Maria Chapdelaine,* not to mention *Pour la patrie,* they wanted to preserve the past and to protect the faith. The new separatism seeks to pour the future into new molds.

Separatism and associated activities form the subject matter of several Canadian novels of the 1960s. *Prochain épisode* (1967)—*The Next Step,* was apparently written while its author, Hubert Aquin (1929–1979), was being detained in a Montreal jail after his arrest for alleged terrorist activities. It is an unusual, highly original novel, interweaving an *apologia pro vita sua* with a spy story and using both threats to present symbolic and direct commentaries on the malaise of Quebec.

This malaise is eloquently sung from the beginning to the end of the book. In a vicious circle it is tied in with the narrator's personal frustration. "The wages of a defeated warrior," says Aquin, "are depression. And the wages of a depressed nation are my defeat." A little later he says that Quebec has no history, that it will not have a history until it is inaugurated in the blood of a revolution, suggesting that French Canada must follow the pattern of the United States and France in order to forge an identity.

But the novel has another aspect. Interwoven with the narrator's agonized protestations is a description of events that made up the "first episode," or at least the one that precedes what is to be *le prochain épisode.* These events constitute an allegory. The character H. de Heutz in his several guises of historian, financier, and government agent is a symbol of the Canadian power structure. K., the girl with the long blonde hair whom the narrator passionately loves and who is presumably his accomplice in the plot to eliminate H. de

Heutz, is symbolic of Quebec and its people. In the usual spy-thriller way, the narrator follows the trail of de Heutz, becoming fascinated as he picks up bits of information about his many-sided quarry. When eventually he finds de Neutz in Geneva, he is himself overpowered and taken prisoner. Inventing a ridiculous sob story, he manages to throw his captor off guard, but when he takes him to a forest to execute him, to the narrator's mystification de Heutz pleads for his life with exactly the same sob story. Before the narrator can steel himself to shoot, a friend of de Heutz's has crept up behind him. Having received instructions to return to Montreal after his failure, the hero is finally captured in Montreal's famed Notre Dame Church.

The allegory implies that the narrator and H. de Heutz are really very much alike. At one point the narrator even mentions that he feels he is almost a spiritual medium for his chosen adversary. In short, the hero (and by extension all those who performed various acts of terrorism in Quebec) is a failure because he cannot identify his intended victim with an enemy who should be destroyed. He has developed a Hamlet complex. Moreover, he has been betrayed by K., symbolizing how the populace of Quebec did not rally to the terrorist cause in the 1960s.

There are a number of parallels between Aquin's book and *Ethel et le terroriste* (1964) by Claude Jasmin (1930–   ), who like Aquin has written several novels. Jasmin, however, takes an objective approach, analyzing the psychology of a young man, Paul, who plants a bomb then goes to New York in an attempt to escape the police. Paul becomes a terrorist because of the same sense of personal and group frustration that torments the hero of *Prochain épisode*. The revolutionary cause offers him a chance to do something significant for the first time in his life; and like so many of the desperate people who jump from bridges or hyjack airplanes, Paul has his brief moment in the sun.

Jasmin's story, however, goes beyond the simple delineation of a character unbalanced by the need for recognition. The book suggests that some of the other members of the terrorist organization fit into that category, but Paul, like the hero of *Prochain épisode,* has enemy-identification problems. He finds it easier to love than to hate, especially with regard to his girlfriend, Ethel, who happens to be Jewish. Ethel shares his feelings of frustration, his moments of childlike joy. But she cannot endorse racist group hatred and murder, and naturally the terrorist group is dependent on group hatred. Paul is told that he must abandon Ethel, something he cannot and will not do. Thus, he ends up alienated from the gang and being propositioned by the police to save himself by turning informer. His only sympathizer besides Ethel is an American Negro professor called Slide, who had been collaborating with the Quebec revolutionaries, but who has become disillusioned by the group's drift from Third World idealism to gutter xenophobia. Paul, then, is another failure as a terrorist.

Similar failures are found in a number of other novels, including Pierre Gravel's *A Perte de Temps* (1969)—*Wasting Time,* James Bacque's *The Lonely Ones* (1969), and Jacques Godbout's *Le Couteau sur la table* (1965). All of these books suggest that the malaise that is at the root of violence and terrorism in Quebec is a part of a universal unrest, which of course it is. Moreover, it has to do with the disintegration of traditional values and the desperate search for a substitute raison d'être.

Like Aquin and Jasmin, Jacques Godbout gives symbolic meaning to his protagonist's deep involvement with a girl. K. is *la patrie,* the motherland, and Ethel is the negation of racism and intolerance, but Patricia in *Le Couteau*—rich, blonde, beautiful, the ultimate in female sensuality and accommodation—represents the affluent North American society, the land of the Lotus Eaters from which the protagonist cannot easily withdraw. She is the Jet Set, gourmet food, flashy motels, and Florida vacations. When the hero speaks to her of the struggles of oppressed peoples, of the threat of nuclear destruction, or of his own bitter existential vacuum, she responds by offering him her spendid body, showered and perfumed. Being half Jewish and half Irish in origin, Patricia combines two ethnic traditions that have long had special significance in French Canada. Each of the two groups, as compared with the Québécois, has successfully penetrated the Anglo-Saxon or WASP power structure, and each has had a love-hate relationship with the people of Quebec. It has been possible to identify with the Jews as a cultural-religious entity surviving against great odds, and with the Irish as Roman Catholic Celts victimized by English oppression. On the other side of the coin, French Canadians have thought themselves exploited by Jewish businessmen (Cf. Richler's *The Apprenticeship of Duddy Kravitz*) and endangered by the assimilation potential of their English-speaking, *vendus* (sold-out) Irish coreligionists. It is, therefore, understandable that Godbout's hero should have a love-hate relationship with Patricia.

Another girl in the novel, Madeleine, symbolizes French Canada, but the quiet, obedient French Canada of days gone by. The hero and the two girls make up a *ménage à trois,* with Madeleine occupying his emotional energy and Patricia his prime time Sunday afternoons. Shortly, however, Madeleine is killed in an accident—decapitated by a truck while rading the hero's motorcycle. A funeral parlor scene symbolizes the death of Quebec's Old Order, which the protagonist can witness with interest but without particular regret. Then he proceeds to seduce Madeleine's little sister.

Godbout's hero does not succeed in finding his vital truth. Like the other novels of the period, *Le Couteau* simply underlines the frustration produced by French Canada's long years of stagnation and the contemporary potential for violence. Although the hero does not harm Patricia, he lets her know that the knife is on the table, and he tells her that it will do no good to struggle and shout or to talk about their good times together in the past. Nothing, therefore, is resolved.

Dramatizing many of the same ideas but also exploring other dimensions of the new, multilateral Canadian nationalism, Hugh MacLennan's *Return of the Sphinx* (1967), as the title indicates, does not pretend to resolve the situation either. Daniel Ainslie, son of the protagonist, is a would-be terrorist who fails for the same reasons as do the heroes of Aquin and Jasmin. But MacLennan includes a gallery of other characters both francophone and anglophone and can thus examine the whole spectrum of ideas associated with separatism. His presentation of English-Canadian attitudes is especially significant. Herbert Tarnley, the prototype of the Anglo businessman, is concerned only about one thing—the security of his investments; he can state categorically that if an independent Quebec were to try to nationalize industry, it "would find itself an appendage on the Latin American desk of the State Department" in Washington. Like so many of his real-life counterparts, Tarnley is a capable man, the sort of person one would want to organize a blood drive or a charity campaign. He believes in solutions, and his solution for the unrest in Quebec is that the authorities should be firm and show no weakness. Clearly everyone benefits from a stable society; therefore Quebec should be maintained as such. As MacLennan subtly implies through Tarnley's relationship with his own sons, his deficiency is that he cannot understand spiritual and psychological aspirations.

Neither can the mighty politician, Moses Bulstrode. Fearless, absolutely honest, competent, built like a bear, and Bible bred, Bulstrode is the epitome of all the old warrior values. He suffers no nonsense from anyone. His attitude to Quebec is neatly summed up in a remark he makes to protagonist Alan Ainslie: "What gives the French Canadians this idea they've had it so tough? It was twenty times tougher in the Yukon than it ever was in Quebec." Not that Bulstrode is anti-Quebec, but as a strict matter of principle he refuses to believe that French Canadians should be accorded any special consideration. Through the character of Bulstrode, Hugh MacLennan poses a major riddle of the Canadian nation: What is equality? The egalitarian attitude of English Canada is that each individual should receive the same treatment. French Canadians, on the other hand, think of themselves first as a group or nation rather than as individuals. In Quebec, equality signifies equal treatment for French Canadians as a cultural entity. Concluding that there may be no way to resolve this and other attitudinal differences, MacLennan's hero, Alan Ainslie, finally decides to take a trip across the country, to lose himself in the vastness of the land.

Some Canadian novelists of the 1960s, incidentally, explore the *Search* theme outside the framework of nationalism.

Marie-Claire Blais, Réjean Ducharme, and Roch Carrier are all in the naturalistic school of the early-twentieth-century novelist previously mentioned, Albert Laberge, and all three lean toward a Faulknerian use of the grotesque. Blais (1939–   ), who was highly praised by Edmund Wilson in his book *O Canada* and lived for several years in the United States as his protégé, has written several novels portraying a phantasmagoric world of cripples and misfits. None of her characters succeeds in the search for meaning, but their anxieties are described with striking imaginative power. Roch Carrier's (1937–   ) novels also display a powerful imagination, but the dark scenarios he paints are tempered by a diabolical sense of humor. His *La Guerre, yes sir* (1968), the story of a funeral wake in a small Quebec village, is often hilariously funny.

Both Alice Munro (1931–   ) and Réjean Ducharme (1941–   ) have written excellent novels about a girl growing into adolescence, although it is difficult to imagine two books and girls so different. Munro's *Lives of Girls and Women* (1971) is about a resaonably normal child in a small Ontario Town. *L'Avalée des avalés* (1966)—*The Swallower Swallowed,* is presented from the point of view of a love-starved, emotionally crippled young girl of mixed Jewish-Christian parentage who builds an elaborate shell around herself. At the other end of the female road of life stands *The Stone Angel* (1965), an engaging portrait of an old lady struggling to cope with senility and maintain her self-respect, written by Margaret Laurence (1926–   ). Among Laurence's other achievements are *A Jest of God* (1966), the story of a prairie schoolteacher that was made into the movie *Rachel, Rachel,* a long identity-search novel called *The Diviners* (1974), and three books based upon the author's experiences in Africa.

Africa, incidentally, has been used by some Canadian writers as a setting to examine the changing nature of Canada. The technique, to be sure, is not new. When Americans were beset with problems of definition and identity similar to those in Canada today, Henry James used European settings in the same way. There is, moreover, a good measure of Jamesian sensitivity and intricacy in *The New Ancestors* (1970) by Dave Godfrey (1938–   ), who has also distinguished himself as an editor and publisher, and *You Can't Get There from Here* (1972) by Hugh Hood (1928–   ), two novels set in Africa that develop into complex allegory pertaining to contemporary Canada. A third novel, David Knight's (1926–   ) *Farquharson's Physique and What It Did to His Mind* (1971), is a straightforward narrative about the death of a Toronto professor in Nigeria.

A highly original treatment of the *Search for Vital Truth* theme is Leonard Cohen's *Beautiful Losers* (1966). Cohen (1934–   ) uses Catherine Tekawitha, the venerated Iroquois virgin who was converted by the Jesuits and who died in 1680 from self-inflicted mortification of the flesh, as a symbol of absolute conviction. This conviction is morbid and perverse, but it is nevertheless the antithesis of the existential vacuum, and the protagonist's impossible desire for congress with the saint is an arresting and effective device to dramatize man's need for spiritual values. Cohen, who is known throughout North America as a poet and singer, employs his poetic skills in *Beautiful Losers* to communicate his hero's spiritual bankruptcy, at the same time ingeniously epitomizing the devolution of the *Divine Order*: "O Father, Nameless and Free of Description," says the book's narrator, "lead me from the Desert of the Possible. Too long I have dealt with Events. Too long I labored to become an Angel. I chased Miracles with a bag of Power to salt their wild tails. I tried to dominate Insanity so I could steal its Information. I tried to program the Computers with Insanity. I tried to create Grace to prove that Grace existed. . . . We could not see the Evidence so we stretched our Memories . . . we did not train ourselves to Receive because we believed there wasn't Anything to Receive and we could not endure with this Belief."

Leonard Cohen published four volumes of poetry during the 1960s, and he typifies the general fertility. Established poets such as Giguère, Cogswell, Grandbois, Layton, Gustafson, Glassco, Birney, and Lapointe continued to produce regularly, while numerous other poets built reputations for themselves. Among the latter are Gwendolyn MacEwan, Ron

Everson, Paul Chamberland, Eli Mandel, Margaret Atwood, Al Purdy, Jacques Brault, D. G. Jones, Milton Acorn, and dozens more. Once again quantity precludes anything more than a few selective glimpses.

Gaston Miron (1928–), by virtue of his own poetry and his promotion of the poetry of others through his Hexagon Press in Montreal, has become a major figure in the Quebec literary world. His work can be satirical and heavily engagé, but it can also be a celebration of the positive potential of life. Like so many other Quebec poets, he sees the former static culture of Quebec as smothering and life denying, while art and the imagination are the agencies to create a new order. Here is part of C. R. P. May's translation of his "Les Années de déréliction" ("The Years of Dereliction"):

> The darkness of this place which clouds the sun itself
> Seeps into my soul, insidious as creeping imbecility.
> Each day in my life repeats the one before
> And I succumb without ever quite dying altogether. . . .
>
> As I have lost, like most of those around me,
> My memory worn down by affliction,
> My dignity, long having had to demean itself,
> And my self-respect, out-mocked by cruel laughter. . . .
>
> Poem, eyes of mine, I have striven to bring you into
>   being
> Fighting against my unreality in this world.
> Here we are, tossed on a destiny adrift
> Clutching still at signs now foreign to us.
> Our faces once lost, your images will go too.
>
> But rising to the surface of that void where live
> Lives sapped of their being, long kept unmindful of what
>   man is,
> Sometimes I seem to glimpse
> A history and a time which will be theirs
> As after a dream when the dream is reality. . . .

Miron has been compared with Toronto poet Raymond Souster (1921–), who also combines writing poetry with publishing. Both men are concerned with the suppressive as-

pects of life, the urban experience, and the problems of communication between human beings. Souster's three-line poem,
dedicated to Gaston Miron, called "The Tragedy," poignantly
epitomizes the nation's problems of communication:

> After the hand-shake
> "Je ne parle pas anglais"
> "Je ne parle pas français"

Like Miron's, Souster's poetry can be robust and senuous,
and it also has a sense of the life-suffocating effects of former
Canadian values and attitudes. Here is his "Colonial Saturday
Night":

> "You're the best audience in the world,"
> Big T says as the last kick of jazz dies
> on the stand and we gulp our drinks
> and spill down into the street:
>
> Yonge Street twelve o'clock Saturday night
> all the bars emptying
> up and down the block
> color suddenly filling
> the sidewalks, everyone hurrying—
> where?—to find girls for the night
> an alley to be sick in
> a copy to pick a fight with?—
>
> or maybe like the four of us
> just walking northward, savoring the night air
> after the cigarett haze, going really nowhere
> in no particular hurry, looking for nothing
> we haven't already put hands or minds around,
>
> > with a little jazz still singing in our heads
> > as we greet the new day, Christ's day,
> > but not yet our own.

Poet and critic Douglas Gordon Jones (1929–   ) says
of Gaston Miron that he "has articulated a world, a land,
where the Quebecois can settle in with his own language
. . . has installed in his body not an iron cross but a green

space." As a poet, Jones himself articulates a vision of a world redeemed by glimpses of regeneration—small girls who "litter the air with color," "the naked figure of a girl" that is "a rumor that must grow." Here is his "Poem a Little Chinese":

> Why, I've nearly stepped on
> A brand new butterfly
> Sunning himself in the sand.
> And I'll be damned,
> Here on a young oak limb,
> Looking like a monkey in a llama skin,
> Is a baby porcupine.
> And not knowing which—
> Whether the one in the hairy coat
> Or the one with yellow wings—
> Is Loo Tse, I bow to them both.

Jones can also be ironic, and his poetry is marked by allusion, philosophical speculation, fertile imagination, and crispness of language, as can be seen in an excerpt from "Faculty Party":

> How easily life can shrink
>   to a gasp
>   between the office and the easy-chair,
> at most
>   as a matter or oral adventure
> with cocktails, cigarettes
> and verbal chatter . . .
>
> What if, a great wave engulfing the room,
>   this girl's hair
>   should like a Venus-flower-basket
> grow long, and I
>   upon the impulse of the wave grow black
> and drive, a shark-
> length, into her womb?
>
> Or with sudden clarity the shrunken man
>   in tweeds
>   outlined a theory which encompassed life?

Neither
  is quite real, and would not suit
the economy of
this living room.

Along with John Glassco, Frank Scott, Louis Dudek, Fred Cogswell, and other Canadian poets, D. G. Jones has translated the work of his francophone counterparts, including the well-known "Speak White," a long poem by Michèle Lalonde (1937–   ) that articulates Quebec anxieties and the fear of being engulfed by "Anglo-Saxon" culture and the North American technological-consumer society. Italicized phrases being in English in the original, the poem reads in part:

We are a rude and stammering people
but we are not deaf to the genius of a language
speak with the accent of Milton and Bryon and
     Shelly and Keats
speak white
and please excuse us if in return
we've only our rough ancestral songs
and the chagrin of Nelligan

Speak white
speak of places, this and that
speak to us of the Magna Carta
of the Lincoln Monument
of the cloudy charm of the Thames
or blossom-time on the Potomac
speak to us of your traditions
we are a people who are none too bright
but we are quick to sense
the great significance of crumpets
or the Boston Tea Party

But when you *really speak white*
when you *get down to brass tacks*
to talk about *Better Homes and Gardens*
to talk of a standard of living
and of the *Great Society*
a little louder then *speak white* . . .

We know now
that we are not alone.

Quite different from that of either Jones or Lalonde is the poetry of Nova Scotian Alden Nowlan (1933–　　), who writes of small-town life with harshness and often startling frankness. Some of his poems convey a sense of horror and impending doom, as for instance "The Execution":

On the night of the execution
a man at the door
mistook me for the coroner.
"Press," I said.

But he didn't understand. He led me
into the wrong room
where the sheriff greeted me:
"You're late, Padre."

"You're wrong," I told him. "I'm Press."
"Yes, of course, Reverend Press."
We went down a stairway.

"Ah, Mr. Ellis," said the Deputy.
"Press!" I shouted. But he shoved me
through a black curtain.
The lights were so bright
I couldn't see the faces
of the men sitting
opposite. But, thank God, I thought,
they can see me!

"Look!" I cried. "Look at my face!
Doesn't anybody know me?"

Then a hood covered my head,
"Don't make it harder for us," the hangman
    whispered.

The preceding selections are intended to provide some idea of the variety of poetry being produced in Canada since 1960. Were it possible to include examples of the work of all the recognized contemporary poets of English and French Canada—Eldon Grier, Michael Ondaatje, Jay MacPherson, Nicole Brossard, Yves Préfontaine, Pierre Nepveu, Dennis

Lee, Margaret Avison, Claude Péloquin, Daryl Hine, and others swelling the ranks with each new publishing season—the full extent of this rich variety could be more properly conveyed. In short, the search for new meanings, the tensions, excitement, and unrest of the 1960s have had the effect of greatly stimulating literary activity in prose and poetry.

The theater, too, has been imbued with a new vitality. James Reaney, George Ryga, David Freeman, John Herbert, Michael Cook, and David Fennario are among several English-Canadian dramatists being successfully played and published. In French Canada, the prolific Michel Tremblay has maintained a steady production, followed by Jean Barbeau, Robert Gurik, Françoise Loranger, Marie-Claire Blais, and Antoine Maillet, whose single-actress play, *La Sagouine,* has received extraordinary acclaim in both Franch and Canada.

The New Hero (1970–   )

The year 1970 might well in the future be known as the year that Canada lost its innocence. It was the year, certainly, that Canadians temporarily lost their civil liberties as a result of the application of the War Measures Act, which was the government's reaction to the kidnapping of the senior British trade commissioner in Quebec and the provincial minister of labor by a terrorist organization called the FLQ (Quebec Liberation Front). The organization had earlier been thwarted in plots to kidnap the Israeli and U.S. consuls.

The body of Minister Pierre Laporte, who had been choked to death with a religious chain he wore around his neck, was found in the trunk of a car on October 17, 1970, one day after the declaration of the War Measures Act, establishing martial law across the land and according police extraordinary powers of arrest and detention. It was not until December 3 that Commissioner James Cross was discovered, and his kidnappers accepted an offer of free passage to Cuba in exchange for his release. Shortly afterward the abductors of Laporte were captures, tried, and sent to prison.

The "October Crisis" produced an almost immediate reaction in the world of literature—articles, poems, plays, even novels were written in both French and English. The *Search* theme of the 1960s became an attempt to analyze why the crisis had taken place, its significance, and its implications for individuals and groups. The War Measures Act and the general public approval of it, convincingly established by opinion polls, suggested strongly that despite the fading of the Old Order, Canadians were still basically system people. Unfamiliar with the evolution of Canadian values, American draft evaders and other exiles in Canada were apparently shocked by the situation. One young American author in Montreal at the time of the October Crisis, Roger Neville Williams, wrote an article called "Strong-Arm Rule in Canada" for the Washington magazine *The New Republic* (January 1971) in which he marveled at how Canadians, in contrast to Americans, "trust their government." It seems likely, however, that Canadians, surprised and shocked by an unprecedented and violent turn of events, simply fell back on habit. Not that they should have been surprised, for had they been paying attention to the serious literature since the 1940s, they would have seen the October Crisis as a climax to a quarter century and more of malaise and transformation of values. And undoubtedly, like a Greek tragedy, it has had the ultimate effect of purging the emotions. Writers in particular, after the first wave of Crisis works, seem almost to have been liberated, given the freedom to examine life and ideas with more objectivity, less self-consciousness, and less personal involvement.

If anything, the literature of the 1970s in Canada is becoming increasingly imaginative and diversified. Robertson Davies has produced a trilogy of brilliant novels—*Fifth Business* (1971), *The Manticore* (1972), and *World of Wonders* (1975)—related to the life of a magician. Clarke Blaise (1939–   ), who was born and reared in the United States, has written two volumes of short stories that often blend his American and Canadian experiences. Poet Margaret Atwood (1939–   ), with three novels in eight years—*Surfacing* (1972), *Lady Oracle* (1976), and *Life Before Man* (1979)—has made a notable mark in Canadian fiction and achieved international recognition. *Le Deux-millième étage* (1973)—*Floor 2000*, by Roch Carrier, is a shift away from the past to the urban dispossessed of the present. My own *Lark des Neiges* (1971) explores the psychology of a young woman of mixed French and Scottish parentage caught between the two Canadian cultures; my *Where Do the MacDonalds Bury Their Dead* (1976), set in Montreal, Detroit, and California, is a seriocomic story of a Canadian trying to come to grips with his own manhood, cultural identity, and salient aspects of North American society, including a Charles Manson-like family. Robert Kroetsch, Victor-Levy Beaulieu, John Buell, Jacques Ferron, Rudy Weibe, Marian Engel, Sylvia Fraser, Hugh Hood, Yves Thériault, Gérard Bessette, and Richard B. Wright are only a few of the other authors who continue to build their reputations, probing new techniques and subject matter and generally broadening the horizons of Canadian literature.

So far, however, the major phenomenon of the 1970s is the emergence in finished form of the *New Canadian Hero*. And what is especially intriguing is that remarkable examples of the new hero can be found in three novels, all published in 1974, by novelists who had previously created classic examples of the traditional Canadian protagonist.

Sinclair Ross's *As For Me and My House* has already been discussed. The protagonist of his latest novel, *Sawbones Memorial,* is a complete and striking contrast to the self-effacing, guilt-ridden Philip Bentley of the earlier book, even though he is also a professional man in a small prairie town. "Sawbones" Hunter is a country doctor retiring at the age of seventy-five after nearly a half century of practice. The town has finally built a hospital, which will be known as the Hunter Memorial, but it will be in charge of a young doctor. A local boy, Dr. Nick Miller is still familiarly referred to by some as "Nick the Hunky." His mother was a Ukrainian charwoman known as Big Anna.

Doc Hunter has never been able to adapt to the system, the code of behavior, and attitudes expected of a doctor by the general public. Actually he has simply ignored the system, doing his job and living his life in his own way, despite the gossip about his drinking and womanizing. Unlike Philip Bentley, he is self-confident and independent, even to the point of making personal, nonmedical decisions that govern the very lives and deaths of people around him. When asked by the local newspaper editor if he ever had doubts, Hunter replies, "If anything ever kept me awake it was for having hesitated, held back, not the other way." On one occasion he performed what amounted to euthanasia for a farm woman in the final stages of cancer. On another, when a farmer fatally pitchforked a man who had tried to rape his daughter, Doc Hunter declined to inform the police, deciding that justice had been done and that a court case would only cause needless suffering for all. On still another occasion, he aborted a young girl pregnant by her father, then managed to rehabilitate both the man and his daughter.

Like earlier protagonist Philip Bentley, Doc Hunter has an illegitimate child. But instead of the child becoming a symbol of guilt and misery, Hunter's son is his triumph. When Big Anna, who came to clean the Hunter home, had said "You vant?" he took without hesitation. Then he kept tabs on the boy as Anna raised him, paying the bills, smoothing his way in school and in the community, taking him along on his doctor's rounds. The reason that Doc Hunter has no regrets upon leaving Upward when at last a hospital has been built, is not only that he is satisfied with himself and his long career, but also that his practice and the hospital will be, as Doc alone now knows, in the hands of his own son—Nick.

Hunter has never had an internal struggle. Questioned by the local clergyman about his religious beliefs, he replies that he has been too busy "with the practical problems" of being a doctor to worry about other things. He thinks of the world as a failed experiment, since abandoned by God: "No help and no interference either. Strictly on our own—sink or swim in our infested mud-bottomed little Here and Now." Believing that he is on his own, therefore, Doc Hunter must be self-reliant and independent. As mentioned in the Introduction, one is tempted to say that the *New Hero* is more like an American than a Canadian, especially when he is taking the law into his own hands frontier fashion. In fact, however, Hunter is perhaps peculiarly Canadian. Although he is obviously listening to his own drummer, he presumes no transcendental metronome to set the beat of his drum, and he symbolizes total escape from the notion of a *Divine Order*. Doc Hunter is independent and self-reliant, not because of prescribed and inculcated national values, but rather in spite of them.

The protagonist of Adele Wiseman's 1974 novel, *Crackpot,* is Jewish like Abraham in her earlier *the Sacrifice,* but that is the limit of what the two have in common. Hoda is the fruit of a bizarre, ritualistic marriage between a blind man and a humpbacked woman. During a time of plague in Russia, when Christians appeared to be stricken more severely than Jews, there was danger of a pogrom arising to add to the threat of the disease itself. The Jews were consequently obliged "to restore the forces of life when only the forces of death reigned before," and the traditional rite was to pick the two poorest and most helpless members of the community and stage a wedding in a cemetery. Thus it came about that Danile and Rahel, parents of Wiseman's heroine, were joined in marriage. Eventually the family find themselves in Winnipeg, Canada, supposedly to be cared for by Danile's uncle. The uncle, however, has been tricked—he did not realize that Danile and Rahel were handicapped when he agreed to sponsor them. His insulting remarks and resentment lead the two immigrants to attempt to support themselves, Rahel laboring as a charwoman and Danile weaving baskets. When Rahel dies, the burden of actually making ends meet falls on daughter Hoda.

Big for her age and grossly overweight, Hoda does housework as her mother had done before her, but she finds out that there are easier ways for a girl to make money. The local butcher gives her soupbones and scraps of meat in return for small sexual favors, and it is not long before she slips into neighborhood whoring. She pretends to her sightless father that she is tutoring the boys who come to her home; he repeatedly calls out to them to study (occasionally causing alarm "because the word for 'study' in Hebrew sounds like the word for 'pig' in Yiddish"). Hoda is a boisterous girl full of good cheer, and she prospers reasonably well. Early in her career, before she becomes truly professional, she gets pregnant, but she is so fat normally that she does not realize she is with child until the last moment. Wiseman achieves a masterpiece of description in the scene where Hoda gives birth, then wrapping herself and the infant, deposits it at the door of a Jewish orphanage.

The climax of the novel, again handled masterfully by the author, is when Hoda's own son turns up with a group of youths to sample her services, and to pay the treat with the money his unknown mother has secretely been sending him! After the episode, significantly, Hoda is not beset by feelings of guilt, only remorse. In order to spare the boy the knowledge that his mother is a notorious whore, Hoda suppresses her natural desire to claim her son. In fact, having found out who he is, she allows him to come to her a second time, again to spare his feelings—a truly amazing yet totally believable chain of events.

Like Doc Hunter, Hoda has been too busy with day-to-day practical matters to become preoccupied with philosophical issues. Like the country doctor, she is tough when she has to be, but she is essentially good, genuinely concerned about others to the disregard of her own interests. She is also self-conficent and self-reliant, capable of turning aside insults and of ignoring the system. On one occasion during a demonstration she pulls a mounted policeman off his horse.

The third novel of the *New Hero* is André Langevin's *Une Chaine dans le parc—A Chain in the Park*. Again the protagonist of the new book, a young boy called Pierrot, is a striking contrast to Langevin's Dr. Alain Dubois in *Poussière sur la ville,* discussed earlier. The novel covers a short period when Pierrot is living with an uncle and three aunts in central Montreal, after he has become too old for the orphanage where he was raised. It does not take long for the relatives to decide to send Pierrot to another institution, a live-in trade school. Their reason, evidently, is that the boy is too independent and self-reliant for them to handle.

And there can be no doubt that Pierrot is a budding Doc Hunter rather than a Docteur Dubois. Despite his orphanage training with nuns, he insists on making up his own mind, even in matters of religion, and he is ready to fight furiously for what he believes to be his rights. He can no more be pushed around than Hunter or big Hoda—as a child in the orphanage Pierrot once broke the nose of a bully who had been tormenting him. Yet he has sympathy and understanding for other people, including a youth called Gaston "le Rat"—"Dogs, it's not their fault, they can't help biting. The same with Gaston."

Pierrot absolutely refuses to occupy himself with unjustified feelings of guilt, even when his aunts go out of their way to make him feel sorry and somehow responsible for his mother's death. He is attracted to Jane, a little blonde girl who wears expensive, dainty dresses (compensation from a mother whose character and profession leave her with not much loving to spare), and he defies everyone to become her companion and protector. Yet he remains independent. Jane is like a young Madeleine, the wife of Dubois in *Pouissière*—she is a wild thing, all sensuality and physical appetite, but Pierrot knows just how to handle her. At ten, he seems to understand more about the opposite sex than Dubois does as a grown man. Or at least he is more capable of acting upon what he undetstands.

Pierrot, Doc Hunter, and Hoda, then, are all strong, independent individualists. The character type has been in Canadian fiction before, lurking in the work of Margaret Laurence, Hugh MacLennon, W. O. Mitchell, and others, but not fully developed, or else keeping out of the way, playing a secondary role. Now he or she is the *New Hero* playing a dominant role. At long last, it seems after decades of conscious effort to define the Canadian identity, to find out what a Canadian is rather than what he is not, the Canadian character has spontaneously begun to define himself.

It was observed at the beginning of this perspective on Canadian writing that a national literature reflects the spiritual quality and growth of a nation. Any country's good authors have their finger on the collective pulse; they are the diagnosticians of a nation's health and the prophets of a nation's destiny. Canadian authors, as has been demonstrated, have traced the spiritual growth of Canada through many stages. They have analyzed the psychology of Canadians from colonial or garrison mentality to a new state of multilateral independence and individualism, the full implications of which remain to be examined and articulated. Canadian writers, therefore, are faced with a brand-new beginning, perhaps the first genuine Canadian beginning. And it might well happen that all the literary works discussed in this survey are mere preludes to what Canadian literature is destined to become in the not-too-distant future.

Chapter 7

An International Perspective:

The Foreign Policy of

Adjustment

ROGER FRANK SWANSON*

Introduction

IN AN INCREASINGLY interdependent world, few would deny that a comprehensive understanding of any country requires the study of international relations as they affect that country. Such a study should set forth clarifying concepts and organizing principles to provide meaning and discipline to a complex mass of detail. Naturally, the scholar's approach to international relations reflects his or her background, inter-

* Dr. Roger Frank Swanson is Executive Secretary, U.S. Section, Committee on Canada–United States Relations of the Chamber of Commerce of the United States, and a former director of the Center of Canadian Studies of the Johns Hopkins School of Advanced International Studies. He is author of *Intergovernmental Perspectives on the Canadian-U.S. Relationship* (1978), *Canadian-American Summit Diplomacy 1923–1973* (1975), and coauthor of *Canadian Foreign Policy: Options and Perspectives* (1971). His articles have appeared in such journals as *Proceedings of the Academy of Political Science, International Organization,* and *International Journal.* He is a founding member of the Association for Canadian Studies in the United States (ACSUS), has been both Secretary-Treasurer and President of that Association, and served as the first editor of the *ACSUS Newsletter* (now the *American Review of Canadian Studies*).

ests, biases, and analytical preferences. Further, these approaches vary over time, so that one can discern several phases through which the study of international relations in the United States has come over the last half century.[1]

Until the mid-1940s, the conventional approach assumed that the search for a peaceful world order was the driving force behind the U.S. role in world affairs. Given the continuing scale of international conflict during these years, this interpretation is often termed "idealistic" or "utopian." Those scholars and statesmen who expressed this traditional outlook shared a moralistic vision of a new international system that was explicitly recognized by their support for the League of Nations and for the 1928 Briand-Kellogg pact to outlaw war. Not infrequently, such interpretations were prescriptive in tone, often selecting for analysis those features that best supported the views of the authors as to what should be the future course of government policy.

By the late 1940s, authors who could point to the recurrence of global war within twenty years of Woodrow Wilson's "war to end all wars" argued for a more "realistic" assessment of international relations. Emphasizing the importance of power in the pursuit of national interests, these "realists" sought to portray their subjects in descriptive terms, relying heavily on empirical research. Their attention was directed at the real world and those forces that propel nations to act as they do; these writers implied that the idealists overlooked or underestimated the extent to which economic self-interest, political strategy, ideological values, and military power all play a role in determining national policy.

By the 1960s, yet another phase in the study of international relations was under way as American scholars, trained in the methodology and techniques of the behavioral and social sciences, began to apply these to the study of foreign affairs. Dissatisfied with the limitations of the more traditional approaches, they believed that the quantitative tools of the "behavioralists" would allow them to be more systematic in delineating units of analysis, laying down hypotheses, gathering data, and verifying their models. They borrowed heavily from other disciplines, including mathematics, economics, psychology, and sociology. Their writing was marked by its heavy reliance on analytical models and theoretical arguments.

Finally, by the 1970s, the study of international relations seemed to be moving into a fourth phase, which might be termed "postbehavioralist." Unhappy with the limitations and rigidities of their predecessors, contemporary scholars attempt to bridge the gap between theory and practice, while seeking to enhance the predictive and explanatory power of policy analysis.

In a similar manner, the study of international relations in Canada has also evolved from a largely prescriptive, historical, and legal orientation to an empirically oriented behavioralism and beyond. Much early writing on Canada's relations with other countries described its evolution within the British Empire and Commonwealth, its involvement in international conflict and in the League of Nations and United Nations, and its role as a "peacekeeper/middle power." Much traditional writing has been in the form of biographical or narrative accounts of participants and events. This is now being supplemented by more analytical appraisals of the decision-making (or decision-avoiding) processes, the interaction of domestic and foreign policy, and the myriad of formal and informal interactions that far outweigh Canada's government-to-government relationship with other nations, especially the United States.

In speaking of the study of international relations in either the United States or Canada, we are in the most general sense speaking of the study of governmental and nongovernmental interactions that take place across the boundaries of nation-states. Although studies have increasingly been done on such nongovernmental actors as multinational corporations, the field of international relations has generally concentrated on nation-states as actors and their interactions with other nation-states.

In examining the role of nation-states in the international system, there is a tendency for Americans not to see Canada as a distinctive actor. If thought of at all, Canada's international experience is usually regarded as a replication, if not an extension of, the U.S. international experience. While there has been a high degree of complementarity between Canadian and U.S. policies, Canada's international experience nevertheless has a distinctive quality that is well worth examining for several reasons.

First, in a policy sense, the fact that Canada and the United States share a forty-five-hundred-mile border, and the fact that the degree of Canadian-U.S. interdependence exceeds that of any other two sovereign nations in history, means that Canadian policies are of tremendous importance to Americans. One need only visualize a worst-case scenario— a Canada that is politically unstable and uncooperative or hostile to the United States—to illustrate this importance. Economically, Canada's trade and investment policies, coupled with the policies of the United States, have resulted in an unprecedented movement of goods and capital. Strategically, Canada is a member of NATO and NORAD (The North American Air Defense Command) and has extensive defense production-sharing agreements with the United States. Moreover, Canada's role in such international organizations as the United Nations, and in such regions as the Middle East through peacekeeping, have a significant impact on U.S. policies. Perhaps it is because Canada has frequently pursued parallel policies, and has cooperated with the United States in so many important ways, that most Americans have failed to appreciate, not only the significance of Canada, but also the fact that Canad' has an international approach and interests that are not identical with those of the United States.

A second reason for studying Canada as an international actor concerns its size. Canada is a medium-sized or "middle power." If we rank nations according to the conventional four-fold criteria of size, population, military, and economic capabilities,[2] we can identify the two superpowers who dominate the international system, several great powers (such as Germany and Japan), as well as a majority of small powers whose international impact is essentially confined to their immediate neighbors. Those nations that are in between, such as Canada, Brazil, and India, are certainly not small in terms of their capabilities, and in some respects they are almost great powers.

Americans are citizens of a superpower, with a tendency to concentrate on the superpower and great-power level at the expense of the intermediate range of nations, except when there is a crisis involving one of the lesser powers that affects U.S. interests. Yet intermediate powers constitute a significant dimension of the international system, playing important roles in international organizations, in international conflicts, and in the resolution of international issues. It is therefore interesting and instructive to examine Canada as a case study of a middle power. Indeed, no other medium-sized nation in the international system has been as conscious of its middle-power status. The very term "middle power" became a symbol for Canadians in that it was associated with mediation and peacekeeping, thereby representing a distinctive and positive international role for Canada.

A third reason for studying Canada as an international actor is the simple fact that Canada is a significant actor because it has the capabilities to influence facets of the international system. Indeed, although Canada does not play a dominant role in the international system, its impact upon it is by no means negligible.

Canada played a significant role in the creation and development of the United Nations, and was also one of the major forces in the growth of the postwar British Commonwealth of Nations and in the creation of the North Atlantic Treaty Organization (NATO). In fact, article II of the NATO treaty became known as the "Canadian Article" because of Canada's insistence that there be included a pledge by alliance members to strengthen free institutions, encourage economic collaboration, and in general create an Atlantic community. In addition, Canada has been an active member of other international agencies that seek to bring order into the international economic system. Canadians supported such institutions as the International Bank for Reconstruction and Development (the World Bank), the International Monetary Fund, and the General Agreement on Tariffs and Trade (GATT). Moreover, by the 1960s Canada, through the initiatives of Quebec, became increasingly involved in the support of a francophone community in Africa. To many, of course, the word "peacekeeping" has become synonymous with Canada. Canadian Minister of External Affairs Lester B. Pearson received the Nobel Peace Prize for his efforts during the 1956 Suez crisis, and Canada has participated in every major UN peacekeeping initiative ranging from the Congo to Lebanon.

Methodologically, there are many ways to examine and analyze Canada's international experience. For the purposes of this book, however, the more traditional, survey-oriented approach is appropriate. To understand Canada's international experience, one must understand five dimensions: Canada's evolution as an international actor, the domestic sources of Canadian foreign policy, the objectives and principles of Canadian foreign policy, the range of relations that Canada has with other nations, and the role of the Canadian-U.S. relationship in this range of relations. These five dimensions explain not only why there has been a great deal of complementarity between Canadian and U.S. policies but also why there have been differences in such areas as Canadian trade with Cuba and recognition of the People's Republic of China.

The theme unifying these five dimensions is the theme of adjustment: Canadian foreign policy must adjust, not only to international forces, but also to internal forces. All nations must of course adjust to international developments in varying degrees, but demands on Canada are especially great, given its vulnerability due to its open economy. In addition, Canada is geographically isolated in North America, which it shares with a superpower. This confers both benefits and constraints upon Canada's international role. While all nations must adjust to internal or domestic forces, the demands on Canada are especially compelling, given its vast geographical expenses, limited number of people, and its profoundly multicultural society. Readers of this book will already know that the internal factor of national unity has become a matter of the highest priority for Canadians.

Divided into six sections, this chapter begins by showing how Canada acquired an autonomous international personality, including the right to make treaties and the right of diplomatic representation. Here we see Canada's gradual emergence from under British tutelage in a long evolutionary process culminating in its complete autonomy. To understand the international experience of a nation, we must identify the domestic factors that define a nation's international personality. The second section of this chapter therefore examines the four factors of geography, demography, political institutions, and economics.

The third section examines the objectives and principles of recent Canadian foreign policy, as defined by the Canadian foreign minister in 1947 and the Canadian government in 1970. In addition, the main thrusts of Canadian foreign policy are identified and examined—the economy, strategic matters, peacekeeping, disarmament/arms control, development assistance, and Law of the Sea. This is followed by a fourth section that examines the range of Canada's relations with other countries and regions, including the Western Hemisphere, Europe, the Soviet Union, Middle East, Africa, Asia and the Pacific, and the People's Republic of China.

Given the extraordinary importance of the United States in Canada's external relations, the entire fifth section is devoted to an examination of the Canadian-U.S. relationship. Here the historical ingredients of the bilateral relationship, including annexation, coexistence, and interdependence, are identified and assessed. A concluding section presents an overview of Canada as an internal actor and summarizes the process of adjustment as a theme in the Canadian foreign policy experience.

What emerges from this chapter is the picture of a medium-sized nation that plays a role in world affairs far in excess of what its real power or close interdependency with the United States would suggest. Moreover, Canada plays this role with defined foreign policy objectives and principles, while adjusting both to the demands of domestic unity and to the changing nature of the international system. The 1970 Canadian foreign policy review captured well this triad of indigenous values and domestic and international forces:

> Foreign policy can be shaped, and is shaped, mainly by the value judgments of the Government at any given time. But it is also shaped by the possibilities that are open to Canada at any given time—basically by the constraints or opportunities

presented by the prevailing international situation. It is shaped too by domestic considerations, by the internal pressures exerted on the Government, by the amount of resources which the Government can afford to deploy.[3]

The essence of Canada's international experience, and the sense of national pride and resiliency inherent to it, were well illustrated by a Canadian author writing in 1938: "Whatever our fate, it is to be hoped that our own government shall decide it."[4]

Canada's Evolution as an International Actor

It is useful to begin a discussion of Canada's international experience with a survey of the Canadian drive for autonomy, since the Canadian acquisition of a sovereign status in effect constitutes the history of Canada's pre–World War II international experience. Canada's achievement of independence as a nation was an evolutionary rather than a revolutionary process. By way of contrast, the U.S. experience consisted of a formal Declaration of Independence, armed conflict, negotiation, the recognition by other nations of an autonomous status with full treaty-making power, and the creation of a diplomatic infrastructure of embassies and consular posts to further U.S. interests in dealing with other nations. If America's acquisition of independence was violent, dramatic, and abrupt, however, Canada's was peaceful, undramatic, and so gradual that at times there seemed to be no movement at all. And yet, Canada did become an autonomous nation, although at times it was difficult for other nations to determine where Great Britain stopped and Canada began.

This Canadian acquisition of sovereign nationhood was neither simple nor automatic, but rather was a complex process involving political/legal, economic, and strategic forces. Legal autonomy for any nation means two things—the right to make treaties and the right of diplomatic representation.[5] It should be emphasized that while Canada's drive for autonomy reflected a concern with status (e.g., full recognition by other nations of Canada as a distinctive and independent state), it was by no means a purely symbolic or representational achievement. That is, as Canada matured economically and politically, it found that its national needs, ranging from commercial to immigration matters, could not adequately be pursued as an adjunct of Great Britain utilizing British embassies and consular posts. Propelling the Canadian drive for autonomy was the increasing conviction on the part of Canadians that if their particular interests were to be preserved, especially those that involved the United States, they must have in their own hands the treaty-making power (as they did not, for example, in the 1903 Alaskan boundary dispute).

From Canadian Confederation in 1867 to World War I we can see the Canadian government defining and asserting the ingredients of autonomy. Canada began to participate as a principal in formal diplomatic negotiations, beginning with the 1871 Treaty of Washington that marked the first time a colonial statesman (the Canadian prime minister) was included in an imperial delegation. This was followed by the 1907 Canadian-French commercial treaty in which a Canadian conducted the negotiations and signed jointly with the British; Canadians negotiated with Japan concerning anti-Japanese riots in British Columbia; and 1909 saw the establishment of the U.S.-Canadian International Joint Commission that created the first formal mechanism for ongoing Canadian-U.S. negotiations. By 1923, with the signing of the U.S.-Canadian halibut treaty, Canada was negotiating and signing treaties without the British, a practice that was confirmed at the imperial conference in the same year.

A second ingredient of the Canadian drive for autonomy in international affairs was the development of a Canadian organizational capacity to handle its own affairs in dealing with other nations. The original Canadian representatives abroad were immigration agents, first appointed in the 1860s. In 1880 the Office of High Commissioner for Canada was created in London, and in 1882 an Agent General was appointed in Paris. By the late 1880s, Canadian commercial agents were posted abroad, and the Canadian Department of

Commerce and Trade (now the Department of Industry, Trade and Commerce) was created in the early 1890s with its own commercial "foreign service." In 1907 commercial agents were elevated to trade commissioners, and in 1909 the Canadian equivalent of a state department or foreign office, the Department of External Affairs, was established.

A third ingredient of Canadian autonomy involved Canadian resistance to British attempts at greater imperial centralization, which included the attempts to form a commercial and defense union. Beginning with the first Colonial Conference in 1887 (by 1907 its successors were called Imperial Conferences), Canada consistently resisted British centralizing tendencies. A fourth and related ingredient of Canadian autonomy was Canada's right to determine the degree of its participation, if any, in British conflicts. This can be seen in the 1885 Sudan expedition, in which Canada did not become involved, and in the 1899 Boer War in which volunteers were recruited and equipped by the Canadian government, although paid for and commanded by the British in South Africa.

FROM WORLD WAR I TO WORLD WAR II
While Canadian autonomy in foreign affairs was, as has been illustrated, an evolutionary development, it is nonetheless true that certain events that gave rise to important and rapid changes in the conduct of Canada's external relations warrant special comment. One such monumental event was World War I.[6] Although the Department of External Affairs had been created in 1909, it was not accorded recognition as the main agency of Canadian foreign policy so long as Britain held, and was seen by other countries to hold, the major responsibility for Canada's relations abroad.

When war broke out among the European powers in August 1914, Canada, as part of the British Empire, was officially at war. Nevertheless, because Canada had full internal autonomy, it was left to the Canadian Parliament to determine the extent of Canada's contribution. A wave of imperial sentiment swept over English Canada, and the country, then only with a population of 6 million, raised an army of six hundred thousand to fight in France and Belgium. In 1917, with casualties rising in Europe, the government brought in conscription (with serious results for domestic unity—see Chapter 2). In 1918 English Canada emerged from the war with an enhanced pride in the country's remarkable contribution to the Allied victory.

Interestingly, however, English Canada's support of the war effort did not lead to blind approval of Britain's conduct of the war. As casualties mounted, Canada began to demand a voice in imperial war policy. Accordingly, in 1917 the British Prime Minister, David Lloyd George, called together the Imperial War Cabinet, which included the prime ministers of the Dominions (South Africa, New Zealand, Australia, and Canada). For Canada, this marked an important symbolic step in its evolution as autonomous actor on the international stage, as did the creation of a distinctive Canadian Army Corps during the war. By virtue of its important military and economic contribution to the war effort, Canada had earned increased international status. This pattern would be repeated both during and after the next world war.

Every Canadian prime minister of the interwar period (most notably Mr. King) used the meetings of Commonwealth heads of state to assert Canadian autonomy in foreign and defense matters. There was particular sensitivity to suggestions of greater policy coordination among the Dominions and London. While continuing to proclaim its support for the Commonwealth, Canada would often point to its position in North America, indicating that it had to consider its relations with the United States and therefore would oppose any overall imperial strategy that might place the United States in opposition to London, with Canada caught in the middle.

During the interwar period, Canada pursued an active foreign policy of cautious noninvolvement. Every effort was made to use the international stage as a forum in which Canada could assert its independence. However, it was the firm policy of Prime Minister Mackenzie King, who also served as Secretary of State for External Affairs, that while Canada would be an active member of the international community, it would avoid making commitments that might draw it into another European war. This inclination was most apparent in the context of Commonwealth relations and with regard to the League of Nations.

The League of Nations provided Canada with a convenient forum in which to demonstrate its growing autonomy in foreign policy. Despite some objections from other countries, Canada had separate representation during the 1919 Paris Peace Conference (although its spokesmen were members of the British Empire delegation). Canada signed the Treaty of Versailles separately from Britain, but under the heading of the British Empire; and it took a separate seat at the League of Nations. In 1921 Canada was elected to the governing body of the International Labor Organization; in 1924 a Canadian senator from Quebec, Mr. Dandurand, was elected president of the assembly of the League; and in 1927 Canada was voted one of the nonpermanent members of the League Council. But while Canada was prepared to use the League as a forum to further its own international stature and to contribute to some of the League's less controversial agencies, it avoided taking any kind of leadership position and was wary of being drawn into war. When Italy attacked defenseless Ethiopia in 1935, the League met to consider sanctions against the aggressor. During its deliberations, the Canadian representative, Mr. Riddell, without the consent of Ottawa, proposed that sanctions be applied. Prime Minister King quickly overruled Riddell, and Canada abandoned the initiative.

However, as the European situation deteriorated in the late 1930s, Canada's relations with Britain again became increasingly important. Despite a trend toward more autonomy, the question of Canada's response should war break out remained unclear (an ambiguity largely due to King's own diplomacy). It is significant that Canada gave its full support to the policy of "appeasement" that saw Britain (and the United States) accede to German demands in the hope that war could be avoided or at least postponed. On the other hand, when the Prime Minister met the German dictator, Adolf Hitler, in the late 1930s, he took special care to say that should a European war break out in which Britain was threatened, Canada would not stand idly by. When Britain declared war on Germany on September 3, 1939, King was determined that Parliament should formally decide whether to join in the struggle or not. Public sentiment, strongly anti-Nazi, predetermined the outcome. However, the independent Canadian declaration of war, coming a week after the British declaration, symbolically confirmed—through an all but unanimous vote in the House of Commons—that Canada was fully in control of its own foreign policy.

Early Canadian hopes that its role in the war might be restricted to supplying material and naval convoy support came to an end with the collapse of France in the spring of 1940. During the dark days when Britain stood alone facing Germany, Canada had the only fully equipped division in England with responsibility for defense against invasion. As the war widened with the inclusion of the United States and the Soviet Union, the Canadian contribution also grew, out of all proportion to its population. The Canadian forces, which at their height had more than 1 million men and women under arms, saw action in every European theater of the war. In particular, Canadian ground forces were engaged in Italy and in the liberation of Holland. The war cost the country forty-five thousand lives. The vast majority of the Canadian forces were raised without resorting to conscription; once again, however, as the casualties mounted in Europe, the government was forced to initiate a draft. Although many French Canadians were already serving, there was a good deal of oppositon to conscription in Quebec, especially given the memories of World War I. As it turned out, very few of those drafted saw combat.

THE POST–WORLD WAR II PERIOD

As did World War I, World War II increased Canada's international standing. While Mackenzie King was certainly eclipsed by the "Big Three" of the Alliance (Churchill, Roosevelt, and Stalin), Canada emerged from the struggle—and remained for a number of years thereafter—in some ways a great power. Canadian leaders stressed the principle of "functionalism" suggesting that a nation's influence in the pursuit of peace at the United Nations would be commensurate with its wartime contributions. With Europe in ruins, Russia devastated, and China in the throes of civil war, only Canada and the United States could boast healthy economies and sufficient financial, industrial, and agricultural resources to reconstruct a viable international order. In addition, Canada had become, because of its wartime collaboration with the United States and Britain and its vast reserves of uranium, a leader in the development of nuclear power. The end of the war also brought about an important shift in the attitude of Canada toward international commitments, and collective security in particular. Owing to the influence of men such as Secretary of State for External Affairs Louis St. Laurent, and his deputy minister, Lester B. Pearson, Canada was prepared to assume greater international obligations. Appropriately, therefore, Canadian diplomacy centered on the establishment of the United Nations. Speaking to the first meeting of the General Assembly in San Francisco, External Affairs Minister St. Laurent announced that "The Government and the people of Canada are anxious to know what armed forces . . . Canada should maintain as our share of putting force behind world law."[7]

To the dismay of Canadians, the growing antagonism between the United States and the Soviet Union soon came to be reflected in the United Nations. In particular, the Security Council was made ineffectual as a genuine instrument of collective security as a result of the Soviet's repeated use of its veto rights. By 1947 the Canadian government was already serving notice on the General Assembly that it could not "accept an unaltered Council." "If forced to," St. Laurent continued, Canada would "seek greater safety in an association of democratic and peace-loving states willing to accept international obligations in return for a greater measure of national security."[8]

Canada did in fact seek greater security in exchange for greater obligations through the North Atlantic Treaty Organization (NATO), founded in 1948, and it is important to note that Canada was one of the forces behind the formation of the Atlantic Alliance. Canadian leaders, reflecting a widely held public view, regarded the Soviet Union as a threat to European security and equated Canadian security with that of Western Europe. The strategy was to rely on deterrence—seeking to prevent war by threatening a would-be aggressor with unacceptable damage. As St. Laurent put it:

> We feel that should war break out that affected the United Kingdom and the United States we would inevitably be involved and that there might be great value in having consummated a regional pact . . . whereby these West European democracies, the U.K. and the U.S., and ourselves agreed to pool for defence purposes our respective potentials and coordinate right away our forces, so that, it would appear to any possible aggressor that he would have to overcome us all if he attempted any aggression.[9]

Although Canada shared the American view of a Soviet threat to Western Europe, Canadian diplomats seemed to have adopted a somewhat more subtle view of that threat that went beyond the military aspect. Of key importance in the minds of those Canadians who helped fashion NATO was the "threat of Stalinism to the virtues and values of western civilization."[10] It was believed that a weak and demoralized Europe would be easy prey for Soviet agitation. By giving it an explicit formal guarantee of protection, NATO would help the region regain the confidence it needed to resist communism. For Canada, then, NATO was to be more than a military alliance. Article II of the treaty, which became known as the "Canadian Article" because of Canada's insistence that it be included, pledged the alliance members to strengthen free institutions "by bringing about a better understanding of the principles upon which these institutions are founded." In the economic sphere the parties pledged to "eliminate conflict in their international economic policies and . . . encourage economic collaboration."[11] For Canada, then, NATO was a framework wherein its interests could flourish in an atmosphere of regional harmony and military security.

Although Canada insisted that reference be made to economic cooperation among the NATO allies, the country was already an active member of other international agencies which sought to revitalize the international economic order. (the International Bank for Reconstruction and Development, the International Monetary Fund, and the General Agreement on Tariffs and Trade). Indeed, as one of the wealthier nations of the postwar world, Canada was able to take an active role in these agencies which were creating an emerging economic order. Since Canada depends heavily upon its exports for the maintenance of a high standard of living, after World War II it actively sought markets and membership in world organizations that would have a bearing on the international trade system. Canada's role in the United Nations Relief and Rehabilitation Administration (UNRRA) and the extensive Canadian relief to a distraught Europe can thus be seen as products of enlightened self-interest.

Nor did membership in NATO mean a reduced Canadian commitment to the United Nations. The world body continued to provide a major focus for Canadian foreign policy. When North Korea attacked in 1950, Canada supported an American-sponsored resolution in the General Assembly, authorizing the United Nations to give military assistance to South Korea. As a reaffirmation of the principle of collective security, Canada joined in those military operations by sending some twenty-three thousand men, all of whom were volunteers, many of which were French Canadians. However, Canada did become concerned with the possible widening of the war to include China and perhaps even the Soviet Union. Attempts were made to restrain the United States, into whose hands the conduct of the war largely fell. The Korean experience did reveal the extent to which the United Nations could become drawn into the growing tensions of the cold war.

While Canadian leaders came to have doubts about U.S. actions in Korea and especially about the leadership of General MacArthur, they appear to have supported the need to build up NATO forces in Europe. At the beginning of the alliance Canada had not envisioned the permanent stationing of troops in Europe. However, a war, even if it was a cold one, necessitated an active military alliance. Consequently, in 1951 Canada was called upon to contribute forces to an integrated European defense force under a supreme allied commander. So long as the Soviet Union was widely perceived as constituting a threat to Canadian security, there was no strong objection to military contributions for Europe in the name of collective security—the government and electorate accepted them as necessary. Mindful of past difficulties with conscription, the Canadian government called for an increase in manpower through volunteers and had little difficulty in meeting its commitments.

The acceptance by Canada of an active role in NATO and of increased defense spending was consistent with its postwar willingness to undertake additional international commitments. Moreover, in 1951 Canada was still one of the few NATO members capable of so doing. Its support for an integrated command was significant. "We and our allies believe," the minister of defence told the House of Commons, "that the fact of participation by the Canadian army will show more emphatically . . . that we stand together with our allies."[12]

Perhaps Canada's greatest contribution to the alliance, and to world peace, came during the Suez crisis of October–November 1956. Earlier that year, President Nasser of Egypt had nationalized the Suez Canal over the objections of Britain and France. These two NATO allies then conspired with Israel, which had been disturbed over raids into its territory from Egypt. Thus, when Israel opened a massive attack across the Sinai Desert, both France and Britain, as had been arranged, called on both sides to halt the fighting. Failing a cease-fire, the two countries proceeded to occupy the Canal area. This, however, brought swift condemnation from the United States, and allied unity seemed to be faltering.

Key to the Canadian solution of the Suez crisis was Lester Pearson's proposal for a United Nations peacekeeping force to be positioned between Israel and Egypt while a political settlement to the Middle East dispute was worked out. Canada offered to contribute troops and logistical support to the force which was known as United Nations Emergency Force (UNEF). UNEF was the first attempt at large-scale peacekeeping—the stationing of neutral multinational forces between potential combatants for the purpose of keeping the two sides at peace while a political settlement was being concluded.

Because the idea had come from a Canadian, and because Canada was willing to supply troops and materiel to UNEF, Canada was henceforth closely linked to United Nations peacekeeping. The country had already been involved in peace observation in Palestine and in Kashmir under United Nations auspices, and had also been asked to serve as a member of the International Control Commission in Indochina (Vietnam). After Suez, Canada accepted an active role in every major peacekeeping operation mounted by the United Nations: in the Congo (1960–64), in Cyprus (1964–present), in the Sinai (1973–present), and between Israel and Syria (1974–present). In addition, Canada has contributed to United Nations peace observation missions in Palestine (1947–48), Lebanon (1958 and 1978), West Iran (1962–63), and along the Indian-Pakistan border (1949–present).[13] Canada also served on the International Control Commission in Indochina until 1973.

Although the importance and implications of peacekeeping and peace observation were perhaps exaggerated in Canada, they did provide the country with the opportunity to play a highly visible role in international politics. And while it is also true that all major peacekeeping operations were mounted with the diplomatic and material support of the United States and were in line with American interests, Canada came to be regarded by a majority of U.S. members as an important part of UN peacekeeping efforts. With its small but well-trained and highly sophisticated armed forces, Canada was able to provide the UN with the kind of expertise in communications, logistics, transportation, and support that are essential for peacekeeping operations. Indeed, Canada itself became so involved with UN peacekeeping that in a major defense review in 1964 the government of Canada listed peacekeeping as the number one defense priority.

In May 1967 tensions began to rise in the Middle East with Egypt threatening Israel with war. President Nasser ordered UNEF out of the Sinai; and because of the vague nature of the consent agreement between Egypt and the

United Nations, U Thant, then secretary general, agreed to withdraw UN forces. The demise of UNEF was taken particularly hard in Canada, especially since Nasser had singled out Canadian troops for withdrawal. It should be borne in mind, however, that peacekeeping represents but one aspect of Canada's mediatory role in the United Nations and in other international forums. Other examples include the International Atomic Energy Commission, the Palestine Commission, and the diplomatic readjustment of the status of India and Pakistan in the Commonwealth. Such tasks constituted the essence of Canadian diplomacy epitomized by Lester B. Pearson.

Domestic Framework

Having surveyed the evolution of Canada as an international actor, it is useful to now direct our attention toward the domestic framework that underpins the formulation and implementation of Canadian foreign policy. In their conduct abroad, not only must all states adjust to the changing nature of the international system, they must also, in varying degrees, adjust to domestic requirements imposed by their internal orders.[14] For the student of international politics, no less than for the student of Canadian studies, Canada offers a revealing case study of the importance of the fourfold domestic sources of foreign policy: geography, demography, political institutions, and economics. Indeed, in its 1971 review of the country's international posture, the government of Canada itself stated unequivocally that Canadian foreign policy must be, and would be, the extension abroad of domestic priorities.

The enduring nature of these four domestic sources of foreign policy cannot be overemphasized in the Canadian context. It is no accident that a Canadian author writing in 1932, one year after the Statute of Westminster that legalized Canada's formal independence, identified essentially the same four factors that to him determined Canada's "relations with the outside world."[15] Although the international system has changed dramatically since 1932, as has Canada's place within this system, these "permanent bases" of Canadian foreign policy continue to exert a crucial influence on the formulation and implementation of Canadian foreign policy.

To a large extent, of course, the close connection between domestic realities and Canada's foreign policy is itself a function of another theme that informs all the chapters of this book. To cite the Canadian government: the "inescapable realities" of all Canadian policies, *domestic and foreign*, are the necessity of maintaining national unity at home and living "distinct [from] but in harmony with the world's most powerful and dynamic nation."[16]

GEOGRAPHY
Canadians built a "distinct" nation across a vast territory, much of which remains uninhabited frozen wilderness most of the year. As was seen in Chapter 1, most of the early settlement and the later urban growth took place in a relatively narrow band of land along the American border. It was in this narrow space that Canada strove to maintain its separateness. Moreover, geography imposed strains on national unity owing to the long distances between regions. Vast territory, therefore, coupled with harsh climatic conditions, exacerbated the political or man-made problems which militated against the survival of a united country, distinctive from the United States.

If today the threat of actual absorption by the United States has abated, the vastness of the country continues to pose problems for an independent, but sparsely populated, nation. Canada has claimed sovereignty over its immense Arctic areas, and when the American oil tanker *Manhattan* crossed through the Northwest Passage in 1969, a Canadian icebreaker was conspicuously sent as an escort. Yet Canada does not really have the resources, on its own, to guard its vast land mass. This (along with the requirements associated with the need to defend the American nuclear deterrent) means that in strategic terms North America is considered a single unit.

While communications between the various Canadian regions are no longer a problem, the legacy of widely diverse and separated settlement has contributed to the regionalism that dominates Canada today. Indeed, the vastness of the country still works against efforts to promote national unity, particularly when regionalism finds an outlet in strong provincial governments. As will be shown below, the tendency on the part of the provincial governments to jealously guard (if not to expand) their constitutional powers complicates the formation and execution of some aspects of foreign policy.

DEMOGRAPHY

Demography also has an important impact on Canadian foreign policy. This is particularly the case with regard to the French-English division. Between the two world wars, Prime Minister Mackenzie King's tepid support of the League of Nations and of imperial defense schemes was due in part to his concern with healing the breach between English- and French-speaking Canadians created by the introduction of military conscription in 1917. "To him inaction was frequently the price of national unity."[17] During the 1960s President De Gaulle's appeals to francophone solidarity, and his injudicious "Vive le Québec libre" gesture in Montreal in 1967, brought forth a wave of indignation from English Canada that strained Canada's relations with France. In a more positive sense, however, there has been an effort on the part of Canada to have its foreign policy and conduct reflect the bilingual nature of the country. The business of the Department of External Affairs, even in Washington and London, is carried on in both French and English. In addition, aid to French-speaking underdeveloped countries has dramatically increased since 1963.

While the French (30.4 percent) and English (43.8 percent) constitute the vast majority of Canada's population, a full 22.6 percent is of other European origin. This is a widely diverse group, and thus its impact on foreign policy is not as great as that of the French and English groups. However, in its dealings with the Soviet Union and Communist countries, the government has been sensitive to some of the concerns of Canadians of East European origin, the Ukrainians in particular. Religious factors have occasionally had some impact on Canadian foreign policy—the Anglican Church of Canada traditionally supported imperial policies. More recently the denunciation of communism by the Catholic church did affect Canada's role in the cold war and was in part responsible for the delay in the recognition of the People's Republic of China. Generally, however, the distribution of population in Canada makes it difficult for the Canadian public as a whole to be effectively mobilized on foreign policy issues.

POLITICAL INSTITUTIONS

The diverse geographic and demographic Canadian environment is presided over by a parliamentary government that is the focal point of Canadian unity. Indeed, from a theoretical viewpoint, parliamentary-style government is most conducive to a unified foreign policy. As was seen in Chapter 3, the head of the government is the prime minister, who is the leader of the party with the most number of seats in the House of Commons (either a majority in the case of a majority government, or a plurality in the case of a minority government). The Prime Minister is also the head of a Cabinet selected (for the most part) from members of his party sitting in the House. Thus there is no sharp separation of powers as in the United States. Ultimately it is the Prime Minister, the Secretary of State for External Affairs, and other relevant ministers in their roles as Cabinet ministers who determine foreign policy. An illustration of the implications of this can be found in comments made by American Secretary of Defense James Forrestal in 1948 after he had met with the Canadian Cabinet's defense committee: "One of the deep impressions that I had as a result of this meeting was the contrast to the functioning of our government. . . . This group not merely was the Defence Committee of the Cabinet . . . but they represented the control of the Parliament, because they are the chosen Ministers of the Liberal Party now prevailing in power, as well as the chiefs of their respective agencies (departments).

Therefore expressions of policy at this meeting are the statements of a responsible government."[18]

This does not mean that the House of Commons itself cannot influence foreign policy. Because all members of the Cabinet, including the Prime Minister and the Secretary of State for External Affairs, normally sit in the House, they may be subject to direct questioning by members of the opposition parties. In addition, there is a Standing Committee on External Affairs and National Defence that has the power to call witnesses and issue reports. Lacking the extensive staff of the U.S. Senate Foreign Relations Committee or the House International Relations Committee, this Commons committee has lately been assisted by the privately run Parliamentary Centre for Foreign Affairs and Foreign Trade. In general, a Prime Minister with a majority in the House of Commons faces no serious challenge to the foreign policies he adopts. However, it is part of the political culture of Canada that the House be informed on matters of foreign policy and given a chance to debate issues, thereby bringing them to the public's attention.

While Canada's style of parliamentary government may lend itself to a unified approach to foreign policy, Canadian federalism does not. Although the intent of the Canadian constitution (the British North America Act) was to create a strongly centralized federation, subsequent judicial decisions reinforced by regionalizing political dynamics have made for a highly decentralized political structure. In terms of foreign policy, the judicial decisions of the Judicial Committee of the British Privy Council, until 1949 the final Canadian court of appeal, established the principle that the federal government may not by itself make—or at least implement—binding commitments with other countries except with regard to the subjects allocated to it in 1867 by the BNA Act. Among the subjects of provincial jurisdiction are human rights, education, and cultural affairs. Increasingly, and principally through the United Nations, these are becoming subjects of international negotiations.

Canada has responded by inviting provincial representatives to international conferences and allowing provincial officials to lead delegations. This naturally complicates the work of foreign service officials who often have to carry on two sets of negotiations, one with other countries and one with provincial representatives. While all Canadian provinces now act externally (Ontario was the first to have an office in London), it has been Quebec that has been most aggressive in asserting provincial autonomy in subjects of international negotiations that come under provincial jurisdiction (in particular, cultural and educational matters). Quebec has also sought to associate itself with other French-speaking countries, occasionally with awkward results. There was, for example, a mutual recall of ambassadors between Canada and Gabon when the latter approached the Quebec government directly without going through normal diplomatic channels. Such contretemps notwithstanding, even moderate Quebec leaders who advocate that the province remain in the Canadian Confederation call for an increased role for Quebec, and for all provinces, in foreign affairs.

ECONOMICS
Intrinsic to Canada's survival as a distinct national entity has always been the creation and maintenance of a viable domestic economy. Here, too, internal considerations have a bearing on foreign policy. While wealthy in terms of resources, Canada has always been short on the necessary capital to exploit those resources. At first, the country was dependent on Britain to provide that capital. Gradually, however, most especially since the 1920s, Canada had relied on massive inflows of American capital. The result has been extensive American ownership in certain key sectors of the Canadian economy such as petroleum, mining and smelting, and secondary manufacturing. Some Canadians see this as a threat to Canadian independence and ultimately to Canada's survival as a distinct national entity. However, attempts by the government to protect Canadian economic independence must necessarily be tempered by concern for continued economic growth and the demands of Canadians for an ever higher standard of living.

Another long-standing feature of the Canadian economy

that has affected foreign policy is its open economy. Canada's first international dealings were to secure markets for its staples. Roughly 50 percent of the GNP is involved in imports and exports. Here again, Canada is dependent on the United States which bought 67.5 percent of all the country's exports in 1976 (up from 65 percent in 1970). This heavy dependence on the American market inevitably produces calls for a more nationalistic foreign economic policy aimed at decreasing this dependency. The "contractual link" signed with the European Economic Community in July 1976 was a concrete manifestation of the Liberal government's intention of diversifying Canadian trade. Yet the sheer volume of the transborder flow with the United States makes it unlikely that any appreciable shift will occur, thus placing a premium on other efforts to assert Canadian distinctiveness.

Canadian Foreign Policy Objectives

It is always difficult to identify the foreign policy objectives of a nation without becoming so general and platitudinous as to render the entire exercise meaningless. And yet, it is important to understand the objectives and principles that serve as both a conceptual foundation and a prescriptive framework for a nation acting in the international community. All nations of course have such objectives and principles, if only implicitly. However, in the case of Canada, we are more fortunate, for Canadian governmental officials have themselves publicly attempted to explicitly identify and define their objectives in 1947 and 1970. While discussing these as exemplars, however, it should be remembered that we are dealing not just with stated principles and objectives but also with domestic forces (as discussed in the preceding section) and international forces (which will be discussed in the next section).

CANADIAN OBJECTIVES IN 1947
In 1947 a Canadian leader boldly and publicly put forth what he saw as Canada's postwar role in the international com-

munity. The occasion was the first Duncan and John Gray Memorial Lecture at the University of Toronto, and the speaker was the Right Honourable Louis St. Laurent, Secretary of State for External Affairs. The lecture was entitled "The Foundations of Canadian Policy in World Affairs," and in it Mr. St. Laurent enunciated five basic principles that guided Canada in its dealings abroad.[19] Significantly, the first principle was that Canada's "external policies shall not destroy our unity." The second guiding principle was a commitment to "political liberty," while the third was respect for the "rule of law." Fourth, Canadian foreign policy would be in accordance with the "conceptions of good and evil which emerge from Hebrew and Greek civilizations and which have been transformed and transmitted through the Christian traditions of the Western world." The fifth basic principle was a "willingness to accept international responsibilities," for as St. Laurent stated, "security" for Canada lay in the "development of a firm structure of international organization."

Mr. St. Laurent then went on to outline the practical application of the basic principles of Canadian foreign policy. First, referring to the uniqueness of the Commonwealth and to the special pride Canadians could take in its achievements, he stated that Canada would seek to preserve it as "an instrument through which we, with others who share our objectives, can co-operate for our common good in peace as in war." Mr. St. Laurent pointed to the informal nature of the Commonwealth arrangements and noted that Canada would resist any efforts to "reduce to formal terms or specific commitments the common understanding upon which it is based." Nor would Canada allow its Commonwealth ties to prevent the country from participating fully "in the task of building an effective international organization on a wider scale."

Within the Commonwealth, Mr. St. Laurent pointed to Canada's relations with the United Kingdom as having "a very special value and significance." Remembering the "imaginative collaboration of British and Canadian leaders . . . who laid the political foundation for the modern Commonwealth," and the Canadian political heritage as well as the common struggle during the "dark days" of 1940, Canada would now work together with Britain for the establishment of a world order based on the principles of freedom.

The second application of the principles underpinning Canadian external relations concerned the United States and the U.S.-Canadian relationship. Mr. St. Laurent outlined the two main characteristics of Canadian policy toward the United States. The first was to settle by negotiation, compromise, and arbitration the problems that may arise between the two countries. Second, Canada recognized its responsibility as a North American nation to contribute to the welfare of the continent. While acknowledging that "regionalism" would not provide the answers to the problems of world security, Mr. St. Laurent stressed that "people living side by side" on the same continent could not ignore each other's interests. As with the United States, Canadian relations rested upon principles that "have emerged clearly from our history." As one of the "fountainheads" of Canadian cultural life, France formed an integral part of the framework of Canadian international life.

The third practical application of Canadian foreign policy principles concerned the support of constructive international organizations. Mr. St. Laurent noted that while Canada was willing to take its part in constructive international action, it had to bear in mind the limitations upon the influence of any secondary power. "No society of nations," he went on, "can prosper if it does not have the support of those who hold the major share of the world's military and economic power. There is little point in a country of our stature recommending international action, if those who must carry the major burden of whatever action is taken are not in sympathy."

Nevertheless, Canada was willing to play its role when international action was taken. St. Laurent went on to list the forums in which Canada had already demonstrated its willingness to support international actions, ranging from the World Bank, UNESCO, and the Civil Aviation Organization (whose headquarters was located in Canada), to the work of the International Atomic Energy Agency. Canada had also been a large contributor to international relief agencies such as UNRRA. Worldwide economic revival was important for

Canada itself, for it was "dependent on markets abroad for the large quantities of staple products we produce and cannot consume," and "on supplies from abroad of the commodities which are essential to our well being." Thus, Canada would give its support "to every international organization which contributes to the economic and political stability of the world."

Mr. St. Laurent went on to note the fourth application of Canadian foreign policy principles—the development of an effective diplomatic service. He noted that Canada had expanded its representation abroad and was building up the Department of External Affairs in Ottawa. He called for a foreign policy that would not be a matter of political controversy at home. In its external relations the government would strive to speak and to act on behalf of the whole of Canada and with the support of all Canadians. Above all, Canada must act abroad as a united people, a people "who, through reflection and discussion, have arrived at a common understanding of our interests and our purposes."

Foreign Minister St. Laurent's identification of the five principles of Canadian foreign policy (national unity, political liberty, rule of law, values of Christian civilization, and the acceptance of international responsibility) served Canada well throughout the post–World War II period of "Quiet Diplomacy." The application of these principles (in the Commonwealth, in dealings with the United States, in support of international organizations, especially the United Nations, and in the development of an effective and growing diplomatic service) resulted in a Canadian international role that was as active as it was constructive. Indeed, Canada came to be identified, both by its own citizens and by foreign observers, as a "middle power" par excellence. This meant that although Canada was not a super or great power, it certainly was not a small power, and had a unique role to play as a mediator in international disputes, most clearly illustrated in Canada's contribution to peacekeeping.

CANADIAN OBJECTIVES IN 1970

By the mid- and late 1960s "some of the safe assumptions of the post-war decades were crumbling away as the world changed," to quote the Trudeau foreign policy review begun early in 1968.[20] The ideological rigidities and power groupings of the cold war began to soften; the Third World began to exert itself with vigorous demands; science and technology had made startling advances in such areas as weapons, communications, and space travel; social attitudes seemed to be tending toward greater confrontation; and institutions were increasingly troubled by divergences and criticism. Nor were these changes confined to the international system. Internally, Canada had its own need to respond to changes in the economy, to regional disparities, and to the ramifications of the "Quiet Revolution" in Quebec. Increasingly, there was a renewed sense of Canadian nationalism coupled with a crescendo of complaints about U.S. cultural and economic influences on Canada, which in turn was fed by Canadian disenchantment with the protracted American involvement in Vietnam and the ensuing social disorders in the United States. In short, Canada's traditional postwar role in a rapidly changing international system had to be reevaluated, in the late 1960s, in the light of significant alterations in the international system as well as in North America. The Trudeau foreign policy review perhaps best captured all this with its observation:

> Policy had not remained static since the war; it had been adjusting to the changing world and to Canada's changing needs. It had served the country well. But an empirical process of adjustment cannot be continued indefinitely. There comes a time for renewal and in 1968 the Government saw that for Canada's foreign policy the time had arrived.[21]

Pierre Elliott Trudeau became Prime Minister in 1968. Upon taking power, one of his first acts was the initiation of a comprehensive foreign policy review, in fulfillment of his campaign promise that "We shall seek a new role for Canada and a new foreign policy based on a fresh appraisal of this rapidly-changing world and on a realistic assessment of Canada's potential."[22] In June 1970, twenty-five months after the inception of the foreign policy review, the Canadian government published the results of its reexamination in the form of a collection of booklets with the overall title, *Foreign Policy*

for Canadians. The collection consisted of a general booklet
that laid out the conceptual framework that was to serve as
the basis for future foreign policy, and five sector booklets
entitled *Latin America, Europe, Pacific, United Nations,* and
International Development.

The foreign policy review first identified three fundamental national aims that encompass the primary preoccu-
pations of Canada and Canadians:

— that Canada will continue secure as an independent political entity;
— that Canada and all Canadians will enjoy enlarging prosperity in the widest possible sense;
— that all Canadians will see in the life they have and the
   contribution they make to humanity something worthwhile
   preserving in identity and purpose.[23]

The review then proceeded to identify six policy themes
that constitute the broad aims of Canadian foreign policy:
foster economic growth, safeguard sovereignty and independence, work for peace and security, promote social justice, enhance the quality of life, and ensure a harmonious natural
environment.[24] These six policy themes, although general in
nature, are extremely significant on two counts. First, having
noted that "There is no natural, immutable or permanent role
for Canada in today's world,"[25] the review argued that Canada's role abroad is to be determined by the emphasis which
Canadian policymakers place on these six themes (coupled of
course with Canadian capabilities and the constraints that
prevail at any given time within Canada and within the international system). Second, these themes are significant in
that they both emphasize and illustrate the point that "foreign
policy is the extension abroad of national policy."[26] Rather
than being preoccupied with exerting international influence,
foreign policy is now internationally oriented, so that the
touchstone of the success of Canadian foreign policy will be
the extent to which it contributes to Canada's national well-
being, including especially the need for national unity.

At the time of its publication in 1970, the Trudeau foreign

policy review met with criticism on two counts—it said nothing new, and it downgraded Canada's relations with the United States by not having a separate booklet on Canadian-U.S. relations. Although partly justified, the first criticism somewhat missed the point. One of the purposes of the review was to systematically and publicly identify the conceptual bases of Canadian foreign policy in a changing international system; and this aspect of the review has an enduring quality. It is impossible to study contemporary Canadian foreign policy seriously without examining the concepts and principles contained in the 1970 review. In addition, the process involved in the review was in itself important in that the entire nation became a sort of classroom of foreign policy where different groups, ranging from scholars to businessmen, made representation. Policy themes were struck, for example, with the rejection of a "helpful fixer" role and the necessity of identifying "countervailing" forces to offset the predominance of the United States. Subsequently, significant changes in Canadian foreign policy, not perhaps direct products of the review, occurred in an atmosphere of reexamination the review very much helped to create. Examples include Canadian recognition of the People's Republic of China (in effect before the review was published), the Canadian 50 percent force reduction in NATO, the establishment of diplomatic relations with the Vatican, and the establishment of an observer status at the Organization of American States in lieu of full membership. Indeed, the entire period of the early 1970s was a period of reassessment, with the government producing such papers as the 1971 defense review, the 1972 Gray Report on direct foreign investment in Canada, and reevaluations and new policies in the cultural sector.

Moreover, the Trudeau review had a major organizational impact on the formulation and implementation of Canadian foreign policy. It stated that "there should be maximum integration in its [Canada's] foreign operations that will effectively contribute to the achievement of national objectives."[27] This has had several implications for the conduct of Canada's foreign policy, both at home and abroad. An Interdepartmental Committee on External Relations was created and made responsible for guiding the process of managerial integration as well as synthesizing departmental planning and allocating resources of foreign operations. Departmental reorganizations followed, and the predominance of the ambassadors as heads of post abroad was reaffirmed.

The second criticism of the Trudeau foreign policy review—that it ignored the United States as the most important external component of Canadian foreign policy—was shortly corrected. In the autumn of 1972, an entire issue of *International Perspectives*, the periodical of the Department of External Affairs, appeared under the authorship of Secretary of State for External Affairs Mitchell Sharp, entitled "Canada-U.S. Relations: Options for the Future." Although this extremely important synthesis will be discussed in the section on Canadian-U.S. relations, suffice it to say at this point that the "third option" was chosen, "a comprehensive long-range strategy to develop and strengthen the Canadian economy and other aspects of our national life and in the process to reduce the present Canadian vulnerability to the United States."[28] Although this paper was successful in articulating the historic Canadian concern about the impact of the United States, it proved to have a short life as a policy paper. Even the term "third option" was dropped from the Canadian foreign policy lexicon as the decade of the 1970s progressed, a process that was hastened with the November 1976 electoral victory of René Lévesque in Quebec with his commitment to national sovereignty. Quite simply, distinctiveness from the United States seemed then to be less important than the maintenance of national unity—an enigma, since the latter surely rests partly on an awareness of the former.

CANADIAN OBJECTIVES AND CANADIAN ACTION

While it is useful to survey the objectives of Canadian foreign policy in 1947 and in 1970, the question remains: How have these objectives been reflected in Canada's international posture? In the most basic sense, we can identify six areas in which Canada has been, and continues to be, an active international actor: the economic (including energy), strategic, peacekeeping, disarmament/arms control, development assistance, and Law of the Sea.

Economically, the fact that nearly one half of the Canadian gross national product is accounted for by imports and exports means that Canada has a vital interest in trade and in the larger international economic system. Perhaps more important, in 1976 Canadian imports came from three major trading blocs. The United States accounted for the bulk of Canada's imports (68.7 percent). Next came the countries of the European Economic Community, led by Britain and West Germany, with the EEC as a whole supplying 8.5 percent of Canada's imports. Although Canada's trade with Japan had increased rapidly, it still accounted for just 4.1 percent of all imports. Significantly, in 1976 the rest of the world accounted for only 18.7 percent of all Canadian imports. On the export side, the United States was overwhelmingly dominant, taking 67.6 percent of all Canadian exports. Once again, Europe was second, absorbing 11.9 percent while Japan took 6.3 percent of Canadian exports, mainly in the form of raw materials. The rest of the world took only 14.2 percent of all Canadian exports. It is obvious therefore that Canada's main economic area of interest is first with the United States, followed by the other industrialized countries in the world, a fact that holds not only for trade but also direct Canadian investment. On the energy side, it is not so certain that Canada and the United States share similar needs and goals—recent pipeline agreements for transporting natural gas from the Alaskan north slope and the Canadian Mackenzie Delta, including the Canadian decision in July 1980 to proceed with the southernmost "prebuild" section of the line, have revealed deep disagreement, even within Canada, on this score. Energy resources, and their pricing, are likely to be a source of controversy and hard negotiating between the provinces and Ottawa, and between Ottawa and Washington, for years to come. From the Canadian standpoint, however, the United States will probably continue to be an important source of capital for the development of Canadian energy resources.

Strategically, we have seen that Canada can be classified as a significant international actor. Because of its proximity to the United States, and its interests in collective security (which includes its formal military ties through NATO and NORAD), Canada has a vital interest in the prevention of conflicts that may lead to a confrontation between the United States and the USSR. This concern extends well beyond North America, since with the assumption of U.S. leadership in the West, anything the United States does anywhere in the world can affect Canadian interests.

We have also seen that Canada contributes to international order through peacekeeping. Throughout the post–World War II period, Canada has been a major contributor to peacekeeping under the auspices of both the United Nations and the International Control Commission in Indochina. By the late 1960s and early 1970s, however, the Canadian government had taken a closer look at Canada's role in peacekeeping and had concluded that "a major factor affecting the Government's decision would be the existence of realistic terms of reference."[29] Nevertheless, in 1973 Canada was asked by the United States to help supervise the shaky Paris Peace accords that ended the Vietnam War. It will be recalled that Canada had been involved in truce supervision in Indochina since 1954. These earlier efforts had largely collapsed by 1968. It was therefore with great reservation that Canada accepted, and was to withdraw within six months with a sense of frustration. Still, Canada did agree to participate in the United Nations forces that went into operation in the October 1973 Arab-Israeli War and in Lebanon in 1978. Government statements in the late 1970s were significantly devoid of the kind of rhetoric that accompanied past peacekeeping operations, perhaps reflecting a more sober, experienced approach. Speaking before the Canadian Arab Federation in May 1976, former External Affairs Minister MacEachen stated that the Canadian objective was simply to do "whatever it can to make a positive contribution to a possible peaceful solution."[30] This is a limited objective, but one that is realistically in line with the nature and scope of modern peacekeeping.

The Canadian commitment to international order goes beyond peacekeeping to include disarmament and arms control. Canada has been extremely active at the Conference of the Committee on Disarmament that has been in progress in Geneva since 1962. This committee is one of the major forums for negotiating multilateral arms control agreements, and from it have come such developments as the 1963 limited test ban treaty, the 1968 nonproliferation treaty, the 1971 seabed arms control treaty, and the 1972 biological-weapons convention. The approach of the Canadian government to arms control was well stated by Canada's former representative to Geneva:

> The aims of Canada at Geneva have been pragmatic and have had to recognize the limitation imposed on Canadian initiative which results from being an ally of the United States, both in Europe as well as for purposes of North American defence. . . . Thus in pursuit of our pragmatic but catalytic course, Canada has put first priority on ending the nuclear arms race, and first and foremost on ending nuclear testing, which is the outward and visible sign of the ongoing contest.[31]

Short of arms control, Canada has also been a significant actor in encouraging a greater degree of détente in the international community. Canada was not only involved in the Conference on Security and Cooperation in Europe (CSCE), which culminated in the August 1975 Helsinki agreements; it has also pursued a lessening of cold war tensions unilaterally through, for example, the diplomatic recognition of the People's Republic of China, the reciprocal 1971 visits of the Canadian prime minister and the Soviet premier, and the subsequent signing of a protocol of understanding with the USSR.

Canada also has a profound commitment to peaceful and orderly development in the Third World. Indeed, Canada was one of the first Western nations to develop a comprehensive developmental assistance program with other Commonwealth countries in the early 1950s through the Colombo Plan. Since then, the Canadian aid program has increased dramatically.[32] By 1974–75, Canadian official development assistance represented 0.52 percent of the GNP ($742 million), while the official United Nations target stands at 0.7 percent of the GNP. Canada's aid was disbursed as follows: 45.7 percent bilateral; 24.5 percent multilateral; 23.6 percent food aid; 6.2

percent other forms of disbursement. As of 1974–75, 49.5 percent of Canadian aid went to Asia; 22.1 percent went to Commonwealth Africa; 20.1 percent went to francophone Africa; 4.5 percent went to the Caribbean; while 4.3 percent went to Latin America.

Two major targets for Canadian developmental assistance are the Commonwealth and *la francophonie*. The first Dominion in the Empire, Canada had of course been a leader in the evolution of the Commonwealth in this century. One period of crisis occurred just after World War II, when long frustrated desires for independence exploded in India and Pakistan. Canada played a major role in the redefinition of the Commonwealth, whereby India could become a republic and yet remain within the Commonwealth. During the 1960s, former African colonies also became independent, thereby adding to the Commonwealth's membership and reinforcing its multiracial character. A crisis was averted in 1961 when South Africa decided to withdraw from the Commonwealth owing to criticism of its apartheid racial policies from other members (including Canada). Canada has been active in Commonwealth developmental plans from the beginning, and also is involved in such functional bodies as the Commonwealth Fund for Technical Cooperation, the Commonwealth Foundation, the Commonwealth Young Program, and the Commonwealth Games.

Of more recent origin, but of equal importance to Canada's foreign policy, is the development in the late 1960s of *la francophonie*—countries that are either wholly or partly French- speaking. The Canadian government became increasingly involved in *la francophonie* in an attempt to reflect Canada's bilingual nature abroad. Aid programs dramatically increased, and Canada and Quebec played major roles in such multilateral organizations as the Agency for Cultural and Technical Cooperation, founded in 1970 in Niger. The agency remains the keystone of the French community's international organization, although there are such other active bodies as the Conference of Education Ministers and the Conference of the Ministers of Youth and Sports from French-speaking countries. The *francophonie* dimension is also reflected on the provincial level, Quebec (as well as Ontario, New Brunswick, and Manitoba) having participated in the convention establishing the agency, Quebec has the status of "participating government" in the agency's institutions and programs.

In addition to developmental assistance, Canada has been especially active in framing an international law governing all aspects of the use of the sea, including such dimensions as the extent of a nation's sovereignty over the sea, the extent of a nation's exclusive rights over fishing and other resources, marine pollution and the protection of marine life against extinction, the settlement of maritime disputes, the exploitation of the areas beyond a nation's jurisdiction, and the role of developing countries in deep-sea exploration. Beginning in 1958 the United Nations organized major conferences on the Law of the Sea in an attempt to establish an international regime that would deal with these dimensions. Canada has been a major actor in all three conferences (1958, 1960, 1974 to the present) and has taken the initiative in other international forums as well as implementing its own national legislation. Canada's overall approach to Law of the Sea has been described by the word "functional," meaning that there should be specific jurisdictions for specific purposes (e.g., a fishing zone, a pollution zone, etc.) rather than full sovereignty for all purposes on the part of the coastal state's declared territorial sea.

In January 1977, Canada's extension of its jurisdiction over fisheries to the two-hundred-mile limit came into effect. This means that Canada is the "owner and manager" of all fisheries within two hundred miles of its coasts. Similarly, Canada has been especially active in national and international pollution controls. In 1970 Canada passed the Arctic Waters Pollution Prevention Act by which it claimed jurisdiction for the prevention and control of pollution within one hundred miles of its Arctic coasts, and through similar legislation it acquired jurisdiction over special areas off Canada's east and west coasts. At the same time, Canada favored a more comprehensive approach than was provided by the Intergovernmental Maritime Consultative Organization, which administers several international conventions regulating oil pollution from shipping. A significant step was the Declaration on the Human Environment that resulted from the 1972 United Nations' Stockholm Conference. Canada's position is that while there must be internationally agreed upon pollution standards, the coastal states including Canada must themselves be enpowered to adopt and enforce their own standards above international rules when necessary.

With this as background, it is useful to now explore individually the regions of the world to assess Canadian interests and levels of activity.

The Range of Canada's External Relations

For Americans accustomed to thinking of their country as a superpower with interests throughout the world, it may be difficult to appreciate the fact that a medium-sized nation like Canada has a range of foreign relations that are also global in scope. The difference between American and Canadian external relations lies not so much in the number of geographic areas in which the two countries have interests, as in the intensity of interests and the extent to which each country can influence the course of events in other areas of the globe. Canada does not have as many areas of "vital interests" as does the United States, nor does it have the means to play a major role in the resolution of diverse international issues. Nonetheless, as this review of the range of Canada's relations will illustrate, Canada is highly active internationally.[33]

WESTERN HEMISPHERE

Before the United States was a global power it was a Western Hemispheric power, and it continues to dominate that hemisphere (including Latin America). Because of this, coupled with Canada's geographical isolation within the Western Hemisphere, it is not surprising to find that the range of Canada's relations and interests with Latin America are relatively limited. Trade between Canada and Latin America amounts to less than $1.3 billion (as compared with more than $60 billion between Canada and the United States). In part the lack of relations between Canada and Latin America is the product of divergent histories.[34] It was not until World War II, when the lines of communication with Europe were ruptured, that Canada began formal diplomatic relations with South America.[35] For a number of years the United States was opposed to Canadian membership in the Pan-American Union (largely on the grounds that at that time, that is, 1928, Canada was not a fully sovereign nation and was still closely tied to England). When the Pan-American Union became the Organization of American States, Canada refused the invitation to join. The country was already a member of a number of international organizations; its natural orientation was toward Europe; and there was a concern that membership in the OAS would have restricted Canadian freedom of action, particularly concerning Cuba (with whom Canada, unlike the United States, continued diplomatic relations with the advent of Castro). At present, Canada is a permanent observer to the OAS along with a number of other countries from outside the hemisphere. Canada also contributes to the Inter-American Development Bank.

In 1975, of Canada's total South American trade, 82.4 percent was with Brazil and Venezuela, the latter constituting the bulk of Canada's trade with South America in the form of crude oil, the former being the location of long-standing Canadian direct investment. On the diplomatic front there is a good deal of interaction with Latin American countries through international agencies associated with the United Nations. Canadian and South American diplomats very often find themselves cooperating as moderators at the United Nations. However, in recent years the level of direct diplomatic contacts through Canadian representation in Latin America has been reduced. This has largely been a result of budgetary restrictions and the increased Canadian interest, because of domestic politics, in the developing countries of francophone Africa.[36]

The major area of Canadian interest in the Western Hemisphere, apart from the United States, is the Caribbean, particularly with those communities that are (or were) British dependencies.[37] Trade relations with this area go back well before Canadian Confederation in 1867. At that time there were close commercial links between the Maritimes and the British West Indies. Today trade is relatively small (roughly $200 million in 1974), although Canada has been active in the fields of transportation and education, and there is a great deal of tourism. Some Canadian development assistance goes to the Caribbean, and there are a number of cooperative and reciprocal programs in the area of national defense.[38]

It is interesting to note that since the 1880s there have been various movements to bring some of the British Caribbean into the Canadian Confederation. As late as 1968, there were resolutions in the Canadian Parliament calling for political union.[39] In part such movements, which originated in some Caribbean nations as well as in Canada, were motivated by commercial investment considerations. Lately, however, as a number of Caribbean states began to identify with the demands of the Third World, there have been difficulties in Canadian-Caribbean relations. Canadians, so accustomed to voicing concern over American corporate imperialism in Canada, were themselves accused of imperialistic actions through large Canadian-owned direct investments, in particular in banks and aluminum production, in the Caribbean. The situation was exacerbated when difficulties arose in Canada because of the perceptible increase in immigrants from the Caribbean.

EUROPE
If in the Western Hemisphere Canada is a regional power without a region, the country is nevertheless a vital part of what has been referred to as the "North Atlantic Community." This region is composed of Canada, the United States, and the industrial democracies of Western Europe, with the latter mostly having membership in the European Economic Community. In 1976 the EEC was Canada's second-largest trading partner, accounting for 11.9 percent of exports and 8.5 percent

of imports. The countries of the EEC are part of the Organization for Economic Cooperation and Development (OECD), which also includes other industrial nations outside Europe including Canada, the United States, and Japan. As has been discussed above, Canada was one of the initiators and continues to support the North Atlantic Treaty Organization.

Historically, Canadian ties to Europe have run through Great Britain. Canadian political institutions are based on an adaptation of the British model, and the British monarch also serves as symbolic Canadian head of state and the link to the Commonwealth. Canadians, of course, have on their own accord elected to retain the Crown, which still continues to symbolize "a common heritage, common institutions and a common approach to public affairs."[40] Since World War II, however, and more particularly since Britain entered the European Community, the actual conduct of Anglo-Canadian relations has tended to be less "special." Although Canada is represented in Britain by a High Commission, its function is the same as all other Canadian diplomatic posts abroad. There remains, nevertheless, one particular constitutional link between the two countries that has of late come to the fore because of the recent Canadian efforts to adjust the British North American Act (the constitution). Amendments to certain sections of the BNA Act still require the consent of the British Parliament. The reason why this anomaly has not been removed is simply that the Canadian provinces and the federal government have not been able to agree on the method to amend the act. In 1980 Prime Minister Pierre Trudeau vowed to "repatriate" the constitution by unilateral federal action if a series of summer meetings and conferences failed to end this stalemate. By mid-September that failure was a fact.

Although like Britain, France is one of the "mother countries" of Canada, relations with France have never attained the same degree of intimacy as with Great Britain.[41] This was largely due to the fact that after the British Conquest in 1763, metropolitan France had little interest in the French-speaking people of Quebec. Current Canadian relations with France largely originated in the post–World War II era when Canada, through NATO and with contributions to European reconstruction, took an active interest in Europe. Today relations with France are mainly the result of that country's culture and language, and its leading place in the European Economic Community.

During the 1960s relations between France and Canada became strained as a result of the rise of nationalism in Quebec and concurrent demands for an increased international role for that province. General De Gaulle extended welcomes to visiting Quebec governmental officials usually accorded only to representatives of national governments. On a visit to Montreal, made in conjunction with Canada's centenary celebrations, De Gaulle shouted the Quebec separatist slogan "Vive le Québec libre" (long live a free Quebec), thereby initiating a diplomatic crisis. It is instructive of the Canadian paradox to note that the Canadian counteroffensive to General De Gaulle's strategy was directed by French-Canadian Prime Minister Pierre Eliott Trudeau and his francophone associates. Whereas De Gaulle had sought to bring Quebec into the larger French-speaking world, the federal government, through the Department of External Affairs, sought to bring Canada as a whole into *la francophonie*.

The early 1970s saw an improvement in relations with France and an effort on the part of French leaders to avoid exacerbating Canadian unity problems. It was at this time also that Canada began to seek closer economic ties with the European Community as part of its Third Option policy. However, in the fall of 1977 René Lévesque, the separatist Premier of Quebec, was given a lavish state welcome by Giscard d'Estaing, who presented him with the Legion of Honor. While it would seem that the French president was motivated more by wanting to gain support within France from the Gaullist faction of his coalition than by a desire to promote French-Canadian nationalism, the action was seen in English Canada as needlessly provocative.

As with France, Canada's relations with the Federal Republic of Germany are in the context of NATO and trade with the EEC. In the late 1960s there appeared to be an identity of interests with regard to NATO when German Chancellor

Willy Brandt began to implement his *Ostpolitik* aimed at reducing tensions between East and West Europe. This was complementary to Canadian reductions in its contribution to NATO forces. However, in recent years the Germans have been demanding that Canada increase its NATO commitment to the army on the Rhine. While Germany is Canada's fourth-largest trading partner, Germany constitutes only 4.2 percent of Canada's total trade, quite small indeed given the size of the respective economies.

Canada also has good relations with other Western European countries. Relations with Holland are particularly warm owing to the fact that former Queen (then Princess) Juliana and her family spent their years of exile during World War II in Canada, and Canadian troops played a leading role in the liberation of Holland. At the United Nations, Canadian and Scandanavian diplomats frequently work together in a mediating capacity. Belgium, like Canada, is a bilingual nation; and Canada's ties with Italy have been strengthened by the massive immigration from that country.

Canada's two main ties to Europe, trade and NATO, have been given particular emphasis in Canadian foreign policy. Stronger trade links to the European Community were regarded as an important component of Canada's third option approach (whereby the country attempts to expand relations with other areas of the world in order to reduce the overwhelming dependency on the United States). While it remains questionable whether or not Canada can appreciably reduce its vulnerability to the United States, it is evident that only the European Economic Community offers the trade potential necessary. Accordingly, in June 1976 Canada and the EEC signed a "contractual link" whereby the two parties pledged themselves to closer commercial and financial cooperation and went so far as to establish a joint committee to further increase economic links. The substantive results of the agreement have yet to be realized because of the general malaise affecting both economies. Another aim of the link, however, was to force the European allies to recognize that Canada had to be dealt with independent of the United States—a familiar use of diplomacy to promote recognition of status. It was also hoped that this would offset a growing European tendency to see NATO as divided into two components—European and (North) American.

Canada appears to have paid a price for this link and recognition. In the early 1970s Canada cut back its commitment to the army on the Rhine, leaving there only one armored brigade (roughly five thousand troops) and a tactical jet fighter squadron. It allowed the equipment for these units to fall behind the times. Germany in particular was concerned about Canada's faltering commitment to Europe, and there are indications that Canada was given its contractual link only after it had agreed to upgrade substantially the quality of its equipment. Canada has now begun to resupply its troops in Europe with the latest German Leopard tank; will shortly purchase new fighter aircraft; will build six new destroyer naval craft, which will be used to fulfill commitments to NATO's Supreme Allied Command Atlantic (SACLANT); and has recently purchased a new long-range patrol aircraft, the Lockheed P-3 Aurora. As expensive as this reemphasis on NATO is, it is not inconsistent with Canada's long-standing commitment to collective security through the North Atlantic Alliance. So long as Canada desires to diversify its external relations, the best opportunity for this seems to rest in closer ties with Europe, regardless of the apparent failure of the Third Option per se.

THE SOVIET UNION AND EASTERN EUROPE

Canada's introduction to the Soviet Union took place during the Allied Siberian intervention in World War I, when Canada acceded to the British request that it supply forces to help overthrow the Communist government. During the interwar period, the Canadian approach toward the Soviet Union was distant and cautious, although there was limited trade and for a short period trade representatives were exchanged.[42] In the 1920s Canada granted *de jure* recognition, but later in the decade severed relations. In the 1930s Canada applied an economic embargo against several Soviet products, which it repealed later in the decade. It was during the World War II period that Canadian-Soviet relations substantially improved; Canada gave a significant amount of aid assistance to the Soviet Union, and diplomatic representatives were exchanged.

Canadian postwar policy toward Moscow was complementary to that of the United States and other Western nations, and followed the ups and downs of the cold war period from the "Spirit of Geneva" to the post–Cuban missile crisis thaw. In the immediate postwar period, Soviet espionage activities in Canada resulted in a serious deterioration of the bilateral relationship. Nevertheless, Canada was more inclined than the United States to transcend the ideological differences between the West and the USSR. Canadian External Affairs Minister Lester Pearson was the first NATO foreign minister to visit the Soviet Union in 1955, and in 1956 a Canadian-Soviet trade pact was concluded. Other wheat sales followed—in 1963 the largest annual sale of Canadian wheat in Canadian history went to the Soviet Union. By 1971 Canadian Prime Minister Trudeau could visit Moscow (the first Canadian Prime Minister to do so), with Premier Kosygin visiting Canada in return. Political, technological, and cultural protocols were signed, followed by the establishment of a joint Canadian-Soviet fisheries commission and political consultations on a number of multilateral issues. Yet in spite of the normalization of Canadian-Soviet relations, such problems as human rights continue to plague the relationship, and the frequent cultural and scientific exchanges have not been without difficulties. Canada's approach toward the Soviet Union has evolved, therefore, from one of suspicious hostility to suspicious coexistence.

The same can be said for Canada's approach toward the countries of Eastern Europe. Canada's relationship with Eastern Europe changed in the context of East-West relations, passing through the wartime alliance, the cold war, and détente. Although not extensive in a relative sense, Canada's ties with Poland constitute the greatest single set of trade and cultural interactions. For example, Canadian trade with Poland makes up more than 40 percent of Canadian exports to Eastern Europe. On the import side, Canadian trade with

Eastern Europe is very small, with Czechoslovakia being the largest single country of origin (constituting some 25 percent of Canada's imports from Eastern Europe). Overall, Canadian trade with Eastern Europe constitutes less than 0.6 percent of total Canadian trade. Affecting Canada's relations with Eastern Europe has been a large number of refugees who sought asylum in Canada, thereby constituting a vocal, anticommunist constituency of some consequence to politicians.

THE MIDDLE EAST

Canada's involvement in the Middle East dates back to the post–World War II period and the beginning of the Middle East crisis. From 1946 to 1948, Lester Pearson and other Canadian diplomats were active on the United Nations' Palestine Commission, which attempted to settle the Arab-Jewish dispute. After the Israeli War of Independence in 1948–49, Canada contributed to the Truce Supervisory Organization established by the United Nations. In the years following, Canada accorded recognition to Israel and supplied some military equipment. As we have seen, the Suez crisis of 1956 brought about increased Canadian involvement in the region through United Nations peacekeeping efforts.

Peacekeeping represents Canada's determination to aid the ongoing diplomatic efforts to arrive at a just solution in the Middle East. It is a limited commitment, but one entirely consistent with the limited influence Canada can bring to bear (even though Canada, like most of the Western nations, has a very important overall interest in a peaceful solution to this long-standing international dispute). The fact that a new round of fighting in the region could lead to a confrontation between the superpowers is of key importance to Canada.

With respect to the Arab-Israeli conflict itself, the government, generally reflecting public sentiment, has always supported the continued existence within secure borders of a Jewish state in Israel. At the United Nations, Canada has opposed efforts to isolate Israel, and there have been significant resolutions passed in the House of Commons in support of Israel, that is, the condemnation of the UN's "zionism equals racism" resolution. As in the United States, the Canadian Jewish community constitutes an important pressure group. Although only numbering 265,000, it is well organized and overwhelmingly pro-Zionist. Despite this fact, perhaps due to energy considerations, Canadian policy has become more sensitive to the Palestinian problem and supports moderate efforts to resolve it which do not threaten Israel's security. However, the scope for Canadian influence remains limited.[43]

Since 1973 Canada has also expanded its economic ties with the Middle East's wealthy oil-producing states. By 1975, total Canadian trade with the Middle East was $2.64 billion, making them the sixth- and seventh-largest Canadian trading partners. Petroleum from the Persian Gulf was temporarily cut off when Canada became a target of the Arab oil embargo, and although the oil is now reaching Canada, its high price has compelled the country to seek greater exports to the oil producers as a means to pay for this energy.

AFRICA

Because of its colonial heritage, with many countries being either former British or French colonies, Africa offers Canada a unique opportunity to conduct a foreign policy reflective of the bilingual nature of the country. In fact, Canada's involvement in Africa results less from direct Canadian interests in the region than it does in broader concerns. As one author has nicely pointed out, Canadian policies toward Africa concerned such generic issues as the desires to maintain a strong Western alliance against the Soviet bloc, encourage the growth of the Commonwealth, locate markets for Canadian goods and outlets for Canadian investment, and create a favorable image of Canada as a nonracist state.[44] Certainly it is difficult to make the case that trade is a significant factor for Canadian-African relations, for Canada's trade with that region consists of some 1 percent of Canada's total world trade. The same holds true for Canadian investment in Africa (which accounts for only some 2 or 3 percent of Canada's total foreign investment).

Prior to the late 1950s, Canada had little interest in the region apart from its historical Commonwealth ties, and generally followed the lead of other Western nations. However, with the emergence of independent nations from former British colonies, Canada's interest increased. Canada not only became a contributor to UN peacekeeping operations in the Congo; Canada also began to place increased emphasis on development assistance to the Commonwealth countries of Africa. Significantly, Canada sided with the black African states of the Commonwealth in their opposition to South Africa. During the 1960s, in response to domestic considerations, ties with the francophone African states were increased, although there was a break in relations with Gabon when that country sought to deal with Quebec without going through Ottawa.

Canadian direct aid to both Commonwealth and francophone countries in Africa is now about equal and, taken together, exceeds $100 million a year. Trade, however, is small (amounting to less than $850 million in 1974). Significantly, Canada's largest trading partner in Africa, and the location of the greatest amount of Canadian direct investment, is South Africa. In 1975 total Canadian trade with Africa was some $875 million, of which South Africa accounts for $328 million, or approximately 38 percent.

Recently, the Canadian government decided to stop giving assistance to private Canadian businesses wishing to trade with South Africa. In its effort to contribute to a peaceful solution of the South African problem, Canada has joined with five other Western nations at the UN in seeking the peaceful separation, with free elections, of Namibia, which is now a South African protectorate. As with the Middle East, the scope for Canadian influence is limited. However, acting in concert with other Western countries through the United Nations, Canada can make a useful contribution consistent with its overall objective of peaceful and orderly development in Africa.

ASIA AND THE PACIFIC

Canadian developmental assistance to the former British colonies of South Asia (India, Pakistan, Sri Lanka, and Bangladesh) began with the Colombo Plan of the 1950s. With the new emphasis on Africa, this region has declined in relative importance. While during the 1950s and early 1960s there was something of an Ottawa–New Delhi axis on some international issues, relations between the two countries were strained when India used a Canadian nuclear reactor to extract fuel for the production of its first atomic weapon. Canadian observers are still along the Indian border with Pakistan. Given the interest of the superpowers in this region, however, it would appear that the scope for Canadian influence has declined. Moreover, as India itself seeks to act as a middle-sized world power and a regional power, areas of common interest with Canada will also become limited.

Canadian involvement in Southeast Asia and Korea also dates back to the 1950s, the cold war era in particular. When the Korean War broke out in 1950, Canada supported American efforts through the United Nations to drive back the North Korean invasion. While Canadian troops participated in the war (on a small scale), Canadian diplomats attempted to influence American policy toward a peaceful settlement and especially to avoid widening the war to include China. Further to the south, in Vietnam in 1954, Canada became a member of the International Control Commission that attempted to supervise the peaceful division of that country into a north and a south. These efforts, although successful at first, were defeated by the growing conflict that eventually involved the United States in a major land war. Early Canadian support of the United States waned when it became apparent that no victory could be achieved and, more important, that American actions, such as the mining of Haiphong Harbor, could well lead to a superpower confrontation. In 1973 Canada again took up peacekeeping duties at the request of the United States, only to withdraw in frustration within six months.

Canada's main interests in the Pacific center around the developed countries of the rim, New Zealand, Australia, and Japan. The latter is Canada's third-largest trading partner, accounting for 4.1 percent of imports and 6.4 percent of exports. Moreover, Japanese investment in western Canada has provided an increasingly important source of capital in the resource industries—by 1980 a developing source for "nationalist" concerns. Therefore in terms of both trade and investment, Japan serves as Canada's most important link to Asia and the Pacific with great potential for growth.

THE PEOPLE'S REPUBLIC OF CHINA

Although Canada had been involved in China before World War II through missionaries, trade and commercial agents, and trading transactions, it was not until the war itself that Canada established diplomatic relations with China. Legations were established in the two capitals, and in 1943 they were elevated to the rank of embassies. During the war, Canada gave China significant assistance, and a warm bilateral relationship seemed to be developing. Madame Chiang Kai-shek visited Ottawa in 1943, addressing both houses of Parliament. However, as China was plunged into an increasingly bitter civil war, the Canadian government was confronted with a dilemma. The Canadian Embassy remained in Nanking after the city fell to Mao's forces, although the Canadian ambassador returned to Canada for consultations and did not return. With Mao's victory and formation of the People's Republic of China in October 1949, it seemed at first as if Canada would follow the British lead of granting recognition to the new government. However, Canada did not do so for a variety of reasons—lack of Canadian public consensus on recognition, lack of consensus among other Commonwealth nations, U.S. resistance to any form of recognition during and after the Korean War, and of course the Korean War itself.

Unlike the United States, Canada did not participate in a trade embargo of the People's Republic. On the contrary, Canada became involved in grain sales to China to the extent that by 1961, China ranked second only to the United Kingdom as an importer of Canadian wheat. The year 1961 saw a colossal grain deal, which included the use of large-scale credit sales (prior to which Canadian sales to China had been cash transactions). Of course the U.S. government strongly disapproved of these Canadian sales, even though the sales were of a nonstrategic nature (by 1969 the U.S. government itself lifted restrictions prohibiting U.S. firms from selling nonstrategic goods), but Canada saw no reason to modify a policy so clearly in its national interest.

The Canadian government decided to seek the exchange of diplomatic representatives with the People's Republic of China in 1969, and did so by 1971. In the text of the agreement, reference was made to the claim of the People's Republic to the island of Taiwan (whereby Canada would "take notice" of the PRC's claim, implying neither agreement nor disagreement). On that island, of course, the Nationalist Chinese government, after nearly thirty years, still claims to be the sole legitimate government of all of China. This reference to Taiwan caused difficulties for Canada with other Western countries. (Further difficulties arose during the 1976 Olympic Games in Montreal, when Canada refused entry to Taiwan's athletes on the grounds that because Canada now recognized only the Peking government, the passports of the Taiwanese athletes were no longer valid for entry into Canada as long as they claimed to be Chinese nationals.)

Generally, the move to recognize the Communist Chinese was seen in Canada as a further demonstration of Canada's intention to adopt a foreign policy more distinguishable from that of the United States. It is perhaps ironic, therefore, that the Canadian move was followed so quickly by the Nixon opening to China and visit to Peking in 1972. In one important sense recognition of the Peking regime was academic, for Canada had traded with the Communists long before it recognized their government; and Canada continues to trade with Taiwan although it no longer accords that government formal recognition.

Canada and the United States

Prime Minister Trudeau himself once observed that as much as 70 percent of Canada's foreign policy is determined by its interdependent relationship with the United States.[45] Many would argue that this is an extremely modest estimate.

Economically, the sheer bulk of bilateral trade exceeds that between any other two nations in history—nearly $60 billion a year. No less than 67 percent of Canada's exports go to the United States, while 69 percent of its imports come from the United States (nor are the figures insignificant from the U.S. standpoint: 21 percent of all U.S. exports go to Canada, and 25 percent of its imports come from that nation). In terms of direct investment, Canada has more than $5 billion in the United States (more on a per capita basis than the United States has in Canada), while the United States has over $25 billion worth of direct investment in Canada.

Strategically, Canada and the United States are locked in a continental embrace through the North American Air Defense Command (NORAD), collaborative antisubmarine warfare (ASW) and coastal surveillance, and defense production-sharing agreements. Moreover, Canada constitutes an integral component of the overall Western deterrent under the leadership of the United States through its participation in NATO. Culturally, Canadians and Americans have much in common: not only through television, radio, movies, books, and magazines; but also through the fact that the Canadian-U.S. border is crossed 72 million times a year.

The list of interdependence could go on, from shared transportation facilities (highways, pipelines, hydroelectric power lines) to Canadian membership in U.S.-based labor unions. Because of the importance of the United States as a component in Canada's international experience, an entire section of this chapter is devoted to the Canadian-U.S. relationship and its historical and contemporary ingredients.

To Americans, the "undefended border" between the United States and Canada serves as a monument to the friendliness and good neighborhood shared by the American and Canadian peoples. There is, however, an even more fundamental reality that is often forgotten. The fact that there is a border to share is a monument to the fact that Canadians did not and do not want to be Americans. As has been emphasized throughout this book, the story of Canada is the story of a people attempting to create a unified and distinct nation in North America. This is the very essence of the Canadian national experience.

To Canadians, Americans have long been guilty of "taking Canada for granted" or "ignoring Canada." Here again, there is a more fundamental reality that is often forgotten, since Americans have always been very much preoccupied with Canada. This preoccupation, however, has been in terms of U.S. interests. Americans have "ignored Canada" when basic U.S. interests were not involved, but when U.S. interests were affected, Americans have had an overwhelming interest in Canada. In fact, at those times, Canadians might well have wished that Americans would take them more for granted.

This is all another way of saying that there are two different national actors involved in the Canadian-U.S. relationship. From a Canadian standpoint, the theme of the bilateral relationship is the Canadian attempt to build a nation in the face of the U.S. colossus. From the U.S. standpoint, the theme involves a process spanning two centuries in which the United States, in the pursuit of its interests, attempted to adjust to a separate nation on its northern border. This adjustment was neither easy nor automatic and involved nothing less than a repudiation of the motto of the United States, *e pluribus unum* (out of many, one). The division of North America along the 49th parallel irrevocably altered the history of the continent and created a set of unresolved dynamics that are still active today.

These dynamics result from the different perceptions and priorities of the Canadian and American people. Americans have been traditionally unconcerned about, or puzzled by, the Canadian goal of separateness and distinctiveness. They have also had difficulty in understanding that Canadians are rather different from Americans, and are often suspicious of arrangements with the United States that are too intimate. To this day, Americans continue to have difficulties in adjusting to a Canadian presence in North America in terms of defining policy options that will meet U.S. interests but that, at the same time, will be acceptable to Canadians as they seek their own interests in the pursuit of a national distinctiveness.

This is not of course to deny the extraordinarily harmonious development of the bilateral relationship, for the United States and Canada can in a sense be viewed as a model of two nations slowly but surely solving their disputes in an enlightened and amicable manner. However, this harmoniousness must be kept in perspective, for we are still dealing with two nations, not rhetorical "neighbors," and nations are engaged in the pursuit of interests, not rhetorical "friendship."

In the broadest sense, a review of the Canadian-U.S. relationship over time suggests that it could possibly have developed in three directions: by absorption or annexation toward a single state; toward coexistence as separate, truly independent entities; or toward the interdependence of two sovereign but deeply interrelated countries. In this analysis, coexistence would involve the nations pursuing their own national policies with no concerted attempt to establish ongoing interdependent arrangements. On the other hand, formalized interdependence would involve highly defined ongoing intergovernmental arrangements (such as the 1964 Columbia River Treaty and the 1977 pipeline agreement) and the creation of joint institutions (such as the 1909 International Joint Commission and the 1940 Permanent Joint Board on Defense).

An understanding of these three alternatives is especially important for Americans, who tend to accept as natural and inevitable the extraordinary amount of interdependence which has prevailed since World War II. However, it is essential that the reader be able to place the current bilateral relationship in an overall historical perspective, for the fundamental question facing Canada and the United States remains the same now as it has been for two centuries: How much separateness and how much togetherness should each country seek in the pursuit of their respective interests, and what policy options will be most effective in this endeavor? The historical record offers some insight.

Annexation ultimately proved unfeasible. Neither attempts at persuasion nor military invasions resulted in the incorporation of Canada into the United States. Americans had therefore to acknowledge, and attempt to adjust to, a *de facto* division of North America. But if too much togetherness did not work, neither did too much separateness. Mere coexistence also proved to be ultimately unfeasible: the economic and strategic requisites of sharing a continent necessitated something more than peaceful coexistence. Having acknowledged the fact of a separate Canada in North America, Canadians and Americans found that they could not simply coexist on an absolutely independent basis.

Formalized interdependence therefore came to the fore, and at first glance seemed to be an ideal solution. Recognizing the existence of two distinct nations living side by side, it also allowed them to create bilateral institutions and selectively to integrate aspects of their national policies when this seemed mutually beneficial. It can be argued, although Canadians might dispute the proposition, that from the Reciprocity Agreement of 1854 to the Auto Pact in 1965, from the establishment of the International Joint Commission in 1909 to the 1971 creation of the Joint Committee on Trade Statistics, formalized interdependence proved to be of considerable value in meeting the respective needs of the two nations.

There was, however, a "Catch-22" in formalized interdependence. If allowed to proceed to its logical end, as it seemed to be doing in the post–World War II period, interdependence could come back full circle to peaceful, unofficial annexation. That is, if bilateral coordination is too integrative and too intimate, the distinctiveness of Canada could be lost—given the disparity of the two countries, Canada could be absorbed by the United States. This fact accounts for the traditional Canadian ambivalence toward formalized interdependence with the United States. The Canadian policy dilemma has been how to sip from the cup of interdependence with the United States without drowning in it.

ANNEXATION

For Americans, annexation would have satisfied both practical and ideological ambitions. From a practical standpoint, it seemed only logical that the newly created revolutionary federation would and should include Britain's remaining North American colonies. A continuing British military presence along their northern border constituted a threat to the Thirteen Colonies. Moreover, both economically and politically, it made sense to regard all the colonies as one unit. Annexation also had a high ideological content. As the people who fired the "shot heard around the world," seeking to create a new political order in North America, Americans simply could not understand why Canadians, especially French Canadians, would not automatically respond to this universal call for liberty by throwing off the yoke of their British oppressors. American misperception was considerable and resulted in a consistent underestimation of the Canadian sense of self-interest and solidarity.

As the winds of revolution stirred in the Thirteen Colonies, many Americans were convinced that Canada should be incorporated into the United States, peacefully if possible, but if not peacefully, then by armed force. In varying degrees, this U.S. sentiment persisted up to the Civil War period. In fact, the U.S. pursuit of annexation was not without its irony, since the net effect of every U.S. attempt to annex Canada was the coalescence of Canadian nationalism, thereby making annexation increasingly less viable as a policy option.[46] Annexation became a catalyst encouraging a distinctive and independent Canada and thus, from the American perspective, counterproductive.

It should be added that some annexationist sentiment could be found in Canada at certain times and in varying degrees, the difference being of course that Canadian and British officials never officially endorsed annexation as public policy. Annexationist sentiment in Canada never reflected more than a minority view and was most evident when Canada faced severe economic and political difficulties. Perhaps its most dramatic expression occurred in October 1849, when a group of Montreal merchants published a formal call for union with the United States. Observing that Canada was "in decay" and in "humiliating contrast" to the United States, this *Annexation Manifesto* concluded that the only complete remedy for Canada's ills was a "friendly and peaceful separation from British connection and a union upon equitable terms with the great North American Confederacy of sover-

eign states."[47] But annexationists in Canada met with little
success at this time and did no better in 1867–71 and 1884–93
when the movement revived.[48]

Gradually, Americans had to adjust to the *de facto* division of North America, but they did so only after exhausting
the possibilities of peaceful persuasion, military power, and
diplomatic negotiations. Three early attempts to enlist Canada in the cause of rebellion all proved unsuccessful. In 1774
the First Continental Congress drew up an address to be distributed in Canada, inviting assistance in opposition to Great
Britain. (Ominously, the document suggested that Canada
would be punished were it disinclined to assist the United
States.) In February 1775, the Boston Committee of Correspondence drew up a letter for the merchants of Montreal,
listing grievances and denouncing the Quebec Act. A third,
similar letter was distributed to the "oppressed inhabitants
of Canada" in May 1775. It soon became clear that no assistance would be forthcoming. Peaceful annexation had failed;
the only recourse was now invasion.

Montgomery and Arnold's invasion of Canada in 1775
failed, and at no time after January 1777 was the safety of
Canada at stake. Even France, an ally of the United States,
did not favor U.S. invasions of Canada. When Washington
pressed them for a joint invasion of Canada, the French declined, saying that the object of their alliance with the United
States was to "secure the independence of the United States,
not to make territorial conquests for them."[49]

Americans, however, did not entirely give up hope of an-
nexing Canada. Article XI of the Articles of Confederation
significantly, if irrelevantly, addressed itself to Canada, af-
firming that Canada would automatically be "entitled to all
the advantages of this Union" should it wish to join. And with
the failure of peaceful persuasion and military invasion, the
Americans turned to diplomacy. Congress instructed the
American representatives to the Paris peace negotiations to
include the cession of Canada to the United States as an item
in the peace treaty ending the Revolutionary War. The American rationale was simple, if unacceptable to the British. The
cession of Canada, according to Franklin, would "promote

sweet reconciliation of a durable nature by at once removing possibilities of all further frictions." U.S. policy clearly represented a continuation of the logic of the annexationist option—division of the continent was unnatural and could lead only to future difficulties for all concerned.

During the period from the 1783 Treaty of Paris to the War of 1812, it was not so much that U.S. and Canadian interests were harmonious; rather, Americans were preoccupied with other matters. This situation changed during the War of 1812, when the annexation option again surfaced as a matter of national U.S. policy. In June 1812, Congress declared war on Great Britain, and again North America witnessed unsuccessful invasions of Canada. The Treaty of Ghent in 1814 essentially confirmed prewar boundaries and established procedures for the resolution of U.S.-British disputes in North America.

For Americans, the period between the 1814 Treaty of Ghent and the Civil War was marked by territorial expansion and internal consolidation. During this half century, the United States seemed more like a flood than a nation, about to spill over and engulf every nook and cranny of the North American continent. Canadians increasingly had difficulty in viewing the vigorous United States with any degree of equanimity. Although annexation of Canada did not become official U.S. policy, there was no shortage of respectable Americans who dreamt of the United States absorbing an entire continent.

Beginning in April 1861, the Civil War soon strained the U.S.-British entente, which in turn strained relations between the United States and Canada. After the ending of hostilities in April 1865, many Canadians feared that the newly reunited Republic would use its built-up military and industrial strength to end the political division of North America. Some Americans felt that Britain should cede Canada to the United States as compensation for the damages caused by unfriendly acts committed during the war. Finally, the abrogation of the Reciprocity Treaty in 1866 threatened to undermine the economic benefits Canada had enjoyed since 1854. Many Canadians believed that Congress deliberately sought to induce economic collapse in Canada and thus hasten voluntary annexation.

For some years, a group of Irish Americans known as Fenians had organized themselves into a paramilitary organization and conducted a series of armed attacks on Canada, some involving as many as eight hundred men.[50] All of the attacks were easily repulsed, and to many the situation had a certain comic quality; but not to Canadians. Although the Fenians were not implementing U.S. policy (in fact, the U.S. government eventually interceded and arrested leaders and members of the movement), the Canadians felt that U.S. authorities were derelict in not preventing obviously blatant violations of Canadian territory.

The British government, while realizing that it could defend Canada only with great cost, could not let it go without a struggle. Even Queen Victoria noted that in their disunited state the colonies of North America invited annexation, an eventuality that was unacceptable to both Britain and her Canadian colonists. The solution seemed to rest in a union of the colonies into an independent nation under the British Crown. Readers of Chapter 2 are familiar with the details of the achievement of Canadian Confederation in 1867.

From the U.S. standpoint, Confederation seemed to be the worst of all solutions, for it further emphasized both the *de facto* and *de jure* division of the continent; it united certain important colonies into a nation; and it did not remove the British presence from North America. Annexationist rhetoric in the United States abounded. The Foreign Relations Committee of the U.S. Senate passed a resolution expressing "its 'extreme solicitude' that a rival confederation was to be formed on the continent and 'founded upon Monarchical principles.'"[51] Similar views were expressed by state legislatures and private citizens. Yet forceful annexation was now at best a remote possibility. Having achieved the military capability to take Canada, the United States now found it politically not in its interest to do so. Part of this was due to the ambiguity of the Canadian Confederation: while Canada was in a sense an independent nation, it was still a part of the British Empire and still strategically and economically dependent on Britain.

Samuel Bemis, commenting briefly on Canadian Confederation in his classic history of American diplomacy, concluded that annexationist tendencies in the United States were "quieted forever by the successful British experience in nation-building—the creation of the Dominion of Canada in 1867."[52] The fact is, however, that the success of Canada's nation building had not been assured in 1867—had this been the case, U.S.-Canadian relations since then would have been entirely different. More accurately, the Canadian nation-building experience would not be completed until well into the twentieth century (many would maintain that it remains an ongoing process to this day). Certainly in 1867, and for some years after, Canada's internal position was precarious and its international position ambiguous. Because of this, annexationist ambitions in the United States were not quieted, although they never again surfaced as governmental policy. Those such as Secretary of State Seward who entertained thoughts of bringing Canada into the Union now looked toward voluntary annexation. In the same vein, while Americans could regard the purchase of Alaska as "Seward's Folly," that event reinforced Canadian determination to hasten incorporation of British Columbia and the Hudson's Bay Company's territory into the Dominion. At any rate, after 1867 there was now a new Canadian central government seeking to extend its authority across its half of North America, in an effort to establish a sovereign and secure independence. For practical purposes, annexationism was a dead horse.

FROM COEXISTENCE TO INTERDEPENDENCE

If, after 1867, Canada would not be territorially annexed to the United States, how would two independent states learn to coexist on the continent? Their coexistence was complicated by the fact that Canada had to be dealt with on two fronts. Americans had to resolve issues peculiar to the North American continent, such as boundary and environmental problems, but at the same time, they had to deal with the British as well as with the Canadians in resolving these issues. Second, Americans had to deal with extracontinental issues resulting from the roles of Great Britain and the United States as international actors, and these issues in turn affected the stability of the Canadian-U.S. relationship (e.g., the Anglo-

U.S. controversies during the Civil War and the 1895 Venezuelan dispute both resulted in Canadian border preparations for war). In short, not only was there a complex bilateral dimension to the U.S. approach toward Canada, there was also an extracontinental, international dimension. If to Great Britain, Canada was a potential hostage for U.S. interests, then to the United States, Canada was a potential stalking horse for British interests.

Nonetheless, the coexistence option proved to be a useful one. In reality, it was nothing more than a means of defining in what framework Canada and the United States would address their common bilateral and multilateral problems. The continent had to be defined in terms of delineating political boundaries and maritime jurisdictions. Continental resources also had to be shared in terms of two entities coexisting side by side, and this involved economic, political, and strategic considerations.

The most significant difference between the boundary settlements of the pre-Confederation period and those which came after 1867 was that the latter not only defined the division of the continent, they also established an international boundary between two sovereign states. If prior to 1867 the Americans could view border settlements as perhaps temporary measures, after Confederation the settlements increasingly took on a new note of finality. Not only would they shape the contours of the American Republic, they would also define the area in which the Dominion of Canada would henceforth exercise its own sovereignty as it assumed more and more of the responsibilities and obligations of an independent nation.

Defining and sharing the continent were not merely abstract concepts in the development of Canadian-U.S. relations.[53] A line between two separate entities had to be drawn from the Atlantic to the Pacific. Nor did the process end at the water's edge, for the fishing grounds, particularly those off the eastern coast of Canada, had to be shared as well. As mundane and tedious as these matters may appear to the casual observer, the process of issue resolution that led to the formalized division of the continent represent the focal points of coexistence.

It took well over a century for the United States to settle the location of its northern border. In part this was due to the process of westward movement as the Republic spread over the plains and pushed toward the Pacific, paralleling, in direction but not in time, the westward expansion of Canada. Another reason for the longevity of the U.S.-Canadian border negotiations can be found in the nature of the coexistence approach itself. It was a pragmatic and "issue-specific" approach. That is, the United States was willing to settle on the location of a disputed part of the border only as the need for a settlement arose. And implied in coexistence was the fact that the United States would be either unwilling or unable to act unilaterally to achieve its aims. Thus, it generally did not resort to military force, but rather to an array of awkward negotiating mechanisms for settling the location of the border.

In the simplest sense, the movement toward coexistence was evident in seven border disputes that, taken together, defined the northern territorial limits of the United States: St. Croix River, Passamaquoddy Islands, Northeastern Frontier (all three involving the border with New England); St. Lawrence to Lake Superior; Oregon; Juan de Fuca (defining the channel that separated the continent from Vancouver Island); and Alaska. In resolving these disputes, four separate methods of issue resolution were ultimately successful: commissions (St. Croix River in 1789 and Passamaquoddy Islands in 1817), direct negotiations (Northeastern Frontier in 1842, St. Lawrence to Lake Superior in 1842, and Oregon in 1846), arbitration (Juan de Fuca in 1872), and tribunals (Alaska in 1903). Although these methods of issue resolution were all temporary and expedient techniques confined to specific issues, their collective application resulted in a permanent border.

By the turn of the century, it was increasingly clear that this ad hoc approach to resolving boundary and related problems was insufficient. In 1905 a Waterways Commission was created to regulate the use by the two countries of the Great Lakes system for transportation and other purposes, and in 1908, a treaty was signed between the United States and Great Britain that provided for an entire resurvey of the border from the Atlantic to the Pacific (with the exception of the Great Lakes) by an international boundary commission. The field work of the commission lasted until the early 1920s, and in 1925 a permanent Canadian-U.S. commission was established to maintain boundary markers and hence to avoid further disputes. Moreover, the International Waterways Commission gave way to the International Joint Commission in 1909, a permanent body created under the Boundary Waters Treaty. In this way policymakers discovered that ostensibly independent coexistence in practice required a degree of formalized interdependence. From ad hoc techniques of issue resolution, there gradually emerged integrative arrangements whereby the two nations relinquished sovereignty in establishing ongoing, coordinated institutional procedures and structures.

The implications of coexistence for dealing with fisheries disputes were similar to those involved in the resolution of boundary issues. In the years prior to the American Revolution, not only had all the lands under British rule been united; so too were the rich fishing grounds, including particularly the North Atlantic fisheries off Newfoundland. As with the border, the division of the continent in 1783 led to disputes over the use of these fishing grounds; in settling these disputes, the United States and Britain/Canada resorted to similar ad hoc bilateral mechanisms to settle issues as they arose. Repeatedly, a settlement would determine how the fisheries were to be shared; disputes would arise, boats would be harassed, angry words spoken and sometimes warships dispatched; and then negotiations would follow, leading to another settlement, sometimes in an international context with arbitration at the Hague. No permanent bilateral authority to manage the sharing of the fisheries could be set up at first. Significantly, however, as with boundary disputes, the fisheries sector also produced formalized interdependence. The International Joint Fisheries Commission was established in 1923; a Pacific Salmon Commission was established in 1930; and a Great Lakes Fisheries Commission was created in 1955.

In addition to boundary and fisheries, the overall Canadian-U.S. relationship witnessed other types of issues that necessitated resolution. For example, arbitration was resorted to, particularly from the 1860s through the 1890s, to settle quotas for the harvesting of fur seals in the North Pacific. In the 1920s treaties and agreements were conducted between the United States and Canada on issues ranging from aviation and shortwave bands to the smuggling of alcoholic beverages into the United States, the erosion of Niagara Falls, and the clarification of the Alaskan boundary. In some cases, however, Congress refused its consent to that which the executive branch had agreed. Such was the case with the proposed treaty to jointly construct a St. Lawrence Seaway signed in 1932, which the Congress found unnecessarily integrative and refused to ratify. Similarly, a series of arbitrations concerning maritime violations (such as the case of the *I'm Alone*, a Canadian ship suspected of carrying illegal alcohol into the United States, sunk in the Gulf of Mexico) proved equally trying. Even in 1980 an East Coast Fisheries Agreement had been delayed for a year awaiting Senate ratification (which now seems unlikely).

It was one thing to resolve boundary and related disputes; it was quite a different matter when it came to economic considerations.[54] Here the basic question was: To what extent could Canada and the United States be economically self-sufficient? Or, to state the question in another way: Would the political independence of Canada be crowned with economic independence?

By the late 1870s, Canada had embarked on its "National Policy" of railway construction, high tariffs, and in time an emphasis on immigration. Canada sought to foster its growth and development in order to live separate and apart from the American economic system, just as it had rejected political integration. For the most part, the United States could be indifferent to Canada's attempts at economic self-sufficiency. However, as the American frontier was closed, as raw materials were exhausted, as industry looked for new markets and as those who had accumulated vast capital looked for a place to invest, Canada took on new importance for those groups in the United States who were found to favor closer economic ties.

In 1911 reciprocity was again seriously considered, an idea that in fact had been considered by the United States as early as 1898 when it suggested the Joint High Commission to look into the matter. Reciprocity was ultimately rejected in Canada as the Americans again underestimated the desire on the part of Canadians to avoid measures that would, they believed, lead to the end of Canada as a separate entity. However, the rejection of reciprocity did not entail a return to the status quo. Economic relations between the two countries grew in spite of, and because of, the high tariffs Canada continued to impose on American goods. Between 1900 and 1914, American exports to Canada grew from $102 million to $396 million.

More important, Canada was becoming an outlet for American venture capital both in the raw materials industry and in manufacturing. By 1914, American direct investment in Canada had reached $700 million. Although British investment was then near $2.5 billion, it was mostly in railway securities and government bonds. World War I hastened the Americanization of Canadian industry, not only in terms of ownership (by 1918, 30 percent of all Canadian industry was American owned), but also in terms of the technology used and the organizational and managerial approaches employed. Thus, by the 1920s, coexistence served American needs. The raw materials of Canada were being tapped; U.S. branch plants had opened the Canadian market; exports to Canada were increasing. However, coexistence fostered tariff wars, especially with the onslaught of the Great Depression, and it was not until the Hull Agreements of 1935 and 1938, later translated into GATT arrangements, that the two nations were able to stabilize their commercial relations. Mere coexistence proved as unviable in the economic sphere as it had in the political sphere, and the Canadian-U.S. relationship embarked upon a journey of unprecedented economic interdependence.

It was not just in economic matters that the United States experimented with coexistence. Like many new revolutionary nations, the United States was particularly sensitive about its strategic position. As long as annexation remained possible, the United States constituted a strategic threat to Canada; but Canada was also of strategic concern to the United States. The presence in Canada, for nearly a century after the American Revolution, of regular British troops was viewed by the United States as a possible threat to U.S security. Even after the British withdrew in the 1870s, Canada would continue to have a place in U.S. strategic calculations. Coexistence proved to be a useful approach, but only up to a point.

From the standpoint of Canadian history, the withdrawal of British forces has been said to have marked the beginning of the transfer of strategic dependence from England to the United States. In reality, what happened was something less dramatic. From 1871 to 1940, with the exception of the American participation in the Great War, Canadian and American strategic interests for the most part did not mesh. Indeed, until World War II they were, at times, worlds apart.

In 1914 Canadian ties to the Empire meant that it was at war when Britain declared war on Germany and Austria on August 4. While Canada exerted itself to produce war materiel, and while its armies suffered heavy casualties on the battlefield, the United States remained neutral. This was coexistence with a vengeance. But the United States was no longer just a North American power, and when its interests clashed with those of a Germany at war, it joined the battle. A Canadian war mission was established in Washington, and a spirit of cooperation emerged. However, once the war ended, the two nations once again went their separate strategic ways; that is, until World War II.

As Europe drew closer to war in the 1930s, the American president (if not his people) began to think in terms of North American defense. In 1938 a famous exchange of declarations took place. In Kingston, Ontario, Franklin Roosevelt declared that: "The Dominion of Canada is a part of the sisterhood of the British Empire. I give you an assurance that the people of the United States will not stand idly by if domination of Canadian soil is threatened by any other Empire."[55] Two days later, Prime Minister Mackenzie King replied that: "We, too, have our obligations as a good and friendly neighbour, and one of these is to make sure that our country is made as

immune from attack or possible invasion as we can reasonably
be expected to make it, and that, should the occasion ever
arise, enemy forces should not be able to pursue their way
either by land, sea or air, to the United States across
Canada."[56]

The tone of these two statements bespoke an interdependent approach to North American defense. In fact, however,
the very genuinely friendly atmosphere in which they were
given notwithstanding, both merely reaffirmed the essence
of coexistence. Roosevelt's statement, read in the cold light of
dawn, merely echoed the Monroe Doctrine, promising not to
aid a Canada sucked into a European conflict, but rather to
ensure that Canadian territory (and, by extension, the United
States itself) would not be threatened by European invasion
and/or occupation. Mr. King's reply equally did not pledge
Canada to an integrated North American defense scheme.
Indeed, he suggested that should Canada be threatened, Canada alone would see to it that enemy forces did not cross the
Dominion to attack the United States (at least he implied that
Canada was in no need of American assistance to deter such
an attack). When in 1939 World War II began, then, the two
North American nations demonstrated their determination
to go their separate, yet complementary, strategic ways, much
as they had done since 1812. Canada declared war on Germany, but the United States remained neutral.

With the fall of France and what many believed to be the
impending fall of Britain, the United States began to have
doubts about the Canadian ability to make itself "immune"
from an attack that might threaten the security of the United
States. Canada too realized that if Britain fell there would be
need for greater coordination of North American defense. On
August 17, 1940, in Ogdensburg, New York, the two countries,
by a simple exchange of notes, implemented not just the coordination of continental defense but the permanent integration of Canada and the United States into a single strategic
unit. A Permanent Joint Board on Defense was established.
As the war progressed, this arrangement permitted further
integration in all strategic areas. This process would soon
extend into the economic sphere; with the Hyde Park Decla-

ration of 1941, both governments agreed that the two economies should be meshed in order to obtain the greatest possible efficiency and productivity from the war effort. Thus, because of the war and the common external threat it entailed, in many extremely important areas—not the least of which was the psychological one—coexistence came to be superseded by interdependence.

INTERDEPENDENCE

As has been seen in the previous sections, neither annexation nor coexistence proved to be adequate options in meeting Canadian and U.S. interests. U.S. territorial absorption of Canada proved to be unacceptable to the Canadian people, and the very attempt to take over Canada simply served to strengthen and consolidate the Canadian sense of independent nationhood. Coexistence was acceptable to both Canadians and Americans and was useful in resolving bilateral problems without long-range integrative commitments. However, mere coexistence was not enough; therefore, coexistence gradually developed into increasing interdependence. Canadians and Americans concluded binding bilateral commitments in which both nations surrendered some sovereignty in the interests of achieving their respective goals.

It was during and after World War II that Canadian-U.S. interdependence became the dominant characteristic of the bilateral relationship. Indeed, the degree of interdependence now exceeds that between any other two nations in history. Economically, we have seen the origins of the current Canadian-U.S. relationship. During the 1950s (especially 1950–57), there was a northward economic expansion marked by massive flows of U.S. capital, accompanied by a rise in U.S. exports to Canada. Economic intimacy increased (for details, see Chapter 4).

Strategically, we have seen how the current Canadian-U.S. relationship dates back to 1940 (with the Ogdensburg Declaration that established the informal bilateral defense alliance) and the 1941 Hyde Park Declaration (which was the economic counterpart of Ogdensburg). There followed a host of wartime committees and boards and unprecedented strategic/economic integration. After the brief postwar euphoria about a new and peaceful international order, U.S. and Canadian perceptions of the increasing threat, and the technological military advances that made this threat ever more compelling locked Canada and the United States into an intimate strategic embrace. During the early 1950s, the two nations developed integrated subarctic and airborne radar systems. In the late 1950s, North American Air Defense Command and an elaborate defense production-sharing arrangement became operable. The defense production program continues, and NORAD has been renewed several times. Although Canadian territory is now relatively less essential to the strategic defense of North America with the advent of new weaponry, Canada and the United States nonetheless share an indivisible defense necessity.

This increasing Canadian-U.S. interdependence also extended to other spheres. Culturally, Canadians vigorously enjoyed American movies, television programs, books, and magazines. Politically, an elaborate system of seventeen joint Canadian-U.S. organizations, in varying degrees active, has evolved, including six commissions, nine committees, an integrated air defense command structure, and an interparliamentary group. In addition, formalized bilateral arrangements were concluded. Examples include the 1959 St. Lawrence Seaway agreement involving navigation procedures along the St. Lawrence Seaway and Great Lakes, the 1964 Columbia River Treaty that involved bilateral use of water power, the 1972 Great Lakes Water Quality Agreement that attempted to jointly solve environmental concerns, and the 1977 pipeline agreement that involved the transportation of resources.

Moreover, this increasing interdependence occurred not just in the national governmental sector but also in the state/provincial and private sectors. Indeed, interdependence has often—perhaps most often—been furthered by the actions of private corporations and businesses. In addition, the Canadian provinces were playing a greater role in the Canadian-U.S. relationship, initiating arrangements within those areas over which the provinces have jurisdiction. Examples include

British Columbia Hydro's decision to sell power to the United States and the more recent large sales of Quebec hydroelectricity to New York.

In short, this increasing interdependence was not the result of a grand design on the part of the Canadian and U.S. governments, but rather reflects the incidental, rational pursuit of national interests. Nor was this pursuit of interests without problems. As early as 1951, Lester Pearson could solemnly and prophetically declare:

> The days of relatively easy and automatic political relations with our neighbor are, I think, over. They are over because on our side, we are more important in the continental and international scheme of things, and we loom more largely now as an important element in U.S. and in free world plans for defense and development.[57]

Similarly, in 1949 the Canadian government had reflected its concern about U.S. cultural influences overwhelming Canada by appointing the Royal Commission on National Development in Arts, Letters and Sciences (the Massey Commission). Its 1951 report stated that there is "the very present danger of permanent dependence" on the United States, and that Canadians are "spending millions to maintain national independence which would be nothing but an empty shell without a vigorous and distinctive cultural life."[58] From this came the Canada Council, whose purpose it was to promote Canadian culture (including that of academia) by means of government grants and subsidies.

In broadcasting the 1957 Fowler Commission Report on radio and television voiced similar cultural concerns; the Broadcast Act of 1958 established a board of broadcast governors "to control the character of any and all programs broadcast by any stations in Canada." Another Fowler Report (1965) was in turn followed by the revised Broadcast Acts of 1966 and 1968. The latter established the Canadian Radio-Television Commission (later called the Canadian Radio-Television and Telecommunications Commission, or CRTC). In 1970 the report of Senator Keith Davey's special Senate Committee on Mass Media resulted in the deletion of U.S. commercials carried on Canadian television. Most recently the attempt to prevent Canadian advertisers from placing ads on American border TV stations (beamed all over Canada by cable hookups) has created a considerable diplomatic crisis.

The 1957 Gordon Royal Commission Report is the economic parallel of the 1951 Massey cultural report, evincing a high degree of concern about U.S. economic impact on Canada. This degree of concern was not immediately shared by the Canadian government, but it did gradually take steps to alleviate that impact. Key sectors in which it was felt that Canadians must maintain control were identified. In 1971 the Canadian Development Corporation was created to encourage the investment of Canadian funds in Canadian enterprises.

Overlapping with this key-sector approach was the competitive phase, a major emphasis introduced by the Watkins Report of 1967. Here the emphasis was on disclosure, extra-territoriality, and competition policy. Moreover, after the 1972 Gray Report on foreign direct investment in Canada, screening procedures were emphasized. This is a major development in that wider attention was paid to political implications as well as economic ones. While the Watkins phase treated these elements as problems of structure in the Canadian economy (while playing down special effects of foreign ownership), the Gray Report's view on foreign ownership was different. Gray urged the government to deal with it more directly.

Nor was the Canadian-U.S. strategic relationship immune to problems. If there had been a feeling of mutuality between Canada and the United States on strategic matters during the 1950s, by the 1960s this mutuality was eroded for several reasons: (1) the Vietnam War demonstrated for the first time during the postwar period that the United States might be involved in a conflict in which Canada would not be an ally; (2) technological advances were taking place which made Canadian territory seem less vital to American defense; (3) international changes such as the increasing détente in East-West relations; and (4) there was an increasing generalized Canadian concern about U.S. economic and cultural domination. Thus, although the defense relationship continued to be intimate, it was not without its problems. The 1962 Cuban missile crisis, for example, resulted in Canadian irritation because Canadians felt insufficiently consulted, while the Americans were distressed at Canada's hesitation in putting its air defense forces on alert. In 1963 the matter of Canadian acquisition of nuclear weapons became an extremely destabilizing issue. American and NATO officials insisted that Canadian officials could meet their defensive obligations to the Western alliance only by acquiring nuclear weapons. The already weak Diefenbaker government was defeated in a general election, partly because of its defense policy. There were Canadian charges of U.S. intervention in Canada's domestic affairs, and there was U.S. irritation at Canada's vacillation regarding continental defense priorities. Of course, many bilateral problems have occurred since the Diefenbaker days; and doubtless they will continue to crop up in the future.

What was happening to the Canadian-U.S. "good neighborhood"? Quite simply, as the bilateral interdependence increased, many Canadians were getting increasingly nervous. The Canadian concern was that this interdependence might be going too far in terms of eroding Canada's distinctiveness as a nation and in terms of constraining Canada as an international actor. It was not that Canadians were categorically in favor of rejecting their interdependent relationship with the United States, for they themselves were delighted with many of the benefits that were accruing from their interdependent arrangements. Instead, the question was a matter of degree—how much interdependence, and how much separateness? (It must be emphasized that Americans did not share this concern about the dangers of unlimited interdependence: because the United States predominates in the bilateral relationship, there is no danger of a loss of U.S. sovereignty stemming from an intimate relationship with Canada. This fact alone seems chilling to many Canadians.)

The 1970 Trudeau foreign policy review captures the complex nuances involved in Canadian concern about the United States. Acknowledging that the United States "will continue to have a heavy impact on Canada, with political, economic and social implications," the review observed that:

> Perhaps the hardest choice in this area of policy . . . will be to maintain a proper balance of interest and advantage between Canada's essential needs in ensuring health and growth in its economy and Canada's determination to safeguard its sovereignty and independence. Nor are these necessarily in conflict at all points, for economic growth is essential to sovereignty and independence.[59]

As mentioned above, the Autumn 1972 *International Perspectives* was a special issue, issued under the signature of Secretary of State for External Affairs Mitchell Sharp and entitled "Canada-U.S. Relations: Options for the Future." According to Mr. Sharp, there were three options: (1) "Canada can seek to maintain more or less its present relationship with the United States with a minimum of policy adjustments"; (2) "Canada can move deliberately toward closer integration with the United States"; and (3) "Canada can pursue a comprehensive long-term strategy to develop and strengthen the Canadian economy and other aspects of its national life and in the process to reduce the present Canadian vulnerability."[60] This delineation of options was not exactly neutral, and Mr. Sharp opted for the now famous third option. "Counterweight" and "diversification" became the new buzz words emanating from Ottawa.

By 1975 the Canadian Secretary of State for External Affairs could officially declare the old "special relationship" to be over. In a January speech in Winnipeg, Mr. MacEachen observed: "What we have witnessed since the early seventies has been the ending of one era and the beginning of a new period in Canada-U.S. relations."[61] Apparently, U.S. officials did not entirely agree. U.S. Ambassador to Canada William J. Porter had observed in a September 1974 speech, also delivered in Winnipeg, that "we are neighbors for better or worse," and since previous Canadian and U.S. officials "made the U.S.-Canadian relationship something special in this world, it's up to us to keep it that way."[62] Whether the Canadian-U.S. "special" relationship is alive or dead of course depends upon how one defines "special." However, few Canadians or Americans would deny that Canadian-U.S. relations have been unique in the postwar period.

The Canadian rhetorical declaration that the special bilateral relationship is over contained two very important and useful conceptual points. First, because of the differences in power and strength between the United States and Canada, Canada as the weaker unit should not expect special favors. If it does, this involves dependence, with concomitant vulnerability and a lessening of national dignity rather than interdependence. Second, Mr. MacEachen implied that both Canada and the United States will now be more concerned with their own interests rather than with their joint interests. Nor would U.S. officials disagree with this assessment. In fact, President Nixon said the same thing, and more eloquently, during his April 1972 address before the Canadian Parliament:

> It is time for Canadians and Americans to move beyond the sentimental rhetoric of the past. It is time for us to recognize— that we have very separate identities—that we have significant differences——and that nobody's interests are furthered when these realities are obscured.[63]

As U.S. and Canadian officials are now willing to acknowledge, there are very real differences between the United States and Canada, as well as diplomatic difficulties. The fundamental question now facing Ottawa and Washington is: What consultative techniques can be utilized to resolve issues, given very real differences in interests?

No one should be surprised by fluctuations of the Canadian-U.S. relationship. In 1816 John Quincy Adams wrote in a diplomatic dispatch to Monroe of "continual tendencies to bad neighborhood" between the United States and Canada.[64] He saw these tendencies as proceeding from three causes: the Indians, the "temper of the British local authorities," and the British armaments on the Great Lakes. Americans are now concerned more about economics than Indians; they are more concerned about the temper of Canadian officials than British authorities; and they are more concerned about pollution in the Great Lakes than armaments on it. This merely suggests that details change but that problems persist. After all, there are two distinct sets of national interests in North America, and there are perceptions of both, Canadian and American.

How, then, does the Canadian-U.S. relationship fit into the overall context of Canada's range of foreign relations with other nations and regions? Unfortunately, ever since the promulgation of the third option approach to Canadian foreign policy, there has been a tendency to oversimplify and to see Canada's relations outside North America as only serving to counterbalance the inherently (mostly inadvertent) hegemonic impact of the United States. This simplistic approach is conceptually unhelpful. It is unhelpful because the other two options were not options at all in the realistic sense of the word. The second, that Canada would seek greater integration with the United States, is entirely in opposition to what Canada is all about—the attempt to create a separate and distinct nation on the North American continent. Moreover, as has been seen, that integration that has already taken place was not the result of a conscious policy of integration but the outgrowth of the pursuit of national interests on the part of both the Canadians and the Americans. When the history of such integrative steps as the Columbia River Treaty, the St. Lawrence Seaway Agreement and the Auto Pact are reviewed, it becomes clear that integration was neither easy nor automatic (nor, perhaps, lastingly successful). Always creating difficulties in the negotiations of interdependence in a given area were the differing interests of the two countries.

As to the first option, a status quo approach, suffice it to say that no nation can carry out a status quo foreign policy. Canada cannot freeze its relations with the United States because, quite simply, it may well be in Canadian interests, as was the case with the Alcan pipeline, to enter into another set of integrative arrangements.

Even the third option, that of strengthening and expanding Canada's ties in other areas of the world, is not so much an option as it is a statement of the facts of international life.

As a sovereign nation, in an increasingly interconnected system of sovereign nations, Canada must adopt policies toward, and conduct relations with, all other countries in order to secure its national interests. Yet it is unhelpful to regard those relations simply as counterweights to the North American interdependency. Canada seeks to expand trade and upgrade its military commitment to Europe because these policies in and of themselves are thought to be in the best interests of the country. Canada seeks to expand development aid to francophone nations because, in addition to assisting orderly and peaceful development, this policy is in the interest of national unity. Canada seeks active participation in UN agencies because these agencies can provide forums in which Canada may conveniently pursue its interests.

It may well be true that some Canadian conduct abroad complements American policy, as in the case of United Nations peacekeeping in the Middle East. However, this is only an indication of what cannot be denied as a broad identity of interests between Canada and the United States on many international problems such as the search for a lasting peace in the Middle East or, more recently, a peaceful solution to the Rhodesian and Namibian problems. After all, as noted above, Canada's main area of interest lies with those of the developed Western democracies. The frequent concurrence of Canadian and American foreign policies outside North America can often be explained for reasons quite apart from the close interdependency that exists on this continent.

Conclusion

This chapter has shown that Canada's international experience is not "just like" that of the United States. Indeed, the obstacles Canada has surmounted in acquiring and maintaining an international personality are difficult to comprehend for Americans, citizens of a superpower born in revolution. First, Canada was isolated in a North America dominated by the overwhelming presence of the United

States. Second, Canada was attempting to reconcile this North American position with its position in the British Empire while simultaneously engaging in a drive for autonomy from Great Britain. Third, Canada was subject to all the domestic constraints of a fragmented, pluralistic society spread across a vast geographical expanse.

In short, Canada accomplished an extraordinary feat by taking its recognized place in the international community. The core elements of Canada's international experience include: the drive for autonomy and the maintenance of sovereignty as a North American nation separate and distinct from the United States; the pursuit of national interests abroad in an ever changing international system; and the Canadian need to preserve national unity in its external endeavors. It is no wonder that Canada's international experience can be characterized as a process of adjustment.

The irony is that just as Canada was demonstrating its full independence in the international system immediately after World War II, it was at the same time becoming increasingly interdependent with the United States in both an economic and a strategic sense. Active in the formation of the postwar international order, Canada was also becoming increasingly active with the United States in a continental context, especially during the 1950s. Meanwhile, the international system had polarized itself between two ideologically hostile blocs, led by the United States and the Soviet Union.

By the late 1960s and early 1970s, Canadian concern about the U.S. hegemonic impact on Canada had dramatically increased, and the international system itself had become more fluid. The Trudeau foreign policy review, and subsequent governmental papers and policies, attempted to absorb and reflect these forces. However, by the middle and late 1970s, still other changes were taking place. Internally, Canada was stunned by the electoral victory of the separatist party in Quebec, which challenged the most basic assumptions about the viability of a unified Canada. The demands of national unity, coupled with economic difficulties, forced the Canadian government and people to turn their energies inward. Canadian-U.S. relations improved, although there were still highly abrasive issues such as the fisheries and cable TV disputes, and Canada continued to meet its international responsibilities including those arising from its NATO commitment. Meanwhile, the international system seemed to be oscillating wildly between confrontation and cooperation as the Soviet Union continued its military buildup and its surrogates undertook adventures in Africa.

As for the future, Canada will, for reasons of necessity as much as choice, continue to be active in the areas of economic and strategic matters, peacekeeping, disarmament/ arms control, development assistance, and Law of the Sea. Moreover, Canada's international experience will continue to be grounded in the fourfold domestic framework of geography, demography, political institutions, and economics. In short, Canada's international experience, and all the ingredients of this experience, are characterized by a process of adjustment tempered by a strong sense of continuity that has emerged out of Canada's evolution as an independent and distinctive nation-state.

Notes

1. This interpretation is from James E. Dougherty and Robert L. Pfaltzgraff, Jr., *Contending Theories of International Relations* (New York: J. B. Lippincott Company, 1971), pp. 379–385.

2. See Michael Brecher, Blema Steinberg, and Janice Stein, "A Framework for Research on Foreign Policy Behaviour," *Journal of Conflict Resolution*, vol. XIII (1969), p. 90.

3. *Foreign Policy for Canadians* (Ottawa: Department of External Affairs, 1970), p. 19.

4. A. R. M. Lower, "Canada Can Defend Herself," *Canadian Forum*, vol. 17 (January 1938), p. 355.

5. See A. Jacomy-Millette, *Treaty Law in Canada* (Ottawa: University of Ottawa Press, 1975). See part I, "Historical Background and Definitions," pp. 5–45.

6. Ibid.

7. D. Milsten, "Canadian Peacekeeping," Ph.D. diss., University of Michigan, Ann Arbor, 1968, p. 60.

8. Ibid., p. 70.

9. Reid Escott, "The Birth of the North Atlantic Alliance," *International Journal*, vol. XXII, no. 3 (Summer 1967), pp. 431–432.

10. Ibid., p. 434.

11. Ibid., p. 435.

12. J. Gellner, *Canada in NATO* (Toronto: Ryerson Press, 1970), p. 26.

13. *Canada's Contribution to the UN*. Reference Paper No. 93, Department of External Affairs, Ottawa, August 1977, p. 15.

14. This survey section is based upon Dale C. Thomson and Roger F. Swanson, *Canadian Foreign Policy: Options and Perspectives* (Toronto: McGraw-Hill Ryerson 1971), chap. 2, pp. 9–19.

15. F. R. Scott, "The Permanent Bases of Canadian Foreign Policy," *Foreign Affairs*, vol. 10, no. 4 (July 1932).

16. *Foreign Policy for Canadians*, op. cit., pp. 20–21.

17. Thomson and Swanson, op. cit., p. 9.

18. Thomson and Swanson, op. cit., p. 14.

19. See "The Foundations of Canadian Policy in World Affairs," an address by Secretary of State for External Affairs Louis St. Laurent, University of Toronto, January 13, 1947, in R. A. Mackay, *Canadian Foreign Policy 1945–1954: Selected Speeches and Documents*, The Carleton Library No. 51 (Toronto: McClelland and Stewart Ltd., 1971), pp. 388–399.

20. *Foreign Policy for Canadians*, op. cit., p. 6.

21. *Foreign Policy for Canadians*, op. cit., p. 8.

22. Policy Statement by Prime Minister Trudeau, May 29, 1968.

23. *Foreign Policy for Canadians*, op. cit., p. 10.

24. *Foreign Policy for Canadians*, op. cit., p. 14.

25. *Foreign Policy for Canadians*, op. cit., p. 8.

26. *Foreign Policy for Canadians*, op. cit., p. 9.

27. *Foreign Policy for Canadians*, op. cit., p. 39.

28. Mitchell Sharp, "Canada-US Relations: Options for the Future," *International Perspectives*, Special Issue (Autumn 1972), p. 13.

29. H. Wiseman, "Peacekeeping Debut or Denouement?" *Behind the Headlines*, vol. XXXI, nos. 1–2 (Toronto: Canadian Institute of International Affairs), p. 12.

30. Speech to Canadian Arab Federation, May 16, 1976. Transcript provided by Canadian Embassy, Washington, D.C., p. 4.

31. George Ignatieff, "Canadian Aims and Perspectives in the Negotiation of International Agreements on Arms Control and Disarmament," in R. St. J. Macdonald et al., eds., *Canadian Perspectives on International Law and Organization* (Toronto: University of Toronto Press, 1974), p. 696.

32. See Canada, International Development Agency, *Strategy for International Development Cooperation, 1975–1980* (Ottawa, 1975).

33. This survey is based largely on Dale C. Thomson and Roger F. Swanson, op. cit., and Peyton V. Lyon and Tareq Y. Ismael, eds., *Canada and the Third World* (Toronto: The Macmillan Co. of Canada, 1976).

34. See J. C. M. Ogelsby, "Canada and Latin America," Lyon and Ismael, op. cit., pp. 162–199.

35. Thomson and Swanson, op. cit., p. 100.

36. Thomson and Swanson, op. cit., p. 104.

37. H. MacQuarrie, "Canada and the Caribbean," in Lyon and Ismael, op. cit., p. 200.

38. H. MacQuarrie, in Lyon and Ismael, op. cit., p. 200.

39. H. MacQuarrie, in Lyon and Ismael, op. cit., p. 215.

40. Thomson and Swanson, op. cit., p. 34.

41. Thomson and Swanson, op. cit., p. 31.

42. See Aloysius Balawyder, *Canadian-Soviet Relations Between the World Wars* (Toronto: University of Toronto Press, 1972).

43. See also T. W. Ismael, "Canada and the Middle East," in Lyon and Ismael, op. cit., pp. 240–276.

44. See Robert O. Mathews, "Canada and Anglophone Africa," and Louis Sobaurin, "Canada and Francophone Africa," in Lyon and Ismael, op. cit., pp. 60–161.

45. Thomson and Swanson, op. cit., p. 126.

46. This material survey is largely based upon Hugh Keenleyside and Gerald S. Brown, *Canada and the United States* (New York: Alfred A. Knopf, 1952), chaps. I–IV.

47. See Donald F. Warner, *The Idea of Continental Union* (Kentucky: University of Kentucky Press, 1960), pp. 17–18.

48. Idem.

49. Samuel F. Bemis *The Diplomacy of the American Revolution* (Bloomington, Ind.: Indiana University Press, 957; eighth printing, 1975), p. 196.

50. See Keenleyside and Brown, op. cit., pp. 122–125.

51. Van Alstyne, *The Rising American Empire* (New York: W. W. Norton and Co., 1960), p. 122.

52. Samuel F. Bemis, *A Diplomatic History of the United States* (New York: Holt, Rinehart and Winston, 1936), p. 382.

53. See Keenleyside and Brown, op. cit., chaps. V–VII.

54. See Keenleyside and Brown, op. cit., chap. VIII.

55. As quoted in James Eayrs, *In Defence of Canada*, vol. II, *Appeasment and Rearmament* (Toronto: University of Toronto Press, 1965), p. 183.

56. Ibid.

57. As quoted in Keenleyside and Brown, op. cit., p. 392.

58. As quoted from 1957 Royal Commission Report and excerpted in J. M. Bliss, ed., *Canadian History in Documents* (Toronto, 1966), p. 372.

59. *Foreign Policy for Canadians*, op. cit., pp. 24–25.

60. *International Perspectives*, op. cit., p. 13.

61. Remarks by Secretary of State for External Affairs Allan J. MacEachen to the Winnipeg Branch of the Canadian Institute of International Affairs, January 23, 1975. Embassy of Canada Report, Washington, D.C.

62. Text of Speech by U.S. Ambassador to Canada William J. Porter to a dinner sponsored by the Canadian Institute of International Affairs in Winnipeg, Manitoba, September 25, 1974. News Release, U.S. Information Service, U.S. Embassy, Ottawa, Ontario.

63. Addresses of President Richard Nixon to both houses of Parliament in the House of Commons, Ottawa, April 14, 1972. *House of Commons Debates*, Official Report, 4th sess., 28th Parliament, vol. II (1972), p. 1328.

64. J. Q. Adams to Monroe, February 8, 1816, Diplomatic Dispatches, Great Britain, General Records of the Department of State, Record Group 19, National Archives, Washington, D.C.

Appendix A

Questions for Discussion and Study

Chapter 1: Geography

1. Did Canada become a nation despite its geography? Before answering, clarify what you mean by geography. If you consider geography to concern only the natural environment, you will come up with a different answer than if you give it the broader definition given in the first section of this chapter.

2. It has been said that an external threat does more to weld a country together and keep it unified than any internal force. Discuss Canada's evolution to national unity in relation to the above idea. Consider the impact on Canada of the attacks on Canada during the American Revolutionary War, the various offers of annexation by the United States, the various boundary disputes, the War of 1812, the two world wars, and the threats of economic and cultural domination by the United States.

3. In what way is the Canadian Shield the "cornerstone" of Canada's physiographic structure? In what ways has the Canadian Shield affected the settlement pattern and economic development of Canada?

4. Despite its huge size, the problem of urbanization of agricultural land in Canada is a greater problem than it is in the United States. Explain why. Consider landforms, soil, climate, and urbanization patterns.

5. Concerning energy supplies, nature has played a trick on Canadians; the greatest supply is where the need is least. Explain the reason for the location of the various energy resources and the reasons for the location of the most densely populated areas.

6. What are some of the limitations of the staple export theory for explaining Canada's current settlement pattern and economic development?

7. In most countries there is usually one primate city that is at least twice the size of the next largest city. In Canada this is not the case. Toronto and Montreal are about the same size. Explain why this is so.

8. Predict what the settlement pattern and population density pattern

will be like in a hundred years' time. Will the population growth continue in the urban-industrial heartland? Or will economic development and population growth spread out into much of the hinterland? Give reasons for your predictions.

9. Discuss the environmental problems and regional disparities implications of continued increase in concentration of economic growth and urbanization in Canada.

10. Transportation networks and governmental transportation policies are extremely important to the economy and unity of Canada. Discuss, using specific examples.

11. Explain why Canada is the highest energy user per capita in the world.

12. Compare and contrast regionalism in Canada and the United States. What factors explain the difference?

13. Compare the economic disparity between the Atlantic Region and the Great Lakes–St. Lawrence Lowlands in Canada with the economic disparity between the manufacturing belt and Appalachia in the United States. Compare and contrast the reasons for the economic gap in each case.

14. Make a list of the factors encouraging national unity in Canada and another list of factors tending to reinforce regionalism and separatism. Assign a relative weight to each factor in order to come up with a balance sheet.

15. Assume that you could start from scratch in drawing a new political map of Canada, complete with provinces and capital cities. Draw a map showing new provincial boundaries and capital cities. Explain what criteria you used. If there are any anomalies, explain them.

(R. K.)

Chapter 2: History

1. What features of colonial development in New France influenced the course of Canadian history after 1763?

2. Analyze the role of the fur trade in Canadian and U.S. history. How did the French and English contest for control of the continent in the seventeenth and eighteenth centuries affect North American development?

3. In what ways is the Conquest a central event in Canadian history?

4. Why did the northern colonies refuse to join in the American Revolution? What were the consequences?

5. Discuss the significance of the War of 1812 from the Canadian and the U.S. point of view. How accurate is the phrase "three thousand miles of undefended border" as applied to northern North America in the nineteenth century?

6. Examine the evolution of colonial society in the half century after 1815. What institutions, values, beliefs, and the like were important?

7. What factors account for the rebellions of 1837, and the adoption of "responsible government" in British North America?

8. How and why was Confederation achieved in 1867?

9. What problems did the BNA Act seek to resolve, and how successfully did it do so? Why or why not?

10. What was the "National Policy" and how was it developed under Macdonald and Laurier?

11. Explain the emergence of "provincial rights" as a political issue after 1885. What are the implications for nationalism in Canada?

12. What is meant by the "North Atlantic Triangle," and how has it evolved in the last 150 years?

13. In what ways has Canada become a North American nation, and how has this been reflected in its relations with the United States and Britain?

14. What has been the impact of external events upon internal unity in Canada?

15. How did Canada become a major industrial nation by 1945? What have been the political and social consequences of this development?

16. Why are Canadians sensitive about "sleeping next to an elephant"?

17. What is meant by the "Quiet Revolution" and what are its implications for Canada as a whole?

18. What are the challenges to Canada's survival as a separate and distinct nation "from sea to sea"? How well has their historical experience prepared Canadians to confront these challenges within their federal system?

19. "Canadian history can best be understood by examining three interlocking relationships: Canada and the United States, Canada and the provinces, and English and French Canada." Discuss.

20. What have been the consequences of economic interdependence and technological development for Canadian autonomy in the twentieth century?

(G. C.)

Chapter 3: Politics

I. CONSTITUTIONAL BASES

1. What advantages and disadvantages are inherent in having an "unwritten" constitution?

2. What are the essential elements of the Canadian constitution? That is, what are the elements whose alteration would result in a *fundamental* change in the Canadian system of government?

II. FORMAL INSTITUTIONS

1. Does the monarchy play any significant role in contemporary Canadian politics?

2. An essential principle of representative, parliamentary democracy is that governments are accountable to an elected assembly. How effective are the constitutional procedures at the disposal of the House of Commons to enforce the accountability of the government of Canada?

3. Evaluate the proposition that the "presidentialization" of the Canadian system of parliamentary government has been a welcome transformation that is necessary for the effective government of Canada.

4. Does debate in the House of Commons serve any useful purpose, or does it merely distract the people's attention from the real centers of power in the political system?

5. "Responsible government would appear to have suffered a strange and alarming inversion: the cabinet is no longer responsible to the Commons; the Commons seems to have become responsible to the cabinet." (R. M. Dawson, *The Government of Canada.*) Discuss.

6. What are some of the resources the prime minister has at his disposal in conflicts with his own Cabinet or with the House of Commons?

7. It is sometimes argued that power has passed in large measure from the hands of our elected representatives into the hands of the nonelected civil service. What is the basis of this argument? Do sufficient safeguards exist to ensure control of the administration by elected representatives?

8. Is it desirable to isolate the judiciary from partisan political influence? If so, does the Canadian system of judicial appointment perform this task adequately? If some political influence is desired, how might it be accomplished most effectively?

9. "The oft-repeated statement that Canada has inherited adequate guarantees to civil liberties from British traditions of common law is an invalid, even a dangerous, assumption." Discuss this contention in light of the suggestion that Canada should have a constitutionally entrenched Bill of Rights.

III. INFORMAL INSTITUTIONS

1. It has been said that the origins and development of Canadian parties have caused them to be arenas for brokerage among regional elites, unconcerned with the key economic issues that most affect the mass public. In this regard, one theorist (Gad Horowitz) has suggested that, for democracy to be served, "our party system must be polarized on a left-right basis, and the main issues raised for discussion in the political arena must be class issues." How satisfactory is the description of Canadian parties offered above? How satisfactory is the prescription offered by Horowitz?

2. Political parties in Canada are often charged with two apparently incompatible functions. On the one hand, they are asked to articulate pol-

itical and social cleavages, making grievances clear in the arena of public debate. On the other hand, they are asked to aggregate cleavages and in part resolve grievances within their own ranks. Are these functions genuinely incompatible? How well do Canadian parties appear to perform either function?

3. How much internal democracy exists in Canadian political parties? To what extent are policymaking, fundraising, campaign organization, and candidate/leadership selection democratically administered in the various parties?

4. Given the criticisms of the single-member, simple plurality electoral system, what advantages would accrue if a proportional representation electoral system were used in Canada? What disadvantages would such a system have?

5. How important is it, for the maintenance of parliamentary democracy, that voters choose their parties or candidates on the basis of clearly defined policy issues?

6. An important premise of at least one common view of politics is equal opportunity of access to political power. To what extent does the current pattern of interest-group activity in Canada impede or facilitate the realization of this ideal of political equality?

7. It has been said that there is no such thing as "public opinion," but rather many "publics" and hence many "public opinions." Moreover, these opinions are sometimes very changeable. What consequences do these contentions have for the measurement and political impact of public opinion in Canada?

8. What functions should the mass media perform in a political democracy? To what extent is the performance of these functions by the Canadian mass media affected by patterns of media ownership and U.S. influence?

9. What are the consequences for Canadian national unity of the regionalized nature of its media system?

10. Can something become a political issue if the mass media do not recognize it as such?

IV. THE CANADIAN FEDERAL SYSTEM

1. Does the historical evolution of the Canadian federal system of government reflect the extent to which Canada is a federal society?

2. Discuss the contention that "the federal aspects of the Canadian constitution, using the latter term in its broadest sense, have come to be less what the courts say they are than what the federal and provincial cabinets and bureaucracies, in a continuous series of formal and informal relations, determine them to be."

3. It is sometimes argued that the best solution for the strains presently experienced by Canadian federalism would be substantial decentraliza-

tion—giving increased powers to all the provinces. Is this a practicable arrangement in contemporary Canada?

4. Does Quebec have a special status in the Canadian federal system? Should Quebec have such a special status?

5. Which of the following has been most significant in adapting the Canadian constitution to changing conditions: formal amendment, judicial interpretation, or political bargaining?

6. "The main beneficiary in Canada from the beginning has been the French-speaking minority, whose dissidence was the original occasion for adopting federalism and is the justification for retaining it today." (William Riker, *Federalism.*) Is Riker correct?

7. Are there as many political issues uniting the provinces in Canada as there are dividing them from one another?

8. Which is more important in determining the policy outputs of provincial governments—the social and economic problems facing each province, or the party ideologies of the provincial governments?

9. To what extent are the problems of municipal governments in Canada related to their reliance on the property tax as a means of funding local administration? What roles could the other levels of government play in tackling local government issues in Canada?

(R. D.)

Chapter 4: Economics

1. When studying the question of whether there ought to be a government-owned corporation involved in exploration for petroleum, does it matter whether one takes an "economics" or a "political economy" approach? If so, how would you expect these approaches to differ in methodology or analysis?

2. In terms of the staples theory, how would you expect different societies to be built on the basis of a slave-plantation economy and a single-family farm economy? What sorts of linkages would be found in each case?

3. Of Canada's great staples, which has had the most beneficial long-run impact from the standpoint of economics? from that of political economy?

4. Can you think of four or five reasons why one country might not wish to be a "satellite" of another country?

5. Did Canada have any real option to becoming a satellite of the U.S. economy in 1850? in 1950?

6. To what extent do economic factors such as trade and investment relations "determine" political, cultural, and social relations?

7. Imagine how you would view central Canada and the federal gov-

ernment in Ottawa if you lived in (a) Halifax, Nova Scotia; (b) Trois
Rivières, Quebec; and (c) Regina, Saskatchewan.

8. Alberta is rich in petroleum. Who should benefit from that wealth?
Albertans? Canadians? How would you go about making that decision?

9. Do you think there is much possibility of Canadians resolving their
regional problems by adopting the same policy approaches used by the U.S.
government? Why?

10. Do the objectives of society and of a private corporation always
coincide? What should be done if they do not? How does this relationship
between society and the corporation differ in Canada from that in the United
States?

11. Specifically, why is it not possible to treat questions of trade, foreign investment, and economic performance as separate, isolated issues?

12. If "comparative advantage" suggests that Canada should concentrate on exports of staples, but Canadians do not want to live in that kind
of a society, what should they do? What is the cost to a society of not doing
that which is "most efficient"?

13. If you were the Canadian minister of finance, would you try to
bring about a free trade treaty with the United States? Why?

14. Does Canada have any options today to an increasingly close economic relationship with the United States?

15. In what ways does it matter, if at all, whether Canadians or foreigners own Canadian manufacturing plants? Would it bother you if Canadians or Germans or Saudi Arabians owned 50 or 60 percent of America's
industry?

16. Should Canada's resources be used to create industrial jobs in Canada, or should the resources be sold to the highest bidder on world markets?
To what extent should the corporations that owned the resources be allowed
to make that decision?

(P. K.)

Chapter 5: Anthropology

1. Do Canadians need their own brand of anthropology to analyze their
own particular social and cultural phenomena?

2. Is the melting pot, as opposed to the cultural mosaic, a negative or
positive way to integrate minorities into society?

3. Should the French and English, as founding peoples of Canada, have
special privileges and prerogatives?

4. Economically, it would be advantageous for Canada to become part
of the United States. Why doesn't it?

5. Is it possible for a nation to identify its own individual character

without contrasting itself with another nation as Canada does with the United States?

6. Does the distinction "native Canadians" as opposed to "Amerindians" have any particular relevance?

7. What impact have the specific environments of Canada had on the development of the traditional cultures and societies of Canada?

8. The vision quest, like some other cultural patterns, appears to be a cultural universal for the Indians of Canada. What does that suggest?

9. What impact has the European contact had on the traditional cultures of Canada?

10. What has been the impact of native Canadian culture on Euro-Canadian culture and society?

11. Can the phrase "the culture of poverty" be applied to the modern Canadian Indian and Inuit?

12. What role did the seigneurial system play in the development of French-Canadian culture and society?

13. What possible personality clashes can arise from the dual role of farmer and lumberjack?

14. What role did the church play in the maintenance of traditional values and life style?

15. What role can the church play in modern Quebec today?

16. What are some of the important institutions that aid in the maintenance of an immigrant's cultural traditions?

17. What are the most important factors leading to assimilation of the immigrant into mainstream Canadian culture and society?

18. Should immigrants in Quebec be required to send their children to French schools in Quebec?

19. When all is said and done, are Canadians different from Americans?

20. Given the experience of Spanish Americans in the United States, what do you foresee for the ethnic minorities of Canada in the next twenty years?

(P. W.)

Chapter 6: Literature

I. PHILOSOPHICAL BACKGROUND

1. What in your opinion are the national values of the United States? What works of American literature reflect these values? What works reflect national concerns or problems?

2. What could account for the duality in the Canadian attitude toward Americans? Can you think of any general attitudes in the United States

toward Canada and Canadians? Do you know of any works by American writers that reflect an awareness of Canada?

3. What is Puritanism? How did it influence the United States?

4. Are there differences between Puritanism and Calvinism? How did the effects of Puritanism and Calvinism (and its Jansenist version) differ in the United States and Canada? How are these differences related to each nation's origin and history?

5. What is the meaning of self-reliant individualism? How is it related to general patterns of behavior in the United States and Canada?

6. What is materialism? conformism? Discuss the implications of materialism and conformism in American and Canadian society and literature.

7. What are the distinguishing features of traditional heroes in Canadian and American literature? Give examples.

8. What is a national myth? Describe national myths of the United States. Why is there a dearth of positive national myths in Canada?

9. Why should there be parallels between the works of black American authors and Canadian authors? Do you know of any such parallels?

10. What are the major comprehensive themes of Canadian literature, and how are they related to the nation's history and philosophical evolution?

II. COLONIAL PERIOD

1. What are the three areas of Canada where literature developed during the Colonial Period?

2. Who were the United Empire Loyalists? What effect did they have on Canada? What other kinds of immigrants did Canada receive?

3. What types of literature were produced during the Colonial Period in Canada? Do you know of similar American works?

4. What stimulated the development of literature in French Canada? Explain and give examples.

5. Why would the theme of exile be popular among Canadian poets? Can you think of American works that treat the same theme?

6. What were the significant aspects of the works of Thomas Chandler Haliburton and Antoine Gérin-Lajoie?

III. CONFEDERATION PERIOD

1. What were some of the motivations for, and what is the nature of, Canadian Confederation? Compare Canadian Confederation with the founding of the United States.

2. Who were the six major Confederation poets in English and French? What kind of poetry did each one write?

3. By the end of the nineteenth century, Canadian Confederation was already in trouble. Speculate on possible reasons.

IV. EARLY TWENTIETH CENTURY

1. What characterized the major writers of this period?

2. Robert Service and William Henry Drummond wrote popular verse rather than serious poetry. Can you think of other examples? Do you think such verse has a place in literary studies?

3. The "Ecole littéraire de Montréal" is known today mainly because of two of its members. Who were they and what kind of poetry did they write?

4. Compare Louis Hémon and Stephen Leacock.

5. What does the term "naturalism" mean in literature? Discuss the implications of Albert Laberge's career as a naturalistic writer.

V. MODERN PERIOD

1. What were the aftereffects of World War I on Canada?

2. The rapid development of the paperback trade has changed the nature of book publishing and marketing. What effect has this development had on Canadian writers? Can you suggest any solutions to the problem?

3. Mazo de la Roche wrote sixteen novels that constitute the saga of the Whiteoaks family of Jalna. Can you think of similar sagas in literature?

4. What are the novels of the soil, and how are they related to the first comprehensive theme of Canadian literature? Who were the two writers who brought the novel of the soil to a climax?

5. Morley Callaghan, Sinclair Ross, and Roger Lemelin all wrote novels with "traditional" Canadian protagonists. What are the characteristics of the typical Canadian protagonist? Explain with reference to the novels.

6. What does modernism mean in poetry? Name some Canadian poets who were involved in the modernist movement in Canada.

7. Comment on the meanings of A. J. M. Smith's poem "The Sorcerer" and F. R. Scott's "Saturday Sundae."

8. What is distinctive about the poetic achievements of E. J. Pratt? of A. M. Klein?

VI. BREAKUP OF OLD ORDER

1. World War II had the effect of weakening traditional systems of values. Explain why this should be so with reference to the novels of Colin McDougall and Jean Vaillancourt and to other war novels you have read.

2. What is the common significance of the characters Rose-Anna Lacasse in Gabrielle Roy's *Bonheur d'occasion* and Abraham in Adele Wiseman's *The Sacrifice*?

3. What is meant by the term "existential vacuum"? What solutions to this state are suggested in the works of Hugh MacLennan and Jean Simard?

4. How do Hugh MacLennan's George Stewart and André Langevin's Alain Dubois resemble each other? Do you see these characters as typically or distinctively Canadian? Explain.

5. Do you think that you would find André Langevin's character Madeleine an attractive individual? Discuss her personality.

6. How is materialism related to the existential vacuum? Explain with reference to Canadian and American literature.

7. What impeded the development of playwriting in Canada? How did native drama eventually become established, and who were the dramatists involved?

8. Explain the meanings of Dorothy Livesay's "The Snow Girl's Ballad," Ralph Gustafson's "The Great Day," Neil Tracy's "I.O.U.," Jean-Guy Pilon's "L'Exigence du pays," and Roland Giguère's "Continuer à vivre."

9. Discuss the meaning of Earle Birney's phrase, "It's only by our lack of ghosts we're haunted."

VII. SEARCH FOR VITAL TRUTH

1. What is nationalism? What are its implications for the United States and Canada?

2. What is the nature of Quebec nationalism, and how has it changed over the last half century? How is it reflected in literature?

3. What would appear to be the major problem of would-be terrorists as presented in Canadian fiction?

4. Discuss the meaning of equality in both American and Canadian contexts and with reference to works of literature.

5. How is the *Search* theme handled by various Canadian novelists and poets of the 1960s? Do you see parallels in American literature?

6. Explain the meanings of the following poems: "Execution" by Alden Nowlan, "Faculty Party" by D. G. Jones, "Colonial Saturday Night" by Raymond Souster, and "Les Années de déréliction" by Gaston Miron.

7. What does poet Michèle Lalonde mean by "speak white"?

VIII. NEW HERO

1. Speculate on the nature and significance of the *New Hero* in Canadian literature. How is he different from the traditional Canadian and American heroes? Do you see any parallels or contrasts in contemporary American literature?

2. In what way is it possible that Canada and Canadians may be experiencing a "new beginning"?

(P. W.)

Chapter 7: International Relations

1. Identify the most important events in the evolution of Canada as an international actor up to World War II and assess their significance.

2. Give four examples of how changes in the international system have affected Canadian foreign policy.

3. Using Canada as an example, explain how a medium-sized power can use multilateral organizations to play a more active and distinctive international role.

4. What has been the impact of Canada's open economy on both the evolution and the scope of Canadian foreign policy?

5. How have Canadian foreign policy objectives changed since World War II, and how do you think they will change in the future?

6. Has the Canadian international experience been one of continuity or discontinutiy?

7. How has the Canadian approach to east-west and north-south relations differed from that of the United States, and why?

8. How has Canada contributed to international peace and security through peacekeeping?

9. Outline Canada's strategic ties with other nations and relate them to Canada's overall foreign policy objectives.

10. Has the French fact in Canada been adequately reflected in the Canadian diplomatic tradition?

11. Has Canada been able to play an international role in excess of its real power as measured in traditional political-military terms?

12. Why did U.S. annexation of Canada prove to be ultimately unfeasible?

13. Contrast coexistence and interdependence in the Canadian-U.S. context, giving specific examples.

14. Why would a Canadian be concerned that Canadian-U.S. interdependence might lead to eventual absorption?

15. In what way is the Canadian "third option" of asserting distinctiveness from the United States a rejection of its foreign policy of adjustment? Is such an option possible in the long run?

16. How does Canada's relationship with the United States fit into its overall range of relations with other nations and regions?

17. Excluding North America, in what regions of the international system is Canada most active, and why?

18. Why have Americans traditionally been unable to view Canada as a separate and distinct international actor?

(R. F. S.)

Appendix B

Bibliographies and Suggested Readings

Editor's Note: These lists are not intended to be exhaustive, definitive, or especially research oriented. They attempt to guide undergraduate students in their pursuit of Canadian studies beyond the scope of this introductory volume. Those who follow the suggestions made here will find extensive, often annotated bibliographies in many of the works they encounter. They should remember, however, that the best guide to recent bibliography in any field is a well-informed, expert teacher.

Each discipline approaches the matter of bibliography differently, and in each field the most important results of recent research appear in different forms and formats. Moreover, to cover the entire sweep of a long-standing discipline such as Canadian history, for example, one needs suggested readings rather different from those intended to illuminate just one aspect of that history. A literary bibliography, mixing creative with critical works, will have a particular appearance and organization. For these reasons we have in general retained each author's own style and format in this appendix.

I. Geography: An Annotated Bibliography

TEXTBOOKS

Warkentin, J. (editor). *Canada: A Geographical Interpretation*. Toronto: Methuen, 1968. A project of the Canadian Association of Geographers for Canada's Centennial in 1967. Each chapter was written by one or more leading Canadian geographers. About half of the book discusses general Canadian topics such as physical geography, economic development, regionalism, and metropolitan dominance. The balance of the book is an historical-geographical account of the regions of Canada. May be heavy reading as an initial exposure to the geography of Canada.

Watson, J. W. *Canada: Problems and Prospects.* Don Mills: Longmans, 1968. The first chapter provides an excellent explanation of how Canada evolved into a nation separate from the United States. Chapters 2 and 3 discuss Canada's physical geography and the human response to it. The balance of the book provides a geographical analysis of the major Canadian regions. The greatest strength of the book is the vivid way in which Watson describes how settlement and development in Canada responded to the natural environment.

Putnam, D. P., and R. G. Putnam. *Canada: A Regional Analysis.* Toronto: Dent, 1970. A very good all-around textbook with numerous maps, photographs, and tables. The regional approach is emphasized. Too much data and detail to make for interesting reading, but it is an excellent reference book.

Tomkins, G. S., T. L. Hills, and T. R. Weir. *A Regional Geography of Canada.* Toronto: Gage, 1970. A thorough regional geography with an abundance of maps and photos including air photographs and colored topographic map sections. The inductive pedagogical approach is used with scores of questions based on data provided in the book.

Hamelin, L. E. *Canada: A Geographical Perspective.* Toronto: Wiley, 1973. An edited translation of Hamelin's book *Le Canada* (Paris: Presses Universitaires de France, 1969). A thematic approach covering the topics of physical geography, settlement, population, economic development, urban affairs, and the Canadian identity. More readable than most textbooks but not as useful as a reference book.

Krueger, R. R., and R. G. Corder. *Canada: A New Geography.* Toronto: Holt, Rinehart and Winston, rev. ed., 1974. A thematic approach to Canada, profusely illustrated with both colored and black-and-white maps and photos. Written for Canadian high school students but useful for college students with little or no knowledge of Canada. Metric measurements and 1976 census data used in the 1978 printing.

Tomkins, D. M., et al. *Canada: The Land and Its People.* Toronto: Gage, 1975. A thematic approach to Canada, written at a similar level to that of the Krueger-Corder book. Profusely illustrated in color as well as in black and white and including air photos and topographic map sections. Metric measurements used.

A number of textbooks on North America produced by U.S. publishers have separate sections on Canada. Of these, the most thorough discussion of Canada is presented in: Starkey, O. P., and J. L. Robinson. *The Anglo-American Realm.* New York: McGraw-Hill, 1969.

CANADIAN REGIONS

Trotier, Louis (general editor). *Studies in Canadian Geography.* Toronto: University of Toronto Press, 1972. A series of six volumes prepared by the Canadian Association of Geographers for the International Geographical Congress held in Canada in 1972. Each book is written by an expert on the region. Extensive bibliographies are included. Authors and titles are: A. G. Macpherson, *The Atlantic Provinces*; F. Grenier, *Quebec*; L. Gentilcore, *Ontario*; P. J. Smith, *The Prairie Provinces*; J. L. Robinson, *British Columbia*; and W. C. Wonders, *The North*.

Robinson, J. L. *The Canadian Shield*. Toronto: Methuen, 1969. A comprehensive and very readable account of the economic geography of the Canadian Shield. The history of the development of each economic sector is traced from its origins to the mid-1960s.

Berger, T. R. *Northern Frontier, Northern Homeland*. Ottawa: Supply and Services Canada, 1977. The report of the Mackenzie Valley Pipeline Inquiry, Volume 1. This is a very thorough and up-to-date description of a section of Canada's North. It succinctly discusses the people, the environment, and a whole array of social and environmental implications of development projects in the North.

Chapman, L. J., and D. F. Putnam, *The Physiography of Southern Ontario*. Toronto: University of Toronto Press, 1966. A description of the physical landscape of southern Ontario, how it evolved, and how man has used it. Illustrated with photos and maps, including a large folded physiographic map in color.

BOOKS OF READINGS

Krueger, R. R., et al. (editors). *Regional and Resource Planning in Canada*. Toronto: Holt, Rinehart and Winston, rev. ed., 1970. Readings based primarily on the Resources for Tomorrow Conference held in Montreal in 1961. Updated and new papers added in 1970. Treats topics such as the regional concept, regional planning and development experiences in Canada, and resource use issues and problems.

Gentilcore, R. L. (editor). *Geographical Approaches to Canadian Problems*. Scarborough, Ont.: Prentice-Hall, 1971. Papers written primarily by Canadian geographers on the topics of population, economic development, cities, and political geography. In the latter section is a paper on "Quebec Separatism and the Future of Canada."

Irving, R. M. (editor). *Readings in Canadian Geography*. Toronto: Holt, Rinehart and Winston, rev. ed., 1972. Papers on geographical diversity, population, settlement, cities, agriculture, resource problems, and regional disparities. Two articles may be of particular interest to Americans: "Foreign Investment in Canada" and "The Location of United States Manufacturing Subsidiaries in Canada."

Bryfogle, R. C., and R. R. Krueger. *Urban Problems (Revised)*. Toronto: Holt, Rinehart and Winston, 1975. Readings on urban problems and urban planning issues in Canada. Includes an extensive bibliography on urban Canada. Edited for easy reading.

McBoyle, G. R., and E. Sommerville (editors). *Canada's Natural Environ-*

ment: Essays in Applied Geography. Toronto: Methuen, 1976. Commissioned papers on the nature of Canada's natural resources and related problems and policy issues. Includes an introductory chapter on "The Role of Geography in Environmental Research, Action and Education."

Krueger, R. R., and B. Mitchell (editors). *Managing Canada's Renewable Resources.* Toronto: Methuen, 1977. Readings on resource management perspectives, assessment, and decision making, and resource management case studies in Canada.

SPECIAL TOPICS

Burke, S., and R. Peterson. *Frog Fables and Beaver Tales.* Toronto: Lorimer, 1973. A hilarious satire on the French-English problem in Canada and Canada-U.S. relations, presented in a children's book format. Can be read in fifteen minutes.

Ray, D. M. *Dimensions of Canadian Regionalism.* Ottawa: Department of Energy, Mines and Resources, 1971. Geographical Paper No. 49. In a series of large colored maps and a few pages of text, this book analyzes the regional social and economic phenomena and relates them to regional disparities. An excellent reference book on Canadian regional dimensions.

Bird, J. B. *The Natural Landscapes of Canada.* Toronto: Wiley, 1972. The best available book on the physiography (regional geomorphology) of Canada. Difficult unless the reader has a sound background in physical geography.

Hare, F. K., and M. K. Thomas. *Climate Canada.* Toronto: Wiley, 1974. A thorough description and explanation of Canada's climates and their interaction with man. The sections on "the regional climates of Canada" and "climate and man in Canada" are easy reading. The section on "general climatology" is difficult reading unless the reader has had an introductory course in climatology.

Simmons, J., and R. Simmons. *Urban Canada.* Toronto: Copp Clark, 1974. A very readable account of the Canadian urban environment: how cities emerged, how they are both different and alike, and how the landscapes within cities vary.

Yeates, M. *Main Street, Windsor to Quebec City.* Toronto: Macmillan, in association with the Ministry of State for Urban Affairs and Information Canada, Ottawa, 1975. A very useful analysis of urbanization in the Great Lakes–St. Lawrence Lowlands. Includes maps of the degree of urbanization by census subdivision.

Krueger, R. R., R. M. Irving, and C. Vincent. *Regional Patterns: Disparities and Development.* Published by Canada Studies Foundation/Canadian Association of Geographers, 1975; distributed by McClelland and Stewart, Toronto. This book, designed for Canadian secondary school teachers and senior students, contains a paper on regional disparities and regional development, one on poverty in Canada, and a third on different approaches to studying the topic of regional disparities.

STATISTICAL DATA

Canada Year Book. Ottawa: Statistics Canada, annual. A huge book of over 1,000 pages filled with basic information and hundreds of tables of statistics. Each year there are special articles about some aspect of Canada. For example, in the 1972 volume an article entitled "Regional Geography of Canada" provides excellent brief descriptions of the different Canadian regions.

Canada Handbook. Ottawa: Statistics Canada, annual. For years up to 1975 it is available from the Department of Supplies and Services, Ottawa. *Canada 1976* is published by, and is available from, Hurtig, Edmonton. Basically a summary of the *Canada Year Book.* It has fewer statistics and is generally more readable than the complete *Year Book.* The centennial edition, *Canada One Hundred 1867–1967* is particularly useful because the description of the evolution of the Canadian nation and the development of the country's major industries.

Perspective Canada. Ottawa: Statistics Canada, 1974. A useful compendium of social and economic statistics with hundreds of tables and graphs and a few maps. Of particular interest to geographers are the sections on population, environmental quality, and bilingualism.

Perspective Canada II. Ottawa: Statistics Canada, 1977. This publication not only updates the information contained in the 1974 volume but also has several chapters of additional data. If only one of the two can be obtained, this second volume is recommended.

Facts from Canadian Maps: A Geographical Handbook. Ottawa: Department of Energy, Mines and Resources, 1974. This small book is filled with statistics about Canada's mountains, rivers, lakes, climate, and cities. It also includes a list of maps, charts, and air photos available from Canadian Government offices. Inside the back cover is a detailed map of Canada at a scale of one inch to 250 miles.

ATLASES

The National Atlas of Canada. Fourth edition. Ottawa: Macmillan Co. of Canada Ltd., in association with the Department of Energy, Mines and Resources, 1974. An excellent reference atlas with maps of almost every conceivable Canadian phenomenon.

Several world atlases published in Canada have good sections on Canada:

Atlas Larousse Canadien. Quebec City: Librairie Larousse, les éditions françaises, 1971.

The Holt World Atlas. Toronto: Holt, Rinehart and Winston, 1970.

The Canadian Oxford Atlas. Toronto: Oxford University Press.

The Canadian Oxford School Atlas. Toronto: Oxford University Press, latest edition, 1976. An inexpensive small atlas that is updated every few years.

TOPOGRAPHIC MAPS AND AIR PHOTOS

Topographic maps are available from the Map Distribution Office of the
  Department of Energy, Mines and Resources, Ottawa; air photos, from
  the National Photo Library, Ottawa. Reproductions of selected topographic map sections and selected air photos along with interpretation
  commentary are available in the following publications:

Blair, C. L., and R. I. Simpson. *The Canadian Landscape, Map and Air
  Photo Interpretation.* Toronto: Copp Clark, 1967.
Chevrier, E. D., and D. F. W. Aitkens. *Topographic Map and Air Photo
  Interpretation.* Toronto: Macmillan, 1970.
Augustine, H. A., et al. *Canadian Stereograms.* Toronto: Dent, 1971.

JOURNALS

The Canadian Geographical Journal. Published by the Royal Canadian
  Geographical Society. A semipopular journal containing numerous well-
  illustrated articles on a wide range of Canadian geographical topics.
The Canadian Geographer. Published by the Canadian Association of Geographers. A journal containing reports of the research of professional
  geographers. Not all of the articles are on Canadian topics.
Maclean's. A newsmagazine with emphasis on Canadian affairs.
Canadian Forum. A magazine devoted to critical articles on issues of Canadian concern. Has a strong Canadian nationalistic emphasis.

FILMS AND SLIDES

The National Film Board, Ottawa, has scores of films on Canadian topics
  of interest to geographers. They (and other information) are available
  in the United States through the Canadian Embassy at Washington,
  D.C., and the following Canadian Consulate offices: Atlanta, Boston,
  Buffalo, Chicago, Cleveland, Dallas, Detroit, Los Angeles, Minneapolis,
  New Orleans, New York City, Philadelphia, San Francisco, and Seattle.

Slide sets with accompanying notes are available for some of Canada's
  major cities from the Canadian Association of Geographers, P.O. Box
  6070, Montreal, P.Q.

II. History: Suggested Readings

Canadian history has been professionally taught in Canadian universities
for nearly a century, and the major English journal in the field—the *Canadian Historical Review,* or *CHR*—dates from 1920. Consequently, the

bibliography facing an American student interested in Canadian history is enormous. The following suggestions are intended as the merest beginning for such a student. Recent work in book form is regularly reviewed by the *CHR, La Revue d'Histoire de l'Amérique du Nord*, the *Journal of Canadian Studies*, the *Journal of Canadian History*, the *American Review of Canadian Studies*, and the more popular but nonetheless scholarly *Canadian Forum*. Students will also want to consult articles in these and other journals for the results of recent research. The lists below deliberately focus on works in English in book form, hopefully such as are likely to be available in undergraduate libraries.

GENERAL

Several textbooks offer a more detailed introduction. Note the dates of publication; there is a dearth of recent substantial texts.

Careless, J. M. S. *Canada: A Story of Challenge*. Revised Edition. New York: St. Martin's, 1963.

Careless, J. M. S. (ed.). *Colonists and Canadians*. New York: St. Martin's, 1971.

Careless, J. M. S., and R. C. Brown (eds.). *The Canadians, Part One*. Toronto: Macmillan, 1967.

Cornell, P. G., et al. *Canada: Unity in Diversity*. New York: Holt, Rinehart and Winston, 1970.

Creighton, D. G. *A History of Canada: Dominion of the North*. Boston: Houghton Mifflin, 1958.

Lower, A. R. M. *Colony to Nation*. New York: Longmans, 1958.

McInnis, E. W. *Canada, A Political and Social History*. Toronto: Holt, Rinehart and Winston, 1969.

McNaught, K. *The Pelican History of Canada*. Baltimore: Penguin Books, 1970.

The following two books are collections of readings:

Bumsted, J. M. (ed.). *Canadian History Before Confederation*. New York: Dorsey, 1972.

Hodgins, B. W., and R. J. D. Page (eds.). *Canadian History Since Confederation*. New York: Dorsey, 1972.

HISTORIOGRAPHY AND BIBLIOGRAPHY

Berger, C. (ed.). *Approaches to Canadian History*. Toronto: University of Toronto Press, 1967.

Berger, C. *The Writing of Canadian History*. New York: Oxford University Press, 1976.

Garigue, P. *A Bibliographical Introduction to the Study of French Canada*. New York: Kraus Reprint, 1976.

Granatstein, J. L., and P. Stevens (eds.). *Canada Since 1967: A Critical Bibliography.* Second Edition. Saratoga, Fla.: Samuel Stevens, 1977.

Lapierre, L. "Historical Studies in French" and Berger, C. "Historical Studies in English." In W. Toye (ed.). *Supplement* to the *Oxford Companion to Canadian History and Literature.* New York: Oxford University Press, 1974.

THE FRENCH REGIME

Eccles, W. J. *France in America.* New York: Harper and Row, 1972.

Frégault, G. *Canada: The War of the Conquest.* New York: Oxford University Press, 1969.

Griffiths, N. E. S. *The Acadians: Creation of a People.* Toronto: McGraw-Hill Ryerson, 1973.

Innis, H. A. *The Fur Trade in Canada.* Revised Edition. Toronto: University of Toronto Press, 1956.

Nish, C. *The French Regime.* Scarborough, Ont.: Prentice-Hall, 1965.

Trudel, M. *Introduction to New France.* New York: Holt, Rinehart and Winston, 1968.

Wade, M. *The French Canadians.* 2 volumes. Revised Edition. Toronto: Macmillan, 1968.

Zoltvany, Y. F. *The Government of New France: Royal, Clerical or Class Rule?* Toronto: Prentice-Hall, 1970.

THE COLONIAL PERIOD

Brebner, J. B. *The Neutral Yankees of Nova Scotia.* New York: Russell & Russel, 1970.

Careless, J. M. S. *Union of the Canadas, 1841–1857.* Toronto: McClelland and Stewart, 1967.

Cook, R. (ed.). *French Canadian Nationalism.* Toronto: Macmillan, 1969.

Craig, G. M. *Upper Canada: The Formative Years, 1784–1841.* Toronto: McClelland and Stewart, 1963.

Creighton, D. G. *The Empire of the St. Lawrence.* Toronto: Macmillan, 1956.

Creighton, D. G. *The Road to Confederation.* Boston: Houghton Mifflin, 1965.

Harris, R. C., and J. Warkentin. *Canada Before Confederation.* New York: Oxford University Press, 1974.

Hitsman, J. M. *The Incredible War of 1812: A Military History.* Toronto: University of Toronto Press, 1965.

Lanctot, G. *Canada and the American Revolution.* Cambridge, Mass.: Harvard University Press, 1967.

MacNutt, W. S. *The Atlantic Provinces, 1712–1857.* Toronto: McClelland and Stewart, 1965.

Morton, A. S. *A History of the Canadian West to 1870–71.* Second Edition. Toronto: University of Toronto Press, 1973.

Morton, W. L. *The Critical Years, 1857–1873*. Toronto: McClelland and Stewart, 1964.

Neatby, H. *Quebec: The Revolutionary Age*. Toronto: McClelland and Stewart, 1966.

Ouelett, F. *Histoire économique et sociale du Québec, 1760–1850*. Montreal: Fides, 1966.

Ouellet, F. *Lower Canada, 1791–1840: Social Change and Nationalism*. Toronto: McClelland and Stewart, 1980.

Rawlyk, G. A. *Revolution Rejected, 1775–1776*. Scarborough, Ont.: Prentice-Hall, 1968.

Winks, R. *Canada and the United States: The Civil War Years*. Baltimore, Md.: Johns Hopkins University Press, 1960.

Wise, S. F., and R. C. Brown. *Canada Views the United States*. Seattle: University of Washington Press, 1967.

Zaslow, M. (ed.). *The Defended Border: Upper Canada and the War of 1812*. Toronto: Macmillan, 1964.

THE NATIONAL PERIOD

Armstrong, E. A. *The Crisis of Quebec, 1914–1918*. Toronto: McClelland and Stewart, 1974.

Berton, P. *The National Dream* and *The Last Spike*. 2 volumes in one. Toronto: McClelland and Stewart, 1974.

Brebner, J. B. *The North Atlantic Triangle*. New York: Russell, 1970.

Brown, R. C. *Robert Laird Borden, A Biography*. Vol. 1, Toronto Macmillan, 1975; Vol. 2, 1980.

Brown, R. C., and R. Cook. *Canada, A Nation Transformed, 1897–1921*. Toronto: McClelland and Stewart, 1976.

Careless, J. M. S. *Brown of the Globe*. 2 volumes. Toronto: Macmillan, 1972.

Craig, G. M. *The United States and Canada*. Cambridge, Mass.: Harvard University Press, 1968.

Creighton, D. G. *John A. Macdonald*. 2 volumes. Toronto: Macmillan, 1952, 1955.

Dawson, R. M., and B. Neatby. *William Lyon Mackenzie King*. 3 volumes. Toronto: University of Toronto Press, 1976.

Levitt, J. *Henri Bourassa and the Golden Calf*. Ottawa: University of Ottawa Press, 1969.

MacIntosh, W. A. *The Economic Background of Dominion-Provincial Relations*. Toronto: McClelland and Stewart, 1964.

McNaught, K. *A Prophet in Politics: A Biography of J. S. Woodsworth*. Toronto: University of Toronto Press, 1959.

MacQuarrie, H. (ed.). *R. L. Borden, His Memoirs*. Toronto: McClelland and Stewart, 1969.

Neatby, B. *The Politics of Chaos*. Toronto: Macmillan, 1972.

Schull, J. *Laurier*. Toronto: Macmillan, 1965.

Stacey, C. P. *Canada and the Age of Conflict: A History of Canadian External Policies, 1867–1921.* Volume 1 of 2. Toronto: Macmillan, 1977.

Stanley, G. *Louis Riel.* Toronto: Ryerson, 1963.

Thompson, J. *The Harvests of War: The Prairie West, 1914–1918.* Toronto: McClelland and Stewart, 1978.

Waite, P. *Canada, 1874–1896.* Toronto: McClelland and Stewart, 1976.

Woodcock, G. *Gabriel Dumont: The Métis Chief and His Lost World.* Edmonton: Hurtig, 1975.

CONTEMPORARY CANADA

Creighton, D. G. *The Forked Road.* Toronto: McClelland and Stewart, 1976.

Dickey, J. S. *Canada and the American Presence.* New York: New York University Press, 1975.

Fraser, B. *The Search for Identity: Canada, 1945–1967.* Toronto: Doubleday, 1967.

Granatstein, J. L. *The Politics of Survival.* Toronto: University of Toronto Press, 1967.

Grant, G. M. *Lament for a Nation.* Toronto: McClelland and Stewart, 1970.

Kilbourn, W. *Canada: A Guide to The Peaceable Kingdom.* Toronto: Macmillan, 1970.

Lévesque, R. *An Option for Quebec.* Toronto: McClelland and Stewart, 1968.

Levitt, K. *Silent Surrender: The American Economic Empire in Canada.* Toronto: McClelland and Stewart, 1970.

Morton, W. L. *The Canadian Identity.* Second Edition. Madison: University of Wisconsin Press, 1972.

Newman, P. *Renegade in Power.* Toronto: McClelland and Stewart, 1963.

Pearson, L. B. *Memoirs.* 3 volumes. Toronto: University of Toronto Press, 1975.

Quinn, H. F. *The Union Nationale.* Toronto: University of Toronto Press, 1963.

Radwanski, G. *Trudeau.* New York: Taplinger, 1978.

Stacey, C. P. *Arms, Men and Governments.* Ottawa: Queen's Printer, 1970.

Thomson, D. C. *Louis St. Laurent, Canadian.* Toronto: Macmillan, 1967.

Trudeau, P. E. *Federalism and the French Canadians.* Toronto: Macmillan, 1977.

REFERENCE

All students should familiarize themselves with the *Dictionary of Canadian Biography*, 6 vols. to date (Toronto and Quebec City: University of Toronto Press and Presses de l'Université Laval, 1966–   ). To be completed in more than twenty volumes, the *DCB* is extraordinarily useful for its bibliography and interpretive essays, as well as for its state-of-the-art biographical content. Volumes I, II, III, IV, IX and X had appeared by late 1980.

(G. C.)

Editor's Note: This chapter has been devoted mostly to political history. Many historians of Canada are now engaged in work on other aspects of history—labor history, economic history, social history, urban history, regional history, business history, women's history—that often involve new methodologies, sometimes borrowed from other disciplines. Their discoveries have so far appeared in papers, monographs, and articles; as yet we are without an adequate synthesis for the nonspecialist. Students may wish to investigate the work of (among others) Gad Horowitz, Anthony Rasporich, Peter Baskerville, Terry Copp, Michael Katz, Brian Young, Viv Nelles, Michael Bliss, John Thompson, Robert Babcock, Greg Kealey, Gerald Tulchinsky, Alan Artibise.

(W. M.)

III. Politics: An Annotated Bibliography

GENERAL TEXTS

The two most detailed and widely used general texts are R. M. Dawson's *The Government of Canada*, rev. Norman War, 5th edition (Toronto: University of Toronto Press, 1970), and J. R. Mallory's *The Structure of Canadian Government* (Toronto: Macmillan, 1971). Both texts have the central government as their main focus, and neither pays much attention to informal institutions other than political parties. The texts both provide excellent and complementary historical overviews of the development of the formal institutions: Dawson is most concerned with parliamentary institutions, while Mallory's strongest sections are on the courts and the administrative machinery. Two shorter, less detailed descriptive texts also exist: Thomas A. Hockin's *Government in Canada* (Toronto: McGraw-Hill Ryerson, 1976) and *Introduction to Canadian Politics and Government* by Walter L. White, R. H. Wagenberg, and R. C. Nelson, 2d edition (Toronto: Holt, Rinehart and Winston, 1977). Hockin pays principal attention to the public service and the development of the policy process, especially in relation to foreign affairs, while White et al. attempt to combine institutional description with some attention to political behavior. The latter text particularly is aimed at the introductory level and is somewhat less sophisticated than Dawson or Mallory. Another major, detailed text enjoying increasingly widespread use is Richard Van Loon and Michael S. Whittington, *The Canadian Political System*, 2d edition (Toronto: McGraw-Hill Ryerson, 1976), which endeavors to provide a more structural-functional and behavioral perspective in contrast to the historical-descriptive style of the earlier texts. This work contains a very extensive bibliography of books and articles on Canadian politics.

GENERAL READERS

In addition to the texts, there are a number of compilations of journal articles and other material of general relevance to Canadian politics. The most introductory and general is Paul W. Fox, ed., *Politics: Canada*, 4th edition (Toronto: McGraw-Hill Ryerson, 1977). Excerpts are usually brief and include not only parts of journal articles but also speeches, newspaper columns, and documents. The variety of material is wide and the quality uneven. A somewhat more specialized collection has been edited by Frederick Vaughan, J. Patrick Kyba, and O. P. Dwivedi and is entitled *Contemporary Issues in Canadian Politics* (Toronto: Prentice-Hall, 1970). The degree of specialization makes this collection less than optimal for the general reader. A more general useful reader, but aimed at a fairly advanced level, is *The Canadian Political Process*, edited by Orest M. Kruhlak, Richard Schultz, and Sidney I. Pobihushchy, revised edition (Toronto: Holt, Rinehart and Winston, 1973). Most of the material in that collection is reprinted from scholarly journals, although some pieces are original for that volume. There are considerable differences in the content of the two editions of the work, but both editions contain extensive bibliographies.

CONSTITUTIONAL BASES

The single best work available on the politics of the Canadian constitution's development is probably R. I. Cheffins and R. N. Tucker, *The Constitutional Process in Canada*, 2d edition (Toronto: McGraw-Hill Ryerson, 1976). Particular attention is paid to the problems posed by the doctrine of parliamentary supremacy in a federal system and by the proliferation of delegated legislation. Also of interest, particularly to students of judicial review, is Peter H. Russell, *Leading Constitutional Decisions*, revised edition (Toronto: McClelland and Stewart, Carleton Library-No. 23, 1973). Valuable historical background can be found in another Carleton Library publication (No. 2), edited by P. B. Waite, *The Confederation Debates in the Province of Canada, 1865* (Toronto: McClelland and Stewart, 1963).

FORMAL INSTITUTIONS

(1) *Executive*: Professor Frank McKinnon has recently produced a work outlining the place of the monarchy in the Canadian system (*The Crown in Canada* [Calgary: The Glenbow-Alberta Institute, McClelland and Stewart West, 1976]), and that may be supplemented by John T. Saywell's now somewhat dated *The Office of Lieutenant Governor* (Toronto: University of Toronto Press, 1957). With respect to the effective executive, two works stand out. The first, Thomas A. Hockin's *Apex of Power* (Toronto: Prentice-Hall, 1971 and 1977), is a collection of essays covering most aspects of the Prime Minister's Office and the operation of Cabinet. The second, W. A. Matheson's *The Prime Minister and the Cabinet* (Toronto: Methuen, 1976), provides a wealth of historical information on the developing Cabinet and Prime Minister's Office, particularly regarding their contribution to accommodation among elites.

(2) *Parliament*: Material on the Senate is understandably scarce. R. A. MacKay's *The Unreformed Senate of Canada*, revised edition (Toronto: McClelland and Stewart, Carleton Library No. 6, 1963), was originally published in 1926, and it is a measure of the Senate's stability that the revised edition could bear the same title more than thirty years later. A somewhat uncritical account of the institution can be found in F. A. Kunz, *The Modern Senate of Canada, 1925–1963* (Toronto: University of Toronto Press, 1965), but a more up-to-date rendering appears in Colin Campbell's book, *The Canadian Senate: A Lobby from Within* (Toronto: Macmillan, 1978). The House of Commons, not surprisingly, has been better served. In addition to the lengthy treatment the House is give in Mallory, Dawson, Hockin, and Van Loon and Whittington, an excellent review of its functioning is provided in Robert J. Jackson and Michael M. Atkinson, *The Canadian Legislative System* (Toronto: Macmillan, 1974). Studies of the House from a legislative behavior perspective include David Hoffman and Norman Ward, *Bilingualism and Biculturalism in the Canadian House of Commons* (Ottawa: Queen's Printer, 1970), and Allan Kornberg, *Canadian Legislative Behaviour: A Study of the 25th Parliament* (New York: Holt, Rinehart and Winston, 1967). Kornberg has collaborated with William Mishler to produce a larger and more recent treatment of the Canadian House of Commons, entitled *Influence in Parliament: Canada* (Durham, N.C.: Duke University Press, 1976).

(3) *Judiciary*: While a number of specialized treatments of constitutional and legal issues exist, there are few book-length studies of the judiciary. The best and most recent is Paul Weiler, *In the Last Resort* (Toronto: Carswell, 1974). A study of the Supreme Court, Weiler's book also deals in general with the administration of justice. A less recent work, but of equally high quality, is Peter Russell's study of the Supreme Court for the Bilingualism and Biculturalism Commission, *Bilingualism and Biculturalism in the Supreme Court of Canada* (Ottawa: Queen's Printer, 1969). A chapter by D. Fouts on the Supreme Court of Canada can be found in Glendon A. Schubert and David J. Danelski, eds., *Comparative Judicial Behaviour* (New York: Oxford University Press, 1969). Most other material on the courts in Canada appears in journal articles, often in legal periodicals.

(4) *Bureaucracy*: Van Loon and Whittington's bibliography contains some eight pages of material on various aspects of the bureaucracy and policymaking in Canada. The most recent and useful book-length treatments of the public service include J. E. Hodgetts, *Canadian Public Service: A Physiology of Government* (Toronto: University of Toronto Press, 1973); W. D. Kenneth Kernaghan, *Bureaucracy in Canadian Government*, 2d edition (Toronto: Methuen, 1973); and Bruce Doern and Peter Aucoin, *The Structure of Policy Making in Canada* (Toronto: Macmillan, 1971). Readers in the field include J. E. Hodgetts and D. C. Corbett, eds., *Canadian Public Administration* (Toronto: Macmillan, 1960), and W. D. K. Kernaghan and A. M. Willms, eds., *Public Administration in Canada: Selected Readings* (Toronto: Methuen, 1971). A worthwhile reader in the area of public policy

analysis is Bruce Doern and V. Seymour Wilson, eds., *Issues in Canadian Public Policy* (Toronto: Macmillan, 1974).

INFORMAL INSTITUTIONS

(1) *Political Parties*: There are a number of books on individual parties, mainly those of social movement or extraparliamentary origin, which provide valuable historical material. They are simply too numerous to list here, but bibliographies of the major texts list the main sources. Two recent general texts on Canadian parties exist. Fred C. Engelmann and Mildred A. Schwartz, *Canadian Political Parties: Origin, Character and Impact* (Toronto: Prentice-Hall, 1975), is more than an extension and updating of their 1967 work, *Political Parties and the Canadian Social Structure* (Prentice-Hall). The authors provide a systems analysis of parties, setting them in the context of their social and economic environment. Also using a systems framework, Conrad Winn and John McMenemy (*Political Parties in Canada* [Toronto: McGraw-Hill Ryerson, 1976]) examine the political parties with particular attention to their contribution to political outputs. They conclude that external exigencies are more important than interparty policy differences in determining government actions. A valuable introductory reader on parties is that edited by Hugh G. Thorburn, and entitled *Party Politics in Canada*, 3d edition (Toronto: Prentice-Hall, 1972). Useful material on particular aspects of party activity can be found in John C. Courtney, *The Selection of National Party Leaders in Canada* (Toronto: Macmillan, 1973), and K. Z. Paltiel, *Political Party Financing in Canada* (Toronto: McGraw-Hill, 1970), but changes in provincial and federal legislation have necessitated some reinterpretation of the financing situation. A summary of the new federal legislation is contained in the chapter by Professor Paltiel in Howard R. Penniman, ed., *Canada at the Polls* (Washington: American Enterprise Institute, 1975).

(2) *Elections*: Information on election practices in T. H. Qualter's *The Election Process in Canada* (Toronto: McGraw-Hill, 1970) is now somewhat out of date with respect to election finance and one or two other details, but the book is still the best compilation of data on the systems of elections in the provinces and at the federal level. An extremely useful descriptive account of national election campaigns from 1867 to 1968 can be found in J. M. Beck, *Pendulum of Power* (Toronto: Prentice-Hall, 1968). Beck includes province-by-province seat and vote distributions for each party in each election. A detailed and generally useful study of one recent federal election (1974) is presented in *Canada at the Polls* (Howard R. Penniman, ed. [Washington: American Enterprise Institute, 1975]). Much of the available information on Canadians' voting behavior is contained in journal articles or conference papers, and there are few good summary treatments of that material. The best review of the literature on Canadian electoral behavior is Mildred Schwartz's chapter in Richard Rose, ed., *Electoral Behavior: A Comparative Handbook* (New York: Free Press, 1974), and two

good attempts to derive generalizations from survey data in connection with specific national election campaigns are S. Peter Regenstreif, *The Diefenbaker Interlude: Parties and Voting in Canada* (Toronto: Longmans, 1965), based on the elections of 1962 and 1963 particularly; and John Meisel, *Working Papers on Canadian Politics*, 2d enlarged edition (Montreal: McGill-Queen's University Press, 1975), based largely on the elections of 1965 and 1968.

(3) *Interest Groups and the Structure of Power*: For many years, the foremost treatment of politically relevant elites in Canada was John Porter's *The Vertical Mosaic* (Toronto: University of Toronto Press, 1965), and that has recently been updated, with respect to economic elites, by Wallace Clement's *The Canadian Corporate Elite* (Toronto: McClelland and Stewart, Carleton Library No. 89, 1975). Treatments of interest groups and lobbying were rare in Canada prior to the late 1960s, but a major study by Robert Presthus has resulted in two recent books—one on Canadian interest-group activity (*Elite Accommodation in Canada* [Toronto: Macmillan, 1973]), and another comparing Canada with the United States on that dimension (*Elites in the Policy Process* [New York: Cambridge University Press, 1974]). Also of value is a shorter collection edited by Paul Pross, *Pressure Group Behaviour in Canadian Politics* (Toronto: McGraw-Hill Ryerson, 1975). Also of interest in this area are readings on the interface between business and government edited by K. J. Rea and J. T. McLeod (*Business and Government in Canada* [Toronto: Methuen, 1969]) and several treatments of the political activity of the labor movement in Canada, including Irving M. Abella, *Nationalism, Communism, and Canadian Labour* (Toronto: University of Toronto Press, 1973); Gad Horowitz, *Canadian Labour in Politics* (Toronto: University of Toronto Press, 1968); David Kwavnick, *Organized Labour and Pressure Politics* (Montreal: McGill-Queen's University Press, 1972); and Robert Laxer, *Canada's Unions* (Toronto: James Lirmer & Co., 1976).

(4) *Public Opinion, Ideology, and Political Culture*: There have been few published analyses of public opinion polls in Canada, and only one major, book-length study—Mildred A. Schwartz, *Public Opinion and Canadian Identity* (Toronto: Fitzhenry and Whiteside, 1967)—that reviews findings of the Canadian Gallup poll. A number of scholars have attempted to deal with the question of Canadian value preferences, ideologies, or political cultures, however. The first chapter of Gad Horowitz's *Canadian Labour in Politics* (see above) makes an argument about the development of Canadian political culture, derived from a critical perspective on Louis Hartz's fragment theory (its application to Canada is outlined in the chapter by Kenneth D. McRae in Louis Hartz, ed., *The Founding of New Societies* [New York: Harcourt, Brace and World, 1964]). Two articles in the September 1974 *Canadian Journal of Political Science* (Richard Simeon and David J. Elkins, "Regional Political Cultures," and John Wilson, "The Canadian Political Cultures," 7 [3], 397–483) provide other bases for measuring political culture—the first uses survey data on attitudes toward government, in the tradition of Almond and Verba's *The Civic Culture;* the

second suggests that the political cultures of the provinces are rooted in their economic development and manifested in the structure of their party systems. Some political views of a potentially important population subgroup are examined in John C. Johnstone's study for the Bilingualism and Biculturalism Commission, *Young People's Images of Canadian Society* (Ottawa: Queen's Printer, 1969). William C. Christian and Colin Campbell have sought to find ideological bases for the national party system but find almost as much division within party ranks as between parties (*Political Parties and Ideologies in Canada* [Toronto: McGraw-Hill Ryerson, 1974]). Some recent attempts to define the normative or ideological foundations of Canadian politics include George Grant, *Lament for a Nation* (Toronto: McClelland and Stewart, Carleton Library No. 50, 1970, originally published 1965); Charles Taylor, *Pattern of Politics* (Toronto: McClelland and Stewart, 1970); and M. Patricia Marchak, *Ideological Perspectives on Canada* (Toronto: McGraw-Hill Ryerson, 1975). Recently a reader has appeared on political socialization in Canada, edited by Jon H. Pammett and Michael S. Whittington (*Foundations of Political Culture* [Toronto: Macmillan, 1970]).

(5) *The Mass Media*: Although a number of articles and collections have addressed the political role of the mass media, most of the available material is summarized in the *Report of the Senate Committee on the Mass Media* (known as the Davey Report [Ottawa: Queen's Printer, 1971], 3 vols.). A useful, though uneven collection is Benjamin D. Singer, ed., *Communications in Canadian Society* (Toronto: Copp Clark, 1972); and two very good introductions to the mass media system and its coverage of politics can be found in articles by Frederick J. Fletcher in H. R. Penniman, ed., *Canada at the Polls* (see above) and D. C. MacDonald, ed., *Government and Politics of Ontario* (see above). For an entertainingly irreverent, popular account of press coverage in the Trudeau years, see Larry Zolf, *The Dance of the Dialectic* (Toronto: James Lewis and Samuel, 1973).

THE CANADIAN FEDERAL SYSTEM

(1) *General*: There is a great wealth of material on Canadian federalism, but the beginning student can best approach the material through four books. The first, Mildred A. Schwartz, *Politics and Territory* (Montreal: McGill-Queen's University Press, 1974), outlines a number of the facts that make Canada a society for whose problems federal solutions seem appropriate. The second, Peter Meekison, ed., *Canadian Federalism: Myth or Reality*, 2d edition (Toronto: Methuen, 1971), is a collection of articles and government position papers that provides a wide variety of material on almost all aspects of the Canadian federal system. The third, D. V. Smiley, *Canada in Question* 2d edition (Toronto: McGraw-Hill Ryerson, 1976), provides an extremely concise overview of Canadian federalism with valuable summaries and criticism of much of the relevant literature. The fourth,

Edwin R. Black, *Divided Loyalties* (Montreal: McGill-Queen's University Press, 1975), provides historical reviews of a variety of conceptions of Canadian federalism and ends with a rather pessimistic account of the future of French-English relations in Canada. A fifth work, extremely useful for a more advanced analysis of the Canadian federal system, is Richard Simeon's *Federal-Provincial Diplomacy* (Toronto: University of Toronto Press, 1972). Simeon examines, using three case studies, some aspects of the conflict among governments in federal-provincial negotiations.

(2) *Provincial Politics*: The government and politics of Canada's provinces remain among the most underdeveloped areas in the study of the Canadian political system. Most of the treatments of individual provinces are now out of date, having been written in the 1950s and early 1960s, although there are one or two exceptions, including S. J. R. Noel, *Politics in Newfoundland* (Toronto: University of Toronto Press, 1971), and Donald C. MacDonald, ed., *Government and Politics of Ontario* (Toronto: Macmillan, 1975). Comparative treatments of the provinces are rare; the party systems are reviewed, but a basis for comparison is not really provided, in Martin Robin, ed., *Canadian Provincial Politics* (Toronto: Prentice-Hall, 1972), while a more explicitly comparative approach to the various provincial systems can be found in David J. Bellamy, Jon H. Pammett, and Donald C. Rowat, eds., *The Provincial Political Systems* (Toronto: Methuen, 1976).

(3) *Municipal Politics*: Local government is also somewhat neglected as a field of study in Canada, although a number of general texts and readers exist. Most useful for the beginning student perhaps is Lionel D. Feldman and Michael D. Goldrick, eds., *Politics and Government of Urban Canada*, 2d edition (Toronto: Methuen, 1972). A fairly critical (and somewhat cynical) analysis of urban politics is provided in James Lorimer's *A Citizen's Guide to City Politics* (Toronto: James Lewis and Samuel, 1972). The successes and failures of various attempts to introduce party politics into municipal government in Canada are reviewed in Jack K. Masson and James D. Anderson, eds., *Emerging Party Politics in Urban Canada* (Toronto: McClelland and Stewart, 1972).

(4) *Judicial Review*: An excellent edition to the material in the texts is an article by Alan C. Cairns on the controversies surrounding the work of the Judicial Committee of the Privy Council ("The Judicial Committee and Its Critics," *Canadian Journal of Political Science*, 4 [1971], 301–345).

IV. Economics: Suggested Readings

This chapter concentrates on a few topics and consequently says little or nothing about the others. Useful general coverage of a broader array of economic issues is found in several collections of readings intended to be

used in introductory economics courses in Canada. Three of the most recently published are: Lawrence H. Officer and Lawrence B. Smith (eds.),
Issues in Canadian Economics (Toronto: McGraw-Hill Ryerson, 1974); John
Chant (ed.), *Canadian Perspectives in Economics* (Don Mills: Collier-Macmillan, 1972); and B. S. Keirsted, J. R. G. Brander, J. F. Earl, and C. M.
Waddell (eds.), *Economics in Canada: Selected Readings* (Toronto: Macmillan, 1974). Very good discussion of the current state of the Canadian
economy can be found in two yearly publications: Government of Canada,
Department of Finance, *Economic Review* (each April), and Economic Council of Canada, *Annual Review*. The most current data can be found in the
Canadian Statistical Review (monthly). A useful collection of data is *Canada
Year Book*, and the longer perspective can be obtained from M. C. Urquart
and K. A. H. Buckley, *Historical Statistics of Canada* (Toronto: Macmillan,
1965).

A most helpful review of the development of the study of economics in
Canada is Daniel Drache's "Rediscovering Canadian Political Economy,"
Journal of Canadian Studies (August 1976), pp. 3–18. Mel Watkins touches
on this too in his discussion of the work of one of Canada's best-known
economists, Harry Johnson, in "The Economics of Nationalism and the
Nationality of Economics: A Critique of Neoclassical Theorizing," *Canadian
Journal of Economics* (November 1978), pp. S87–S120.

The standard texts for the development of Canada's economy are W.
T. Easterbrook and H. G. Aitken, *Canadian Economic History* (Toronto:
Macmillan, 1956), and W. T. Easterbrook and M. H. Watkins (eds.), *Approaches to Canadian Economic History* (Toronto: McClelland and Stewart,
1967). The latter is a collection of readings, and includes Mel Watkins's
"A Staples Theory of Economic Growth," the best statement of the staples
theory. A new text is W. T. Marr and Donald G. Paterson, *Economic History
of Canada* (Toronto: Macmillan, 1980). The most accessible of Harold Innis's
works is his *Essays in Canadian Economic History* (Toronto: University of
Toronto Press, 1956), although I would never restrain anyone from reading
any of his longer works, such as *The Fur Trade in Canada* (Toronto: University of Toronto Press, 1956). Also recommended is an "Innis issue" of
the *Journal of Canadian Studies* (Winter 1977), "Harold Innis, 1894–1952."

Close the 49th parallel, etc. (Toronto: University of Toronto, 1970), edited by Ian Lumsden, was a catalyst for the "nationalist" literature of the
1970s. This book has readings which describe both the historical development and current state of Canada's dependency on the United States. Another, somewhat more recent book along the same lines is Robert Laxer,
Canada Ltd.: The Political Economy of Dependency (Toronto: McClelland
and Stewart, 1973).

The Economic Council of Canada's *Living Together* (Ottawa: Government of Canada, 1978) gives a good selection of current data and some
analysis of Canada's regional disparities. Two recent books that are also
very much worth reading are: N. H. Lithwick, *Regional Economic Policy:
The Canadian Experience* (Toronto: McGraw-Hill, 1978), and Anthony G.

S. Careless, *Initiation and Response: The Adaptation of Canada's Federation to Regional Economic Development* (Montreal: McGill-Queen's University Press, 1977).

Another Economic Council of Canada report heads off the literature on trade relations: *Looking Outward* (Ottawa: Government of Canada, 1975). Its free trade message is given support by R. J. Wonnacott in his Economic Council report, *Canada's Trade Options* (Ottawa: Government of Canada, 1975); but John N. H. Britton provides a good counterargument in his article, "Locational Perspectives on Free Trade," *Canadian Public Policy* (Winter 1977), pp. 4–19.

The Canadian Senate has recently given its support to free trade in a report by the Standing Committee on Foreign Affairs, *Canada-U.S. Relations* (Ottawa: Government of Canada, 1978). The best introductory source is probably W. T. Hunter's review article, "Toward Free Trade? The Dilemma of Canadian Trade Policy," *Journal of Canadian Studies* (Spring 1978), pp. 49–62.

The first popular book in the recent debate on foreign ownership was Kari Levitt's *Silent Surrender: The Multnational Corporation in Canada* (Toronto: Macmillan, 1970). A counterargument is presented in A. E. Safarian, *Foreign Ownership of Canadian Industry* (Toronto: University of Toronto Press, 1973). *The Multinational Firm and the National State* (Don Mills: Collier-Macmillan, 1972), edited by Gilles Paquet, contains several articles that examine the theory and practice of foreign direct investors in Canada. The most recent pro and con books out are: Patricia Marchak, *In Whose Interests* (Toronto: McClelland and Stewart, 1979), and Stephen Globerman, *U.S. Ownership of Firms in Canada* (Montreal: C. D. Howe Research Institute, 1979). The three Canadian government studies are: *The Structure of Foreign Ownership in Canada* (1967); House of Commons, *Canada-U.S. Relations* (1970); and *Foreign Direct Investment in Canada* (1972). Valuable information regarding the current operation of foreign investment policy is found in the Annual Reports of the Foreign Investment Review Agency.

Energy policy seems continually to be in a state of flux as major political events and shifts in supply and demand alter the underlying reality on which policy must be based—thus, sources that are "current" today may be outmoded very soon. Nonetheless, one report that is worth looking at for a basic sense of Canada's energy situation is: Minister of Energy, Mines and Resources, *An Energy Policy for Canada* (Ottawa: Government of Canada, 1973). A critical look is contained in James Laxer's *Canada's Energy Crisis* (Toronto: James Lorimer, 1975).

Finally, there are two collections of papers that give good discussions of the whole spectrum of issues in Canada's relationship with the United States: Annette Baker Fox (ed.), *Canada and the United States: Transnational and Transgovernmental Relations* (New York: Columbia University Press, 1976); and H. Edward English (ed.), *Canada–United States Relations* (New York: Praeger, 1976).

V. Anthropology: Suggested Readings

GENERAL

Few texts deal with the peoples and cultures of Canada in any detail. *The Canadian Family Tree* (Ottawa: Queen's Printer, 1967) contains short histories of many ethnic minorities in Canada, some accomplishments of each minority, and short bibliographies.

Elliott, Jean Leonard. *Minority Canadians*. 2 volumes. Scarborough, Ont.: Prentice-Hall of Canada, 1971. Contains several interesting articles on modern native and immigrant societies. The articles are short but well written and social science oriented. There is little information on traditional native Canadian life, however.

Davis, Morris and Joseph Krouter. *The Other Canadians*. Toronto:. McClelland and Stewart, 1978. Profiles six groups: Indians, Eskimos, blacks, Orientals, Doukhobors, and Hutterites. It deals with the social and political problems of these groups. There is much useful data on the problems of these peoples, but little descriptive ethnography.

Driedger, Leo. *The Canadian Ethnic Mosaic*. Toronto: McClelland and Stewart, 1978. Multidisciplinary and covers a number of groups: French, Indians, Jews, Inuit, Mennonites, and Italians. It deals with specific social, political, and psychological problems.

NATIVE PEOPLES OF CANADA

The best overall introduction to the traditional Indian and Inuit cultures is still Diamond Jenness, *Indians of Canada* (Toronto: University of Toronto Press, 1977). It is rich in detail and soundly based in anthropology. There is some material, however, that is dated. This text should not be confused with Eileen Jenness, *Indian Tribes of Canada* (Toronto: McGraw-Hill, 1966). Ms. Jenness based her short text on her husband's, but it lacks the richness of detail of his book.

Leechman, Douglas. *Native Tribes of Canada*. Toronto: W. J. Gage, 1956. Rich in detail and in illustrations. It appears, however, to be aimed at high school students.

Hawthorn, H. B. *A Survey of the Contemporary Indians of Canada*. 2 volumes. Ottawa: Government of Canada, Indian Affairs Branch, 1967. Presents a series of articles and recommendations concerning modern Canadian native peoples. It deals with the economic, educational, and political characteristics of the Indians of Canada. It also describes the role of the Canadian government in Indian affairs.

For more explicit information see: Abler, Tom, and Douglas E. and Sally M. Weaver. *A Canadian Indian Bibliography, 1960–1970*. Toronto: University of Toronto Press, 1974.

An excellent book of readings is Bruce Cox, *Cultural Ecology: Readings on the Canadian Indians and Eskimos* (Toronto: McClelland and Stewart, 1973). It is a scholarly text containing articles by the best-known anthropologists in the field: Speck, Tooker, Trigger, Leacock, Tanner, Fisher, Steward, Weinberg, Damas, and Smith. The emphasis is on the relationship of environment to Indian and Inuit society and culture.

A very good book on Indians today is Heather Robertson, *Reservations Are for Indians* (Toronto: Lorimer, 1970). Ms. Robertson is a journalist, not an anthropologist, but she provides a rich background for understanding the Indian Act and the reserve system in Canada.

Tremblay, Marc-Adelaid. *The Patterns of "Amerindian Identity."* Laval: Les Presses de l'Université Laval, 1967. Presents the papers given at Laval University in a symposium on Amerindians in 1973. These papers, in English or French, give much information on Indians and Inuit in modern Canadian society: leadership, rights, legal problems, environment, and health.

Algonkian Hunting and Gathering Societies of the Eastern Woodlands: H. F. McGee, *The Native Peoples of Atlantic Canada: A History of Ethnic Interaction* (Toronto: McClelland and Stewart, 1974), is a good scholarly account of the Indians on the eastern seaboard. Norman A. Chance, *Conflict in Culture: Problems of Developmental Change Among the Cree* (Ottawa: Saint Paul University Press, 1968), is an interesting examination of the Cree from a psychological anthropologist's point of view. Alfred G. Bailey, *The Conflict of European and Eastern Algonkian Cultures, 1504–1700: A Study in Canadian Civilization* (Toronto: University of Toronto Press, 1968), is an excellent account of the effect of the fur trade on the Algonkian Indians. Charles A. Bishop, *The Northern Ojibwa and the Fur Trade* (Toronto: University of Toronto Press, 1968), uses ethnohistorical techniques, specifically Hudson's Bay Company records, to provide a wealth of detail on the movements of the Ojibwa in northern Ontario.

Iroquoian Agricultural Tribes: Bruce Trigger, *The Huron: Farmers of the North* (New York: Holt, Rinehart and Winston, 1969), is an excellent example of ethnohistorical research. It is a reconstruction of Huron traditions and culture from historical records. Lewis Henry Morgan, *The League of The Iroquois* (New York: Corinth Books, 1962), is a classic account of Iroquoian culture—although that of New York State.

Indians of the Plains: The classic study is Robert H. Lowie, *Indians of the Plains* (New York: The American Museum of Natural History, 1954). It is a book rich in details on the Plains Indian cultures. It does not, however, separate "Canadian" from American Indians. John W. Bennett, *Northern Plainsmen* (New York: Aldine, 1969), has a good section on the Indians in the Jasper region of western Canada. It is especially good in treating the modern Plains Indian today.

Indians of the Northwest Coast: John W. Adams, *The Gitksan Potlatch: Population Flux, Resource Ownership and Reciprocity* (Toronto: Holt, Rinehart and Winston, 1973), is one of the new series edited by Sally Weaver on native peoples of Canada. It provides information on the contemporary potlatch in today's Northwest coast society. It is scholarly, but may be too advanced for the beginning student. Phillip Drucker,

Indians of the Northwest Coast (Garden City, N.Y.: Natural History Press, 1955), like the Lowie book on the Plains Indians, is rich in anthropological detail. Ronald and Evelyn Rohner, *The Kwakiutl: Indians of British Columbia* (New York: Holt, Rinehart and Winston, 1970), is an excellent study of the effect of acculturation on an Indian group. Wolfgang Jilek, *Salish Indian Mental Health and Culture Change* (Toronto: Holt, Rinehart and Winston, 1974), reports on the resurgence of spirit dancing in the 1960s among the coast Salish of the lower mainland of British Columbia. In the presentation of the psychology of altered states, it is an excellent cross-disciplinary study of native Canadian cultures.

Northern Athabaskan Hunters: A good introduction to the cultures of this area is James W. Vanstone, *Athapaskan Adaptations* (Chicago: Aldine, 1974). The approach is that of cultural ecology, but it is straightforward and easy to read.

The Inuit: There are a number of books written in this area, from the classic study of the central Eskimo by Franz Boas to the popular texts of Farley Mowat. A very good account of the traditional Eskimo is Asen Balikci, *The Netsilik Eskimo* (New York: The Natural History Press, 1970). Balikci has produced a number of films on the Netsilik for the *Macos: Man, A Course of Study*. The text is readable and is an excellent reconstruction. For an excellent account of modern Inuit, see Nelson Graburn, *Eskimos Without Igloos* (Boston: Little, Brown and Company, 1969).

FRENCH CANADA

The classic ethnographic study of rural French Canada is Horace Miner, *St. Denis: A French Canadian Parish* (Chicago: University of Chicago Press, 1939). It is still the best general account of traditional French-Canadian culture.

Another important book is Marcel Rioux and Yves Martin, *French Canadian Society*, Vol. 1 (Toronto: McClelland and Stewart, 1964). It contains many excellent articles on the basic institutions, cultural dynamics, and organization of French Canada.

Gold, Gerlad, and Marc-Adelaid Tremblay. *Communities and Culture in French Canada*. Toronto: Holt, Rinehart and Winston, 1973. Another excellent book that updates Rioux and Martin.

Mallea, John. *Quebec's Language Policies: Background and Response*. Quebec: Les Presses de l'Université Laval, 1977. A good introduction to language issues in Quebec—although it went to press before bill 101 was introduced.

IMMIGRANTS

Chinese: There are several articles, but few available books, on the Chinese of Canada. A good, but sometimes unscholarly, account is Foon Sien,

The Chinese in Canada (Ottawa: Royal Commission on Bilingualism and Biculturalism, 1967), available on microfilm as one of the studies done for the Royal Commission on Bilingualism and Biculturalism.

Blacks: The best historical account by far is Robin Winks, *The Blacks in Canada* (New Haven: Yale University Press, 1971). Professor Winks has background in anthropology and gives a good social-historical account of the blacks. An excellent anthropological account of black Canadians is Donald Clairmont and Denis Magill, *Africville* (Toronto: McClelland and Stewart, 1974). It chronicles the death of a black community.

Ukrainians: A rich account of the early Ukrainian settlements in Canada is Vladimir Julian Kaye, *Early Ukrainian Settlements: 1895–1900* (Toronto: McClelland and Stewart, 1974). See also Paul Yuzyk, *The Ukrainians in Manitoba* (Toronto: University of Toronto Press, 1953).

Italians: The best ethnographic account of Canadian Italians is Jeremy Boissevain, *The Italians of Montreal: Social Adjustment in a Plural Society* (Ottawa: Queen's Printer, 1970). It is scholarly, thorough, and yet easy to read.

Hutterites: There are several good studies in this area; the two following are especially good: John Bennett, *Hutterian Brethren: The Agricultural Economy and Social Organization of a Communal People* (California: Stanford University Press, 1967), and John Hostetler and Gertrude Huntington, *The Hutterites in North America* (New York: Holt, Rinehart and Winston, 1967).

CANADIAN ELITES

The classic account of Canadian elites is John Porter, *The Vertical Mosaic* (Toronto: University of Toronto Press, 1965). A sound sociological account of class and status in Canada. Two other studies that build on Porter's analysis are: Peter Newman, *The Canadian Establishment* (Toronto: McClelland and Stewart, 1975), and Wallace Clement, *The Canadian Corporate Elite: An Analysis of Economic Power* (Toronto: McClelland and Stewart, 1975).

USEFUL JOURNALS

American Review of Canadian Studies
Anthropologica
Canadian Journal of Linguistics
Canadian Review of Sociology and Anthropology
Journal of Canadian Studies
Recherches Sociographiques

VI. Literature: Bibliography

PRIMARY SOURCES

Novels: The novels listed without comment are those already mentioned in the text of this chapter. A few more, with annotations, have been added to make the list more representative. Although the dates indicated in the text are original dates of publication, the editions below are those most readily available and not necessarily first editions. Only French-Canadian novels available in translation are included. The abbreviation NCL is for the New Canadian Library Series of McClelland and Stewart Ltd.

Allister, William. *A Handful of Rice*. London: Secker & Warburg, 1961. A brutally realistic novel about Canadian soldiers in a Japanese prisoner-of-war camp.

Aquin, Hubert. *Prochain épisode/Prochain Episode*. Trans. Penny Williams. NCL, 1967.

Atwood, Margaret. *Surfacing*. Toronto: McClelland and Stewart, 1972.

Atwood, Margaret. *Lady Oracle*. Toronto: McClelland and Stewart, 1976.

Atwood, Margaret. *Life Before Man*. Toronto: McClelland and Stewart, 1979.

Aubert de Gaspé, Philippe. *Les Anciens Canadiens/Canadians of Old*. Trans. Charles G. D. Roberts. NCL, 1974.

Bacque, James. *Big Lonely*. Toronto: New Press, 1970.

Bessette, Gerard. *La Bagarre/The Brawl*. Trans. Marc Lebel and Ronald Sutherland. Montreal: Harvest House, 1977.

Bessette, Gerard. *Le Libraire/Not For Every Eye*. Trans. Glen Shortliffe. Toronto: Macmillan, 1962. About church censorship in pre–Quiet Revolution Quebec.

Birney, Earle. *Turvey*. NCL, 1963.

Blais, Marie-Claire. *Tête blanche/Tête Blanche*. Trans. Charles Fullman. NCL, 1961.

Blais, Marie-Claire. *Une Saison dans la vie d'Emmanuel/A Season in the Life of Emmanuel*. Trans. Derek Coltman. New York: Farrar, Straus and Giroux, 1966.

Buckler, Ernest. *The Mountain and the Valley*. NCL, 1961. A novel about the awakening process of a boy in the Maritimes.

Buell, John. *Four Days*. New York: Farrar, Straus and Cudahy, 1962. Suspenseful story about involvement in the underworld.

Callaghan, Morley. *The Loved and the Lost*. Toronto: Macmillan, 1951. About a white liberal girl who becomes involved with the black community in Montreal.

Callaghan, Morley. *Such Is My Beloved*. NCL, 1957.

Callaghan, Morley. *A Fine and Private Place*. Toronto: Macmillan, 1975. Story of a Toronto author, largely autobiographical.

Carrier, Roch. *La Guerre, yes sir!/La Guerre, Yes Sir!* Trans. Sheila Fischman. Toronto: Anansi, 1970.

Carrier, Roch. *Le Deux-millième étage/They Won't Demolish Me*. Trans. Sheila Fischman. Toronto: Anansi, 1974.

Carroll, Jock. *The Shy Photographer*. New York: Stein and Day, 1964. A bawdy comedy about a Canadian traveling across the United States.

Cohen, Leonard. *Beautiful Losers*. Toronto: McClelland and Stewart, 1966.

Cohen, Matt. *The Disinherited*. Toronto: McClelland and Stewart, 1974.

Cohen, Matt. *Flowers of Darkness*. Toronto: McClelland and Stewart, 1981.

Connor, Ralph. *The Man from Glengarry*. NCL, 1960.

Davies, Robertson. *Fifth Business*. New York: Signet, 1971.

Davies, Robertson. *The Manticore*. Toronto: Macmillan, 1972.

Davies, Robertson. *World of Wonders*. Toronto: Macmillan, 1975.

De la Roche, Mazo. *Delight*. NCL, 1961. A novel not in the Jalna series about a beautiful girl whose looks and goodness cause nothing but trouble.

Ducharme, Réjean. *L'Avalée des avalés/The Swallower Swallowed*. Trans. Barbara Bray. London: Hamish Hamilton, 1968.

Engel, Marian. *Bear*. Toronto: McClelland and Stewart, 1976. A highly imaginative and symbolic novel about womanhood and fantasy.

Engel, Marian. *Lunatic Villas*. Toronto: McClelland and Stewart, 1976.

Fraser, Sylvia. *The Candy Factory*. Toronto: McClelland and Stewart, 1974.

Garner, Hugh. *Cabbagetown*. Toronto: Ryerson, 1969.

Godbout, Jacques. *Le Couteau sur la table/Knife on the Table*. Trans. Penny Williams. Toronto: McClelland and Stewart, 1968.

Godfrey, Dave. *The New Ancestors*. Toronto: New Press, 1970.

Gravel, Pierre. *A Perte de Temps* (bilingual edition). Toronto: Anansi, 1969.

Grove, Frederick P. *Our Daily Bread*. Toronto: Macmillan, 1928.

Grove, Frederick P. *The Master of the Mill*. NCL, 1961.

Grove, Frederick P. *Settlers of the Marsh*. NCL, 1966. About a Swedish immigrant whose puritanical conscience forces him to marry a prostitute, then murder her.

Haliburton, Thomas Chandler. *The Clockmaker*. NCL, 1958.

Harvey, Jean-Charles. *Les Demi-civilisés/Sackcloth for Banner*. Trans. Lukin Barrette. Toronto: Macmillan, 1938.

Hebert, Anne. *Kamouraska/Kamouraska*. Trans. Norman Shapiro. Toronto: Musson, 1973. The story of an affair between an American doctor and a married woman in Quebec.

Hémon, Louis. *Maria Chapdelaine/Maria Chapdelaine*. Trans. W. H. Blake. Toronto: Macmillan, 1921.

Hodgins, Jack. *The Invention of the World*. Toronto: Macmillan, 1977.

Hodgins, Jack. *The Resurrection of Joseph Bourne*. Toronto: Macmillan, 1979.

Hood, Hugh. *You Can't Get There from Here.* Ottawa: Oberon, 1972.

Hood, Hugh. *The Swing in the Garden.* Ottawa: Oberon, 1975. The first of a series of novels, collectively entitled *The New Age*, to deal with the social evolution of Toronto. Others are *A New Athens* (1977) and *Reservoir Ravine* (1979).

Houston, James. *The White Dawn.* New York: Harcourt, Brace, 1971. About the clash of cultures as sailors live for several months with a tribe of Eskimos.

Jasmin, Claude. *Ethel et le terroriste/Ethel and the Terrorist.* Trans. David S. Walker. Montreal: Harvest House, 1965.

Kirby, William. *The Golden Dog.* NCL, 1969.

Knight, David. *Farquharson's Physique and What It Did to His Mind.* London: Hodder and Stroughton, 1971.

Kroetsch, Robert. *The Words of My Roaring.* Toronto: Macmillan, 1966. Story about a boisterous character in the Canadian West.

Langevin, André. *Poussière sur la ville/Dust Over the City.* Trans. John Latrebe and Robert Gootlieb. NCL. 1974.

Langevin, André. *Une Chaine dans le parc/Orphan Street.* Trans. Alan Brown. Toronto: McClelland and Stewart, 1976.

Laurence, Margaret. *Stone Angel.* NCL, 1965.

Laurence, Margaret. *A Jest of God.* Toronto: McClelland and Stewart, 1966.

Lemelin, Roger. *Pierre le magnifique/In Quest of Splendour.* Trans. Harry Lorne Binsse. Toronto: McClelland and Stewart, 1955.

Lemelin, Roger. *Au pied de la pente douce/The Town Below.* Trans. Samuel Putman. NCL. 1961.

MacLennan, Hugh. *Two Solitudes.* Toronto: Collins, 1945.

MacLennan, Hugh. *The Watch That Ends the Night.* Toronto: Macmillan, 1959.

MacLennan, Hugh. *Return of the Sphinx.* Toronto: Macmillan, 1967.

MacLennan, Hugh. *Voices in Time.* Toronto: Macmillan, 1980.

McDougall, Colin. *Execution.* Toronto: Macmillan, 1958.

Marcotte, Gilles. *Le Poids de Dieu/The Burden of God.* Trans. Elizabeth Abbott. Toronto: Copp Clark, 1964. Story of a priest struggling with his doubts about the system.

Marlyn, John. *Under the Ribs of Death.* NCL, 1964.

Mitchell, W. O. *Who Has Seen the Wind?* Toronto: Macmillan, 1947.

Moodie, Susanna. *Roughing It in the Bush.* NCL, 1963.

Munro, Alice. *Lives of Girls and Women.* Toronto: McGraw-Hill Ryerson, 1971.

Munro, Alice. *Who Do You Think You Are?* Toronto: Macmillan, 1978.

Richler, Mordecai. *The Apprenticeship of Duddy Kravitz.* NCL, 1969.

Richler, Mordecai. *Joshua Then and Now.* Toronto: McClelland and Stewart, 1980.

Richler, Mordecai. *St. Urban's Horseman.* Toronto: McClelland and Stewart, 1971.

Richler, Mordecai. *Joshua Then and Now*. Toronto: McClelland and Stewart, 1980.

Ringuet. *Trente Arpents/Thirty Acres*. Trans. Felix and Dorothea Walter. NCL, 1960.

Ross, Sinclair. *As for Me and My House*. NCL, 1957.

Ross, Sinclair. *Sawbones Memorial*. Toronto: McClelland and Stewart, 1974.

Roy, Gabrielle. *Bonheur d'occasion/The Tin Flute*. Trans. Hannah Josephson. NCL, 1957.

Rule, Jane. *Contract with the World*. New York: Harcourt, Brace, Jovanovich, 1980.

Sutherland, Ronald. *The Snow Lark (Lark des Neiges* in hardcover). Toronto: New Press, 1971.

Sutherland, Ronald. *Where Do the MacDonalds Bury Their Dead?* Toronto: General Publishing, 1976.

Wiebe, Rudy. *The Temptations of Big Bear*. Toronto: McClelland and Stewart, 1973. About an Indian chief in the Canadian West.

Wiseman, Adele. *The Sacrifice*. Toronto: Macmillan, 1956.

Wiseman, Adele. *Crackpot*. Toronto: McClelland and Stewart, 1974.

Wright, Richard B. *The Weekend Man*. New York: Farrar, Straus and Giroux, 1970. A young man trying to cope with lack of direction and motivation.

Poetry, Short Stories, and Drama: Listed below are anthologies that provide good selections of poetry, short stories, or plays. These anthologies also contain bibliographical information about separate volumes of the works of individual writers. Separate editions of Canadian plays, including translations of Quebec playwrights such as Michel Tremblay and Robert Gurik, are available through Talon Books Ltd. and other publishing houses.

Birney, Earle (ed.). *Twentieth Century Canadian Poetry*. Toronto: Ryerson, 1953.

Cogswell, Fred (ed.). *One Hundred Poems of Modern Quebec*. Fredericton: Fiddlehead, 1970.

Cogswell, Fred (ed.). *A Second Hundred Poems of Modern Quebec*. Fredericton: Fiddlehead, 1971.

Glassco, John (ed.). *Poetry of French Canada in Translation*. Toronto: Oxford, 1970.

Gustafson, Ralph. *The Penguin Book of Canadian Verse*. Baltimore: Penguin, 1967.

Klinck, Carl, and Reginald Watters (eds.). *Canadian Anthology*. Toronto: W. J. Gage, 1966. Contains both prose and poetry and extensive bibliographical material.

Mandel, Eli (ed.). *Poetry of Contemporary Canada*. Toronto: McClelland and Stewart, 1972.

Pacey, Desmond (ed.). *A Book of Canadian Stories*. Toronto: Ryerson, 1962.

Richards, Stanley. *Canada on Stage*. Toronto: Clarke Irwin, 1960.

Rimanelli, Giose and Roberto Ruberto (eds.). *Modern Canadian Stories*. Toronto: Ryerson, 1969.

Scott, F. R. (ed.). *New Provinces: Poems of Several Authors*. Toronto: Macmillan, 1936.

Smith, A. J. M. (ed.). *The Book of Canadian Poetry*. Toronto: W. J. Gage, 1957.

Smith, A. J. M. (ed.). *The Oxford Book of Canadian Verse: in English and French*. Toronto: Oxford, 1960.

Smith, A. J. M. (ed.). *Modern Canadian Verse*. Toronto: Oxford, 1967.

Stevens, John (ed.). *Modern Canadian Stories*. New York: Bantam, 1975.

Sutherland, John (ed.). *Other Canadians*. Montreal: First Statement Press, 1947.

Weaver, Robert. *Canadian Short Stories*. Toronto: Oxford, 1960.

Wilson, Milton. *Poets Between the Wars*. Toronto: McClelland and Stewart, 1967.

REFERENCE AND CRITICISM

Frye, Northrop. *The Bush Garden*. Toronto: Anansi, 1971. A collection of Frye's essays on various aspects and authors of Canadian literature.

Fulford, Robert, Dave Godfrey, and Abraham Rotstein (eds.). *Read Canadian: A Book About Canadian Books*. Toronto: James Lewis and Samuel, 1972. Contains essays on history, economics, politics, society, and the arts, as well as on literature and publishing. Useful bibliographies and other information.

Jones, D. G. *Butterfly on Rock*. Toronto: University of Toronto Press, 1970. A thematic study mainly focused on poetry.

Klinck, C. F. (ed.). *Literary History of Canada*. Toronto: University of Toronto Press, 1974. A monumental survey of the whole of Canadian literature, invaluable for data on minor authors and little-known works.

Mandel, Eli (ed.). *Contexts of Canadian Criticism*. Toronto: University of Toronto Press, 1970. A selection of critical essays.

McCourt, Edward A. *The Canadian West in Fiction*. Toronto: Ryerson, 1949.

Moss, John. *Patterns of Isolation in English-Canadian Fiction*. Toronto: McClelland and Stewart, 1974. A thematic study, as the title indicates.

New, W. H. *Articulating West: Essays on Purpose and Form in Modern Canadian Literature*. Toronto: New Press, 1972. A collection of essays on individual authors.

Pacey, Desmond. *Creative Writing in Canada*. Toronto: Ryerson, 1961. A general survey of Canadian writing from beginnings to the 1960s.

Phelps, Arthur S. *Canadian Writers*. Toronto: McClelland and Stewart, 1952. A collection of perceptive essays on a number of individual writers.

Story, Norah (ed.). *The Oxford Companion to Canadian History and Literature*. Toronto: Oxford, 1967. Contains capsule biographies and masses of useful information.

Sutherland, Ronald. *Second Image: Comparative Studies in Quebec/Canadian Literature*. Toronto: New Press, 1971. Thematic analysis of the parallel evolution of Canadian literature in English and French, bibliographies, and translation information.

Sutherland, Ronald. *The New Hero: Essays in Comparative Quebec/Canadian Literature*. Toronto: Macmillan, 1977.

Warwick, Jack. *The Long Journey: Literary Themes of French Canada*. Toronto: University of Toronto Press, 1968. Thematic analysis, as the title indicates.

INDIVIDUAL AUTHORS

Several publishing houses have series of books on individual Canadian authors. The following may be useful:

McClelland and Stewart, "Canadian Writers" Series of NCL:

> *Marshall McLuhan*, by Dennis Duffy
> *Margaret Laurence*, by Clara Thomas
> *Frederick Philip Grove*, by Ronald Sutherland
> *Stephen Leacock*, by Robertson Davies
> *Earle Birney*, by Richard Robillard
> *Northrop Frye*, by Ronald Bates
> *Malcolm Lowry*, by William H. New
> *James Reaney*, by Ross G. Woodman
> *E. J. Pratt*, by Milton Wilson
> *Leonard Cohen*, by Michael Ondaatje
> *Mordecai Richler*, by George Woodcock
> *Hugh MacLennan*, by Alec Lucas
> *George Woodcock*, by Peter Hughes
> *Ernest Buckler*, by Alan R. Young
> *Farley Mowat*, by Alec Lucas

Copp Clark, "Studies in Canadian Literature":

> *Charles G. D. Roberts*, by W. J. Keith
> *Frederick Philip Grove*, by Douglas Spettigue
> *Hugh MacLennan*, by George Woodcock
> *Earle Birney*, by Frank Davey
> *Ernest Buckler and Sinclair Ross*, by Robert Chambers
> *Brian Moore*, by Hallvard Dahlie
> *Morley Callaghan*, by Victor Howard
> *A. M. Klein*, by Miriam Waddington
> *Al Purdy*, by George Bowering
> *Margaret Avison*, by Ernest Redekop
> *E. J. Pratt*, by Sandra Djwa

McGraw-Hill Ryerson, "Critical Views on Canadian Writers":

Margaret Laurence, by William New
Archibald Lampman, by Michael Gnarowski
Leonard Cohen, by Michael Gnarowski
The McGill Movement, by Peter Stevens
Morley Callaghan, by Brandon Conron
Ernest Buckler, by Gregory Cook
F. P. Grove, by Desmond Pacey
A. M. Klein, by Thomas Marshall

Gage Publishing Ltd., "Profiles in Canadian Drama":

James Reaney, by James Reaney
Robertson Davies, by Patricia Morley
George Ryga, by G. S. MaCaughey
Gratien Gelinas, by Renate Usmiani

On occasion special issues of journals are devoted to individual writers. Notable here are *Essays on Canadian Writing,* Winter/Spring 1978/79 (Hugh Hood); and the *Journal of Canadian Studies,* Fall 1978 (Margaret Laurence), Winter 1979/80 (Hugh MacLennan), and Spring 1980 (Morley Callaghan).

JOURNALS

Journals of literary criticism and of creative writing are multitudinous. Students should at least be aware of the following, which often contain important bibliographical articles:

Canadian Literature (University of British Columbia)
Canadian Poetry (University of Ottawa)
Essays on Canadian Writing (York University)
Journal of Canadian Fiction (Concordia University)
Queen's Quarterly (Queen's University)
University of Toronto Quarterly (University of Toronto)

VII. International Affairs: An Annotated Bibliography

For a pre–World War II historical overview, a useful source that is available in paperback is G. P. de T. Glazebrook's two-volume set—*A History of Canadian External Relations* (Vol. I: *The Formative Years to 1914,* and Vol. II: *In the Empire and the World, 1914–1939* (Toronto: McClelland and Stewart Ltd., 1966. Carleton Library Series, Nos. 27 and 28). Also helpful is the more recent C. P. Stacey, *Canada and the Age of Conflict: A History of Canadian External Policies*, Volume 1, 1867–1921 (Macmillan, 1977).

Although somewhat dated, there are two textbooks that present comprehensive overviews of contemporary Canadian foreign policy concentrating on the Trudeau foreign policy review, both of which are available in paperback: Peter C. Dobell's *Canada's Search for New Roles: Foreign Policy in the Trudeau Era* (Toronto: Oxford University Press, 1972), and Dale C. Thomson and Roger F. Swanson, *Canadian Foreign Policy: Options and Perspectives* (Toronto: McGraw-Hill Ryerson Ltd., 1971). A more detailed complement to these textbooks, and one of the more useful single books on Canadian foreign policy, is R. St. J. MacDonald et al.'s gigantic *Canadian Perspectives on International Law and Organization* (Toronto: University of Toronto Press, 1974), which covers the major dimensions of Canadian foreign policy by chapter, ranging from peacekeeping to disarmament. A very recent compendium of descriptive analyses of many facets of Canada's foreign policy, past and present, containing useful data on trade and development assistance patterns, is Senior Foreign Service Officer John Stiles's *Developing Canada's Relations Abroad* (Sackville, N.B.: Mount Allison University, 1980).

A useful recent paperback edition is Norman Hillmer and Garth Stevenson (eds.), *Foremost Nation: Canadian Foreign Policy and a Changing World* (Toronto: McClelland and Stewart Ltd., 1977), which updates and reassesses Canada's approach toward regions (e.g., Latin America and Africa) and issues (e.g., energy and an international industrial strategy). Another welcomed recent paperback is *Canada's Foreign Policy: Analysis and Trends* (Toronto: Methuen, 1978), edited by Brian W. Tomlin, which utilizes research strategies in examining aspects of Canadian foreign policy. An absolute must in any listing of works on Canadian foreign policy are the interpretive essays of John W. Holmes, which are especially known for their incisiveness and sense of balance. Fortunately, collections of these essays are now available in two paperback books: *The Better Part of Valour: Essays on Canadian Diplomacy* (Toronto: McClelland and Stewart Ltd., 1970, Carleton Library No. 49), and *Canada: A Middle-Aged Power* (Toronto: McClelland and Stewart Ltd., 1976, Carleton Library No. 98). Such a listing as this must also include the provocative and penetrating analyses of James Eayrs, in, for example, his collection of essays, *Diplomacy and Its Discontent* (Toronto: University of Toronto Press, 1971).

Three edited books are especially useful in capturing the Canadian concern about the U.S. impact on Canadian foreign policy: Stephen Clarkson's (ed.) seminal volume, *An Independent Foreign Policy for Canada?* (Toronto: McClelland and Stewart Ltd., 1968), J. L. Granatstein's (ed.) *Canadian Foreign Policy Since 1945: Middle Power or Satellite?* (Toronto: The Copp Clark Publishing Company, 1970), and John Redekop's *The Star Spangled Beaver* (Peter Martin Associates Ltd., 1971). In addition, George Grant's *Lament for a Nation: The Defeat of Canadian Nationalism* (Toronto:

McClelland and Stewart Ltd., 1965) captures in a powerful and poignant manner the concerns of conservative Canadian nationalists.

For the origins of the Canadian diplomatic tradition and institutions, H. Gordon Skilling's book, *Canadian Representation Abroad: From Agency to Embassy*, is essential (Toronto: The Ryerson Press, 1945). Two volumes are helpful on policy organization and formulation: James Eayrs's *The Art of the Possible: Government and Foreign Policy in Canada* (Toronto: University of Toronto Press, 1961), and R. Barry Farrell's *The Making of Canadian Foreign Policy* (Prentice-Hall of Canada Ltd., 1969). For a highly introductory look at foreign policy formulation during the Trudeau era, Bruce Thordarson's book is useful: *Trudeau and Foreign Policy: A Study in Decision-Making* (Toronto: Oxford University Press, 1972). And for an introductory look at the domestic sources of Canadian foreign policy, see Thomas A. Hockin et al., *The Canadian Condominium: Domestic Issues and External Policy* (Toronto: McClelland and Stewart Ltd., 1972). A useful source in understanding the role of the Canadian provinces in internal relations is Howard A. Leeson and Wilfried Vanderelst, *External Affairs and Canadian Federalism: The History of a Dilemma* (Toronto: Holt, Rinehart & Winston of Canada Ltd., 1973).

For a look at Canada's interwar experience in international organizations, Richard Veatch's book, *Canada and the League of Nations* (Toronto: University of Toronto Press, 1975), is helpful. In terms of Canada's perception of its international role, a classic collection of essays can be found in J. King Gordon (ed.), *Canada's Role as a Middle Power* (Toronto: Canadian Institute of International Affairs, 1966, Contemporary Affairs No. 35). In terms of Canada's relations with other parts of the world, Peyton V. Lyon's and Tareq Y. Ismael's *Canada and the Third World* (Toronto: The Macmillan Company of Canada Ltd., 1976) is helpful in that it is divided into specific regions, including francophone and anglophone Africa, the Middle East, and Latin America. J. C. M. Ogelsby's *Gringos from the Far North: Essays in the History of Canadian-Latin Americans, 1866–1968* (Toronto: The Macmillan Company of Canada Ltd., 1976) is an especially welcome addition.

On the strategic side, John Gellner's paperback *Canada in NATO* (Toronto: The Ryerson Press, 1970) is a useful source in exploring and documenting Canada's NATO involvement, while Colin S. Gray's *Canadian Defence Priorities: A Question of Relevance* (Toronto: Clarke, Irwin and Company Ltd., 1972) surveys the overall Canadian strategic situation. James Eayrs's three-volume set, *In Defence of Canada* (Vol. I: *From the Great War to the Great Depression*; Vol. II: *Appeasement and Rearmament*; Vol. III: *Peacemaking and Detente*) (Toronto: University of Toronto Press), provides a historical perspective. For an understanding of Canada's role in international crises, see Robert W. Reford's *Canada and Three Crises* (Toronto: Canadian Institute of International Affairs, Contemporary Affairs Series No. 42, 1968).

On the economic side, O. J. McDiarmid's book, *Commercial Policy in the Canadian Economy* (Cambridge, Mass.: Harvard University Press, 1946), is an excellent overview, while L. D. Wilgress provides equally useful insights in *Canada's Approach to Trade Negotiations* (Montreal: Private Planning Association of Canada, 1963). A. F. W. Plumptre's paperback, *Three Decades of Decision: Canada and the World Monetary System, 1944–75* (Toronto: McClelland and Stewart Ltd., 1977), is also essential in covering the monetary side, while Hugh G. J. Aitkens et al., *The American Economic Impact on Canada* (London: Cambridge University Press, 1959), is helpful in covering the U.S. influences. Two paperback volumes that pursue these issues in recent years are by H. Edward English et al.: *Canada in a Wider Economic Community* (Toronto: University of Toronto Press, 1972), and *Transatlantic Economic Community: Canadian Perspectives* (Toronto: University of Toronto Press, 1968).

An especially useful collection of volumes is *Canada in World Affairs*, published by the Canadian Institute of International Affairs. The collection consists of twelve volumes to date, divided into two-year periods, and covers the period from the prewar years through 1963, with more volumes forthcoming. Each volume is an interpretive survey of events and is written by a different author. For those interested in primary sources, the Canadian Department of External Affairs publishes an ongoing series (nine volumes to date) entitled *Documents on Canadian External Relations*; similar to FRUS, these now cover the period from 1909, when the Department of External Affairs was established, through the 1940s. There is also a useful collection of documents from the interwar period: Walter A. Riddell's *Documents on Canadian Foreign Policy: 1917–1939* (Toronto: Oxford University Press, 1962). Two paperback volumes covering the postwar period are: R. A. Mackay's *Canadian Foreign Policy 1945–54* (Toronto: McClelland and Stewart, 1971) and Arthur E. Blanchette's *Canadian Foreign Policy 1955–65* (Toronto: McClelland and Stewart, 1977, Carleton Library No. 103).

Biographies offer a useful and enjoyable point of entry into Canadian foreign policy, and this is especially the case with the three-set collection on Lester B. Pearson, who was one of the key architects of Canada's postwar international role (Vol. I of *Mike* covers the period 1897–1948; Vol. II, 1948–57; and Vol. III, 1957–68) (Toronto: University of Toronto Press, 1972, 1973, and 1975).

For those interested in keeping abreast of current developments in Canadian foreign policy, essential and inexpensive reading can be found in *International Perspectives*, which is a bimonthly journal on world affairs consisting of articles of fact and opinion. Published by the Canadian Department of External Affairs, subscription rates in the United States are $5.00 per year (payable to the Receiver General of Canada) and can be posted to Printing and Publishing, Supply and Services, Ottawa, Ontario, Canada K1A OS9.

For those wishing to seriously pursue studies of Canadian foreign policy, the following three publications of the Canadian Institute of International Affairs (Toronto) are essential:

Behind the Headlines. A monthly publication consisting of monographs discussing contemporary international issues and geographical areas.

International Canada. A monthly summary of Canadian government statements and political discussion regarding Canada's international involvements.

International Journal. A quarterly journal, edited by James Eayrs and Robert Spencer. Each issue, consisting of several learned articles, is entirely devoted to one subject.

Subscriptions to all three sources can be obtained by writing to: Canadian Institute of International Affairs, 15 King's College Circle, Toronto, Ontario, Canada M5S 2V9.

For those wishing to explore Canadian foreign policy in a more comprehensive manner, the following two bibliographies are very helpful:

Page, Donald. *A Bibliography of Works on Canadian Foreign Relations, 1945–1970.* Toronto: Canadian Institute of International Affairs, 1973. 442 pages.

Motiuk, Laurence, and Madeline Grant. *A Reading Guide to Canada in World Affairs, 1945–1971.* Toronto: Canadian Institute of International Affairs, 1972. 313 pages, and a second volume covering the period 1971–75.

For those interested in governmental sources, there are several publications covering most aspects of Canadian foreign policy as well as Canada's relationship with the United States. These include:

Foreign Policy for Canadians. Ottawa: Queen's Printer, 1970. Six booklets covering the United Nations, International Development, Latin America, Europe, the Pacific, and a general booklet.

Canada. Department of External Affairs. *Federalism and International Relations* and *Federalism and International Relations Supplement.* Ottawa: Queen's Printer, 1967 and 1969.

Canada. Department of Defence. *Defense in the 1970s.* Ottawa: Queen's Printer, 1971.

Foreign Direct Investment in Canada (The Gray Report). Ottawa: Government of Canada, 1972.

Foreign Ownership and the Structure of Canadian Industry (Watkins Report). Ottawa, 1968.

Canada. International Development Agency. *Strategy for International Development Cooperation, 1975–1980.* Ottawa, 1975.

CANADIAN-U.S. RELATIONS

Two overview books are especially helpful in understanding the Canadian-U.S. relationship. For a historical survey see G. M. Craig, *The United States and Canada* (Cambridge, Mass.: Harvard University Press, 1968). For an examination of the entire range of issues confronting the contemporary relationship, see John Sloan Dickey's *Canada and the American Presence* (New York: New York University Press, 1975, A Council on Foreign Relations book). A classic continues to be the J. B. Brebner paperback book, which was written in 1945, *North Atlantic Triangle: The Interplay of Canada, the United States and Great Britain* (Toronto: McClelland and Stewart Ltd., 1968, Carleton Library No. 30).

There are also useful collections of essays and documents on the Canadian-U.S. relationship. Two books from the 1960s include:

Dickey, J. S. (ed.). *The United States and Canada*. Englewood Cliffs, N.J.: Prentice-Hall, 1964.

Merchant, L. T. (ed.). *Neighbours Taken for Granted: Canada and the United States*. New York: Frederick A. Praeger, 1966.

Two collections of essays from the 1970s are:

Preston, Richard A. *The Influence of the United States on Canadian Development: Eleven Case Studies*. Durham, N.C.: Duke University Press, 1972.

English, H. Edward (ed.). *Canada–United States Relations*. Proceedings of the Academy of Political Science, Vol. 32, No. 2, New York, 1976 (entire issue).

An especially positive development in the literature on Canadian-U.S. relations is the attempt to apply methodologies. For a transnational approach, see Annette Fox, Alfred Hero, and Joseph Nye (eds.), *Canada and the United States: Transnational and Transgovernmental Relations* (New York: Columbia University Press, 1976). For an approach utilizing integration, see W. A. Axline, J. E. Hyndman, P. V. Lyon, and M. A. Molot (eds.), *Continental Community? Independence and Integration in North America* (Toronto: McClelland and Stewart Ltd., 1974).

The Swanson book addresses itself to a half century of meetings between U.S. presidents and Canadian prime ministers: Roger F. Swanson, *Canadian-American Summit Diplomacy 1923–1973, Selected Speeches and Documents* (Toronto: McClelland and Stewart Ltd., 1975, Carleton Library Series No. 81). For those interested in decision making in the Canadian-U.S. context, the following book is useful: Roger F. Swanson, *Intergovernmental Perspectives on the Canadian-U.S. Relationship* (New York: New York University Press, 1978).

In addition, there are useful sources on specific aspects of the bilateral relationship. A book that examines the Canadian-U.S. cultural interface is Janice L. Murray (ed.), *Canadian Cultural Nationalism* (New York: New York University Press, 1977). On the political side, see David R. Diener (ed.), *Canada-U.S. Treaty Relations* (Durham, N.C.: Duke University Press, 1963).

For an expression of Canadian concern about the U.S. economic impact on Canada, see:

Godfrey, Dave, and Mel Watkins (eds.). *Gordon to Watkins to You: The Battle for Control of Our Economy*. Toronto: New Press, 1970.
Levitt, Kari. *Silent Surrender: The Multi-National Corporation in Canada*. New York: St. Martin's Press, 1970.

For a useful exploration of the bilateral business interactions, see:

Litvak, I. A., Maule, C. J., and Robinson, R. D. *Dual Loyalty: Canadian-U.S. Business Arrangements*. Toronto: McGraw-Hill Company of Canada Ltd., 1971.

Index

Many items not listed separately will readily be found under the larger, more general entries which are derived from the particular subject material of each chapter; i.e. History, Geography, International Relations, Political System, Economy, etc. Authors' names and literary titles are found under Literature.

Index